We as an organization fully endorse the purpose and material of *Encountering the World of Islam* and use it and promote it as much as possible as a valuable resource for training people in Muslim evangelism.

Africa Inland Mission

Finally! A counterpart to *Perspectives on the World Christian Movement*, but on Islam! Having taught in various *Perspectives* courses myself and seen their effectiveness, it is my dream that *Encountering the World of Islam* will make a similar impact equipping those already on a path toward lifelong service among Muslims and attracting those…who have still failed to grasp that it is the Muslims' turn to discover Christ's love. Comprehensive but presented in bite-sized chunks, *Encountering the World of Islam* will be widely used as a mobilizing and training tool in the years to come.

Dr. David Lundy, International Director, Arab World Ministries

*Encountering the World of Islam* combines valuable information about Muslim belief and practice with practical approaches to communicating God's love. It is the best introduction to Islam I know. I highly recommend it!

Dr. Rick Love, International Director, Frontiers

This is the most significant training tool of its kind that I have ever seen. All of us who love Muslims will want to study it and try to give the course and the book wider circulation. All of God's people need exposure to this great research and challenge.

George Verwer, Founder, Operation Mobilization

Islam is at the crossroads. The next few years could herald sweeping changes and unprecedented opportunities for Christian witness in the Muslim community. It is imperative that we prepare ourselves with a biblical and historic understanding of Islam that enables us to communicate the gospel to the Muslim heart. *Encountering the World of Islam* is designed to provide this foundation.

Steve Richardson, U.S. Director, Pioneers

The *Perspectives on the World Christian Movement* is one of the best introductions to God's heart for the world and what he is doing around the world. I am thrilled that there is now a similar course focusing on the world of Islam, and I am excited about how God is going to use it to build among God's people a passion to see Muslims come to Christ.

Steve Strauss, USA Director, Serving in Mission(SIM)

We are very encouraged with the amazing breakthroughs that are occurring as the Lord Jesus builds his church among Muslim peoples. We trust that *Encountering the World of Islam* will be an effective tool to encourage many more believers to become involved with what the Lord is doing.

Charlie Davis, Executive Director, The Evangelical Alliance Mission (TEAM)

A very practical and interactive course that will
of Islam and help in developing more effective v
valuable resource for anyone interested in Musli
Trevor Kallmier, Inter
nal

# ENCOUNTERING
# THE WORLD OF ISLAM

Edited by Keith E. Swartley

A ministry of

10 West Dry Creek Circle • Littleton, CO 80120 USA
303.459.5400 (p) • 303.459.5401 (f)
*www.calebproject.org* • *www.calebprojecteurope.org*

Published by

**Authentic**
MEDIA

ATLANTA • LONDON • HYDERABAD

Authentic Publishing
We welcome your questions and comments.

USA    1820 Jet Stream Drive, Colorado Springs, CO 80921  www.authenticbooks.com
UK     9 Holdom Avenue, Bletchley, Milton Keynes, Bucks, MK1 1QR
       www.authenticmedia.co.uk
India  Logos Bhavan, Medchal Road, Jeedimetla Village, Secunderabad
       500 055, A.P.

Encountering the World of Islam
ISBN-10: 1-932805-24-9
ISBN-13: 978-1-932805-24-6

Library of Congress Cataloging-in-Publication Data

Encountering the world of Islam / edited by Keith E. Swartley.
       p.cm.
Includes bibliographical references and index.
ISBN 1-932805-24-9 (pbk.)
1. Missions to Muslims. 2. Islam--Relations--Christianity. 3. Christianity and other religions--Islam. 4. Islam--Essence, genius, nature.
I. Swartley, Keith E., 1964-

BV2625.E54 2005
297--dc22
2005000658

Cover design: John Battenfield
Interior design: Paul Merrill, Amy Battenfield

Printed in the United States of America

# DEDICATION

I dedicate this book to:

My beautiful wife and partner, Ethel. You are priceless, and irreplaceable in my life.

My favorite—and only—daughters, Margaret and Charis. I am so proud of both of you.

My parents, Dick and Anne Swartley. Without your support and patience, this book would have never been written.

And the late Rick Mead, without whom I might never have been in Kenya in 1983, where I encountered Muslims face-to-face for the first time.

# CONTENTS

# THE DEVELOPMENT OF ISLAM

---

** This reading is found at *www.encounteringislam.org/readings.*

# EXPRESSIONS OF ISLAM

** This reading is found at *www.encounteringislam.org/readings*.

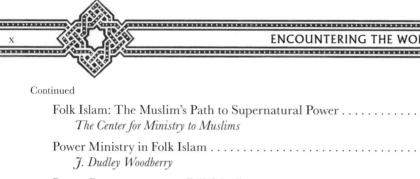

# CHRISTIANITY AND ISLAM

** This reading is found at *www.encounteringislam.org/readings*.

** This reading is found at *www.encounteringislam.org/readings*.

Continued

# OUR RESPONSE TO ISLAM

---

** This reading is found at *www.encounteringislam.org/readings*.

\*\* This reading is found at *www.encounteringislam.org/readings.*

Continued

# APPENDICES

# INDICES

** This reading is found at *www.encounteringislam.org/readings*.

# FIGURES AND TABLES

# MAPS

# HIGHLIGHTS

 ## CONCEPTS

## OUTREACH

## OUTREACH, continued

## PEOPLE GROUPS

## QUOTATIONS

## QUR'AN

## STORIES

## STORIES, continued

## WOMEN

# FOREWORD

As you start to encounter the world of Islam through these pages, visualize your task by looking at how the Muslim faith has been taught for over a millennium at the major training center for missionaries of Islam—al-Azhar Mosque and University in Cairo.

There students gather in a circle around a professor who sits in front of a pillar on a chair which is named for the subject matter taught there—for example, the "Chair of Qur'anic Commentary." Over the centuries as charitable endowments were given to pay the salary of the professor, they became "endowed chairs" and became the model for endowed academic chairs in universities and seminaries around the world. This is the image that can help us visualize our task as we are guided in our study of Muslims through the pages of this book.

As the chair is held up and balanced by four legs, our study must be held up and balanced by four perspectives. First we must see how orthodox Muslims understand their faith and practice. This requires attempting to enter into the experience of Muslims—performing mental ablutions to cleanse away preconceived ideas and sitting at their feet to hear what they have to say. Christian understanding and witness must be willing to deal with Islam as Muslims define it and the ideals it espouses.

The second leg or perspective is to take the best of non-Muslim scholarship from a spectrum of disciplines. Western orientalists have done in-depth analysis using historical and linguistic tools, emphasizing texts rather than behavior. Missionaries and theologians have tended to analyze Islam by the theological categories of the western Christian experience, but, like western orientalists, they have often forced Islam into categories that are not inherent to it. Behavioral scientists, like anthropologists, have used participant observation skills to understand Muslims, but often they lacked textual skills. We need all of these tools to understand Muslims.

The third leg or perspective is the study of the popular beliefs and practices of common Muslims. These are often a blend of formal Islam with beliefs and practices of previously-held indigenous or tribal religions. These include a desire for power or blessing through holy men or women, shrines, or protective amulets. The felt needs of these folk Muslims are somewhat different from those of formal Muslims. They may feel the need for a savior from fear of demonic beings or harmful forces more than they feel the need for a savior from sin. The gospel must be seen as relevant to their felt needs.

To give the chair balance there is need for the fourth leg or perspective—our witness among and to Muslims. The first three require the fourth because understanding without commitment is irresponsibility. As our eyes drift up to the pinnacle of the mosque, we see a crescent moon—the symbol of Islam. The crescent moon reflects light, as Islam

reflects some biblical light, but the crescent is empty or dark in the center. Our task is to fill that center with "the glory of God in the face of Jesus Christ" (2 Cor. 4:6).

In our scene at al-Azhar Mosque and University, the sheikh or professor has a book in his hand or head which represents the information imparted. The students sit in a circle for interaction and reflection. And their shoes are at the door, since the mosque is a place of worship as well as study. These shoes represent their experience and practice in real life. These three must always be kept together—the information, the interaction and reflection, and the experience and practice.

*Encountering the World of Islam*, the book that you are to use as a guide to your learning, is designed to blend these—the information it and your leader offer each week, the interaction and reflection you experience with the other students during the learning sessions, and your experience with Muslims in the intervening days. If you keep these interacting together, this encounter with Islam will be fruitful both in your own lives and the lives of the Muslims you encounter.

J. Dudley Woodberry

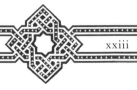

# ACKNOWLEDGEMENTS

No work of this magnitude is achieved without a team effort, and I have been blessed by the talents of many collaborators. I am indebted to Francis Patt and to the U. S. Center for World Mission, whose vision moved this project forward in the years prior to September 11, 2001; and to Craig Simonian who ran the first pilot version of this course in 1992 prior to my involvement. The U. S. Center for World Mission's *Perspectives Study Program* served as our model and inspiration for this course and materials. I also wish to pay tribute to my wife, Ethel, who urged me to develop instructional objectives and helped me expand the integrative assignments to strengthen the mobilization objective of the course. Don and Anne Rodgers, Phil Bruner, Joanne Knipmeyer, Susan Gingrich, and my parents, Dick and Anne Swartley, have also made invaluable contributions to the production and editing of earlier editions of this material, under the name *Perspectives on the World of Islam*. My sincere thanks goes to the students who suffered through initial drafts of the course, and the many others who encouraged us to persevere in this endeavor.

I am especially grateful for my early mentors in ministry to Muslims. Just as I hope this volume will inspire you, these are the men who inspired me, encouraging this work in the 1990s, before Islamic studies came into vogue. They include the late Dr. Harvie Conn, Jim Cooper, the late Dr. William McElwee Miller, the late Woody Phillips, Dr. Larry Poston, Dr. David Shenk, the late Dr. J. Christy Wilson, Dr. J. Dudley Woodberry, and especially Dr. Don McCurry.

Since this ministry transferred to Caleb Project in 2002, many hands have moved this effort forward. A number of key financial partners have enabled us to publish it. Most notably, Frontiers and Mount Paran Church of God of Atlanta, Georgia, made early significant financial contributions, followed by Benjamin and Gwen Burke, James and Kathleen Coler, and Ed and Becky Watt; and Grace Community Church of Columbia, Maryland; Knox Presbyterian Church of Ann Arbor, Michigan; Mars Hill Bible Church of Grandville, Michigan; and Perspectives of Northern California. I also thank our home church, Church of the Saviour in Wayne, Pennsylvania, for upholding me and my family with prayer and generous financial support.

Special thanks to the U.S. Center for World Mission for their generous contribution of articles from the *International Journal of Frontier Mission*, and to the Evangelical Missions Information Service of the Billy Graham Center, for their generous contribution of articles from the *Evangelical Missions Quarterly*.

At Caleb Project, Abby Barnes, John and Amy Battenfield, Harold Britton, Altair Fatton, Gwen Hanna, Catherine Horn, Joanne Knipmeyer, Brad Koenig, Wanda Kolba, Paul Merrill, Daisy Schween, Marti Smith, Dick and Anne Swartley, Ethel Swartley, Carissa Ward, Paul al-Yahya, and Jim Zlogar all played indispensable roles in completing this project. Each deserves his or her own byline, illuminating and memorializing their considerable efforts. I also appreciate the contribution of those who reviewed each lesson's content. Their insights, based on time-tested field knowledge and service, have been invaluable: Jeleta Eckheart, Omar Iskander, David King, Mike Kuhn, Fran Love, Fouad Masri, and Richard McCallum. Lastly, my thanks to our team at Authentic Media: Angela Duerksen, Michaela Dodd, and Volney James.

My sincerest gratitude to all,
Keith E. Swartley
*kswartley@encounteringislam.org*
Spring 2005

# COURSE INTRODUCTION

*Encountering the World of Islam* is the title, both of the book you are reading and a course which uses the book as its primary text. This introduction explains the features of the book, as well as the assignments commonly used in the course. If you are reading the book without attending our course, you may still wish to page through this Course Introduction to learn how to navigate through the features of each chapter (called lessons). You may also enjoy some of the activities which are assigned in the course. You can learn more about *Encountering the World of Islam* as a course at our web site, *www.encounteringislam.org.*

Muslims praying

© Caleb Project

## OUR FUNDAMENTAL ASSUMPTIONS

We have relied on several fundamental assumptions in creating and assembling this material:

1. We believe in Jesus Christ as God Incarnate. It is for him that we do all our work. It is against his example and obedience that we are all compared. Because Christ is our hope, we also have a hopeful view of the future and of our relationships with Muslims. As you evaluate this course, please evaluate us on how well we have reflected the character of Christ, our Lord and Savior.

2. We desire to relate to Muslims as equals. We do not believe in engaging them in argument, for they are not our enemies. We do not fear or blame them, or label them as evil. Compared to Christ, not one of us is righteous; none of us meets God's standard. We seek to overcome patterns of social engagement that have raised walls between us, leading to conclusions based on ideology, politics, and nationalism. We want to establish a base of understanding and empathy, and to tear down barriers by building lasting relationships between us, just as Christ has initiated relationship with us. Where we must evaluate Islam, we have tried to be careful to use

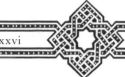

the same criteria of criticism we want applied to ourselves. We believe the first and foremost criterion is Christ. Please evaluate our fairness toward Muslims as compared to Christ's example of justice.

3. We are evangelical. We have something we desire to share—the Good News of salvation through Jesus Christ. We wish to share him while, at the same time, upholding the intrinsic value of all people. We believe we are obligated to share our faith in Jesus Christ, and we choose to exercise our fundamental human right to share our faith.

4. We believe that demonstrating Jesus Christ's love includes addressing all the needs people have. As Christ has transformed us into new beings, our faith, coupled with our empathy for our fellow human beings, compels us to reach out in friendship, evangelism, and the good deeds which minister to the whole person and the community, by addressing medical, educational, social, economic, and political needs.

5. We are practical. While each lesson in this course deserves a full semester of academic study, that is not our purpose. We want to equip Christians with the practical knowledge and experience they need to immediately begin to understand and befriend Muslims. Those who desire to live among Muslims need further study of Islam, Muslim culture, and perhaps language. Muslims are excellent teachers, and other programs exist to provide further training for Christians working with Muslims.

## TO OUR MUSLIM READERS

We are glad that you are reading our materials. We feel that it is very important for Christians to understand their Muslim neighbors, fellow co-workers, and students. Regrettably, too many Christians still hold prejudices against Muslims, because they lack personal knowledge of Islam or experience in Muslim relationships. We discourage argument or debate. We wish to promote a constructive, unbiased view of Muhammad, Islam, and Muslims.

Even though Caleb Project is an evangelical ministry, we do not support proselytism or any other form of coercion or inducement. We actively discourage any negative forms of personal witness which are argumentative, or do not respect the traditions and opinions of others.

We are evangelicals, and, as such, feel an obligation to share our faith. However, we understand this must be done in gentleness, love, and respect, and not on a conditional basis: 1 Peter 3:15 says, "Always be prepared to give an answer to everyone who asks you to give the reason for the hope that you have. But do this with gentleness and respect." The response to our witness is in God's hands, and Christians are not in any way to appear intimidating.

Within the course, we also call on Christians to pray for, and strive for improvements in, the human conditions for Muslims. As you know, many Muslims do not have access to human rights, basic education, healthcare, clean water, or adequate food, and many are not able to freely practice their religion or have a voice in governing their own affairs.

We recognize that our approach may differ from the public response heard from some ministries since September 11, 2001. Sadly, too many have continued to respond in fear of terrorism, and with continued uncritical support for Israel and the denial of equal rights for all members of our society. Others have disparaged Muhammad or Islam, not recognizing the deep debt that all modern societies owe Islamic civilization. As a part of our course, we encourage Christians to regret and apologize for the wrongs carried out against Muslims, however mistakenly, in the name of Christ (the Crusades, slavery, imperialism, and even current forms of political-economic oppression). Christians should not be silent on these issues, or allow the name of Jesus Christ to be besmirched by the sins of opportunistic so-called Christians.

We have been overjoyed to help a number of churches respond constructively to the local and global community of Muslims. In the numerous courses we have held since September 11, 2001, Muslim leaders from the local communities have been invited to speak and have been warmly received. The students in the classes have read from the Qur'an and Muslim authors. We have introduced Palestinian Christians who gave these congregations a more balanced view of the Middle East, and we have encouraged each student to begin an open dialogue with a Muslim acquaintance for the purpose of friendship, not proselytism.

We feel strongly that Christians should listen to Muslims, because Muslims explain their views better than we ever could. We could have chosen materials written by Christian or secular authors to explain the life of Muhammad, Muslim contributions to global civilization, and the diversity of views in the Muslim community. However, we firmly believe that Muslim-authored materials give a superior, more authoritative explanation of these topics. We also think that Christians will benefit from reading these articles, no matter what degree of background knowledge of Islam they possess. We believe our curriculum will help Christians appreciate Muhammad, Islam, and Muslims, as they see points we have in common and, perhaps for the first time, they hear Muslims thoughtfully and reasonably explain their faith. We specifically thank the Royal Embassy of Saudi Arabia, Amana Publications, and Dr. Javeed Akhter for trusting us to include their articles. We sincerely hope—for it is our intention—that all of our materials will prove to be consistently respectful, while at the same time clearly presenting our desire to obediently share our faith in Jesus Christ with Muslims.

## TO COURSE COORDINATORS

We are pleased that you are coordinating a local class using our curriculum. We desire to help you promote and host the class. Further information to assist you in this effort is available on the course's companion web site, including sample promotional materials, advice on selecting instructors, class planning templates, lesson notes, handouts, grading manuals, and other activities. In addition, other services are available to you through Caleb Project: discounts on Caleb Project products, coordinator training workshops, and a web site companion to the course to

organize your class enrollment, submission of assignments, grading, class notices, and so forth. This on-line courseware also hosts audio and video lessons for those students who cannot attend all sessions. Please visit *www.encounteringislam.org/coordinators* to learn more.

## TO COURSE INSTRUCTORS

We are delighted that you are bringing your experience to students studying this material. This course is most often taught by a different lecturer for each lesson. When preparing your lecture, please refer to the specific lesson you will be covering to review the Lesson Objective(s) and the Lesson Introduction. This will give you a quick overview of what you have been asked to teach. Please also note the material being covered by the other lectures, especially those prior to and following yours, so that you will not duplicate material dealt with in other lessons. Lesson plans, student handouts, and audio-visual presentations are posted on our web site, which may be adapted for your presentation: *www.encounteringislam.org/instructors*. We also have audio and video of other instructors covering each lesson. Please adapt your presentation to include your own experience and stories. Your viewpoint is valued, and we do not expect you to cover the material exactly as we have presented it. In fact, we believe that the students will be more engaged by integrating your perspective on the lesson topic into their learning experience.

## LESSON STRUCTURE: ELEMENTS OF INSTRUCTION

This course integrates instructional systems development patterns to enhance adult learning, adapted from the work of Robert Gagne, Leslie Briggs, and Walter Wager (*Principles of Instructional Design*, 1988). Special emphasis has been placed on incorporation of the objectives into the student's worldview and lifestyle. Each Objective is achieved through the following means:

1. Gaining attention: Introductory questions ("Ponder This") and reading assignments about the Objective.

2. Objective: The subject matter of the Lesson.

3. Review of salient, previously covered ideas: Lesson introduction and classroom review.

4. Presentation of new information: Lecture of the week and Lesson Readings assignments.

5. Guidance of learning: Class and on-line forum discussions.

6. Elicitation of performance: Quizzes, final exam, and on-line forum discussions.

7. Provision of feedback: Grading of assignments and on-line forum discussions.

8. Assessment of learning: Final exam and written paper.

9. Enhancement of retention and learning integration: Relationship with a Muslim, field trip to a mosque, on-line forum discussions, and prayer.

Additional activities, lesson plans, presentations, and handouts are available to course instructors and coordinators at *www.encounteringislam.org.* These resources require a brief, one-time registration process.

## COURSE ASSIGNMENTS

Many of you may be reading this book without attending a companion course. In this case, you control your learning. If you are just reading the book but would like to gain from the additional resources we have available, check *www.encounteringislam.org* to see if there is an upcoming class in your area. If there is not, you can still benefit from the learning enhancements on our web site, or you can register to take the class on-line. Several areas of the companion web site are free. Other features may require a nominal one-time fee. If you are attending the companion course, this web fee will be paid as a part of your regular course fees; and your coordinator will give you an enrollment key, which you will need the first time you visit the web site.

Typical assignments for *Encountering the World of Islam* courses include readings, on-line discussions, on-line quizzes, meeting with a Muslim, a mosque field trip, and a final examination, which could include a written paper, an oral report, or both. Each of these typical assignments is described below. However, if you are taking this course for credit, be sure to follow the guidelines in your course syllabus; they supercede the instructions given for assignments in this text. Even if you are not taking a class in association with reading this book, we encourage you to take advantage of our on-line resources, and to try some of the optional activities and assignments.

### Reading Assignments

Each set of Lesson Readings is designed to reinforce and expand the knowledge gained from course lectures. Ideally, the assigned readings should be read *prior* to the lecture that accompanies that lesson. The readings assignments are found in each lesson in this book, under the heading Lesson Readings. Not all readings are found in the book; some are only available on the companion web site, *www.encounteringislam.org/readings.* See page 4 for an example of the readings assigned for Lesson 1. Other supplemental activities and links are also available as free resources on this web site.

In each lesson, the introductory questions titled Ponder This, the Lesson Objective, and the Introduction will help focus your learning as you read. If you do not have time to do anything else, read these three pieces before each lecture because they will help you participate and learn from the lecture. Some readings are controversial; these are designed to stimulate thought, not to force the student's agreement with what is presented. Each set of readings is divided into three parts or load increments:

**Key Readings:** These consist of about twenty pages per lesson. We highly recommend these readings for everyone taking the course. They will give you a grasp of the key points of each lesson. These readings are all found in the book, immediately following the introduction.

**Basic Readings:** These consist of about thirty-five pages per lesson: read both Key and Basic Readings. In addition to the Key Reading assignments, most students will want to continue reading to gain a general understanding of the lesson topic. We highly recommend both the Key and Basic Readings for most students. Students seeking a Caleb Project certificate for completing this course must read all Key and Basic Readings. Basic Readings are all contained within the book directly behind the Key Readings.

**Full Readings:** These consist of about forty-five pages per lesson: read Key, Basic, and Full Readings. Full Readings are not found in this book but are only available on-line in the web-based companion to the textbook. Visit *www.encounteringislam.org/readings* to find these reading assignments. These readings are available free of charge but do require a brief, one-time registration process. We recommend the Full Readings to any student who plans to work with Muslims. Most students taking this course for academic credit will also be required to read the Full Readings. Please note: Full Readings are not found in this book, but on our web site.

Students: If you are taking this course to earn a completion certificate or for academic or continuing educational credit, you may be graded on the readings assignments through your responses to on-line forum discussions, quizzes, and the final examination.

Coordinators: Additional reading—from the Recommended Readings & Activities or the For Futher Study sections—may be assigned to for-credit students, as indicated in your syllabus, to fulfill your academic institution's requirements for academic credit.

## Additional Lesson Features

**Ponder This:** These introductory questions are to help frame your thoughts as you enter the lesson. Take a moment before you begin the lesson to reflect on these questions.

**For Further Study:** This feature identifies additional suggested reading on topics discussed in the lesson which may be used for deeper study of these subjects. Professors using this book as a text may wish to assign some of these readings to their students. For Further Study features can be found periodically throughout the book and provide more detail and context on the subjects to which they are referenced.

**Discussion Questions:** These open questions give you an opportunity to apply the lesson material in a discussion with others. This may be a class activity, or give you ideas for your discussion forum posting, or simply serve as points to mull over on your own.

**Recommended Readings & Activities:** This feature identifies additional readings and activities which may be of interest to you or assigned by your professor. They include reading, watching, praying, visiting, eating, listening, meeting, shopping, or Internet surfing activities. Recommended Readings & Activities are found at the end of each lesson and provide more material on the subject of the lesson.

## THE COMPANION WEB SITE

Caleb Project hosts a companion web site to this book. On this site you will find additional readings, learning activities, courseware for completing assignments, tools to promote a course using this text, and other helps for students, instructors, and coordinators. Visit *www.encounteringislam.org* to learn more about these features. A brief, one-time registration is required. After the initial registration, you can tailor your own path, exploring areas of interest in the order you desire. Plenty of help is available as you navigate the site.

### On-line Discussion Forum

The knowledge acquired from this course is not as important as the way it will affect your view of Muslims and future interactions with them. As a way of demonstrating your integration and application of the ideas encountered in the classroom and Readings, you may be required to participate in an on-line discussion forum. In the forum, you will discuss your experiences and reactions to the world of Islam as you discover it and integrate the course content into your life. Your postings should record your responses to other contacts you have with Islam and Muslims, in addition to the course work. You may react to world news, impressions of Muslims seen or met, new insights about past experiences with Muslims, or reflections on conversations with Muslim acquaintances.

Your posting may be a graded assignment. If so, you will be required to write one posting per lesson. The coordinator will read your entry and may respond to it. He or she will be looking for evidence that you are interacting thoughtfully with the course content and integrating the content into your behavior and thinking. Your posting will be graded for your thoughts and reflectiveness, and your entry must be made prior to the next class session. Late postings may not be accepted. The postings to the discussion forum of your class are made on-line at *www.encounteringislam.org/classforums*. The first time you visit the forum, if you have not already been enrolled by your course coordinator, you may need to complete a brief, one-time registration process using your course enrollment key.

### Responding to Discussion Forum Postings

In addition to posting new entries to the discussion forum for each lesson, you may be required to browse through your classmates' postings and respond to them with your own comments, encouragement, or insights. The coordinator may choose to grade your response postings and require that they be submitted prior to your next class meeting. In large classes, you may be assigned to a small group within your class. Your course coordinator will designate these groups, and you will post discussion responses within this small group. You may also consider working together with this small group for other integration activities and projects.

### On-line Quizzes

At *www.encounteringislam.org/quizzes*, there are four on-line quizzes which your course coordinator may assign. These quizzes are designed to be taken in an open-book format. Your answers should

show that you have thought about the questions and reduced your responses to the most salient points. Be sure to answer all parts of the question. If it asks you to cite two examples, make sure you include two examples. The key to taking these quizzes is to read and think about each question before writing your response. Answers should not be long; a few sentences or a short paragraph is sufficient. Each quiz covers one section of the course, or three lessons. Unless otherwise specified in your syllabus, the due dates of each quiz are as follows:

Quiz 1 – before class session 4.
Quiz 2 – before class session 7.
Quiz 3 – before class session 10.
Quiz 4 – one week after class session 12.

## RELATIONSHIPS WITH MUSLIMS

To just learn about Muslims without meeting and conversing with them would be to miss one of the richest experiences we desire for you in this course. Therefore, one of the primary assignments in an *Encountering the World of Islam* course is for you, with our help, to initiate meeting with a Muslim. The purpose of your two required meetings is for you to interact and learn, by asking questions about what your Muslim friend's life is like, what his or her values are, what he or she thinks, and so forth. Taking this course is the best excuse you may ever have for approaching a Muslim and inviting them to lunch or coffee. Your opening could be:

> I am studying about Islam and Muslims, and one of my assignments is to ask a Muslim to share with me what it means to be a Muslim from their

perspective. Would you be willing to do that with me?

Optimally, your first meeting should take place after the third lecture and before the ninth, with the second meeting prior to completing the course. Following each meeting, your coordinator may require you to post your personal reflections on the meeting as a discussion forum or journal entry. Like other postings, this assignment can be completed on-line at *www.encounteringislam.org/classforums*.

The goal of spending time with a Muslim is to listen and learn. Be sure to be extremely sensitive to his or her views, opinions, beliefs, and culture. Initially, the person may be suspicious, thinking that you only want to "convert" him or her. Your friend may be wary because of previous negative experiences with Christians, and may need to express some frustrations.

Do not focus your conversations on the differences between Christianity and Islam. You should not engage in debate or argument. If the person you are trying to befriend becomes argumentative, listen patiently. If you are able to pose questions, express your desire to learn. If your friend is an immigrant or international student, ask what life is like where he or she is from, what people there eat, how they school their children, what your friend misses from home, what is difficult about living here, and so forth. The reading in your textbook by C. R. Marsh, *Sharing Our Faith with Muslims* (found on p. 302), may be helpful to you as you prepare to meet with your new Muslim aquaintance.

A certain amount of time that your meeting should last has not been specified. However, a brief attempt to converse does not qualify as a meeting. The expectation is that, first, you contact a Muslim to arrange an appointment; then you have a meeting. Two meetings are required.

**Finding a Muslim to Meet:** You may be wondering where to find a Muslim to talk to and how to begin. Here are some suggestions. Often, Muslims whom you have not yet recognized are all around you. What about the family with the different speech who runs the store where you buy gasoline or coffee? If you are on a university campus, listen for accents or look for different patterns of dress (for instance, women who wear head coverings). Ask an English as a Second Language (ESL) teacher whether there are Muslim students who are looking for conversation partners, or call the office of a local Muslim fellowship or mosque and explain your assignment. Wherever you are, pause to observe the people close at hand for clues to the many contacts with Muslims you may already have. Most importantly, ask God to guide you to that Muslim with whom you can build a friendship, and then watch for the person he will send your way.

**How to Begin:** Start your conversation with a Muslim just as you would with any person you just met. Be conscious of the fact that he or she may be tired of being singled out because of a distinctive accent or form of dress. If you are rejected, do not take it personally. Also, be aware of the person's responsibilities; if there is a long line of customers the person must wait on, hang around until after he has served

them before you begin a conversation. If your intended friend is hurrying off to class, do not try to engage him or her in a meeting then; set an appointment. Some examples of conversation openers are:

> Excuse me, but what language were you just speaking with your friend?

> I hear you speak with a slight accent. Do you mind if I ask where you are from?

> Excuse me, but I see that you are wearing a head covering. Are you a Muslim?

Then explain the reason for your inquiry and ask for the assistance you want:

> I am interested in Islam. If fact, I'm taking a course about Islam, and one of our assignments is to talk with a Muslim to find out more about Islamic culture and beliefs. Could we get together sometime to talk? I would really appreciate your help.

If the person agrees, set a time and place to meet. Be sure to exchange phone numbers, or find another way of contacting each other if the person does not show up for the first appointment. He or she may be skeptical about your sincerity and intentions, or might misunderstand the agreement you have made. Call to confirm your appointment. Please do your best not to make the person feel like a "project" whom you have only "targeted" to get what you want. Muslims are very friendly and hospitable people. By showing them respect, you will already have begun to reduce their concerns.

**Women with Women, Men with Men:** Because roles are clearly defined in Islam, choose a Muslim of your same gender whenever possible. If you are a man and make the acquaintance of a Muslim woman, ask her if she has a brother or male friend who would be willing to talk with you. If you are a woman, inquire whether the man you have met has a female relative or friend you could contact.

Other important resources are non-Muslim international students and immigrants you may meet, because internationals often know other internationals from their own countries and from others. Do not be embarrassed if you ask someone if he is a Muslim and he is not. Simply apologize, explain why you asked, and request an introduction to anyone he might know who is a Muslim.

**Following Up with Your Muslim Friend:** Your relationship with your Muslim aquaintance will not always continue past the end of this course, but if it does, you will eventually have an occasion to talk with your Muslim friend about your faith. After getting together a few times, your friend may begin to ask questions about you and your beliefs. Be open in your answers but not pushy. You should probably not invite them to church right away, even if they want to come, because many of the cultural practices of Christians may be offensive to them, unless they have been prepared ahead of time.

A home Bible study or dinner with Christian friends is a better first step. Expose your Muslim friend to Christian community, fellowship, and love rather than to doctrine or teaching in a potentially uncomfortable format. Your relationship with your friend may not continue long enough or go deep enough to share the whole gospel with them. God may be using the temporary connection just to help you grow, or, through your friendship, a seed may be planted that later is watered and harvested by others.

We recognize that this assignment may feel threatening. We encourage you to be courageous. Students from previous courses who befriended Muslims have had positive experiences. You decided to take this course or buy this book to learn about Muslims. Maybe you hope to learn more to be able to pray for them, or because someone special to you works with Muslims or is a Muslim. Maybe you intend to live among Muslims in the future. At some point, you will need the experience and insight of actually sitting down with another person who happens to be a Muslim. Why not now?

## A Field Trip to a Mosque

Just as we would be remiss if we only studied about Muslims without actually meeting them, our understanding of Muslims would be incomplete without witnessing their primary expression of spirituality: ritual prayers together with the Muslim community at the mosque. Another assignment in *Encountering the World of Islam* course is to visit a mosque or Islamic community center and observe Islamic prayers firsthand. Following this field trip, your coordinator may require you to post your reaction to this experience in an additional on-line journal or discussion forum posting.

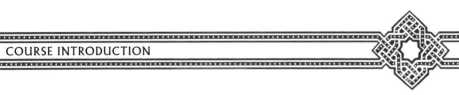
The primary purpose of the field trip is for you to observe, listen, and learn from the worship and conversation with Muslims at the mosque. Be extremely sensitive to their views, opinions, beliefs, and cultures, because, initially, they may be suspicious that you only want to argue with them. The reading in your textbook by C. R. Marsh, *Sharing Our Faith with Muslims* (found on page 302), may be helpful to you as you prepare to visit the mosque.

Do not focus your questions on the differences between Christianity and Islam, or debate or argue with the worshipers or their leaders. If they become dogmatic on something you disagree with, just listen. If you have a chance to pose questions, ask what it is like to be a Muslim, how they practice Islam, and what Islam means to them. The field trip may present an opportunity to make an appointment for your assignment on meeting with a Muslim.

Be careful to guard your behavior during the field trip. Watch what the Muslims do and follow their instructions. If you make a mistake or cause an offense, apologize quickly. Do not try to justify your behavior; just humbly ask what you should have done instead. Be especially alert to remove your shoes at the proper place before entering the mosque's prayer room. Both men and women should dress conservatively in loose-fitting clothing. Women should not wear short skirts, sleeveless dresses, or any otherwise revealing clothing; women will also need to completely cover their hair. Men and women may be required to sit apart from each other in the mosque. Everyone should be quiet and respectful while inside the prayer room. If someone requests that you wash before entering or sit in a particular place, do so without objection. However, you may also ask for instructions, and you do not have to participate in rituals. Your purpose is to respectfully observe. Islam's holy book, the Qur'an, must be treated with respect, and not written in or placed lower than your waist.

If you are invited for a meal after prayers, it is impolite not to accept. Eat and drink at least some of what is offered, even if you are not hungry. If you are sick or allergic to something, explain this, but clearly express your thanks. During the meal, talk quietly with those gathered, being careful not to interrupt or monopolize the conversation. Do not talk only to other classmates, but focus on speaking with those who invited you. Ask questions rather than making statements. Continue to observe and follow your Muslim hosts' leading during the meal and in the conversation that may follow. In particular, if the Muslim men sit in a certain place, then the men from your class should sit among them and talk with them. The same is true for the women.

If the Muslims offer you gifts, accept them with thanks. If they offer materials for sale, you may purchase them if you wish but are not obligated to do so. As you leave the mosque, be sure to express your gratitude personally to your hosts for their hospitality, and their willingness to explain their beliefs, and to include you in their worship.

## FINAL EXAM

In completing the *Encountering the World of Islam* course, different types of students

may be required to complete different kinds of final exams. At a minimum, all students seeking a Caleb Project certificate of completion must submit an oral report to their class during the Lesson 11 class period ("Our Response to Islam"), or to their coordinator. Students seeking academic credit may be assigned a formal final exam, a paper, or both depending on their syllabus requirements. Specific guidelines for oral reports and papers are given below.

### Oral Report

Either as a brief report to the class or in a meeting with the course coordinator, discuss how your course learning and experiences will be integrated into your values, attitudes, and behavior. Discuss how you plan to incorporate your new knowledge and insights into your world-view and lifestyle.

If meeting with the course coordinator, the format will be an informal discussion. The coordinator will discuss your journal and meetings with your Muslim friend, as well as your reactions to the field trips, readings, class lectures, and quizzes. Be prepared to give an evaluation of your personal growth over the span of the course. Preparation for this assignment is important. As is the case with a written exam, your grade will reflect your level of completion of the stated objectives of this assignment:

1. In anticipation of your appointment with the coordinator, review how your personal values, beliefs about Muslims, and attitudes and behavior toward them have changed as a result of the course. List any questions you have for the coordinator. He or she can advise you of other ways to integrate or apply what you have learned about Islam.

2. Formulate and be ready to explain the personal plan you will use (or could use) to communicate the gospel to a Muslim friend. This proposal should include practical examples of how you will use your spiritual gifts, talents, and prayer life to share the gospel in the Muslim world.

### Final Paper

If you are taking this course for credit, it is likely that you will be required to write a paper. You may also be asked to give a brief oral synopsis to your class or to have a longer oral discussion of your paper with the course coordinator. If not otherwise assigned in your syllabus, your assignment will be to write a ten- to fifteen-page ministry plan.

This paper should be a demonstration of your achievement of the objectives of the course and a description of your personal ministry plan for communicating the gospel to a Muslim. In the paper, review how your personal values, beliefs about Muslims, and attitudes and behavior toward them have changed as a result of the course. Include practical examples of how you will (or could) use your spiritual gifts, talents, and prayer life to communicate the gospel in the Muslim world.

After submitting your paper, make an appointment to defend it in an informal discussion with the course coordinator. Be prepared to give an evaluation of your personal growth during the course, and how you plan to integrate your new

knowledge and insights into your world-view and lifestyle.

As in the case of a written exam, the grade you earn will reflect the level of your preparation and completion of the assignment objectives. During the discussion, the course coordinator may also discuss your journal entries and meetings with your Muslim friend, as well as your reactions to the field trips, readings, class lectures, and quizzes. Prior to your appointment, list any questions you have for the coordinator. He or she can advise you of other ways to integrate or apply what you have learned about Islam.

## COURSE CONTINUATION PROJECTS

In order to facilitate continued learning, integration, and personal involvement after the course, we encourage structured follow-up experiences. These could include:

1. A personal prayer plan (refer to Lesson 12).
2. Continued friendships with Muslims.
3. Taking a trip to a Muslim country, with emphasis on relationship building and language learning, possibly living with a Muslim family.
4. An internship in some type of outreach to Muslims.

## COURSE EVALUATION

The *Encountering the World of Islam* course is always being refined. We request and greatly appreciate your comments and suggestions about how to improve the content, emphasis, lectures, readings, and assignments. We believe that all criticism, even when negative, can be used constructively to produce better learning. If you find a more applicable reading or a good instructor, please let us know. And if you do not prefer something we have used, we need to hear your opinion. Let us know. You can e-mail us at *info@encounteringislam.org.*

## BIBLICAL AND QUR'ANIC QUOTATIONS

Throughout the book we have endeavored to properly cite which translations of the Bible or the Qur'an are quoted by using abbreviations in SMALL CAPS following each reference. Where an author has relied on a particular translation throughout an article, we have noted this information at the bottom of the first page of the article, below the bibliographic citation. In some cases, we have been unable to determine which translation the author used (TRANS. UNKNOWN). A key for other abbreviations is found below.

**Bible Translations:** All quotations are from the New International Version (NIV) unless otherwise noted.

> CEV – *Contemporary English Version*
> GNB – *Good News Bible*
> KJV – *King James Version*
> MESSAGE – *The Message*
> NASB – *New American Standard Bible*
> NIV – *New International Version*
> NKJV – *New King James Version*
> NRSV – *New Revised Standard Version*
> RSV – *Revised Standard Version*
> WEYMOUTH – *The New Testament in Modern Speech*

**Qur'an Translations:** Most quotations are from Pickthall, Shakir, or Yusuf Ali. Others are noted. Qur'an versification is not standardized. If the quote referenced does not match when reviewed in a Qur'an tranlation, refer to the adjacent verses to find the reference.

AHMAD ALI – *Koran*, translated by Mir Ahmad Ali

MAULANA – *The Holy Qur'an*, translated by Maulana Muhammad Ali

PICKTHALL – *The Meaning of the Glorious Qur'an*, translated by Mohammed Marmaduke Pickthall

RODWELL – *The Koran*, translated by John Medows Rodwell

SHAKIR – *The Qur'an: Translation*, translated by Mohammedali H. Shakir

YUSUF ALI – *The Meaning of the Holy Qur'an*, translated by Abdullah Yusuf Ali

TRANS. UNKNOWN – The author did not cite which translation he or she quoted.

## NAVIGATION ICONS

Icons are used throughout the book to guide your learning. Some icons refer to reading levels, and guide where to stop reading in each lesson and where to go next. Other icons identify Lesson Highlight topics. A key to all icons is below.

### Reading Icons

 This icon identifies the **Key Readings**, which are highly recommended for all students.

 This icon identifies the **Basic Readings**. The Basic Readings add depth to the Key Readings and are recommended for all students.

 This icon identifies the **Full Readings**, which are not found in the book but are available through the companion web site, *www.encounteringislam.org/readings*. These readings may not be assigned to all students but are available free of charge.

### Highlight Icons

 These brief Highlights identify and discuss important biblical or cultural **Concepts** the student should know.

 These Highlights identify and discuss appropriate ways for **Outreach** to Muslims.

 These are brief overviews of the major Muslim affinity blocks and describe those ethnic groups which are examples illustrating characteristics of the **People Groups** found in each block.

 These are brief **Quotations** that illustrate important lesson points.

 These Highlights explore important verses and concepts from the **Qur'an**.

 These **Stories** give us a window into the lives of Muslims and Muslim-background believers.

These Highlights discuss issues that apply specifically to Muslim **Women**.

## USING THE GLOSSARY

Italics are used throughout the book to denote the first time a glossary word appears in the book. Please refer to the Glossary for definitions of these terms. Also see the Common Word List on page xli. Common Words are not italicized. If you come across an unfamiliar word or concept, check: it is probably in the Glossary. Terms and concepts are thoroughly cross-referenced to assist you.

# ARABIC PRONUNCIATION GUIDE

In this course we have used this simplified guide for pronouncing Arabic terms. Pronunciation advice is found in parentheses after the English transliteration of each word, along with its definition, in the Glossary. Make an effort to learn how to pronounce common words[1] used in this course.

## VOWELS:

- short *a* as in car –> **ah** (kahr)
- short *a* as in ran –> **a** (ran)
- long *a* as in bake –> **ay** (bayk)

- long *e* as in bee –> **ee** (bee)
- short *e* as in get –> **eh** (geht)

- short *i* as in hit –> **ih** (hiht)
- long *i* as in like –> **ie** (liek)
- long *i* at beginning of word/name –> **I**

- short *o* as in on –> **ah** (ahn)
- long *o* as in go –> **oh** (goh)

- short *u* as in but –> **uh** (buht)
- *oo* as in rupee –> **oo** (roo-pee)
- long *u* as in butte –> **yoo** (byoot)
- *er, ir,* or *ur* as in skirt –> **uhr** (skuhrt)
- *ow* as in cow –> **ahw** (cahw)

## CONSONANTS:

- The "**q**" is like the *c* in "cough," made further in the back of throat (a darker quality).
- The "**kh**" is pronounced as the Scottish "ch" in "Loch Ness monster," further back in the throat.
- The "**gh**" sounds like the Arabic ayn ('), but with a hard *g* sound with a constriction at the back of the throat. For example, "ghazi" (**ghah**-zee).
- All other consonants are pronounced as in English.

## DIACRITICS:

- The *ayn* (') is a constriction at the back of the throat as in Ka'aba.
- The *hamza* (') signifies a glottal stop or catch, as found in Scottish English, replacing the *t*, as in "bi'er" (for "bitter"), or "Sco'ish" (for "Scottish").
- The *alif* ('), an exception to the hamza; the alif extends a sound, as in "Qur'an" (kohr-**aahn**).

---

1. See page xli for the Common Word List.

# COMMON WORD LIST

**Abu Bakr** (ah-boo **bah**-kuhr) – first male convert, Muhammad's sponsor; first Caliph

**Aisha** (ah-**ee**-shah) – Muhammad's favorite wife (third)

**Ali** (ah-**lee**) – Muhammad's cousin, successor (Shi'a)

**Allah** (**ahl**-lah) – *God* (Arabic)

**Allahu Akbar** (ah-**lah**-hoo **ahk**-bahr) – *"Allah is the Most Great"*

**amulet** – charm, talisman

**animism** – belief that creation is alive with spirits, worship of spirits

**Arabia** – Southwestern Asian peninsula

**Arabic** – Semitic language; language of Qur'an

**Arabs** – native speakers of Arabic

**aya** – verse of a Sura in the Qur'an

**Ayatollah** (ah-yah-**tohl**-lah) – *sign of Allah*, honorific title for a high-ranking Shi'a legal scholar

**Bedouin** – nomadic desert Arabs

**Believers** – monotheists; believers in Allah

**Bismillah** (bihs-mihl-**lah**) – *"In the name of Allah;"* invocation of Allah

**Byzantine Empire** – Eastern late Roman Empire

**Byzantium** – ancient Greek city (Istanbul)

**Cairo** – capital of Egypt; Islamic center

**caliph** (khah-**lihf**) – former political, spiritual Islamic ruler

**Caliphate** (khah-**lihf**-ate) – Muslim state headed by a caliph

**charismatic** – personal religious experience emphasizing the supernatural gifts

**Christendom** – Christianity as geographical entity

**Constantinople** – former name of Istanbul

**contextualization** – process of biblical, culturally appropriate, indigenous witness

**Creed** – *witness*; Shahada, first Pillar

**Crusades** – Christian campaigns to reconquer Holy Land, Jerusalem (1200s–1300s)

**Dar al-Harb** (dahr ahl-**hahrb**) – territory outside Islamic supremacy (at war)

**Dar al-Islam** (dahr ahl-**ihs**-lahm) – territory of Muslim supremacy (peace)

**da'wa** (dah-**ah**-wah) – *invitation*; calling all people to the path of Allah

**dhimmi** (**thihm**-mah) – protected subjects, usually Jews and Christians

**du'a** (**dah**-ah-wah) – *to call*; supplication, informal prayer

**evil eye** – envious glance bringing evil

**al-Fatihah** (ahl-**fah-tee**-hah) – opening Sura (Qur'an), repeated in salat

**Fatima** (fah-**tee**-mah) – Muhammad's and Khadija's daughter

**fatwa** (**faht**-wah) – religious edict

**folk Islam** – popular Islam

**Gabriel** – archangel Allah sent to reveal Qur'an to Muhammad

**gospel** – Jesus' message; Injil

**hadith, Hadith** (hah-**deeth**) – *traditions*; collection of literature which interprets Islam; sayings of the Prophet

**Hagar** – Ishmael's mother

**Hajj** (**hahj**) – pilgrimage (to Mecca); fifth Pillar

**halal** (hah-**lahl**) – *permitted*, lawful

**hanif** (hah-**neef**) – pre-Islamic Arab monotheist

**haram** (hah-**rahm**) – *forbidden*, unlawful

**Hasan** (hahs-**sahn**) – Ali's son, Muhammad's grandson

**Hegira** (**hihj**-rah) – Hijra

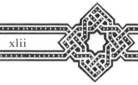
**Hijra** (**hihj**-rah) – Muslim emigration (Mecca to Yathrib [Medina])

**Holy Black Stone** – sacred stone in wall of Ka'aba

**Holy City, The** – Mecca

**Holy House** – Ka'aba (**kah**-ah-bah)

**Husayn, Husain, Hussein** (hoo-**sayn**) – Ali's son, Muhammad's grandson; mourned by Shi'a

**Id al-Adha, Eid al-Adha** (eed ahl-**ahd**-hah) – Feast of Sacrifice, end of Hajj

**Id al-Fitr, Eid al-Fitr** (eed ahl-**fooh**-tihr) – Feast of Breaking the Fast, end of Ramadan

**ijma** (**ahj**-mah) – consensus of legal scholars

**imam** (ee-**mahm**) – spiritual leader, professional cleric

**Imam** (ee-**mahm**) – prominent jurist (Sunni); divinely appointed successor (Shi'i)

**infidel** – non-believer, polytheist, idol worshiper

**Injil** (ihn-**jeel**) – original, uncorrupted Gospel; present-day New Testament

**Isa** (**ee**-sah) – Jesus (Arabic)

**Ishmael** – father of Arabs, Abraham's son

**Islam** (**ihs**-lahm) – *submission*; monotheistic Muslim faith

**Islamist** – radicial Islamic political or social activist

**jihad** (**jee**-hahd) – *struggle*; internal for holiness, external to extend umma, popular media term for holy war

**jinn** (**jihn**) – species of spirits, both evil and helpful

**Ka'aba** (**kah**-ah-bah) – Holy House in Mecca, holds Holy Black Stone, center of Islam

**kafir** (**kah**-fihr) — *ungrateful, unbeliever, infidel*

**Khadija** (khah-**dih**-jah) – Muhammad's first wife

**madrasah** (mahd-**rah**-sah) – Islamic school

**Mahdi** (**mah**-dee) — *the rightly guided one*; the coming Imam, a Messiah-like world leader who will return

**man of peace** – community leader who welcomes Christian witness (Luke 10:5–9)

**masjid** (**mahs**-jihd) – *mosque* (Arabic)

**MBB** – Muslim-background believer

**Mecca** – Islam's holiest city; place of the Ka'aba

**Medina** (mah-**dee**-nah) – Islam's second holiest city

**Messenger of God, The** – Muhammad

**Middle East** – Southwest Asia

**minaret** – tower of mosque for call to prayer

**Monophysite** (mon-**nof**-ih-site) – believed doctrine of Christ's inseparable nature, human-divine

**mosque** (**mahsq**) – Muslim house of worship, prayer

**Muhammad** (moo-**hahm**-mahd) – last Prophet and founder of Islam (570–632)

**mujahid, mujahideen** (moo-**jah**-hihd, moo-**jah**-hah-deen) – holy war fighter(s)

**mullah** (**moo**-lah) – Muslim religious leader or cleric

**Muslim** (**moos**-lihm) – one who submits; follower of Islam

**Nestorian** – believed doctrine that Christ had two distinct natures: one divine, one human

**Ottoman** – Turkish Empire (c. 1300–1922)

**Paradise** – reward after death; heaven

**People of the Book** – Jews and Christians (Qur'an)

**Persia** – remnants of ancient empire in Southwest Asia

**Pillars of Faith** – the five religious duties of Muslims

**pir** (**peer**) – *elder, wise person*; saint, spiritual guide (Sufi)

**popular Islam** – common Muslim practices, addressing problems of fear, powers and spiritual beings

**power encounter** – confrontation of evil powers, through prayer

**prophet** – a warner, divinely inspired

**Prophet, The** – Muhammad, God's Messenger

**Qur'an** (Koran) (**kohr**-aahn) – sacred scriptures of Islam (in Arabic)

**Quraysh** (koor-ray-**ihsh**) – dominant, Arab Meccan tribe (Muhammad's)

**rakat** (sing., **rakah**, **raka**) (rah-**kat**, **roo**-koo-uh) – *set* of ritual prayers

**Ramadan** (**rah**-mah-dahn) – sacred month of the fast

**rasul** (rah-**sool**) — *apostle*; messenger; a prophet; title of Muhammad

**salaam** (sah-**lahm**) — *peace*; a greeting of peace

**salat** (sah-**laht**) – five required, daily, ritual prayer times; second Pillar

**saum** (**suh**-woom) – *the fasting*, third Pillar, especially during Ramadan, cf. p. 526

**Shahada** (shah-**hah**-deh) – Creed, *witness*; first Pillar

**Shari'a, Shari'ah** (shah-**ree**-ah) – ideal Islamic law; God's will expressed in the Qur'an, the Hadith, and the Sunna

**sheik, sheikh, shaykh** (**shaykh**) – *chief*; leader of tribe, religious order

**Shi'i** (plur., **Shi'a**) (**shee**-ee) – minority (15 percent) branch of Islam, followers of Ali

**shirk** (**shuhrk**) – *association* of partners with Allah; considered polytheism

**Sind** – region of Pakistan; a river

**Sufi, Sufism** (**soo**-fee) – Islamic mysticism; seeking awareness of God's presence, relationship to him

**Sunna** (**soon**-nah) – established, normative precedent; based on Muhammad's example, from Hadith

**Sunni** (plur., **Sunnis**) (soon-**nee**) – largest (85 percent) branch of Islam; derived from Sunna

**Sura (Surah)** (soo-**rah**) – chapter of Qur'an

**ta ethne** (**tah** ehth-nay)– *all the nations, people groups* (Greek)

**tawhid** (**tahw**-heed) — term used to express the unity of Allah, the only God

**Traditions** – Hadith

**truth encounter** – confrontation of unbelief with the Bible

**Ulama** (oo-**lah**-mah) – group of Muslim scholars trained in Islamic law

**Umar** (**oo**-mahr) – Muhammad's father-in-law; later, second Caliph

**umma, ummah** (**oom**-mah) – Muslim *community*; the unified, equal people of Islam

**Uthman** (**ohth**-mahn) – Muhammad's cousin, third Caliph

**Wahhabi** (plur., **Wahabiyin**) (wah-**hah**-bee, wah-**hah**-bee-yeen) – conservative branch of Sunni Islam

**worldview** – system of values; one's view of the reality

**Yathrib** (**yehth**-rihb) – destination of emigration (hijra); renamed Medina

**Zaid** (**zah**-eed) – Muhammad's adopted son

**zakat** (**zah**-kaht) – statutory alms tax (for needy); fourth Pillar

# THE DEVELOPMENT
# OF ISLAM

# LESSON 1
# THE FOUNDING OF ISLAM

## PONDER THIS

- What influenced Muhammad to develop into the leader he became?

- What can we appreciate about Muhammad?

- How did the direction of Muhammad's life differ from the course chosen by Christ?

- What should be our Christian attitude toward Muhammad?

# LESSON OBJECTIVE

Describe the founding of Islam and the life of Muhammad. Include:

1. The historical, cultural, and religious setting in Arabia prior to Islam.

2. Muhammad's decision to flee from suffering in Mecca and to pursue success through politics in Medina; in contrast to the course Christ chose, leading to the cross.

3. The growth of Islam from Muhammad's first revelation through the political takeover of Mecca and the death of Muhammad.

4. Muhammad's rejection of the biblical traditions of Judaism and Christianity through confronting the Jews in Medina, changing the direction of prayer, subjugating Mecca, and transitioning the Islamic movement into an Arab religion.

5. Islam's early interactions with Judaism and Christianity, including the lack of a Bible in Arabic at the time of Muhammad.

# LESSON READINGS

# INTRODUCTION

Universally, as fallen creatures, we come equipped with our own cultural grids—sets of biases or lenses through which we view the world. We use these lenses to edit, interpret, and evaluate what we experience. Usually, we are unaware of our own cultural lenses, unless we encounter someone with a different set.

Turkish woman and child

© Caleb Project

To understand Islam, we need to look at the world through a different lens. This will give us a greater understanding and appreciation, even empathy, for Muslims and their world. Points on which we were previously uninformed will be corrected, and our own grid of interpretation will expand. Does this mean we will agree with or accept all that we see? No, for that is not our goal.

*Encountering the World of Islam* is designed not only to develop our interpretation of and respect for Muslim points of view, but also to prepare us for deep and lasting relationships with Muslims. While many things about Muslims and Islam may give us pause, our focus on rapport and relationships emphasizes listening and learning.

## MUHAMMAD'S FIRST REVELATION

Let us begin by looking at Muhammad's first revelation, the experience that gave birth to Islam. One of his wives describes it clearly in the collection of traditions about Muhammad known as the Hadith:

> The commencement of the Divine Inspiration to *Allah's Apostle* was in the form of good dreams that came true like bright daylight; and then the love of seclusion was bestowed upon him. He used to go in seclusion in the cave of *Hira* where he used to worship (Allah alone) continuously for many days before his desire to see his family. He used to take with him the journey food for the stay, and then come back to (his wife) Khadija to take his food

likewise again, till suddenly the Truth descended upon him while he was in the cave of Hira. The angel came to him and asked him to read. The Prophet replied, "I do not know how to read."

The Prophet added, "The angel caught me (forcefully) and pressed me so hard that I could not bear it any more. He then released me and again asked me to read, and I replied, 'I do not know how to read.' Thereupon he caught me again and pressed me a second time, till I could not bear it any more. He then released me and again asked me to read but again I replied, 'I do not know how to read (or what shall I read)?' Thereupon he caught me for the third time and pressed me, and then released me and said, 'Proclaim! (or Read!). In the name of thy Lord and Cherisher, who has created; created man, out of a (mere) clot of congealed blood: Proclaim! And thy Lord is most bountiful'" (Sura 96:1–3, YUSUF ALI). Then Allah's Apostle returned with the Inspiration and with his heart beating severely. Then he went to Khadija and said, "Cover me! Cover me!" They covered him till his fear was over, and after that he told her everything that had happened and said, "I fear that something may happen to me." Khadija replied, "Never! By Allah, Allah will never disgrace you. You keep good relations with your kith and kin, help the poor and the destitute, serve your guests generously, and assist the deserving, calamity-afflicted ones."

Khadija then accompanied him to her cousin Waraqa bin Naufal bin Asad bin Abdul Uzza, who, during the pre-Islamic period, became a Christian, and used to write the writing with Hebrew letters. He would write from the gospel in Hebrew as much as Allah wished him to write. He was an old man and had lost his eyesight. Khadija said to Waraqa, "Listen to the story of your nephew, O my cousin!" Waraqa asked, "O my nephew! What have you seen?" Allah's Apostle described whatever he had seen. Waraqa said, "This is the same one who keeps the secrets (angel Gabriel) whom Allah had sent to *Moses*. I wish I were young and could live up to the time when your people would turn you out." Allah's Apostle asked, "Will they drive me out?" Waraqa replied in the affirmative and said, "Anyone who came with something similar to what you have brought was treated with hostility; and if I should remain alive till the day when you will be turned out, then I would support you strongly." But after a few days Waraqa died, and the Divine Inspiration was also paused for a while.[1]

Something extraordinary seems to have happened to Muhammad in the cave of Mount Hira, near Mecca, something that profoundly changed the direction of his life. Biblical figures had similar experiences. Jacob wrestled for a whole night with the spiritual being he faced in Genesis 32, and Samuel needed Eli's encouragement to listen to the voice of God in 1 Samuel 3. Most angelic visitations recorded in the Bible begin with the angel saying, "Do not be afraid." In this passage, Muhammad was clearly shaken, yet this story includes no such injunction against fear.

## "WHAT DO YOU THINK OF THE PROPHET MUHAMMAD?"

Muslim friends often ask this question, as a test, near the beginning of our friendships. How we answer often affects the direction of our relationships. Muhammad has been accused of being mentally ill, an epileptic, and even demon-possessed. He has been viewed negatively for his behavior toward women and Jews. Yet he is the founder of one of the largest, most enduring, and most powerful movements in history. The honest person, when composing a list of the most influential people in history, would need to include Muhammad. But what do we know about the Prophet of Islam and what shaped him?

As we understand the circumstances in which Islam was born and developed, we will be able to articulate a deeper and fairer understanding of Muhammad. We will need to recognize the weaknesses and failures of Christians and the church at that time. Also, we will explore the shift in early Islam from a reform movement, through its growth and persecution in Mecca, to its creation of a new, distinct society in Medina.

A poor orphan himself, Muhammad became a trustworthy negotiator of disputes and a successful merchant. Later he grew into a religious and social reformer and capable political leader. Muhammad called people to worship the One True God, the Creator of the universe. He stood against idolatry, the mistreatment of the poor, orphans, and widows, and

the usury practiced by the rich. He called on people to submit to God, and to be grateful to God for his provision, lest they suffer God's coming judgment. For these stands he and his followers were brutally persecuted by their own people.

## FROM MECCA TO MEDINA

After twelve years of persecution, Muhammad and his small group of followers fled to Yathrib, which later became known as Medina, and a major shift in the development of Islam took place. Muhammad came to see persecution and suffering as abhorrent, the pursuit of success as his path, and that success as a sign of God's blessing. Islam dates its calendar, not from the birth of Muhammad, or his death, or his first experience in the cave on Mount Hira, but from this flight to Medina. Muhammad saw Yathrib's invitation for him to settle their trible rivalries as God's deliverance from suffering. This migration initiated a new and prosperous Islamic society, including the building of the first mosque in Medina and the establishment of Muslim prayers. Today, as Muslim communities around the world are being called to prayer five times each day, the words that ring out are, "God is great! Come to prayer! Come to success!"

While the new Muslim society grew in power, Muhammad began to show signs he was being corrupted by the influence he wielded. Although he was faithful to Khadija, his first wife, until her death, he later married between nine and eleven women. Most were the widows of his early followers, whom he protected, and political marriages that brought the allegiance of Arab tribes. One was a young girl, several

were slaves, and one was the wife of his adopted son.

Initially, Muhammad sought to identify with the three tribes of Jews of Medina. After they opposed him, he exiled two tribes and killed eight hundred men of the third tribe and sold women and children into slavery (following the common practice of the time). Muhammad and his people also raided caravans and were accused of breaking treaties. We should not assume that the extension of Muhammad's control led either to all forced conversions or all changed hearts. Muhammad saught financial retribution on his enemies by raiding the caravans of the Quraysh, and he fought with Arab tribes that would not submit. This may have set patterns for the future expansion of the Islamic world and its picture of success. However, the levels of violence were nothing compared to that of the *Mongol* invasion, the Crusades, or the global wars and genocides of the twentieth century.

## IN LIGHT OF HIS TIME

What happens when we evaluate Muhammad's accomplishments by the light of the time in which he lived, rather than judging him by present-day standards? How long did it take for the modern world to abolish slavery and give women voting power and other rights? Treating people as property is a part of

## WHAT DOES THE QUR'AN SAY?

The first of the 114 suras (chapters) of the Qur'an is called al-Fatihah, which means *the opening*. In some ways it parallels the Lord's Prayer in the New Testament. "Studying the two prayers side by side ought to remove the foreignness which we feel about prayer in Islam and enable us to appreciate some of the common ground in Christian and Muslim spirituality. Thinking about Muslims at prayer may give us an opportunity to sit where they sit and to enter into something of their relationship with God."[1] Al-Fatihah is recited five times a day at salat (prayers).

Yusuf Ali's translation of al-Fatihah from Arabic reads:

> In the name of Allah, Most Gracious, Most Merciful.
> Praise be to Allah, The Cherisher and Sustainer of the Worlds;
> Most gracious, Most Merciful;
> Master of the Day of Judgment.
> Thee do we worship, And Thine aid we seek,
> Show us the straight way,
> The way of those on whom Thou hast bestowed Thy Grace, Those whose (portion) is not wrath, And who go not astray.

The words with which the Sura begins are the most frequently repeated passage in the whole Qur'an. The first line, called the Bismillah, is said on all kinds of occasions, for instance, to ward off curses, bless a child, before eating, or when starting anything new.

1. Colin Chapman, "Biblical Foundations of Praying for Muslims," in Dudley Woodberry, ed., *Muslims and Christians on the Emmaus Road* (Monrovia, Calif.: Missions Advanced Research and Communications Center, 1989), p. 306.

Source: *Encountering the World of Islam*

## Al-Fatihah–The Opening Sura of the Qur'an

© Caleb Project

history most of our *cultures* share. The Muslim world is not unique. How many of Solomon's wives were young slave girls? How old was Mary when she was married to Joseph? How many of our Judeo-Christian leaders like David and Gideon were corrupted and suffered the outworking of their own unfaithfulness and depravity? If we measure Abraham standing before Pharaoh or Joshua facing his battles, what do we learn about them and their times? What about the failures of our spiritual leaders today? And how about us? How do we find ourselves react-

ing to those who oppose us? If we want to find an example of one who was tempted but did not sin, only the life of Christ can be our model.

Human nature leads Christians to focus on Muhammad's human failures and emphasize his weaknesses without recognizing his strengths. Can we identify Muhammad as a progressive reformer who dedicated himself to preaching against idolatry and the mistreatment of women and orphans? A leader who unified a feudal, tribal society into a com-

munity governed by law? A fellow human being and sinner?

## INTERACTION WITH JEWS AND CHRISTIANS

As a seeker of truth, how is it that Muhammad failed to see Christ displayed in the Christians of his time? They seem to have been divided, focused more on political control of their human empires than on sharing Christ with the people around them. The few bright spots of Christian mission in the seventh century—Nestorians taking the gospel into India and China, and the Celts taking Christ to the Germanic peoples—were far from Arabia. What might have happened if the Christians of Muhammad's time and region were less racist and self-centered? What if they had helped expand his knowledge of God's truth? These theoretical questions have implications for us today: Do Christians bear responsibility for what people around them think of God? To what extent are our interactions with others a negative witness instead of a positive one?

At the time Islam began, Arabia lacked a biblical witness. Muhammad and the Arab peoples lacked the Bible in their language. The few Jews and Christians in the region followed heretical practices and were therefore unable to demonstrate biblical solutions to the societal ills Muhammad sought to correct. The Bible would not be translated into Arabic until A.D. 837, and then not published (beyond a few scholarly manuscripts) until 1516. For the last fourteen centuries, few Christians have reached out to Muslims. Even today, although one-third of all non-Christians are Muslims, perhaps one in twelve missionaries works among them.

Muhammad seems to have expected that the Jews around him would affirm his message. When they did not, Islam increasingly departed from the Judeo-Christian traditions. Then a revelation instructed him to pray facing Mecca instead of *Jerusalem*, and to institute the fast of Ramadan in place of the *Day of Atonement*. The *pilgrimage* to Mecca was adopted to unite the Arab tribes under Islam as they returned to Mecca each year for the Hajj.

*– K.S., Editor*

1. From Sahih Bukhari, *The Collection of Hadith*, narrated by Aisha; trans. M. Muhsin Khan; vol. 1, bk. 1, no. 3. Aisha was Muhammad's favorite wife in his old age.

# HOW ISLAM BEGAN

*by William M. Miller*

 **EDITOR'S NOTE**

As we study the following article, we should ask ourselves, "How could we have a more balanced approach toward the founder of Islam, as well as our own Christian history?" I believe that the difference between Muslims and Christians lies not in our behavior but who we view as our Savior. Moreover, considering ourselves better than others is arrogant, and a biblically illegitimate position from which to witness for Christ.

Dr. Miller was my mentor. I experienced the great blessing of sitting under his teaching and seeing his loving heart for Muslims during the last years of his earthly life. A faithful man of prayer, he kept huge trays of index cards recording the names of Muslims he met, and he continued to pray for each of them for decades. His focus and gentle confidence in the grace of Christ, while choosing not to resort to undue criticism of Islam, impresses me even today. In particular, I remember him at more than ninety-five years of age reciting Hebrews 12:1–3 from memory:

> Therefore, since we are surrounded by such a great cloud of witnesses, let us throw off everything that hinders and the sin that so easily entangles, and let us run with perseverance the race marked out for us. Let us fix our eyes on Jesus, the author and perfecter of our faith, who for the joy set before him endured the cross, scorning its shame, and sat down at the right hand of the throne of God. Consider him who endured such opposition from sinful men, so that you will not grow weary and lose heart.

It is essential that those Christians who would like to tell their Muslim friends and acquaintances about Christ—as well as those who desire to pray intelligently for Muslims, and for those who by word and deed are making Christ known to them—should understand clearly who Muhammad was and what he taught. Though many excellent books have been written by Christian scholars about the history and teachings of Islam, it seems that some Christians have vague ideas about how this religio-political system began and on what doctrines and practices it was established. In this article, the most interesting story of the Prophet of Arabia will be told briefly, as it was related by the early Muslim historians. A sincere effort will be made to "speak the truth in love" (Eph. 4:15). However, it is not possible to tell the story of Muhammad's life with complete historical accuracy, for the sources available consist largely of traditions, some of which originated long after the death of Muhammad. The source that is most reliable is the Qur'an. The facts stated in the following pages are

William M. Miller was a missionary of the Presbyterian church to Iran from 1919 to 1962. He died in 1995 at the age 101, one of the last missionaries of the Student Volunteer Movement.

Adapted from William M. Miller, *A Christian's Response to Islam* (Phillipsburg, N.J.: Presbyterian and Reformed, 1980), pp. 13–40. Used by permission. *www.prpbooks.com*

those on which most of the Muslim and non-Muslim writers agree.

## ARABIA IN MUHAMMAD'S TIME

In the providence of God a baby boy was born in Mecca, in the western part of Arabia, about the year A.D. 570, to whom the name Muhammad (*praised*) was given. Little did those who named the child realize that he was destined to influence the world as few other individuals have, and would indeed be praised by untold millions of people for centuries to come.

Arabia is a vast land, much of which is desert. In the desert regions the Bedouin nomads moved about with their flocks and herds, living in their black tents. There were also cities in which rich merchants carried on their trade, the chief of which was Mecca. Through Mecca passed the camel caravans carrying merchandise between *Yemen* in the south and *Syria* in the north. Mecca was both an important commercial center and a shrine city. In it, from ancient times, had been located the Ka'aba (*cube*), a cubical building which was known as the House of Allah. There was a tradition that when this Holy House was destroyed by a flood, Abraham (*Ibrahim*) and his son Ishmael (*Ismail*) rebuilt it. In the Arabic language Allah means *The God*, and it seems that the Arabs recognized him as the Supreme God. Whether they learned of him from the Jews or inherited this knowledge from their ancestor Abraham is not evident. The name of Muhammad's father was *Abd Allah*, which means *slave of Allah*.

Though the Arabs recognized Allah as supreme they did not consider him to be the only god, nor did they place importance on his worship. They worshiped a number of other deities, and at the time of Muhammad's youth, the Ka'aba was full of the images of other gods and goddesses. When the Arabs came to Mecca to trade at the annual fairs, they also performed the customary rites of the pilgrimage to the Ka'aba, walking around it seven times and kissing or touching the Holy Black Stone (*al-Hajar al-Aswad*) which was built into the wall. This was a meteorite to which great religious significance was attached. Though the Arabs were not a very religious people, the shrine at Mecca and its rituals were precious to them as an important element in their cultural heritage.

## HANIFS, JEWS, AND CHRISTIANS IN ARABIA

Not all the people of Mecca were satisfied with conditions in their country. The political situation was not good, for the many small tribes were frequently warring with one another, and, because of their lack of unity, were in danger of being swallowed up by the great empires about them—those of Persia, Byzantium, and *Ethiopia*. The popular religion did not satisfy those few individuals who wanted to know God. It is said that a small group of intelligent men known as hanifs used to meet together to discuss these political and religious problems.

Were there no people in Arabia who could tell them of the One True God? Yes, from ancient times large numbers of Jews had resided in Arabia, and a few of them were in Mecca. In Medina, which was 280 miles north of Mecca, there were three large tribes of Jews with their synagogues

and their Scriptures. They had prospered materially; they owned camels, houses, and lands, and largely controlled the commerce of the city. Their education and standard of living were higher than those of the pagan Arabs around them. The Arabs knew that the Jews did not worship idols, but were worshipers of Allah, the unseen God. But it is improbable that the Jews made known to the pagans the spiritual treasures which were in their Scriptures.

Also, there were Christians in Arabia. In the north there were several Arab tribes which had become Christian. In the south in *Nejran* were many Christians who had their bishops and priests and their Scriptures in the *Syriac* language. This Nestorian Church of the East, which had previously sent its missionaries into Arabia, had not met with great success in its efforts to convert the Arabs, most of whom had remained pagans. It seems that the Christians lacked the love, purity of life, and spiritual power needed to make them an effective missionary agency in Arabia.

## MUHAMMAD'S YOUTH

Abd Allah, the father of Muhammad, died before the birth of his son (about 570) in Mecca. *Amina*, Muhammad's mother, died when he was six years of age, and the orphaned boy was entrusted to the care of his grandfather. The old man soon died and Muhammad was taken by his uncle, *Abu Talib*, who was kind to him. Muhammad's family was a part of the very powerful tribe called the Quraysh, which was responsible for the Ka'aba. But Abu Talib, though influential, was poor, and it is said that for a time Muhammad served as a shepherd in the desert. It is also said that when he was twelve years of age he accompanied his uncle who went with a trading caravan to Syria.

## MARRIAGE

The youth became a man of ability and good character. At the age of twenty-five he was employed by a wealthy widow in Mecca named Khadija to accompany her caravan to Syria. So successful was he in this business venture that on his return, Khadija, who was forty years of age, made him an offer of marriage.

## WHO WAS MUHAMMAD?

His readiness to undergo persecution for his beliefs, the high moral character of the men who believed in him and looked up to him as leader, and the greatness of his ultimate achievement all argue his fundamental integrity. To suppose Muhammad an impostor raises more problems than it solves. Moreover, none of the great figures of history is so poorly appreciated in the West as Muhammad.

W. Montgomery Watt, *Mohammad at Mecca* (Oxford: Oxford University Press, 1953), p. 52.

## FOR FURTHER STUDY

W. Montgomery Watt, *Muhammad: Prophet and Statesman* (Chicago, Ill.: Kazi Publications, 1996). *www.kazi.org*

Muhammad agreed and his wife gave him love, wealth, and an influential position in Meccan society.

Two sons and four daughters were born to Muhammad and Khadija, and until her death twenty-five years later, he took no other wife. To their great sorrow both sons died in infancy. During these years Muhammad associated with the chief people of Mecca and became well-acquainted with the religious and political situation in his country. Khadija was a relative of one of the hanifs who had become a Christian, and it is probable that Muhammad discussed with him and the other hanifs the problems of Arabia. Muhammad knew that Jews and Christians worshiped Allah and did not worship images. Though he continued to worship at the Ka'aba, it is probable that he had begun to realize that the images in this House of Allah were not gods.

## GROWING INFLUENCE

From what we know of the history of Muhammad, it seems clear that he was a sincere seeker for God. He now had leisure and money for travel. Did it not occur to him that he could go to Nejran or Syria or Ethiopia to inquire from learned Christians what their Scriptures taught about God? It seems that Muhammad never made a serious effort to learn what was written in the Scriptures, which he knew were in the hands of Jews and Christians and which he later attested to as being true. The accounts which came to him of the contents of the Bible were evidently from people who were unable or unwilling to give him correct information. As a result, to the end of his life

Muhammad never learned what the true gospel is. Was he prevented from going to Christian teachers by what he saw of the bitter quarrels among members of the different branches of the church? Did his ethnic pride in being an Arab from Mecca make him unwilling to humble himself and go to Jews or Christians, minority peoples, for guidance? Whatever the cause may have been, it is probable that it was at this point that Muhammad missed the way to God. He failed to seek spiritual help from those qualified to show him Christ, the way to the Father.

## MUHAMMAD'S APPOINTMENT AS THE PROPHET OF ALLAH

It is said that Muhammad and other seekers for God used to go from time to time to a cave three miles from Mecca to meditate and worship. One night in the month of Ramadan, about the year 610, when Muhammad was forty years of age, he and his family were at this cave. According to tradition, the angel Gabriel (*Jibril*) came to Muhammad as he slept and commanded him to recite. The command was twice repeated, and Muhammad asked what he was to recite. The angel replied, "Recite thou in the name of the Lord, who created man from clots of blood" (Sura 96:1–2, RODWELL). When he awoke Muhammad was in great doubt as to what this experience meant. Was it from the jinn, the creatures who inspired the soothsayers, or was it from Allah? Muhammad had heard from the Jews of the prophets whom Allah had sent to the people of Israel. But no prophet had ever been sent to the Arabs. Could this be a message from Allah that he was to be a prophet and apostle to his own people? He confided in his faithful

## The Quraysh Family Tree

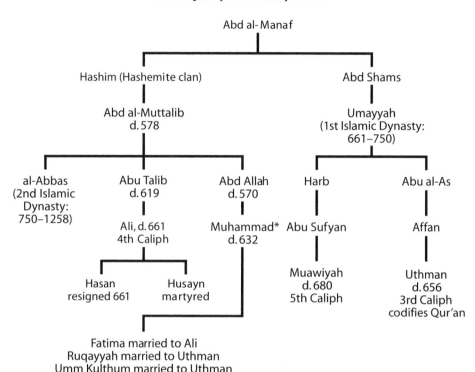

Abd al-Manaf

Hashim (Hashemite clan)

Abd Shams

Abd al-Muttalib
d. 578

Umayyah
(1st Islamic Dynasty:
661–750)

al-Abbas
(2nd Islamic
Dynasty:
750–1258)

Abu Talib
d. 619

Abd Allah
d. 570

Harb

Abu al-As

Ali, d. 661
4th Caliph

Muhammad*
d. 632

Abu Sufyan

Affan

Hasan
resigned 661

Husayn
martyred

Muawiyah
d. 680
5th Caliph

Uthman
d. 656
3rd Caliph
codifies Qur'an

Fatima married to Ali
Ruqayyah married to Uthman
Umm Kulthum married to Uthman

*Note: The first Caliph, Abu Bakr al-Siddiq's (d. 634) daughter, Aisha, and the second
Caliph, Umar Ibn al-Khattab's (d. 644) daughter, Hafsah, were both married to Muhammad.
All dates A.D.

wife, and she comforted him and assured him that this was indeed an appointment to the prophetic office. However, it seems that for some months, during which time no more revelations came to him, Muhammad was deeply depressed, and even considered suicide.

After about two years other revelations began to come in various forms. Sometimes Muhammad saw the angel Gabriel, sometimes he only heard a voice, and sometimes he heard the sound of a bell through which the words of the angel were brought to him. Sometimes the message came in a dream, and at other times it came in his thoughts. When revelation came to him, his whole frame would become agitated and perspiration would pour down his face. He would often fall to the ground and foam at the mouth. The messages always came to him in Arabic, and Muhammad spoke the words that he received, and they were written down by people who heard them from Muhammad's lips. It is generally

## Eight Affinity Groups of Muslim Peoples Today

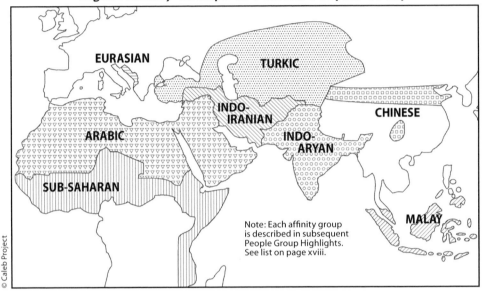

EURASIAN

TURKIC

INDO-IRANIAN

ARABIC

INDO-ARYAN

CHINESE

SUB-SAHARAN

MALAY

Note: Each affinity group is described in subsequent People Group Highlights. See list on page xviii.

© Caleb Project

supposed by Muslims that Muhammad was himself illiterate. After his death these messages were collected and incorporated in the Qur'an, which means *recitation.* Muhammad was convinced that the words which came to him were not his own, but the very word of God, and he was only the "reciter." Thus Muslims believe that the Qur'an is not Muhammad's book, but God's.

## THE MESSAGE THAT CAME TO MUHAMMAD

The heart of the message which Muhammad received was that there is no god but Allah, the One True God, who created heaven and earth and everything in them. Man is God's slave, and it is his first duty to submit to God and obey him. God's goodness and mercy are seen in his provision for all the needs of men, and men must be grateful. A great and terrible

*Judgment Day* is coming, when the earth will be shaken, and God will raise all the dead to life, and will judge them. He will reward with the pleasures of a sensual paradise those who worship him and do good deeds, and will condemn to the fires of *hell* those who do evil deeds, the worst of which is *associating* other gods with God. Where did Muhammad derive this message? Muslims insist that it came to him by direct revelation from God. We may surmise, however, that the truth of the oneness of God had been impressed on his mind by his contacts with the Jews. And possibly the expectation of the *resurrection* and final Judgment, a doctrine repugnant to the materialistic Arabs, had come to Muhammad from the preaching of some Christian missionary. In whatever way these truths came to him, Muhammad proclaimed them with great earnestness, seeking to bring the people of Mecca to repentance and faith in one God.

## Effects of Muhammad's Preaching in Mecca

When Muhammad made the claim that he was a prophet sent by God, there were a few people who at once believed in him. They were his wife Khadija; a young cousin Ali, who was a member of his family later to become his son-in-law; and his adopted son Zaid. Then an honorable merchant, later known as *Abu Bakr*, who was not a relative, professed faith in Muhammad. And others, most of them people of humble origin, joined the movement. But the leading people of the city, whom Muhammad was eager to win, ignored and soon began to ridicule him. Who was he, a common man, to make such a claim for himself? And his message about the resurrection was incredible.

How could dead bones come to life again? They accused him of sorcery and fraud. As Muhammad began to attack the gods in the Ka'aba, saying they were not gods, the men of Mecca became increasingly angry and began to persecute his little band of a hundred followers. They could do nothing to Muhammad, because he was protected by his uncle Abu Talib.

The persecution became so severe that Muhammad sent eighty of his followers to Ethiopia, a Christian country. They were well treated there, until they later joined Muhammad in Medina. The opposition did not stop Muhammad's bitter denunciation of his enemies, whom he threatened with the wrath of God. New converts joined him, and he encouraged

## Where Do Muslims Live?

Many people think that most Muslims are Arab and live in the "Middle East," but the Muslim world is much more diverse. The more than 1.3 billion Muslims alive today live in every part of the globe and make up 21 percent of the world's population. Arabic is the primary language of more than 250 million Muslims across North Africa, the Arabian Peninsula, and Southwest Asia, or 20 percent of Muslims, which makes it the fifth most widely spoken language in the world.

The four countries with the largest Muslim populations are Indonesia (197 million), Pakistan (148 million), India (149 million), and Bangladesh (120 million). Iran, Turkey, Egypt, and Nigeria are each home to between 48 to 74 million Muslims. Altogether, fifty countries have a Muslim majority. Another twenty countries have more than a million Muslims. China has 25 million and Russia has 13 million. While the most Muslims live in Asia (911 million) and Africa (324 million), a growing number make their homes in countries like France, Germany, the United Kingdom, and the United States. Western Europe has 12 million Muslims and the United States has 6 million. The world's Muslim population is growing 2.2 percent per year, largely through high birthrates.

As many as 3,700 Muslim ethno-lingual groups lack a reproducing, self-sustaining, church-planting movement within their own culture. Approximately 4 percent of the world's mission force is focused on Muslims.

Many Muslims suffer from lack of food and clean water, illiteracy and poor education, poor health care, poverty, natural disasters, and a lack of basic human rights. A compassionate response to their welfare should move us to reach out and help them.

Sources: *World Christian Encyclopedia, Operation World.*

them to be strong by telling them stories of the courage of the ancient prophets and believers in times of suffering.

## PROGRESS IN FORMATION OF THE MUSLIM COMMUNITY

During these years Muhammad was engaged in building up a community of people bound together not by blood ties, as in Arab society, but by faith in Allah and his Apostle. Their basic belief, which later became their Creed (Shahada), was: "There is no god but Allah; Muhammad is the Apostle (Prophet) of Allah." Those who submitted in faith to Allah and his Apostle were known as Muslims, since in Arabic Muslim means *one who submits.* From the same Arabic root comes Islam, which means *submission.* This became the name by which the movement was known. From the first, Islam was conceived to be a church-state, a religion expressed in a political society, in which Muhammad was, under God, the ruler in matters both religious and civil. His position resembled that of Moses in the theocracy of Israel. The Quraysh in Mecca realized that a state within their state was being created, and they deeply resented its presence.

In the tenth year of his mission (A.D. 620) Muhammad suffered two great losses. His uncle Abu Talib died, the kind man who had helped him and protected him since his childhood, although he never became a Muslim. Also Khadija, his faithful and able wife, died. After a few months Muhammad sought comfort by marrying the widow of one of the believers. He also married Aisha, the seven-year-old daughter of his friend Abu Bakr, whom

he took to his abode three years later. She became his favorite wife.

## THE HIJRA, OR MIGRATION, TO MEDINA (A.D. 622)

Being unable to make further progress in Mecca, Muhammad saw no alternative to a transfer of his mission to a more favorable location. He decided to go to Yathrib, a city 280 miles north of Mecca, which, after his going there, became known as Medina, the City of the Prophet. The people of Yathrib were more open-minded than were the keepers of the Ka'aba, and about half of the inhabitants of that region were Jews. The *pagan* Arabs looked up to the Jews for their superior culture and wealth but resented their economic success. It is said that in 621 Muhammad met twelve men from Yathrib who had come to Mecca for the annual pilgrimage and converted them to Islam. They made more converts in their city; and at the pilgrimage a year later, seventy-two men and two women from Yathrib met Muhammad and swore allegiance to him, promising to defend him with their lives. He also promised to fight for them. From this alliance we see the nature of the society which Muhammad wanted to establish.

As the time of departure to Yathrib approached, Muhammad had a vision, which must have cheered him as he contemplated his thirteen years of unsuccessful effort to win the people of his native city to his side. He saw himself carried from Mecca to Jerusalem, the city that he and his followers faced in their worship, as did the Jews. From Jerusalem he was carried up into heaven, where he talked with apostles and prophets of the past, and was attested and honored by them. In some of the traditions, this *Night Journey* (*Lailat al-Miraj*) is related as a bodily ascension to heaven. But in another tradition, his wife Aisha stated that on that night Muhammad did not leave his bed. The courage and faith of Muhammad during these years of comparative failure in Mecca, and his assurance of final victory, are indeed worthy of praise. Would that he had thus endured in the service of Jesus Christ!

In his final message to the people of Mecca, Muhammad sternly denounced them for their unbelief and threatened them with terrible punishment, both in this world and in the next. He then bade his followers make their way in small parties to Yathrib, a journey of several weeks by camel. Learning that the Quraysh were planning to prevent him from departing, he and Abu Bakr escaped from the city, hid for several days in a cave, and then, by a safe route, made their way to Yathrib. This migration, called in Arabic *Hijra*, took place in the summer of 622. From this event Muslims date their history, since it is thought that Islam truly began when the Prophet and his followers established their community in Medina. Today in Muslim lands, documents, letters, newspapers, etc., are dated from the Hijra [A.H., *anno Hegirae*, the beginning date of the Muslim lunar calendar].

## BREAK WITH JEWISH-CHRISTIAN TRADITION

During his years in Mecca, Muhammad never claimed that he had performed a miracle to prove that he was a prophet.

However, when asked what sign he could show to convince the people that God had sent him, he replied that his miracle was the Qur'an (the verses [ayat] of its chapters are called *signs* in Arabic), because no one was able to produce the like of it. Muhammad considered the Scriptures of the Jews and Christians to be true, but he thought the followers of these religions had misinterpreted them and had corrupted their religions. He maintained that God had sent him to call people back to the true worship of God, which was the religion of Abraham. In leading his followers in worship, he imitated the Jews in facing Jerusalem, and he was eager to win the Jews' allegiance and support. He never claimed divinity for himself, and said to the people, "I am a man like you." He was aware that he needed to confess his sins and ask pardon of God, as did other men.

When Muhammad rode into Yathrib on his camel, many people of different tribes urged him to become their guest. Not wishing to offend any of them by a refusal, he allowed his camel to decide for him. When the camel sat down of its own accord to permit its rider to dismount, there Muhammad established his residence and built the first mosque ever erected for worship. It is said that his first sermon was preached on a Friday; as a result, Friday became the day for congregational worship in Islam. His son Zaid was sent back to Mecca to bring the family of Muhammad to their new home. The political situation in Medina was confused, as there was no central authority to keep the peace among the various tribes. Soon Muhammad was able to become the civil as well as the religious ruler in the city, as

more and more people submitted to him and became Muslims. It seems that he ruled wisely and brought law and order to his new capital.

Muhammad at first looked to the Jews in Medina to attest and support his claims. It was probably at this time that a revelation came to him directing him to take a conciliatory attitude toward people who had not believed on him, and not forcefully induce them to accept Islam. The command was: "Let there be no *compulsion* in religion" (Sura 2:256,

## SHOULD CHRISTIANS USE "ALLAH" IN BIBLE TRANSLATION?

*by Joshua Massey*

The question of translating "God" as "Allah" is hotly debated in non-Arab lands, where many sincere Christians are convinced Allah is a false god. Ironically, this debate does not exist for Arab Christians, who have continually translated *elohim* and *theos* (the primary terms for God in biblical Hebrew and Greek) as "Allah," from the earliest known Arabic Bible translations in the eighth century till today.

Most scholars agree that "Allah" is the Arabicised form of the biblical Aramaic *elah*, corresponding to the Hebrew *eloah*, which is the singular of *elohim*, a generic word for God used throughout the Old Testament. As in English, the Bible uses *elah* and *elohim*, for both the "Most High God" and "false gods;" English uses an upper or lower case "g" to distinguish between these two. In contrast, Muslims never use "Allah" to refer to a false god, but to only the One True God, the God of Abraham, Isaac, and Jacob.

Muslim writers have been using "Allah" in their quotations of the Christian Bible since the ninth century. Jewish scholars have also been translating *elohim* and *elah* as "Allah" since the earliest known Arabic translations of the *Torah* in the ninth century until today. So, in spite of the apparent differences in how the person of God is understood according to biblical and Qur'anic content, Arabic-speaking Jews, Christians, and Muslims together have been addressing God as "Allah" over the last fourteen centuries.

Nonetheless, many sincere missionaries who strive to be biblical tend to reject all Muslim terminology, culture, and religious forms that they construe as "Islamic"—even elements with biblical Jewish and Christian origins. Issues of terminology for God are significantly convoluted when working with Muslims in non-Arabic-speaking lands where Christians use alternate terms for God. Although millions of Arab and non-Arab Christians (e.g., 30 million Javanese and Sundanese Christians in Indonesia) worship God as "Allah," other non-Arab Christians are prone to strong aversions to using "Allah" for God when unaware of its history and broader usage in the body of Christ. It is all too easy to misunderstand any term when we do not know the language or its wider context of usage.

Similarly, it is equally easy to gloss over the problematic history of many non-Arabic terms Christians use for God. The English word "God," for example, comes from the pagan Germanic *Gott*, which was used as a proper name for the chief Teutonic deity, Odin, who lives on top of the world-tree and created the first humans with his wife, Freya, a blonde, blue-eyed goddess of love, fertility, and beauty. Should English speakers therefore discontinue addressing the Most High as "God"? In spite of its pagan origin and its present use for both false deities and

RODWELL). Later this verse was *abrogated* [repealed, abolished]. Though some of the Jews assured Muhammad that his coming had been predicted in their Scriptures, which was the attestation he sought, most of them remained aloof. They knew he could not be their Messiah, who must be of the family of David (*Dawud*). When Muhammad detected their attitude he called them hypocrites. They then told him frankly that his coming was not foretold in their Scriptures, and he replied by accusing them of misinterpreting their sacred books. He did not charge them with changing the text of the Scriptures, but of omitting the references to him.

(cont. from p. 20)

the Most High, "God" (when capitalized) is generally understood by English speakers as the God of the Bible, and therefore perfectly acceptable to English-speaking Christians. "Allah," in contrast, shares the same Semitic roots as biblical Hebrew and Aramaic, is not presently used for false deities, and is clearly understood by all Arab Christians and Muslims as the God of the Bible. "Allah" is therefore a perfectly acceptable term for Arabic-speaking Christians and Muslims.

While using "Allah" is a non-issue for Arabic-speaking Christians, many non-Arabic-speaking Christians have difficulty separating the term from its meaning, as defined by Islamic teaching. If we do not use a new term, it is believed, Muslims will misunderstand the nature of God in the Bible. Christian advocates for using "Allah" among Muslims in non-Arabic-speaking lands counter that introducing foreign terms for God will create immense hurdles in communication, perhaps even guaranteeing that a truly indigenous church-planting movement will never occur. The task, they say, is not to discard such easily redeemable terms, but to fill them with biblical meaning. The more a Muslim's understanding of Allah is informed by the Scriptures, the more biblical his or her theology of God will become.

Filling familiar words with new meaning, rather than tossing them aside as irreparable, is some-thing the church has wisely done from the beginning. For example, *Logos* (the Word) was long used by pagan Stoics to describe "the divine soul of the world." Like *elohim* and *elah*, non-Jewish usage of the Greek *theos* did not denote a specific deity in the first century, but a polytheistic totality of gods, with Zeus being the father of gods and men (as the Bible testifies, Acts 14:11–12). Nonetheless, New Testament writers did not shy away from using *Logos* (John 1:1, 14) or *theos*, which occur 1,343 times in the New Testament and are translated "God" 1,320 times.

Therefore, if the translator's objective is to furnish the Bible in a way that will be well received as Good News by Muslim readers, the solution to this linguistic predicament is not necessarily to avoid the term "Allah," no matter how vehemently some non-Arabic-speaking Christians may oppose it. "Allah" has been a perfectly acceptable term in Bible translation for millions of Arab and non-Arab Christians for over a millennium and remains so for Muslim readers today.

Joshua Massey is a cultural anthropologist currently residing in the Middle East, where he is coordinating the develop-ment of indigenous media to assist Muslim followers of Jesus, proclaiming God's kingdom, and making disciples.

Adapted from Joshua Massey, "Should Christians Use Allah in Bible Translation?" in *Serving in Mission Together* (104), p. 5. *www.sim.org/mag_104.asp* (cited 9 December 2004). Used by permission.

**Editor's note:** No one gains the friendship of a Muslim through logical arguments alone. Muslims have a different perception of the character of God than that taught in the Bible. Just as we Christians need to grow in understanding who God is, so we must help our Muslim friends better understand him.

## ISLAM, AN INDEPENDENT RELIGIO-POLITICAL SYSTEM

In the second year of the Hijra, the break with the Jews became complete. He had at first observed their holy Day of Atonement, but now instituted in its place the Ramadan month of fasting. He also instituted the Feast of Sacrifice [Id al-Adha] in memory of Abraham's sacrificing the ram instead of his son [thought to be Ishmael]. Until now he and his followers had faced north toward Jerusalem in their worship, but a revelation came to him to change the prayer direction to Mecca. It is said that one day as he was standing in front of the believers in the mosque, leading them in their prayers facing Jerusalem, he suddenly turned about toward the south, and completed the worship facing Mecca. Having failed to win the Jews, he sought in this way to win the favor of the Quraysh. Muhammad justified this radical change by saying that the Ka'aba had been dedicated by Abraham and was the original center for the worship of God. This turnabout in worship was an act of very great significance, for it indicated an abandonment of the Jewish-Christian tradition and the launching forth on a new course which was related to, but in many essentials in conflict with, the teachings of the Bible. Islam had now been established as an independent religio-political system.

## THE DECISION TO USE FORCE

During the second year in Medina, life became very difficult for the immigrants from Mecca. Their funds were exhausted, and probably the hospitality of the believers from Medina was being strained. Something needed to be done if the community was to continue. What solution was provided by Allah? This revelation came to Muhammad: "O Prophet, contend against the infidels...and be rigorous with them" (Sura 9:73, RODWELL). So Muhammad began to do what Bedouin chieftains usually did when in financial difficulties: he began with divine approval to raid the caravans of his enemies in Mecca. He had tried for thirteen years by peaceful means to induce them to submit to him, and had failed. Now he would use the sword, and by capturing their caravans, he would both hurt them and help himself.

Accordingly, Muhammad sent out a party in the sacred months, during which it was the custom of the Arabs to refrain from warfare, to capture a caravan belonging to Mecca. They met with success and divided the booty. The violation of the sacred months was justified by a revelation that came to Muhammad.

Encouraged by this victory, an attempt was made to capture a very large caravan which was about to return from Syria laden with merchandise. Muhammad went forth in person with 350 armed men, and at a place called Badr met and defeated the army of a thousand men that had come from Mecca to protect the caravan. It is said that forty-nine men in the army from Mecca were killed, while Muhammad lost fourteen of his followers. The booty was divided among the warriors, and one-fifth was kept by Muhammad, to be used by him in helping the needy. This became a precedent for the division of the spoils of war. The victory at Badr (*the Battle of Badr*) was of very great importance for Islam. It assured Muhammad that God was with him. It convinced his followers that they were on the winning side and would profit from future victories. It alarmed the Quraysh, who began to fear that they would finally be defeated by Muhammad. It also induced many pagan Arabs to come to Medina and submit to Muhammad as their ruler. And it indicated that [power] was more effective than [verbal persuasion] in making converts for Islam.

## ATTACKS ON THE JEWS OF MEDINA

The Jews were unhappy over Muhammad's victory at Badr, and some of them composed and recited verses in which they ridiculed the people of Medina for submitting to a man who had slain his own people in battle. The Muslim historians tell of at least four Jews, one of whom was a woman, who were assassinated by the zealous followers of Muhammad for this crime. The assassins were not even rebuked by Muhammad for what they had done.

Realizing that the Jews were his enemies, Muhammad determined to get rid of them. He accused one of the tribes, called *Banu Qainuqa*, of breaking a treaty, and informed them they must accept Islam. When they refused, the Muslims besieged them for fifteen days, defeated them, drove them from their homes, and confiscated all their property.

Soon after this, an army of a thousand men came up from Mecca for the purpose of defeating Muhammad. They met the Muslim army at a place near Medina called *Uhud* and there inflicted a defeat on them. Muhammad himself was wounded. But for some reason, the Meccans did

not follow up their victory and went back home. This defeat was a humiliation for Muhammad, and he was comforted by revelations which came to him, explaining that the fault was with the Muslim soldiers who had disobeyed orders, and that the defeat was permitted by God to test their faith. Final victory was promised, and Muhammad was able to encourage his followers to endure their sufferings and their sorrow in the loss of those who fell in the battle.

Having fought and defeated several hostile tribes, Muhammad next attacked another Jewish tribe, the *Banu Nadir*, which had been friendly to some of his enemies. They were ordered to leave all their possessions and depart. On their refusal to do so, a force of Muslims was sent against them, which cut down their date trees and ruined their properties. Seeing they could resist no longer, they agreed to depart and were allowed to take with them only what they could carry on their camels. Their arms and their crops were divided among the Muslims.

After a time Muhammad attacked another large Jewish tribe called the *Banu Qurayza*, which, up to this time, had been friendly to him but had recently failed to participate in one of his battles. Tradition states that Gabriel came to Muhammad and ordered him to arise and strike "the idolaters who are possessors of *the Book*, the Banu Qurayza." At once a large force was sent against this tribe. When their provisions were exhausted and they were unable to resist any longer, they asked permission to emigrate as the Banu Nadir had done. This request was refused, and they were ordered to surrender uncon-

ditionally. This they were forced to do. Then the women and children were sold into slavery, their property was divided among the Muslim soldiers, and their eight hundred men were taken to Medina and there massacred. Thus the Jews in and about Medina were eliminated.

## THE WIVES OF MUHAMMAD

After the death of Khadija, Muhammad took several other wives. After marrying six, he desired to marry Zainab, the beautiful wife of Zaid, his adopted son. According to Arab custom, it was unlawful for a man to marry the wife of an adopted son, even if the son divorced her. However, a revelation came to Muhammad that God had permitted him to have Zainab. Whereupon, Zaid divorced her and she became Muhammad's seventh wife. At the time of his death, according to Muslim historians, Muhammad had between nine and eleven wives and several concubines, one of whom was Mary, a *Coptic* Christian slave who had been given to Muhammad by the ruler of Egypt. Each of his wives had a separate room, and Muhammad slept in their rooms in turn. It is not surprising that peace did not always prevail in the Prophet's household.

## FINAL STRUGGLE WITH MECCA

In the fifth year of the Hijra, the Quraysh made a final desperate attempt to destroy Muhammad and his rule in Medina (*Battle of the Trench*). They approached Medina with an army of ten thousand men. The Muslims dug a trench about the city to defend it, and the Meccans were unable to break through and take the city.

When their provisions were exhausted, they returned to Mecca and never again attempted to fight Muhammad.

But Muhammad was determined to subdue Mecca, the one place in Arabia which he most desired to possess. He longed to make the pilgrimage once more to the House of Allah, and so in 628 he and a group of Muslim pilgrims traveled toward Mecca. However, the Quraysh refused them entrance into the city. Then negotiations were carried on with the Quraysh, and a treaty was made in which both sides agreed not to fight for ten years, and permission was granted for Muhammad and his followers to enter Mecca unarmed the following year. The followers of the Prophet thought they had met with defeat, but Muhammad assured them it was a great victory. A revelation came stating that Islam, the religion of truth, will be "exalted above every religion" (Sura 48:28, RODWELL). Henceforth Judaism and Christianity were to be superseded by Islam.

After winning other victories over rebel tribes, in 629 Muhammad and two thousand of his followers took advantage of the permission granted them in the treaty and came to Mecca for the Lesser Pilgrimage (*Lesser Hajj*). On their approach, the Quraysh vacated the city, and the Muslims entered unarmed. Muhammad performed all the rites of the pagan ritual, going seven times about the Ka'aba, which was still full of images, kissing the Holy Black Stone, and offering the sacrifices. He also married his eleventh wife and won to his side several of his former foes.

## MECCA, CENTER OF ISLAM

Though it had been agreed that there would be no more war for ten years, Muhammad was convinced that he must now conquer Mecca in order to make his control of Arabia complete. And so, as soon as he returned to Medina from the Lesser Pilgrimage, he raised an army of ten thousand men and started back to Mecca. When he reached the city, Abu Sufyan, the leader of the Quraysh and one of Muhammad's bitterest foes, realized that further resistance was useless, came out to meet the conqueror, and became a Muslim. The army entered the city unopposed. Muhammad went to the Ka'aba and ordered that the images be brought out and destroyed. He took over the rule of the very city he had fled eight years before. He declared a general amnesty to the people of Mecca, with the exception of a few individuals who were executed for certain crimes. Mecca now became the center of Islam, with Muhammad as its supreme ruler. It was indeed a day of triumph and great joy for Muhammad and his followers. The new believers in Mecca were rewarded for their submission by being given generous portions of the large booty recently taken in a victory over some

## A CUP OF TEA

You've been watched. By Halima, a young Muslim woman.

She's intrigued with your life. Why would you leave your home country? Why would you want to come here? Why aren't you like the women on TV?

Halima would like to get to know you. But she's afraid you won't understand or accept her. And she's waiting for you to speak.

"What should I say to her?" you ask yourself. You approach her and the words come, to your surprise, naturally.

"Hello. Would you like to come to my home for a cup of tea?"

Later, after Halima has come and gone, you smile and think, "All I had to do was give her a cup of tea."

Muslim women are often in the news today, but usually only the ones at extreme ends, either those who are pitied, such as veiled Afghans under Taliban rule, or those who are admired, such as strong political activists in Indonesia, Bangladesh, and Egypt. We may find veiled women mysterious, but as we get to know them we realize they, like Halima, are similar to us—with their hurts, their dreams, their worship of God, their family obligations, and their jobs and careers. Many Muslim women have encountered Jesus and felt his love for them through the words and actions of those of us who know Jesus. They become essential parts of Christ-centered communities.

Source: *www.frontiers.org*

### FOR FURTHER STUDY

Geraldine Brooks, *Nine Parts of Desire: The Hidden World of Islamic Women* (New York: Anchor Books, 2004).

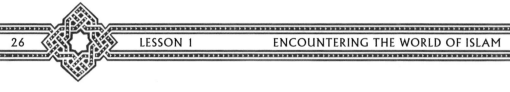
rebel tribes at Hunain. But some of the old believers were not happy about this.

## CONVERSION BY FORCE

During the ninth year of the Hijra, many tribes, realizing that they could no longer resist Muhammad, came and submitted to him. At this time a revelation came which abrogated the previous command not to use force in making converts (Sura 2:256, RODWELL). It was this: "When the sacred months are past, kill those who join other gods with God wherever ye shall find them, and seize them, besiege them, and lay wait for them with every kind of ambush; but if they shall convert and observe prayer and pay the obligatory alms, let them go their way" (Sura 9:5, RODWELL). The purpose of this command was to put an end to idolatry, and it was outwardly, at least, highly successful. Not only were pagans forced at the point of the sword to become Muslims. A Christian prince in the north of Arabia named Ukaider was promised his life if he accepted Islam, [which subsequently he did]. From this we infer that Christians, because of their worship of Christ, were at this time counted as *polytheists.*

However, a different policy was adopted toward the Christians of Nejran in the south of Arabia. Tradition states that when a letter from Muhammad commanding them to become Muslims reached this large Christian community, they were greatly perplexed as to what they should do. Should they submit, or should they fight Muhammad? It was decided that they would send a large deputation to talk with him. Their bishop and a number of their chief men made the long journey to Medina. They found

Muhammad in the mosque, and he welcomed them and permitted them to perform their Christian worship there. After three days, Muhammad invited them to accept Islam. A discussion followed about Isa (Jesus) in which Muhammad said Jesus was his brother and was only a servant of God, by whose permission he had healed the sick and raised the dead to life. But the Christians insisted that Jesus was God's Son, and refused to give up their faith in him and become Muslims.

At this point, a revelation came to Muhammad, instructing him to challenge the Christians to trial by imprecation (invoke evil upon). They would curse one another and let God decide who was right and who wrong. So Muhammad went out, with his daughter Fatima and her husband Ali (Muhammad's cousin) and their sons Hasan and Husayn, and sat under a cloak. The Christians came to meet them adorned in the finest silken garments. Being deeply impressed by the simplicity of the holy family of Islam, and fearful of being destroyed by the curse of Muhammad, they refused to participate in the trial. So relates the Islamic tradition. We do not have the account the Christians gave of this remarkable confrontation.

It is said that Muhammad permitted these Christians to keep their religion and be under his protection, provided they paid a high tribute. They accepted these terms and returned to their homes. This was probably the first time that Muhammad had come face to face with educated and influential Christians. However, it seems that he made no effort to learn from them the true teachings of

their religion and only wished to subdue them. In this he succeeded.

## GREATER PILGRIMAGE AND DEATH OF MUHAMMAD (A.D. 632)

In the tenth year of the Hijra, Muhammad went to Mecca for the *Greater Pilgrimage* (Hajj), which was his last. He took with him all his wives, and it is said that a hundred thousand people accompanied him. He performed all the rites of the pilgrimage according to the ancient pagan customs, thus incorporating them into his religion and setting an example for all future pilgrims. He there delivered an address in which he said: "This day I have perfected your religion for you" (Sura 5:5, RODWELL).

The Muslims of the Shi'a sect have a tradition that on the return journey to Medina, Muhammad halted the caravan in a very hot place in the desert and assembled the people about him. Then he called his son-in-law Ali to his side, appointed him as his successor, and bade the people obey him. This tradition is rejected by other Muslims as untrue.

Not long after Muhammad's return to Medina, he became very ill. Fearing that after his death his followers might quarrel among themselves, he admonished the leaders to be loyal to one another and to obey his successor. He directed Abu Bakr to lead the worship when he was too ill to do so, and it was thought by some that this was an indication that he should succeed Muhammad. Finally, on June 8, 632, death came to Muhammad in the room of his wife Aisha as he rested on her lap. It is said that a grave was dug in that very place and in it the Prophet of Arabia was buried. Later a mosque, called the Prophet's Mosque, was built, and the grave became a place of pilgrimage.

## ISLAM'S ADVANCES

As soon as Muhammad died, a power struggle took place. If Ali had really been appointed by Muhammad as successor, nevertheless he was not chosen to that position by the leaders, for they finally gave their allegiance to Abu Bakr. He became the first caliph (vicegerent [or representative of Allah]). Three others followed, all assassinated by other Muslims. The fourth was Ali. Wars followed, Muslims slaying other Muslims. However, in spite of these serious internal difficulties, the Muslim armies went forth to conquer the world. They met with amazing success, which they believed was proof that God was with them.

In a short time, the Muslim armies, fired by religious zeal and eager for plunder and conquest, defeated the armies of the Persian and Byzantine empires. They conquered Syria and Egypt, moved across North Africa, conquering lands which had been strongly Christian, and occupied Spain. Only in 732 was their westward advance stopped by Charles Martel in the Battle of Tours in France. Eastward they also swept, conquering all the lands to the Oxus and Indus rivers. Islam continued to advance, by peaceful means or by warfare, until it was established all across Asia and Africa. Now one-fifth of the population of the world is proud to be called Muslim.

## MEASURED AND FOUND WANTING

We have attempted to tell accurately and fairly the story of Muhammad, the founder of Islam. What is to be our estimate of him? Every possible opinion about him has been expressed. He has been pictured as God's most perfect and holy prophet. He has also been considered a devil incarnate, who, according to Dante, is to be the chief among the damned because he led many people astray. That he was a man of great ability, who achieved remarkable success in the face of almost insuperable difficulties, cannot be questioned. As a leader he had the outstanding ability to win and hold the allegiance of men. He was a very religious man who hated idols and was passionately devoted to Allah, whom he considered to be the One True God. His courage and perseverance in proclaiming the doctrine of the unity of God are indeed inspiring.

However, when the life of this great man is measured by the standard of Jesus Christ, he is found wanting. It seems that he began his mission as a sincere and obedient proclaimer of the truth as he saw it. But somewhere in his life he lost his way. Having failed to inquire about the way to God from those qualified to guide him, he took the wrong road, which led him and untold multitudes who followed him far from the truth. By ignoring the teachings of Christ, either intentionally or through ignorance, Muhammad never knew how much God loved him and all mankind in giving his Son to save the world.

Not knowing God truly, Muhammad began to place political expedience and even personal preferences above the moral and ethical principles which he had taught. It appears that he used the revelations, which he said came from God, to justify actions which even the pagan Arabs considered wrong. And, in claiming that Islam had taken the place of Christianity, and that he as the *Seal of the Prophets* had supplanted Christ, he rejected God's holy purpose for the salvation of the world through Christ alone. The message of every true prophet of God must be in agreement with the messages of the prophets who preceded him. Since the message of Muhammad is in many important respects contradictory to the Word of God revealed by previous prophets and apostles, and particularly to the truth of Jesus Christ, it is not possible for Christians to consider Muhammad to have been God's prophet. Rather, he is one of those foretold by Christ who would lead many astray (Matt. 24: 24–25). It is for their salvation that we must labor and pray.

**End of key readings for Lesson 1. See** RECOMMENDED READINGS & ACTIVITIES **on p. 40.**

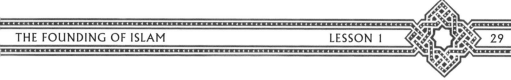
# CHRISTIANITY AND EARLY ISLAM

*by Samuel H. Moffett*

**EDITOR'S NOTE**

Dr. Moffett, like Dr. Miller, is respectful in his tone towards Muslims. He is particularly insightful about the opportunities Christians missed at the beginning of Islam. Both Miller and Moffett were ahead of their time in adopting relatively unbiased attitudes towards Muslims. Yet, as products of earlier generations, they project some western superiority. In particular, the way Dr. Moffett links Muhammad to Christianity's defeat and Charlemagne to Christianity's triumph seems ill-conceived; political and military advance and retreat do not indicate gospel advance and retreat. That would be like claiming God must be behind the people who "win." (And, as we have seen, Dr. Miller also makes several indirect swipes at Muhammad for the discord in his household and his readiness to use the sword.)

When Umar b.'Abd al-Aziz came into power (A.D. 717), they (the Christians of Nejran) complained to him that they were in danger of extinction… that the continual raids of the Arabs overburdened them with heavy taxes for revictualing them, and that they suffered from the unjust treatment (of the governor). By Umar's orders, their census was taken, and it was found that they were reduced to one-tenth of their original number. (Baladhuri [d. 892], trans. by Hitti)

Two men, Muhammad in Asia and Charlemagne in the West, may well have changed the history of the world more decisively and dramatically than anyone else in the second five hundred years of the Christian age (A.D. 500 – 1000). Muhammad is a symbol of Christianity's near defeat in Asia, Charlemagne of its near triumph in the West. In the history of the church, defeat is never final and triumph is never quite complete, but for Asian Christianity, the loss of the Middle East to Islam was more than the loss of its home and birthplace; it marked the first permanent check to Christian expansion in all the previous six hundred years of the history of the church.

The Muslim conquest of the mid-seventh century, which so abruptly terminated the Persian era of Asian church history, was not the end of Persian Christianity. It was a time of upheaval of empires, but it did not bring down upon the church the immediate havoc of religious persecution and massacre with which it is popularly associated. On the contrary, there is considerable evidence that the Nestorians in Persia welcomed the Arabs as liberators from *Zoroastrian* oppression, and that the Arab conquerors in turn found it

Samuel Moffett was born in Korea of American parents. He taught for four years in China, under both nationalist and communist governments, until 1951. He was professor of mission history at Princeton Theological Seminary for many years.

Adapted from Samuel H. Moffett, *A History of Christianity in Asia*, vol. 1. (New York: Orbis Books, 1998), pp. 324–32. Used by permission. *www.orbisbooks.org*

more to their advantage to segregate and use the Christians than to exterminate them. Gibbon's unforgettable metaphor of Christians facing "a Muhammad with the sword in one hand and the Koran [Qur'an] in the other" is doubly misleading. To Muhammad the *Holy Book* was the Bible. The Qur'an appeared only after his death. And a better metaphor than the sword, as far as Muslim-Christian relationships were concerned, would be a net; for, after the conquest, Christians found themselves caught in the web of Islam, but not usually under its sword. The net, if not always comfortable, was at least safer than the sword.

The unknown author of the *Chronicle of Seert*, a history of the Nestorians written perhaps as early as the ninth century, describes the Persian Christian reaction to the victors in very positive terms. Neither Christians nor Jews were required to give up their religion, and although they were heavily taxed, on the whole they were not violently abused. The Christian chronicler says: "The Arabs treated them with generosity, and by the grace of God (may He be exalted), prosperity reigned, and the hearts of Christians rejoiced at the ascendancy of the Arabs. May God affirm and make it triumphant!"[1]

## MUHAMMAD AND THE CHRISTIANS

As the Arab tide rolled in, Christians very early claimed the authority of Muhammad himself in defense of their religious rights. Christian and Arab sources alike preserved copies or excerpts of a treaty said to have been concluded by the Prophet with the Christians of

Nejran (northern Yemen) and all other Christian sects.[2] It is possible that he did indeed reach a special agreement with the church in Nejran, which was well known to the Arabs as the chief Christian center of southern Arabia,[3] and this may have served as a rough model for later arrangements. But details of Muhammad's life are far too uncertain[4] to lend authenticity to any of the formal legal commitments to Christian communities that have been attributed to him. The first comprehensive attempt to outline the status of Christians under Islam is probably the *Covenant of Umar (Omar)*, father-in-law of Muhammad, who ruled as the Prophet's second successor from two years after Muhammad's death (634), to ten years after the Arabs took Seleucia-Ctesiphon, capital of the Persian Empire (644).

But Muhammad did have personal contacts with Christians and had formed a generally favorable opinion of them years before his successors so completely conquered them. The story of his first meeting with a Christian is as unreliable as most of the anecdotes of his early life, but both Arab and Christian historians often repeated it. The earliest and most trustworthy of the Muslim biographers of the Prophet, the eighth-century writer *Ibn-Ishaq*, relates that at the age of twelve, on a caravan trip to Syria with his uncle, the young Muhammad met a Christian [Nestorian] monk named *Bahira* at Basra, which was the seat of the Monophysite bishop of the desert Arabs. The old monk recognized signs of greatness in the boy and protected him from some who would have harmed him.[5] The same biographer names another Christian, Jabr, who was perhaps an Ethiopian, as exerting great

## The Arabian Peninsula and the Surrounding Region in the Sixth Century

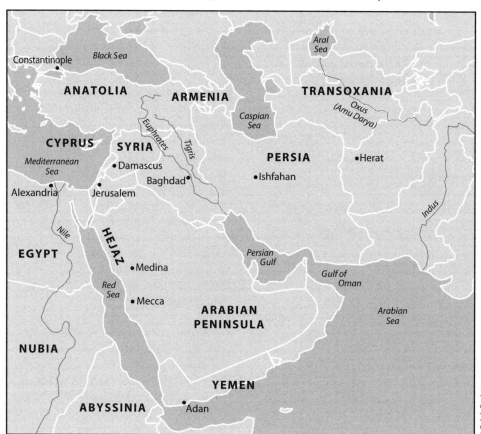

© Caleb Project

influence on the Prophet: "According to my information, the apostle used often to sit at al-Marwa (a hill overlooking Mecca) at the booth of a young Christian called Jabr, a slave of the B. al-Hadrami (tribe), and they used to say, 'The one who teaches Muhammad most of what he brings is Jabr the Christian.'"[6]

Another tradition suggests that a cousin of the Prophet's first wife was a Christian. His name was Waraqah ibn Naufal, and it is true that of all Muhammad's acquaintances, he was the most informed about Christianity. He is described as a "hanif," a term denoting one who has become dissatisfied with paganism and is attracted to vaguely monotheistic ideas.[7] Some say that he did become a Christian before his death.[8] But Muhammad's family, the *Hashim*, who belonged to the Quraysh tribe, had a vested interest in paganism. His great-grandfather, *Hashim*, had won for the Quraysh the right to provide food and water for pilgrims to the Ka'aba, the Holy House in Mecca, which Muslim tradition would later identify as the place where the angel appeared to Hagar in the desert and saved the father of the Arabs, the infant Ishmael (Ismail; cf., Gen. 21:15–20). At the time Muhammad was born, however, the Holy House was still full of idols, the holiest of which were the Holy Black Stone, which according to some traditions had come down out of Paradise, and the Moabite statue of *Hubal*, chief of the many gods of Mecca.

Muhammad was an unlikely leader. His family was poor and declining in power. His father had died before he was born, so by Arab custom he could not even inherit his father's property, and he was brought up by an uncle, the Hashim family chief. But when he was twenty-five his fortunes began to change. He married a wealthy widow fifteen years older than he was, and in the more leisurely life that this brought him, he entered into a period of mystic experiences and meditation. About the year 610, while a triumphant Persia was pushing back the armies of Constantinople through Odessa to Antioch and the Mediterranean, [and when he was] forty-four years old, Muhammad's meditations began to be interrupted by visions and voices he felt were calling him to be the *Messenger of God*.[9]

## SOCIAL AND RELIGIOUS CHANGE

It was a time of social unrest in the Arabian Peninsula. *Rome* and Persia had been slowly but effectively destroying each other in a hundred years of almost incessant war (540–629). As the war continued into the seventh century, the exhausted empires were less and less able to protect their Arab client-states on the desert borders; the *Ghassanid* kings in the northwest, who owed allegiance to Rome, and *Lakhmid* and Yemen in the east and south, who looked to Persia. In those kingdoms, Christian Arab communities had been planted by Monophysites on Rome's southern border and by Nestorians nearer Persia. New wealth was accumulating in the politically neutral center, along the strategic north-south caravan route from Africa to Roman Syria, outside the Arab kingdoms where Christian Arab communities had begun to flourish. But now economic and political power was draining away from the evangelized borders of empire into the unreached center, along the caravan route from Africa to Syria and its pagan trade cities of the desert, Medina and Mecca.[10]

Into this ferment of change, Muhammad's revelations brought two most troubling and divisive pronouncements, one religious, the other social. To the pagans he began to preach against idols and proclaim that there is only one good and all-powerful God. This threatened Mecca's chief source of pride, the Holy House, the shrine of the gods. And to the rich, who were profiting most from both caravans and pilgrims, he preached that wealth must be shared with the poor. This was quite understandably less popular with the rich than with the poor. It weakened clan loyalties, dividing the people not by families but by possessions. It upset the whole city, and in an unforgettable incident, the richer and more powerful members of his own clan, the Quraysh, drove Muhammad out of Mecca as a troublemaker.[11]

With some seventy followers, he found refuge in Yathrib, which was renamed Medina in his honor,[12] about three hundred miles north of Mecca. All Muslim history is dated from this momentous pilgrimage in the year 622, known as the Hijra (or Hegira, which denotes a change of direction; hence the *emigration*, or less accurately, the flight).[13]

In Medina Muhammad continued his crusade against polytheism. His most significant religious contacts there were with Jews, of whom there was a large community in Medina, and he concluded a covenant of mutual toleration with them, for it seemed logical to him to try to draw those two monotheistic groups, Jews and Muslims, together.[14] He began to draw up rules of worship for his own followers and even thought of using a trumpet as the Jews did to call them to prayer. But the Muslim-Jewish alliance all too soon broke down. Muslim tradition implies that it was because too many Jews in Medina began to identify Muhammad with the coming of their messiah and began to join the pilgrims from Mecca.[15]

## MUHAMMAD ACCEPTED AS LEADER

At any rate, it was not in alliance with the Jews but with the pagan communities of Arabic Medina that Muhammad eventually found his place of leadership.[16] Here at last he won acceptance as a prophet of religion, here he learned to rouse his followers to war, and here he honed his political skills as a strategic, politically neutral referee in the tribal rivalries that were tearing the town apart. He began by uniting the quarreling people of Medina against their Arabic commercial rivals (and his own opponents) in Mecca and led them in devastating raids on Meccan caravans. Then he took advantage of his estrangement from the Jewish community to unite the Arabs against the Jews religiously. He urged them to reject the exclusivist claim of the Jews to be the "children of God," and further aroused

## NEED OF THE HOUR

"When he saw the crowds, he had compassion on them" (Matt. 9:36).

Most Muslims today have not experienced the compassion of Christ through believers' actions of friendship and service. The need of the hour is for Christians to relate to Muslims with compassion. A first step is demonstrating friendship. Befriend a Muslim co-worker or greet Muslims in your neighborhood. What might this look like? Jesus Christ shows us the way.

Jesus took the initiative, modeling compassion and service. He left heaven to be with and serve humanity (see Phil. 2:5–11). Motivated by his compassion for us, God took the initiative and reached out to us with a message of love, hope, and salvation.

Just as Jesus had compassion for men and women, God gives us compassion to motivate us to identify with, give aid, and show mercy to others, sharing with them in their situation. Let us ask God to give us his same attitude of love and service, so we may reach out to the Muslims God has placed around us.

Source: Fouad Masri, *www.crescentproject.org.*

## The Life of Muhammad

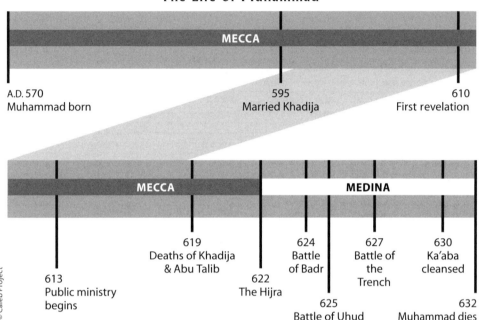

MECCA

A.D. 570
Muhammad born

595
Married Khadija

610
First revelation

MECCA                    MEDINA

619
Deaths of Khadija
& Abu Talib

624
Battle
of Badr

627
Battle of
the
Trench

630
Ka'aba
cleansed

613
Public ministry
begins

622
The Hijra

625
Battle of Uhud

632
Muhammad dies

© Caleb Project

them to jealousy of Jewish prosperity. In a tragic series of episodes for which the Prophet has been greatly criticized, the Jews of Medina were driven from the city by exile, assassination, and execution.[17] Where once he had worshiped toward Jerusalem, he turned his people instead toward Mecca as the Holy City and its holy place, the Ka'aba. The Fast of Ramadan replaced the Day of Atonement. By then, in 630, the armies of a united Medina had occupied Mecca, led in triumph by the religious leader the Meccans had ridiculed and rejected, Muhammad. Islam had become more than the first step toward the unification of the Arabian Peninsula, more than a variation on Judaic religion. It was the beginning of a new and universal vision that would embrace a far greater goal, the conquest of the world.

Late that same year, Muhammad led an army of thirty thousand men north against Persia's southern borders, with what might later have become highly significant help from two largely Christian (Monophysite) Arab tribes, the Bakr banu-Wail and the Taghlib. But two years later Muhammad was dead.

## CHRISTIANITY AND THE QUR'AN

For the most authentic indication of early Muslim attitudes, we must turn first of all to the Qur'an.[18] The 114 suras (chapters) of the Qur'an did not appear in writing in collected form until after Muhammad's death. They were gathered and edited by his secretary during the reigns of the Prophet's successors. An initial collection was attempted under the Caliph Umar, and the accepted canonical version assembled under the Caliph Uthman (644–656). The dating of the various visions and prophecies is highly debatable, and scholars often disagree on which suras can be traced to Muhammad's early period in Mecca and which come from the later Medina period. But, accepting some degree of gradual change in Muhammad's understanding of the Christian faith, and judging from the Qur'an as a whole, it can be said that he was both surprisingly tolerant of Christianity and surprisingly uninformed about it.

Muhammad's general principle concerning the Christian revelation in both the Old Testament and the New Testament was that there is no conflict between the Word of God, as it came to the Jewish prophets and to Jesus and the apostles, and the word of God as it was revealed directly to him.[19] In the Qur'an the influence of the Old Testament is predominant. What references there are to New Testament teachings, though significant, are rather scattered and uneven. The fault was not Muhammad's. As L. E. Browne has remarked, if Christians had seized the opportunity in that age, when Arabia was barely becoming literate, and had "made the first Arabic book the Bible instead of the Qur'an, the whole course of the religious history of the East might have been different."[20] But after at least three hundred years in Arabia, Christians, whether *Chalcedonian*, Nestorian, or Monophysite, had made no translation of the New Testament into Arabic.[21] So when the Prophet sought for a name for *the One True God*, the same God whom he thought Christians and Jews also worshiped, he did not use the Hebrew or the Greek name for God, but "rather

hesitantly" chose the name Arabs used for the pagan supreme being, Allah.[22] Keeping his religion strictly monotheistic by purging it of the clutter of Arabic gods and superstitions, but at the same time keeping it firmly embedded in Arabic tradition, proved to be a master stroke of cultural adaptation.

## JESUS CHRIST

As for Jesus Christ, Muhammad speaks of him with the highest respect, but only as one of the greatest of the prophets. His earliest mention of Jesus in the Qur'an (according to traditional dating)[23] is in Sura 19, where Jesus is described as a prophet of the Book, like Moses. Though Moses is mentioned more often, Muhammad ascribes more titles of honor to Jesus than to any other figure in the history of his "true religion," Islam. Jesus is never criticized. He is Messenger, Prophet, Servant, Word of truth, Spirit of God, Son of Mary, and the Messiah. He was born of a virgin, he worked miracles, and he was taken up alive into heaven.[24] His main mission on earth, however, was to confirm the law that prophets before him had given to the seed of Abraham and to bring "glad tidings of an apostle" who would come after him and "whose name shall be *Ahmad* [Muhammad]" (Sura 61:6, YUSUF ALI).

Many of the details the Qur'an adds to the story of the life and work of Jesus turn into fantasy, with echoes of third-century apocryphal Christian documents. The birth of Christ, for example, takes place under a palm tree in the desert, and an angel instructs Mary to shake the tree and eat its dates. He calls down a feast from heaven, and a table is lowered from the skies. More

serious, in its theological implications, is the manner in which the account of the crucifixion in the Qur'an deviates from that in the New Testament. The Qur'an states that Jesus did not die but was rescued from the cross by a ruse, and a substitute was provided to take his place (Sura 19:22–26; also 3:49; 4:157; 5:112–118).[25]

## REPUDIATION OF CHRISTIAN DOCTRINES

It is impossible to pinpoint chronologically just when and how the differences between Muhammad and the Christians became increasingly obvious to him, for the dating of the chapters of the Qur'an is too uncertain. But the major points of contention are quite clear by the time the Qur'an began to take written shape, perhaps not long before his death in 632. The first collection, as we have noted, was not assembled until the caliphate of Umar (634–644), "from date leaves and tablets of white stone, and from the breasts of men" according to tradition. The final canonical editing was completed under the next caliph, Uthman (644–656).[26]

By that time, the Prophet is represented as explicitly repudiating such central Christian doctrines as the Trinity and the deity of Jesus Christ. He accepts the ascension but bypasses the cross. His differences from those he still calls People of the Book he now explains by rejecting the integrity of the Christian Scriptures, and accuses Christians of altering their own written records of God's revelation. For, since God does not change, his Word to them must originally have been in complete accord with his revelations to the last and greatest of the prophets, Muhammad: "Believe in God and in His apostles. Say

## RASHID'S STORY

When Rashid realizes the book in his hands is written in (Tifinagh), the ancient alphabet of his own language, his wrinkled face lights up. Though he cannot read the words, his identity as a Berber makes these symbols precious to him.

"You have no idea how much this means to me!" he exclaims. Studying the letters for several minutes, his attention turns to the rest of the mysterious booklet he holds. Then he reaches for another copy of the book in Arabic, which he can read more easily. Again, he is thrilled. It is the Gospel of John. "This is the *Injil*!" he says. "I have always wanted to read the Injil (part of the Christians' religious book; see Glossary). The Qur'an talks about it. You have given me the most precious gift."

Rashid is a *Berber* from North Morocco. After retiring several years ago, he dedicated his life to the study of Islam. He lives a quiet life, seldom leaving his house except for prayers, and spends his time reading religious books. He is one of many such men among the Riffi Berbers. As their careers come to an end and their children are grown, they begin to think more of spiritual things. Some are only trying to behave in a respectable way and others want to make up for the sins of their youth. But many, like Rashid, are seeking spiritual truth. May they find what they seek.

Source: Marti Smith, *calebproject.org*

not 'Trinity'…For God is One God:…(Far exalted is He) above having a son (Sura 4:171, YUSUF ALI). O Jesus, son of Mary! Didst thou say unto men, 'Worship me and my mother as gods?'…He will say,…'Never could I say what I had no right (to say)' (Sura 5:116, YUSUF ALI). The transgressors [Christians]…changed the word from that which had been given them (Sura 7:162, YUSUF ALI). Ye People of the Book! Why do you clothe Truth with falsehood, and conceal the Truth?" (Sura 3:71, YUSUF ALI).[27]

Nevertheless, for the most part, the Prophet remained friendly toward the Christian communities he encountered in Arabia. This is in marked contrast to his attitude toward the Jews: "Strongest among men in enmity to the Believers wilt thou find the Jews and Pagans [polytheists]; and nearest among them in love to the Believers wilt thou find those who say, 'We are Christians' [Nazarenes]…These are men devoted to learning [priests] and men who have renounced the world [monks], and they are not arrogant" (Sura 5:82, YUSUF ALI).

But scattered progressively through the Qur'an are hints of a hardening of the Islamic mindset, as differences of belief and teaching became more and more obvious. Then Christians and Jews are berated equally: "Ye who believe! Take not the Jews and the Christians for your friends and protectors; they are but friends and protectors to each other. And he amongst you that turns to them (for friendship) is of them. Verily, God guideth not a people unjust" (Sura 5:51, YUSUF ALI).

It is apparent that by the time of his death, the Prophet saw very clearly that his first hopes of attracting the earlier monotheists, Jews and Christians, to his newer revelation had been an illusion. But by that time also, any substantial Christian hope of converting Islam to Christian monotheism was gone.

## WHY MUHAMMAD NEVER BECAME A CHRISTIAN

Why did Muhammad, who was at first so open to the witness of the Old and New Testaments, not become a Christian? One reason has already been suggested. There was no Bible in Arabic. He was never given the chance to know the Scriptures of the Christian canon in their true, fully accepted form, and what fragments he had heard about its contents were insufficiently persuasive. It is quite possible that underlying and related to this was an element of cultural insensitivity toward Arabs on the part of Christians in imperial Persia and Byzantine Syria. Why had Asian missionaries translated the Scriptures into the tongues of better known cultures, into Syriac and in part into Chinese, but not into Arabic? Did they consider Arabic not worth the effort? They had even at times begun to put portions into some tribal languages of central Asia, but not into Arabic. If this hinted at a cultural, racial prejudice, the Arabs, who were fiercely proud of their identity, could not have failed to resent it.

A second reason may have been the sad spectacle of Christian disunity. As he became aware of the angry divisions in the Christianity of the Middle East—Nestorian, Monophysite, and Chalcedonian, to say nothing of the schisms of the heretical sects—Muhammad may well have concluded that his quest for Arab unity and religious reform could never be accomplished within a Christian framework. A third reason, probably, was the negative effect of Christianity's political connections to Arabia's imperialist neighbors. Byzantium was Chalcedonian orthodox, Persia's largest religious minority was Nestorian, and Ethiopia was Monophysite. Byzantine Syria also had a considerable Monophysite population. "The Qur'an," as W. M. Watt has written, "offered the Arabs a monotheism comparable to Judaism and Christianity but without their political ties."[28]

However, overriding all such rationalizations and conjectures as to why Muhammad never became a Christian is surely the burning certainty in his soul that the One True God, "the Merciful, the Compassionate," had chosen him above all the prophets and had spoken to him directly in a way he had never spoken to any man before or since. Muhammad's power came not in the context of his reaction to other faiths, other social patterns, or other governments; his power was in the transparent sincerity of his own religious convictions. He was a prophet self-authenticated. That was his strength; and to those who did not follow him, that was his weakness.

**End of Basic Readings for Lesson 1. See** RECOMMENDED READINGS & ACTIVITIES **on p. 40.**

**Go to:**
***www.encounteringislam.org/ readings* to find the Full Reading for Lesson 1.**

## ENDNOTES

1. *Histoire Nestorienne* (*Chronicle of Seert*), A. Scher, ed., in PO t. 13, fasc. 4, no. 65, p. 581f. The date of the *Chronicle* is uncertain; internal evidence suggests either after A.D. 828 or 1228.

2. On the Christian side, the treaty, as quoted at length by the *Chronicle of Seert* (pp. 601ff.), extends its provisions to all Christian sects. Mari ibn Suleiman, a Nestorian historian of the twelfth century, gives a different version that attributes the pact to a direct meeting between Muhammad (before his death in A.D. 632) and the Nestorian patriarch Yeshuyab II (A.D. 628–43); cited by L. E. Browne, *The Eclipse of Christianity in Asia from the Time of Muhammad till the Fourteenth Century* (Cambridge: Cambridge University Press, 1933), p. 41. On the Arab side, references to the treaty are found in Baladhuri, a ninth-century Persian historian (*Kitab al-farq bain al-firaq*, P. K. Hitti, trans. [Cairo, 1924]). Six copies of the "Covenant of the Prophet" are still preserved in St. Catherine's Monastery at the foot of Mount Sinai; cited by A. S. Atiya, *A History of Eastern Christianity* (London: Methuen, 1968), p. 268.

3. There are numerous references to Christian Nejran in the early biographies of Muhammad, especially in ibn-Ishaq (707–773), *Sirat Rasul Allah* (as edited by ibn-Hisham in the ninth century), trans. by A. Guillaume as *The Life of Muhammad* (Oxford: Oxford University Press, 1955), pp. 14ff. See Guillaume's comments, p. xviii. See also ibn-Ishaq's lengthy account of the Christian deputation from Nejran to Muhammad in Medina, probably based on later memories, pp. 270ff.

4. Not until at least 125 years after Muhammad's death do the first collections of the historical traditions of his life begin to appear.

5. Ibid., pp. 79–81. Ibn-Ishaq's is the first and best of the early biographies of the Prophet, well documented for the period after the Hijra of A.D. 622 but uncritical about the years before. Muslim historians used the legend to indicate recognition of Muhammad's holiness by a Christian, while Christians referred to it as proof that Christian teaching was the source of the Prophet's inspiration.

6. Ibid, p. 180. These early anecdotes are from the more uncritical section of the biography, the early period at Mecca.

7. R. Bell, *The Origin of Islam in Its Christian Environment* (London: Cass, 1926; reprint, 1968), pp. 57f.

8. K. Cragg, *Muhammad and the Christian* (Maryknoll, N.Y.: Orbis, 1984), p. 18.

9. See the account of his visions in the Qur'an, Sura 53:1–18.

10. "The extraordinary events of the seventh century completely reversed the role of the Arabs. From a peninsular people who had played a marginal and subordinate role in history, they develop into an imperial race and succeed in terminating the Indo-European interregnum in the Near East, reasserting *Semite* political presence in the region, and carrying the Semitic political factor into the medieval world by the foundation of a universal state"; Irfan Shahid, in P. M. Holt, et al., eds., *The Cambridge History of Islam*, vol. 1 (Cambridge: Cambridge University Press, 1970), pp. 25f.

11. Ibn-Ishaq, pp. 112–231.

12. *Madinat al-Nabi*, i.e., "city of the Prophet."

13. A.H. (anno Hegirae) 1, therefore, is A.D. 622. On the problem of correlating the Qur'anic and western calendars and fixing the date, see E. J. Brill, *First Encyclopedia of Islam*, "Hidjra (Hijra)," (Leiden, 1987).

14. "The Jews have their religion and the Muslims have theirs…Each must help the other against anyone who attacks the people of this document," Ibn-Ishaq, p. 233.

15. Ibid., pp. 239–70.

16. The best critical analysis of this period is W. M. Watt, *Muhammad at Medina* (Oxford: Clarendon, 1956); I follow his interpretation.

17. See the account and analysis in Watt, pp. 204–20. Also Ibn-Ishaq, pp. 239–47.

18. In the later development of Islam, however, it must be remembered that, as Goldziher noted long ago, "The Sunna [*tradition*] is the judge over the Koran [Qur'an], and not the Koran judge of the Sunna"; I. Goldziher, *Mohammedanische Suidien*, vol. 2 (Halle: Niemeyer, 1889), p. 19.

19. See Bell's discussion of Christian and Jewish influences on Muhammad, pp. 100ff.

20. Browne, p. 14. Historians are uncertain about the degree of Muhammad's own literacy. He used secretaries. One of his wives (Hafsa) could read and write; two others could read but not write.

21. It is not known when the first translation of the gospels into Arabic was made. A tradition, repeated by Bar Hebraeus (Abu'l Faraj) in the thirteenth century, relates that an Arab prince ordered "a Monophysite named John" to make a translation around the year A.D. 635, but the earliest surviving fragments cannot be dated earlier than the ninth century; see B. Spuler, *The Muslim World*, pt. I (Leiden: Brill, 1960), p. 26, n. 1. Whatever Muhammad may have learned directly of the Christian Scriptures must have come from oral communication. See Brill, *First Encyclopedia of Islam* (Leiden, 1987), pp. 1913–1936ff, on *Injil* (or *Indjil*, gospel). Injil in the Qur'an refers primarily to the revelation of God to Jesus, and secondarily to the Christian Scriptures.

22. Spuler, p. 117.

23. References and quotations from the Qur'an are from the translation of A. Yusuf Ali, *The Meaning of the Glorious Quran: Text* [in Arabic], *Translation* [in English], *and Commentary* (Cairo, Beirut, and Lahore, 1938ff.), which is the work of a committed Muslim. For felicitous English phrasing, compare A. J. Arberry in Oxford's the World's Classics series, *The Koran Interpreted* (Oxford, London, New York: Oxford University Press, 1964). Verse numbering varies slightly in other translations.

24. See especially Suras 3, 5, and 19, which are named for events connected with Jesus. Other scattered references should be noted, particularly Sura 2:87, 253; 4:157–159, 171; 9:30–31; 43:57–65; 57:26–27; and 61:6. For extended treatments of Jesus as portrayed in the Qur'an, see G. Parrinder, *Jesus in the Qur'an* (New York: Sheldon, 1965); S. M. Zwemer, *The Moslem Christ, An Essay on the Life, Character, and Teachings of Jesus Christ According to the Koran and Orthodox Tradition* (New York: American Tract Society, 1912); and Cragg, pp. 100–120.

25. Muslim commentators have never quite been able to correlate the statement in Sura 4:157 that Jesus did *not* die, with that in Sura 3:55, where God says (in literal translation), "I will make thee die." Muslim translations soften this in English to, "I will take thee."

26. W. Muir, *The Life of Mohammed* (Edinburgh: Grant, 1923), pp. xxff.

27. Some, like T. P. Hughes, in *A Dictionary of Islam* (Lahore: Premier Book House, 1885; reprint, 1964), argue that the Qur'an never disputes the genuine inspiration of the New Testament text, but only refers to its distortion by Christians in their reading of it; see article on "Injil."

28. Holt, et al., eds., *The Cambridge History of Islam*, vol. 1, pp. 33–35. See also Bell, p. 12ff.

# DISCUSSION QUESTIONS

1.     Reflect on what you have learned about Muhammad. What things have increased your understanding about Muhammad and Islam? Has your respect for him also changed?

2.     Reflect on Christianity in Muhammad's time. What kind of interaction did Muhammad have with Jews, Christians, and their holy books? What impression did they give him, and why?

3.     What implications does what you have learned have for Christians today?

# RECOMMENDED READINGS & ACTIVITIES*

Read:    Karen Armstrong, *Muhammad: A Biography of the Prophet* (New York: Harper Collins, 1992).

Watch: *The Message: The Story of Islam*, starring Anthony Quinn (Anchor Bay Entertainment, 1976).

Pray:    Pray for unreached people groups using Caleb Project prayer cards.

Order:   A free Qur'an on the Internet.

Surf:    Discover related web sites at *www.encounteringislam.org/lessonlinks*.

# LESSON 2
## EXPANSION OF ISLAM

## PONDER THIS

- What benefits did Islam bring to the cultures into which it expanded?

- What are some of the historical reasons that have attracted people to Islam?

- How has the world benefited from Islamic contributions to global civilization?

- How have today's conflicts been influenced by past confrontations between "Islamic" and "Christian" societies?

# LESSON OBJECTIVE

Describe, from the Muslim point of view, the expansion of Islam:

1. Briefly describe the geographic and demographic spread of Islam—west to Spain; east on the Silk Road through Central Asia to China, India, the Philippines, and Indonesia; to Africa; and eventually to western Europe and North America.

2. Illustrate how Islam's expansion was not only in politics, but also in culture, trade, and the advancement of knowledge.

3. Illustrate how, in many cases, Islamic governance was welcomed as deliverance from oppressive rule by the communities it conquered, and how the religious conversion was more gradual than forced.

4. Describe how these early interactions set the stage for future conflicts: political and cultural clash wrapped in religious garment. Include past European reaction to Islam's expansion, today's prejudice against Muslim countries, and Muslims' prejudices against the West. Note that these mutual distortions occur in political, economic, and military actions. In particular, take into account the Crusades and colonialism.

# LESSON READINGS

# INTRODUCTION

Within one hundred years of Muhammad's death, Muslims ruled the area from Spain to Afghanistan. How and why did Islam expand so rapidly, and what were Islamic societies like? Many times history is taught in such a way that over emphasizes conquest. The political and economic leadership of Muslims, plus advances in science, technology, law, and art, are often neglected. My high school history text compared the advance of Muslim forces into Spain and France with the sack and burning of Rome by the Goths.

An Uzbek man wearing a Doppa (hat)

© Caleb Project

It did not occur to me as a student to question what I was taught. Nor did I pause to wonder who was preserving the knowledge of the Greeks for "rediscovery" during the Renaissance, or why Columbus was motivated to find a new route to India and China. I never learned about the vast Islamic civilizations of Africa and Asia, including the empires of Delhi, Hausa, Suanusiya, Turkestan, or Yunnan. Not until I went to East Africa and later studied in Turkey did I discover the omissions from my education.

Like others, every time I heard that Islam was "spread by the sword," I assumed Muslim subjugations were very bloody and entailed wholesale destruction. True, early Muslim conquests were indeed wars, and Muslims even called them "jihad." However, they were benign in comparison to the Crusades and the Mongol invasions. Early generals were exiled by the caliph if they treated Christians and Jews brutally. Many Muslim armies did not put even true pagans to death, but gradually converted them with economic and political pressure. Islam was also spread by trade relationships and evangelism, instead of by forceful rule. For example, the Mongols were converted to Islam by evangelism, not by battlefield victories.

## Independence and the End of Western Imperialism

A surprising number of the countries where Muslims live did not become independent of colonial powers until the twentieth century. They are listed here with their dates of independence and occupying powers:

Be-Belgium
Br-Britain
F-France
G-Germany
Is-Israel
It-Italy
M-Morocco
N-Netherlands
P-Portugal
R-Russia
S-Spain
T-Turkey
US-United States
Y-Yugoslavia

| Year | Country (Power) |
|------|-----------------|
| 1918 | Saudi Arabia (Br, T) |
| 1921 | Turkey (F, R, It) |
| 1925 | Iran (Br) |
| 1932 | Iraq (Br) |
| 1936 | Egypt (Br) |
| 1943 | Lebanon (F) |
| 1945 | Albania (It) |
| 1946 | Jordan (Br), Philippines (US), Syria (F) |
| 1947 | India, including Pakistan and Bangladesh (Br) |
| 1948 | Myanmar (Br), Sri Lanka (Br) |
| 1949 | Indonesia (N) |
| 1951 | Libya (F) |
| 1953 | Cambodia (F) |
| 1954 | Laos (F), Vietnam (F) |
| 1956 | Morocco (F, S), Sudan (Br), Tunisia (F) |
| 1959 | Guinea (F) |
| 1960 | Benin (F), Burkina Faso (F), Cameroon (F), Chad (F), Central African Republic (F), Congo (F), Ivory Coast (F), Cyprus (Br), Ghana (Br), Madagascar (F), Mali (F), Mauritania (F), Niger (F), Nigeria (Br), Senegal (F), Somalia (Br, It), Togo (F), Democratic Republic of Congo (Be) |

Though Muslims also have their own biases, many times failing to acknowledge their debt to Greek philosophy, science, and astronomy, the world owes much to the cultural achievements of Muslim civilizations. An appreciation for these accomplishments should affect our relationships with Muslims today. Are we willing to lay aside our myths and prejudices in order to understand Muslims' perspective on the world? It is an issue of fairness, is it not?

English speakers today still use many Arabic terms, like "alchemy," "alcohol," "algebra," "algorithm," "alkali," "antimony," and "azimuth," and those are just the As! Arabic terms fill our technical language all the way to zero and zenith. Personally, I am quite grateful that I do not balance my checkbook using Roman numerals but benefit from the Arabic numeral system. Christopher Columbus used maps and instruments derived from Muslim technology when he sailed to the New World. Roger Bacon (1214–1294), regarded as the father of the European Renaissance and the scientific method, credited the Islamic world as his most valuable source; Muslims had already discovered what he explained to Europeans. And, contrary to popular opinion, tulips did not originate in Holland—they came from Turkey.

As Muslim rule extended through the world, populations did not immediately convert en masse. Often non-Muslims (called "dhimmi") were protected, but they paid for this protection through higher taxes, a common practice of regimes at the time. Many of those under Muslim rule preferred this relatively benevolent system over the oppression they faced under "Christian" Byzantines. Certainly these non-Muslims were second-class citizens with few rights. Over time many did convert, either to secure lower taxes or to alleviate their oppression. Other peoples continued to flee "Christian" rule for the protected minority status under Muslim rulers (for instance, the Jews' escape of the Spanish Inquisition).

Islam flowered during Europe's Dark Ages, making progress in learning, art, medicine, law, engineering, and military arts. Muslim scholars brought back to light the works of antiquity and advanced their own theories, though their names are forgotten by many today: Al-Battani, Ibn al-Baytar, Al-Biruni, Al-Idrisi, Hunayn ibn Ishaq, Al-Khawarazmi, *Omar Khayyam*, Ibn Rashud (Averroes), Al-Razi, Ibn Sina (Avicenna), Abu al-Qasim al-Zahrawi, and Al-Zarqali. One scholar of history describes the true origin of Europe's renaissance.

It was under the influence of the Arabian and *Moorish* revival of culture, and not in the fifteenth century, that the real renaissance took place. Spain, not Italy, was the cradle of the rebirth of Europe. After steadily sinking lower and lower into barbarism, Christian Europe had reached the darkest depths of ignorance and degradation when the cities of the *Saracenic* world, Baghdad, *Cairo*, Cordova, Toledo, were growing centers of civilization and intellectual activity. It was there that the new life arose which was to grow into a new phase of human evolution. From the time when the

| 1961 | Kuwait (Br), Sierra Leone (Br), Tanzania (G) |
| 1962 | Algeria (F), Burundi (Be), Rwanda (Be), Uganda (Br) |
| 1963 | Kenya (Br), Malaysia (Br) |
| 1964 | Malawi (Br), Malta (Br), Zambia (Br) |
| 1965 | Gambia (Br), Maldives (Br), Singapore (Br) |
| 1967 | Yemen (Br) |
| 1968 | Equatorial Guinea (S) |
| 1971 | Bahrain (Br), Qatar (Br), United Arab Emirates (Br) |
| 1974 | Guinea-Bissau (P) |
| 1975 | Gabon (P), Mozambique (P), Western Sahara (S), Comoros (F) |
| 1976 | Seychelles (Br) |
| 1977 | Djibouti (F) |
| 1983 | Brunei (Br) |
| 1989 | Afghanistan (R) |
| 1991 | Azerbaijan, Kazakhstan, Kyrgyzstan, Tajikistan, Turkmenistan, Uzbekistan (R) |
| 1992 | Slovenia, Croatia, Bosnia-Herzegovina (Y) |

Still Occupied: West Bank and Gaza (Is), Western Sahara (M), Mayotte (F)

Adapted from: Don McCurry, *Healing the Broken Family of Abraham* (Colorado Springs, Colo.: Ministry to Muslims, 2001), pp. 349–50. Used by permission. *www.mtmsims.org*

influence of their culture made itself felt began the stirring of new life.[1]

Islam continued to spread, even during the Crusades and the takeover of Muslim lands by the Mongols, through missionary efforts by tradesmen and mystics. Muslims came to hold much of the world's wealth and power, with monopolies and control of the trade routes for silk, slaves, and spices. Not until Cortez came to the New World and acquired all the gold he could locate for Spain did the economic scales shift in favor of Europe. Even as its Sultan's leadership faltered back in Asia, the Ottoman Empire maintained supremacy for another four hundred years, as did other Muslim rulers in Sub-Saharan Africa, South Asia, China, and Indonesia.

Only in the latter half of the nineteenth century did European powers truly catch up to the Muslim world economically, militarily, and culturally. Unfortunately, that European imperialism left a powerful imprint on the Muslim world. Even at this later stage, the rift between Christian and Muslim societies continues to be as much political and cultural as it is religious.

Most Muslim peoples did not gain autonomous governance from European colonial powers until the 1960s. The last Muslim nations were not freed from colonial rule until the 1990s. Today, sixty percent of the world's poorest people are Muslims. Eighty percent of the world's refugees are Muslims. Eighty-one percent of predominantly Muslim countries do not have direct elections.

Whatever the reasons, Muslim societies are not as glorious now as they once were. Some Muslims blame this entirely on the greed and power of the West. Others identify ways in which Muslims have not been faithful to Islam and ask if part of the problem is God's chastening. In response to such challenges, today's Muslims have experienced reforms and revivals.

As citizens of Christ's kingdom, how do we interpret history and how do we respond? For one thing, we can recognize that Jesus Christ came to overturn the logic of the world and establish God's spiritual kingdom. Power, wealth, success, and even knowledge are not sure signs of God's blessing or of being on "God's side." Both Christian and Muslim societies make this misjudgment. Jesus said, "My kingdom is not of this world. If it were, my servants would fight to prevent my arrest by the Jews" (John 18:36).

– *K.S., Editor*

## ENDNOTE

1. Robert Briffault, *Rational Evolution: The Making of Humanity* (New York: MacMillan, 1930), p. 138.

# A BRIEF HISTORY OF MUSLIM CIVILIZATION

*by Bruce Sidebotham*

## THE UMAYYAD PERIOD OF CONQUEST (A.D. 632–732)

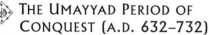

Islam spread rapidly after the death of Muhammad. Political rule was extended to Syria, *Mesopotamia*, Persia, Palestine, Egypt, North Africa, and the Iberian Peninsula. Major centers of cultural Christianity like Antioch, Alexandria, Jerusalem, and Carthage came under Muslim rule.

At certain times in some places Islamic rule offered more than the rule of Christendom. The rival Byzantine and Persian empires, racked with internal feuds, gave way rapidly to the new overlords who could arbitrate their feuds impartially. Rome and Constantinople remained centers of Christian rule, though much of Europe was in its "Dark Ages."

## THE ABBASID PERIOD OF CONSOLIDATION (A.D. 732–1250)

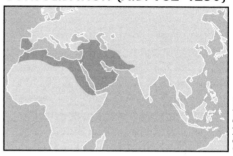

Islamic influence, strongly felt in Spain, did not expand into France and surrounding Europe because *Charles Martel*, general of the Franks, stopped the Muslim Berber advance at Poitiers and then *Tours*, France.

Islamic civilization experienced a Golden Age for several hundred years. Learning flourished in Arab and Persian communities and cities like Cordoba and the new city of Baghdad, which became one of the world's largest cities. Great cultural advances were made based on earlier Greek works in science, law, philosophy, and medicine; and in art, architecture, and poetry. Political power migrated from Arabia to Egypt, Baghdad, Persia, and eventually Turkey.

To the East, many people were suffering under the rapidly expanding Mongol empire, which also brought Turks into

Dr. Bruce Sidebotham spent seven years in cross-cultural ministry in Indonesia. He directs a branch of Mission to Unreached Peoples, called Operation Reveille, which trains and equips service personnel for cross-cultural ministry.

Adapted from *The Reveille Shofar*, 6, No. 1 (first quarter 2002). Used by permission. *www.oprev.org*

Byzantine Asia Minor and today's Central Asia. Both Mongols and Turks were eventually converted to Islam and subsequently spread Islam into India and China, establishing empires there in the next period.

During the period of the Crusades (1095–1272), Christians captured Jerusalem and significant parts of Palestine. Events surrounding the Crusades left huge scars on Muslim-Christian relations, but were not particularly disruptive of overall Muslim rule. The beginning of the Renaissance in Europe was greatly influenced by new knowledge and advancements brought back from Muslim civilization by returning Crusaders.

## THE OTTOMAN PERIOD OF RESURGENCE (A.D. 1250–1700)

© Caleb Project

The Muslim empire of the Ottoman Turks was the largest empire of its day, dominating the region for 650 years. The Ottomans took the Crusader cities of Antioch in 1268, and Acre (Syria) in 1291, and the Byzantine's Constantinople in 1453. Ottoman conquest of Europe was halted at Vienna in 1683. Islam's entry

to the Balkans during this period set the stage for World War I and modern crises in Kosovo and Bosnia.

Islam reached into India and East Africa between the tenth and twelfth centuries through both conquest and trade. In West Africa, Timbuktu became a center of Islamic learning. Missionaries, mystics, and merchants took Islam into the Malay Peninsula and Indonesia between the thirteenth and fifteenth centuries. Mongol conquests facilitated the spreading and strengthening of Islam throughout the regions of Central, South, and East Asia. Known in South Asia as the *Mughals*, these Central Asian rulers controlled much of India until the nineteenth century. The first of India's Mughal rulers, *Babur* (1483–1530) was a descendant from both Central Asia's *Timur* (1336–1405) and *Genghis Khan*. Shah Jahan, another Mughal ruler, built the Taj Mahal at the height of Islamic prosperity in India.

Muslims dominated much of the global trade that increased during this time. Their monopoly of the spice trade led Columbus to seek alternate trade routes in 1492, which brought him to America and led to the growth of the Spanish, Portuguese, and other rival Western European empires. In the same year Muslim Moors were driven from Spain and Portugal.

## THE COLONIAL PERIOD OF DECLINE (A.D. 1700–1979)

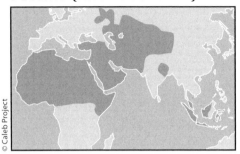

In the seventeenth and eighteenth centuries the once invincible but now corrupt and bureaucratic Ottoman Empire became more decentralized and eventually disintegrated. The Ottoman Empire officially ended in 1922 following an alliance with Germany in World War I. Imperialistic western powers came to rule almost the entire Muslim world. Henceforth, the "Christian" West would dictate international relations and set the political boundaries of the modern Muslim world.

Some Muslims blame the "Christian" West for the resulting disunity, instability, and relative weakness of the Muslim world as it went into political decline. Booming populations in many Muslim areas, wealth from oil, and resentment toward the West fueled the growth of Islamic missionary and political activities. These entrenched feelings, plus economic instability, primed parts of the Muslim world for change, whether in the form of revival, reform, resurgence, or even revolution.

## THE MODERN PERIOD OF INTERNAL CRISIS (A.D. 1979 TO THE PRESENT)

The 1979 deposition of Iran's moderate Shah by more conservative elements marks a turning point in modern Islamic history. "Islamist" Muslims in many countries have been struggling to reunite the Muslim community under Shari'a law, with some success. Islamists seek to defend and liberate Muslims from foreign ideas and influence, sometimes through extreme means. Yet many Muslims prefer moderate or secular ideals. From Algeria to the Philippines, and from Chechnya to the Sudan, Islamist groups are fighting secular governments and their own moderate brethren. For various Islamists, the struggle is more a political rallying cry and a symbol of past glories than a religious movement.

# THE SPREAD AND DEVELOPMENT OF ISLAM

*by Colin Chapman*

It is impossible to begin to understand Islam today without some idea of how it has developed since the time of the Prophet. This is especially important for Christians, since for fourteen centuries Islam has developed alongside Christianity, and for much of this time has not enjoyed an easy relationship with Christendom.

This is how Kenneth Cragg sums up some of the difficulties that Christians are likely to encounter in reflecting on this history:

> Among the factors contributing to the rise of Islam was the Christian failure of the church. It was a failure in love, in purity, and in fervor, a failure of the spirit. Truth (as often before and after), was involved—to its hurt—in the spiritual fault of its trustees. Islam developed in an environment of imperfect Christianity, and later, by its own inner force, gathered such strength as to become, and remain, essentially at odds with the pure [Christian] faith....

This is the inward tragedy, from the Christian angle, of the rise of Islam, the genesis and dissemination of a new belief which claimed to displace what it had never effectively known. The state of being a stranger to the Christian's Christ has been intensified by further failures of love and loyalty on the part of institutional Christianity, in the long and often bitter external relations of the two faiths through the centuries.[1]

## THE EARLY SPREAD OF ISLAM

These are the main dates (all A.D.) and events which we need to note:

| | |
|---|---|
| 632 | Muhammad dies. |
| 632–61 | The first four caliphs rule in Medina. |
| 661–750 | The *Umayyad* Dynasty rules in Damascus. |
| 661 | Sunnis and Shi'a split. |
| 710 | Muslim forces reach the Indus. |
| 711 | Muhammad ibn Qasim conducts campaigns in the Sind (southeast Pakistan). |
| 714 | Muslims occupy Spain. |

Colin Chapman has worked with the Church Missionary Society (CMS) and the International Fellowship of Evangelical Students in Egypt, Lebanon, and Cyprus. He is an authority on Islam and is now principal of Crowther Hall, the CMS Training College in Birmingham, England.

Adapted from Colin Chapman, *Cross and Crescent: Responding to the Challenge of Islam* (Leicester, UK: InterVarsity Press, 1995), pp. 127–38. Used by permission. *www.ivpress.com*

## The Arab World

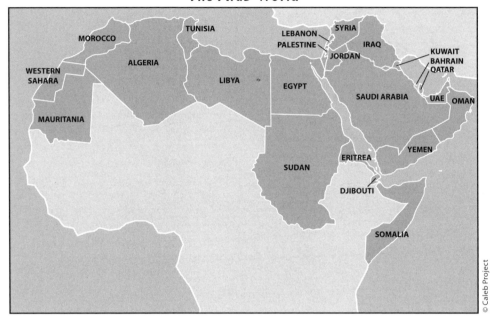

© Caleb Project

## THE ARABIC-SPEAKING WORLD

Many people associate Muslims with the Arab world. Although the majority of Muslims world-wide are not Arab, Islam is rooted in the Arab culture and language of its founder, Muhammad. Islam's holiest cities, Mecca and Medina, to which millions of Muslims make pilgrimage each year, are in the Arabian Peninsula.

North Africa, the Arabian Peninsula, and the Middle East contain 22 Arabic-speaking countries, with almost 280 million people. The countries which compose the Arab world are home to diverse people groups—including Arabs, Berbers, and Bedouin groups, the Tuareg peoples, and the Egyptians—for a total of 209 people groups.

Egypt had a Christian majority until a few hundred years after the beginning of Islam. Today it is 87 percent Muslim. Most of its 74 million people live in the fertile Nile Valley, creating some of the highest population densities in the world. The majority of Egyptians are still *fellahin*, or farmers. While some Egyptians still wear traditional dress of ankle-length tunics, many men in the cities have adopted blue jeans and athletic shoes.

Other significant Arab concentrations are found in Australia, Canada, Iraq, Israel, Libya, Oman, Saudi Arabia, Sudan, the United Arab Emirates, the United Kingdom, the United States, and Yemen.

Sources: *Operation World*, *www.joshuaproject.net*.

| 732 | One hundred years after Muhammad's death, Islamic Empire stretches from Spain to Persia. |
| 732 | Charles Martel defeats the Muslim forces at Poitiers and Tours in France. |
| 750–1258 | The *Abbasid* Dynasty rules in Baghdad; a Golden Age of Islam. |
| 909–1171 | The *Fatimid* Dynasty rules in Egypt. |
| c. 1000 | *Mahmud of Ghazna* invades the Punjab (northwest India); Muslim governor is set up in Lahore. |

In studying the spread of Islam in the first few centuries, we need to take special note of the position of Jews and Christians under Islamic rule, and comment on certain stereotypes in the minds of many about the use of force in the spread of Islam.

First, in several cases Christians welcomed the spread of Islamic rule. In Syria, for example, it brought relief from Byzantine rule, while in Egypt it helped the Copts to depose a puppet patriarch and recall their own exiled patriarch. The Copts joined forces with the Muslims to drive out the Byzantines.

Second, all non-Muslims living under Islamic rule paid a land tax (*kharaj*). Jews and Christians were treated as dhimmi, members of a protected community, and paid in addition a poll tax (*jizyah*). They were not allowed to do military service or pay the Muslims' alms tax.

Third, in the Indian subcontinent, in East Asia, and in West and East Africa, Islam was spread by traders, many of whom came originally from Arabia. Sufis also played an important role in spreading Islam.

Fourth, it is a dangerous oversimplification to say that Islam was "spread by the sword." Since this is such a controversial issue, it is worth comparing the accounts of the spread of Islam in the first four hundred years, given by four writers who approach the subject from different perspectives, and who are writing about the spread of Islam in a particular area at a particular time.

## DIFFERING ACCOUNTS

The first account is written by a Muslim, Hammudah Abdalati, explaining the kinds of pressures that were brought to bear on those who refused to embrace Islam in its earliest years in Arabia:

> Those who rejected Islam and refused to pay tributes, in collaboration with other sectors to support their state, made it hard for themselves. They resorted to a hostile course from the beginning, and meant to create trouble, not so much for the new Muslim comers as for the new Muslim converts and their compatriots, the tribute-payers. In a national sense, that attitude was treacherous; in a human sense, mean; in a social sense, careless; and in a military sense, provocative. But in a practical sense

it needed suppression, not so much for the comfort of the newcomers as for the sake of the state in which these very traitors were living. This is the only time force was applied to bring such people to their senses and make them realize their responsibilities: either as Muslims by accepting Islam freely, or as loyal citizens by being

© Caleb Project

Waiting for the bus in Java

## THE HIJAB

"And say to the believing women that they cast down their looks and guard their private parts and do not display their ornaments except what appears thereof, and let them wear their head-coverings over their bosoms…" (Sura 24:31, SHAKIR).

She was completely covered in a black flowing robe. Her eyes were all I could see. She looked my way. I smiled and stuttered a greeting. Her eyes lit up and we connected. We were both foreigners visiting this Asian country, but we found a friend in each other. We shared and laughed about husbands and marriage. I also spoke about trusting God.

I would have missed this opportunity if I had done what others do—simply passed, and looked anywhere but *at* the veiled Muslim woman. Is it because we are afraid or don't know what to say to them? Maybe we just don't understand why they are dressed differently.

The veil is worn proudly by Muslim women who strongly believe in female modesty. It is also called the *hijab*, *burqa*, *chador*, or *abaaya*. It covers the hair and sometimes the face. Depending on local custom, Muslim dress may include the full-length flowing Saudi *chadris*, a head scarf tied closely to the head (revealing only the face) worn with a modern suit popular in Egypt, or a silky shawl tossed loosely on the head (with the *salwar kameez*, baggy trousers and tunic) worn by Pakistanis. Women wear the veil as a political statement, a sign of religious or cultural identification, a demonstration of family honor, or a way to stay safe and respectable.[1]

A twenty-nine-year-old woman from Saudi Arabia, educated in London, says,

> I think that it is very wrong to believe that the veil…is a sign of oppression, retardation, or subjugation as the West believes.… I wear the veil because, for me, it is a sign of personal and religious choice. It is because I lived in the West, and I saw all the corruption and immorality.… Now I am more convinced of our local traditions and I am more attached to them. I want to preserve my Arab-Islamic identity, and, for me, this is a way to show it.[2]

1 Phil and Julie Parshall, *Lifting the Veil: The World of Muslim Women* (Waynesboro, Ga: Gabriel Publishing, 2002), p. 58.
2 Mona Al Munajed, *Women in Saudi Arabia Today* (New York: St. Martin Press, 1997), p. 57.

Source: Annee W. Rose, *www.frontiers.org.*

## The Holy Injil

© Caleb Project

Cover of an Arabic Bible

tribute-payers, capable of living with their Muslim compatriots and sharing with them equal rights and duties.[2]

The second is an account written by a Christian Islamic scholar, Michael Nazir-Ali, describing some of the campaigns within Arabia itself that were led by *Khalid*, the great military leader in power immediately following Muhammad's death:

Much of the credit for this expansion must go to Khalid, who contributed more than any other man, apart from Muhammad, towards the creation of Islam as a world power. However, although we can admire his military prowess, the same, unfortunately,

cannot be said of his morality. His perfidious treatment of Malik Ibn Noweira is a case in point. Malik's tribe had surrendered to Khalid, and Malik had professed Islam. He was, nevertheless, taken prisoner along with his wife and family, and, in the middle of the night, was treacherously murdered. Khalid forcibly married his widow on the spot. This caused a rebellion in the Muslim ranks, and a formal complaint against Khalid was laid before Abu Bakr. Khalid was only slightly rebuked, although Umar, later the second caliph, had advocated harsher punishment. When Umar became caliph, he relieved Khalid, first of his command in the east, and ultimately of all command. Khalid, so far as we know, spent his last days in great poverty and in obscurity.[3]

The third is an account of the main conquests in the Middle East and North Africa, also written by a Christian Islamic scholar, John Taylor:

When Islam spread rapidly over much of the civilized world, it spread first as a military and political success story; yet it was sometimes centuries before the inhabitants of the conquered lands voluntarily became Muslims. On the other hand, the motive in the minds of the caliphs behind the military and political expansion was that ultimately there should be those conversions to Islam. In the minds of the soldiers, as in every other genera- tion, there was the desire for the spoils of war; but the Muslim conquests were remarkable for their discipline and lack of wanton destruction.[4]

The fourth is an account of the conquests in North India in the tenth century, written by Trevor Ling, a professor of comparative religion at the University of Manchester:

> The purpose of Mahmud, the ruler of Ghazna, in carrying out these raids was to seize the treasure that was known to be available in the form of gold and jewels in the Hindu temples of the Punjab. It so happened that the Islamic concept of jihad, now interpreted as "holy war," provided a religious motivation for the raids, for, as Mahmud's own account of his activities makes clear, he regarded himself as engaged in a war against infidels and idolaters. The nature of his operations has earned him the title of "Mahmud the idol smasher." He is said also to have ordered the slaughter of many Brahmin priests. The part which he played in the coming of the Muslim Turks to north India is of the kind which has too often been taken

## HOLY BOOKS

Muslims refer to the Qur'an and Hadith, as well as the *Torah*, *Psalms*, and the *Gospels*, as holy books. The Qur'an also confirms the teaching of these earlier books:

> Say: "We believe in Allah, and in what has been revealed to us and what was revealed to Abraham, Ismail, Isaac, Jacob, and the Tribes, and in (the Books) given to Moses, Jesus, and the Prophets, from their Lord: We make no distinction between one and another among them" (Sura 3:84, YUSUF ALI).

> If thou wert in doubt as to what we have revealed unto thee, then, ask those who have been reading the Book from before thee: The Truth hath indeed come to thee from thy Lord; so be in no wise of those in doubt (Sura 10:94, YUSUF ALI).

However, Muslims do not trust the Bible since they believe it has been corrupted:

> But because of their breach of their Covenant, we cursed them, and made their hearts grow hard: they change the words from their (right) places and forget a good part of the message that was sent them, nor wilt thou cease to find them—barring a few—ever bent on (new) deceits. But forgive them, and overlook (their misdeeds): for Allah loveth those who are kind. From those, too, who call themselves Christians, We did take a Covenant, but they forgot a good part of the Message that was sent them; so we estranged them, with enmity and hatred between the one and the other, to the Day of Judgment. And soon will Allah show them what it is they have done. O People of the Book! There hath come to you our Messenger, revealing to you much that ye used to hide in the Book, and passing over much (that is now unnecessary): there hath come to you from Allah a (new) light and a perspicuous [easy to understand] Book (Sura 5:13–15, YUSUF ALI).

But Muslims are encouraged to read the Bible for themselves:

> And recite (and teach) what has been revealed to thee of the Book of thy Lord: none can change His Words, and none wilt thou find as a refuge other than Him (Sura 18:27, YUSUF ALI).

Source: *Encountering the World of Islam*

## Where Is the Middle East?

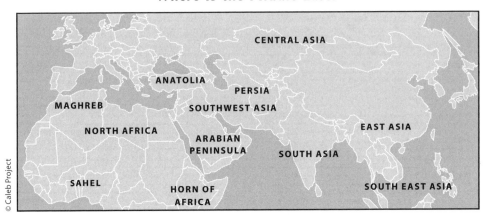

© Caleb Project

to be typical of the advance of Islam everywhere—by the sword. It was against this view that T. W. Arnold's account of the expansion of Islam in 1913 in *The Preaching of Islam* provided so valuable a corrective.[5]

## THE CRUSADES AND MEDIEVAL MUSLIM—CHRISTIAN RELATIONS

It should not take Christians long to discover that the Crusades have left a deep scar on the minds of Muslims all over the world. Although they ended more than seven hundred years ago, for many Muslims it is as if they happened only yesterday. And recent events such as the *Rushdie Affair*, the Gulf War, and the Bosnian conflict have made many feel that the Crusades have never ended. These are some of the key dates and events:

| 1060 | Beginning of campaigns to drive the Moors out of Spain. |
| --- | --- |
| 1096–1291 | The Crusades. |
| 1169 | Capture of Jerusalem from Christians by *Salah al-Din (Saladin)*. |
| 1206 | Invasion of Muslim Turks into North India; set up of sultanate of Delhi. |
| 1220–49 | Mongol invasion of Persia under Genghis Khan; destruction of Baghdad. |
| 1291 | Fall of *Acre*. |
| 1390 | The *Mamluk* Dynasty in Egypt; Cairo now center of Muslim world. |
| 1396 | Eastern Europe entered by the Turks. |
| 1453 | Fall of Constantinople to Ottoman Turks. |
| 1503–1722 | *Safavid* Empire in Persia. |

| | |
|---|---|
| 1512–1918 | Ottoman Empire; centered in Turkey. |
| 1526–1858 | The Mughal Empire in North India. |
| 1565 | Repulse of Turkish attack on Malta. |
| 1683 | Repulse of Turkish attack on Vienna. |

The legacy of the Crusades is accurately summed up in a single sentence by Ling: "An enduring result of the Crusades was the embittering of relations between Christians and Muslims for many generations, and a vast amount of misrepresentation and misunderstanding on both sides."[6]

Albert Hourani speaks similarly about the legacy of suspicion and enmity that has been left by the struggle between the Christian world and Islam over many centuries:

It is easy to see the historical relationship of Christians and Muslims in terms of holy war, of Crusade and jihad, and there is some historical justification for this. The first great Muslim expansion in Christian lands—Syria, Egypt and North Africa, Spain, and Sicily; the first Christian reconquests—in Spain, Sicily, and the Holy Land; the spread of Ottoman power in Asia Minor

## WHERE IS THE MIDDLE EAST?

*The Far East, the Sub-Continent, the Near East,* and *the Middle East.* Each of these terms has been used to specify parts of Asia and even Africa. But such designations do not have commonly accepted meanings and often carry negative connotations for the peoples who live in the areas described. Territories labeled "the Far East" and "the Sub-Continent" are better described as East Asia and South Asia. However, "the Near East," and especially "the Middle East," do not have clear, alternative names.

At times "the Near East" is said to include Central Asia (the "-stan" countries) and Iran (Persia). Sometimes Iran, Pakistan, and Afghanistan are included as part of "the Middle East," although they are linguistically, historically, and culturally distinct. Because of North Africa's linguistic ties and Turkey's historic connections (through the Ottoman Empire), they also are mislabeled part of "the Middle East," though Turks (and Iranians) typically do not care to be referred to as Middle Easterners.

Modern Turkey does have a distinct geographic name: *Anatolia.* So do Saudi Arabia, Yemen, and the other Arab Gulf States: the Arabian Peninsula. Terms like Anatolia, Arabian Peninsula, Central Asia, North Africa, and Persia are accurate for these geographic regions and acceptable to their inhabitants. Updating our nomenclature is appropriate. (For example, Westerners no longer call Southeast Asia "Indochina"). Though referring to Iraq (ancient Mesopotamia), Israel, Jordan, Lebanon, Palestine, and Syria as *"Southwest Asia"* may seem awkward, this designation is more accurate than "the Middle East."

Source: *Encountering the World of Islam*

and the Balkans; and then the spread of European power in the last two centuries: All these processes have created and maintained an attitude of suspicion and hostility on both sides, and still provide, if not a reason for enmity, at least a language in which it can express itself.[7]

Hourani goes on to explain, however, that the relationship between the two faiths in Western Europe has been more complex than this:

> But Crusade and jihad do not cover the whole reality of political relations between Christendom and the world of Islam, and still less do they explain the attitude of Christians to Islam, and of Muslims to Christianity. The communities which profess the two religions have faced each other across the Mediterranean for more than a thousand years; with hostility, it is true, but with a look of uneasy recognition in their eyes.

> When Western Europe first faced the challenge of Muslim power, it did so without any real knowledge of what it was fighting, and the combination of fear and ignorance produced a body of legends, some absurd and all unfair.[8]

## AGAPE LOVE

God showed his boundless love for all people by sending his Son to die for them, to redeem them. This act proved that all men are loved by God. His *agape* love is unconditional love, a love that does not demand or expect reciprocation. God's love impels us to love others with the same selfless love God showed us in Christ.

Since love is a choice—an action (not a response or affection)—we can demonstrate this love by showing respect for our Muslim neighbors. We may not hold the same opinions as Muslims do, but we should not belittle Muhammad, Islamic teachings, or its religious leaders. We can use our words and deeds (such as greetings, dress, and mannerisms) to express our respect for our Muslim friends, their culture, and their worldview. We can let them teach us about their uniqueness. By deciding not to let politics, religion, or nationality get in the way, we can find ways to relate to one another.

While the Qur'an says God is merciful and compassionate, many Muslims view God primarily as judge and king. As a result, Islam can be a religion of law and regulations. Muslims live in fear, not sure if God cares for them, and yearning to experience his loving grace. Agape love can open the door.

The Holy Spirit can help us love. The first fruit of his indwelling power is agape love (see Gal. 5:22–23) —the same love with which God loves us, the same love by which we are to be known (see John 13:35). Ask the Holy Spirit to motivate you with a special love for Muslims. We are the hands and feet of Jesus. Through us, Muslims can experience Christ's love. If we say we love him, we must love as he loves.

Source: Fouad Masri, *www.crescentproject.org*.

## EUROPEAN COLONIALISM AND THE MISSIONARY MOVEMENT

Some will no doubt object to the idea of linking Western Colonialism with Christian mission. They probably feel uncomfortable about some of the links between the missionaries on the one hand, and the soldiers, the traders, and the administrators on the other. The perception of the Muslim world, however, is that these two movements came basically from the same source, the desire of the Christian West to dominate the world.

| | |
|---|---|
| 1757 | British expansion in India begins. |
| 1792 | *William Carey* begins his work in India. |
| 1798 | Napoleon arrives in Egypt. |
| 1805–1812 | *Henry Martyn's* work takes place in India and Persia. |
| 1857 | The Indian Mutiny and War of Independence occurs. |
| 1910 | Edinburgh Missionary Conference held. |
| 1917 | British General Allenby enters Jerusalem. Ottoman Turks are defeated. Ottoman Empire ends. |
| 1922 | The Caliphate abolished by *Ataturk*. |
| 1948 | State of Israel established. |

Coming after centuries of uneasy relationships between Muslims and Christians in Europe and the Mediterranean, the colonial era, beginning in the middle of the eighteenth century, created a further crisis for the Muslim world. This is how Kenneth Cragg explains what over two centuries of "Christian" imperialism meant to the Muslim world:

> Islam was largely under non-Muslim government in wide areas of its dispersion. Western imperial control did not, by and large, affect the practice of religion. It did not close mosques, forbid Ramadan or pilgrimage, or proscribe belief. By all these "religious" tests (as a Westerner might see them), Islam was altogether free. But, politically, in many areas, Muslims did not rule themselves. Recall the basic conviction, arising from its origins, that Islam must rule. Recall the long caliphal history when Islam did rule. From the Hijra on, Islam had bound religion and rule into one.
>
> Not, then, to have Muslim rule, however free the rituals, is not to be Islam in a full sense. It is a state of exile, the puzzle and pain of which caused much debate in the nineteenth century. In India, for example, Islam was bewildered and dismayed.[9]

## REFORM AND RENEWAL MOVEMENTS IN ISLAM

Against this background of despair and defeat, we can begin to understand the significance of the following nine people who led movements for the reform and renewal of Islam. But we must bear in mind that it is not always easy to determine the extent to which the impulses towards revival have come from outside influences and to what extent they have come from within.

**1. Shah Wali Allah** (1702–62) of Delhi worked for the renewal of Islam in India. For him, this meant getting rid of Hindu elements which had crept into Islam and encouraging the hope that Muslim government would once again be restored. In Wali Allah's view of Islam, "A broad, humanistic sociological basis is overlain by a doctrine of social and economic justice in Islamic terms, and crowned by a Sufi worldview" (Fazlur Rahman). According to S. M. Ikram, a Pakistani historian, "More than anyone else he is responsible for the religious regeneration of Indian Islam."[10]

**2. Muhammad ibn Abd al-Wahhab** (1703–92) was an Arab sheik who, after years of travel in Iraq and Persia, returned to Arabia at the age of forty and began a movement for the purification of Islam. The main targets of his attack were: (1) aspects of popular Islam, such as the veneration of saints, visiting the tombs of saints, belief in the intercession of the Prophet and saints, and other forms of what he regarded as "superstition"; (2) the lowering of moral standards among Muslims; and (3) additions to basic Islamic beliefs and practices from the Sufis, philosophers, and theologians. He appealed to the Qur'an and the Sunna as the only sources of authority and rejected all other later Muslim authorities.

The legacy of the movement which al-Wahhab began is summed up by Trevor Ling as follows: "The challenge of the Wahhabi movement to moral corruption within Islam, and its emphasis upon the importance of the moral element in Muslim life and thought, had a lasting effect, in that this became an almost universal feature of subsequent reform movements, both in Arabia and elsewhere in the Muslim world."[11]

**3. Sayyid Ahmad Khan** (1817–98) of Delhi was much more positive than many other Muslims toward modern scientific knowledge and argued that it was fully compatible with Islam. He also tried to convince fellow Muslims that Islam and Christianity have much in common. "It is to him," says Trevor Ling, "that a great deal of credit must be given for the awakening of the Muslims of India to a new understanding of the possible place of Islamic religion in the modern world."[12]

**4. Jamal al-Din al-Afghani** (1839–97) was more concerned with the social and political issues facing Muslims and protested against the intrusion of alien elements in the areas of politics, culture, and religion. In his concern to unite the Muslim world, he became the leader of the *Pan-Islam* movement, which called for the creation of an Islamic world state.

**5. Muhammad Abduh** (1849–1905), an Egyptian theologian who taught at the *al-Azhar University* in Cairo, was critical of the rigidity and conservatism of many orthodox theologians whose minds seemed closed to everything in the modern world. He stood for a liberal and open kind of Islam, arguing that faith and reason were

compatible, and that there need be no contradiction between faith and modern knowledge. He wanted to see greater flexibility in the formulation of Islamic law, believing that traditional laws should in certain cases be replaced by new laws that were more appropriate to the social context. He was not, however, prepared to apply modern critical methods to the study of the Qur'an. As a result of his teaching, a new kind of secular modernism grew up in the Middle East, some of whose adherents called for the separation of religion and state. At the same time, there was opposition from *fundamentalist* groups which wanted to return to the Qur'an and Sunna.

**6. Muhammad Iqbal** (1873–1938) was for many years the leader of the *Muslim League*, a movement which was founded in 1906 to focus the political aspirations of Muslims in India. From 1930 he began to argue for a separate Muslim state in India, and because of his widespread influence, he is generally regarded as "the spiritual founder of the state of Pakistan" [nine years after his death, Pakistan gained independence].[13] In discussions about Islamic law, he believed that the interpretation of the law needed to be opened up in a radical way. He is also well known for his writings as a poet and philosopher.

**7. Mawlana Abu al-Ala Mawdudi** (1903–79) was a journalist and a self-taught Islamic scholar who founded the organization called *Jamaat-i Islami* (Community of Islam) in 1941. Although at first he opposed the idea of establishing a separate Muslim state, when the state of Pakistan came into existence in 1947, his main aim became "the

thorough Islamization of the government of Pakistan and its purging from all western moral, spiritual, and political values and practices."[14]

**8. Hasan al-Banna** (1906–79) was brought up in a small village in the Nile Delta in Egypt and learned much of his Islam from his father who was a graduate of the al-Azhar University in Cairo. While working as a teacher in Ismailiyya on the Suez Canal, he became acutely aware of the depressed state of the Muslim world—politically, culturally, and economically. He and some friends bound themselves together by an oath and called themselves the *Muslim Brothers* (*Ikhwan al-Muslimun*).

During the 1930s and 1940s the movement grew rapidly, in spite of being officially banned at times by the government for demanding that the Shari'a should be established as the law of the country. After a member of *The Brotherhood* assassinated the prime minister who had banned the movement, Banna himself was assassinated by the secret police. The Brotherhood, although officially suppressed in some Arab countries, is still very active, and continues to call for the restoration of Shari'a law, sometimes by peaceful means and sometimes through revolution and violence.

**9. Ayatollah Ruhollah Khomeini** (1900–89) was born into a family in which both his father and grandfather had been religious scholars. At the age of nineteen he began his studies in the religious sciences under Shi'i scholars, mostly at the holy city of Qom to the south of Tehran. He soon attracted the attention of his

teachers and colleagues because of the way he combined a deep spirituality and mysticism with a passionate concern for social and political issues.

He found himself in opposition to the Iranian monarchy, which he saw as a totalitarian dictatorship determined to eliminate Islam as a cultural, social, and political force. After his first public statement against the government in 1943, he became a popular leader who expressed the aspirations of his people. He was arrested in 1963 after protesting against a series of measures which he believed would bring the country further under foreign influence, and was later released.

During periods of exile in Turkey, Iraq, and France (1964–79), his sermons and lectures were distributed widely through the network of mosques within Iran, both in print and on cassette, and he received a rapturous welcome when he returned to Tehran in 1979 after the Shah had left the country. In a special ruling (fatwa) some months after the publication of the book *The Satanic Verses* in 1988, he pronounced the death sentence on its author, Salman Rushdie. He remained the leader of the Islamic revolution in Iran until his death in 1989.

With this summary of movements of revival and reform within Islam, we should be in a position to appreciate some of the issues facing the Muslim world today.

**End of key readings for Lesson 2. See** RECOMMENDED READINGS & ACTIVITIES **on p. 75.**

## ENDNOTES:

1. Kenneth Cragg, *The Call of the Minaret* (London: Collins, 1986), p. 219.
2. Hammudah Abdalati, *Islam in Focus* (London: World Assembly of Muslim Youth, 1980), p. 150.
3. Michael Nazir-Ali, *Islam: A Christian Perspective* (Carlisle, UK: Paternoster, 1984), pp. 35–36.
4. John Taylor, *Introducing Islam* (Cambridge: Lutterworth Press, 1971), p. 33.
5. Trevor Ling, *A History of Religion East and West* (New York: Macmillan, 1982), p. 300; he cites T. W. Arnold, *The Preaching of Islam* (publisher unknown, 1913).
6. Ling, p. 302.
7. Albert Hourani, *Europe and the Middle East* (Berkeley: University of California Press, 1980), p. 4.
8. Ibid., p. 9.
9. Cragg, *Islam and the Muslim* (Maidenhead, Berkshire, UK: Open University Press, 1978), pp. 78–79.
10. Author did not source Rahman or Ikram.
11. Ling, p. 300.
12. Ibid., p. 384.
13. Ibid., p. 387.
14. Ibid., p. 395.

# ISLAM AND THE DEVELOPMENT OF KNOWLEDGE

*by The Royal Embassy of Saudi Arabia*

Islam is a religion based upon knowledge, for it is ultimately knowledge of the oneness of God, combined with faith and total commitment to him, that saves man. The text of the Qur'an is replete with verses inviting man to use his intellect, to ponder, to think, and to know, for the goal of human life is to discover the truth, which is none other than worshiping God in his oneness.

The hadith literature is also full of references to the importance of knowledge. Such sayings of the Prophet as "Seek knowledge even in China," "Seek knowledge from the cradle to the grave," and "Verily, the men of knowledge are the inheritors of the prophets," have echoed throughout the history of Islam and incited Muslims to seek knowledge wherever it might be found. During most of its history, Islamic civilization has been witness to a veritable celebration of knowledge. That is why every traditional Islamic city possessed public and private libraries, and some cities like Cordoba and Baghdad boasted of libraries with more than 400,000 books. Such cities also had bookstores, some of which sold a large number of titles. That is also why the scholar has always been held in the highest esteem in Islamic society.

## ASSIMILATION OF PRE-ISLAMIC SCIENCES

As Islam spread northward into Syria, Egypt, and the Persian Empire, it came face to face with those sciences of antiquity whose heritage had been preserved in centers which now became a part of the Islamic world. Alexandria had been a major center of sciences and learning for centuries. The Greek learning cultivated in Alexandria was opposed by the Byzantines who had burned its library long before the advent of Islam. The tradition of Alexandrian learning did not die, however. It was transferred to Antioch, and from there farther east to such cities as Edessa [Urfa in Turkey], by eastern Christians who stood in sharp opposition to Byzantium and wished to have their own independent centers of learning. Moreover, the Persian king Shapur I had established Jundishapur in Persia as a second great center of learning, matching Antioch. He even invited Indian physicians and mathematicians to teach in this major seat of learning, in addition to the Christian scholars who taught in Syriac, as well as the Persians whose medium of instruction was *Pahlavi*.

Once Muslims established the new Islamic order during the Umayyad period, they turned their attention to the centers of learning which had been preserved and sought to acquaint themselves with the knowledge taught and cultivated in them. Therefore, they began a concerted effort to translate the philosophical and scientific works available to them, from not only Greek and Syriac (which was the

Adapted from "Islam and Knowledge," *Islam: A Global Civilization* (Washington, D.C.: The Royal Embassy of Saudi Arabia, n.d.), pp. 20–27. Used by permission.

language of eastern Christian scholars), but also from Pahlavi, the scholarly language of pre-Islamic Persia, and even from *Sanskrit* (classical literary language of India). Many of the accomplished translators were Christian Arabs, such as Hunayn ibn Ishaq, who was also an outstanding physician, and other Persians, such as Ibn Muqaffa, who played a major role in the creation of the new Arabic prose style conducive to the expression of philosophical and scientific writings. The great movement of translation lasted from the beginning of the eighth to the end of the ninth century, reaching its peak with the establishment of the House of Wisdom (Bayt al-Hikma), by the caliph al-Ma'mun at the beginning of the ninth century.

The result of this extensive effort of the Islamic community to confront the challenge of the various philosophies and sciences of antiquity, and to understand and digest them in its own terms and according to its own worldview, was the translation of a vast corpus of writings into Arabic: most of the important philosophical and scientific works of Aristotle and his school, much of Plato and the Pythagorean school, and the major works of Greek astronomy, mathematics, and medicine (such as the *Almagest* of Ptolemy, the *Elements* of Euclid, and the works of Hippocrates and Galen), were all translated into Arabic. Furthermore, important works of astronomy, mathematics, and medicine were translated from Pahlavi and Sanskrit. As a result, Arabic became the most important scientific language of the world for many centuries, and the depository of much of the wisdom and the sciences of antiquity.

The Muslims did not translate the scientific and philosophical works of other civilizations out of fear of political or economic domination, but because the structure of Islam itself is based upon the primacy of knowledge. Nor did they consider these forms of knowing as "un-Islamic" as long as they confirmed the doctrine of God's oneness, which Islam considers to have been at the heart of every authentic revelation from God. Once these sciences and philosophies confirmed the principle of oneness, the Muslims considered them their own. They made them part of their worldview and began to cultivate the Islamic sciences based on what they had translated, analyzed, criticized, and assimilated, rejecting what was not in conformity with the Islamic perspective.

## MATHEMATICAL SCIENCES

The Muslim mind has always been attracted to the mathematical sciences, in accordance with the abstract character of the doctrine of oneness. The mathematical sciences have traditionally included astronomy, mathematics itself, and much of what is called physics today. In astronomy, the Muslims integrated the astronomical traditions of the Indians, Persians, the ancient Near East, and especially the Greeks, into a synthesis which began to chart a new chapter in the history of astronomy, from the eighth century onward. The *Almagest* of Ptolemy (treatise on astronomy, geography, and mathematics, A.D. 150), whose very name in English reveals the Arabic origin of its Latin translation [from the Arabic *al-majisti*, or the greatest], was thoroughly studied, and its planetary theory criticized by several astronomers of both the eastern and western lands of Islam, leading to the major critique of the theory by Nasir al-Din al-Tusi and his students, especially Qutb al-Din al-Shirazi, in the thirteenth century.

The Muslims also observed the heavens carefully and discovered many new stars. The book on stars by Abd al-Rahman al-Sufi was in fact translated into Spanish by Alfonso X el Sabio, and had a deep influence

A Madurese boy studies the Qur'an

upon stellar toponymy (place names) in European languages. Many names of the stars in English, such as Aldabaran [from *dabaran*, or following (the Pleiades)], still recall their Arabic origin. The Muslims carried out many fresh observations which were contained in astronomical tables called *zij.* One of the acutest of these observers was al-Battani. His work was followed by that of numerous others. The zij of al-Ma'mun (observed in Baghdad), the Hakimite zij of Cairo, the *Toledan Tables* of al-Zarqali and his associates, the Il-Khanid zij of Nasir al-Din al-Tusi (observed in Maraghah), and the zij of Ulugh-Beg (from Samarqand) are among the most famous Islamic astronomical tables. They wielded a great deal of influence upon western astronomy up to the time of Tycho Brahe. The Muslims were in fact the first to create an astronomical observatory as a scientific institution, this being the observatory of Maraghah in Persia, established by al-Tusi. This was indirectly the model for the later European observatories. Many astronomical instruments were developed by Muslims to carry out observation, the most famous being the astrolabe (observes

position and determines altitude of a celestial body). There even existed mechanical astrolabes perfected by Ibn Samh, which must be considered the ancestors of the mechanical clock.

Astronomical observations also had practical applications, including not only finding the direction of *Makkah* (Mecca) for prayers, but also devising almanacs (the word itself being of Arabic origin). The Muslims also applied their astronomical knowledge to questions of timekeeping and the calendar. The most exact solar calendar, existing to this day, is the Jalali calendar, devised under the direction of Omar Khayyam in the twelfth century and still in use in Persia and Afghanistan.

As for mathematics proper, like astronomy, it received its direct impetus from the Qur'an, not only because of the mathematical structure related to the text of the sacred book, but also because the laws of inheritance delineated in the Qur'an require rather complicated mathematical solutions. Here again, Muslims began by integrating Greek and Indian mathematics. The first great Muslim mathematician,

© Caleb Project

Turkish gentleman

such figures as al-Karaji until it reached its peak with Khayyam, who classified by kind and class algebraic equations up to the third degree.

The Muslims also excelled in geometry as reflected in their art. The brothers Banu Musa, who lived in the ninth century, may be said to be the first outstanding Muslim geometers [geometry experts], while their contemporary Thabit ibn Qurrah used the method of exhaustion, giving a glimpse of what was to become integral calculus. Many Muslim mathematicians, such as Khayyam and al-Tusi, also dealt with the fifth postulate of Euclid, and the problems which follow if one tries to prove this postulate within the confines of Euclidean geometry.

al-Khwarazmi, who lived in the ninth century, wrote a treatise on arithmetic whose Latin translation brought what is known as Arabic numerals to the West. To this day, *guarismo*, derived from his name, means figure or digit in Spanish, while "algorithm" is still used in English.

Al-Khwarazmi is also the author of the first book on algebra. This science was developed by Muslims on the basis of earlier Greek and Indian works of a rudimentary nature. The very name "algebra" comes from the first part of the name of al-Khwarazmi's book, *Kitab al-jabr wa' l-muqabalah*. Abu Kamil al-Shuja' discussed algebraic equations with five unknowns. The science was further developed by

Another branch of mathematics developed by Muslims is trigonometry, which was established as a distinct branch of mathematics by al-Biruni. The Muslim mathematicians, especially al-Battani, Abu'l-Wafa, Ibn Yunus, and Ibn al-Haytham, also developed spherical astronomy and applied it to the solution of astronomical problems.

The love of the study of magic squares and amicable numbers led Muslims to develop the theory of numbers. Al-Khujandi discovered a particular case of Fermat's theorem that "the sum of two cubes cannot be another cube," while al-Karaji analyzed arithmetic and geometric progressions such as, $1^3+2^3+3^3+\ldots+n^3=(1+2+3+\ldots+n)^2$. Al-Biruni also dealt with progressions, while Ghiyath al-Din Jamshid al-Kashani brought the study of number theory among Muslims to its peak.

## PHYSICS

In the field of physics, the Muslims made contributions especially in three domains. The first was the measurement of specific weights of objects and the study of the balance, following upon the work of Archimedes. In this domain, the writings of al-Biruni and al-Khazini stand out. Secondly, they criticized the Aristotelian theory of projectile motion and tried to quantify this type of motion. The critique of Ibn Sina, Abu'l-Barakat al-Baghdadi, Ibn Bajjah, and others led to the development of the ideas of impetus and momentum and played an important role in the criticism of Aristotelian physics in the West up to the early writings of Galileo. Thirdly, there is the field of optics, in which the Islamic sciences produced Ibn al-Haytham (the Latin Alhazen), who lived in the eleventh century, the greatest student of optics between Ptolemy and Witelo. Ibn al-Haytham's main work on optics, the *Kitab al-manazir*, was also well known in the West as *Thesaurus opticus*. Ibn al-Haytham solved many optical problems (one of which is named after him), studied the property of lenses, discovered the camera obscura, explained correctly the process of vision, studied the structure of the eye, and explained for the first time why the sun and the moon appear larger on the horizon. This interest in optics was carried on two centuries later by Qutb al-Din al-Shirazi and Kamal al-Din al-Farisi. It was Qutb al-Din who gave the first correct explanation of the formation of the rainbow.

## "I HAVE TO THINK OF ETERNITY"

Murat was born in a Muslim family in Uzbekistan. As a young man he played soccer with some foreign Christians and eventually began studying the Bible with them. When Murat was in the hospital, sick with severe pain, his Christian friends visited him. "They prayed for me in the name of Jesus and I was delivered," reasoned Murat. "I still like Islam, but I can see the power in Jesus' name."

Although Murat began to grow in his understanding of and commitment to Christ, he experienced setbacks when his father died. As a son, his family duty was to carry out extensive local Islamic funeral rituals. Living at home, he faced great pressure to study and practice only Islam. Murat's widowed mother opposed his continued interest in Christ, and he wanted to do anything to please her. He knew she was wiser than he. Several years earlier she had warned him not to marry the classmate he loved, and their marriage had ended in divorce. Now she told him not to follow Christ.

Eventually, Murat realized he would have to follow Christ even if it meant bringing pain and trouble to his family. "If I follow my mother's ways, she will be happy, but I will go to Hell. I have to think of eternity. I can follow her all this life, but then what will I do for eternity?"

Source: Marti Smith, *www.takeitglobal.org*

© Caleb Project

Shir Dar Madrasa in Samarkand, Uzbekistan; religious school founded between 1619–36

It is important to recall that, in physics as in many other fields of science, the Muslims observed, measured, and carried out experiments. They must be credited with having developed what came to be known later as the experimental method.

## MEDICAL SCIENCES

The hadiths of the Prophet contain many instructions concerning health, including dietary habits. These sayings became the foundation of what came to be known later as prophetic medicine (*al-tibb al-nabawi*). Because of the great attention paid in Islam to the need to take care of the body and to hygiene, early in Islamic history Muslims began to cultivate the field of medicine, turning once again to all the knowledge that was available to them from Greek, Persian, and Indian sources. At first, the great physicians among Muslims were mostly Christian, but by the ninth century Islamic medicine, properly speaking, was born with the appearance of the major compendium, *The Paradise of Wisdom (Firdaws al-hikmah)*, by Ali ibn Rabban al-Tabari. He synthesized the Hippocratic and Galenic traditions of medicine with those of India and Persia.

His student, Muhammad ibn Zakariyya al-Razi (the Latin Rhazes), was one of the greatest of those physicians who emphasized clinical medicine and observation. He was a master of prognosis, psychosomatic medicine, and also of anatomy. He was the first to identify and treat smallpox, to use alcohol as an antiseptic, and to make medical use of mercury as a purgative. His *Kitab al-hawi (Continens)* is the longest work ever written in Islamic medicine, and he was recognized as a medical authority in the West up to the eighteenth century.

The greatest of all Muslim physicians, however, was Ibn Sina, who was called the "prince of physicians" in the West. He synthesized Islamic medicine in his major masterpiece, *al-Qanun fi'l-tibb (The Canon of Medicine)*, the most famous of all medical books in history. It was the final authority in medical matters in Europe for nearly six centuries and is still taught wherever Islamic medicine has survived to this day, in such lands as Pakistan and India. Ibn Sina discovered many drugs and identified and treated several ailments such as meningitis, but his greatest contribution was in the philosophy of medicine. He created a system of medicine, within which medical practice could be carried out and in which physical and psychological factors, drugs, and diet are combined.

After Ibn Sina, Islamic medicine divided into several branches. In the Arab world, Egypt remained a major center for the study of medicine, especially ophthalmology, which reached its peak at the court of al-Hakim. Cairo possessed excellent hospitals, which also drew physicians from other lands, including Ibn Butlan, author of the famous *Calendar of Health*, and Ibn Nafis, who discovered the lesser or pulmonary circulation of the blood long before Michael Servetus [Spaniard, 1511–1553], who is usually credited with the discovery.

The western lands of Islam, including Spain, benefited from the appearance of outstanding physicians such as Sa'd al-Katib of Cordoba, who composed a treatise on gynecology, and the greatest Muslim figure in surgery, the twelfth century Abul-Qasim al-Zahrawi (the Latin Albucasis) whose medical masterpiece, *Kitab al-tasrif*, was well known in the West as *Concessio*. One must also mention the Ibn Zuhr family, which produced several outstanding physicians, and Abu Marwan 'Abd al-Malik, who was the *Maghreb's* most outstanding clinical physician. The well-known Spanish philosophers, Ibn Tufayl and Ibn Rushd, were also excellent physicians.

Islamic medicine continued in Persia and the other eastern lands of the Islamic world under the influence of Ibn Sina with the appearance of major Persian medical compendia, such as the *Treasury* of Sharaf al-Din al-Jurjani, and the commentaries upon the *Canon* by Fakhr al-Din al-Razi and Qutb al-Din al-Shirazi. Even after the Mongol invasion, medical studies continued, as can be seen in the work of Rashid al-Din Fadlallah, and, for the first time, there appeared translations of Chinese medicine and interest in acupuncture among Muslims. The Islamic medical tradition was revived in the Safavid period when several diseases, such as whooping cough, were diagnosed and treated for the first time, and much attention was paid to pharmacology. Many Persian doctors, such as Ayn al-Murk of Shiraz, also traveled to India at this time to usher in the golden age of Islamic medicine in the subcontinent and to plant the seeds of the Islamic medical tradition which continues to flourish to this day in the soil of that land.

The Ottoman world was also an arena of great medical activity derived from the

## QUOTES

When Abu Bakr spoke, Umar sat down. Abu Bakr praised and glorified Allah and said, "No doubt! Whoever worshiped Muhammad, Muhammad is dead, but whoever worshiped Allah, Allah is alive and shall never die."

Sahih Bukhari, *The Collection of Hadith*, trans. M. Mubsin Khan; vol. 1, bk. 57, no. 19. Narrated by Aisha.

"Better the Sultan's turban than the Cardinal's Hat" (from an Orthodox church leader at the time of the Crusades).

Michael Llewellyn Smith, "The Fall of Constantinople," in *History Makers* (London: Marshall Cavendish, Sidgwick & Jackson, 1969), p. 189.

heritage of Ibn Sina. The Ottoman Turks were especially known for the creation of major hospitals and medical centers. These included not only units for the care of the physically ill, but also wards for patients with psychological ailments. The Ottomans were also the first to receive the influence of modern European medicine, in both medicine and pharmacology.

In mentioning Islamic hospitals, it is necessary to point out that all major Islamic cities had hospitals. Some, like those of Baghdad, were teaching hospitals, while some, like the Nasiri hospital of Cairo, had thousands of beds for patients with almost any type of illness. Hygiene in these hospitals was greatly emphasized, as al-Razi had written a treatise on hygiene in hospitals. Some hospitals also specialized in particular diseases, including psychological ones. Cairo even had a hospital which specialized in patients having insomnia.

Islamic medical authorities were also always concerned with the significance of pharmacology, and many important

## GOD'S PROMISE TO MUSLIMS

Three great world religions—Judaism, Christianity, and Islam—trace their beginnings to a man of strong faith, Abraham (Heb. 11:11, 17–19). God made a covenant with Abraham, promising to bless his offspring and all the peoples of the world through him (Gen. 12:1–3; 15:1–19). In the New Testament we are told that, through faith in Jesus, we are "Abraham's seed and heirs according to the promise" (Gal. 3:26–29). Abraham is called *Friend of God* in Scripture (2 Chron. 20:7; Isa. 41:8; James 2:23); in Islam he is known by the same name, *Khalil Ullah* (Sura 4:125). The tribes of Muhammad's Arabia, and Muslims to this day, trace their ancestry back to Ishmael, Abraham's son by Hagar, not to Isaac, Abraham's son by Sarah.

Unfortunate circumstances led Hagar to flee her home, but God had great compassion for her. When Ishmael was born, God promised Hagar that her descendants would be too numerous to count (Gen. 16:9–11; 17:20; 21:8–21; 25:13–16). Today more than 1.3 billion Muslims (one of every five people) identify with her.

When Hagar cried out, God named her child Ishmael, which means *God hears* (Gen. 16:11). Moreover, "God was with the boy as he grew up" (Gen. 21:20). God's relationship with Hagar and Ishmael exemplifies God's boundless love for mankind. Even today, God has not forgotten millions of Hagars and Ishmaels. He still hears their cries.

Isaiah describes (in chapters 60 and 61) a glorious sight, all the peoples of the earth being gathered into heaven: "Lift up your eyes and look about you: all assemble and come to you" (60:4). This passage and many others promise hope for our Muslim friends. Ishmael's sons will bring their flocks to worship the risen Christ: "All *Kedar's* [section of Arabian desert] flocks will be gathered to you; the rams of Nebaioth [Ishmael's firstborn son] will serve you; they will be acceptable as offerings on my altar" (60:7).

### FOR FURTHER STUDY
Adapted from: Don McCurry, *Healing the Broken Family of Abraham* (Colorado Springs: Ministry to Muslims, 2001). *www.mtmsims.org*

works, such as the *Canon*, contain whole books devoted to the subject. The Muslims became heir not only to the pharmacological knowledge of the Greeks, as contained in the works of Dioscorides, but also the vast herbal pharmacopoeias of the Persians and Indians. They studied the medical effects of many drugs, especially herbs. The greatest contributions in this field came from Maghrebi scientists such as Ibn Juljul, Ibn al-Salt, and the most original of Muslim pharmacologists, the twelfth-century scientist, al-Ghafiqi, whose *Book of Simple Drugs* provides the best descriptions of the medical properties of plants known to Muslims. Islamic medicine combined the use of drugs for medical purposes with dietary considerations. A whole lifestyle derived from the teachings of Islam created a synthesis which has not died out to this day, despite the introduction of modern medicine into most of the Islamic world.

Tending sheep in Aleppo, Syria

© Stuart Brown / Saudi Aramco World / PADIA

## NATURAL HISTORY AND GEOGRAPHY

The vast expanse of the Islamic world enabled the Muslims to develop natural history, based not only on the Mediterranean world, as was the case of the Greek natural historians, but also on most of the Eurasian and even African land masses. Knowledge of minerals, plants, and animals was assembled from areas as far away as the Malay world [island group of Southeast Asia, from the mainland to Australia, separating the Indian and Pacific oceans], and synthesized for the first time by Ibn Sina in his *Kitab al-Shifa'*

(*The Book of Healing*). Such major natural historians as al-Mas'udi intertwined natural and human history. In his study of India, al-Biruni likewise turned to the natural history and even geology of the region, describing correctly the sedimentary nature of the Ganges River basin. He also wrote the most outstanding Muslim work on mineralogy.

As for botany, the most important treatises were composed in twelfth-century Spain with the appearance of the work of al-Ghafiqi. This is also the period when the best-known Arabic work on agriculture, the *Kitab al-falahah*, was written. The Muslims also showed much interest in zoology especially in horses, as witnessed by the classical text of al-Jawaliqi, and in falcons and other hunting birds. The works of al-Jahiz and al-Damiri are especially famous in the field of zoology and deal with the literary, moral, and even theological dimensions of the study of animals, as well as the purely zoological aspects of the subject. This is also true of a whole class of writings on the wonders of creation, of which the book of Abu Yahya al-Qazwini, *Aja'ib al-makhluqat* (*The Wonders of Creation*), is perhaps the most famous.

© Seana Yee

La Mezquita de Cordoba founded in A.D. 786

Likewise, in geography, Muslims were able to extend their horizons far beyond the world of Ptolemy. As a result of travel over land and by sea, and the facile exchange of ideas made possible by the unified structure of the Islamic world, and the Hajj, which enables pilgrims from all over the Islamic world to gather and exchange ideas (in addition to visiting the House of God), a vast amount of knowledge, of areas from the Pacific to the Atlantic, was assembled. Starting with al-Khwarazmi, who laid the foundation of this science among Muslims in the ninth century, the Muslim geographers began to study the geography of practically the whole globe, minus the Americas, dividing the earth into the traditional seven climes, each of which they studied carefully from both a geographical and climactic point of view. They also began to draw maps, some of which reveal with remarkable accuracy many features, such as the origin of the Nile, not discovered in the West until much later. The foremost among Muslim geographers was Abu Abdallah al-Idrisi, who worked at the court of Roger II in Sicily (1093–1154), and who dedicated his famous book, *Kitab al-rujari* (*The Book of Roger*), to him. His maps are among the great achievements of Islamic science. It was, in fact, that with the help of Muslim geographers and navigators, Magellan crossed the Cape of Good Hope into the Indian Ocean. Even Columbus made use of their knowledge in his discovery of America.

## CHEMISTRY

The very word "alchemy," as well as its derivative "chemistry," came from the Arabic *al-kimiya*. The Muslims mastered Alexandrian—and even certain elements of Chinese—alchemy, and very early in their history, produced their greatest alchemist, Jabir ibn Hayyan (the Latin Geber), who lived in the eighth century. Putting the cosmological and symbolic aspects of alchemy aside, one can assert that this art led to much experimentation with various materials, and, in the hands of Muhammad ibn Zakariyya al-Razi, was converted into the science of chemistry. To this day, certain chemical instruments, such as the alembic (*al-anbiq*, used in distillation), still bear their original Arabic names; and the mercury-sulfur theory of Islamic alchemy remains the foundation of the acid-base theory of chemistry. Al-Razi's division of materials into animal, vegetable, and mineral is still prevalent, and a vast body of knowledge of materials accumulated by Islamic alchemists and chemists has survived over the centuries in both East and West. For example, the use of dyes in objects of Islamic art, ranging from carpets to miniatures or the making of glass, have much to do with this branch of learning, which the West gained completely from Islamic sources, since alchemy was not studied and practiced in the West before the translation of Arabic texts into Latin in the eleventh century.

## TECHNOLOGY

Islam inherited the previous millennium's experience in various forms of technology from the peoples who entered the fold of Islam and the nations which became part of Dar al-Islam. A wide range of technological knowledge, from the building of water wheels by the Romans, to the underground water systems by the Persians, became part and parcel of the technology of the newly founded order. Muslims also imported certain kinds of technology from the Far East, such as paper, which they brought from China, and whose technology they later transmit-

ted to the West. They also developed many forms of technology on the basis of earlier existing knowledge, such as the metallurgical art of making the famous Damascene (highly decorated metalwork from Damascus) swords, an art which goes back to the making of steel several thousand years before on the Iranian Plateau. Likewise, Muslims developed new architectural techniques of vaulting, methods of ventilation, preparations of dyes, techniques of weaving, technologies related to irrigation, and numerous other forms of the applied sciences, some of which survive to this day.

In general, Islamic civilization emphasized the harmony between man and nature, as seen in the traditional design of Islamic cities. Maximum use was made of natural elements and forces, and men built in harmony with, not in opposition to, nature. Some of the Muslim technological feats—such as dams which have survived for over a millennium, domes which can withstand earthquakes, and steel which demonstrates incredible metallurgical skill—attest to the exceptional attainment of Muslims in many fields of technology. In fact, it was such a vastly superior technology that first impressed the Crusaders in their unsuccessful attempt to capture the Holy Land, and much of this technology was taken back to the rest of Europe by the Crusaders.

## ARCHITECTURE

One of the major achievements of Islamic civilization is architecture, which combines technology and art. The great masterpieces of Islamic architecture, from the Cordoba Mosque and the *Dome of*

*the Rock* in Jerusalem, to the Taj Mahal in India, display this perfect wedding between the artistic principles of Islam and remarkable technological skill. Much of the outstanding medieval architecture of the West is in fact indebted to the techniques of Islamic architecture. When one views the Notre Dame in Paris, or some other Gothic cathedral, one is reminded of the building techniques which traveled from Muslim Cordoba northward. Gothic arches, as well as interior courtyards of so many medieval and Renaissance European structures, remind the viewer of the Islamic architectural examples from which they were originally drawn. In fact, the great, medieval, European architectural tradition is one of the elements of Western Civilization most directly linked with the Islamic world. Islamic architecture can be directly experienced in the Moorish style, found not only in Spain and Latin America, but in the southwestern United States as well.

## INFLUENCE OF ISLAMIC SCIENCE AND LEARNING UPON THE WEST

The oldest university in the world, still functioning after eleven hundred years, is the Islamic university of Fez, Morocco, known as the Qarawiyyin.... Islamic learning influenced the West greatly through Spain, where Muslims, Christians, and Jews lived, for the most part peacefully, for many centuries. Translations began to be made in the eleventh century, mostly in Toledo, of Islamic works into Latin, often through the intermediary of Jewish scholars, most of whom knew Arabic and often wrote in Arabic. As a result of these translations, Islamic thought, and through it much of Greek thought, became known to the West, and western schools of learning began to flourish. Even the Islamic educational system was emulated in Europe. To this day, the term "chair" in a university reflects the Arabic *kursi* (literally seat) upon which a teacher would sit to teach his students in the madrasah (school). As European civilization grew and reached the high Middle Ages, there was hardly a field of learning or form of art, whether it was literature or architecture, where there was not some influence of Islam present. Islamic learning became, in this way, part and parcel of Western Civilization, even as, with the advent of the Renaissance, the West not only turned against its own medieval past, but also sought to forget to acknowledge the long relationship it had enjoyed with the Islamic world, one which was based on intellectual respect despite religious opposition.

**End of Basic Readings for Lesson 2. See** RECOMMENDED READINGS & ACTIVITIES **on p. 75.**

**Go to:**
*www.encounteringislam.org/ readings* **to find the Full Reading for Lesson 2.**

# DISCUSSION QUESTIONS

1. As Islam expanded from its original context, it was received by other cultures. How did it change those cultures?

2. In what ways did Islam preserve and benefit those cultures and the world at large?

3. What are some of the reasons people in non-Muslim societies are attracted to Islam today?

4. What is the meaning of modesty in your culture and how is it practiced?

5. How would you respond to foreign domination of your society, regardless of its benefits?

# RECOMMENDED READINGS & ACTIVITIES*

Read: Karen Armstrong, *Islam: A Short History* (New York: Modern Library, 2000).

Paul Marshall, Roberta Green, and Lela Gilbert, *Islam at the Cross-roads* (Grand Rapids: Baker Books, 2002).

Watch: "Islam: Empire of Faith," PBS Home Video, 2001.

Pray: Prayer-walk through ethnic neighborhoods, specifically praying for Muslims.

Listen: Visit your local library and check out some traditional Arabic music.

Surf: Discover related web sites at *www.encounteringislam.org/lessonlinks*.

* For expanded details on these Recommended Readings & Activities, visit *www.encounteringislam.org/lessonlinks*.

# Lesson 3
## Islamic Beliefs

## PONDER THIS

- What are some of the beliefs that Muslims and Christians have in common?

- Which elements of faith are most important to Muslims?

- As a Christian, what elements of your faith are most important to you?

# LESSON OBJECTIVE

Describe the basic practices and beliefs of Islam from a Muslim point of view. Include:

1.  Practices of confession, prayer, fasting, alms, and pilgrimage.

2.  Belief in monotheism, angels, holy books, prophets, the Day of Judgment, and predestination.

3.  The role of the umma in putting into practice the Qur'an and Hadith, leadership and elder rule, consensus and analogy, interpretation of Shari'a law, and jihad.

# LESSON READINGS

# INTRODUCTION

When I, the editor, first shared my faith with Muslim friends, I believed that when I proved that Christianity was true, my friends would change. I failed to recognize that people rarely change because of logical arguments. Likewise, as I grew in my understanding and appreciation of Muslim history and culture, my friends certainly approved of my efforts, but they also had difficulty reconciling my knowing more while remaining unconvinced of the logic of becoming a Muslim. Most of us fail to understand that a change of heart is a spiritual matter. Indeed, my Muslim friends agree that no one can change another person's belief. The Qur'an says, "There is no compulsion in religion" (Sura 2:256, PICKTHALL). After all, we do not expect that fans of one sports team, even when confronted with their team's poor record, will switch their allegiance to another club. Their investment in supporting their team is not swayed by the logic of who is winning.

Giving zakat to the poor

© S.M. Amin/Saudi Aramco World/PADIA; "Alms to Poor"

While we each desired the other to agree to our convictions—particularly our spiritual beliefs—it was easier for me to value my friends' culture and history than it was for me to comprehend their religious persuasions and reasoning. Part of the difficulty was that I was not familiar with Islam's belief system, logic, and vocabulary. Also, I had not recognized that my Muslim friends sincerely accepted what Islam teaches. Another obstacle was that I kept describing my position in idealized particulars—as they did theirs—but in reality we did not observe one another following these ideals. What was needed was for each of us to stop trying to convince the other and to disavow the presumption that our lives demonstrated the perfect version of our religion. After all, the lives of most so-called Muslims and Christians do not match their religions' teachings anyway.

## The Heart of the Muslim World

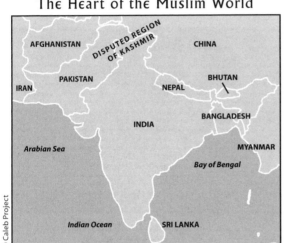

© Caleb Project

religion, with comprehensive and convincing logic. Many are of the opinion that Islam provides simple, clear guidelines for people to follow in fulfilling God's requirements for mankind, and they find great meaning in their Islamic practices. In addition, the Qur'an and the Hadith may influence their everyday living, as they seem to provide an answer to every question of how to manage daily life. While we would not "switch teams," sitting with Muslims "on their bench," so to speak, understanding more about their religion, will benefit us in our communication. We may also find new bridges to help explain our faith to Muslims.

After making these attitudinal changes, we could relate as peer counterparts.

## MEETING A THOUGHTFUL MUSLIM

Part of our goal in this lesson is to appreciate Islam as an attractive and reasonable

At some point in your life, you will meet an attractive, thoughtful Muslim. Our hope is that you will be prepared to admire and respect him or her, to

## INDO-ARYAN PEOPLES

The *Indo-Aryan peoples* of South Asia, numbering more than a billion people and forming 2,573 people groups, live in the countries of Bangladesh, India, Nepal, and Pakistan. These four countries range from 5 to 96 percent Muslim, for a total of almost 390 million adherents. South Asia is truly the heart of the Muslim world, as it has three of the four largest Muslim populations. Like the Hindus, Muslims of South Asia are divided by caste.

One significant Muslim people group of this region is the Ansari, estimated to be between 11 and 16 million. Historically, the Ansari are weavers. They create the silks and carpets, as well as other handicrafts, for which their lands are famous.

Most of the Ansari live in small towns and villages in the northern states of India where they form close-knit, stable communities. Some work at skilled crafts such as brass and woodworking, while others farm or run small businesses. Like most of India's Muslims, they tend to be poor and considered low in caste, and they perform rituals of spiritism in order to ward off evil. Traditionally, an Ansari home is led by the eldest male who makes decisions involving his sons and their wives and children.

Sources: *Operation World, www.joshuaproject.net.*

converse gracefully, agree where you can, and not be offended or offensive even though you do not perceive Islam the same way. This is only fair: I expected my Muslim friends to extend these courtesies to me. Sadly, they often exhibited this behavior better than I did.

## CHRISTIAN AND MUSLIM LEGALISMS

Some forms of Islam can be rigid and legalistic, and they do not adequately address the real problem of the human heart: a broken relationship with God. If we Christians contrast our superficial assumptions and religious behavior point-for-point with those of Muslims, we can easily project a similar rigidity and equally simplistic opinions about God. Our religious persuasion is—or should be—radically different. It begins with God's solution to the condition of our sinful hearts and not with our external behaviors. What might happen if we changed how we express our beliefs? Instead of saying, "I do this or that because I am a Christian," we would say "I have been graciously adopted by God as his dearly loved child through my trust in him. He is transforming my identity and my behavior from my heart outward as he remakes me into the image of his Son, Jesus Christ." Biblical Christianity is a trust relationship, not a system of rules to follow: it is "God felt by the heart, not reason" (Blaise Pascal). In this sense, the difference between my Muslim friend and me is not an issue of behavior but of my Savior. In fact, many people (not just

Ansari weaver

Muslims) perceive Christianity poorly as a result of looking at our behavior rather than being directed to look at Christ himself.

## SHARING EFFECTIVELY

That said, we may still feel the urge to jump ahead to the part where we speak of those convictions about Christ with which Muslims disagree. We will get to that in Lesson 8. That may seem like a long delay, but there is good reason: when we do voice our views with our Muslim friends, we want to be prepared to share our faith effectively.

As we learn about Islam and begin to understand the worldview of Muslims, we will discover both bridges between our beliefs and places where the tender love of Christ is needed. Much of Islamic belief focuses on external conduct. We will

observe the basic practices and stated religious convictions of our Muslim friends. But, as we do, and as we study, we should probe for a deeper understanding. Why do they do what they do? What is it that they value? How do they perceive themselves, the world around them, and even reality itself? In studying their religion, we unfold a map with which to begin this journey. Future lessons will delve further into their world, past the exterior impressions.

By the time we examine our disagreements, we hope to have corrected our misperceptions, achieved a greater appreciation for their lives, and narrowed our differences. Having moved beyond misunderstanding and communication on a theoretical level, we will be prepared to relate to our friends from the reality of their values and perceptions. Since we are inquiring about Muslims' religion, much of what we learn will come through their voices without rebuttal. As the Native American proverb advises, we must "first walk in their moccasins."

*– K.S., Editor*

# QUR'AN, HADITH, AND SHARI'A

*by Keith E. Swartley*

To conceptualize the place of Shari'a law in the Muslim world, we must first understand its sources, as well as their significance and influence. The weightiest authority is that of the Qur'an.

## THE QUR'AN, MIRACLE FROM GOD

The Qur'an, the Holy Book of all Muslims, is considered to be a miracle from God, eternal and uncreated, sent down from heaven (*ijaz al-Qur'an*) in Arabic by direct dictation. Its existence was used by Muhammad as proof of his apostleship (see Sura 10:37–39). Its contents are binding on the conduct of faithful Muslims.

Since the Qur'an came to be in a chiefly oral culture, it was not collected into book form during Muhammad's lifetime. It was preserved by his *Companions* who recited, memorized, practiced, and transcribed it. The first caliph, Abu Bakr, instructed *Zayd*, Muhammad's aide, to gather and assemble the text (in A.D. 634) from all written and oral sources, especially from Muhammad's closest companions and earliest converts. During the reign of the third caliph, Uthman, the text was compiled and approved as an official version of the Qur'an. In 657, all previous written versions were condemned and burned.

## STRUCTURE AND STYLE OF THE QUR'AN

The Qur'an is divided into 114 chapters, called suras or revelations, each with a distinct name. The suras are not arranged topically or chronologically, but from longest to shortest, with the exception of the first (see "What Does the Qur'an Say?" p. 8). The earliest suras, dating from Muhammad's years in Mecca, are the most lyrical and full of feeling.

> Muslims have continually insisted that the internal proof that the Qur'an is the word of God is its literary majesty: "If you could just understand it, and hear it being chanted in Arabic, you would know it is the truth."[1]

Later revelations from the years in Medina tend to be less poetic and have a stronger emphasis on ethical teaching. Earlier suras display a more tolerant attitude toward Christians and Jews, while later suras reflect the shift from identifying with the traditions of Jews and Christians to establishing Islam as a distinct religion (with Mecca as its center of worship). Often, a copy of the Qur'an will include an index or table showing which suras are from which period. Muslim scholars do not apply historical or textual criticism to the Qur'an, so the historicity and textual consistency of the Qur'an has not been examined

Keith Swartley works for Caleb Project and is the editor of *Encountering the World of Islam*. Keith first befriended Muslims in 1983. Since then he has enjoyed learning from and sharing with Muslims in Indonesia, Kazakhstan, Kenya, Kyrgyzstan, South Korea, Turkey, United Kingdom, and the United States.

from within Islam in the same way that Christians have examined the Bible.

## TRANSLATIONS OF THE QUR'AN

Muslims believe that a true translation of the Qur'an is not possible. Only the general meaning, lacking the perfection of the original, can be given in other languages. Muslims, regardless of their native languages, therefore read the Qur'an in Arabic. Nevertheless, there are translations of the Qur'an in many other languages. These are viewed as commentaries or interpretations of the Qur'an, and may be given titles like, *The Meaning of the Glorious Koran: An Explanatory Translation*, by Mohammed Marmaduke Pickthall (d. 1936).

Most Muslims (80 percent worldwide) do not speak Arabic as their native tongue,

and many Muslims are illiterate. In spite of these obstacles, faithful Muslims often memorize the whole Qur'an from hearing it in Arabic. In Muslim preaching, it is common for the teacher to read or quote the Qur'an in Arabic first, and then explain the meaning in the local language. This paraphrase of the Qur'an shapes the hearers' understanding of the Arabic phrases.

> Great reverence and awe of a somewhat mystical quality is given to the Qur'an by Muslims. It is treated as something almost worthy of worship. It is commonly read from an ornate stand made for holding it.... Muslims often comment on the beauty of the Arabic text, particularly as it is chanted. Merit is acquired from the rote reciting or reading of it, without any need for understanding.[2]

## WHAT IS PERMITTED?

The very word "halal" in Arabic simply means "loosed," meaning that it is free from restrictions. Most Muslims accept the teaching that everything is halal (permissible) unless specifically prohibited by a reference in the Qur'an or Hadith.[1]

The Qur'an has many instructions on how a Muslim should live his life in a holy manner so as to be pleasing to God. Muslims are required to perform more good works than bad works so that their good works will outweigh their bad on the Day of Judgment when their deeds are weighed on a scale.

> Then, he whose balance (of good deeds) will be (found) heavy, will be in a life of good pleasure and satisfaction. But he whose balance (of good deeds) will be (found) light, will have his home in a (bottomless) pit (Sura 101:6–8, YUSUF ALI).

Halal most often refers to the use of food, beverages, medicines, cosmetics, and other products. Halal guidelines in Islam are very similar to the kosher principles of Judaism. However, the Qur'an allows flexibility when Muslims find themselves in circumstances beyond their control:

> Eat what they catch for you, but pronounce the name of Allah over it (Sura 5:4b, YUSUF ALI).

1   See Highlight "What Is Forbidden?" page 102.

Source: Annee W. Rose, *www.frontiers.org*.

## THE HADITH

In addition to the Qur'an, Muslims rely on the Sunna (the straight path, manner of life), as these are expressed in hadith. Collections of hadith record all that Muhammad and the early Muslims (the Companions of the Prophet) are known to have done or said. Muhammad's example is considered the best model of Islam. There are six major collections of hadith (traditions, or sayings of the Prophet). Each was gathered, evaluated for reliable transmission, and organized by an early Islamic scholar, for which each collection is named: al-Bukhari, *al-Muslim, al-Tirmidhi, Abu Daud al-Sijistani, al-Nasai,* and *al-Qazwini*. There are also other Hadith collections relied upon by various Muslim groups. The most respected and often quoted is the collection made by al-Bukhari (810–870). Bukhari examined more than 600,000 potential hadith and retained as authentic 7,397 (divided into 97 chapters). Muslim preachers and writers freely quote from the Hadith and use them to define appropriate actions, elucidate portions of the Qur'an, or express theological points.

Since Islam seeks to answer questions and establish guidance for many details of life, these collected traditions cover all sorts of subjects, including moral teaching, religious duties, and legal problems. Although Muslims generally believe the Hadith are secondary to the Qur'an, they often refer to the Hadith itself for daily guidance. For example, the Qur'an explains the times of two of the five daily prayers. Muslims look to the Hadith for explanation of the other three times.

Abu Barza said, "The Prophet used to offer the *Fajr* (prayer) when one could recognize the person sitting by him (after the prayer), and he used to recite between sixty to one hundred ayat (verses) of the Qur'an. He used to offer the *Zuhr* prayer as soon as the sun declined (at noon), and the *Asr* at a time when a man might go and return from the farthest place in Medina and find the sun still hot. (The sub-narrator forgot what was said about the *Maghrib* [prayer]). He did not mind delaying the *Isha* prayer to one third of the night or the middle of the night."[3]

## THE SHARI'A

The rules and principles derived from the Qur'an and the Hadith were subsequently codified in a set of judicial precedents and law, better known as the Shari'a. The Shari'a is the fundamental law of Islam, the constitution of the Islamic community, and is considered the application of the divine will to every situation in life. Several Islamic countries base their governing constitutional law on Shari'a (for instance, Saudi Arabia and Iran). How to respond in each situation is determined by the legal interpretation of Islam (*fiqh*). Different groups rely on differing methods and sources in determining Shari'a through fiqh. In general, after the Qur'an and the Hadith, other methods or sources in determining Shari'a are ijma, the consensus of the community (often as represented by religious scholars or judges); *qiyas*, the application of principles from past cases, usually by analogy; and *ijtihad* or independent reasoning. In some Muslim groups only a religious scholar or officially appointed *mufti* may translate

or give interpretations of the Qur'an, such as the supreme council of al-Azhar University for most Sunnis and the *Aga Khan* for Ismailis.

## SCHOOLS OF INTERPRETATION

Although most Muslims emphasize unity and adherence to the law, they may differ on how to interpret the law, just as do members of other religious communities. There are four main schools of interpretation, or *Madhhabi*, within Islam. Sunnis, Shi'a, and Sufis are found within each school and each school has many subgroups.

**1. The *Hanafi* school** (the earliest and most widespread), founded by al-Numan ibn Thabit ibn Zuta Abu Hanifah (d. 767), is followed by about one third of all Muslims, especially in Turkey and Central Asia. It permits a liberal interpretation of the Qur'an by analogical reasoning (*qiyas*), resulting in interpretations which could be (and are often) made by the personal opinion (*ray*) or preference (*istihsan*) of the average person.

**2. The *Maliki* school** was founded by Malik ibn Anas al-Asbahi (d. 795) and is predominant in North Africa as well as some Arabian Gulf states. It developed law emphasizing the Hadith, especially those attributed to Muhammad's closest Companions. In fact, it relies on the practices of the Medinan companions in developing law. This school uses ray and qiyas.

**3. The *Shafi'i* school** was founded by Muhammad ibn Idris ibn al-Abbas ibn Uthman ibn Shafi'i (d. 819) and is the principal authority in Egypt, Palestine, and Jordan as well as a significant influence in Pakistan, India, and Indonesia. It also applies a more liberal interpretation to the Qur'an and stresses the rights of the community (umma), determined by the consensus (ijma) of community leaders (Ulama), often a body of religious judges (*quda*). These leaders issue legal rulings (*fatawi*). This school prefers the Hadith which are directly attributed to Muhammad over all others and denies istihsan and ray as sources of law.

**4. The *Hanbali* school** was founded by Abu Abdillah Ahmad ibn Hanbal (d. 855) and is the official school in Saudi Arabia and Qatar with many adherents in Palestine, Syria, and Iraq. It is the smallest and most conservative school. It rejects legal innovation beyond the literal use of the Qur'an and the Hadith. Even the *Sultan* and the Caliph were not to interfere with the decisions made by the religious judges. The Wahhabis of Saudi Arabia are of the Hanbali school.

## IMPLICATIONS FOR CHRISTIANS

As we learn more about the Qur'an, Hadith, and Shari'a from our Muslim friends and the different interpretations among Muslims arises, we should remember that many Christians disagree on the interpretation of the Bible and major theological issues. Even though our faith is biblically based, humility regarding our ability to understand and apply the Bible to our lives is essential. We should present our identity as Christians as being based on our faith in Jesus Christ, not on our adherence to a particular interpretation of Christianity and the Bible.

## For Further Study

Mateen Elass, *Understanding the Koran: A Quick Christian Guide to the Muslim Holy Book* (Grand Rapids: Zondervan, 2004). *www.zondervan.com*

Caesar E. Farah, *Islam* (Hauppauge, N.Y.: Barrons Educational Series, Inc., 2003), Chap. 8–9. *www.barronseduc.com*

Steven Masood, *The Bible and the Qur'an: A Question of Integrity* (Waynesboro, Ga.: Authentic Lifestyle, 2001).

## Endnotes

1. Greg Livingston, *Planting Churches in Muslim Cities* (Grand Rapids: Baker, 1993), p. 183.
2. Bruce McDowell and Anees Zaka, *Muslims and Christians at the Table* (Phillipsburg, N.J.: P & R, 1999), p. 72.
3. Sahin Bukhari, *The Collection of Hadith*, narrated by Abu al-Minhal; vol. 1, bk. 10, no. 516.

## Take the Initiative

When we work with Muslims, see them in shops, or sit next to them on airplanes, we should not wait for them to take the initiative to start a friendship. We should take the first step. While their modest dress and behavior might seem like barriers, Muslim women may make friendships more easily than men; many are lonely and have never experienced the love of Christ. Out of respect, only women should build friendships with Muslim women. Our initial step could be to invite our Muslim acquaintance to lunch or for coffee or tea. Perhaps other Christians could join.

Whenever I meet a Muslim, I pray silently, "Lord Jesus, I am ready to share about you. Please open the door for me." Christ has never failed to provide an entry! Once I sat by a Lebanese student on a flight from Beirut to Istanbul. As we put our seat belts on, I prayed, "Lord Jesus, I am ready to share. Please open the door," which, of course, he did!

We might even have the opportunity to build a relationship with a whole family. If we let them adopt us and share their way of life with us, our friendships may be deep and meaningful. Through us, God can show our Muslim friends what faith in Christ and Christ's love are really like. The Muslim culture and life are all about relationships. That means they are open to new relationships and will not likely rebuff any initiative we may take to speak to them.

God commands us to be hospitable, to welcome people into our lives, families, and homes, and to share our time, service, and experiences. Our acts of hospitality and kindness will speak volumes as we share our faith in Christ. If you pray the prayer I do, be ready for God to answer!

Source: Fouad Masri, *www.crescentproject.org.*

# ISLAMIC RELIGIOUS PRACTICES: THE PILLARS OF FAITH

*by C. George Fry and James R. King*

An old gospel hymn admonishes believers to "trust and obey." For Muslims too, religious commitment involves trust (or faith that God is, that he reveals himself, and that he cares for mankind), and obedience (good works that please God, serve man, and express values). In fact, submission, or obedience, is the very essence of Islam. As Frithjof Schuon has observed, there is about Islam a "vertical dimension" of intelligence, intellect, and reason, and a "horizontal dimension" of will, ethics, and commitment. There is power in the world, and it is to be used justly; there is a duty to the community to be fulfilled; there is a harmony, a cosmos, a design about the world that is to be sensed and expressed; there are bodily desires to be felt and brought under control.[1] By deeds or good works (*din*), a Muslim does what he can to express his commitment to Allah and to nurture and support the community to which he belongs.

For Old Testament Jews, the moral, civil, and ceremonial law was summed up in the Pentateuch. For early Christians, the law was expressed in the Sermon on the Mount and in the Pauline letters. The moral and ritual obligations of Muslims are summed up in five, or possibly six, Pillars of Faith (*Arkan*) which provide the moral and ethical counterbalance for the several theological tenets which comprise the doctrinal part of Islam.

## CONFESSION OF FAITH

In all of the Abrahamic religions, the first and foremost duty—both in time and in importance—is to confess the faith. The recitation of the creed indicates that one has understood, appreciated, and internalized the theological message. The recitation of the creed is also a test of orthodoxy, and it becomes as well a covenant between oneself, the deity, and the community. These points apply with equal force to Islam, Judaism, and Christianity. All rest on a conviction that expresses itself through a confession.

The key Islamic concept here, in Arabic, is *sh-h-d*, which carries with it the idea of being present or of witnessing. *Tashahhud* means "a giving of one's testimony," or "professing the faith," and the city of Meshed (Iran) is a spot where the faith is professed in a peculiarly intense way. The testimony, the *Shahada*, is phrased in a liturgical form, one of the most famous liturgical expressions in all world religions: *La ilaha illa Allah, (wa) Muhammad rasul Allah.* (There is no god but God, [and] Muhammad is the Prophet of God.) Since

C. George Fry is associate professor of historical theology and director of missions education at Concordia Theological Seminary. James R. King is a professor of English at Wittenberg University. Dr. Fry and Dr. King are coauthors of *The Middle East: Crossroads of Civilization*.

Adapted from C. George Fry and James R. King, *Islam: A Survey of the Muslim Faith* (Grand Rapids: Baker, 1982), pp.71–87. Used by permission. *www.bakerbooks.com*

no formal method of entry into Islam is prescribed, except the recitation of this confession, some fairly rigid guidelines exist as to the manner of this act of witness: the Shahada must be repeated aloud, with total comprehension (i.e., it must be understood intellectually, emotionally, and volitionally); it must be recited with sincerity, genuine love in the heart, and no reservations or hesitations in the mind; it must be assumed that the faith will be maintained until death; it must be recited correctly, in the orthodox form, without heterodox changes. If one can confess this creed in sincerity of heart and with integrity of mind, one is a Muslim. How strikingly simple and direct this is—in contrast with the elaborate statements of belief that have developed in the Protestant, Roman, and Orthodox Christian churches.

The Creed begins with an affirmation of God: "There is no god but God." This simple and austere affirmation of monotheism further establishes Islam within the Abrahamic tradition. It is reminiscent of the opening sentence of Genesis, "In the beginning God…" (Gen. 1:1), and of the opening of the Apostles' Creed, "I believe in God…" With a single brief phrase, Islam wipes out a host of heresies that have tormented the Christian faith—atheism (there is no God), agnosticism (whether God exists cannot be ascertained), materialism and naturalism (the material

world is the only reality), pantheism (God is identical with the world), deism (God does not intervene in human affairs), and polytheism (there are many gods). The Islamic Confession asserts theism in its boldest sense: there is a God, the Creator, the Merciful, the Provider, the Judge, the Revealer of himself. Jews and Christians could utter this part of the Shahada with a clear conscience, for what Muslims affirm here is what the *Shema* and the Apostles' Creed also affirm in their own way.

The Muslim Creed continues with a description of the terms by which God reveals himself to man: "and Muhammad is the Prophet of God." We note the audacity with which Islam places God and Muhammad together in a single sentence, a bold stroke that has caused many in the West to misname this faith "Mohammedanism." But this is a serious mistake: though Muslims do indeed revere Muhammad as the supreme revelator of God in human history, they do not worship him. Islam is a religion of submission to God, not a religion about a man. Yet, apart from the message carried to man by Muhammad, full knowledge of God would not be possible.

The confession of faith is made on all kinds of occasions: at birth it is whispered into the ear of the baby; at death it is spoken over the body of the deceased; in time of battle

## Is Allah God?

I have never met a Muslim-background believer who regards the God he previously sought to worship as a wholly false god. Instead, he is filled with wonder and gratitude, that he has now been brought to know that God as he really is, in Jesus Christ our Lord.

John D. C. Anderson, "The Missionary Approach to Islam," *Missiology* 4, no. 3 (1976), p. 295.

Ritual purification or wudu

a root meaning "to call," and it involves supplication, calling upon, or asking for.

The Qur'an gives no specific rules for prayer. We know that Muhammad experimented with a variety of practices and that from earliest times Muslims have shared certain fixed prayer customs. It is now assumed that Allah instructed Muhammad in these practices during his Ascension or Night Journey, Lailat al-Miraj.

it is a call to courage; in times of peace it is heard from the minarets of the city, both early in the morning and late at night. There is no time in a Muslim's life when the Creed is far from his lips or his heart.

## ADORATION AND PRAYER

Worship is the second great duty of a Muslim. Worship is ascribing to God that which is due to him as Creator, Preserver, and Judge of the universe. While worship includes many elements—preaching, teaching, reading of the scriptures, rejoicing, and fellowship, the essence of worship in all religions is adoration (or the praise of God) and conversation (or prayer). Christian worship makes a prominent place for the sacraments (baptism and the Lord's Supper in Protestantism). In Islam, however, the place of such experience is taken by prayer, especially ritual prayer or salat, a format of liturgical texts and fixed gestures performed either in a mosque, [the place of public worship, or in private.] Informal prayer is known as du'a, from

One feature of Muslim prayer is that it is carefully scheduled. An orthodox Muslim ought to pray five times a day, though originally Muhammad himself prayed twice daily—morning and evening. Jews in the time of Jesus prayed thrice daily—morning, noon, and night—and in medieval Christian monasteries prayer was offered eight times a day. Islam has traditionally prescribed five periods of daily prayer—at sunrise, at noon, in mid-afternoon, in the evening, and at night. While these prayers may be either public or private, it is thought desirable that the believer make his way to a nearby mosque for prayer if that is at all possible. Attendance at the Friday noon service is incumbent on Muslims. This service lasts about an hour, and it includes a sermon by the *khatib* of the mosque. Before and after this service, Muslims can be found at their secular tasks, Saturday often being reserved as a day of rest and—ideally—as a day when the faithful meditate on spiritual matters.

# The Postures of Prayer

1. Takbir i-Tahrimah

2. Ruku

3. Tasmi'

4. Takbir as-Sijdah

5. Salam

6. Munajat

Another feature of Muslim prayer is that it is strictly liturgical, all features being carefully established by tradition. The prayer itself is preceded by the call to worship (*adan*) given by a cantor (*muezzin*) from the minaret of the mosque. All too often today the beautiful call is tape-recorded and broadcast from the minaret by loudspeakers. Before entering into prayers, a Muslim must remove his shoes, lest the carpet on which he prays be dirtied for others. Also before prayer, the believer undertakes ritual purification with water if it is available, but otherwise with sand. One must wash the feet up to the ankles, and the arms to the elbows, and the face, including the inside of the ears.

Upon purification, a believer joins the community for prayers. Because various postures are involved in ritual prayer, men and women do not pray together, but in separate groups. Prayer takes place on the great carpets which are spread on the floor of the mosque, or on a small prayer rug if the ritual is undertaken in a private home or place of business. Prayer is directed toward Mecca, guidance in this matter being provided by the *qibla* wall of the mosque, into which prayer niches or *mihrabs* are built. (Muslim tour guides often misname such niches "altars.") The qibla wall also contains the *minbar* or raised pulpit from which the preacher delivers the Friday sermon.

Following the call to worship—which in Islam is done with the human voice, not as in Judaism with a ram's horn, or as in Christianity with bells—the congregation gathers behind the leader of the prayers, who is variously known as the imam (in Arab countries), mullah (in Iran), or *hoja*

(in Turkey), and the liturgy begins. Prayer includes ascriptions of glory to God, recitations, and various bodily movements and gestures. The prostrations (*sujud*) and bowings (*ruku*) comprise a rakah, and a number of rakahs compose a particular service. The postures involved include: (1) the *Takbir i-Tahrimah*, standing with arms partly raised; (2) the *Ruku*, bowing; (3) the *Tasmi,* standing; (4) the *Takbir as-Sijdah*, prostration, knees and arms bent; (5) the *Salam*, kneeling; and (6) the *Munajat*, kneeling, arms partly raised.

Emphasis on prayer posture may at first glance seem novel to the western Christian, yet a moment's consideration will remind us that Episcopalians kneel, Lutherans stand, Presbyterians sit, and Pentecostals raise their hands to pray. Total prostration is known in parts of the Russian Orthodox Church and in Roman Catholicism during certain ceremonies. So while the postures of prayer which Islam prescribes may seem strange, there are certain parallels within Christianity.

## MINISTRATION AND ALMSGIVING

If the first of the Five Pillars of Islam meets the human need for proclamation and confession of one's faith, and the second meets the human need for adoration and worship, the third of the Pillars, the requirement of *alms*giving, appears to fill yet another need, the need to minister to the physical and spiritual needs of other persons. In fact, ministry or service is central to the three great religions which trace their origins to Abraham. There are many provisions in the Old Testament for the care of the poor and the suffering. In the early Christian church the office of deacon was established for the care of the poor; and in the Qur'an, it is repeatedly made clear that man must respond to the abundance which God has given him by sharing it with the less fortunate. It is worth noting that the root meaning of *kafir*, usually translated as "unbeliever," is actually "ungrateful."

There are two important words in Arabic that have to do with almsgiving. The more common of these is *zakat*, from a root that

Takbir as-Sijdah (posture of prayer)

means "to grow" or "to be pure"; it seems to imply that the giving of alms is a means of purifying one's soul—perhaps from the guilt that inevitably accompanies the accumulation of property. The other term is *sadakat*, from a root that means "true" or "sincere"; the reference is to whatever is sanctified to God's service. Some authorities find in these two words a distinction between obligatory and voluntary giving; and, indeed, this is a critical issue in Islam, for the question is a natural one: does almsgiving which is required really benefit the soul? Thus, in some countries, almsgiving amounts to what is virtually a state tax (zakat stamps can be purchased in post offices), whereas elsewhere it is a matter of voluntary payments to mosque personnel or direct contributions to the poor.

Yet another significant reflection of the command to give alms is the institution of *waqf* (in Turkey, *evkaf*), the Arabic root implying "to stop," and thus, "to commit to" or "to dedicate to." A waqf is an endowment left by a wealthy (or not so wealthy) Muslim on his death for a specific purpose—pens and paper for scholars in

a library, a street fountain where animals may drink, a yearly treat for the children in a grammar school on the Prophet's birthday, a hospital, a university. The gifts can be large or small, but so complex is the administration of such gifts in the modern world that nearly every Islamic country now has a Ministry of Waqfs, which functions somewhat like the U.S. Department of Health and Human Services, supervising endowments so that available funds are invested wisely and distributed appropriately.

The obligation to give alms is one of the most treasured of all the Pillars of Islam. For Islam is thus revealed as a middle ground between what it regards as the twin evils of capitalism and communism. Muslims feel that almsgiving would discipline capitalism into a sense of social responsibility and correct communism by insisting that the only valid reason for sharing one's wealth is to express gratitude for God's bounty. Muhammad would have agreed on this point with James, who wrote: "Religion that God our Father accepts as pure and faultless is this: to look

after orphans and widows in their distress, and to keep oneself from being polluted by the world" (James 1:27).

## FASTING

The fourth duty that falls to every good Muslim is the practice of ritual fasting during the month of Ramadan, "the best of all months."[2] The Arabic word for fasting, *saum*, implies "abstinence," as well as all the moral inspiration which abstinence can bring. Ramadan is believed to be the month during which Muhammad began to receive the revelation of the Qur'an, but the rituals celebrated at this time also

## WHAT DOES THE BIBLE SAY ABOUT THE FIVE PILLARS OF ISLAM?

The Bible contains Christian disciplines that Islam's Five Pillars parallel. These disciplines provide us with yet another way to build bridges in our relationships with Muslims.

### 1. Confession (Shahada)
"Hear, O Israel: The LORD our God, the LORD is one!" (Deut. 6:4).

### 2. Prayer (Salat)
"Pray continually" (1 Thess. 5:17).

"And when you pray, do not be like the hypocrites, for they love to pray standing in the synagogues and on the street corners to be seen by men.… They have received their reward in full. But when you pray, go into your room, close the door and pray to your Father, who is unseen. Then your Father, who sees what is done in secret, will reward you" (Matt. 6:5–6).

### 3. Fasting (Saum)
"When you fast, do not look somber as the hypocrites do, for they disfigure their faces to show men they are fasting.… But when you fast, put oil on your head and wash your face, so that it will not be obvious to men that you are fasting, but only to your Father, who is unseen; and your Father, who sees what is done in secret, will reward you" (Matt. 6:16–18).

### 4. Giving (Zakat)
"Just as you excel in everything—in faith, in speech, in knowledge, in complete earnestness and in your love for us—see that you also excel in this grace of giving" (2 Cor. 8:7).

"When you give to the needy, do not let your left hand know what your right hand is doing, so that your giving may be in secret. Then your Father, who sees what is done in secret, will reward you" (Matt. 6:3–4).

### 5. Pilgrimage (Hajj)
"Beloved, I beg you as sojourners and pilgrims, abstain from fleshly lusts which war against the soul, having your conduct honorable among the Gentiles, that when they speak against you as evildoers, they may, by your good works which they observe, glorify God in the day of visitation" (1 Peter 2:11–12, NKJV).

"Let us throw off everything that hinders and the sin that so easily entangles, and let us run with perseverance the race marked out for us" (Heb. 12:1).

Source: *Encountering the World of Islam*

seem to have roots in Christian and Jewish asceticism (especially the Jewish Day of Atonement). Moreover, the idea of a holy month was known in pre-Islamic Arabia.

During the daylight hours of Ramadan, a good Muslim allows no solid food or liquid to pass down his throat, including, if possible, his own spittle. The inhaling of tobacco smoke is also covered by this prohibition, as are such discharges as vomiting and bloodletting. If the code is broken, even on the orders of a physician, the day of fasting must be made up at another time. During the hours of darkness, eating and drinking are permitted. It appears to be a matter of the personal piety of the believer whether this time will be spent in feasting or simply in eating what is necessary to survive. Daylight is said to have arrived when a black thread can be distinguished from a white thread (see Sura 2:187).

Since the Muslim calendar is based on the phases of the moon, the months are movable (it takes about thirty-five years for a month to pass all the way around the calendar), and thus Ramadan sometimes falls in the cool seasons, sometimes in the hot months. Ramadan means "the scorcher," and this suggests that it originally fell in the summer. When this is indeed the case, the prohibition against drinking can work a terrible hardship on the faithful, straining their endurance to the breaking point and making tempers very short. Usually work and school hours are shortened during this time so that people can spend more time in their homes, and very devout Muslims might spend the last ten days of the month in a mosque.

The month of fasting begins with the sighting of the new moon. If there is a cloud cover, the moon's appearance may be delayed. The announcement is made by hanging lamps in the streets and by gunfire. Ramadan ends with the great feast of Id al-Fitr, "the breaking of the fast," a time of general celebration, a time for new clothes, the exchange of greeting cards, gifts, and visits, feasting, and movie-going. There is a general feeling that human beings have tested their powers of endurance by self-denial and have overcome their own baser instincts. The powers of evil have been set back, the gates of hell have been closed; the way to Paradise has been opened. Not to keep the fast is seen by many believers as just as serious as—or more serious than—neglecting the daily prayers. It is an act of defiance of the communal moral code; it is an assertion of atheism.

## PILGRIMAGE TO MECCA

The fifth obligation, which every devout Muslim tries to fulfill at least once in his or her lifetime, is the duty of making the Hajj or pilgrimage to Mecca. The phenomenon of pilgrimage to a specific religious shrine is to be found among all peoples and all religions—Christians, Hindus, Buddhists, and Jews—and at all periods of history. Even in pre-Islamic times Mecca was a holy city, the object of visitation by pagan Bedouins. The Qur'an, however, gave the practice increased emphasis and much sharper focus, and Muhammad himself established the specific rituals to be carried out by the pilgrims. As it has evolved over the centuries, the Hajj has become an incredibly complex social phenomenon, involving pilgrims from all over the world,

## Diagram of Culture

Source: Lloyd E. Kwast, "Understanding Culture" in Ralph D. Winter and Steven C. Hawthorne, eds. *Perspectives on the World Christian Movement: A Reader*, rev. ed. (Pasadena, Calif.: William Carey Library, 1992), pp. C3–C6.

and we can do no more here than sketch out the broader outlines.[3] The authoritative description of the Hajj is to be found in Sura 2, the source of much important religious guidance.

The goal is the city of Mecca, the birthplace of Muhammad, the scene of his early life, and the place where the revelations which make up the Qur'an began. The focus of interest, even in pre-Islamic times, was the celebrated Holy Black Stone and the shrine, the Ka'aba, in which it was lodged. According to Islamic tradition, this shrine was constructed originally by Adam, perhaps damaged or destroyed by the great flood with which *Noah* is linked, and repaired by Abraham and Ishmael. Before the time

of Muhammad, it had housed numerous images of pagan gods, which Muhammad destroyed; and in early modern times, the adherents of one fanatically iconoclastic Islamic sect, believing that the Ka'aba itself had become an object of worship, tried to dismantle it. Modern scholarship identifies the stone as a meteorite. Folk religion regards it as a talisman of supernatural power. In the last year of his life, Muhammad made the pilgrimage from Medina to Mecca; after his death the practice continued and was formalized. Eventually, houses around the Ka'aba were torn down to make way for a mosque (*Al Masjid al-Haram*); this mosque has been enlarged time and again across the centuries.

During the month specifically set aside for pilgrimage, *Dhu al-Hijja*, pilgrims flock to Mecca from all over the world, those who are wealthy flying into Jidda by plane. Others come by freighter or bus, often in huge caravans; the poor make their way painfully and patiently on foot. Many suffer incredible hardships during this journey, which might last for several years, but to meet death en route or in Mecca is, as might be expected, regarded as a special blessing.

In Jidda, on the coast, about forty miles from Mecca, all male pilgrims, rich and poor alike, put on the two seamless sheets

[*izar* and *rida*], and they seek to establish peace within themselves and with others around them. Both the seamless sheets and the peaceful state are referred to as the *Ihram*. Normal pleasures are prohibited at this time. Along the road to Mecca, the credentials of the pilgrims are checked by Saudi Arabian police, so that only genuine Muslims actually enter the Holy City. Here accommodations are available that range from the most Spartan to the most lavish. Apparently, the fleecing of pilgrims, which for many centuries was the main source of revenue for natives of the area, has now been brought under control by the government. The Saudi government also exercises rigorous control over sanitary conditions.

The ceremonies of the pilgrimage begin with the ritual cleaning of sanctified parts of the body, after which the pilgrim enters the sacred area around the Ka'aba, through the Gate of Peace (*Bab as-Salaam*), passing to the Place of Abraham, and then to the awe-inspiring Ka'aba itself, the central object of the pilgrimage, to which he has been addressing his prayer all his life. Some pilgrims are able to enter the Ka'aba itself, while others press their faces to the wall. All seek to kiss the Holy Black Stone, which is mounted at an appropriate height in a massive silver holder.

## How Do You See the World?

Each of us evaluates the world through the eyes of our culture. Judgments about things we own, ways we interact, and what we feel is acceptable are influenced by our culture.

Below our exterior behaviors lie our true values and beliefs. Our values are what we esteem; our beliefs are what we hold as true. These values and beliefs may be different from our ide-als—standards we may profess but which do not accurately reflect how we live day to day.

Underneath our societal values and beliefs, at the core of our beings, lies our worldview, our definition of reality. All our choices, reactions, and decisions are shaped by our worldview. So is our language and our sense of beauty. It is easy to describe our behavior but more difficult to describe why we do what we do. Our worldview is so much a part of us that we function without being conscious of it. We are like fish who cannot describe water because we have never lived outside of it.

In some African societies one wife cannot have enough children and many children die during childhood. Do these societies view many children as their wealth and future? In other cultures, an equally expensive practice provides each child his or her own room. Is it that in this world-view privacy and personal autonomy are valued so highly that parents will work to provide for bigger homes?

When Christ enters our lives, he begins to transform our worldview. Often well-intentioned Christians seek to change external behavior without allowing for people's hearts to change first. This results in legalism. As Christ came to live within the culture of the Middle East, so we must adopt the worldview of our Muslim friends in order to be his witnesses. We also need to believe that God can work in every societal worldview in order to transform hearts and lives.

Source: *Encountering the World of Islam*

Then follows the ceremony of *Tawaf*, the sevenfold circumambulation of the Ka'aba, symbolic of the way Muslims turn their thoughts to Allah at this time. After this first of three prescribed Tawafs, pilgrims visit *Al-Hijr*, the spot from which Muhammad began his celebrated Night Journey, and then they run between certain hills outside of Mecca in the ritual known as the *Say*. This peculiar ceremony honors Abraham's slave wife, Hagar, and her son Ishmael (Ismail), who, at the insistence of Sarah, were abandoned in the wilderness. In her distress at her plight and her son's thirst, Hagar is said to have run back and forth between these hills until Allah caused water to spring from a spot known now as the *Well of Zamzam*.

Midway through the pilgrimage rites, pilgrims move into tents outside the city of Mecca for the ceremony of standing in the Valley of *Arafat* at the foot of the Mount of Mercy. This celebrated *"standing ceremony,"* which lasts throughout an entire afternoon, creates in the minds of the devout a profound sense of the presence of God in their lives and of divine forgiveness of their *sins*. They remember, too, that Muhammad visited this spot and preached here on his final pilgrimage. So meaningful is this ceremony that many authorities regard it as the climactic or central event of the entire pilgrimage. In the evening, pilgrims gather forty-nine small stones, which they take to *Mina* the next morning in order to hurl them at one of three stone pillars representing the devil and his powers of temptation. By this rite (*Jamra*) they recall the way Ishmael, on his way to be sacrificed by his father Abraham (some Muslim scholars substitute Ishmael for Isaac as the son

whom Abraham nearly sacrificed), turned back the suggestions of *Iblis* that he flee.

The slaughtering of a small animal on the field of sacrifice is a way of remembering that Allah accepted Abraham's sacrifice of a ram in place of his son. Following this ritual, male pilgrims have their hair cut and are released from many of the prohibitions that marked the earlier phases of the pilgrimage. Now all pilgrims return to Mecca for a second circumambulation of the Ka'aba, and then hasten back to Mina for a second ritual of stoning the devil. The final return to Mecca occurs on the thirteenth day; a third set of circumambulations of the Ka'aba is made, and the pilgrimage is complete after the pilgrims pass through the Farewell Gate.

However, there is an hadith that instructs pilgrims to visit Medina while they are in the Hejaz, and many do, since Muhammad is buried beneath the dome of the Medina mosque. While in Medina, pilgrims also visit the burial ground of Muhammad's wives and Companions, offering prayers on their behalf. After this, the pilgrim is urged to return home as quickly as possible, lest over-familiarity with holy things lead to a lessening of their power. The pilgrim will return home to the heartfelt congratulations of family and friends and to a prestige which he or she did not enjoy before.

## JIHAD

Sometimes regarded as another duty of Muslims, even a possible sixth Pillar, jihad is popularly interpreted as the act of fighting for the faith against unbelievers, but the more basic meaning is "struggle for the

faith." The basic stipulations are outlined in Sura 2:190–193 (TRANS. UNKNOWN):

> On behalf of God, fight whoever fights you, but do not be the aggressor: indeed, God does not like aggressors. Kill them when they advance on you and force them out of the places from which they forced you.... Fight them until there is no persecution and religion belongs to God, and if they abandon their ways, there is to be no hostility—except against evildoers.

Elsewhere, two kinds of people are cited as being particular objects of such activity—those who do not believe in God at all and pay no regard to what he has prohibited (Sura 9:29), and Christians, who "ascribe *partners* to God" (Sura 2:135, TRANS. UNKNOWN). However, it must be noted that over the years there has been just as much stress put on the original, root meaning of jihad—struggle or the expenditure of effort in the Way of Allah—as there has been on the militant suggestion of the term. The popular image of Islam converting unwilling victims by the sword is not confirmed by history, and even recent efforts to see war against Israel as jihad have not met with enthusiasm. However, the rebirth of Islamic fundamentalism in such countries as Libya and Iran may mean a return in our times to the more militant significance of this term. Finally, it should be noted that many authorities regard jihad as a specific form of the first obligation, the duty to witness to the faith, rather than as a separate duty in its own right.

 **End of Key Readings for Lesson 3. See** RECOMMENDED READINGS & ACTIVITIES **on p. 111.**

## ENDNOTES

1. Frithjof Schuon, *Understanding Islam* (Baltimore: Penguin Books, 1972), p. 29. [See Glossary for a fuller explanation of *din*.]
2. A useful account of some major Islamic rites is Gustave von Grunebaum's *Muhammadan Festivals* (New York: Henry Schuman, 1951).
3. Classic account by a Westerner who made the pilgrimage safely is Richard Burton's *Personal Narrative of a Pilgrimage to Al-Madinah and Meccah* (1855–56). A two-volume set of the 1893 edition is available from Dover. The Nov.–Dec. 1974 issue of *Aramco World* is devoted to the pilgrimage. Also see an article in *National Geographic*, Nov. 1978. Most recent account is Mohammed Amin's *Pilgrimage to Mecca* (London: Macdonald and Jane's, 1978).

# THE FUNDAMENTAL ARTICLES OF FAITH IN ISLAM

*by Hammudah Abdalati*

 The true, faithful Muslim believes in the following principal articles of faith:

**1. One God.** He believes in one God, supreme and eternal, infinite and mighty, merciful and compassionate, creator and provider. This belief, in order to be effective, requires complete trust and hope in God, submission to his will, and reliance on his aid. It secures man's dignity and saves him from fear and despair, from guilt and confusion.

**2. Messengers of God.** He believes in all the messengers of God without any discrimination among them. Every known nation had a warner or messenger from God. These messengers were great teachers of the good and true champions of the right. They were chosen by God to teach mankind and deliver his divine message. They were sent at different times of history and every known nation had one messenger or more. During certain periods, two or more messengers were sent by God at the same time to the same nation. The Holy Qur'an mentions the names of twenty-five of them, and the Muslim believes in them all and accepts them as authorized messengers of God. They were, with the exception of Muhammad, known as "national" or local messengers. But their message, their religion, was basically the same and was called Islam, because it came from one and the same source, namely, God, to serve one and the same purpose, and that is to guide humanity to the Straight Path of God. All the messengers, with no exception whatsoever, were mortals, human beings endowed with divine revelations and appointed by God to perform certain tasks. Among them Muhammad stands as the Last Messenger and the crowning glory of the foundation of prophethood. This is not an arbitrary attitude, nor is it just a convenient belief. Like all the other Islamic beliefs, it is an authentic and logical truth. Also, it may be useful to mention here the names of some of the great messengers like Noah and Abraham, Ishmael and Moses, Jesus and Muhammad, may the peace and blessings of God be upon them all. The Qur'an commands the Muslims thus:

> We believe in God, and the revelation given to us, and to Abraham, Ishmael, Isaac, Jacob, and the Tribes; and that which was given to Moses and Jesus, and that which was given to all prophets from their Lord. We make no discrimination between one and another of them, and we bow to God (Sura 2:136, TRANS. UNKNOWN; cf., 3:84; 4:163–65; 6:84–87).

---

Hammudah Abdalati was director of the Canadian Islamic Center of Alberta, associate professor at Syracuse University, and recognized Islamic expert. He was a renowned lecturer and scholar who served as a resourceful consultant and advisor for many organizations, including al-Azhar University, and individuals both in North America and abroad.

Adapted from Hammudah Abdalati, *Islam in Focus* (Beltsville, Md.: Amana Publications, 1998), pp. 11–22. Used by permission. *www.amana-publications.com*

In addition, the Qur'an states in clear terms that the message of Islam as a religion is the culmination of previous revelations. God says:

> The same religion has He established for you as that which He enjoined on Noah—which We have sent by inspiration to you—and which We enjoined on Abraham, Moses and Jesus: namely, that you should remain steadfast in religion, and make no divisions therein; to those who worship other things than Allah, hard is the (way) to which you call them. Allah chooses those whom He pleases, and guides to Himself those who turn (to Him). (Sura 42:13, TRANS. UNKNOWN)

**3. Scriptures and Revelations.** The true Muslim believes, as a result of article two, in all the scriptures and revelations of God. They were the guiding light which the messengers received to show their respective peoples the Right Path of God. In the Qur'an a special reference is made to the books of Abraham, Moses, David, and Jesus. But long before the revelation of the Qur'an to Muhammad, some of those books and revelations had been lost or corrupted, others forgotten, neglected, or concealed. The only authentic and complete book of God in existence today is the Qur'an. In principle, the Muslim believes in the previous books and revelations. But where are their complete and original versions? They could be still at the bottom of the Dead Sea, and there may be more scrolls to be discovered. Or perhaps more information about them will become available when the Christian and Jewish archaeologists reveal to the public the complete original findings of their continued excavations in the Holy Land. For the Muslim, there is no problem of that kind. The Qur'an is in his hand, complete and authentic. Nothing of it is missing and no more of it is expected. Its authenticity is beyond doubt, and no serious scholar or thinker has ventured to question its genuineness. The Qur'an was made so by God, who revealed it and made it incumbent upon himself to protect it against interpolation and corruption of all kinds. Thus it is given to the Muslims as the standard or criterion by which all the other books are judged. So whatever agrees with the Qur'an is accepted as divine truth, and whatever differs from the Qur'an is either rejected or suspended. God says, "Verily, we have, without doubt, sent down the Qur'an, and we will assuredly guard it" (Sura 15:9, TRANS. UNKNOWN; cf., 2:75–79; 5:13–14, 41, 45, 47; 6:91; 41:43).

**4. Angels.** The true Muslim believes in the *angels* of God. They are purely spiritual and splendid beings whose nature requires no food or drink or sleep. They have no physical desires of any kind, nor material needs. They spend their days and nights in the service of God. There are many of them, and each one is charged with a certain duty. If we cannot see the angels with our naked eyes, it does not necessarily deny their actual existence. There are many things in the world that are invisible to the eye or inaccessible to the senses, and yet we do believe in their existence. There are places we have never seen, and things like gas and ether that we could not see with our naked eyes, smell or touch or taste or hear; yet we do acknowledge their existence. Belief in the angels originates from the Islamic

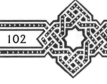
principle that knowledge and truth are not entirely confined to the sensory knowledge or sensory perception alone (Sura 16:49–50; 21:19–20. See also the references in article two above).

**5. Day of Judgment.** The true Muslim believes in the Last Day of Judgment. This world will come to an end some day, and the dead will rise to stand for their final and fair trial. Everything we do in this world, every intention we have, every move we make, every thought we entertain, and every word we say, all are counted and kept in accurate records. On the Day of Judgment they will be brought up. People with good records will be generously rewarded and warmly welcomed to the heaven of God, and those with bad records will be punished and cast into hell. The real nature of heaven and hell and the exact description of them are known to God only. There are descriptions of heaven and hell in the Qur'an and the Traditions of Muhammad, but they should not be taken literally. In heaven, said Muhammad, there are things which no eye has ever seen, no ear has ever heard, and no mind has ever conceived. However, the Muslim believes that there definitely will be compensation and reward for the good deeds, and punishment for the evil ones. That is the Day of Justice and final settlement of all accounts.

If some people think that they are shrewd enough and can get away with their wrong doings, just as they sometimes escape the penalty of the mundane laws, they are wrong; they will not be able to do so on

## WHAT IS FORBIDDEN?

Like the prohibitions of the Old Testament law, Islam has practices which are forbidden (haram). A Muslim must combine faith and action (belief and practice) to work out his salvation through the guidance of God. His commitment to din (way of life or religion) includes avoiding certain behaviors and engaging positive practices, including the Five Pillars.

To protect man from insanity and degeneration, from weakness and indulgence, from indecency and temptation, Islam has prohibited certain things pertaining to food, drinking, recreation, and sex. Among these are the following:

- All kinds of intoxicants (wines, spirits, beer, liquors, drugs, etc.) (Sura 2:219; 4:43; 5:93–94).
- The meat and products of swine (pork, bacon, ham, lard); of wild animals that use claws or teeth to kill their victims (tigers, wolves, leopards, etc.); of all birds of prey (hawks, vultures, crows, etc.); of rodents, reptiles, worms, and the like, of dead animals, and of birds that are not slaughtered properly (Sura 2:172–73; 5:3–6).
- All forms of gambling and vain sports (Sura 2:219; 5:93–94).
- All sexual relations out of wedlock and all manners of talking, walking, looking, and dressing in public that may instigate temptation, arouse desire, stir suspicion, or indicate immodesty and indecency (Sura 23:5–7; 24:30–33; 70:29–31).[1]

1. Hammudah Abdalati, *Islam in Focus* (Beltsville, Md.: Amana Publications, 1998), p. 43.

Source: Annee W. Rose, *www.frontiers.org*.

the Day of Judgment. They will be caught right on the spot defenseless, without any lawyer or counsel to stand in their behalf. All their deeds are visible to God and counted by his agents. Also, if some pious people do good deeds to please God and seem to get no appreciation or acknowledgment in this temporary world, they will eventually receive full compensation and be widely acknowledged on that day. Absolute justice will be done to all.

Belief in the Day of Judgment is the final, relieving answer to many complicated problems of our world. There are people who commit sins, neglect God, and indulge in immoral activities, yet they seem to be "superficially" successful in business and prosperous in life. And there are virtuous and God-minded people, yet they seem to be getting less rewards for their sincere efforts and more suffering in the present world. This is puzzling and incompatible with the justice of God. If the guilty people can escape the mundane law unharmed and, in addition, be more prosperous, what is, then, left for the virtuous people? What will promote the cause of morality and goodness? There must be some way to reward goodness and arrest evil. If this is not done here on this earth—and we know that it is not done regularly or immediately—it has to be done some day, and that is the Day of Judgment. This is not to condone injustice or tolerate mischief in this world. It is not to sedate the deprived or comfort their exploiters. Rather, it is to warn the deviants from the Right Path, and remind them that the justice of God shall run its full course sooner or later (see the previous references).

### 6. God's Infinite Power and Plan.

The true Muslim believes in the timeless knowledge of God and in his power to plan and execute his plans. God is not indifferent to this world, nor is he neutral to it. His knowledge and power are in action at all times to keep order in his vast domain and maintain full command over his creation. He is wise and loving, and whatever he does must have a good motive and a meaningful purpose. If this is established in our minds, we should accept with good faith all that he does, although we may fail to understand it fully, or even think it is bad. We should have strong faith in him and accept whatever he does, because our knowledge is limited and our thinking is based on individual or personal considerations, whereas his knowledge is limitless and he plans on a universal basis.

This does not in any way make man fatalist[ic] or helpless. It simply draws the demarcation line between what is God's concern and what is man's responsibility. Because we are by nature finite and limited, we have a finite and limited degree of power and freedom. We cannot do everything, and he graciously holds us responsible only for the things we do. The things which we cannot do, or things which he himself does, are not in the realm of our responsibility; he is just and has given us limited power to match our finite nature and limited responsibility. On the other hand, the timeless knowledge and power of God to execute his plans do not prevent us from making our own plans in our own limited sphere of power. On the contrary, he exhorts us to think, to plan, and to make sound choices, but if things do not happen the way we wanted or planned them, we should not lose faith or surrender ourselves to mental strains and shattering worries. We should try again and again, and if the results are not satisfactory, then we know that we have tried our best and cannot be held responsible for the results, because what is beyond our capacity and responsibility is the affair of God alone. The Muslims call this article of faith the belief in *qadaa* and *qadar*, which simply means, in other words, that the timeless knowledge of God anticipates events, and that events take place according to the exact knowledge of God (Sura 18:29; 41:46; 53:33–62; 54:49; 65:3; 76:29–31).

**7. Life's Purpose.** The true Muslim believes that God's creation is meaningful and that life has a sublime purpose beyond the physical needs and material activities of man. The purpose of life is to worship God. This does not simply mean that we have to spend our entire lives in constant seclusion and absolute meditation. To worship God is to know him, to love him, to obey his commandments, to enforce his law in every aspect of life, to serve his cause by doing the right and shunning the evil, and to be just to him, to ourselves, and to our fellow human beings. To worship God is to live life, not to run away from it. In brief, to worship God is to imbue ourselves with his supreme attributes. This is by no means a simple statement, nor is it an oversimplification of the matter. It is most comprehensive and conclusive. So if life has a purpose and if man is created to serve that purpose, then he cannot escape the responsibility. He cannot deny his existence or ignore the vital role he has to play. When God charges him with any responsibility, he provides

him with all the required assistance. He endows him with intelligence and power to choose his course of conduct. Man, thus, is strongly commended by God to exert his utmost to fully serve the purpose of his existence. Should he fail to do that, or misuse his life or neglect his duties, he shall be responsible to God for his wrong deeds (Sura 21:17–18; 51:56–58; 75:37).

**8. Dignified Status of Man.** The true Muslim believes that man enjoys an especially high-ranking status in the hierarchy of all the known creatures. He occupies this distinguished position because he alone is gifted with rational faculties and spiritual aspirations, as well as powers of action. But the more his rank excels, the more his responsibility grows. He occupies the position of God's viceroy on earth. The person who is appointed by God to be his active agent must necessarily have some power and authority, and be, at least potentially, endowed with honor and integrity. And this is the status of man in Islam; not a condemned race from birth to death, but a dignified being potentially capable of good and noble achievements. The fact that God chose his messengers from the human race shows that man is trustworthy and capable, and that he can acquire immense treasures of goodness (Sura 2:30–34; 6:165; 7:11; 17:70–72, 90–95).

**9. Islam Universal.** The true Muslim believes that every person is born Muslim. This means that the very course of birth takes place in accordance with the will of God, in realization of his plans and in submission to his commands. It also means that every person is endowed with spiritual potentialities and intellectual inclinations that can make him a good

Muslim, if he has the right access to Islam and is left to develop his innate nature. Many people can readily accept Islam if it is properly presented to them, because it is the divine formula for those who want to satisfy their moral and spiritual needs as well as their natural aspirations, for those who want to lead a constructive and sound life, whether personal or social, national or international. This is so because Islam is the universal religion of God, the maker of human nature, who knows what is best for human nature (Sura 30:30; 64:1–3; 82:6–8).

Qur'an lesson in Delhi

© Caleb Project

### 10. Freedom, Responsibility, and Sin.

The true Muslim believes that every person is born free from sin and all claims to inherited virtue. He is like a blank book. When the person reaches the age of maturity, he becomes accountable for his deeds and intentions, if his development is normal and if he is sane. Man is not only free from sin until he commits sin, but he is also free to do things according to his plans on his own responsibility. This dual freedom—freedom from sin and freedom to do effective things—clears the Muslim's conscience from the heavy pressure of inherited sin. It relieves his soul and mind from the unnecessary strains of the doctrine of original sin.

This Islamic concept of freedom is based upon the principle of God's justice and the individual's direct responsibility to God. Each person must bear his own burden and be responsible for his own actions, because no one can expiate for another's sin. Thus, a Muslim believes that if Adam had committed the first sin, it was his own responsibility to expiate for that sin. To assume that God was unable to forgive Adam and had to make somebody else expiate for his sin, or to assume that Adam did not pray for pardon, or prayed for it but it was not granted, would be extremely unlikely and contrary to God's mercy and justice, as well as to his attribute of forgiveness and power to forgive. To assume the said hypothesis would be an audacious defiance of common sense and flagrant violation of the very concept of God (see the references in article nine above; Sura 41:46; 45:15; 53:31–42; 74:38).

On this rational basis, as well as on the authority of the Qur'an, the Muslim believes that Adam realized what he had committed and prayed to God for pardon, as any other sensible sinner would. It is also on the same basis, the Muslim believes, that God, the forgiving and merciful, granted Adam pardon (Sura 2:35–37; 20:117–22). Hence, the Muslim cannot possibly accept the doctrine that Adam, with the whole human race, had been condemned and unforgiven until Jesus came to expiate for their sins. Consequently, the Muslim cannot entertain the dramatic story of Jesus' death on the cross just to do away with all human sins once and for all.

Here the reader must be cautioned against any wrong conclusions. The Muslim does not believe in the crucifixion of Jesus by his enemies, because the basis of this doctrine of crucifixion is contrary to divine mercy and justice, as much as it is to human logic and dignity. Such a disbelief in the doctrine does not in any way lessen the Muslim's reverence for Jesus, or degrade the high status of Jesus in Islam, or even shake the Muslim's belief in Jesus as a distinguished prophet of God. On the contrary, by rejecting this doctrine, the Muslim accepts Jesus but only with more esteem and higher respect, and looks upon his original message as an essential part of Islam. So let it be stated again, that to be a Muslim, a person must accept and respect all the prophets of God without any discrimination.

### 11. Salvation by Beliefs and Practice.
The true Muslim believes that man must work out his salvation through the guidance of God. This means that in order to attain salvation, a person must combine faith and action, belief and practice. Faith without action is as insufficient as action without faith. In other words, no one can attain salvation until his faith in God becomes dynamic in his life and his beliefs are translated into reality. This is in complete harmony with the other Islamic articles of faith. It shows that God does not accept lip service, and that no true believer can be indifferent as far as the practical requirements of faith

are concerned. It also shows that no one can act on behalf of another or intercede between him and God (Sura 10:9–10; 18:30; 103:1–3).

### 12. Unreached Not Responsible.
The true Muslim believes that God does not hold any person responsible until he has shown him the Right Way. This is why God has sent many messengers and revelations, and he has made it clear that there would be no punishment before giving guidance and sounding the alarm. So, a person who has never come across any divine revelations or messenger, or a person who is insane, is not held responsible to God for failing to obey the Divine instructions. Such a person will be responsible only for not doing what his sound common sense tells him to do. But the person who knowingly and intentionally violates the law of God or deviates from his Right Path will be punished for his wrong deeds (Sura 4:165; 5:16, 21; 17:15).

This point is very important for every Muslim. There are many people in the world who have not heard of Islam and have no way of knowing about it. Such people may be honest and may become good Muslims, if they find their way to Islam. If they do not know and have no way of knowing, they will not be responsible for failing to be Muslims. Instead, the Muslims who can present Islam to such people will be the ones responsible for failing to invite them to Islam and show them what Islam is. This calls upon every Muslim throughout the globe not only to preach Islam in words but also—and more importantly—to live it in full (Sura 3:104; 16:125).

**13. Goodness of Human Nature.**
The true Muslim believes that in human nature, which God created, there is more good than evil, and the probability of successful reform is greater than the probability of hopeless failure. This belief is derived from the fact that God has tasked man with certain assignments and sent messengers with revelations for his guidance. If man were by nature a hopeless case, impossible to reform, how could God with his absolute wisdom assign him responsibilities and invite him to do or shun certain things? How could God do that, if it were all in vain? The fact that God cares for man and takes a stand in his interest proves that man is neither helpless nor hopeless, but is appreciative of and inclined to good. Surely with sound faith in God and due confidence in man, miracles can be worked out, even in our own times. To understand this properly, one has to carefully study the relevant passages in the Qur'an and reflect on their meanings.

## FAMILY AND CHILDREN

> Your Lord has decreed that you worship none but Him, and that you be kind to parents. Whether one or both of them attain old age in your life, say not to them a word of contempt, nor repel them, but address them in terms of honor. And out of kindness, lower to them the wing of humility and say, "My Lord! Bestow on them Your mercy as they cherished me in childhood" (Sura 17:23–24, YUSUF ALI).

Muslims value interdependence within the family and community. Extended families may live together, and many Muslims work in businesses owned by their families. Decisions are frequently made by the group and primarily by the men. Muslim women are free to make independent decisions if they are not contrary to the leadership of the family.

Marriages may be arranged within the extended family to ensure that single women are not left alone. Among the women and children, a matriarchal system often prevails; stress in the home can be high, especially with the mother-in-law who is honored by the son above his wife.

Many Muslim women feel honored to spend their time in the home caring for the needs of the entire family. [See Honor and Shame, p. 119.] Women have great influence in rearing the children in the ways of Islam. Boys are generally favored above daughters. A man is dishonored if his wife remains childless, whereas the birth of a son is cause for great celebration.

Despite many apparent restrictions, millions of Muslim mothers are loved and respected by husbands and children, even into old age. Muslims find it difficult to understand why older women would be put into nursing homes, separated from their families, to be cared for by strangers. Muslim children are responsible for caring for their aging parents, for making their lives as comfortable as possible.

Source: Annee W. Rose, *www.frontiers.org*.

### FOR FURTHER STUDY
Miriam Adeney, *Daughters of Islam: Building Bridges with Muslim Women* (Downers Grove, Ill.: InterVarsity Press, 2002). *www.ivpress.com*

**14. Faith Completed by Convictions.**
The true Muslim believes that faith is not
complete when it is followed blindly or accepted unquestioningly unless the believer
is reasonably satisfied. If faith is to inspire
action, and if faith and action are to lead
to salvation, then faith must be founded
on unshakable convictions without any
deception or compulsion. In other words,
the person who calls himself a Muslim
because of his family traditions, or accepts
Islam under coercion or blind imitation,
is not a complete Muslim in the sight of
God. A Muslim must build his faith on
well-grounded convictions, beyond any
reasonable doubt and above uncertainty.
If he is not certain about his faith, he is
invited by God to search in the open book
of nature, to use his reasoning powers, and
to reflect on the teachings of the Qur'an.
He must search for the indisputable truth
until he finds it, and he will certainly find
it, if he is capable and serious enough
(Sura 2:170; 43:22–24).

This is why Islam demands sound convictions and opposes blind imitation. Every
person who is duly qualified as a genuine
and earnest thinker is enjoined by Islam
to employ his faculties to the fullest extent.
But if a person is unqualified or uncertain
of himself, he should pursue his thinking
only as far as his limits can take him. It
will be quite in order for such a person to
rely only on the authentic sources of religion, which are sufficient in themselves,
without applying to them any critical
questioning of which he is incapable. The
point is that no one can call himself a
true Muslim unless his faith is based on
strong convictions and his mind is clear
from doubts. Because Islam is complete
only when it is based on strong convictions

and freedom of choice, it cannot be forced
upon anybody, for God will not accept
this forced faith. Nor will he consider it
a true Islam if it does not develop from
within or originate from free and sound
convictions. And because Islam insures
freedom of belief, many non-Muslim
groups lived and still live in the Muslim
countries, enjoying full freedom of belief
and conscience. The Muslims take this
attitude because Islam forbids compulsion
in religion. It is the light which must
radiate from within, because freedom of
choice is the cornerstone of responsibility.
This does not exempt the parents from
responsibility for their children; nor does
it condone their being indifferent to the
spiritual welfare of their dependents. In
fact, they must do everything possible to
help them to build a strong inspiring faith.

To establish faith on sound grounds,
there are various parallel avenues. There
is the spiritual approach, which is based
mainly on the Qur'an and the Traditions
of Muhammad. There is also the rational
approach, which eventually leads to faith
in the Supreme Being. This is not to say
that the spiritual approach lacks sound
rationality. Nor is the rational approach
deprived of inspiring spirituality. Both approaches, in fact, complement one another
and may well interact. Now if a person is
sufficiently equipped with sound rational
qualities, he may resort to the rational
approach, or to the spiritual approach,
or to both, and may be confident that his
conclusion will be right. But if a person
is incapable of profound inquiry or is
uncertain of his reasoning powers, he may
confine himself to the spiritual approach,
and be contented with the knowledge he
can derive from the authentic sources of

religion. The point is that, whether one uses the spiritual approach or the rational technique or both, one will in the end come to faith in God. All these avenues are equally important and accepted by Islam, and when properly channeled, lead to the same end, namely faith in the Supreme Being (Sura 5:16–17; 12:109; 18:30; 56:80–81).

### 15. Qur'an: God's Only Perfect Word.

The true Muslim believes that the Qur'an is the word of God, revealed to Muhammad through the agency of the angel Gabriel. The Qur'an was revealed from God piece by piece on various occasions to answer certain questions, solve certain problems, settle certain disputes, and to be man's best guide to the truth of God and eternal happiness. Every letter in the Qur'an is the word of God, and every sound in it is the true echo of God's voice. The Qur'an is the first and most authentic source of Islam. It was revealed in Arabic. It is still and will remain in its original and complete Arabic version, because God has made it his concern to preserve the Qur'an, to make it always the best guide for man, and to safeguard it against corruption (Sura 4:82; 15:9; 17:9; 41:41–44; 42:7, 52–53).[1]

### 16. Traditions of Muhammad: Second Source of Islam.

The true Muslim believes in a clear distinction between the Qur'an and the Traditions of Muhammad. The Qur'an is the word of God, whereas the Traditions of Muhammad are the practical interpretations of the Qur'an. The role of Muhammad was to convey the Qur'an as he received it, to interpret it, and to practice it fully. His interpretations and practices produced what is known as the Traditions of Muhammad. They are considered the second source of Islam and must be in complete harmony with the first source, namely the Qur'an, which is the standard and the criterion. If there be any contradiction or inconsistency between any of the Traditions and the Qur'an, the Muslim adheres to the Qur'an alone and regards everything else as open to question, because no genuine Tradition of Muhammad can ever disagree with the Qur'an.

## REMARKS

In this discussion of the cardinal articles of faith in Islam, we have deliberately differed from the traditional presentation on the subject. We did not confine them to five or six articles. Instead, we tried to include as many principles as was possible. But it should be pointed out here that all the articles of faith mentioned above are based upon and derived from the teachings of the Qur'an and the Traditions of Muhammad. More verses from the Qur'an and many parts of the Traditions could have been quoted to show the foundation of these articles of faith. This was not done because of the limitations of space. However, the Qur'an and the Traditions of Muhammad are available references for any detailed study.

We have also kept to a minimum the use of western terminology and technical language like "predestination," "fatalism," "free will," and so on. This was done deliberately because we wanted to avoid confusion and technicalities. Most of the technical terms used in religion among non-Arabic speaking people lead to

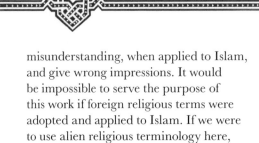

misunderstanding, when applied to Islam, and give wrong impressions. It would be impossible to serve the purpose of this work if foreign religious terms were adopted and applied to Islam. If we were to use alien religious terminology here, we would have to add many qualifications and comments to clarify the picture of Islam. This also would have required much more space than is available. So, we have tried to explain things in ordinary, plain language.

**End of Basic Readings for Lesson 3. See** RECOMMENDED READINGS & ACTIVITIES **on p. 111.**

**Go to:**
*www.encounteringislam.org/ readings* **to find the Full Reading for Lesson 3.**

## FOR FURTHER STUDY

John L. Esposito, *What Everyone Needs to Know about Islam* (New York: Oxford University Press, 2002). *www.oup.com*

## ENDNOTE

1. In testimony to God's conservation, the Qur'an is the only scripture in human history that has been preserved in its complete and original version, without the slightest change in style or even punctuation. The history of recording the Qur'an, compiling its chapters and conserving its text, is beyond any doubt, not only in the minds of the Muslims, but also in the minds of honest and serious scholars. This is an historical fact which no scholar from any faith—who respects his knowledge and integrity—has ever questioned. As a matter of fact, it is Muhammad's standing miracle that if all mankind were to work together they could not produce the like of one Qur'anic chapter (Sura 2:22–24; 11:13–14; 17:88–89).

# DISCUSSION QUESTIONS

1.  In this lesson, did you learn anything about what Muslims believe that surprised you? What elements of the lesson helped you understand Muslims better?

2.  What aspects of God's character does Islam seem to emphasize?

3.  What is Islam's judgment of the nature of man?

# RECOMMENDED READINGS & ACTIVITIES*

Read:   Phil Parshall, *Understanding Muslim Teachings and Traditions: A Guide for Christians* (Grand Rapids: Baker Books, 2002).

        Hammudah Abdalati, *Islam in Focus* (Beltsville, Md.: Amana Publications, 1998).

Watch:  *Inside Mecca*, National Geographic DVD (2000), and *Inside Islam*, History Channel DVD (2002).

Pray:   Pray for Muslims everyday during the month of Ramadan. A thirty-day Ramadan prayer guide is published each year.

Meet:   If your community has an international student center or English language center, ask if they have any Muslim students seeking conversational English tutoring.

Surf:   Discover related web sites at *www.encounteringislam.org/lessonlinks*.

* For expanded details on these Recommended Readings & Activities, visit *www.encounteringislam.org/lessonlinks*.

# EXPRESSIONS
# OF ISLAM

# LESSON 4
## MUSLIMS TODAY

## PONDER THIS

- There have been many changes in the world since Islam was established in the seventh century. How have Muslims responded to these changes?

- How can we express empathy for Muslims and the challenges they face today?

- What does the gospel require of Christians in responding to the suffering of others?

- What attitudes are Christians called to have in responding to change?

# LESSON OBJECTIVE

Describe the movement of Islam from its crystallization in seventh-century Arab culture to the development of the various kinds of Islam present today. Include the following issues:

1. Islam's beginnings as a small, persecuted, and suffering reform movement.

2. Islam's transformation to an all-encompassing social system during Muhammad's lifetime.

3. Islam's enforcement of dominance and power after the Hijra.

4. Islam's struggle to define its leadership, with codification of the Qur'an by Uthman and the political-moral leadership debate under Ali.

5. Islam's transformation into a multicultural religion and the causes of the Sunni-Shi'i and other divisions.

6. Islam's three main responses to the forces of the modern world:

   a. returning to militant, political, and violent roots

   b. modernizing and becoming ecumenical through reform and secularization

   c. attempting to find a middle road between radical entrenchment and liberal dilution.

# LESSON READINGS

Full:    Islamic Fundamentalism: Implications for Missions
The Growth of African-American Islam
Full Readings are found at *www.encounteringislam.org/readings.*

# INTRODUCTION

The Qur'an is rooted in seventh-century Arabian culture. Yet expressions of Islam have changed as the Muslim umma, or community, has grown and as its relevance has been challenged. In response to these challenges, Muslim communities have either accommodated to the changes or become entrenched in old patterns. These responses have fragmented the umma into various branches and subgroups (for example, Sunni and Shi'i, Wahhabi, *Ahmadiya*, *Nation of Islam*, and so forth).

Morroccan men gather for prayer

© Caleb Project

Islam's character first changed when the umma fled persecution in Mecca and began to form a successful society in Medina. The newly dominant umma began to subjugate non-Muslims, including the Jewish tribes of Medina. At this time, the umma shifted its focus and became an Arab-focused religion. Rather than celebrating the Jewish Day of Atonement and praying toward Jerusalem, now both the Hajj and prayers were directed toward Mecca. Another shift occurred soon after Muhammad's death as cultural differences and disagreements over how to choose a leader caused rebellion and civil war in the umma. Muslims still struggle with these tensions today. In fact, more social, political, technological, and economic changes have taken place in the past century than in all the years of Muslim history since the time of Muhammad. As a result, and just as is true of all societies, the Islam of today is more diverse and is struggling with change more than ever before.

For all of the umma's diversity, Muslims share a spiritual kinship and a similarity of forms. All Muslims adopt equivalent styles of politeness, cleanliness, and clothing. Most use Arabic names. Muslims around the world celebrate the same feasts and festivals and repeat the same prayers. They demonstrate, and take pride in, solidarity with the global umma of Islam. Only two communities are recognized

in Islam: Dar al-Islam (*Dar as-Salaam*), the house of peace, and Dar al-Harb, the house that is not yet Muslim. This oneness of purpose—to defend their community and to seek to extend it—fleshes out the oneness of the umma and Muslims' shared belief in one God.

Tawhid, or oneness, also stands as a rejection of a dichotomy between the secular and the sacred. Muslims believe that God should rule all of one's heart and life, not just a portion of either. Personal, religious, economic, social, and political spheres of life are all to be submitted to God via Islam. In the words of Muhammad Iqbal, "Religion is not a departmental affair; it is neither mere thought, nor mere feeling, nor mere action; it is an expression of the whole man."[1]

While this idealistic vision of a united and successful umma inspires Muslim da'wa, or outreach, much of the umma is suffering under oppressive "Islamic" governments which fall short of the ideal. The Muslim empires of earlier centuries have faded, and the Caliphate has been dissolved. Many Muslims live in pluralistic cultures or have immigrated into western societies. In light of these factors, what exactly is the umma today?

While there is not, in reality, one Islam or one type of Muslim, there are several common genres. Some are actively religious and deeply concerned about the moral drift of their cultures toward modernism, while others are modern and western in their orientation. Some Muslims are nationalistic, proud to be who they are (which is synonymous with being Muslim), but the vast majority are just common people, needing housing, food, education, healthcare, and more job opportunities. These broad categories are fluid and freely overlap.

So, whereas Lesson 3 may have helped us understand the religious practices of Muslims, and Lesson 5 the everyday life of common Muslims, we also need to appreciate Muslims' approach to dealing with the world Islam faces today. Islam has both religious and secular reform movements seeking to modernize the faith. Islam has resurgent revival efforts attempting to reunite the umma and return it to its ideals. While these undertakings may be either too western or too Arab for the average followers of Islam, their aspirations are affecting our world. As we cover these broad themes, we must bear in mind that we are to listen to our Muslim friend's opinion, and respond to his or her needs, while not giving in to responding or thinking in terms of stereotypes.

Muslims live in a world that has been newly rocked by nationalism, capitalism, socialism, modernism, materialism, secularism, and racism. Muslims' failed experiments with these philosophies have left them disillusioned. Many are asking, "Has God forsaken us? Perhaps he is chastening us to return to Islam." This message appeals to many types of Muslims, whether wealthy youth disillusioned with modern life; poor women suppressed by too few opportunities; economically constricted, middle-class business people; or African-American males imprisoned for urban crimes.

Muslims' disillusionment sometimes turns to anger toward those they perceive

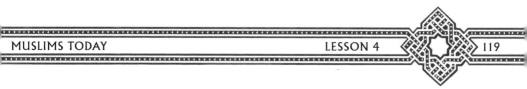
as the cause of their failure. They may believe nations of the West—wealthy, consumer-oriented, and self-interested—are largely responsible for creating their suffering or, at least, for initiating little to alleviate it. In the eyes of many Muslims, the imperialism of the twentieth century continues today, in the form of economic and cultural oppression through the West's commerce and exported television, movies, and pornography. Muslims are afraid that their children will adopt godless western values because of exposure to these things. They fear for the future of their families and communities.

Some Muslims have decided that the International Monetary Fund and the World Bank are puppets of multinational companies, forcing austerity on the poor, pursuing their own economic interests, and never paying for the bad investments they make in dictatorial regimes. Many Muslims have observed western nations instituting policies that suit the West's interests and giving financial aid and exporting

## HONOR AND SHAME

"Nothing cleanses the shame except blood" (Arab proverb).

In every culture, families, communities, and governments teach their children that certain behaviors are acceptable and should be rewarded, while other behaviors are unacceptable and must be punished. These values and how they are taught vary from one society to the next. Many western cultures focus on truth, honesty, right and wrong, guilt and innocence. Children are told "No!" when scolded. Legal systems protect freedoms and rights. Cheating is not permitted because it is not fair. It is not polite, respectful, civil, or courteous to distort or conceal the truth: one cannot trust a liar.

However, in most non-western cultures children are scolded with *shame*, and they are taught to politely hide the truth rather than be discourteous. Shame may also be used as punishment for criminal behavior, and legal systems may defend actions taken to protect one's *honor*. Honor may demand that one gives gifts to authorities, out of respect. To the Westerner, these practices appear to be lies and bribes. But, in non-western communities, those who neglect these duties may be considered impolite, disrespectful, uncivil, or discourteous: one cannot trust a dishonorable person.

Honor and shame are powerful social motivators. In many cultures, honor is held collectively by the family or community; shame is an offense against all and must be avenged. Someone who dishonors his family may be shunned, or, in extreme cases, murdered to restore the honor of the family name. Much of the Bible reflects a culture of honor and shame: "He who ignores discipline comes to poverty and shame, but whoever heeds correction is honored" (Prov. 13:18; see also Num. 12:14; 2 Sam. 13:1–32; and Heb. 12:1–3).

### FOR FURTHER STUDY
Roland Muller, *Honor and Shame: Unlocking the Door* (Philadelphia, Pa.: Xlibris, 2000). *www. xlibris.com*

Source: *Encountering the World of Islam*

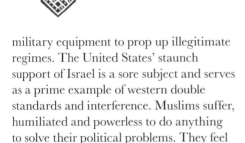

military equipment to prop up illegitimate regimes. The United States' staunch support of Israel is a sore subject and serves as a prime example of western double standards and interference. Muslims suffer, humiliated and powerless to do anything to solve their political problems. They feel that shame cannot be hidden but which, they feel, must be avenged.

How would we react in their situation? While I, the editor, do not agree with all Muslim views on current events, I empathize with their plight. I agree that godlessness, apostasy, and infidelity are often hallmarks of modernity. I recognize how angry I become over small insults, and wonder whether I would resort to violence if I saw no other alternatives. But when I hear my Muslim friends express disillusionment with the indiscriminate violence that murders women and children, the weak, and fellow Muslims, I realize they too long for an alternative.

## THE TRUE FACE OF DEMOCRACY

While in a Bengali neighborhood of London, I saw a poster which proclaimed, "Democracy Is Slavery." On the ground beneath it was a stack of flyers which read:

- Democracy represents a way of life where man is sovereign. Man controls his life the way he wants. He makes the laws for himself, judging good and bad according to his desires. Democracy means man is independent from the Creator.

- Homosexuality, promiscuity, and illegitimate children are considered normal values in the free and democratic societies of the West.

- Democracy means the people are slaves to the laws made by incompetent politicians who only seek to secure their own interests.

- The culture of freedom and democracy teaches us that there is no difference between Muslims and the Jews, Christians, Hindus, atheists, idol worshippers, and so forth.

- The West, by brainwashing you to believe in democracy, aims to keep you away from the powerful truth of Islam.

- Islam follows the law of God, not man.

- The Muslim submits his will to the perfect will of God.

## DO YOU STILL BELIEVE IN DEMOCRACY?

While this particular Muslim political group has a different view of democracy than I do, I also realize that many democracies fall short of the ideal and entail unintended, problematic consequences. Like many Muslims, I too strive to submit myself first to God and not to imperfect human systems.

Radical groups like *HAMAS* often appeal to Muslims by contributing to their community, feeding the poor, and ministering to orphans and widows. The Bible challenges us to do the same. Muslims need human rights, social welfare, economic opportunity, and religious freedom, which

## The Paths of Muhammad and Christ

| Following the Hijra | Following the Cross |
|---|---|
| Flee persecution. | Persevere. |
| Suffering abnormal. | Suffering normal. |
| Seek statehood. | Reject statehood. |
| Bring reform through law. | Bring reform through leaven, salt, and light. |
| Need power. | Need a savior. |
| Deny the cross: Reject weakness and vulnerability. | Pick up the cross: Be transformed through weakness and vulnerability. |

Source: David W. Shenk, "Islam and Christianity: A Quest for Community," unpublished paper, 14 January 1983.

© Caleb Project

are Christians' responsibility to endorse and pursue. So many Muslims ask, "Where are the Christians who follow Jesus?" This is why David Shenk's article on p. 133 is so important.

We need to make an informed response. But before that, we need to assess: How are our various denominations presenting Muslims with a divided and conflicting image of Christ? How are these forms of Christianity tied to our cultures? How is biblical Christianity able to adjust to different times and places? How should our churches adapt to change in the world, without falling into legalism or license? Carl Ellis, co-author of *The Changing Face of Islam in America*, says that we often present Christ wrapped in the plastic bag of western culture. No wonder the intended recipients are choking on the bread of life!

Christ's path is different from the path of this world. Jesus did not seek success, wealth, or power. He humbled himself and went to the cross for us. Now he calls us to follow in his steps, not building an earthly community but an eternal spiritual kingdom. Muslims would never criticize Jesus. His reputation is unimpeachable. The problem is our failure to act as Jesus would, so that Muslims can see Christians acting as Jesus would. What do we do about this?

– *K.S., Editor*

### FOR FURTHER STUDY
Jacob M. Fellure, *The Everything Middle East Book: The Nations, Their Histories, and Their Conflicts* (Avon, Ma.: F+W Publications, 2004).

### ENDNOTE
1.  Muhammad Iqbal, *The Reconstruction of Religious Thought in Islam* (Lahore, Pakistan: Ashraf Press, 1968), p. 2.

# DIVERSITY WITHIN MUSLIM UMMA

*by Phil Parshall*

The Prophet foresaw the schisms that would arise among his disciples. In one of the most famous Traditions, Muhammad is reported to have said: "Verily, it will happen to my people even as it did to the children of Israel. The children of Israel were divided into seventy-two sects, and my people will be divided into seventy-three. Every one of these sects will go to hell, except one sect."[1]

The assumption by Muhammad was that heresy would be easily identifiable. All deviants would be consigned to hell by the umma. Only true Muslims would be privileged to enter paradise. In reality, heresy in a religion or ideology has never been easy to identify. There are many admixtures of doctrine, interpretation, and practice within any group. Purity is relative.

Within Islam, homogeneity and heterogeneity, unity and discord, love and hate all merge into that which is at once a religion, a worldview, a community, a ritual, and a code. For all, an overriding unity is a sought-after but elusive phenomenon. Most Muslims experience frustration that the umma of Islam falls short of the ideal of unity set forth by the Prophet.

## SHI'A WITHIN ISLAM

The torches and weirdly lit banners, the bunch of black chains in the right hand of every man, the black garments, the glazed and exhausted eyes of the performers, and their drenched, sweating bodies signified a religious experience with which I was totally unfamiliar. Intense yet deliberate, the rhythm of the slow, liturgical chant never varied, its tempo ruled by the downward sweep of the chains, by the long, sustained cries of the leaders, by the thud of metal on flesh. In ancient and dignified figures, these young men were spelling out once more for a million pilgrims the renunciation, the humility, and penitence which lie at the heart of Shi'i Islam.

"Ohhhh—Husayn, most great, most honored, we grieve for thee," called the leader, walking backward, step after measured step down the cleared aisle of the street. At this signal, the chains were swung like incense burners, across the body, out to the side; a silent half beat, marked by the thump of bare feet marching in unison, passed before the score of chains swung back to thud on the bared shoulders.

"Yaaaa—Husayn," answered the young men. Their shoulders were bruised blue from the ritual beatings, the kerchiefs around their heads

---

Phil Parshall is one of today's leading authorities on ministry to Muslims. He and his wife, Julie, have lived among Muslims since 1962, in Bangladesh and the Philippines. He is the author of nine books on Christian ministry among Muslims.

Adapted from Phil Parshall, *Beyond the Mosque* (Grand Rapids: Baker, 1985), pp. 47–63. Used by permission. *www.bakerbooks.com*

blotched from perspiration. Still they kept up the sustained note, the measured beat, and the chains swung again like censers. The chains thudded, the chant swelling higher from a score of throats, from a hundred, as the *taziyas* awaiting their turn

Shi`a self-flagellation

inside the mosque were heard in the distance, in the silent half beats of the continuing ritual.

"Ohhhhhh—Husayn, our beloved martyr, we grieve for thee," cried the leader. Tears streamed down the faces of sobbing men standing near me, and the piercing, wailing cries of the women spoke of loss and pain and grief and lamentation.[2]

Such was the experience of Elizabeth W. Fernea as she visited Husayn's tomb at the huge Shi'i pilgrimage center in *Karbala*, Iraq. A similar ritual occurs among Shi'i Muslims throughout the Islamic world on the anniversary of the death of Husayn, their leader, hero, and, most importantly, martyr.

## THE QUESTION OF MUHAMMAD'S SUCCESSOR: THE SUNNI-SHI'I SPLIT

It is important to realize that the initial and fundamental split between Sunnis and Shi'a was over the question of succession. The issue was of a political nature. Today approximately 85 percent of all Muslims are Sunnis, while 15 percent are Shi'a.

Muhammad made no provision for his successor. This created the climate for Islam's first major crisis, as it tried to constitute itself as a major political-cum-religious combined force following the decease of its autocratic and charismatic leader.

Abu Bakr, Umar, and Uthman followed Muhammad successively in leadership. Upon the assassination of Uthman, Ali became the caliph. He was a first cousin of Muhammad's, as well as a son-in-law of the Prophet through his marriage to Fatima. Immediately, Ali came into conflict with *Muawiyah*, the governor of Syria, who was also a relative of Uthman. It is at this point the divergence between Sunnis and Shi'a takes place. Ali is recognized by Shi'a as the first legitimate caliph. Ali's son, Hasan, according to Shi'a, should have been the rightful leader, followed by Ali's other son, Husayn. In the critical historical moment when Husayn might actually have assumed such leadership, Muawiyah's loyalists killed Husayn and seventy of his followers at the battle of Karbala.

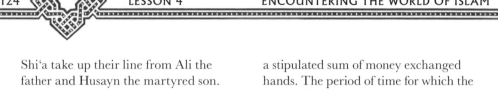
Shi'a take up their line from Ali the father and Husayn the martyred son. Sunnis, on the other hand, recognize the line of Abu Bakr, Umar, Uthman, Ali, and Muawiyah.

Shi'a give the successors of Muhammad the title "Imam" rather than "Caliph." These Imams are historically regarded as infallible guides to all truth. The largest group of Shi'a believes that there were twelve of these Imams. The last one in the lineage was Muhammad al-Mutazar, who was also known as al-Mahdi (the rightly guided one). He was reputed to have disappeared (occultation) into the mosque of Samarra, Iraq, in A.D. 878. The "Twelver" Shi'a believe him to be still alive and actively engaged in guiding the believers. At the end of the age he will reappear and convert the world to Islam. Allegiance to him is a cardinal doctrine among those Shi'a who are specifically called the *Twelvers*.

## SHI'I DISTINCTIVES

Over the years of Islamic history there developed a number of Shi'i distinctives that have put some distance between them and other Muslim traditions. For instance, their Qur'an contains a few variants when compared to the Qur'an used by the rest of the Islamic world.[3] Also, the Shi'a "have their own collections of hadith, composed during the tenth century, at a time when the Buyid *amirs* were masters of Baghdad."[4] A practice that separates some Shi'a from Sunnis has been that of *muta* or temporary marriage. This has particularly taken place among soldiers who were fighting a war far from family and home. A contract was drawn up and a stipulated sum of money exchanged hands. The period of time for which the marriage would be valid was written into the contract. Orthodox Sunni leaders have condemned the practice as tantamount to adultery.[5] The Qur'anic citation of Sura 4:28 has been interpreted as supporting the practice of muta: "Allah desires that he should make light your burdens, and man is created weak" (SHAKIR).

## AYATOLLAH KHOMEINI ON DISSENSION BETWEEN SUNNIS AND SHI'A

It is appropriate to give equal time to Iranian Ayatollah Ruhollah Khomeini [d. 1989], the most famous of all contemporary Twelver Shi'a, to present his case for the necessity of brotherhood among all Muslims, as they together wage war against the "agents of America and Zionism."

> More saddening and dangerous than nationalism is the creation of dissension between Sunnis and Shi'a, and diffusion of mischievous propaganda among brother Muslims. Praise and thanks be to God that no difference exists in our Revolution between these two groups. All are living side by side in friendship and brotherhood. The Sunnis, who are numerous in Iran and live all over the country, have their own Ulama and shieks; they are our brothers and equal with us, and are opposed to the attempts at creating dissension that certain criminals, agents of America and Zionism, are currently engaged in. Our Sunni brothers in the Muslim world must know that the agents of the satanic superpowers do not desire the

welfare of Islam and the Muslims. The Muslims must disassociate themselves from them, and pay no heed to their diverse propaganda. I extend the hand of brotherhood to all committed Muslims in the world and ask them to regard the Shi'a as cherished brothers and thereby frustrate the sinister plans of foreigners.[6]

It could be stated that Khomeini is an advocate of pragmatic umma. He is looking on it as a unifying force to further his revolutionary goals. In actuality, current political alienations in the Muslim world contribute to religious divisiveness. In 1983, I visited a Shi'i mosque in Detroit. A huge portrait of Khomeini was hung in the outer room. Revolutionary literature was spread over a large table. It is obvious that no Iraqi Sunni Muslim would feel comfortable worshiping in the mosque, even though he has religious affinity on most doctrinal issues with his Iranian coreligionists. I could not help but contrast this with the spirit of brotherhood I observed during the 1974 Lausanne Congress on World Evangelization. At the conference, Bangladeshis and Pakistanis, South Africans and Zimbabweans, East and West Germans, all believers in Christ, transcended normal political antagonisms and freely demonstrated the reality of the oneness of Christ that is commanded in John 17.

One further quote from a Muslim Seyyed Hossein Nasr who minimizes Sunni and Shi'i differences is given here with the aim of investigating primary sources, and allowing Muslims of varying traditions to speak to the issues under consideration:

Sunnis and Shi'a, both belonging to the total orthodoxy of Islam, do not in any way destroy its unity. The unity of a tradition is not destroyed by different applications of it, but by the destruction of its principles and forms, as well as its continuity. Being "the religion of unity," Islam, in fact, displays more homogeneity and less religious diversity than other worldwide religions. Sunnis and Shi'a are dimensions within Islam, placed there, not to destroy its unity, but to enable a larger humanity and differing spiritual types to participate in it. Both Sunnis and Shi'a are the assertion of the Shahada, *"La ilaha illa Allah [(wa) Muhammad rasul Allah],"* expressed in different climates and with a somewhat different spiritual fragrance.[7]

## WAHHABIS

Muhammad Ibn Abd al-Wahhab was born at Ayinah in North Arabia in 1691. He was carefully instructed in Islamic doctrine according to the Hanbali school, the strictest of the four schools of law. Ibn Abd al-Wahhab traveled extensively and studied at Mecca, Baghdad, and Medina. For a year he was recognized as an exponent of Sufism. In the end, he became a disciple of the ideas of Ibn Taimiyyah, a fourteenth century Hanbalite theologian who was a proponent of meticulously observing Islamic law and ritual.

Ibn Abd al-Wahhab was expelled from his hometown. He then took refuge in the village of Dariya, under the patronage of the local chief, *Muhammad bin Saud.*

© Caleb Project

Sumatran boy

This association was to determine the whole course of Arabian history. The Wahhabis, with the patronage of the Saud family, began to attack neighboring towns and tribes, and, as each town was reduced, Wahhabi doctrines were imposed upon it. By the end of the nineteenth century, the Wahhabis controlled most of what is now called Saudi Arabia. The name itself is suggestive: "The Arabia belonging to the Saud family." The Saudi family has controlled important parts of Arabia ever since, with two important interruptions. The first was the Turkish occupation (1818–33); the second was Muhammad bin Rashid's reign between 1891 and 1901.[8]

The aim of Ibn Abd al-Wahhab was to purge Islam of any accretions which were added later than the third century of the Muslim calendar. He was horrified to note in his travels the aberrant practices of Muslims. The following list of rituals, beliefs, and prohibitions set forth by Ibn Abd al-Wahhab indicates his concerns regarding the Islam he observed:

- The four schools of law and six books of Hadith must be acknowledged.
- All objects of worship, other than Allah, are false, and all who worship other gods are worthy of death.
- To visit the tombs of Muslim saints seeking to please God and win his favor, is prohibited.
- Introducing the name of a prophet, saint, or angel into a prayer is an act of polytheism.
- Intercession may be made only to Allah.
- No vows may be made to any human being.
- It is unbelief to profess knowledge which is not based on the Qur'an and the Sunna.
- Attendance at public prayers is mandatory.
- Smoking tobacco is forbidden and can be punishable by up to forty lashes.
- The shaving of one's beard and the use of abusive language are prohibited.
- Alms are to be paid on all income.
- The use of the rosary is forbidden. Names of God are to be counted on the knuckles of one hand.
- Wahhabi mosques are built with great simplicity; no minarets or ornaments are allowed.
- Muhammad's birthday is not celebrated.
- The use of silk, gold, and silver is forbidden.
- Music is also disallowed.
- Anthropomorphic concepts of God are believed. Qur'anic texts about God's hand, his hearing and seeing, along with his ascent to the throne, are literally interpreted.
- Jihad or religious war is regarded as an obligation to be engaged in

## Southeast Asia

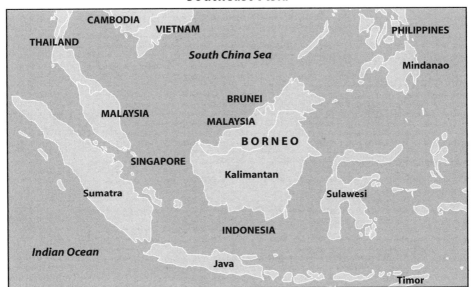

CAMBODIA
VIETNAM
THAILAND
PHILIPPINES
South China Sea
Mindanao
BRUNEI
MALAYSIA
MALAYSIA
BORNEO
SINGAPORE
Kalimantan
Sumatra
Sulawesi
INDONESIA
Indian Ocean
Java
Timor

© Caleb Project

## MALAY PEOPLES

The Malay peoples—more than 300 million people in hundreds of people groups—live in the Southeast Asian island nations of Brunei, Indonesia, Malaysia, and the Philippines, as well as Singapore and southern Thailand.

Political policy toward religion in these nations is surprisingly diverse. While Islam is the state religion in Brunei, the government of Singapore allows relative freedom of religion. In the Philippines, which is 5 percent Muslim, the Catholic Church holds considerable influence. Even though Sunni Islam is the official religion in peninsular western Malaysia, Muslims are a minority in eastern Malaysia. In Indonesia, where 80 percent are at least nominally Muslim, the government dictates that all citizens choose one of five religions: Buddhism, Protestant or Catholic Christianity, Hinduism, or Islam.

The three million Aceh on the northern tip of Indonesia's island of Sumatra are nearly 100 percent Muslim. They live both in rural areas, as rice farmers and fishermen, and in cities as low-paid manual laborers up to high-profile government officials.

In 1976 some of the Aceh formed a movement campaigning for an independent state. Thousands of lives have been lost in the subsequent, sporadic guerilla war against the Indonesian military. The Aceh also face mounting tensions between a traditional Islamic culture that values high moral standards and community (including an active responsibility for neighbors), and the materialistic western lifestyle, increasingly familiar to them through the media. In December 2004, the Aceh were devastated by a tsunami.

Sources: *Operation World, www.joshuaproject.net.*

when necessary.
• Use of tombstones is not allowed.[9]

## STRICT LEGAL INTERPRETATION

Wahhabis are dedicated to the strict interpretation and application of Islamic law. At times Wahhabis have gone beyond the Qur'an in seeking to implement strict social codes. An illustration of this is the execution of the Arabian princess and her boyfriend for the sin of adultery. Such a stern and extreme punishment is not prescribed in the Qur'an. It would be accurate to perceive present-day Wahhabism as, most of all, a movement that favors conservative legal interpretation. Libya, Iran, Saudi Arabia, and Pakistan are a few examples of states in which radical Islamic fundamentalism has been dominant. These countries are seeking to return to the original purity of early Islam. Oil funds are pouring out of Libya and Saudi Arabia for the support of Muslim missionaries. The worldwide program of building mosques is unprecedented in the modern era. If Ibn Abd al-Wahhab himself were alive today and could observe the "Islamic Revolution," he indeed would be pleased.

## AHMADIYA

The founder of the Ahmadi movement, *Mirza Ghulam Ahmad*, was born in 1839 at Qadian in Punjab, India. The title *mirza* indicates his ancestors came into India with the conquering Mughals. Ahmad received a good education in Arabic and Persian. He also meditated and pursued religious study. He was said to have frequently had a mystical experience of hearing voices which came from an unknown source. About 1880, he concluded that he was called of God for a special mission in life. Shortly thereafter, he published *Barahini Ahmadiyya*, which, in the initial instance, was well received by fellow Muslims.

On March 4, 1889, Ahmad announced he was the recipient of a divine revelation that authorized him to initiate disciples of his own. From that time forth, he began to expound a series of new doctrines. Soon he had attracted a very able group of followers. Opposition to Ahmad was quickly generated by traditional Muslims. This controversy raged until his death in 1908.

The Ahmadis teach several distinctive doctrines:

• No verse in the Qur'an is, or can be, abrogated. If one verse appears to be inconsistent with another, that is due to faulty exegesis.
• Jihad (or holy war) has lapsed, and coercion in religion condemned.
• To say that Muhammad is the Seal of the Prophets does not mean that he is the last of them. A seal is a hallmark and he embodies the perfection of prophethood; but a prophet or apostle can come after him as did the Hebrew prophets after Moses.
• Jesus is dead, as are the rest of the prophets, and he did not ascend bodily into heaven.
• Hell is not everlasting.
• Apostasy is not punishable by death.
• Any innovation in religious practice is culpable. The worship of saints is an invasion of the prerogative of God.
• Ijma or catholic consent is generally limited to the Prophet's Companions.

- Revelation will always remain a privilege of the true believer.
- Belief in Mirza Ghulam Ahmad al-Qadiani as the Messiah-Mahdi is an article of faith. Faith is incomplete without it.
- Spirituality in religion is more important than legalism. An Ahmadi need not belong to any particular madhab or school of law.
- The medieval Ulama need not be followed in the interpretation of the Qur'an and the Hadith.[10]

## AHMADIYA'S CONTROVERSIAL CLAIMS

Within this set of doctrinal beliefs is to be found the most controversial of all of Ahmad's claims. In reflecting on the Muslim teaching of the Imam-Mahdi, he noted that the scriptures of Zoroastrians, Hindus, and Buddhists all prophesied the coming of a great teacher. Over a period of time, Ahmad came to feel that he was a *mujaddid* (renewer) sent by God for the purpose of restoring the true faith of Islam. He thus professed to be both the promised Messiah, the Mahdi, and a mujaddid. "Likewise, on the ground that God, at intervals, sends renewers of religion, he claimed that, in his capacity of Mahdi, no other than Muhammad had made his second advent. He was, in fact, an 'image of the Holy Prophet.'"[11]

As Kenneth Cragg has observed, Ahmad's "most serious potential heresy was the precise import of his claims to Islamic revelation."[12] But what was Ahmad really saying regarding his prophethood or messiahship? Muhammad Ali postulates that Ahmad never claimed prophethood

in the technical sense. Ali saw Ahmad's usage of words like prophethood, revelation, and disbelief to be in Sufi allegorical and metaphorical terms.[13] Once Sufi esoteric language is introduced into the controversy, we have moved into an area that prohibits any type of specificity. Sufi words can carry many different meanings. The main issue is that present-day Ahmadis firmly perceive Mirza Ghulam Ahmad as a prophet of God.

## OUTSIDE MAINSTREAM ISLAM

The Ahmadiya thus proceeded to raise up a new structure of religious beliefs and practices, outside of the mainstream of Islam. They developed a new prophet, a new focus of devotion, a new mission, a new spiritual center, new rituals, and new religious leadership. These are the features which raise Ahmadiism to the level of a new religion. Muslims who choose to convert to the Ahmadi fold must reject old institutions and personalities.

> Moreover, it is also to be noted that the Mirza raised the standard of the prophethood, and declared all those who did not accept his claim as kafirs (unbelievers) in a Muslim world which was already torn by dissensions. By so doing, however, the Mirza raised an iron wall between himself and the Muslims. On the one side of this wall there are a few thousand followers of the Mirza, and on the other side is the rest of the Muslim world, which stretches from Morocco to China, and has great personalities, virtuous movements of reform, and valuable institutions. They stand isolated from and opposed to the whole of this

world. Thus, he unnecessarily added to the difficulties of Muslims, further aggravated their disunity, and added a new complication to the problems facing them.[14]

Ahmad was said to be a severe and unyielding person. The overwhelming force of his personality and sense of mission seemed to draw disciples. He had a magnetic quality about him that would cause men in significant numbers to forsake all and follow him. He is said to have performed many miracles. He was also able to "will" evil upon his detractors through imprecation and curses. A documented sample of his violent attacks upon traditional Muslim leaders has been preserved: "Of all animals, the filthiest and most repellent is the pig. But filthier than pigs are those, who, owing to their base desires, conceal the evidence of reality. O corpse-eating Maulvis! O filthy spirits! Pity on you that you concealed the true evidence of Islam out of hostility. O worms of darkness! How can you hide the radiant rays of truth?"[15]

## BRANDED NON-MUSLIMS

As a result of such inflammatory rhetoric, Ahmad was branded a heretic, blasphemer, enemy of the faith, and imposter. He was ostracized and was forbidden the use of mosques. Subsequently, a number of Ahmadiya in Afghanistan have suffered

## BE YOURSELF

The Great Commission commands Christians to go and make disciples. Looking at the text more closely, we see that "going" and "disciple-making" together constitute our obedience: "As you go, make disciples."

We need to remember to communicate our commitment to Christ's teachings in our daily activities at home, school, and work. We can let others see our passion to love and obey our Savior Jesus, and make it our goal to show people the love of Christ regardless of their response to the gospel.

Wherever we go, we should involve our Muslim friends. Invite them to picnics or to attend your children's school play. If they share your interest in sports, invite them to a game or watch one on television. Don't assume some kind of unrealistic piety is required to impress the Muslims you know. Be yourself and look for ways to share your life.

At the same time, we should ask our Muslim friends to teach us about their culture. It is alright to confess our ignorance, because our questions will show our interest, build understanding, and identify common ground. "In what city were you born? For what things is your homeland known? What kinds of things does the government there do for the people? How is it that you came to this country? What are some of the cultural differences you see here? What do you miss the most? Please tell us about your family."

Muslims will talk more about their home culture than their religion, and they may see the two as one. As we learn from our Muslim friends, the Lord Jesus will lead us in how to share the Good News.

Source: Fouad Masri, *www.crescentproject.org.*

the penalty of death for their heresy. In Pakistan in 1953, there were riots between Sunnis and the Ahmadiya. The campaign of mutual antagonism continued to be waged until 1974, when the Ahmadiya were formally declared non-Muslims by an act of the Pakistan Parliament. An article in *Arabia* updates the situation in Pakistan:

> The Pakistani government has banned the use of Muslim nomenclatures by the Qadianis [one faction of Ahmadiya]. The new ordinance, passed in April 1984, provides a punishment of three years imprisonment and a fine for a person of the Qadiani group or the Lahori group [the other faction], who, by words either spoken or written, or by visible representation, refers to the successors or companions of Mirza Ghulam Ahmed, or Sahaba, his wife, as an ummul-Momineen, or a member of his family as "Ahle-Bait," or calls his place of worship a Masjid.

> The same penalty is provided for any Qadiani who directly or indirectly poses himself as a Muslim, or refers to his faith as Islam, or preaches or propagates his faith, or invites others to accept his faith. The ordinance empowers the provincial government to confiscate any newspaper, book, or other document printed by the Qadianis.[16]

According to their own figures, there are 500,000 members of this group, half of them living in Pakistan. The headquarters of the movement is in Rabwah, Pakistan, where there is a strong ruling secretariat. Ahmadis give very generously through expected gifts and donations. They have a strong publishing program that disseminates their propaganda throughout the Muslim world. In addition, they have emphasized the establishment of schools and colleges. The people of their former center, Kadiyan, are some of the most educated in all of India.

There is a sect of the Ahmadiya in Lahore that is relatively small. The group accepts Ghulam Ahmad as mujaddid, but not as a prophet. It too has emphasized the publication of tracts and books in its outreach program.

## ANTI-CHRISTIAN ORIENTATION

Ahmadiya are extremely anti-Christian in orientation. They believe that Jesus journeyed to Kashmir, and today they can point to his grave in Srinagar. I spent some time seeking to trace down another of their claims by searching for the reputed grave of Mary, the mother of Jesus. It is said to be located on a mountainside near Murree, Pakistan. I was, however, unsuccessful in my quest.

There was a small, fanatical group of Ahmadiya living in the town where I was resident for several years in one particular Muslim country. They were not a significant force in the community. But they were able to give our small group of missionaries a difficult time. Once, their leaders went to talk to one of our new missionaries who was engaged in language study. He, not knowing their identity, was gracious to them and sought to answer honestly their many queries. A few days after that visit, an article in the district newspaper accused our missionary of being an agent of the Central Intelligence

Agency. It was evident that his Ahmadi guests had been the informants.

In that town, the Ahmadiya had their own small mosque, exclusively for their own use. They did not participate in any Muslim ritual with Sunnis.

The zeal of this sect amazes me. They are highly motivated people who are willing to endure even death for their beliefs. In fact, they seem to thrive on persecution. Are they members of the umma of Islam? That is a question of persisting irritation throughout the Muslim world. It is important to note that they consider themselves to be Muslims.

## FOR FURTHER STUDY

David Zeidan, *Sword of Allah: Islamic Fundamentalism from an Evangelical Perspective* (Waynesboro, Ga.: Authentic Media, 2003). *www.authenticbooks.com*

## ENDNOTES

1. *Mishkatul-Misabih*, bk. 1, chap. 6, pt. 2.

2. Elizabeth W. Fernea, *Guests of the Sheik* (Garden City, N.Y.: Anchor, 1965), pp. 242–43.
3. Maurice Gaudefroy-Demombynes, *Muslim Institutions*, trans. John P. Macgregor (London: George Allen and Unwin, 1950), p. 38.
4. Ibid., p. 39.
5. L. Bevan Jones, *The People of the Mosque* (Calcutta: Baptist Mission Press, 1932), p. 135.
6. Imam Khomeini, *Islam and Revolution: Writings and Declarations of Imam Khomeini*, trans. Hamid Algar (Berkeley, Calif.: Mizan, 1980), p. 302.
7. Seyyed Hossein Nasr, *Ideals and Realities of Islam* (New York: Praeger, 1967), pp. 147–48.
8. Michael Nazir-Ali, *Islam: A Christian Perspective* (Exeter: Paternoster, 1983), p. 96.
9. Samuel M. Zwemer, *Islam: A Challenge to Faith* (New York: Student Volunteer Movement for Foreign Missions, 1907), pp. 150–51.
10. Alfred Guillaume, *Islam* (Baltimore: Penguin, 1954), pp. 126–27.
11. L. Bevan Jones, *Christianity Explained to Muslims* (1937; Calcutta: Baptist Mission Press, 1964), p. 169.
12. Kenneth Cragg, *Islamic Surveys 3: Counsels in Contemporary Islam* (Edinburgh: University Press, 1965), p. 156.
13. Abul Hasan Ali Nadwi, *Qadianism: A Critical Study*, trans. Zafar Ishaq Anseri (Lahore: Shaikh Muhammad Ashraf, 1965), p. 121.
14. Ibid., pp. 136–37.
15. Ibid., p. 86.
16. "Qadianis—Non-Muslim," *Arabia* (June 1984), p. 72.

# CANDID CONFRONTATION: THE MUSLIM UMMA, THE CHRISTIAN CHURCH

*by David W. Shenk*

"Why don't Christians follow the way of Jesus?" a Muslim asked. I was dining with a close friend, a Muslim, in the Blue Nile Restaurant in Washington, D.C., when he leaned close and asked that disturbing question.

He continued, slowly, pensively: "When I read the gospel, I am overjoyed. The life and teachings of Jesus are wonderful, wonderful, really truly wonderful. But, please show me Christians who are willing to follow in the *sunna* (way) of Jesus."

We sipped our cardamom-spiced tea in reflective silence and then he continued. "I have met a few, very few people who try to follow Jesus. But they follow him only in their private lives. Consequently, your American society has become very evil. It seems to me that you Christians really do not believe that the sunna of Jesus is practical. That makes me very sad."

These comments reminded me of a similar conversation an acquaintance and some of his clergymen colleagues had with Ayatollah Khomeini on Christmas Day, 1979. The Ayatollah implored these churchmen to take Jesus more seriously, and then added that, if the Christians in America really believed in and followed Jesus, the tragedy of American injustice against Iran would not have happened.

## THEOLOGICAL AND PRACTICAL ISSUES

Both the Muslim umma and the Christian church are communities of God-fearing believers. Both believe they have received from God a mission in the world. In meeting one another, we experience commonality and pain. In fact, Islam is a profound challenge to Christian perceptions and commitment to be the people of God. There are several reasons for this.

### Muslims as God-fearers

Islam is a post-Christian movement of God-fearing people. Within the New Testament, God-fearing Gentiles were recognized with appreciation as people who had moved closer to the truth than their polytheistic contemporaries (see Acts 10:34–36; 13:26). These pre-Christian God-fearers were exceptionally receptive to Christian faith. Islam, on the other hand, presents a theological problem which has no precedent in the New Testament, a monotheistic faith which is

Dr. David W. Shenk is global missions consultant with Eastern Mennonite Missions in Salunga, Pennsylvania. He was born into a missionary family in Tanzania and has worked in Somalia, Kenya, and the United States, and taught in Lithuania. He has authored more than a dozen books related to missions and the relationship of the gospel to other religions.

Adapted from David W. Shenk, "Islam and Christianity: A Quest for Community," unpublished paper, 14 January 1983. Used by permission.

post-Christian, and which was birthed in a Christianized environment.

In Islam, we see the etchings of aspects of Christian faith. Islam is like a form of Arian Christianity,[1] but unlike Arianism, Islam has flourished outside the modifying discipline and witness of Christian experience and biblical revelation. Therefore, although Arianism within the church finally withered into oblivion, Islam has thrived as a movement outside the bounds of churchly discipline.

## Islam's Inclusiveness

Islam began as a quest of a people for inclusion in the people of God. Islam seeks to embrace and be embraced by all God-fearers. It began as a quest by the Arab people for inclusion, and now invites all people to participate in the blessing of that inclusion.

In the seventh century, Arabia, island of the Arabs, was largely encircled by Christian peoples. The advanced Christianized cultures, Ethiopian, Egyptian, and Syrian, on the Arabian periphery, had the Bible in their native languages. The pagan, nomadic Arabs were living in ignorance (*jahiliyyah*), an ignorance perpetuated through exclusion from the community of the People of the Book. For nascent Islam, the Arabic Book (Qur'an) and Arabian Prophet proclaimed the good news that the Arab peoples were now also included. The da'wa (invitation) of Islam is the good news that all other peoples are also invited to enjoy inclusion in the community of peace, the people of God. The inclusiveness of the invitation, as well as the detestation for all forms of exclusivism, is revealed in the Muslim conviction that everyone everywhere is born a Muslim. The success of Islamic mission is therefore not statistically measurable. All are born Muslim; Islamic mission is to invite people to affirm the reality of inclusion.

## Islam's Expansion in Christian Areas

Islam's most rapid early missionary expansion has been through the Islamization of Christianized societies. Within one century of its birth, Islam had gained control of half of the Christianized world. In all Christianized societies ruled by Muslim governments, there has been a steady flow of converts from the church to Islam. Political techniques, such as the dhimmi (protected) status for the church, or the application of forms of the law of apostasy to Muslims who would convert to Christianity, have combined to assure that the net flow of conversions always favored Islam. In all countries ruled by Muslim governments, contracting Christian communities (in relationship to Islam) have been the norm. Muslims refer to the regions under Muslim political control as the Dar al-Islam (house of peace). Where the Dar al-Islam is established, the church is confronted with church growth in reverse.

## Islam's Claim to Be the Faith of All True Prophets

Muslims believe that Islam is the primal, middle, and final religion of mankind, given as a mercy for all people. It is the faith of Adam, Abraham, and Muhammad. In fact, all true prophets are Muslims. All necessary truth is succinctly summarized in the Qur'an, which is the criterion of all truth. God-fearers weep

with joy when hearing the Qur'an recited. From an Islamic perspective, the fundamental test as to whether one is a person of faith is one's personal response to the Qur'an and belief in the Prophet of Islam. In relationship to professed believers in God, the foremost question in the mind of Muslims is this: "What do you believe concerning the Qur'an and the Prophet?" A lack of commitment to the Prophet and the Book suggests that one's professed faith commitment is not genuine, and the dialogue is subsequently often broken (see Sura 84:20–25).

### Islam's Emphasis on God's Oneness

The Islamic commitment to tawhid (the unity of God) profoundly affects the Muslim commitment to community. Belief in the unity of God is pragmatically reflected in the unity and harmony of the community which lives under the law of God. According to Dr. Ali Shariati (Iranian Shi'i, d. 1977), belief in tawhid is commitment to the exorcism of all aspects of disequilibrium. All forms of disharmony are shirk, that is, the adding of associates to divinity. The umma is commanded by God to protect the community of faith from *shirk*. The community must be protected from all forms of disharmony, including the destabilization which can occur through unregulated religious pluralism, or the dichotomization of life into secular and spiritual realms. Tawhid is the experience and expression of personal and social integration and harmony under the revealed will of God. Within the framework of tawhid, church growth—which in any sense seems to threaten the integrity of the umma or the political authority of the Dar al-Islam—is normally perceived as contributory to disharmony; it is a form of shirk. (Note: The umma is the Muslim community and the Dar al-Salaam is Muslim political and territorial authority.)

How should the church respond theologically to the Islamic worldview as briefly outlined above? It is tempting to sidestep the issues. It is interesting that contemporary church growth writings are heavily oriented toward communication theory and anthropology, with a parallel dearth of theological reflection. At the Colorado Springs Consultation on Muslim Evangelization (1978), only one of the thirteen foundation papers attempted an in-depth probe of the theological issues. Seven of the papers related to cultural

## DIVERGENT VALUES

The subjugation of 90 percent of the Muslim world by western *colonial* rule in the early part of this century—up to the period of the Second World War—has left an indelible imprint on the minds of Muslim peoples. Today the Muslim world struggles with the question of how to acquire western technology without accepting the philosophical assumptions behind it. This interaction of *western cultural* values with Islamic values has given birth to a wide variety of Muslim responses, which stretch across a spectrum from extreme accommodation to total rejection.

Don McCurry, *Healing the Broken Family of Abraham: New Life for Muslims* (Colorado Springs: Ministry to Muslims, 2001), p. 103. *www.mtmsims.org*

dynamics. The underlying assumption seemed to be that the fundamental objection of Islam to the gospel is western culture, that if the gospel is clothed in appropriate cultural forms, the theological objections will be easily surmounted. Is this really the case? It is noteworthy that at that Colorado Springs Consultation all of the case studies came from marginally Islamicized peoples. There was no serious reflection on how to share the gospel with devout Muslims living under orthodox Muslim governments.

## QUESTION FROM THE UMMA TO THE CHURCH

Could it be that we hesitate to accept theological or community engagement with Islam because we are embarrassed by the questions which the umma addresses to the church? Yet, if we would listen, we might discover that, through the questions which Islam addresses to us, our own perceptions of the gospel will be purified. And in the purification process, the gospel itself will become more attractive and

## VIEW OF WESTERN WOMEN AND CHRISTIANITY

What do Muslim women conclude when they compare themselves to western or Christian women? One Lebanese Muslim woman's thoughts:

> Compared to Muslim women, Christian [western] women are privileged. We didn't have schools; we couldn't go to university; we couldn't get jobs. So we had a cause to fight for. Compared to this, Christian women were born in "Paradise." What did they have to fight for? Many western countries speak in their name, but none speaks in our name.[2]

But Muslim women believe that the western women's privileges have come at too great a cost. An Arab woman says: "The western woman has lost her family. When we sit all together around the table to eat, I feel I am the happiest person on earth. Western women miss this precious feeling…We are happy to be able to give so much to our homes and families."[3]

Christian women are guilty by association with western culture, which—because of its demands for the abortion rights, divorce, government-funded childcare, equality with men, and immodest public dress and behavior—has led many Muslim women to reject western attempts for their "liberation." In blurring distinctions between men and women, western women admittedly have gained many rights, but, in the eyes of Muslim women, they have lost their honor, and, ultimately, their unique and powerful contributions to society. Muslims are frustrated with the West's mindset that Islam is to be scorned because of its treatment of women.

How can Christian women distance themselves from the negative images of western womanhood? Bridges of trust are built as Christian women focus on the concerns they share with Muslim women: the future of the family unit in a world that doesn't protect it. "Talk to us; see us," says a Saudi woman. "It's true we may not have many rights. But we deal with the same problems you do."[4]

Source: Fran Love, *www.frontiers.org*.

### FOR FURTHER STUDY

Leila Ahmed, *Women and Gender in Islam* (New Haven, Conn.: Yale University Press, 1992).

life-changing for Christians, and also for our Muslim friends.

There are a number of disturbing questions which the umma presents to the church. I will address the one already alluded to in the introductory conversation: "Why don't you follow Jesus?" Said another way, "Why don't you who believe in Jesus commit yourselves to the kingdom of God as lived and practiced by Jesus?"

Confronting western culture

© Caleb Project

Many Muslims suspect that we really do not believe in the practicality of Jesus. "How can anyone love his enemy?" I have often been asked. Frequently I have gone to mosques in East Africa and listened to the sermons. It is surprising how often Muslim preachers proclaim Islam as the practical faith, in contrast to Christianity, which is far too idealistic. The question, "Why don't you follow Jesus?" is a form of Muslim witness, actually a subtle invitation to follow Muhammad, the pragmatic prophet.

Nevertheless, the question also reflects the Muslim commitment to tawhid, the unity of every dimension of life under the rule of God. Muslims who know Christians are often disturbed at the easy manner in which many western Christians violate tawhid by cozily dividing life into secular and sacred, public and private, temporal and spiritual.

Jesus also commanded tawhid. In fact, from a biblical perspective, he is the perfect revelation of tawhid. He is the breakthrough into history of the fullness of the kingdom of God. From a Muslim perspective, the unitary will of God has been marvelously revealed in the Qur'an, whereas the biblical witness is that the eternal Word is revealed in Jesus himself. The divergence between the Book (Qur'anic guidance) and the Person (Jesus, the Redeemer) is the issue which drives a theological and practical wedge between Islam and Christianity. This divergence propels Islam toward a nomistic (law-based) organization of society, whereas the New Testament Christian is more pneumatically (spirit) oriented. In Islam, there is tremendous concern about submitting to codified guidance, whereas, in the Christian experience, one is called to live in the Spirit of Jesus Christ.

## JESUS AS LORD?

Islamic perplexity concerning Christian life and commitment, however, is not necessarily contingent on the different views of the essence of revealed peace. Rather, the umma asks why we so often fail to commit ourselves to the one whom we profess as Lord and the peace he has revealed. Jesus, who is the dramatic

breakthrough of the kingdom of God, announced at the beginning of his ministry that he had come to preach Good News to the poor, freedom for the prisoners, sight for the blind, and release for the oppressed (Luke 4:16–21). In his life, Jesus revealed that this radically new kingdom order is effectuated through redemptive, suffering love, supremely demonstrated in his crucifixion and resurrection. The kingdom of God as revealed in Jesus is a total commitment to love, even one's enemies. But one cannot live that way without suffering. That is the issue.

Western Christianity, especially, has developed neat theological escape hatches. For multitudes of Christians, the kingdom life applies only to private life; it is not applicable to public life. We have developed a dual citizenship theology. We dichotomize life into spiritual and secular. Jesus is Lord of the spiritual but not of the secular.

The Islamic question is really a plea, an invitation to Christians to take tawhid seriously, to really reflect the kingdom of God in every area of life. This invitation is expressed frequently, as was true during a dialogue between Muslims and Christians in a forum adjacent to the United Nations in New York City. Dr. Ala Eddin Kharafa addressed us. At that time he was director of the Muslim World League of North America and the representative of the League to the United Nations. He pointed out that an absolutely foundational commitment of the League is the transcendence of the umma over nationalism. He assured us that there is only one Muslim nation. All nationalisms that segment the unity of the nation of Islam are aberrations of the reality of Islam.

The nation state is a recent phenomenon for Muslims. It is a residual consequence of western imperial intrusions into the nation of Islam and the overthrow of the Caliphate during the Turkish revolution (1924). In spite of the blessings of independence, there is deep disquiet among many Muslims, because the nation state represents a fractured umma. Dr. Kharafa pointed out that, for the Muslim, any national allegiance that supersedes loyalty and commitment to the total community of faith is wrong. The Shi'i theologian, Dr. Ali Shariati, refers to nationalistic division in the umma as shirk, or idolatry. Tawhid is harmony; it is the participation in fraternal commitment to one another; it is participation in the Dar al-Islam that is not fractured by nationalism.

Biblical faith also teaches that national loyalties dare not supercede loyalty to the kingdom of God; when the two conflict, the follower of Jesus has only one option, that is, the Jesus way. Justice, peace, righteousness, the cause of the dispossessed and poor, the urgent invitation to participate in a redeemed and joyous relationship with God and the believing community—all are aspects of the kaleidoscope of kingdom living. Jesus dramatically proclaimed the transnational nature of the kingdom of God by calling his disciples to seek the kingdom rather than those things that the nations seek (Luke 12:30–31). And on the night of his arrest, he said, "My kingdom is not of this world. If it were, my servants would fight" (John 18:36).

The Islamic plea to take tawhid seriously should rekindle within Christians a sincere commitment to live in the light

of, and give witness to the fact that, God's intention is "to bring all things in heaven and on earth together under one head, even Christ" (Eph. 1:10). The church in mission is called by God to be an authentic sign that God's intention for the cosmos has already broken into history. The church, as the most authentic global community, with congregations or fellowships present in all nation states around the world, is uniquely positioned to give witness that Christ is creating a redeemed community that transcends the divisions of the nation state.

## INVITATION FROM THE CHURCH TO THE UMMA

Although both Christians and Muslims should ideally perceive of the kingdom of God as tawhid, there is a significant divergence in their respective perceptions of the nature of mission, community, and the kingdom of God. For the sake of simplicity, let me suggest that this divergence is revealed in the Hijra versus the cross.

The Hijra is the flight from suffering in Mecca to the triumph of Medina. While Muhammad was still in Mecca, the Medinans invited him to become statesman of their city. The Hijra was his acceptance of this invitation. In Mecca, Muhammad was a persecuted, lonely prophet, but in Medina he became both prophet and statesman. In Mecca the umma was incomplete; it possessed no symbols of power. In Medina all the mechanisms of political, economic, cultural, and religious power were brought under the rule of God through the statesmanship of the prophet. In Mecca the prophet was victimized by his enemies,

but in Medina he was triumphant over his enemies; military victory over the enemies of the Muslims became a sign of the favor of God upon the umma.

The Hijra represents the great theological divide between Islam and Christianity. It is a theological movement in the opposite direction from that chosen by Jesus of Nazareth six centuries earlier. The Hijra is the affirmation that the will of God is invulnerable to the devices of evil men. It is a profound denial of the way of the cross in God's dealings with man. Jesus, similarly to Muhammad, was also offered the handles of political and economic power by the Galilean zealots. They also desired to make him captain of their incipient umma, a community dedicated to the establishment of freedom and the rule of God through political power. But Jesus explicitly and deliberately rejected the statesmanship road to establishing the rule of God. On the contrary, he thereafter "set his face" to go to Jerusalem, where he met the cross. He chose to lay down his life in an act of total vulnerability, rather than save his life through political or military means. The cross is the ultimate sign of God's total redemptive vulnerability. God establishes his rule through redemptive love.

## THE CROSS VERSUS THE HIJRA

This is the fundamental theological impasse between Islam and Christianity. The impasse is so profound that Islam is lured into, and consequently, explicitly yields to, the temptation of denying the crucifixion of Christ. The denial of the crucifixion is not based on historical criteria, but rather on theological necessity.

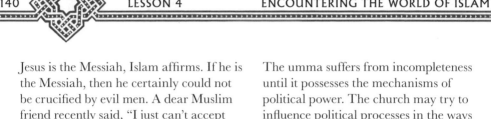
Jesus is the Messiah, Islam affirms. If he is the Messiah, then he certainly could not be crucified by evil men. A dear Muslim friend recently said, "I just can't accept that Jesus died on the cross. He is too good a man for that. It seems to me that the Cross suggests weakness, vulnerability by God. I cannot, I just cannot, believe that God would permit the Messiah to suffer in that way."

The Hijra and the cross are fundamental theological directions that explicitly and implicitly inform the Muslim umma's and the Christian church's perceptions of themselves and their respective missions in the world. A few examples will suffice.

The umma suffers from incompleteness until it possesses the mechanisms of political power. The church may try to influence political processes in the ways of justice; however, the New Testament vision of the church rejects possessing political structures. The umma attempts to reform society through the application of Islamic law, the Shari'a. The New Testament church attempts to transform society from within by being a leaven and a light to the society. The umma considers the suffering of righteousness to be abnormal, a situation that needs to be rectified. The church perceives the suffering of love as being fundamentally central to the manner in which God redeems the

## OVERCOMING THE PAST

"When I see a cross, I shudder." The attractive young woman acknowledges that nothing makes her as nervous as the ancient symbol. The cross represents everything foreign which tried to destroy her people, the Tatars. Perhaps this is why the gospel has made so little difference in her Russian city, Kazan.

Dominated by foreign powers since the time of Genghis Khan, the people of Kazan have endured an open wound from 1552, when Ivan the Terrible and his missionaries tried to force the people to become Christian. "People were taken to a river in the winter, a hole made through the ice, and any person unwilling to be baptized was drowned with his children," explains a local Muslim leader.

"What Ivan the Terrible did was a bad thing because it wounded the heart of Tatar people, and put an obstacle in the way to Jesus Christ," says Rahim, a local Muslim-background believer. "When my uncle learned that I had believed in Jesus Christ, he came to our house and said, 'You are a traitor of your people. If you believe in Jesus Christ, you have betrayed our grandfathers, our religion; you betrayed me.'"

A scattering of "baptized" Tatars claim descent from those converts centuries ago, but they fit in with neither Russians nor Tatars. Considered traitors to their culture, they are a people unto themselves, their name used as a curse. Even for the nominal Muslim, betraying Islam by joining them seems unthinkable. Visiting a Russian Orthodox church is also forbidden. Living as a Christian Tatar is an inherently confusing combination, especially if one has never seen anyone try. Rahim feels like a pioneer as he tests new models for following Christ in ways his people can understand.

Source: Marti Smith, "The Volga Tatars," *Echo Magazine* (winter 1999).

nations. The church is truest to its calling when it gives of itself in suffering love.

Yet, no congregation fully reveals the fullness of God's love revealed in Jesus; the church is a fellowship of redeemed sinners. Our witness as Christians is that we are forgiven sinners, that we celebrate the grace of forgiveness—offered by Jesus in his crucifixion as he cried out in forgiveness for those who had crucified him. All humanity is accomplice to his crucifixion; forgiveness is offered to all.

We must repent of the temptation to become "Islamicized Christians." The two communities are established on different theological foundations. And these fundamentally different origins inform their respective approaches to a wide variety of issues: human rights and freedoms, religion and state, ministries to the poor and dispossessed, human and economic development, secularization and attitudes toward enemies of the community, approaches to mission and conversion, progress and change, and even marriage and family. Most significantly, the Hijra and the cross speak to the nature of the human condition, the nature of the kingdom of God, and the nature of forgiveness and salvation.

## A Sign of the Lamb

Although the Hijra and the cross invite us to travel in opposite directions, there is an aya (sign) of the cross in the soul of Islam. The Qur'an affirms that when Abraham was about to sacrifice his son in obedience to God's command, God provided a "tremendous" sacrifice as a substitution. The son of Abraham was redeemed from death by that sacrifice. Every year during the annual Hajj to Mecca, all pilgrims and Muslims around the world offer sacrifices of animals, in commemoration of the ransom from death of a son of Abraham through a substitutionary sacrifice.

"Why have you become a believer in the Messiah?" I asked a former Muslim.

He replied, "A friend gave me the Gospel of John. In the first chapter I read that Jesus the Messiah is the Lamb of God. Immediately a mystery in the soul of Islam was unlocked. I knew that the millions of animals we sacrifice at the annual pilgrimage are a sign pointing to the Messiah who is the sacrificial Lamb of God."

"Who explained that to you?" I asked.

"The Holy Spirit!" my friend responded simply and profoundly.

 **End of Key Readings for Lesson 4. See** RECOMMENDED READINGS & ACTIVITIES **on p. 153.**

### ENDNOTES

1.  Arianism, the heresy taught by Arius, of fourth century Alexandria, who held that Jesus was not of the same substance as God, that he was only the best of created beings.
2.  Bouthaina Shaaban, *Both Right- and Left-Handed: Arab Women Talk about Their Lives* (Bloomington and Indianapolis: Indiana University Press, 1991), p. 97.
3.  Ibid., p. 113.
4.  "Voices from behind the Veil," *Christian Science Monitor* (cited 22 December 2001). *www.csmonitor.com*

# DIVERSITY AMONG MUSLIMS: AN ANALYSIS

*by Javeed Akhter*

One of Islam's major objectives is to achieve unity of mankind through the unity of God. The first and essential step toward unity of mankind is the unity of the Muslim community (umma). The Qur'an's exhortations to Muslims to remain united are stated in clear and unambiguous terms: "And hold fast, all together, unto the bond with Allah, and do not draw apart from one another" (Sura 6:159).[1] "And remember the blessings, which Allah has bestowed upon you: how you were enemies; he brought hearts together, so that through his blessings you become brethren" (Sura 21:92–93). Islam's annoyance at those who tear apart the unity of the community, "wide asunder, piece by piece" (Sura 23:52–53), is unmistakable. The condemnation of previous communities who have broken apart into sects also appears forcefully on multiple occasions (Sura 6:159; 21:92–93).

It is therefore surprising and perplexing to see the extent of division in the Muslim community. Heterodoxy, or departure from the original religious point of view of the Qur'an and Sunna (the way) of Prophet Muhammad, appears to be the rule rather than the exception. In fact, sometimes it is difficult to identify a group that is universally accepted as truly representing the tenets of Qur'an. Nevertheless, most scholars would concede that the Sunni community, which constitutes more than 80 percent of all Muslims, is the identifiable orthodoxy [seen as orthodox]. Currently, there are a multitude of Islamic and quasi-Islamic sects. In one instance, a heterodox sect has evolved into an entirely new religion, *Bahaism*. This old and continuing phenomenon of discord and heterodoxy deserves close scrutiny and analysis.

## CAUSES OF ISLAMIC SECTS AND MOVEMENTS

Although chronological and descriptive accounts of the various movements and sects in Islam are available and useful, it would be more instructive to look at what causes them. An attempt at understanding the reasons which led to the departures from the norm would be more meaningful than a mere cataloging of beliefs and practices. Each category will be discussed below, later, lessons learned from each will be discussed.

1. Political discord about succession: the *Khariji* and the Shi'a.
2. Differences of opinion about "freedom of action" versus "will of Allah": Ashari and *Mutazali*.
3. Mystic influences: Sufis and *Barelvis*.

Javeed Akhter is the executive director of the Chicago-based International Strategy and Policy Institute, established by a group of American Muslims in 1994. He is the author of the book, *The Seven Phases of Prophet Muhammad's Life*.

Adapted from Javeed Akhter, "Schisms and Heterodoxy among Muslims: An Etiological Analysis and Lessons from the Past." (23 November 2003). *www.ispi-usa.org/currentarticles/schism.html* (cited 10 December 2004). Used by permission.

4. Back-to-the-roots movements: Wahhabis and *Salafis*.
5. Reform movements: Sayyid Ahmad Khan's *Aligarh Muslim University* in India and Mohammed Abduh's original Salafi movement in Egypt.
6. Followers of charismatic leaders and groups looking for a savior: *Hashashians* were followers of Hasan Salah and Ahmadiya follow Mirza Ghulam Ahmad; groups looking for a savior or caliph, like the Hizb ut Tahrir.
7. The suicidal militants.
8. The evangelists: *Tablighis.*
9. Miscellaneous: Qarmatians, were people of a communistic faith; Bahaism, which started out as an offshoot of Islam but is now a distinct and separate faith.

**Political Discord about Succession**
In the first civil war fought among Muslims, at Siffin in A.D. 669 (A.H. 37) [other sources 657], Ali and Muawiya agreed to settle the dispute about succession by arbitration. A group of puritans among the followers of Ali disagreed and broke away, forming the first heterodox group in the history of Islam. They believed only Allah could decide the issue of succession. (How this could be accomplished is a mystery to me.)

One of the beliefs of this group, the Exitors [or Seceders, Kharijis], was that any Muslim who committed a major sin became de facto an apostate and earned the death penalty. Though sincere in their beliefs, the Exitors were uncompromising and dogmatic and were responsible for much violence in early Islam. Their descendants are called *Ibadis*, after an early leader, Abdullah bin Ibad, and are much more moderate in their views.

Political discord about succession also led to the formation of the party of Ali (*Shi'at Ali*) now simply called the Shi'a. The Shi'a account for approximately ten to fifteen percent of Muslims. They believe that their religious leader, or Imam, has to be a direct descendant of Ali and is infallible. The Imam is the only source of religious instruction and guidance. There are many sub-sects among the Shi'a. The sub-sects are based largely on the number at which the chain of Imams is believed to have broken, with the occultation rather than death, of the last Imam in the chain. Iranians (*Ithna Asharis*, or twelve Imamers Twelvers) believe the chain broke with the twelfth Imam. The *Ismailis*, on the other hand, claim the chain broke with the seventh Imam. The Ismailis consecrate the number seven and point out that there are seven heavens, seven orifices in the head, seven stages of knowledge, seven major prophets, and the world goes around in cycles of seven thousand years.

Shi'i philosophy is highly chiliastic (belief in the coming millenium), awaiting the return of the "occulted Imam." In the absence of the Imam, his surrogate, for example the Ayatollah, has absolute authority.

As a result of the massacre of Imam Husayn (Ali's son and Prophet Muhammad's grandson) and his followers at Karbala, there is also a pervasive sense of martyrdom. Annual commemoration of this massacre occurs in the first ten days of *Muharram*, the first month of the Islamic lunar calendar.

## "Freedom of Action" Versus "The Will of Allah"

Wasil ibn Ata broke off from his mentor, Hasan al-Basari, a famous teacher, and founded the Mutazalite movement. *Italaza*, the root word for Mutazila, means to secede. The issue at hand was the status of a Muslim who had committed a major sin. Was he, as the Kharijites claimed, an apostate who should be killed, or was he merely a hypocrite as Hasan al-Basari taught? Wasil ibn Ata felt the status of that category of sinner was somewhere between those two positions.

Mutazalites were essentially rationalists and believed man had free will. They proclaimed the Qur'an to have been "created in time and that it was not the uncreated word of Allah." Heavily influenced by Greek (Hellenistic) philosophy, they applied reason to solve all problems. They were ascendant in the time of Caliph al-Mamun in 844 (A.H. 212), and persecuted others. The next caliph, in whose reign *Asharism* took hold, in turn persecuted them.

*Al-Ashari*, a former Mutazalite, formed an anti-Mutazalite movement named after him. This school proposed that "man has no power over his will, but has control over his responsibilities, even though they are willed by Allah." The famous *Nizamiyah School* was founded to propagate the Ashari viewpoint. Asharism is the prevalent viewpoint on man's free will in Islam today.

## Mystic Influences

Sufism is a reactive movement that arose to counter and soften the rigid ritualism of orthodox Islam. It injected a heavy dose of mysticism and is widely accepted as the "inner dimension" of Islam. Sufis are ascetic in their practices and their language is veiled and allusive. There is a liberal use of metaphors of wine and love in Sufi discourse. *Dhikr* (trance, remembering Allah) sessions are important in their practice. There are many Sufi sects in South and Central Asia and Iran. Most Sufis are Sunnis. Some Sufi practices appear to be influenced by Persian *shamanism* and Indian Hinduism. In the Indian subcontinent, the Barelvis follow many Sufi practices, including use of music (*qawwali*) and intercession by their teacher or pir.

## Back-to-the-Roots Movements

Founded a little over two hundred years ago, Wahhabism rejects all innovation in Islam after the Prophet Muhammad's time in the seventh century. Wahhabis attack saint worship and believe in divine decree (qadaa) in all human endeavors. They are rigid in their interpretation of the Shari'a (Islamic jurisprudence) and are notoriously intolerant of Sufism and of innovation. One major reason for Wahhabism's continued influence is its patronage by the Saudi royal family: Wahhabism is the official creed of Saudi Arabia. An example of the literalist Wahhabi interpretation of Islam is that women are denied the right to drive a car, to "protect their dignity." The Deobandi movement of the Indian subcontinent is a watered-down version of Wahhabism.

The Salafi reform movement was established at the beginning of the twentieth century, with the objectives of overcoming stagnation and abandoning the mindset of *taqlid*, or automatic obedience of precedence, for the ijtihadi

approach. See number 5 in Progression to Violence (below).

Many of the politically active movements like the Muslim Brotherhood have back-to-the-roots philosophy as their driving force. The rationale of these movements is that the way out of the current decline of the Muslim community is to go back to its origins.

## Reform Movements

Other reformers feel that Muslim renaissance will come by way of modernization and finding creative solutions to new problems based on old principles (ijtihad).

Sayyid Ahmad Khan, popularly known as Sir Sayyid, formed the Aligarh Muslim University, with the intent of bringing western education to Muslims. He was much vilified in his time but was remarkably successful. At the time of its

## PROGRESSION TO VIOLENCE

How and why do people who have historically lived peaceably together suddenly become violent toward one another? Whether a population lives under an oppressive government, a minority group feels that those in power do not understand their needs, or a majority group racially blames their problems on a minority, the steps toward violence are the same.[1]

1. An external group is stereotyped.
2. There is a long period of verbal complaint against that external group.
3. Discrimination against the external group grows.
4. The in-group goes through social strain because of economic deprivation or other oppression.
5. The oppressed people come to distrust rational means to deliver them from their problems. Irrational explanations and solutions become appealing.
6. The discontented organize.
7. Individuals gain courage from the organization which validates their violent impulses.
8. Precipitating incidents occur: trivial provocations cause an explosion of violence.
9. Mob psychology sustains destructive activities by overcoming individuals' reluctance to participate in violence.

Before 1776, while England controlled her colonies in America, most colonists did not desire to revolt against King George. But after many appeals to the king for fair treatment were ignored, the radical rhetoric of those in favor of revolution attracted a large following. This led ultimately to the Declaration of Independence and the American Revolutionary war. Unlike wars of independence, terrorism (attacks on non-combatants) is an inexcusable form of violence. Yet people who feel desperate take action to preserve themselves, and we cannot defend a lack of empathy for the poor and the oppressed.

1 Nabeel T. Jabbour, "Islamic Fundamentalism: Implications for Missions," *International Journal of Frontier Missions*, 11, no. 2 (April 1994), p. 85; adapted from Gordon Allport's classic analysis on prejudice: Gordon Allport, *The Nature of Prejudice* (New York: Doubleday Anchor Book, 1958), pp. 56–58.

Source: *Encountering the World of Islam*

Praying at the mosque

formation, many of the ruling elite in Pakistan were graduates of Aligarh.

Another important reformer, Mohammad Abduh, and his disciple, Rashid Rida in Egypt, formed the Salafi movement. They ascribed Qur'anic verses about human institutions to the Prophet's thinking, rather than to the word of Allah. The Salafi movement has metamorphosed into a clone of Wahhabism.

There have been a number of other reformers like Ali Shariati, in the Shi'i tradition; Jamaluddin Afgahani, who was a charismatic speaker but wrote little; the Pakistani scholar of Islamic thought, Fazlur Rahman, who did much of his work at the University of Chicago; and, among current scholars, Khaled Abu Fadl, who lives in California. However, these reformers have been unable to generate populist reform movements and influence only a minority of Muslims.

**Followers of Charismatic Leaders and Groups Looking for a Savior**
Hashashians (*Assassins*, "consumers of hashish"), were the followers of Hasan al-Salah. The followers of this creed were

heavily indoctrinated in the Ismaili brand of Shi'i Islam. Active in 1112 (A.H. 480), they were believed to follow their leader's instructions unto death. The stories about them claim that they would take hashish and go unhesitatingly on missions of assassination, as well as suicide. Most of these stories appear to be fiction perpetrated by the Crusaders, who were constantly harassed by daring raids from this group. The survivors of Hashashians are called *Khojas*, whose titular head is the Aga Khan. They would be considered a quasi-Islamic sect.

Mirza Ghulam Ahmad (d. 1908) started out as reformer. Later he declared himself many things at different times, including Prophet, Mahdi of Islam, the promised Messiah of Christians and Krishna of Hindus. The Ahmadi movement is basically a personality cult and has broken onto Qadiyani and Lahori factions. The state of Pakistan has declared it un-Islamic. However, this has been successfully challenged in South African courts. It is quite likely that, just as the Bahais did earlier, the Ahmadis may declare themselves a separate religion.

The *Hizb al-Tahrir* is a relatively new group that has as its main goal the establishment of the Caliph (Khalifa), who will be the savior for the Muslims. They feel Muslims should unite in one Islamic state that is administered by Shari'a. Anyone who governs by non-Islamic law is considered either a transgressor (*fasiq*) or a disbeliever (kafir). Their economic system calls for the state revenues to be collected

from multiple sources, including booty of war (*maal-e-ghanimat*). It is an important and largely peaceful resistance movement in the Russian "Stans." In the United States and the West, the Hizb al-Tahrir have a small but vocal following, known for their tactic of disrupting meetings of other groups and organizations that they consider hypocritical.

## The Suicidal Militants

Islam's rejection of suicide is clear and categorical. This rejection is based on the belief that life is a sacred gift from God that man may not end even if he is in pre-terminal distress. Islam's rejection of killing, or even harming, the innocent is equally clear and forceful:

> If one slayeth another for other than manslaughter or for spreading disorder in the land, it shall be as if he hath slain all mankind. But if one saveth a life of a single person, it shall be as if he hath saved the life of all mankind. (Sura 5:32, TRANS. UNKNOWN)

It is therefore all the more surprising that the twenty-first century has seen the use of suicide attacks by militant Muslims to fight oppression. The desire to fight oppression is understandable, as is the sense of powerlessness and humiliation in the face of hypocrisy and remorseless brutality. However, the use of suicide attacks, that additionally have caused many innocent deaths, is difficult to understand.

These groups justify attacks on the military and civilians by designating the target groups or nations as those that are spreading "disorder" (*fasad*) on earth. One scholar, citing civilian Palestinian deaths,

including the killing of large numbers of children, has rationalized suicide attacks within the state of Israel, but not outside. The suicide attackers see themselves as martyrs to a noble cause, and the act of suicide as altruistic. They appear to have rejected many other political and economic non-violent means available to bring about change. They forget that Prophet Muhammad never sent anyone on a suicide mission. Islam honors bravery and martyrdom; however, Prophet Muhammad always prayed for the safe return of those who had to go into combat.

## The Evangelists

The second largest congregation of Muslims, after the Hajj, is the gathering (*ijtema*) of the followers of the Tablighi Jamaat. Formed in the mid-nineteenth century in India to evangelize new Muslims in the villages of North India, it has become immensely popular and claims a following in the millions. The Tablighis follow a very structured routine that is simple, though demanding. They are very particular about how they dress, eat, sleep, and interact with others. Their program has six steps to it that include bearing witness (*kalimah*), performing ritual prayers (salat), acquisition of knowledge and remembrance of Allah (*ilm-o-zikr*), social conduct that requires respect of all Muslims (*ikram-e-muslimeen*), sincerity of intent (*ikhlas-e-niyyat*), and sparing time for Allah (*tafriq-e-waqt*). This last requirement demands that the followers go away in groups for days to weeks at a time, evangelizing other Muslims as well as rejuvenating their own faith. It is not uncommon to hear an announcement that a Tablighi Jamaat is visiting the local masjid, and a sermon from one of

the leaders of the group will follow the prayer service.

### Miscellaneous

There have been many different movements in Muslim history that defy easy stratification. An example is the Qarmatians who were a communist sect. They shared property and wives by way of initiation into the group. Their claim to infamy lies in stealing the Black Stone (al-Harjar al-Aswad) of the Ka'aba and hiding it for more than twenty years.

Islam influenced many of the local religions and traditions and sparked monotheistic movements in Hinduism. However, a new religion Bahaism (also called *Baabism*), also emerged from it. Syed Ali Mohammad (d. 1850), the charismatic founder of Bahaism, had a Muslim background. Later he declared himself the gateway or Baab, through which the divine truth is revealed. At various times, he also called himself Mahdi, Buddhist Maitrya, and Shah Behram of Zoroaster.

## LESSONS LEARNED

A retrospective review of the various schisms leaves one with the impression that, although some of these movements were truly bizarre, most were an understandable result of the growth of a community. They were a result of diversity and vigor in religious discourse, and the influence of the faiths and traditions Islam came into contact with during its spread.

## WHAT IS JIHAD?

In Arabic, "jihad" means to struggle, strive, exert, or fight, depending on context. The original religious meaning was to "struggle against one's evil inclinations" or "an exertion to convert unbelievers."[1] Since the days of Muhammad, Muslims have struggled to improve the Islamic community and to bring all people into Islam (submission to God).

> And strive hard in (the way of) Allah, (such) a striving is due to him…. Therefore keep up prayer and pay the poor-rate and hold fast by Allah. (Sura 22:78, SHAKIR)

> The (true) believers are those only who believe in Allah and his Messenger and afterward doubt not, but strive with their wealth and their lives for the cause of Allah. Such are the sincere. (Sura 49:15, PICKTHALL)

Although the popular media often uses "jihad" to mean "holy war," it is only in the past fifty years that a very small faction of Muslims has promoted jihad outside of their own lands, with violence and terrorism against Muslims and non-Muslims. "To justify the struggle against their coreligionists, extremists branded them unbelievers for their neglect in adhering to and enforcing a particular interpretation of Islam."[2] Most Muslims believe war is reserved for the defense and protection of Islam.

> Fight in the way of Allah against those who fight against you, but begin not hostilities. Lo! Allah loveth not aggressors. And slay them wherever ye find them, and drive them out of the places whence they drove you out, for persecution is worse than slaughter. (Sura 2:190–91a, PICKTHALL)

It is also striking how poorly these variances from the norm were tolerated. The extent of persecution the heterodox groups were subjected to was sometimes extreme. In many instances, the persecution drove the heterodox group to break away completely from the mainstream and form a different cult or even a new religion. It is also apparent that most of these schisms could have been prevented, or at least modulated, if the larger orthodox community of the time had practiced simple tolerance and compassion.

### Political Discord about Succession

Political discord is avoidable by the exercise of compromise, for politics is indeed the art of compromise. Shi'i and Sunni discord may, with good justification, be called an accident of history. There are many areas of commonality between these two communities. The challenge is to focus on these areas of commonality and unite.

Political discord is not just a historical phenomenon. There are many areas of political discord in today's Muslim world. It is worth noting that states with representative governments are best able to deal with the political discord.

### Conceptual Differences

Honest conceptual disagreements will predictably occur in any large religious community. It is the intolerance of the other's point of view that results in much discord and sometimes bloodshed. By cultivating the simple art of respecting honest differences of opinion, much of this discord could have been avoided. Arguably, honest differences of opinion

---

(cont. from p. 148)

> Then, when the sacred months have passed, slay the idolaters wherever ye find them, and take them (captive), and besiege them, and prepare for them each ambush. But if they repent and establish worship and pay the poor-due, then leave their way free. Lo! Allah is forgiving, merciful. (Sura 9:5, PICKTHALL)

> Fight those who believe not in Allah, nor the Last Day, nor hold that forbidden which hath been forbidden by Allah and his Messenger, nor acknowledge the religion of truth, (even if they are) of the People of the Book, until they pay the jizya with willing submission, and feel themselves subdued. (Sura 9:29, YUSUF ALI)

A Muslim who dies performing jihad is guaranteed salvation and instant entrance into Paradise. These martyrs do not have to wait for the Day of Judgment to hear if their good works outweigh their bad.

> And (as for) those who are slain in the way of Allah, he will by no means allow their deeds to perish. He will guide them and improve their condition. And cause them to enter the garden which he has made known to them. (Sura 47:4–6, SHAKIR)

1. John L. Esposito, ed., *Oxford Dictionary of Islam*, (Oxford: Oxford University Press, 2003), pp. 159–60.
2. Ibid., p. 160.

Source: *Encountering the World of Islam*

are healthy in the growth of any community. The challenge, as has been observed, is to disagree without being disagreeable. This is an area where Muslims may learn valuable lessons, both from the ethics of disagreement the early Companions of Prophet Muhammad practiced, as well as from the prevalent culture in the West that respects differences of opinion. A true paradox is that Muslims have shown more tolerance toward non-Muslims than toward each other.

### Mystic Influences

Sufism is the vehicle through which Islam spread in most of South Asia and Central Asia. It remains an important vehicle for the spread of Islam in the United States and the West. It continues to provide spiritual solace to millions. Its contributions to Islam are massive and it is clearly a part of Islam.

Nevertheless, it is worth noting that the poet-philosopher Muhammad Iqbal (d. 1938) considered it one of the major weaknesses affecting Muslims. Many orthodox Muslims share this viewpoint. Nonetheless, Sufis should be accepted in the mainstream of Islam. The followers of Sufism should feel comfortable in all mosques (masjids), and their leaders should share the Friday podium with others. Sufis tend to be intolerant of Wahhabi or Salafi Islam. They should take a hard look at some of their rituals, which are heavily influenced by Hindu and shaman practices as well reevaluate their doctrines of intercession and self-annihilation.

### Back-to-the-Roots Movements

It is easy to understand the evolution of the back-to-the-roots movements. These are a reaction to the mutations that have arisen in Islam over time, as well as a yearning for Islam's ascendant past. If they are able to modulate their extremism, they could play a healthy role in the evolution of the Muslim community. The Sufi-Salafi divide is one of the major areas of friction among today's Muslims.

### Reform Movements

Though diametrically opposed to the Wahhabi-Salafi movements in their approach, the modernizing movements share the objective of reforming the community and restoring its strength. Their approach to reforming Islam is completely different from the Wahhabi group. They use the innovative or ijtihadi (independent reasoning) approach, as opposed to the literalist or taqlidi (unquestioning imitation of precedence) approach of the Wahhabi-Salafi groups. The modernist approach provides the best chance of reenergizing Muslims. The modernist scholars, however, have been singularly unsuccessful in producing a populist movement and have remained largely elitist. If they could spawn a populist movement or teaching institution, it would be of immense benefit to Islam and Muslims.

### Followers of Charismatic Leaders

As long as there are gullible and naïve people around, charismatic leaders can find fertile ground for their maverick ideologies. Additionally, many Muslims are looking for a charismatic leader, in some instances, a Caliph, to be their savior. These charismatic leaders and sects exploit this popular yearning in establishing their hold on their followers. The only antidote to this is increasing the level of education and sophistication

among the general populace. The orthodox mainstream should keep lines of communication open with these fringe groups, rather than spend its energies in unproductive confrontation. The more we reject these groups, the more likely it is that they will break off completely.

### The Suicidal Militants

The suicidal militants spring from among young men with seething and legitimate anger toward the oppressors of Muslims all over the world. These violent followers of the nonviolent religion of Islam are an anachronism. Their suicidal missions are reactive to the injustice they are faced with, and not the result of an accepted theology or philosophy. Restoration of justice and fair play within nations and in international relations will largely vaporize the motivation for suicidal missions.

### The Evangelists

Some form of evangelism is an inevitable part of any religion. The intellectual leaders of this group have the opportunity to channel its enormous energy to practical piety, like building homes for the homeless, teaching the illiterate, and running food kitchens and shelters.

## Conclusions

Will Muslims ever reach the degree of education and sophistication necessary to avoid schisms? The answer is unclear. However post–9/11 Muslims do not have the luxury of remaining divided.

The best chance for a moderate movement to emerge, that would overcome disunity and heterodoxy among Muslims, may still be in the West. The level of education among Muslims in the West is higher than in any Muslim-majority country. They have free access to literature and varied opinion. This allows them to examine differing ideologies firsthand, without the filter—of a biased opinion, or censorship of the state, or the intellectual oppression of the community—that is present in most Muslim-majority states. Muslims in the West are also influenced by the local traditions of freedom of expression and defense of the other's point of view. A maverick in the West is often tolerated, and sometimes even celebrated, rather than ostracized.

The solution for heterodoxy does not merely lie in an attitudinal change. The emergence of a model Muslim state that is just, pluralistic, and successful economically, and has clout and dignity in world affairs, practices democracy based on Islamic principles (Shuracracy), would be the best antidote for many of the extreme trends among Muslims. Muslims would look to this successful role model and may stop trying to replicate the past.

Would the monumentally self-centered and often Machiavellian worldview of the dominant political culture in the West allow that to happen? Would a Muslim state overcome its internal challenges and emerge as a role model for Muslims today? Once again, the answers are unclear. Currently, the only candidate state for this role is Malaysia. Turkey, under the leadership of modernist Muslims and not the illiberal secular military that rules it currently, also has a remote chance.

A united Muslim community (umma) clearly is the first step, before Muslims

may fulfill the Qur'anic mandate of uniting the entirety of mankind.

## FOR FURTHER STUDY

Colin Chapman, *Islam and the West: Conflict, Co-existence or Conversion?* (Carlisle, UK: Paternoster, 1998).
*www.paternoster-publishing.com*

**End of Basic Readings for Lesson 4. See** RECOMMENDED READINGS & ACTIVITIES **on p. 153.**

**Go to:** *www.encounteringislam.org/ readings* **to find the Full Readings for Lesson 4.**

## ENDNOTE

1　The translation of the Qur'an used throughout this article was not noted by the author.

# DISCUSSION QUESTIONS

1.  How has Islam changed over the centuries, and how has it stayed the same? What unique challenges has it faced?

2.  How has Christianity been able to adjust to different times and places? Are there ways in which it needs to adapt more—in order to reproduce around the world—or less—to preserve its purity and unity?

3.  How do Muslims view the many divisions within Christianity? How can we promote Christian unity without falling into legalism or license? See Colossians 1:9–14 and 3:12–17.

# RECOMMENDED READINGS & ACTIVITIES*

Read:  Colin Chapman, *Whose Promised Land?* (Grand Rapids: Baker Books, 2002).

Don McCurry, *Healing the Broken Family of Abraham* (Colorado Springs: Ministries to Muslims, 2001).

Watch: *Malcolm X*, starring Denzel Washington (Warner Studios, 1992).

*Kandahar*, starring Nelofer Pazira (Makhmalbaf Films, 2001).

*Frontline: The Muslims* (PBS, 2002).

Pray:  Locate articles about Muslims or Muslim countries in a newspaper. Pray specifically for the individuals and families involved in those situations. Watch for answers to your prayers in the news.

Surf:  Discover related web sites at *www.encounteringislam.org/lessonlinks*.

\* For expanded details on these Recommended Readings & Activities, visit *www.encounteringislam.org/lessonlinks*.

# Lesson 5
## THE EVERYDAY LIFE
## OF MUSLIMS

## PONDER THIS

- What is family life like in a typical Muslim community?

- What makes Muslim families strong?

- How are Muslim families similar to Christian families?

- What roles do honor and shame play in a Muslim community? How do honor and shame affect life in your community?

- How has the role of women of the West changed over the last 100 years?

# LESSON OBJECTIVE

Describe the everyday practices of people in a particular Muslim community, as they are lived out within their communities and these families, from their point of view. Include:

1.  Eastern worldview and group identity.

2.  Family life: extended family and community roles, women and children.

3.  Holidays, rites of passage, and other special events.

4.  Wealth and poverty, education and illiteracy.

5.  Community values: respect for elders; hospitality, including food and entertainment; honor and shame.

6.  Role of the Qur'an and Hadith in everyday life.

# LESSON READINGS

# INTRODUCTION

For most Muslims, Islam is as much a way of life as a system of beliefs. In fact, the daily lives of the majority of Muslims may bear little resemblance to the formal practices of Islam. Partly this is because 80 percent of Muslims do not speak Arabic or come from an Arab background. They are like the many people who call themselves Christians but do not read the Bible or attend church except at Christmas, Easter, weddings, and funerals. The rituals of birth, engagement, mar-

School friends

riage, death, and annual feasts may be the core religious experiences for those in a Muslim community. But, for almost all of them, day-to-day living consists primarily of family and neighbors, meals and rest, work and commerce, and the ordinary activities of its men, women, children, extended families, and community leaders. These provide the context for planting and harvest, hospitality, reciprocity, rivalries, honor, gifts, music, poetry contests, and sports.

Muslim families' particular ethnicity, customs, values, and language mix with the teachings of Islam to form a local community's culture. While each locale's expression demonstrates many similarities with Islam elsewhere, the area's flavor, color, richness, and diversity may also seem contradictory to the Islam exhibited in other contexts. If we ask a Muslim to describe Islam, he may accurately articulate its basic tenets. But if we invite him to describe his family, community, or customs, a richer world will unfold—which

our friend does not see as separate from the Islam he previously described.

While we may perceive Muslims as wealthy, even in Saudi Arabia, most are not. In fact the average standard of living in Saudi Arabia is 23 percent of that in the United States. Nearly all Muslims suffer economic privation; the average Muslim's standard of living is less than one-tenth that of people living in Europe or North America. Hence, more of their time and energy is spent on meeting the basic needs

of their families for water, food, clothing, and housing. Numerous Muslims also live in regions where war, disease, famine, or natural disasters can and do disrupt life at any time. Many are refugees, forced to flee their homelands. Those with means have migrated to urban areas or to wealthier countries in search of better economic conditions. Yet, their hopes and dreams, doubts and fears, needs and wants, are remarkably similar to our own.

We recognize that our day-to-day life is the frame of reference in which we must live out our faith, and this is true for Muslims as well. Therefore, in order to truly understand Muslims and minister to them, we need to appreciate the forces affecting their daily lives. Much of the time we will spend with our Muslim friends will likely be over meals, with groups and with families. Our learning how to relate to Muslims through their familial relationships may prove more significant than simply discussing the content of theological beliefs.

The main keys to deeper comprehension of Muslims are language and family. Language involves far more than the exchange of technical information. The native tongue expresses the stories, idioms, proverbs, poetry, music, and gestures of a culture. Whereas travel directions can be obtained in an international medium like English, or a purchase can be arranged in a regional trade lingo like Swahili, only the local vernacular can reveal the intimate details of relationships that we most desire to understand. Without a solid grasp of its language, we may miss what a culture identifies as beautiful, enjoyable, unspoken, or forbidden.

Much of our lives is carried out in the foundational unit of human society, the family. Our perceptions of love, loyalty, respect, truth, spirituality, and basic values are formed within this circle. In its close bonds also occur the deepest pains of distrust, rejection, gossip, abuse, unforgiveness, bitterness, divorce, violence, and death. Unemployment, alcoholism, gambling, and immorality attack and destroy Muslim families just as they besiege all families. And this holds true whether they live in villages or cities, or are professionals, religious leaders, political activists, or nomads.

Rival in importance to language and family in most Muslim cultures is the value of honor and its twin, shame. Honor is the motivator of behavior, the arbitrator of justice, and the currency of exchange. The binding force of honor brings hope and life to the individual, family, and community; a person's honor is tied to the group and vice versa. The group may so determine the identity of the self that he or she does not have a strong sense of individuality apart from it. As Muslim communities change, coming under modern influences, and disrupting traditions, a great feeling of loss can arise.

Because Muslims have a strong sense of group identity, Christians need to do more than simply understanding Muslims' way of life. We need to allow them to see us as more than distant aliens with an unknown language and family structure. If our Muslim friends do not see that we have similar needs, problems, and struggles, why would they want to relate to us? To share Christianity with our Muslim friends, our values must be observable

## A Visual Model of the Muslim Worldview: Boat in the "Ummah Sea"

**Family Name**

**Arabic Language:**

Superiority

Exaggeration

Shading Truth to
  Protect Family

Over-assertion

Repetition

Shaming

**Islamic Values:**

Finality of Qur'an
  and Hadith

Determinism

Fatalism

Resistance to
  Change

Anchor to the Past

Popular Islam

**Bedouin Ethic:**

Group Solidarity

Mutual
  Responsibility

Hospitality

Generosity

Courage

Self-respect

Protection of Women

# HONOR

**Floating on the Sea of the Muslim *Ummah***

© Common Ground Consultants, Inc.

and we must be willing to receive. For example, many people will not ask for help even when it is offered, yet some of the best friendships are started when we ask Muslims for help as Jesus did when he asked the woman at the well for a drink of water (John 4:7). Through these relationships, we can learn many things about hospitality, loyalty, and honor. We can receive as much as we give.

Moreover, if we hide our real lives and struggles, retreating behind walls of external religious behavior, we will be, in fact, as unapproachable and foreign to Muslims as they may seem to us. If we want to demonstrate the saving work and power of Christ in our lives, our friends must see it by observing it in our imperfect daily living. This is how relationships work. Words have little meaning without the valid lives to explain them: words, unless demonstrated by a changed life, can be dangerous.

Paul's approach is commendable:

> When I came to you, brothers, I did not come with eloquence or superior wisdom as I proclaimed to you the testimony about God. For I resolved to know nothing while I was with you except Jesus Christ and him crucified. I came to you in weakness and fear, and with much trembling. My message and my preaching were not with wise and persuasive words, but with a demonstration of the Spirit's power, so that your faith might not rest on men's wisdom, but on God's power (1 Cor. 2:1–5).

*– K.S., Editor*

## WORLDVIEW PICTURED IN EVERYDAY LIFE

"Suppose one of you has a friend, and goes to him at midnight and says, 'Friend, lend me three loaves of bread; because a friend of mine on a journey has come to me, and I have nothing to set before him'" (Luke 11:5–6).

In their everyday lives, most Muslims would be more concerned with maintaining traditions and relationships than with their schedule and how much they get done. Greetings and exchange of news matter much more than accomplishments and progress. Even among the most impoverished Muslims, visiting and hosting take priority over other things. To Westerners, Jesus' words in Luke make little sense. If our neighbors came to our door at midnight demanding bread, we may might call the police. In western culture, neighbors ask for very little. But for Muslims, life is full of such events. It is common for neighbors to ask for help, food, or even money. A neighbor would not be sent away empty-handed, because the one he asked will certainly have a similar need in the future.

This loyalty and cooperation with others is required for larger community events, such as holiday celebrations. Muslim neighborhoods often have women's groups in which the women pool their resources to make large purchases and collaborate on community projects. Many businesses are conducted in much the same manner. Moreover, a prudent business owner might retain an unproductive worker on the payroll simply because the worker's family reciprocates his retention by patronizing the business.

Source: *Encountering the World of Islam*

# MUSLIM SOCIAL PRACTICES

*by Phil Parshall*

## EDITOR'S NOTE

Parshall describes Muslims' social practices in terms of sensitivity on the part of the church planters to local culture and the needs of Muslim-background believers (MBB). He lists a number of suggested contextual adaptations and bridges, a little early for our consideration, but worth noting.

 ## FESTIVALS

Festivals are central in Muslim society. Popular observances indigenous to particular areas enhance regional unity, while times of rejoicing commemorated throughout the Islamic world promote social identity and solidarity. They include Id al-Adha, Id al-Fitr, *Maulid al-Nabi*, and *Lailat al-Baraa*:

- Id al-Adha (*Qurbani Id*), Feast of Sacrifice, on the tenth day of Dhu al-Hijja, marks the end of the Hajj. It celebrates Abraham's willingness to sacrifice Ishmael and Allah's provision of a ram instead. The sacrifice is obligatory for any Muslim who can afford it, of a ram or other animal, and is part of the Hajj rituals, as well as being made in every Muslim community. The meat is shared with the poor.

- Id al-Fitr, "the festival of the breaking of the fast," is the major three-day festival to mark the end of the month's fast of Ramadan. There is a significant amount of visiting from home to home, and new clothes are worn.

- The Maulid al-Nabi, the celebration of Prophet Muhammad's birthday, occurs on the twelfth day of Rabi al-Awwal. The extent of the celebration will vary among Islamic nations. Generally, it is not a public holiday. Religious groups arrange special seminars on the Prophet's life. Poems (*qasida*) are read that extol the behavior and accomplishments of Muhammad.

- Lailat al-Baraa (*Shab-i-Barat*, Persian, "the night of records") is observed on the fourteenth night of Shaban. Muhammad is alleged to have said that annually on this night God registers in the *barat* (or record) all the actions men are to perform in the ensuing year, and that all the children of men who are to be born and to die in the year are recorded. Muhammad enjoined his followers to stay awake the whole night, to repeat certain prayers, and to fast the next day. (Frequently, this night is marked more by feasting and merriment than by fasting—at least on the part of the younger people.)[1]

---

Phil Parshall is one of today's leading authorities on ministry to Muslims. He and his wife, Julie, have lived among Muslims since 1962 in Bangladesh and the Philippines. He is the author of nine books on Christian ministry among Muslims.

Adapted from Phil Parshall, *Muslim Evangelism: Contemporary Approaches to Contextualization* (Waynesboro, Ga.: Authentic Media, 2003), pp. 223–31. Used by permission.

## The Muslim Calendar

**Years are counted since the Hijra when Muhammad migrated to Medina, which is assumed to have been 16 July 622 A.D. On that date A.H. 1 started (A.H. stands for Anno Hegirae or year of the Hijra).**

**The Muslim year follows a lunar calendar of 354 days which is 11 days shorter than the Gregorian year.**

| Name of the Month | | Events |
|---|---|---|
| 1. | Muharram | Islamic New Year (1st) |
| | | Ashura (10th) |
| 2. | Safar | |
| 3. | Rabi al-Awwal | Maulid al-Nabi (12th) |
| 4. | Rabi al-Thani | |
| 5. | Jumada al-Awwal | |
| 6. | Jumada Athani | |
| 7. | Rajab | Lailat al-Miraj (27th) |
| 8. | Sha'ban | Lailat al-Baraa (15th) |
| 9. | Ramadan | Lailat al-Qadr (27th) |
| 10. | Shawwal | Id al-Fitr (1st) |
| 11. | Dhu al-Qa'da | |
| 12. | Dhu al-Hijja | Hajj (7th -10th) |
| | | Id al-Adha (10th) |

© Caleb Project

Several observations need to be made concerning these Muslim celebrations:

- They are all religious in nature. People performing the rituals identify these ceremonies with fasting, feasting, and almsgiving.

- Festivals perform a sociological function. These times of celebration are greatly anticipated by all of society. Nominal Muslims enter into the ritual with great zest, much as nominal Christians celebrate Christmas.

- It is difficult for the new MBB from Islam not to participate to some measure in these celebrations. There should be understanding toward those believers who feel they must ostensibly follow the dictates of Muslim society during these observances.

- The foreigner should respect Muslim celebrations. For instance, it is not considerate to eat in public during the month of fasting. It is probably wise to close offices and institutions on the major commemoration days.

- Christmas, Good Friday, and Easter can serve as functional substitutes for Muslim religious days. These days should be celebrated in ways that are culturally appropriate. The MBBs will want to structure the form of celebration as closely as possible to societal norms. The emphasis must be on the spiritual significance of the particular observance. (For instance, I question Santa Claus giving out gifts to Christian national children in a predominantly Muslim country.)

- In some Muslim countries, Christians are allowed to put on special Christmas and Easter radio and television programs at government expense. These should be prepared with cultural and spiritual content so as to best communicate Christ to the Muslim heart.

## BIRTH CUSTOMS

There are no special injunctions in the Qur'an regarding customs to be observed at the birth of an infant. Circumcision is found only in the Traditions.

The following practices are common among Muslims:

- At the birth of a child, he is wrapped in swaddling clothes and presented to a gathering of family and friends. A Muslim priest recites the summons to prayer in the infant's right ear. Alms are distributed to the poor. According to the Traditions, the amount of silver given in alms should be of the same weight as the hair on the child's head. Friends and neighbors visit the home and bring presents for the infant.

- On the seventh day, the sacrifice called *aqiqa* is performed. In the case of a male, two sheep or a goat is required, but, in the case of a female, one sheep or goat is needed for the sacrifice. The animals must be without blemish. At the time of the sacrifice the infant's father prays, "O Allah! I offer this in the stead of my son, its blood for his blood, its flesh for his flesh, its bone for his bone, its skin

for his skin, its hair for his hair. O God! I make this as a ransom for my son from the fire, in the name of Allah, Allah the Great." The animals are skinned and divided into three equal parts. One part is given to the midwife, one part to the poor, and the remaining third is used by the members of the household. The reasons for this ceremony have been listed by Bevan Jones.

Muhammad is believed to have warned parents that, if this ceremony is not performed, God will not, at the last day, call up the child by its parent's name. Neglect of it will mean that all through life the child's "hand" will not be "good." Moreover, there are positive benefits accruing therefrom. It ensures effective deliverance from all manner of misfortune in this life, and is a safeguard against the influence of Satan. The body is purified by this rite and will be found pure on the day of Resurrection. The child that might have otherwise died in infancy will, after the ceremony, certainly live. Yet should it die in childhood, it will go to heaven and, though its parents might go to hell, the child's prayers to God on their behalf

## MUSLIM RHYTHM OF LIFE

There are four movements in the Muslim rhythm of life. The first is common to all human beings—eating, sleeping, working, and everything else that goes with normal living. The second is the ritual form of Muslim faith—praying five times daily, fasting annually, pilgrimage once in a lifetime, and so on. The third movement stems from the calendar of Muslim festivals. The fourth and final movement is provided by the rites of passage in Muslim families, from birth to death. These four movements, interwoven with each other, make up the rhythm of Muslim life.

Adapted from Roland Miller *Muslim Friends: Their Faith and Feeling* (St. Louis, Mo.: Concordia Publishing House, 1995), p. 290.

will gain entrance to Paradise for them also.[2]

- Considerable importance is attached to the naming of the child. It is common for the child to be given his name on the seventh day. The name may be given by the eldest male member of the family, or by some pious man who recites the Qur'an and then chooses a name from the Holy Book.

- As soon as the child is able to talk, or when he reaches the age of four years, four months, and four days, he is taught the Bismillah, that is, "In the name of God, the Merciful, the Gracious."

## WOMEN PROTECTING HONOR

Daily life in a Muslim family reflects community standards of honor and shame. To act in a way that might seem immodest or disobedient is to weaken the family and endanger its integrity. A family's honor rests upon the chastity of its females, who must maintain their virginity until marriage and be faithful to their husbands after marriage. If a woman does not protect the family honor by her good behavior, the family may feel that it needs to disown, maim, or kill her in order to reestablish the family's reputation. Even if women behave appropriately, they still live in the fear that the community will *perceive* that they were involved in illicit sexual behavior.

The Qur'an and Hadith provide parameters which believing Muslims see as divine guidelines for marriage and the ideal wife. Husbands are to love, provide for, and protect their wives. Wives are to make family their first priority. As each member obeys the following Islamic laws, their actions bring honor to the family and the larger community:

- Women dress and behave modestly.
- Women are never alone with a male who is not from the extended family.
- Young ladies marry according to the wishes of the family.
- Children honor and obey their parents, even as adults.
- Women and children respect male authority.
- Bearing a son brings honor; bearing no sons, shame.
- Pregnancy outside of wedlock is the ultimate shame.

So much shame is brought upon the family if a member breaks away from the faith and traditions, that some consider an early death better than for the rebellious member continuing to bring shame upon the community. Fear of bringing shame and punishment on oneself and family is a powerful motivator of conformity.

To some outsiders, this tight bond of family may seem unusually restrictive, a loss of personal choice and individual identity. Yet it also brings the benefits of security, safety, and a sense of belonging.

Source: Annee W. Rose, *www.frontiers.org.*

### FOR FURTHER STUDY

Mary Ann Cate and Karol Downey, *From Fear to Faith: Muslim and Christian Women* (Pasadena, Calif.: William Carey Library, 2002). *www.wclbooks.com*

- In the opinion of Sunni doctors, the circumcision of the child should take place in his seventh year, the operation being generally performed by a barber. But the date of circumcision varies greatly throughout the Muslim world. Not until the child arrives at puberty is he required to observe all of the customs of Muslim law, but it is incumbent on parents to teach the child prayers and the Qur'an.

Aceh wedding

Animistic practices sometimes accompany childbirth:

> During the first seven days the mother must not strike a cat or she and the child will both die. Candles are lit on the seventh day and placed in a jug of water near the head of the child to guard it against evil spirits. Before the child is born, a special amulet is prepared, consisting of seven grains each of seven different kinds of cereal. These are sewn up in a bag, and, when the infant is born, it is made to wear it. The mother also has certain verses of the Qur'an written with musk water or ink on the inside of a white dish. This is then filled with water, the ink being washed off, and the contents are taken as a potion.[3]

Animism aside, how should the MBB relate to birth ceremonies that have been common to his society for generations?

- The Muslim birth ceremony should be closely followed. It is a time of joyous celebration. The name of God and Jesus could be whispered in the baby's ear. I know of one missionary who followed this custom with his first-born child.

- The aqiqa sacrifice presents more of a problem. Instead of an animal being offered so that God will protect the child from Satan, could not a feast be given for family and friends? During the feast, Bible verses that speak about the once-and-for-all sacrifice of Jesus could be read. The baby could then be prayed over and dedicated formally to Christ.

- Naming the child with an Old Testament name could be a part of the seventh-day ceremony. This name could be spelled and pronounced as in the Qur'an.

- Circumcision should be carried out on all male children. This is an important part of the identification the MBB's children are to have with Muslims.

## MARRIAGE CUSTOMS

Marriage customs and ceremonies vary somewhat throughout the Muslim

world. We will attempt to define those practices that are generally representative. The place of the woman in Islam is in submission to her husband. Muhammad is quoted as saying, "The best woman is the one who is loved by her husband and her relatives, who is humble in her husband's presence, and who always listens to him, who adorns herself and is cheerful solely to be his joy, and who is virtuous and modest and retiring before others."[4]

Almost all Muslim women marry. A woman who is single past college age is a rarity. The average age of marriage for the female is approximately fourteen. Muslims are permitted to marry up to four wives. Surah 4:3 (RODWELL) states, "Of women who seem good in your eyes marry two, or three, or four; and if ye still fear that ye shall not act equitably, then one only." Marriage practices can include elaborate ceremonies and customs of engagement:

- Legally binding arrangement of marriage may also be made by the families years before the actual marriage. Sometimes family difficulties result from rebellious children not desiring to fulfill these family obligations.

- Marriage, according to Muslim law, is simply a civil contract. The consent of both parties in the presence of witnesses is necessary. An imam preaches a sermon which enunciates the mutual rights and duties of the husband and the wife. After the sermon, the man and woman are asked if they accept the new relationship; and upon an affirmative reply, the marriage ceremony is concluded. A feast follows in the home of the husband's parents.[5]

- A Muslim marriage is not conducted in the mosque but rather in a home or other convenient place. The imam injects religious content by having the bridegroom repeat:

  - "I desire forgiveness from God."
  - Four chapters of the Qur'an. These have nothing to do with marriage, but seem to have been selected because of their brevity.
  - "There is no god but God and Muhammad is his Prophet."
  - A profession of belief in God, the angels, the Qur'an, the prophets, the Resurrection, and the absolute decrees of good and evil.[6]

The marriage customs of Christians in Muslim lands and Muslims are similar, but there are a few differences:

- Christians prefer to have wedding ceremonies in the church. The Christian minister will ask the couple to sit together for their vows, but, in the case of the Muslims, the couple will sit in different rooms. The imam will go separately to each for the vows.

- The Muslim bridegroom promises the bride that he will give her a certain amount of money if he divorces her. This is not true among Christians, except in isolated instances.[7]

- The Persian wedding ceremony described earlier is full of deep and meaningful symbolism. Such ritual can be retained. The MBB should seek to be original in constructing a wedding ceremony that incorporates the best of Muslim culture and also includes truths from the Bible and witness. This will take on varying distinctives from culture to culture. The one thing to be avoided is a ceremony that is full of western practices which are meaningless and unintelligible to the Muslim community.

Muslim funeral in India

© Caleb Project

## FUNERAL CUSTOMS

Again, funeral customs vary according to locality, but there are some common threads:

- As a Muslim approaches death, he is encouraged to repeat his affirmation of faith in Allah. If he is unable to do this because of the advanced state of his illness, a friend or relative may do it for him. At the moment of death, all those who are nearby begin to wail and recite the Qur'an. The dead person's feet must then be turned so they face Mecca. The mouth and eyes are closed properly. Perfume is sprinkled on the body.

- The washing of the body is extremely important. It may be done by relatives or by specially appointed people. There are customs that regulate which parts of the body must be washed first and how many times the body is to be turned over. All is done very carefully, as it is believed that the body is still sensitive to pain in the first hours after death.

- The religious funeral service will generally not be held in the mosque. It can be conducted in an open field near the mosque or close to the person's home. Prayers are said on behalf of the departed soul.

- When a person dies, the angels come to ask him about his earthly deeds. He must therefore be buried as soon as possible, lest they be kept waiting. The grave is dug in accordance with certain specifications concerning direction, length, and depth. Coffins are seldom used. The dead person is buried in a white shroud.

  After the funeral ceremony, the family of the deceased is supposed to remain at home for ten days while friends and relatives come to visit them. On the third day, a special service is arranged called kol. The Qur'an is read out loud by many people in concert for the benefit of the dead person's soul. Then food is distributed among the children. Another ritual is held on the tenth day, and also on the fortieth day. During these forty days it is necessary to give food to the Muslim priest. It is believed that the food goes to the dead person.[8]

Several years ago a close Muslim friend's mother died very unexpectedly. At my

friend's request, I went and stayed for three days and nights with him. Because his father, who had died some years previously, had been a high government official, the death of his mother was on the front pages of all the daily newspapers. The elite of the city came to the home to offer condolences.

One of the first acts was to bathe the body. Following this, "professional" priests were hired to come to the home, recite the Qur'an, and say prayers for forty days and nights. There was a time of serious negotiation regarding the price these men demanded for their services. Finally an agreement was reached, and they took up their task of praying for the departed soul with intense seriousness.

The funeral was delayed for several days until the older son could arrive from

## THE FEAST OF SACRIFICE

Every year Muslims around the world celebrate the feast of Id al-Adha, also known as the Feast of Sacrifice or Great Feast (*Id al-Kabir*), in South Asia as *Bakr Id*, and in the Turkic world as *Kurban Bayram*. At this time, many Muslims sacrifice a sheep or a goat to commemorate how God redeemed the son of Abraham, as recorded in the Qur'an (Sura 37:99–113).

Judaism teaches about this same event: "When Abraham was about to sacrifice his son, the angel of the Lord stopped him. Abraham…saw a ram caught in the thicket by its horns which he sacrificed…as a burnt offering" (Gen. 22:1–19).

Although Jews do not commemorate this specific event with a feast, its meaning is preserved in Passover. Passover is when Jews observe the night that God spared their firstborn from being slain in Egypt. The angel of death "passed over" the houses of those who put the blood of a slaughtered sheep on their doorposts (Ex. 12:1–14).

Since Christians believe in both the Abrahamic sacrifice and the Passover, why don't they celebrate them? Is there a Christian Passover too? The Injil says that human beings are spiritually dead. Sin is the gulf that separates us from God. Jesus Christ was crucified and died as a righteous sacrifice for the human race. Just as God redeemed the son of Abraham by the sacrifice he provided, the blood of a ram, God redeemed the world through the blood of Jesus Christ. Jesus became the true *Adha*: he was the Lamb of God, sacrificed to set us free from sin, by whom God bridged the gulf that separated us from him.

The events of Adha and Passover were object lessons God used so we could understand true redemption. The Bible says that the blood of calves and sheep will not wash away sins (Heb. 10:14), and that all our good works are like filthy rags compared to God's righteousness (Isa. 64:6). No one can possibly pay the huge debt that is owed to God. The good news is that God sent Jesus Christ to be the perfect sacrificial lamb of God who takes away the sins of the world. Adha and the Passover are remembered in one glorious celebration of the Crucifixion and Resurrection of Jesus Christ, known in English as *Easter,* and in Arabic as *Id al-Qiyama.* Jesus Christ is the Adha for people of all nations and races. Through him we can have fellowship with God and experience his love and redemption.

Adapted from Fuad Issa, *Adha in the Injeel* (Indianapolis: Arab International Ministry, 1995). Used by permission.

England. Approximately one hundred men lined up in the yard, faced the coffin, and prayed together for the woman's soul. Following this, I drove the coffin in a pickup truck to the airport, where the government had provided a helicopter to fly the body to the village home for burial. On the way to the airport, the two sons exhorted me to drive slowly and to avoid any bumping or jerking. On the fifth day, the ritual of saying 125,000 prayers for the deceased took place. More than two hundred people came and participated in this special service.

Funeral services for MBBs should be evaluated in the light of Muslim practices:

- Simple things (like holding a religious service in an open field close to the person's home) can easily be adopted. Rituals such as saying prayers for the dead will, of course, be omitted. Appropriate substitutes can be found.

- Meetings to remember the dead could be held on the same days when Muslims would traditionally hold some ritual. These meetings would be for the purpose of honoring the life and witness of the loved one. If these are not held, the Muslim community will conclude there was no love or respect for the departed person.

Rather than offering specific guidelines, these suggestions have been made to demonstrate that the Christian communicator will need to make relevant applications within his or her particular situation.

## ENDNOTES

1. L. Bevan Jones, *The People of the Mosque* (Calcutta: YMCA Publishing House, 1939), p. 129.
2. Ibid., pp. 411–12.
3. Samuel M. Zwemer, *Across the World of Islam* (New York: Fleming H. Revell, 1929), pp. 127–28.
4. Bess Donaldson, *The Wild Ruc: A Study of Muhammadan Magic and Folklore in Iran* (New York: Arno Press, 1978 reprint of 1938 edition), p. 48.
5. Maulana Muhammad Ali, *The Religion of Islam* (Lahore: The Ahmadiyya Anjuman Ishaat Islam, 1936), pp. 628–29.
6. Thomas Patrick Hughes, *A Dictionary of Islam* (London: W. H. Allen and Company, 1895), p. 318.
7. Anwar M. Khan, "Strategy to Evangelize Muslim Jats in Pakistan" (Th.M. thesis, Fuller Theological Seminary, 1976), p. 22.
8. Ibid., p. 29.

# FASTING AND FEASTING

*by Marti Smith*

 Every year Muslims worldwide observe Ramadan (or Ramazan), the sacred month of saum or religious fasting. Ramadan is the ninth month of the Islamic lunar calendar and is ten days earlier each year, so it may occur in spring, summer, fall, or winter. Sura 2:183–88 provides guidelines for the fast, which begins with a hearty predawn meal: "Eat and drink, until the white thread of dawn appear to you distinct from its black thread; then complete your fast till the night appears; but do not associate with your wives while ye are in retreat in the mosques. Those are limits (set by) Allah" (Sura 2:187, YUSUF ALI).

Especially when it falls during the hottest months of the year, the fast can last up to fifteen hours a day and be quite difficult. The fast is strict, prohibiting all eating and drinking during daylight hours for all adults, except pregnant or menstruating women, nursing mothers, and those who are sick or too elderly. Smoking is also forbidden, and, in some places, Muslims refrain from bathing or swallowing their own saliva during the hours of daylight. Young children and those who are traveling may be exempt from the fast, although they may choose to, or be expected to, make up the missed days later. After sundown, communities break the fast together. Islamic fasting is a public, community event, and so is the feasting that follows. Especially during the first three days of Ramadan, schools and businesses may close so that families can be together.

The streets may be nearly deserted during the days of Ramadan, but, in the evenings when the fast is broken, Muslim cities come to life. People who are often too busy to get together will plan special gatherings during this time. Particularly in Arab countries, the feasting may last late into the night. Many of those who can will sleep for much of the following day, radically changing the patterns of life during the month of Ramadan and reducing the fast's hardships. Day becomes like night, and night like day.

Keeping the fast in a more secular community, or where Muslims are in the minority, is much more challenging: it requires going about one's ordinary tasks without making accommodations for the difficulties of fasting. For those who have to work or carry on with daily life, weariness and irritability are common. Tempers may flare. Though fasting can be a point of pride, it can also teach patience and humility, revealing one's weaknesses and building self-control. Those who are fasting may pray together and encourage each other, knowing someone will notice if they are tempted to slip away for a drink of water or to smoke a cigarette.

## A TIME FOR HOLINESS

The rituals and prohibitions of Ramadan go beyond eating and drinking; everyone

---

Marti Smith is part of the staff of Caleb Project. She trains and serves short-term teams which do ethnographic research among the cultures of people groups around the world.

must be especially careful to abstain from sinful thoughts and behavior during this holy month. Indulging in morally questionable practices such as gossip or anger, going out with a girlfriend or boyfriend, or watching certain kinds of movies are all discouraged. Ramadan is a time to look within oneself, pray, and draw close to God and the community of Muslims. Older men, especially, may feel the need to abstain from worldly conversation and devote themselves to praying and reciting the Qur'an. Some Muslims believe that prayers and righteous acts are worth more during Ramadan. More people join in ritual prayers, and extra prayer times are scheduled. The prospect of gaining rewards in heaven for good works done during Ramadan encourages Muslims to persevere.

Food and hosting

© "Hosting" – Kristie Burns/Saudi Aramco World/PADIA

Many secular Muslims who neglect the duties of Islam at other times will observe the fast, or at least part of it. Sharing the hardship of fasting knits Muslims together and builds their sense of community. On the other hand, more conscientious Muslims sometimes look down on those who live ungodly lives all year but pretend to be holy during Ramadan, or those who cheat and make excuses not to participate in the fast.

## A TIME FOR HOSPITALITY

The elaborate meals that characterize hospitality in many Muslim communities are a special focus during the Ramadan month. Common practice is to invite friends, relatives, and neighbors to gather, pray, and break the fast together. A western convert to Islam describes such gatherings:

I'll never forget the first few times I was invited to dinner at Muslims' homes. The generosity was overwhelming. I was uncertain what to make of it all. They really seemed to put into practice the hadith, "Whoever believes in Allah and the Last Day should be generous to his visiting guest."

Consider what Muslims do during the month of Ramadan. It is truly a thing to see: the tables laid with soups

and dates; then three or four main dishes of lamb, chicken, and beef, curries, rice, pastas and couscous; then side dishes of salads, hummus, and vegetables; not to mention the desserts, cakes and pastries, tea and coffee.

When I entered Umm Mohammad's house the first time ten years ago, having been greeted at the door by her oldest daughter, I remember being overcome by the mélange of wondrous smells, bright smiles, infectious laughter, and pure happiness that I found in the room. Lively conversation, all the food you could want, refreshing drinks, and bonhomie permeated every nook and cranny. There were many conversations in other languages, but the smiles gave me a sense of welcome.[1]

## BREAKING OF THE FAST

At the end of Ramadan, Muslims break the fast with an extravagant feast called Id al-Fitr, which may last for several days. In many Muslim communities, this is the biggest holiday and social gathering of the year. The customs of Id al-Fitr vary from culture to culture, but usually celebration, eating, and giving gifts are involved. In Uzbekistan, women prepare great batches of the national dish, a kind of pilaf, and exchange bowls of it with their neighbors. Uyghurs of China and Central Asia make homemade noodles. In Malaysia, everyone returns to his or her hometown or village. In many places, Id al-Fitr is a time for families to come together in unity. Tui, an Indonesian Muslim, gives this description:

> Id al-Fitr is a time of rebirth or new beginnings. It is a time to visit parents and friends, asking forgiveness of wrongs done. You must approach them humbly, on your knees, as an expression of submission, gratitude, and honor. It is a relief to be forgiven and return to a purer, unburdened state. Once everyone has forgiven each other, then God is willing to forgive them. But it does not last forever. It is only temporary, and that is why this must be done every year.[2]

## A CHRISTIAN RESPONSE

Some Christians in Muslim countries observe the fast in order to identify with the Muslims they would like to reach. After all, fasting is a godly discipline

## CULTURAL ASSUMPTIONS

[It is not] sufficient simply to supply western Christians with a list of guidelines as to the customs and etiquette of Muslims, helpful through such contributions can be. Rather, an understanding of the assumptions about reality that lie behind such surface behavior is needed. Communication too often fails to get off the ground, or develop appropriately, precisely because different assumptions are being made about what is going on in the relationship between the western Christian and non-western Muslim.

Bill Musk, "To Save a Soul," *Touching the Soul of Islam: Sharing the Gospel in Muslim Cultures* (East Sussex, UK: Monarch Publications, 1995), p. 18.

appropriate for Christians. On the other hand, the Muslim approach to fasting conflicts with biblical injunctions and examples on a number of points. Some believers in Christ feel that participating in the Ramadan fast sends the wrong message to their Muslim friends. (See "What I Learned by Keeping the Fast," by Erik Nubthar, p. 387.)

Regardless of whether or how the fast is kept, the month of Ramadan provides many opportunities for Christians to pray for and with Muslim friends, to participate in social and spiritual gatherings, and to engage Muslims in discussions about spiritual things. Muslims may be seeking God and examining their own hearts during Ramadan; they may also be more open to dreams and visions from God. Christians see Christmas and Easter as excellent times to reach out to Muslims and other non-believing friends. Ramadan and other Muslim holidays may provide just as many open doors. Pray together with Christian friends, and ask God for opportunities to understand, experience, and respond to what happens in a Muslim community during this important season.

## ENDNOTES

1.  Debra Hewly, "Hosting amongst Muslim Homes," *Al Jumuah* 13, no. 4 (July 2001), pp. 14–15.
2.  Caleb Project, *The Madurese of Indonesia* (Littleton, Colo.: Caleb Project, 1996), p. 18.

# HONORING STRANGERS

*by Gregg Detwiler*

### EDITOR'S NOTE

As we learn about Muslim community values of hospitality and honor, we must remember our biblical responsibility to minister through mercy, offering help, hospitality, compassion, and other deeds.

In Deuteronomy 26:1–13, God gave his people, freshly redeemed from the bondage of Egypt, a ritual that would remind them of their former captivity. The Israelites were to bring their offering of first-fruits to the priest. They were to declare aloud the history of their salvation and to express their joy in every good thing the Lord had given them. Then they were to share their offerings with the Levites and the aliens among them.

> You shall give it to the Levite, the alien, the fatherless and the widow, so that they may eat in your towns and be satisfied. Then say to the LORD your God: "I have removed from my house the sacred portion and have given it to the Levite, the alien, the fatherless and the widow, according to all you commanded." (Deut. 26:12b–13a)

An alien, or stranger, was a non-Jew who lived with the Jews. He could be likened to an immigrant who is a permanent resident of a country not his own. The sojourner (a word used in some translations) might parallel someone who is a temporary resident of a foreign land. From the beginning, God intended that the Gentiles (non-Jews) would be part of his people, a revelation more fully expressed in the New Testament, but also glimpsed in the Old Testament. One such glimpse is found in God's instructions to practice hospitality and service to aliens and strangers. That service was an expression of gratitude and obedience.

Today, with the light of the New Testament, we see the spiritual symbolism in these instructions. We, too, were once slaves in a land of captivity. We, too, suffered the bondage of sin. We were liberated from the domain of darkness and ushered into our promised land, the kingdom of God. What, then, is to characterize those who have made this journey by God's grace?

In Matthew 25:31–46, Jesus paints a word picture of a heavenly judgment scene in which "all the nations will be gathered before him" (v. 32), and he will separate the sheep from the goats. What distinguishes the sheep from the goats? They are distinguished by their response to the hungry, the thirsty, the stranger, those in need of clothing, the sick, and those who are in prison. The righteous, seemingly almost without thinking about it, feed the hungry, supply drink for the thirsty, invite the stranger in, clothe the needy,

---

Gregg Detwiler is the multicultural ministries coordinator at Emmanuel Gospel Center in Boston, Massachusetts.

Adapted from Gregg Detwiler, "Honoring Strangers," *Discipleship Journal*, 137 (2003), p. 31. Used by permission. *www.navpress.com/magazines*

look after the sick, and visit the prisoner. They are commended and rewarded for their hospitality and service to the disenfranchised and the alien. The wicked, on the other hand, apparently oblivious to the opportunity and need around them, suffer God's judgment.

The description of the needy in Jesus' story sounds very much like what refugees and immigrants often experience today. Aliens are often those who, due to global political unrest and economic hardship, find themselves hungry, thirsty, sick, imprisoned, and so on. At the very least—even if they have the necessities of food, drink, and clothing—they are strangers in a foreign land who need hospitality and friendship.

 **End of Key Readings for Lesson 5. See** RECOMMENDED READINGS & ACTIVITIES **on p. 188.**

## INDO-IRANIAN PEOPLES

Like the Turkic peoples, the Indo-Iranian peoples are spread across Central Asia in Iran, Iraq, Syria, Turkey, Uzbekiststan, Tajikistan, Kazakhstan, Afghanistan, Pakistan, and India. Some Indo-Iranian people groups have substantial populations in Azerbaijan, China, Georgia, Kuwait, Oman, Qatar, Serbia, Montenegro, and Russia. Two Indo-Iranian Muslim groups in Argentina, the Northern Pushtun and the Iranians, have between 80 and 100 thousand people each.

Indo-Iranians number more than 130 million people, including the Afghans, Kurds, Persians, and Tajiks. Of the 171 Indo-Iranian people groups, 110 are predominantly Muslim.

The Kurds, an estimated 25 million people, live in a region they call Kurdistan, which straddles Iran, Iraq, Turkey, Syria, Armenia, and Azerbaijan. They are the world's largest ethnic group without a homeland. Most Kurds live apart from others, in mountainous areas where they can retain their own culture, traditions, and languages. Traditionally nomadic herders, most are now semi-nomadic or settled. The majority practice devout Sunni Islam. As a people, they lack political unity, yet have usually withstood subjugation by other nations without losing their identity. However, in vying for autonomy in the last half of the twentieth century, the Kurds have been used as pawns in war and have suffered genocide multiple times in the hands of the region's governments; thousands now live in North America and Europe. Recent openness has resulted in a young but growing church-planting movement among the Kurds of northern Iraq.

Sources: *Operation World, www.joshuaproject.net.*

### FOR FURTHER STUDY
Robert Blincoe, *Ethnic Realities and the Church: Lessons from Kurdistan* (Pasadena, Calif.: Presbyterian Center for Missions Studies, 1998).

# COMMUNITY AND CUSTOMS

*by Caleb Project*

What is real, daily life like for a Muslim man, woman, or child? What are the most important, underlying beliefs, values, and traditions that shape family and community life? Many of these influences vary from culture to culture, even within a culture, according to education levels, urbanization, or other factors. However, certain customs are commonly shared between Muslim cultures because of the same influences. What follows is a series of snapshots which demonstrates some of these customs, both shared and varied. These snapshots are composites, based on the work of ethnographic research teams in three different, largely Muslim, countries: Azerbaijan, Indonesia, and Syria.

## "OUR GREATEST TREASURE": FAMILY AND COMMUNITY LIFE IN AZERBAIJAN

Tofiq is a young man from a traditional family in Azerbaijan.[1] Tofiq's strongest relationships will be with the same people all his life: relatives, neighbors, and local friends from school or work. His attitudes are the same as those of his parents, grandparents, and neighbors. Tofiq tells his story in his own words:

### Portrait of a Traditional Family

Our city of Ganja is the second largest in Azerbaijan. Many of us live in the grey cement apartment complexes you see throughout the city, but there are many more beautiful buildings and houses of many sizes. Walking along the dirt and gravel road, you will notice that each house is surrounded by stone or brick walls with large steel doors. Do not let these fool you into believing we are a people who hide or close ourselves off from one another. Nothing could be less true. You will see.

As you enter our gates we greet you with a warm welcome. If you are a woman, your greeting comes with kisses on the cheek from my mother and sister. If you are a man, my father and brothers will extend their hands to you in welcome. After you remove your shoes, you are invited inside. My mother and sister will prepare tea for us while we talk.

### Responsibilities in Familial Relationships

Most problems, large or small, are brought to my father's attention and submitted to him for counsel. Little is or can be hidden from him. Although more than two hundred thousand people live here, when I do something without my parents' knowledge on one end of the city, news of my deed always reaches home before I do. Nothing can be kept secret. We sometimes say, "The ground has ears."

Caleb Project is a mobilization ministry based in Littleton, Colorado. For the past twenty-five years Caleb Project has sent ethnographic research expeditions around the world. *Encountering the World of Islam* is a ministry of Caleb Project. *www.calebproject.org*

While children are young, they give respect first to the father, then to the mother. But I am twenty-four. When I am twenty-five, I will have authority over my mother. She must listen to me when I ask her to do something. My brother and sister must also respect me. Even now, if I asked my sister to wash my clothes, she would do so without arguing.

As the oldest, in my father's absence, I am responsible to protect the home, the women, and the honor of our family. As a brother, I am especially responsible for defending my sister's honor. If a boy to whom she is not engaged approaches her on the street, touches her, or even speaks to her, I am bound to seek out this offender and fight him. I will be shamed if I neglect this duty, and others will say I have no honor.

If my father's brother visits, the women in our family must show respect by standing when he comes into the room, never turn their backs on him, interrupt, or speak loudly. Their pose must be respectful, never crossing legs or slouching in his presence. Among men, preference is given to the oldest. My grandfather is respected and sought for counsel because of his age and wisdom. My father is shown respect by his younger brothers, and my younger brother Sanan must respect me.

Azerbaijani bread is typically offered to guests

The majority of our relatives live near our home, one uncle and his family next door. Relatives commonly visit one another two or three times a week, but some we see every day. We drink tea and talk, enjoying one another's company even to the early hours of the morning. Family is our greatest treasure, our greatest priority. We will protect, defend, and support one another every way possible. We may only see our distant relatives for weddings or funerals, but if anyone is in need, we strive to meet that need. If it is financial, we will give money. If it is physical, we work to find a cure.

Traditionally, a family's children will marry in their order of birth. A high expectation is placed on girls and boys alike to be married before the age of

© Caleb Project

twenty-five, and families will work hard to find appropriate spouses.

**Shame and Social Problems**

Because relationships are an Azerbaijani's greatest treasure, broken relationships are a great grief. The most significant social problems are those that hurt relationships, betray trust, or destroy family honor, such as divorce, crime, and drug abuse.

Ideally, a marriage will be approved and supported by both sets of parents, but this does not always happen; few families escape the strain of at least one rebellious engagement and marriage. This temporarily breaks family relationships but damage is seldom irreparable. One woman told of her family's trouble:

> I was already married, caring for my son Hagan and pregnant with my second, when my sister Gulla left. She always enjoyed her studies, so, with some reluctance, my father allowed her to attend the Institute of Foreign Languages in Baku. There she met and fell in love with Suleman. Not only was he not from our region, but we learned that his family was less traditional and considerably less educated than ours. With thought and counsel, my father refused to allow Gulla to marry him. In spite of this they married. None of us attended the ceremony. Two years (and two children) later, Suleman's parents came to my father and mother to ask them to reconsider, bringing to their attention that they had grandchildren they had never seen. As is expected in such a situation, my parents conceded, and there was a second wedding.

Great social stigma is associated with drunkenness. An Azerbaijani man should never be seen drunk in public. Most would rather crawl home on hands and knees at

## LEARNING TO FORGIVE

As Aigul, a believer from Turkmenistan, follows Christ, she's learning to live out his character. But it isn't easy. She explains, "I have never seen my parents apologize, or my brothers and sisters either. To be humble is difficult for all the people in our country. Pride is the worst thing. They say, 'No, I'm not going to forgive, to bow down!' So they don't talk to each other for months. In the end one of them has to humble themselves, but it's very hard.

"For a while I lived with Christina, a foreign Christian. She asked me to translate something for her, and when I gave it to her she was frustrated with my bad handwriting. 'You should have written it nicely,' she said. My feelings were really hurt when she said that, and I didn't want to talk. I was still angry the next day, but she wrote me a card apologizing and gave me a box of chocolates. That was the first time I knew someone who said they were sorry.

"Then last year I had an argument with my mother because I did not want to get married. She was offended and would not talk to me. My old habit came back and said, Don't apologize! but after two or three hours I knew I had to. So I prayed and prayed, and God gave me the desire to apologize. My mom was so surprised, she cried and cried."

Source: Marti Smith, *calebproject.org*.

night than be found in the morning, lying drunk in a doorway, one person said. The shame of alcoholism in Azerbaijan adds to its horror: upset with themselves for lacking self-control, men take out their frustrations on their wives and families, leading to abuse, which sometimes leads to divorce and whole families losing their honor and dignity.

## Passing on Traditions: Stories, Poems, and Songs

In most societies children learn values and traditions from their parents and grandparents, as well as at school and through religious education, through listening to, memorizing, and reciting stories and proverbs, and singing songs. Many of the world's Muslims grow up with a preference for oral learning, and they will understand, trust, and remember what they are told—especially through narrative—over what they read or hear through propositional truth. Through these forms they can also express ideas and emotions they might not otherwise articulate. Two Azerbaijanis explain:

> We do not like to speak about bad things. We do not let people see us cry. If we cry, we go into our bedrooms so no one can hear us. We cry only in music. Our music lets us express things we cannot express otherwise.[2]

> We love poetry very much. It is the language of our hearts. Even if a person in Azerbaijan does not write poetry on paper, poetry is written on all our hearts. It helps us understand life better.[3]

In most Muslim cultures, children study and memorize poetry, as well as learning proverbs and stories. Particularly in the Persian and Turkic worlds, people speak with pride of "our national poets" and other great thinkers. Their words are passed down to children as part of family life. "We call them *atalar soz*, which means 'the words of our fathers,'" explains Merhaba, an Azerbaijani woman. "I can hear my mother's sayings ringing in my ears at this very moment."[4]

## Struggling to Learn New Ways

Economic problems hit Azerbaijan's men at their point of pride. Many find life much more difficult now than it was under the Soviet Union, and they grieve over the changes more than they celebrate the new opportunities:

> I used to be a tractor driver. I enjoyed my job and was paid seventy rubles a month. My father taught me to drive when I was young and ever since then I have loved to drive. When the Soviet Union broke up, I lost my job. There was no one to pay me. Since Azerbaijan has become independent, I have not had a good job. Now I sell things in the bazaar. I buy them cheaply and then resell them at a higher price. I am embarrassed to have such a job, but there is no other way to earn money. There is no way out. I work very hard and can just barely support my family.[5]

## INSIDE THE KAMPUNG: MEET THE ACEHNESE

To understand the culture of the Acehnese of Indonesia,[6] understanding

the *kampung* or neighborhood is essential. It is one of their most important social structures, a source of community, support, and accountability.

The size of kampungs varies; ranging from one hundred to one thousand people. Kampungs are found in both rural and urban localities. In cities they resemble neighborhoods, while in rural areas they resemble villages. Each kampung is named, sometimes after a person or landmark. Every kampung has a *meunasah*, a community building used for prayer, Islamic teaching, and civil meetings, and a *pos* (a small elevated hut), a significant meeting place where young men often go to relax on the benches there, to talk or play dominoes.

### A Wedding in the Kampung

Today has been a busy day in Dewi's neighborhood. It started like any other day, with the 5 A.M. call to prayer, but attendance at the mosque was a bit sparse; many people had worked hard through the night in preparation for a wedding reception.[7] For several days many people from the tightly knit kampung have been working with Dewi's family to prepare for this special day. Though grueling, participation in the all-night preparations is a privilege for those involved because it shows they are very close to the couple getting married. As the bride, Dewi sits ready, like a princess in the new house her parents have given her in accord with Acehnese tradition.

Many more of the couple's closest friends and relatives had received an invitation to come this morning for the big moment when Ismail, the groom, arrived from his kampung with seventy of his friends and family. All are welcomed into the new house and shown to their places. Later in the afternoon a group of around two hundred people come from all over town, mostly from Ismail's and Dewi's kampungs, to share an impressive feast. Not surprisingly, nearly every family in Dewi's kampung visits, since almost 40 percent of these people are directly related to her parents.

Present to make sure everything goes well is the *lurah* of Dewi's kampung, who enjoys a position in the community like a combined mayor and sheriff, and who has been involved in the wedding preparations from the beginning. Weeks before, he met with Dewi's and Ismail's parents to make official their agreements about bride price and to help make plans for the huge reception. It is important that his kampung host a proper, traditional wedding reception, or people will notice. The imam also ensures that the religious details are in order. Both families are happy for the advice and help as it is important to them, too, that their children have a respectable Muslim wedding.

For Dewi's and Ismail's parents to go to any less trouble and expense would be stingy, not only to their children but to all the people in the community. After all, they will be looking out for Dewi and Ismail: the men will work to maintain the roads and ditches in front of the house, just as they care for their own; the women will visit in the afternoons and help Dewi learn to cook for her new husband and future children. So it is a must for this young couple to include their future com-

munity from the very beginning of their life together.

In a society which, like this one, is *matrilocal* (where couples live with wife's kin group), women's relationships preserve a sense of family heritage. In most cases they live in the same neighborhoods as their grandmothers and great-grandmothers. Today, especially in the cities, one can find some kampungs in which people are not related or even all of the same ethnicity, but residents still form close relationships and describe their neighbors as "like family."

**Community Leadership**

Returning from a semester at the university to find her father Muhammad's house full, Hati felt a mixture of pride and concern. Her father was teaching the Wednesday evening lessons to women of the kampung, and nodded to Hati as she slipped past a dozen ladies singing

## MUSLIM COMMUNITY

Umma (community) is a unifying element of Islamic societies. It is the primary source of identity for Muslims, superseding language, culture, and geographic location.[1] The Qur'an declares the umma to be superior and universal:

> Ye are the *best community* that hath been raised up for mankind. Ye enjoin right conduct and forbid indecency; and ye believe in Allah. And if the People of the Scripture had believed, it had been better for them. Some of them are believers; but most of them are evil-livers (Sura 3:110, PICKTHALL).

> This day have I perfected your religion for you, completed my favor upon you, and have chosen for you Islam as your religion. But if any is forced by hunger, with no inclination to transgression, God is indeed oft-forgiving, most merciful (Sura 5:3b, YUSUF ALI).

The umma is to be a witness to all humanity:

> Thus, have we made of you an Ummat justly balanced, that ye might be witnesses over the nations, and the Messenger a witness over yourselves (Sura 2:143a, YUSUF ALI).

The umma is to protect its members:

> The believers, men and women, are protectors one of another. They enjoin what is just, and forbid what is evil: they observe regular prayers, practice regular charity, and obey God and his Messenger. On them will God pour his mercy, for God is exalted in power, wise (Sura 9:71, YUSUF ALI).

Many times Muslims fail to see Christians acting as a community, either politically (as in the Protestant-Catholic conflicts of Northern Ireland), or in fellowship between our churches and denominations. On the other hand, Muslims will admit that they also do not always stand together (for instance, in aiding the Kurds or the Bengalis).

1. John L. Esposito, *What Everyone Needs to Know About Islam* (London: Oxford University Press, 2002), p. 15.

Source: *Encountering the World of Islam*

passages from the Qur'an to unpack in the next room.

Her father's health had been failing this last year, but he still kept his busy schedule, teaching Islam and Arabic every day at a nearby secondary school as well as teaching community classes four nights a week and twice on Saturdays. Often neighbors would ask him to come pray at special occasions in their homes. His employer at the school had given him Friday afternoons off so he could lead prayer and teach lessons at the mosque.

The people of the kampung often came to him with questions about religion and everything from how to conduct their business to how to raise children. Because Muhammad's answers were based on the Qur'an, they were unquestionably the most reliable. Indeed, though he had no official government position, Muhammad was the most influential man in the kampung. He received unequaled respect and honor from his neighbors.

When the kampung observed funerals, circumcisions, infant dedications, weddings, and Islamic holidays, they almost always wanted Muhammad's presence. At the request of new parents he had even chosen names for most of the young people in the kampung.

Almost all the important and recognized leaders in the kampung are good Muslim men.[8] Some focus on civic duties, while others have primarily religious responsibilities. Acehnese kampung culture does not sharply distinguish its secular leaders from religious, perhaps because religion plays a central role in all of life, and all are servants of the kampung.

**The Poor**

"Just once more," thought Ahmad as he swung his machete. A sudden rush, followed by a crash and cloud of dust and leaves seventy-five feet below, brought down Ahmad's quarry, a bunch of coconuts. Ahmad descended the palm tree slowly to gather his harvest, then brushed the slivers from his chest and arms. He could hardly feel them through his thick calluses, badge of his many years harvesting coconuts for a living. He did not make much money, but could usually provide the bare essentials of life for his family of six. During lean times, when there were no coconuts to harvest or he was too sick to climb, the local mosque provided them with food and money in accordance with Islamic teachings.

Wheeling the day's harvest home on a cart, Ahmad passed his wife squatting on a large concrete slab at the edge of the muddy river, scrubbing clothes with a stiff brush. As she and other kampung women worked, their children played in the river.

Ahmad's simple, one-room thatched hut stood in the shadow of a beautiful five-bedroom stucco house with Spanish-tile roof and ceramic-tile floors. Sometimes he wished he could provide a house like that for his family, but he knew that would never be. Making that kind of money took connections. Education might provide a way out, but Ahmad felt he was too old for that and had come to accept his position: it was better to enjoy his lot than to struggle for more.

Like Ahmad, many Acehnese men lack money, connections, and education, and cannot hope for better jobs or more money.[9] Some resign themselves to a life of poverty, knowing the community will never allow them to go hungry. They live in a place with abundant food, and Islam urges those with money to share with poor neighbors.

Transportation in Turpan, China

© "Cart in the City" Nik Wheeler/Saudi Aramco World/PADIA

Ahmad's friends would agree that being pious was more important than being rich. Ahmad knew his understanding of Islam was quite limited. Learning the Arabic language to read and understand the Qur'an was as beyond his reach as was a university education, but he felt he could attain heaven through prayers, fasting, and reciting the Creed. In the same way that he had come to accept his poverty, he had decided to commit himself to the way of Islam, without thinking about it very much. Every person he knew was also a Muslim, and none of them had ever read the Qur'an either.

### The Younger Generation

As a popular American rock band blared from the television, Ida pulled herself away from the sights and sounds of MTV to pray. She ceremonially cleansed herself and covered her body with a long white veil. As she recited the words and followed the well-practiced movements of the prayers, she heard the phone ringing.

After she finished prayers, she returned the phone call to her "friend." Her other close friends know that this is actually a boyfriend, but she has been careful not to let her family know. After they made

a date to meet at the movie theater after school tomorrow, Ida settled back down in front of MTV to study for college entrance exams.

Ida's older brother, Abang, turned off the radio that had been blaring simultaneously from his room. He reached for his jacket and left for the pos to meet his friend. Abang did not leave very often to play cards or dominoes; he was busy with university classes, with the prospect of getting a job as a lecturer there. Some young Acehnese men in the kampung spent almost every evening at the pos. Usually they were the ones without jobs or money to finish school. The young men he met at the pos are the same ones with whom Abang has prayed, played soccer, and performed community service: even though pursuing different goals, they were still tied together through the brotherhood of Islam and their community.

Abang and his friends are comfortable being Muslims in the modern world. Sometimes they discuss the Qur'an and other Islamic teachings, but find it easy to fulfill the law's requirements and still

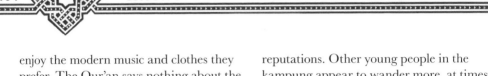
enjoy the modern music and clothes they prefer. The Qur'an says nothing about the movies they like to watch.

Ida, on the other hand, struggles with what it means to be a good Muslim. Though many of her friends do not, she has been taught to wear the *jilbab* (head scarf) in order to avoid the wrong kind of relationships with boys. She hesitates to forsake her boyfriend and their secret dates, but wonders if her friends could be right when they claim to be more honest than she.

Both Ida and Abang seem to be model teenagers in the kampung. The children of respectable parents, they understand their responsibility to keep up their families'

reputations. Other young people in the kampung appear to wander more, at times seeming to even turn their backs on the Muslim way of life.

Forces that are changing societies all over the world are affecting the younger generation of Acehnese.[10] Increasing numbers of young men and women are receiving higher education, which equips them with a heightened awareness of the world outside the kampung. People who have not attended university tend to be closest to neighbors of their kampungs, but university graduates, who want to talk about things only the educated can understand, will also make close friends in the workplace.

## PRAYER

On my first visit to an Iranian restaurant, I discovered that the owner's wife was sick. When I asked if I might pray for her physical healing, the man was grateful. When I explained that I would be asking in the name of Jesus, he responded, "I believe Jesus is the healer." The Lord is great, for he healed the owner's wife, and a week later I gave him a New Testament.

We should pray for the Muslims in our community. If we know their names, we may pray daily for them and ask the Lord to make "divine appointments." We will be pleasantly surprised as the Lord orchestrates events for us to be witnesses.

What if we don't know the names of Muslims in our community? A friend of mine in London has a creative solution: he prays for Muslims with different common names each day of the week. For example, on Mondays he prays for everyone named Ali; on Tuesdays for those named Muhammad. He asks God to send someone to tell each about Jesus. What a great idea! Beseeching God to awaken the hearts of Muslims!

Besides praying *for* Muslims, we can pray *with* them. Our concept of prayer as a conversation with our heavenly Father is not found in Islamic theology or practice, but there are two other kinds of prayer: ritual prayer (salat) and personal appeal (du'a). Salat is performed individually or in a mosque five times a day, but du'a is an informal request for blessing and protection, such as, "May your house be prosperous," or "May our children grow up well." As we build friendships with Muslims, they will share their needs with us. Then we may ask for permission to pray with them, that God will meet these needs.

Source: Fouad Masri, *www.crescentproject.org*.

A number of Acehnese young people believe that sexual immorality and drinking alcohol are part of being modern, impressions from television programming—which glamorizes wealth, technology, and sexual freedom—grouping the three in the minds of some. Adoption of this negative side of modernization is most pronounced among those who are not strong Muslims. Many Acehnese discern that not all of what the West has to offer is good; they want to absorb the technology without giving up their moral standards. So the modernization of Aceh does not mean the Acehnese mind is becoming more westernized or secular: they want to integrate their Islamic worldview with living in the modern world.

### Knowing the Rules

The Acehnese, like other Indonesians, are aware of the differences between the customs of their communities and endeavor to uphold these traditions. They describe the local guidelines, as *adat*, something between law and custom, the system that governs their ceremonies, holidays, and rites of passage. "If a person breaks adat," explains one Acehnese, "all people will be stranger to him and separate from him, and maybe ask him to leave.… He will be unhappy because no one will share with him or help him any more."[11] Adat plays an important role in Acehnese life, as is true in most Muslim communities.

In places where few understand Arabic, people may believe that all their local traditions are part of Islam. If disagreement about a tradition ever arises, those who are the eldest, most pious, or well-versed in the Qur'an are consulted. A shared commitment to listen to community leaders keeps traditions in place. But modernization is having an effect. Throughout the Muslim world, whatever rules are in place are followed, strictly by some, more permissively by others. In few Muslim cities is there just one way of life.

## DYNAMICS OF POWER: WAYS OF LIFE IN THE CITY OF DAMASCUS

Damascus[12] is the economic and political center of Syria. Three of the world's major religions, Judaism, Christianity, and Islam, were born in the region, and their growth and development has affected that of Damascus. Perennial wars among neighboring countries and tenuous relationships with the rest of the world place Syria in a precarious position. Also, war refugees from Palestine, Lebanon, Iran, and Iraq have flooded the city, swelling its population from a half million to more than four million in a period of twenty-five years.

### Original Inhabitants of Damascus: Shaamee

Damascus, the capital of the Southwest Asian country of Syria, is part of a region once known as Ashshaam. Descendents of its original inhabitants, a group of Arabs called the Shaamee, can trace their family heritage in the city back for hundreds of years. Though their power and prestige have waned under socialism, the Shaamee still control a large portion of the economic power base in Damascus. Many come from long lines of wealth, much of which has passed from one generation to another. Others have made money on their own. The majority are businessmen, known for their hard work and love of money. Many own family businesses which have been passed down for generations. Shaamee do not like working for the government and resist being controlled by outsiders. They would rather control their own destinies.

Khalid and Abudul are Shaamee. Although young, they work many hours in their father's shop. Soon the shop will be Khalid's, since he is the firstborn son. Because of his long working hours, he has little time for Islam. He works hard and saves his money in order to start a family some day.

Khalid must wait to marry because a Shaamee father will not consent to the marriage of his daughter until the suitor can afford a house. This expectation weighs heavily on Khalid as spiraling inflation pushes the possibility of purchasing a house further and further away. If he becomes rich, Khalid believes, he will be able to rest and be truly happy.

## Newcomers to the City:
## Village Migrants

In strong contrast to the power-holding Shaamee are the newcomers to the city from other places. An astounding number of families have migrated to Damascus from Syrian villages in search of work. Brightly colored traditional dress and customs passed down by ancestors highlight diverse groups of villagers in Damascus. They try to hold on to village ways by living together and visiting their home towns regularly. Even so, the modern urban way of life pulls strongly. Many try to get ahead through education, but they feel caught between the need to adapt to city life and the desire to maintain the simplicity of village life.

Hala is studying English at Damascus University, and she is best friends with a Shaamee girl, Minal. Although Hala's daydreams frequently take her back to her village in the North, she has been exposed to new customs, traditions, and ways of thinking through her relationship with Minal.

Leyla has village ties as well. She has grown up in Damascus, but each summer she returns with her family to their village. Since her family is well-to-do and respectable, in Damascus they blend into the large middle class, but back in the village, they are held in high esteem. Leyla's village is known for its staunch devotion to Islam. Everyone there is Muslim.

## Refugees and Immigrants

Political turmoil and Syria's role in maintaining a regional balance of power have created a climate of fear and mistrust in Damascus. Secret police watch carefully, questioning anyone who might pose a threat to national security and rewarding those who report the group activities of their neighbors and friends. This atmosphere has strengthened people's desire for trustworthy friends. When choosing a friend in the city, he or she will observe carefully to make sure the prospective friend is reliable.

Among the non-Syrian people groups settling in the country is a large community of Palestinians. A series of government laws facilitated their integration into Syria but allowed them to maintain their own national identity. "If you are Palestinian, then you do not consider yourself Syrian. Once Palestinian, always Palestinian," explained one young man. Another said,

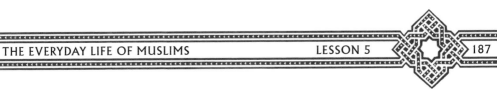

"Of course my wife must be Palestinian! It is important to have someone who understands our problems, not just sympathize with me."

Palestinians in Damascus can be found in almost all walks of life. The educated take professional jobs with the government as teachers, doctors, and lawyers. While Syrian Arabs morally support the Palestinians in their political struggles, some, like the powerful Shaamee, may not be able to understand or relate to the sufferings the Palestinians have faced. "We love the villagers more than the Shaamee, because our customs are closer to those of the villagers," explains a Palestinian man. "The Shaamee don't treat you honestly. They are friends with you only for the money."

Khalid was three years old when his father decided to flee Palestine to escape the fighting between Israelis and Palestinians in 1948, so they fled to the Golan Heights. Like most other Palestinians who left, his father expected to return to their village within a week or two, but the family was still in the Golan Heights when it was invaded and annexed to Israel in 1967. This time his father decided to stay and fight and was killed in battle. After his father's death, Khalid and his family moved to Lebanon, where they lived until 1980, when escalating war forced them to move again, this time to Damascus. Now Khalid, his wife, and their five children live in the largest refugee camp in Damascus. Khalid's mother, as he explains with emotion, is "without her mind" because of all the things which have happened to her. These circumstances keep Khalid's pain fresh.

## CONCLUSION

Is there a Muslim way of life? The strong influence of the Qu'ran and Hadith certainly create patterns and instill values that can be found all across the Muslim world. But the diversity of Muslim cultures and unique circumstances have fostered the development of a great variety of local customs which determine the shape of families and communities.

### FOR FURTHER STUDY

David W. Shenk, *Journeys of the Muslim Nation and the Christian Church* (Scottdale, Pa.: Herald Press, 2003). *www.heraldpress.com*

 **End of Basic Reading for Lesson 5. See** RECOMMENDED READINGS & ACTIVITIES **on p. 188.**

 **Go to:** *www.encounteringislam.org/ readings* to find the Full Reading for Lesson 5.

### ENDNOTES

1. Caleb Project, *The Azerbaijanis: A Cultural Description and Strategy Report* (Littleton, Colo.: Caleb Project, 1995), pp. 56–60, 70.
2. Ibid., p. 98.
3. Ibid., p. 100.
4. Ibid., p. 101.
5. Ibid., p. 41.
6. Caleb Project, *The Cross and the Rinceong* (Littleton, Colo.: Caleb Project, 1993), p. 31.
7. Caleb Project, *A Prayer for Indonesia* (Littleton, Colo.: Caleb Project, 1993), pp. 10–12.
8. Ibid., pp. 12–13.
9. Ibid., pp. 20–21.
10. Ibid., pp. 16–17.
11. Ibid., p. 57.
12. Caleb Project, *The Muslims of Damascus*, pp. 19–20, 105–108, and *Damascus from Darkness to Light* (Pasadena, Calif.: Caleb Project, 1988).

# DISCUSSION QUESTIONS

1. The western worldview sees life as being easily compartmentalized into different, separate sections. We may have different communities and adopt different behaviors depending on whether we are at work, home, or church. In the eastern worldview, where life is seen as an integrated whole. Is one way more "biblical" than the other? Why or why not?

2. How might the gospel that Christians preach seem disconnected from the lives of the Muslims they are trying to reach?

3. At what points does your life fail to be integrated with your faith?

# RECOMMENDED READINGS & ACTIVITIES*

Read: Christine Mallouhi, *Mini-Skirts, Mothers, and Muslims* (Grand Rapids: Monarch Publications, 2004).

Edward J. Hoskins, *A Muslim's Heart* (Colorado Springs: Dawson Media, 2003).

Pray: For specific members of Muslim families (mothers, fathers, aunts, and so forth). If possible, involve your own family members in prayer for those in these roles and for families that are similar to yours. For example, your family might pray for Muslim families with the same number of children.

Eat: Visit a Middle Eastern, Indonesian, or African restaurant and try a dish you have never sampled before. Ask the restaurant staff to tell you when and how this dish is eaten. Is it an everyday dish, prepared and eaten at home? Is it a special food, prepared for holidays or family celebrations?

Surf: Discover related web sites at *www.encounteringislam.org/lessonlinks*.

---

* For expanded details on these Recommended Readings & Activities, visit *www.encounteringislam.org/lessonlinks*.

# LESSON 6
# THE SPIRITUAL WORLD
# OF MUSLIMS

## PONDER THIS

- How do Muslims attempt to find effective spiritual solutions to their problems?

- How do we Christians try to manipulate the supernatural world?

- What does the gospel offer the person who struggles with fear?

# LESSON OBJECTIVE

Describe and analyze how these everyday practices (as they are expressed in Muslims' cultural, ethnic, and spiritual worldviews) could be reoriented to a biblical worldview that includes the supernatural realm. Include:

1. Dreams and visions, powerful places and objects, supernatural beings and controlling forces, and sufism.

2. Transcendence (God is greater than, and independent of, mankind) versus immanence (God is intimately involved with mankind).

# LESSON READINGS

# INTRODUCTION

The vast majority of Muslims function within a worldview—an understanding of the universe—that encompasses unseen supernatural beings and forces which affect daily life. A Muslim might not ask, "What made me sick, and how do I get better?" but might frame the question, "Who made me sick, and why?" While this explanation of life is accepted and prevalent among Muslims, how such beliefs are applied varies widely. Popular Islam may have developed

Counting repetitions with prayer beads

© Caleb Project

in response to the barrenness of classical forms of Islam, which do not meet the heart needs of Muslims. Or, popular Islamic beliefs may echo pre-Islamic, animistic, and Hindu beliefs. Either way, most Muslims attempt, through human activity, to influence God and other unseen powers in order to fulfill their needs. Muslims are not the only group with this worldview; animists and other folk religions also operate from similar viewpoints.

## MISLEADING LABELS

To describe popular Islam, many authors have used the term "folk Islam," a misleading label which implies that rural or uneducated Muslims are its main adherents. However, anthropologists and other experts examining Islamic cultures tend to avoid the term "folk Islam." Popular Islam is not limited to villages or to local regional customs; and virtually all formulations of Islam include local or *occultic* elements. Even modern, educated, urban, or intellectual Muslims are committed to assumptions and remedial disciplines which deal with the supernatural forces and beings affecting their lives.

Christians—not Muslims—have used terms like "folk Muslim," animist, spiritist, occultist, or shamanistic in describing this customary behavior. But, as stated in the last lesson, ethnicity and notions of ethnic identity—its associated indigenous customs, meanings, and folklore—are probably more important in understanding and relating to Muslims than any "Islamic" characteristics.

## The Caucasus Mountain Region

© Caleb Project

## OTHER CHOICES

Bill Musk calls popular Islam "ordinary Islam." While "ordinary" and "popular" accurately describe the nature of these Islamic forms, several of the authors chosen for this lesson continue to refer to this diversity of expressions collectively as "folk Islam." Please note that their use of the term "folk" fuses three separate notions: animism, mysticism, and unique local manifestations of Islam.

Animism is probably the wrong designation, because that would be a religion of spirit worship. While many Muslims recognize, even dabble in, the spirit world, they are not animists nor animistic because they do not deify spirits. Muslims, no matter how occultic, are monotheists.

Mysticism in Islam covers several subsets of popular Islamic usage. Identifying all of these popular representations as mystical would not adequately explain some of the practices covered in this lesson. In addition, when we classify customs mystical, we may subconsciously but erroneously be labeling them "superstitious," judging such beliefs irrational, illogical, anti-intellectual, and trusted by the naïve and credulous.

## INVALID DICHOTOMY

Some portray popular Islam as informal, unorthodox, or "low" Islam. However, many Muslims actively involved in the spirit realm also follow all the formal requirements of Islam. Certainly, many Muslims have adapted Islam to their own cultures and needs, an apparent differentiation between "popular" expressions and Islam as classically represented. But the dichotomy between "classical" and "popular" formulations is no longer accepted in anthropological circles or in Islamic studies programs. For example, support for amulet use appears in the Qur'an and the Hadith. So, are charms and talismans a "popular" or a "classical" aspect of Islam? Furthermore, who decides which modes of Islam are "popular" and which are "orthodox"?

Overall, Muslims are seeking a connection with the spiritual world and with God. In Islamic theology, God is primarily transcendent: He is distant and uninvolved in human affairs. But we were created with an internal hunger for an intimate relationship with our Creator. This heartfelt need for connection with God (immanence) is a driving force in popular Islam. Moreover, many Muslims are fearful of the pressures affecting their daily lives: sickness, death, jealousy, infidelity, and privation, to name a few. They have mounted an unrelenting search for supernatural influence to counteract these forces. Understanding the reality of

## EURASIAN PEOPLES

While Christianity is the religion of the majority of most Eurasian peoples, Bosnians, Albanians, and forty Caucasian people groups are Muslim. The Northern *Caucasus* region, which lies between the Black Sea and the Caspian Sea, is made up of eight Russian republics and is inhabited by more than fifty people groups of Caucasian, Iranian, and Turkic origin. A number of Caucasian and Siberian peoples lost half of their populations through Russian conquest, genocide, and deportations under Stalin. All non-Russian peoples in the region suffered severely from Communist oppression, cultural control, and the enforcement of Russian Orthodoxy during the nineteenth and twentieth centuries. The people of the Northern Caucasus, who are predominately Muslim, have long resented the Russian domination.

The Chechen are an indigenous Eurasian people of mountain herdsmen and farmers who have lived in the Caucasus for thousands of years. They are Sunni Muslims who practice Sufi mysticism, and they speak a distinct Caucasian language. Chechen communities traditionally form around a clan structure, and their population of more than a million is predominately rural.

A declaration of independence, issued by a separatist Chechen movement in 1991, triggered the 1990s wars between the Russian Republic of Chechnya and Russia. These wars officially ended in 1996 with a Russian retreat, but, by 1999, Russia had regained control, and the violent battle over Chechnya resumed. Already one of the poorest regions in the former Soviet Union, the entire area has been destabilized by this conflict, and power, heat, and water to most towns have been cut off. More than 100,000 Chechen have died, and 500,000 have fled to surrounding states and republics, leaving the nation traumatized and devastated.

Sources: *www.joshuaproject.net, www.peopleteams.org, www.tconline.org.*

fear and spiritual power in their lives is important in relating to Muslims.

## BIBLICAL WORLDVIEW

If finding an appropriate name by which to identify this Muslim belief system is one difficulty, the other is our poorly conceived worldview. Western Christians need a reorientation to the perception of the universe as it is biblically described—including the reality of unseen spiritual forces and beings (2 Cor. 10:3–5; Eph. 6:12). Maybe we do not employ animistic attempts to manipulate God to meet our needs. But do we turn to God with everything? Are we demonstrating our total dependence on his supernatural, supreme command of our lives, spiritually, emotionally, mentally, and physically? One reason both Muslims and Christians[1] everywhere continue to visit fortunetellers and other "spiritually powerful" people is that so doing addresses needs seemingly not met in other religious experience. Another is that sinful people choose action over asking, trusting, or waiting on their confessed Sovereign.

One of Christians' regrettable failures has been that they did not accept or under-stand biblically described spiritual beings and forces, even though claiming to sub-cribe to the authority of the Bible. Magic, witches, miracles, demons, dreams, and the like were viewed as archaic concepts from an unenlightened time, and not germane to their work. Some went so far as to limit biblical accounts of such influences and personages to being "mere" stories rather than historical realities. Other individuals trivialized the true power of the supernatural realm, as well as of prayer, failing to emphasize the full

range of spiritual gifts (besides preaching). Providentially, many Christians have returned to Scripture and reclaimed the biblical worldview of an authentic, active spirit world.

## REAL ENEMY, POWERFUL WEAPONS

In this lesson, our assumptions about what is real will be questioned. Which line of thinking have we been following? Have we been functioning with an incomplete and inadequate biblical worldview? Christ's death and resurrection not only save us from our sins and heal us from our shame, but break the power of the kingdom of darkness, transferring us into the heavenly realm, arming us with Christ's supernatural authority.

If we relate to Muslims only through our own cultural lenses, we may not notice indications of popular Islamic cosmology. Moreover, to enter the real worldview of our Muslim friends, we may first need to help them understand that we too acknowledge a world of such forces and beings affecting our lives, and have to cope with pervasive evil. We believe that our enemy, Satan (*Shaytan* for Muslims), is alive and powerful, and controls many demons skilled at deception, oppression, manipulation, and temptation. In the early church, exorcism was a normal part of baptism, and renouncing Satan was a part of communion. Biblical Christianity has both a defensive and an offensive theology for dealing with the spirit world. Praying for our Muslim friends has super-natural force, conferring potent *baraka*, spiritual blessing, in the name of Jesus. If—until now—we have not understood

our responsibility, our prerogatives, or our partnership with the church, we need to arm ourselves.

We may be inexperienced in handling the weapons of divine power—in asking Jesus Christ to use his authority to save or heal, to perform miracles, or to speak to people through dreams and visions—but these are the events through which most Muslims come to Christ. Or, we may not have used prayers of protection, for instance, when interacting with people, entering places, or receiving objects. However, the summons is compelling: "Pray in the Spirit on all occasions with all kinds of prayers and requests. With this in mind, be alert and always keep on praying for all the saints. Pray also for me, that whenever I open my mouth, words may be given me so that I will fearlessly make known the mystery of the gospel, for which I am an ambassador in chains. Pray that I may declare it fearlessly, as I should" (Eph. 6:18–20).

*– K.S., Editor*

## FOR FURTHER STUDY
Rick Love, *Muslims, Magic and the Kingdom of God* (Pasadena, Calif.: William Carey Library, 2000). *www.wclbooks.com*

## ENDNOTE
1. Many cultures in the world have embraced Christianity syncretistically.

# FOLK ISLAM: THE MUSLIM'S PATH TO SUPERNATURAL POWER

*by The Center for Ministry to Muslims*

While Muslims confess the greatness of God, many live in fear of evil spirits. Their religion teaches that there is one God and that there is no mediator between God and humankind. Yet countless Muslims seek someone to manipulate magical powers.

The Qur'an acknowledges that Allah is closer than one's jugular vein; yet he seems so distant, so unreachable, and so inaccessible. Numerous times each day, devout Muslims recite *Bismillah al-Rahman al-Rahim* (In the name of Allah, the Merciful, the Compassionate). They desperately want God to be merciful and compassionate, yet countless Muslims dread his unpredictable acts. Followers of Islam worldwide greet one another with *As-salaam alaikum* (Peace be upon you). They talk much about peace, but without Jesus the soul is not at rest. Powerless people are in need of supernatural power.

People all over the world—rich and poor, sophisticated and illiterate—at times feel a desperate sense of weakness in the face of overwhelming problems common to humanity. The helpless and hopeless often take desperate actions to get in touch with supernatural powers. This phenomenon among Muslims is often referred to as folk Islam.

## WHAT IS FOLK ISLAM?

Folk Islam is a broad, catch-all phrase that describes the mixing of formal or orthodox Islamic practices with primitive, animistic practices. Animism is the belief that all of creation is pervaded or inhabited by spirits or souls, that all of creation is in some sense animate or alive. People try to influence these spirits by using magic or rituals intended to harness their supernatural power for human ends. These practices involve efforts to appease these spirits, to bring blessings to themselves, or to put curses on their enemies.

Think of orthodox or "ideal" Islam as a shopping mall which consists of neatly organized shops, and a colorful and clearly marked directory with names and numbers, established patterns, prices, and schedules. Folk Islam is like an open market or bazaar, a fluid, free-flowing maze that sprang up without careful pre-planning. It developed as the need arose.

In practice, Muslims range from the strict orthodox who reject all forms of magic, to those who overtly and consistently involve themselves in magical practices. Between these extremes are perhaps the majority, who covertly visit a shaman during a time of crisis or secretly use charms for protection. The actual life of most Muslims is quite different than the "advertised" Islam.

Adapted from The Center for Ministry to Muslims, "Folk Islam: The Muslim's Path to Supernatural Power," *Intercede* 18, no. 5 (September–October 2002), pp. 1, 4–5. Used by permission. *www.cmmequip.org*

Folk Islam is about solutions—not concerned so much about life after death, but rather focused on solving the everyday problems of the here and now. Since overwhelming afflictions are common to humans everywhere, most Muslims are involved in some forms of magical practices, in search of supernatural solutions. Folk Islam is generated by the need of powerless people to use power to overcome the problems of this life. If the spiritual well of Islam satisfied their thirst and met their felt needs, Muslims would not be involved in animistic practices.

## Folk Islamic Experiences

Let us examine some common experiences Muslims encounter in everyday life and their search for supernatural power to resolve their situations.

Aisha is about to give birth to her first child. Suddenly, and for no apparent reason, she is overcome with the thought that something is seriously wrong. She is paralyzed with fear, believing her baby will die at birth. Desperately wanting to hear a word of hope that everything will be all right, Aisha frantically calls for the neighborhood fortune teller, an elderly woman who mysteriously knows the secrets of Aisha's heart and future.

Fatima, Aisha's neighbor and friend, has been married for six years and has been unable to conceive. She feels painful shame that it is all her fault. Fatima has been saying her prayers faithfully and has regularly visited the tomb of a saint to say special prayers. She believes this shrine is a place of power, but she is still barren. She is lonely and vulnerable. Then she hears about an elder of the community who is considered a holy man, a living saint, with supernatural powers. He is not highly educated in religion, but friends say he possesses baraka, special blessings or powers to bring results. Fatima is told that this man has magically helped others with this "positive spiritual force" he possesses. She gathers money that ought to buy food for her family, approaches the practitioner, kisses his hand, and tearfully tells him her troubles.

From another person of power, Samira received an amulet to ward off the effects of the evil eye of a jealous neighbor. Samira lives in fear that someone will put a curse on her or her newborn son.

One of Saida's greatest fears is that her husband might be unfaithful to her. She knows she cannot be with him at all times to monitor his behavior, so Saida puts a few drops of her urine in his tea. She hopes this specially blessed "love potion," this object of power, will magically keep him faithful to her.

Daoud has a law degree from his country's esteemed university and is a respected superior court judge. His eldest son, Ahmed, is not developing properly and is barely able to talk. Little Ahmed's condition occupies Daoud's mind during the day, and it consumes his time and energy in the evenings and on weekends. At work he possesses authority to render difficult decisions in complex criminal cases, yet at home Daoud feels so helpless because of his inability to find a solution for his son, whom he loves dearly. He feels shame that his six-year-old child is not mentally ready to start school. Judge Daoud secretly visits the sheik, a respected scholar who has made the pilgrimage to Mecca and who eloquently teaches the great traditions of Islam. After explaining many mystical insights, this spiritual leader gives Daoud several instructions, which include fasting on certain days, saying special prayers, and memorizing and reciting certain verses of the Qur'an. Then Daoud is given a folded piece of paper which contains carefully selected verses of the Qur'an. This he inserts into a small leather pocket.

Ahmed must wear this amulet, an object of power, on his body. However, if Daoud is to truly witness the healing of his beloved son, he must make a vow and kill an animal as a sacrifice.

Young Azamat has dreamed for years of becoming an accomplished architect. He envisions designing beautiful homes and functional office buildings. However, he knows if he does not pass the final exam, these dreams will never become a reality.

## WOMEN AND POWER

While popular Islam permeates all regions and social classes in the Muslim world, it has its strongest hold on those to whom official Islamic teachings are least available, including those living in rural areas, the uneducated, and women. Women have limited access to the mosque and few are instructed in the Qur'an. Therefore, most do not realize when they have wandered from the orthodox faith, and believe that they are being good Muslims when they follow the folk beliefs taught them by their grandmothers.[1] While some rich and educated women will reject all forms of magic, the majority of Muslim women either will engage blatantly in animistic practices or resort to them in times of desperation.[2]

Usually Muslim women are responsible for perpetuating this system of beliefs and practices. An educated man may scoff at the superstitions of popular Islam while his wife carefully pins a charm to her daughter's dress. Fathers take their sons to the mosque and teach them how to pray, but mothers fill their children with stories of jinn and the evil eye, and show them how to protect themselves against malevolent forces. In this way, through example and stories, rather than through formal education, women pass the beliefs of popular Islam on to the next generation.

While leadership in formal Islam is restricted to men, many women have proved to be powerful practitioners of popular Islam and are accorded great authority, respect, and sometimes fear in the community. They may be the very old, masseuses, fortune-tellers, midwives,[3] exorcists, sorcerers, washers of the dead, and *shaykhas*.[4] These powerful women play an extremely important role in the religious lives and life-cycle events of women who practice popular Islam. The services of those who deal with infertility, protection of the unborn, and birthing practices are often considered to be indispensable. Most village women believe that they cannot have a healthy baby without following their instructions.[5]

1. Bill Musk, *The Unseen Face of Islam,* rev. new ed. (London: Monarch Books, 2003), p. 182
2. Rick Love, *Muslims, Magic, and the Kingdom of God: Church Planting among Folk Muslims* (Pasadena, Calif.: William Carey Library, 2000), p. 24.
3. Ibid., p. 29.
4. Musk, *Unseen Face,* pp. 108–109.
5. Julia Colgate, "Muslim Women and the Occult: Seeing Jesus Set the Captives Free," *Ministry to Muslim Women: Longing to Call Them Sisters,* ed. Fran Love and Jeleta Eckheart (Pasadena, Calif.: William Carey Library, 2000), p. 41.

Source: Amy Bennett, *www.christar.org.*

Azamat visits a holy man, a person of power, who burns incense and prays. Azamat is instructed to take a bath at midnight with seven types of flowers in the water. While bathing he must repeatedly mention the name of the headmaster of the school where he is going to take the exam. Following these directives will guarantee positive results on this critical exam.

Amulets for protection against the "evil eye"

Musa keeps having the same horrible nightmare over and over. He wakes up trembling in fear. He believes that jinn are troubling him and causing this horror in his life. He is convinced there is great agitation in the unseen world among evil spirits at this time of the year. Due to lack of sleep, he has become extremely irritable and difficult to work with. He has not been able to concentrate on his accounting duties at the bank. After visiting a practitioner, Musa now wears a white thread around his wrist and an amulet attached to his pillow at night.

Aisha, Fatima, Daoud, and the other individuals described above represent Muslims around the world. They believe in supernatural powers—persons of power, objects of power, power places, power times, and power rituals. Though these individuals may have vastly different ethnic and social backgrounds, they all have something in common: when faced with difficult situations, they all recognize their need for supernatural power, and they look for someone perceived to be in touch with the spirit world.

## PRESENTING THE GOSPEL OF CHRIST AS THE ANSWER

This is the spirit world in which the average Muslim lives. However, this phenomenon represents a marvelous backdrop for the presentation of the gospel of Christ to Muslims. How appropriate for a follower of Jesus to reassure Samira that she does not have to worry about the "evil eye" if God's eye is on her.

The suffering of some is so severe that they have given up all hope for recovery. Perhaps you have a Muslim friend whose life is filled with unhappiness to the point of despair, or one who is anxious about something that has happened. They may be asking themselves, "Is this truly the purpose of life? Did God create us to live with such anxiety, hopelessness, and fear of evil spirits? Is this the fate of the human race, with no hope of deliverance and inner peace? Is this the desire of him who is al-Rahman al-Rahim, the Merciful, the Compassionate?" The answer, of course, is no. Spirit-anointed followers of Jesus

have the answers to the desperate search of their Muslim friends, for ultimate power is in Christ.

The Qur'an gives Jesus the unique title *al-Masih* (the Christ), without explaining his significance as the Anointed One. The message to our Muslim friends must be "how God anointed Jesus of Nazareth with the Holy Spirit and power, and how he went around doing good and healing all who were under the power of the devil, because God was with him" (Acts 10:38).

All the people described above demonstrate that Muslims long for real and lasting solutions to real-life problems. The baraka (power to bring results) they are searching for when they go to a mediator to manipulate magical powers is illusive, deceptive, and short-lived.

The anointing that Jesus possessed, and passes on to his followers, is the true baraka that people are seeking today to meet the desperate needs of their souls. Through Jesus, Muslims can find equilibrium in a shaky, unstable, and hostile world. Muslims are seeking a mediator—someone who is in touch with God. They must know that the Holy Spirit is at work today. Will we be God's instruments to display true, biblical baraka—the anointing of the Holy Spirit?

### For Further Study
Bill Musk, *The Unseen Face of Islam,* rev. new ed. (London: Monarch Books, 2003).

## "I Saw Him in a Dream"

Sokrat woke up sweating from a nightmare. In his dream he saw Shaytan (Satan) coming for his soul. Then he saw a flaming sword between himself and the devil. A voice seemed to come from the sword saying, "Sokrat, I am Isa. I have the power to save you if you believe in me."

Sokrat is a Uyghur, part of the large Muslim community living in China. He has not yet decided how to respond to his dream. Will Sokrat accept the power of Jesus to save him? Will he be open to learning more about the man in his dream?

Although most Christians in Sokrat's area emphasize biblical teaching and character building over emotional experiences, they recognize that God is at work in supernatural ways. Many Muslims who come to Christ tell the Christians who share the gospel with them that they recognized the truth from their dreams. Pray that God's Spirit will continue to speak to Uyghurs like Sokrat and other Muslims around the world in dreams, as well as through his messengers.

Source: *The Uyghurs of Central Asia* (Littleton, Colo.: Caleb Project, 2003), p. 26.

# POWER MINISTRY IN FOLK ISLAM

*by J. Dudley Woodberry*

Jesus lived in a world concerned with power, similar to the world of folk Islam that we have observed. There were spirit powers which he exorcized (Luke 9:37–43). The woman with an issue of blood treated the hem of his garment as a power object (Luke 8:41–56). The pool of Bethesda was a power place, and when the water was stirred, it was a power time (John 5:1–47). Anointing the sick with oil (Mark 6:13) or exorcising by believing prayer and command (Mark 9:14–29), might be seen as power rituals. Our Lord himself was a power person (Luke 5:17–26).

## JESUS' APPROACH

Jesus' sending out of the disciples in a power ministry in Luke 10 suggests what he would do with similar folk Muslims. From his example we can take away thirteen principles of a power ministry.

**The first principle** we see is that he would go in partnership. We read that the Lord sent them out "two by two" (v. 1). Although he originally faced his adversary alone, he developed an approach of partnership. The powers are real, and discernment is needed. The most significant work among folk Muslims in South Asia has placed a couple in each village.

**Second**, Jesus would have the way prepared for himself. The passage goes on to say that the Lord sent them ahead of him into every place prior to his arrival (v. 1). Every major advance of the church has had a period of preparation, of preevangelism. A man named Inayat, who has an effective power ministry in Pakistan, finds that healing and salvation usually come gradually after preparation in teaching.[1]

**Third**, Jesus would pray for reinforcement as he entered the spiritual warfare. He continues: "Pray...the Lord of the harvest to send out laborers" (v. 2). The most effective power ministries among folk Muslims in South Asia are team ministries. One team is made up of fifteen believers from Brethren, Roman Catholic, Pentecostal, and Episcopal backgrounds.[2] This is spiritual warfare so prayer is essential. In another country in which there was flooding and erosion of the river bank, a naked madman called for five Christian couples to pray that the erosion would stop. They waded into the river and prayed from 8:30 A.M. until noon, with villagers watching and jeering. Then the wind changed, the water calmed, and the erosion stopped. Two villagers accepted Christ, and others still point to the place on the bank where the erosion stopped.

J. Dudley Woodberry's love for Muslims and his knowledge of their beliefs and culture have long been acknowledged. He has served in Lebanon, Pakistan, Afghanistan, and Saudi Arabia.

Adapted from J. Dudley Woodberry, "The Relevance of Power Ministries for Folk Muslims," *Wrestling with Dark Angels*, ed. C. Peter Wagner (Ventura, Calif.: Regal Books, 1990), pp. 321–31. Used by permission. All Scripture quotations in this article are from the RSV.

**Fourth**, Jesus would enter the encounter with a power expressed by vulnerability, by the cross. "I send you out as lambs in the midst of wolves," Christ said (v. 3). Our Lord conquered the cosmic powers on the Cross (Col. 2:15), and we can expect to be "partakers of Christ's sufferings" (1 Peter 4:13, KJV). This year in a South Asian country, a Muslim leader became a follower of Christ. A mob gathered to kill him. He prayed and someone shouted that someone else had been critically injured. The mob disbanded and ran to the other man's house.

**Fifth**, Jesus would alter his approach according to the timing and the context. Christ's instructions included, "Carry no purse" (Luke 10:4), yet elsewhere the disciples are told to take one and even to get a sword (Luke 22:35–36). We see historical cycles in the more extraordinary signs and wonders, with the greatest concentrations being when there are major expansions of the Church.

**Sixth**, Jesus would focus on the receptive but still leave a witness with those who are not. Jesus goes on to tell the disciples: "Whenever you enter a town and they receive you,…heal,…and say,…'The kingdom of God has come near to you.'" Conversely, they are told to leave any place that does not receive them while announcing that "The kingdom of God has come near" (Luke 10:8–11). Currently, folk Muslims are more receptive than the orthodox, suggesting that we should focus on the former while we still give a witness to others.

## ANOTHER SOURCE OF POWER

*by Dale Fagerland*

Bokoum was born in Mali, West Africa, perhaps forty or fifty years ago. No one knows for sure. Through a revelation or a dream, Bokoum's Muslim parents were told that their son would grow up to be a very evil man. Thus, when he was a baby, his parents put out one of his eyes. If he were handicapped, they reasoned, surely he wouldn't become too wicked. The parents' fear must have led them to treat their child horribly, and Bokoum did indeed grow up to be evil. He was big, strong, and violent.

Eventually he went to Djibo, Burkina Faso. There he would stake out a path leading to the market and lie in wait for his victims. Attacking several people at a time, he would beat them, rob them, and leave them for dead. He was the most feared outlaw in the region.

Whenever Bokoum went on a rampage, the police tried to arrest him. At least ten or twelve men were needed to capture and confine him. They drained blood from his veins to weaken him; then they put him in jail. But when Bokoum's blood replenished itself and his strength returned, he broke out of jail and planned his next attack.

Bokoum trusted amulets and fetishes for his power. He collected a pebble from ninety-seven different hills and had a Muslim spiritual leader bless them. This act, he believed, gave him power over all the land among the hills.

However, as time went on, Bokoum gradually became aware of another source of power. My wife and I were working with a small group of Christians in Djibo. When Bokoum heard that we were

**Seventh**, Jesus would engage in a holistic ministry of healing and announcing God's rule, of demonstration and proclamation in which healing is a sign of the kingdom. The disciples' instructions were to "heal the sick" and proclaim the nearness of the kingdom (v. 9), and they reported that the demons were subject to them (v. 17). In South Asia, country doctors declared a three-year-old girl to be within hours of death. A Christian couple prayed for her and she was healed. Four followed Jesus. The villagers were given instruction during the next few months and nine more believed. With the subsequent combination of demonstration and proclamation in the area, the numbers have mushroomed into the thousands.

**Eighth**, Jesus would note that power ministries lead to opposition as well as faith. The unresponsive are told, "Woe to you!... For if the mighty works done in you had been done in Tyre and Sidon, they would have repented" (v. 13). As in our Lord's day, both responses are still found. Where hundreds became Christians in a South Asian locality, a mob estimated at ten thousand came with petrol to kill a convert. They got sidetracked on learning of an imam in the area who had also become a follower of Jesus. The latter was able to calm all but two, who then began rolling on the ground in pain and had to be hospitalized. The news led about two hundred more to follow Christ.

**Ninth**, Jesus would point out that worldviews need to be expanded to include the spirit world and the cosmic battle there. The disciples returned and reported that: "Even the demons are subject to us in your name." Jesus responded: "I saw Satan fall like lightening from heaven" (vv. 17–18). This omission in most western worldviews

(cont. from p. 202)

building a church, he was curious. He went to the work site and talked to the Christians who were volunteering their labor. God had already begun to deal with his heart, and he was not as violent with the church people as he was with others. In fact, he began to warm up to them.

To construct the building, we had to mix the cement by hand and make every block individually from a mold. Bokoum wanted to help, so we gladly hired him. He could do the work of four men. As they worked, the Christians talked to Bokoum about his soul. Later, Jim Bryant and his family joined us in the work at Djibo. Because I had lived there for several years, Jim asked if I knew anyone who would serve as a night guard for his family.

"Yes," I replied. "I know someone who is better than a German Shepherd, a Doberman Pinscher, or a Pit Bull Terrier." Jim hired Bokoum to be his night guard, and the Bryant family continued to talk to him about salvation. They explained that God wanted to change his life. Little by little Bokoum came to realize that he needed this change, and finally the Bryants led him to the Lord.

Immediately Bokoum's life began to change dramatically, and he burned his fetishes. Today one would never know that he was once a feared criminal. He now has a wife and family, and he tells everyone, even Muslim leaders, what God has done in his life. He knows that true power does not come from fetishes or fists, but from the Spirit of God.

Source: *Intercede* 17, no. 1 (January–February 2001), p. 5. Used by permission. *www.cmmequip.org*

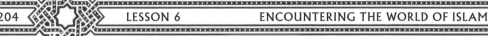
## Types of Magic

Practitioners of popular Islam seek supernatural power through four different types of magic:

| Types of Magic | Description | Example |
|---|---|---|
| Productive | Seeking blessing and success | Visiting a shaman |
| Protective | Seeking protection from things that make them afraid and sick | Using amulets, charms, or potions for protection |
| Destructive | Seeking revenge and ways to hurt their enemies | Placing a curse on someone or something |
| Divination | Seeking to learn about the future or things that may be hidden | Consulting a fortune teller |

Adapted from: Rick Love, *Muslims, Magic, and the Kingdom of God* (Pasadena, Calif.: William Carey Library, 2000).

is what Paul Hiebert has called "the flaw of the excluded middle."[3]

**Tenth**, Jesus has given, and continues to give, authority in both the physical and the spiritual realms. He gave the disciples authority over "serpents and scorpions, and over all the power of the enemy" (v. 19). The story above, of Christians praying for the flooding and erosion to stop, illustrates how God responded to prayer concerning the physical elements. One of the lessons that Christians who are oppressed by spirits need to learn is that they have authority to command them to leave.

**Eleventh**, he would prioritize evangelism over exorcism. The disciples are warned: "Do not rejoice in this, that the spirits are subject to you; but rejoice that your names are written in heaven" (v. 20). Some of those involved in a ministry of exorcism

have found it monopolizing so much of their time that other areas of ministry like evangelism have suffered.

**Twelfth**, Jesus would demonstrate that, instead of being overrun with potentially harmful beings and forces, the universe is under the control of a personal, loving Father. Then Jesus addressed God as "Father, Lord of heaven and earth" (v. 21). Analysis of folk Islam has previously demonstrated that the folk Muslim lives in fear.

**Finally**, Jesus would observe that, for understanding such spiritual realities, simple faith and teachableness are more important than erudition. Christ's prayer recognizes that God has "hidden these things from the wise and understanding and revealed them to babes" (v. 21). Most of us in academia or in foreign missionary

service have had to learn about the spirit world and spiritual warfare from the common people we serve. Richard DeRidder observed how unprepared his formal training in traditional reformed theology left him for dealing with the spirit world in which his people lived. he concluded: "This is a chapter of reformed theology that has still not been written, and perhaps which cannot be written by the West."[4]

## PAUL'S APPROACH

As described in Acts 19, the Ephesus of Paul's day contained the major elements found in folk Islam. It had spirit powers (vv. 11–20) and power objects in the silver shrines of Artemis (v. 24) and the sacred stone that fell from heaven (v. 35), a meteorite like the Black Stone in the Ka'aba in Mecca. It had a power place, the temple of Artemis (v. 27), and power times when there were celebrations in honor of the goddess. There were power rituals performed by the Jewish exorcists who tried to use the name of Jesus as a power word (v. 13). Other rituals would have been used by those who practiced the magic arts (vv. 18–19). We can infer from what Paul said and did in the Ephesian context fifteen principles he would use among folk Muslims.

**The first principle** is that he would engage in power ministries in the context of teaching. In Ephesus, Paul "entered the synagogue and for three months spoke…about the kingdom of God." Then he "argued daily in the hall of Tyrannus. This continued for two years, so that all…heard the word of the Lord" (vv. 8–10). The spiritual effectiveness of Inayat's power ministry in Pakistan, to which we have referred, is that it is always carried on in the context of teaching. Healings and exorcisms that do not occur in the context of extended teaching seldom make much permanent impact on the church. Such teaching was necessary in an African country when a folk Muslim sorcerer followed Christ. Deception had become such a way of life for him that it was a difficult habit to break, a task needing all the spiritual reinforcement possible.

**The second principle** has already been seen in Luke 10; Paul would focus on the receptive. "When some were stubborn and disbelieved, speaking evil of the Way before the congregation [of the synagogue], he withdrew" (v. 9).

**Third**, God would use him in the miracles, but God would be the one accomplishing the task. The account continues: "God did extraordinary [literally, not the ordinary] miracles [literally, powerful deeds] by the hands of Paul" (v. 11). Conversely, folk Muslims tend to focus on the human instrument as the power person.

**Fourth**, the word "extraordinary" reminds us that there is also an ordinary way that God works. So, we may note, God would also use Paul in ordinary ways. We need to remember that the God who does extraordinary things is also the one who established the works through the laws of nature, such as healing through medicine. Even the gift of grace to endure unchanged suffering is a work of God.

**Fifth**, God might let objects convey the power, but the power would be God's, not that of the objects. "Handkerchiefs or

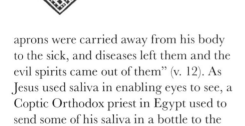

aprons were carried away from his body to the sick, and diseases left them and the evil spirits came out of them" (v. 12). As Jesus used saliva in enabling eyes to see, a Coptic Orthodox priest in Egypt used to send some of his saliva in a bottle to the sick who could not come to him, and God would sometimes heal them.

**Sixth**, real evidence of the power of God is often accompanied by counterfeits. "Itinerant Jewish exorcists," Luke reports, "undertook to pronounce the name of the Lord Jesus over those who had evil spirits" (v. 13). Here, and elsewhere where the activities of those other than Paul are described, the principles are stated without reference to Paul. Folk Muslims have fabrications of the works of the Spirit. Some exorcise spirits in the *Zar* cult, speak in tongues, prophesy concerning the future, or collapse in unconsciousness in a state like being "slain in the Spirit." Discernment is required for deciding between what is real and what is an illusion; what is of God and what is of the devil; and what has a physical, or psychological, or spiritual cause, or any combination of these.

**Seventh**, spirits recognize the authority of Jesus and those in whom he resides.

The evil spirit answered the exorcists: "Jesus I know, and Paul I know, but who are you?" (v. 15). Folk Muslims try to appease or threaten spirits, but the Christian can speak with authority because Christ is over all such powers (Eph. 1:20–21). God's superior power was evident in an African country where a Muslim tried to put a curse on a Christian convert. It backfired, and the Muslim got deathly sick. No medicine man could help him, so he had to contact the Christians, who prayed for him. He was healed and became a Christian.

**Eighth**, spirits have real power, using the bodies they inhabit. The passage continues: "The man in whom the evil spirit was leaped on them, mastered all of them, and overpowered them" (v. 16). In the same African country just described, a sorcerer put a curse on three people who became insane, though they were later restored to mental health through Christian prayer.

**Ninth**, evidence of power elicits fear, which can only be balanced when God is seen as a loving Father. The result in Ephesus was that "fear fell upon them all" (v. 17). As has been demonstrated previously, the everpresent state of mind of folk Muslims is that of fear.

## BELIEF AND PRACTICE

It is plain that the beliefs and practices of ordinary Muslims contradict many formal aspects of the Islamic faith. They indicate a commitment by the masses to popular religion. Unfortunately, that commitment has remained mostly hidden from, or ignored as irrelevant by, western missionaries to Muslims.

Bill Musk, *The Unseen Face of Islam* (Grand Rapids: Monarch Books, 2003), p. 202.
*www.lionhudson.com*

**Tenth**, signs of the power of the kingdom should lead to the exalting of the King. The verse continues: "And the name of the Lord Jesus was extolled" (v. 17). This is often not the case, since folk Muslims just want healing and usually do not care where it comes from. In Mindanao, the sick may go to the Muslim Shaman, the Catholic priest, the government hospital, and the Protestant missionary.

**Eleventh**, Christian converts often continue magical practices.

Ethnographic researcher discovers needs of Muslim women

In Ephesus, many new believers confessed their practices of magic and burned their books on magic (vv. 18–19). In Faisalabad (formerly Lyalpur), Pakistan, people cast off their Muslim amulets at an evangelistic meeting, but once outside, bought St. Christopher's medals as "stronger" Christian amulets. A Christian holy woman in the capital city of Islamabad wrote Bible verses, rather than qur'anic verses, for amulets.

**Twelfth**, magic seeks to manipulate mechanically rather than to submit to the will of God. This is a temptation for Christians as well as Muslims.

**Thirteenth**, materials associated with magic must be destroyed. If a former Muslim sorcerer in an African country had not burned his paraphernalia, he said he probably would have used it to discover and curse those who stole his boat and fishing net, his only means of support for himself and other converts who had lost their jobs and homes.

**Fourteenth**, the demonstration of God's power should lead to the increase of the message rather than be an end in itself. The result in Ephesus was that: "The word of the Lord grew and prevailed mightily" (v. 20). This is why significant church growth has only resulted when power ministries have been combined with teaching.

**Last**, "the powers" with which the Christian must contend are not only spirits but human institutions, be they commercial, religious, legal, or governmental. These are included in the biblical definition of "the powers."[5] The story (in Acts 19) concludes with the silversmiths, who, because of their economic interests, stir up the populace by appealing to their religious concerns and civic pride. Then the legal and governmental institutions are identified as means of expressing complaints or redressing wrongs (vv. 24–39).

Current converts in the countries described have lost their jobs, their families,

and, in some cases, their lives. They have been called disbelievers and have faced court cases to deprive them of their property. In such situations, those Christians with means of livelihood have provided for others. In another case, they have tried to form a cooperative. Though the New Testament leads Christians to expect suffering with no guarantee of escape in this life, God did avenge such treatment in one African town where Muslims have been persecuting Christians. A friend, whose judgment I trust, personally saw and reported that, for five months this year, in daylight, balls of fire struck the fences, and later the homes, of Muslims who persecuted the Christians. God's power comes in judgment as well as mercy.

Last year my wife, youngest son, and I visited Ephesus. The Temple of Artemis, one of the seven wonders of the ancient world, had all sunk into the marsh, except one pillar which bore witness to the glory that had been. Nearby stands the Isa (Jesus) Mosque, representing the orthodox faith that has replaced the old paganism. Yet the mosque is surrounded by homes in which are hung glass replicas of blue eyes (*nazars*) to ward off the evil eye—reminders of the folk beliefs and practices that are mixed with the orthodox. Yet, like the temple before, these too will pass away. All that will be left is the name on the mosque—Jesus—since, as the previous residents were told, he sits "far above all...power" (Eph. 1:21).

## FOR FURTHER STUDY

Rick Love, *Muslims, Magic and the Kingdom of God* (Pasadena, Calif.: William Carey Library, 2000). *www.wclbooks.com*

**End of Key Readings for Lesson 6. See** RECOMMENDED READINGS & ACTIVITIES **on p. 222.**

## ENDNOTES

1. Vivienne Stacey, "The Practice of Exorcism and Healing," *Muslims and Christians on the Emmaus Road*, ed. J. Dudley Woodberry (Monrovia, Calif.: Missions Advanced Research and Communications Center, 1988), pp. 317–31.
2. Ibid., p. 322.
3. Paul Hiebert, "The Flaw of the Excluded Middle," Missiology 10 (January 1982), pp. 35–47.
4. Richard R. DeRidder, *Discipling the Nations* (Grand Rapids: Baker Book House, 1975), p. 222.
5. Walter Wink, *Naming the Powers: The Language of Power in the New Testament* (Philadelphia, Pa.: Fortress Press, 1984).

# POWER ENCOUNTER AMONG FOLK MUSLIMS

*by Rick Love*

Greg Livingstone (co-founder of Frontiers) likes to tell a humorous story from the early days of Frontiers. Greg asked one of his Pentecostal missionaries how he was planning to reach Muslims. The missionary replied, "I'm going to raise the dead!" Shaking his head, Greg queried, "Do you have a Plan B"? People usually laugh at this story. But the majority of missionaries working among folk Muslims wrestle with the supernatural issues that confront them.

More than three-fourths of the Muslim world, approximately 800 million people, are folk Muslims, doctrinally Muslim but animist in practice. Folk Muslims confess Allah but worship spirits. They are more concerned with magic than they are about Muhammad. Frontiers missionaries have shared accounts with me of folk Islam in every region where we serve: North Africa, the Middle East, Central Asia, South Asia, and Southeast Asia. I have interviewed workers in other missions agencies as well, and they give further confirmation of these phenomena.

For example, there is a widespread fear of curses among folk Muslims. Tunisians are afraid that someone will find their fingernail trimmings and use those to curse them. In Yemen, they prefer using a person's hair to curse someone. (Both cases illustrate what is known as *contagious magic.*) In Jordan, one worker talks about "blood blessings" as a frequent practice. If someone buys a car, they will sacrifice a lamb and place the blood on the bumper of the car for protection from the forces of darkness. When a new house is built, they also sacrifice a lamb and apply its blood to the door frames. Morocco actually has "occultic fairs" called *moussem*, which draw as many as twenty thousand people! During these "satanic signs and wonders conferences," people gather in small groups all over the countryside to witness supernatural feats, to offer blood sacrifices, and to receive baraka (blessings). One friend told me of people who, possessed by spirits, would slash themselves with knives without cuts or bleeding. Others would dance in trances, take bites of bread, and then throw the bread out so the crowd could receive the baraka. Two other veteran workers described certain people possessed by animal spirits (like a lion or tiger spirit), who would actually kill a live animal (like a cow) with their bare hands and devour it.

But there is a lighter side to folk Islam. A love potion in Morocco is used to keep

Dr. Rick Love is the international director of Frontiers, a mission agency devoted to glorifying God by planting churches among all unreached Muslim peoples.

Adapted from, Rick Love, "Power Encounter among Folk Muslims: An Essential Key of the Kingdom," *International Journal of Frontier Missions* 13, no. 4 (El Paso, Tex.: International Student Leaders Coalition for Frontier Missions, 1996), pp. 193–95. Used by permission. *www.ijfm.org*

Snake charmer in Marrakesh, Morroco

men faithful to their wives. This magical potion is served in tea and includes the wife's urine. With a hearty laugh, an Arab worker told me that "Every man in Morocco has drunk his wife's urine, from the king down to the poorest peasant!"

After interviewing one worker from Egypt about various types of magical practices among folk Muslims (including weekly, all-night exorcism ceremonies), he exclaimed, "Dallas Theological Seminary didn't prepare me for this!" To be fair, however, most seminaries do not.

Regardless of seminary background or denominational heritage, the issues of signs and wonders challenge everyone involved in reaching folk Muslims.

Demons and magicians are no respecters of theological heritage! For example, one non-charismatic missionary with Frontiers in Central Asia (a Baptist by denomination and a Campus Crusader by training), led a Muslim shaman to Christ. Even though this Muslim convert wanted to serve Christ, he was still drawn to shamanistic practices. Truth encounter alone was not enough! When some non-charismatic Frontiers leaders came to encourage and coach this missionary, they were questioned about spirit realm issues, and signs and wonders. Since they had not dealt with this issue before, they encouraged him to contact other Frontiers missionaries who had experience. He sent out an e-mail to a number of our missionaries and within twenty-fours hours received counsel from five other team leaders. This missionary to Central Asia told me recently that every time their Muslim convert church meets, they have a healing service!

A Presbyterian missionary in Central Asia describes his experiences of power encounter:

> You may find it interesting to know that we have seen more cases of "demonization" here than anywhere we have ever been before. [He has served in two other Muslim countries.] We see cases weekly in cell meetings and on Sundays. The stories I could tell would really shock some of you. But this is reality here. We are

making inroads into a people group where the gospel has never existed before....Have you ever seen a demonized person scream and yell because the written Word of God was being read or spoken? We have! (Taken from a missionary's prayer letter.)

Although once the exclusive domain of Pentecostal and charismatic Christianity, the issue of power encounter is now a major concern of the broader evangelical world. It is an important aspect of reaching folk Muslims. Power encounter—the demonstration of God's power over Satan (primarily in healing and exorcism)—plays an essential role in reaching folk Muslims. Power encounter certainly is not *the* key to the kingdom (as some from signs and wonders backgrounds seem to assume), but it is an essential key to unlocking doors in reaching folk Muslims.

Those from a more traditional evangelical background often fail to realize this fact.

It would seem that signs of the kingdom (power encounter) should lead to the exalting of the King. This is often not the case, however, since folk Muslims want healing and usually do not care where it comes from. In other words, people seeking power do not necessarily seek the Savior. God has used many people in Frontiers in a ministry of signs and wonders. But few of those healed came to Christ! (We do believe they are much more receptive to Christ, however). A coworker of mine estimates that one out of ten who are healed are now following Christ. He compares this with the healing of the ten lepers, only one of whom returned to give thanks to Jesus. One reason for this lack of conversion is the folk Muslim's worldview. Because they live in a world of magic and

## WHY IS BARAKA NEEDED?

Muslims believe God confers *baraka* (blessing) upon humankind. Certain individuals possess the power of baraka, which is manifested in their ability to affect spiritual outcomes. Baraka and its opposite force, curses, are often associated with places, things, words, or gestures.

The Muslim greeting *"As-salaam(u) alaikum(u)"* ("Peace be upon you") is the most common blessing between Muslims. Repeating the first line of each sura in the Qur'an, *"Bismillah al-Rahman al-Rahim"* ("In the name of Allah, the Merciful, the Compassionate") is another common blessing, used to protect and ward off curses and jinn (evil spirits).

Many Muslims live in constant fear of curses and jinn, which they believe God created along with man. "He created man of clay like the potter's, and the jinn did he create of smokeless fire" (Sura 55:14–15, PICKTHALL).

Muslims also believe in Iblis, the one ejected from heaven, who was responsible for Adam and Eve's disobedience. The name Iblis is used interchangeably with *Shaytan* (or Satan), which means "adversary" in Arabic. "'Behold!' We said to the angels, 'Bow down to Adam': They bowed down except Iblis. He was one of the jinn, and he broke the command of his Lord. Will ye then take him and his progeny as protectors rather than me? And they are enemies to you! Evil would be the exchange for the wrong-doers!" (Sura 18:50, YUSUF ALI).

Source: Annee W. Rose, *www.frontiers.org.*

miracles, they are not always awestruck by demonstrations of God's power. On the other hand, if we demonstrate no power, they are even less impressed!

When I first went to the field, I was looking for that dramatic power encounter that would lead to a major breakthrough among the Sundanese. I had the encounter, but not the breakthrough! It happened during martial arts training (known as *pencak silat*).

I was preparing to go to America, and my instructor, Mr. Agus (the founder of Manderaga) was giving me a personal lesson. He started teaching me breathing exercises that were linked to a shoving-type motion. In between exercises, he was telling me stories about the power to knock people over (from a distance without touching them, known as *tanaga dalam*, inner power), as well as the power to heal. He said he himself had often experienced these things. So, I asked him if he would give an example, since I had heard many stories but had never experienced it. He told me to get into a certain stance, and then he started to give me the tanaga dalam shove (from a distance). As he did this, I was praying against the powers of darkness in the name of Jesus. When nothing happened, he asked me to get in another stance. Again, the same shove, the same prayers, and the same results. After trying this for a number of times, he asked me if I wanted to try. Since I had never done this before, I copied the tanaga dalam shove that I had seen. He stood about five feet in front of me. I gave him the

shove, simultaneously praying in the name of Jesus. To my shock, he went flying backwards as if Mike Tyson had hit him. I hadn't touched him at all, and yet a power surged from me that knocked him backwards. This happened a few more times. Finally he stopped, shook his head, prayed, and with a pale, flustered look,...said meekly, "Let's continue our exercise." (Taken from author's field notes.)

This encounter did not lead Mr. Agus to Christ, but because of my experience, I take great comfort in 2 Corinthians 12:12: "The signs of a true apostle were performed among you with all perseverance, by signs and wonders and miracles" (NASB). Paul, the great pioneer church planter, describes his ministry in terms of power encounter. His ministry was characterized by the supernatural. It was also characterized by "all perseverance." Many reject our message from the start. Even those who are healed often reject Christ. But with power and "all perseverance," we will see churches established among folk Muslims.

Some of my closest friends and coworkers in Southeast Asia have had similar experiences. They had often prayed for the sick. Some were healed, some were not. But even when there were manifestations of power, people did not repent. Nevertheless, this couple has persevered, and within the last couple of years, they have seen breakthroughs because of signs and wonders. In one case, a national couple serving with them cast numerous demons out of a Muslim who then repented, along with his family. The man

delivered from demons has become the bridge into the community:

> Samson, a local shaman, unable to sleep due to the occult forces in his life, made the rounds from shaman to shaman, seeking to be delivered of his powers. However, none were able to free him. One evening some time later, Samson went on a rampage, tearing his house apart and shouting wildly. Priscilla and Aquila, the national couple working with our colleagues, ran to his home (two hundred yards away), and began to cast out demons in the name of "The Lord Isa al-Masih." Not experienced in this, they were amazed to observe many different entities leave him, each with its own name and voice. That night all of his amulets and weapons were burned and buried. Beginning the next day, this shaman, who was once feared by all the neighbors, and who had in the past committed hideous sins, was now asking forgiveness of neighbors and witnessing to his family. Several months later, in September 1993,

## PREPARED TO GIVE A DEFENSE

"But in your hearts set apart Christ as Lord. Always be prepared to give an answer to everyone who asks you to give the reason for the hope that you have. But do this with gentleness and respect, keeping a clear conscience, so that those who speak maliciously against your good behavior in Christ may be ashamed of their slander" (1 Peter 3:15–16).

Does this admonition leap to mind when Muslim friends raise objections? "The Bible has been changed." "The Trinity is idolatry." "Jesus is not the Son of God." "God would not let Jesus die." Does our angry frustration mount as our most treasured beliefs are denied? As we prepare a biting reply, God's Spirit reminds us to answer only in gentleness and reverence. After all, Christ commanded us to turn the other cheek. The Spirit whispers, "Only God can truly change hearts. Christ suffered worse indignities on your behalf." We may need to suffer injustice to demonstrate the meaning of his grace and sacrifice.

How do we give an answer, or as other translations put it, a defense or argument for our beliefs? In a court of law, the defense attorney is charged with the responsibility of presenting the client's case with diligence. If the attorney were to quarrel with the judge, his or her license to practice law may be revoked, the client might be afforded a new trial, and the attorney could even be jailed—all for not providing the client with an adequate defense. To advocate properly, the lawyer prepares for the case, researching the judge's previous opinions of the relevant law and decisions in similar cases. The attorney does not start to "argue" the case from the client's perspective but instead begins his presentation from the point of view of the judge or jury. Then step by step, without ever offending those who must decide, the attorney builds a case. Rapport is built with the jury, and the judge is given time to consider the possibility that the client's case has merit from the judge's own point of view. Only when the decision is sure does the attorney ask for a verdict, entrusting the client's fate to the judge and jury.

How much greater is our hope in Jesus Christ than that of a client in a criminal case! Therefore, how much more gently must we build our case in giving a defense for the gospel!

Source: *Encountering the World of Islam*

A Kyrgyz man in a doorway

© Caleb Project

Samson and his wife, his daughter and son-in-law, and one of Aquila's nieces who now lived with him were baptized. They have become the nucleus of a small...fellowship. (Taken from author's personal correspondence.)

The issue of power encounter, or signs and wonders, is not just necessary for evangelistic breakthroughs. It is also a crucial part of the building up of the church. Two things frequently happen in a folk Islamic context that make power encounter a central part of the pastoral process. First of all, I believe "deliverance" needs to be a part of the rite of baptism. People who come out of folk Islam are immersed in spirit powers, charms, and amulets. We cannot simply ask them to repent in a general way and believe that this is sufficient. I find it more than just an interesting historical fact that exorcism was a part of baptismal preparation in the early church.

In April 1995, I had the privilege of participating in a baptism of a folk Muslim convert that included deliverance. The baptism ceremony began with a prayer of renunciation prior to the actual baptism. Everyone being baptized made a public renunciation of any type of magic. They publicly declared, "I renounce every act of seeking power for myself through magic, charms, or amulets of any kind." Then the pastor asked each baptismal candidate if they had been involved in magic of any kind. Only one man admitted that he had. (In this particular baptism, many of the candidates were teenagers who had not been involved in magic.) Next, the leaders of the church took the man into a different room and had a special deliverance for him. The pastor challenged him to say, "Jesus is Lord of my life." At first he could not. We prayed against the forces of darkness, and continued to tell the man being prayed for to submit himself fully to the Lord. He then confessed Jesus as Lord, along with renouncing every form of occultic practices. Finally, he convulsed, the spirits left, and he was set free.

This leads to a second point about power ministry among converts from folk Islam. It is very typical for those converted from folk Islam to revert and go to a shaman in times of crisis. Another man in this same congregation had gone to a shaman just prior to the baptismal service described above. When this man heard the prayer of renunciation and the testimony of the other man's deliverance, he confessed his sin in this area and was also prayed for.

A close friend of mine, who has served more than eight years in Southeast Asia among folk Muslims, has seen much fruit.

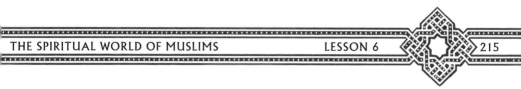

But he has also experienced his share of suffering and setbacks. His Navigator training and Baptist heritage have not prepared him for the spiritual warfare he has encountered. He says that the powers of darkness are the hardest things he has had to face in his ministry. He believes that most of the young converts he works with still suffer from various levels of demonization. Because of this, he now sets aside time at the end of almost every public meeting for repentance and prayers of deliverance.

Repentance in a folk Islamic context must involve both renunciation of occultic practices and deliverance from these forces. The texts that have been most helpful to me in this regard are Deuteronomy 18:9–15 and Acts 19:18–20. In Deuteronomy, spiritism of any kind is described as detestable and forcefully denounced. Instead of going to a shaman, Moses called the people of God to listen to the coming prophet, the prophet Jesus (*Nabi Isa*). Acts 19 deals with these issues in a complementary fashion by illustrating the nature of repentance for folk Muslims. There needs to be public confession of occult practices, along with the destruction of every charm and amulet (regardless of monetary value).

But there are other, more positive types of power encounters as well. In my early days on the field, I met a Muslim named Pono who had heard the gospel and told me he wanted to be saved. With great enthusiasm I shared the gospel with him, but he was not impressed. He said he understood, but he wanted to be sure of his salvation. So I suggested the possibility that Pono had already accepted Christ, but he was just struggling with sin. I turned to passages in the New Testament about the flesh and the spirit and explained those to him. Pono just shook his head. All of a sudden, I realized that this was not an issue of truth encounter. It was an issue of power encounter.

I told Pono that I was going to lay hands on him and pray that the Holy Spirit would come upon him and fill him. As I laid my hands on Pono and prayed, the Holy Spirit came upon him. The power and presence of God filled the room. Pono met God that day and he has never been the same (see Acts 19:16 for a similar experience). Pono had a power encounter. After this experience, I patiently (and sometimes impatiently) discipled him. Pono has become the pastor of a Muslim convert church. "Signs and wonders—with all perseverance!"

Folk Muslims believe they are at the mercy of spirits, demons, evil eye curses, and sorcery. Because of this, they are more preoccupied with magic than they are with Muhammad. Folk Muslims push the issue of power encounter to the forefront. The sick need healing. Will they be healed by magic or by Christ? The demonized need deliverance. Will the shaman or the missionary do it? The fearful need protection. Will it come through a charm or through him who came to destroy the works of the devil (1 John 3:8)? Power encounter is not the only key to reaching the hearts of folk Muslims, but it needs to be an essential factor in effectively evangelizing them, and in planting the church of Jesus Christ in their midst.

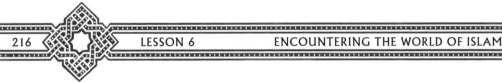

# MYSTICISM: ESCAPE FROM THE LAW

*by Don McCurry*

Sufism is the English word derived from the Arabic word for mysticism. The word has an interesting history. Most scholars agree that "Sufi"came from the Arabic word *suf* for wool. Sufis were ascetics who adopted a simple lifestyle in protest against the opulence of their godless Muslim rulers. In a sense, they renounced the world and went seeking God. They wore rough woolen garments from which they got their nickname "wooleys" or Sufis.

## THE DEVELOPMENT OF SUFISM

There were several reasons for the birth of this movement. Muslim caliphs were no exception to the rule that "power corrupts, and absolute power corrupts absolutely." Following the great success of the Muslim armies in the early centuries of Islam, a great gap developed between the rulers who became corrupt and the pious scholars who were powerless against them. Among the pious scholars there was a division between those who thought they could own property and lead normal lives, and those who wanted to renounce the world, follow a path of physical self-denial, and seek God. The Sufis were those who renounced the world and became seekers.

Sufism received a further impetus from the bitter wars over orthodoxy and law. These endless controversies led to a great sterility of the spirit. In reaction to this, many pious Muslims sought to have experiences with God rather than debates about him. Sufism was further stimulated by the daring thought that, if Muhammad could receive revelations from God, so could others. Without creating new scriptures, they wanted to replicate Muhammad's experiences of direct contact with God. In addition, Michael Nazir-Ali points out, "Sufism developed as a result of stimulus which Muslims received from the Christian monasticism of the Middle East"[1]

Islamic mysticism, at its best, could be represented by the sayings of Rabiah al-Adawiyya (713–801) of Basra:

> I exist in God and am altogether his. I live in the shadow of his command....To a royal Husband am I betrothed, and to him do I minister; and if I leave his ministry, my Betrothed will be wroth with me and will write me a letter of divorce and will dismiss me from his house.[2]

> I have loved thee with two loves, a selfish love and a love that is worthy

---

Don McCurry is currently the director of the Summer Institute of Muslim Studies, president of Ministries to Muslims, and the acting director of the Ibero-American Institute of Transcultural Studies in Spain. He is a veteran missionary who has worked in Pakistan and pioneered work in Central Asia with Open Doors. Additionally, he has prepared Egyptian missionaries for the Arab world. Dr. McCurry edited *The Gospel and Islam*.

Adapted from Don McCurry, *Healing the Broken Family of Abraham* (Colorado Springs: Ministries to Muslims, 2001), pp. 89–94. Used by permission. *www.mtmsims.org*

of thee. As for the love which is selfish, therein I occupy myself with thee, to the exclusion of all others. But in the love which is worthy of thee, thou dost raise the veil that I may see thee. Yet is the praise not mine in this or that, but the praise is to thee, in both that and this.[3]

## SUFI BELIEFS

Gradually, Sufism developed both structurally and metaphysically. What was at first a form of religion adopted by individuals and communicated to a small circle of companions gradually became a monastic system, a school of saints, with rules of discipline and devotion. Sufi novices (*murids*) learned these from spiritual directors (pir, *ustadh*, or *murshid*), to whose guidance they submitted themselves absolutely.[4]

The development of theosophical thought in the movement is most noteworthy.

Theosophy is any of various forms of philosophical or religious thought based on supposed insights into the divine nature. Fazlur Rahman explains:

> The early ascetic piety, with its emphasis on the interiorization of the motive, was a reaction to the external development of the law. During the ninth and tenth centuries, Sufism developed a doctrine of "gnosis," of an inner experiential knowledge (*marifah*), which it progressively came to oppose to the intellectual knowledge (*ilm*) of theology, which developed during the same period.[5]

Thus, in the course of a century, Sufism, which was initially little more than asceticism, became first mystical and then theosophical, and even ran the risk of being confused with pantheism.[6] Still later, Sufism bred all kinds of disorderly and frenzied rituals involving self-inflicted

## "WHICH PIR DO YOU FOLLOW?"

"Henry" is a local believer who serves alongside SIM missionaries in a ministry of compassion in Asia. One day Henry was walking in his home area. A middle-aged stranger called to him "Peace on you, brother." "And on you be peace," replied Henry.

The stranger invited Henry to come over and chat for a while. A few moments of typical friendly conversation over a cup of sweet tea followed. Then the stranger said: "I have been watching you for a long time, and you are different. Your behavior is different, your family is different, your way of life is different. Which pir do you follow?"

A pir is a folk Muslim spiritual leader, living or dead. Many pirs, or their gravesites, are reputed to have magical powers. Some estimates say that more than 70 percent of the people of this particular country are adherents of a pir.

The stranger correctly surmised that Henry's life was different because he was a follower of a different teacher. Realizing this as a God-given opportunity, Henry led the man to a more private place, and bit by bit started to tell him about the "other holy books" (the Law, Prophets, and Gospels). As a result, this new friend is now meeting weekly with Henry to study the Bible.

Source: *Serving in Mission* 102, p. 12, *www.sim.org*.

wounds, swaying chanters falling unconscious to the floor, or members whirling themselves into religious ecstasy, only to be hung up by their feet until they returned to their senses. Such scenes were graphically described by eyewitness John A. Subhan.[7]

All of the orders of Sufism do not follow the same stages of discipline. Each order sets its own rules. Below, Subhan describes the steps or stages of the mystic journey laid out for the disciple in the Sufi Order to which he formerly belonged[8]:

1. Repentance: Awakening from indifference to evil and developing a sense of contrition for sin.

2. Love: The adept gives himself to remembrances of the names of God and seeks to exclude all thoughts except of God.

3. Renunciation: The aspirant is urged to observe poverty and renounce all worldly desires. Ultimately, he renounces all but God himself.

4. Knowledge: The aspirant contemplates the nature, attributes, and works of God, until God is all he thinks about.

5. Ecstasy: By remembering and reciting the names and attributes of God, a state of mental excitement or ecstasy is induced.

## ASK GOOD QUESTIONS

The worldviews and attitudes of the Muslims we meet may be influenced by their religious and educational backgrounds, politics, and how much they understand the Christian faith. Asking good questions will show us where our Muslim friend is coming from and help us build a relationship. Our questions can help us understand the other person's worldview, feelings, and aspirations—touching his heart, and not just his mind. Questions we might ask include:

> Can you tell me about where you are from?
> What is the best thing about your country?
> What did you like and dislike about growing up there?
> What do you like about this country?
> What did you like about being raised a Muslim?
> Who is Jesus, in your opinion?
> What have you heard about him, and how do you know it is true?
> Have you read the Injil the New Testament, which is the revelation given to Jesus?
> Why do you think there are different religions?

I was distributing copies of the Injil to passengers in cars waiting for a ferry from Europe to North Africa. When I offered one man an Injil, he told me he was a Muslim and an imam. Excited, I was led to focus my communication on one issue, pointing out that Islam teaches about the Prophet Jesus, and that his message, the Injil, was sent by God. He asked me if I had read the Qur'an. "Yes," I was able to answer, "twelve times." In turn, I asked him if he had read the Injil. When he said he had not, I exclaimed, "You are the religious teacher and have never read the Message given to Prophet Jesus?" Convicted, he took a copy and promised to read it. I believe the Word of God will not return void and will do its work with this man.

Source: Fouad Masri, *www.crescentproject.org*.

6. Reality: The heart is now supposed to be illuminated with the true nature of God. At this point, the aspirant is to seek to be utterly dependent on God—to trust him.

7. Union: At this stage, the mystic believes he "sees" God face-to-face. The mystic believes his old self is annihilated, and he is utterly satisfied with God and God is utterly satisfied with him.

The Sufi emphasis on the inner experience was coupled with the deep desire to escape from one's self, or as the Sufi would put it, the annihilation of self, thus making possible one's absorption into God. In addition to offering a supposed "seeing" of God, or union with God, Sufism was characterized by the spontaneity with which local groups could spring up around an itinerant preacher or a homegrown mystic of great piety. In the course of its development, the heads of these orders (or their followers) felt it necessary to trace the divine light resident in their leader (pir or sheik) back to Muhammad himself.[9]

Sufis meet either in established meeting houses, or informally wherever it is convenient. Natural groupings of people can voluntarily come together. For example, farmer types in rural communities, men gathered together in military units, men of similar professions and trades, women in local neighborhoods, and units of like-minded people within a city. In short, any natural grouping of people could unite anywhere around a pious leader.

## THE RECOVERY OF MUSIC

Sufi orders encouraged the use of poetry and music. Talented composers wrote beautiful music for their love songs to God. Some brotherhoods encouraged dancing as part of worship. Since music and dancing were never permitted in the mosque, Sufis built their own lodges or met outdoors.

It was Zephaniah, the prophet, inspired by God's Spirit, who has revealed to us that God sings. "The Lord your God is with you; he is mighty to save. He will take great delight in you he will quiet you with his love; he will rejoice over you with singing" (Zeph. 3:17). And why would he not? After all, we are made in his image and we sing. He loves to hear us sing. And he has given us his Spirit to assist us in singing: "Be filled with the Spirit. Speak to one another with psalms, hymns, and spiritual songs. Sing and make music in your heart to the Lord, always giving thanks to God the Father for everything, in the name of our Lord Jesus Christ" (Eph. 5:18b–20). Muslims therefore, have turned to romantic and folkloric music. The Sufis could not help but "borrow" religious music from their neighbors—God made us musical. We Christians have so much to offer Sufis in our rich tradition of music.

It was the "singing Sufis" who led so many pagans into the folds of Islam. Now it is our turn to lead the Sufis into the arms of Jesus with music and song. "Let us come before him with thanksgiving and extol him with music and song" (Ps. 95:2). Dancing, too, to the music of many instruments, is to have its place in the winning

## Hierarchy of Powers and Beings in a Popular Islamic Worldview

| POWERS | BEINGS OR PERSONS | UNIVERSE |
|---|---|---|
| Fate | God | "Otherly" Universe |
| Qur'an | Angels | Realm of God (Eternal) |
| | | |
| Magic, Sorcery | Satan, Devils | Spiritual Universe |
| Astrology, Divination | Jinn | Realm of Angels (Eternal) |
| Baraka (Blessing) | Prophets | |
| Dhikr | Dead Saints | |
| Evil Eye | Spirits | |
| Omens | Ancestors | |
| Vows, Curses | Souls of Recently Dead | |
| | Dreams – Visions – Sleep | |
| Herbs | Holy Men | Temporal Universe |
| Drugs | Humans | Realm of People and |
| Natural Forces | Animals | Things (Not Eternal) |
| | Plants | |

Source: Bill Musk, *Unseen Face of Islam* (Grand Rapids: Monarch Books, 2004) p. 174.

of the Sufis, for some Sufi orders dance in search of ecstasy. The psalmist writes:

> Let them praise his name with dancing and make music to him with tambourine and harp. For the Lord takes delight in his people; he crowns the humble with salvation (Ps. 149:3–4).

> Praise him with the sounding of the trumpet, praise him with the harp and lyre, praise him with tambourine and dancing, praise him with the strings and flute, praise him with the clash of cymbals, praise him with resounding cymbals Let everything that has breath praise the Lord. Praise the Lord (Ps. 150:3–6).

Let us help the Sufis discover their real roots in Jesus. Let us use their very strength in music and song to woo them to the true God.

## THE SPREAD OF SUFISM

From humble beginnings in the eighth and ninth centuries, these Sufi orders swept the Muslim world and constituted a highly successful, missionary movement in the centuries that followed. It is generally conceded that the "singing Sufis" did as much to convert pagans to Islam as did

the Muslim armies. Sufism could exist as a highly organized secret order, or individuals could meet in loose, unorganized associations. A member could be residential or attend as a volunteer.

Along with all the strengths and advantages that this movement offered its members, Sufism suffered many weaknesses. By offering the devotee supposed direct access to God, it weakened the place of the law, lessened the position of the Qur'an and the Hadith, and led to a great deal of nominalism and, in many cases, moral laxity.

One of the unusual things one will notice about Sufism is that it is so pervasive. In one variety or another, it is found throughout the Muslim world. Theoretically, one can be a member of most Muslim sects and still be a member of a Sufi order, although offering a seeker "direct access to God" renders the need for a Shi'i-type imam or ayatollah unnecessary. This

belief in direct access to God, by the way, allowed many Shi'a to defect to Sufism and the Sunni branch of Islam.

**End of Basic Readings for Lesson 6. See** RECOMMENDED READINGS & ACTIVITIES **on p. 222.**

**Go to:**
***www.encounteringislam.org/readings*** **to find the Full Readings for Lesson 6.**

## ENDNOTES

1. *Frontiers in Muslim–Christian Encounter* (Oxford: Regnum Books, 1987), p. 22.
2. Margaret Smith, *Studies in Early Mysticism in the Near and Middle East* (Oxford: Oneworld Publications, 1995), p. 186.
3. Ibid., p. 223.
4. R. A. Nicholson, *Studies in Islamic Mysticism* (Cambridge: University Press, 1907), p. 392.
5. Fazlur Rahman, *Islam*, 2d ed. (Chicago: University of Chicago Press, 1979) p. 141.
6. Nicholson, *Studies*, p. 391.
7. John A. Subhan, *Sufism: Its Saints and Shrines* (Lucknow, India: Lucknow Publishing House, 1938), pp. 1–4.
8. Ibid., pp. 68–72.
9. Phil Parshall, *Bridges to Islam* (Grand Rapids: Baker Book House, 1983), p. 57.

# DISCUSSION QUESTIONS

1. What needs are Muslims trying to meet by practicing popular Islam?

2. What are some of the things that you, or people you know, do or say that might seem like attempts to manipulate God into fulfilling your needs or desires?

3. When faced with difficulties in your life and the reality of supernatural forces, what would it look like if you plainly demonstrated trust in God's love and sovereignty?

# RECOMMENDED READINGS & ACTIVITIES*

Read: Rick Love, *Muslims, Magic, and the Kingdom of God* (Pasadena, Calif.: William Carey Library, 2000).

Bill Musk, *The Unseen Face of Islam*, new ed. (London: Monarch Books, 2003).

Watch: View an American or western movie or TV drama. Note the role of spiritual icons or powers. How do these unstated beliefs compare to popular or ordinary Muslims' beliefs?

Pray: Use some or all of the six postures of prayer Muslims use in salat in your own prayers. See "The Postures of Prayer" on page 91.

Visit: Shop in an international market, asking shopkeepers about unfamiliar foodstuffs. Try unusual dishes in an ethnic restaurant, engaging the manager or waitperson in friendly conversation.

Surf: Discover related web sites at *www.encounteringislam.org/lessonlinks*.

---

\* For expanded details on these Recommended Readings & Activities, visit *www.encounteringislam.org/lessonlinks*.

# CHRISTIANITY
# AND ISLAM

# LESSON 7
## CULTURAL BARRIERS

## PONDER THIS

- What are some misconceptions Muslims and Christians have about each other?

- Why is community life so important to Muslims?

- What role did your family play in your coming to Christ? How might a Muslim's family influence his or her decision to follow Christ?

- What values do Muslims have that are attractive to you?

# LESSON OBJECTIVE

Describe the perception of cultural expressions of Christianity which are barriers to Muslims coming to Christ. Include:

1.  Our mode of interaction (theological focus rather than relational).

2.  Historical barriers (including the Crusades and colonialism).

3.  Muslim and Christian ideas of community and relationships.

4.  Sociological and cultural misunderstandings (behavioral differences in dress, diet, family, and morals; for instance, drinking, movies, and TV).

5.  Economics and politics.

# LESSON READINGS

# INTRODUCTION

Making friends in India

Are we beginning to commend ourselves again? Or do we need, like some people, letters of recommendation to you or from you? You yourselves are our letter, written on our hearts, known and read by everybody. You show that you are a letter from Christ, the result of our ministry, written not with ink but with the Spirit of the living God, not on tablets of stone but on tablets of human hearts.

Such confidence as this is ours through Christ before God. Not that we are competent in ourselves to claim anything for ourselves, but our competence comes from God. He has made us competent as ministers of a new covenant—not of the letter but of the Spirit; for the letter kills, but the Spirit gives life (2 Cor. 3:1–6).

Like the Corinthians to whom Paul was writing, Muslims will recognize the truth in our witness when our communication issues from within our deep and lasting friendship relationships with them.

A person's reluctance to put his trust in Jesus usually does not rest primarily on theological doubt. A Muslim considering Christianity will wonder, "How will my family react? What will be the consequences of my decision culturally, politically, economically, or socially within the community? How will this affect my allegiance to my family and community? Who will be my friends? Who will I marry?" These questions affect the decision to follow Jesus even in societies that are not community-oriented.

Similarly, a person's hesitations about the message of the gospel cannot usually be overcome by a one-time decision to follow Christ. Attitudes toward new messages change incrementally, and a premature focus on contrasting Islamic beliefs over against new, unfamiliar theology can quickly entrench those we witness to in their presuppositions about Christianity. Lifelong adherence to Christ may start with a personal decision, but life choices are rarely made in response to rational arguments for or against beliefs, values, and behaviors. The West's model of

direct communication and emphasis on undeniable proof may show thoughtless lack of respect for a culture in which indirect forms of communication are more persuasive in changing their attitudes and building consensus decisions.

## Dimensions of Response to Christ

| | |
|---|---|
| **Cognitive:** | **Knowledge of the gospel** |
| **Affective:** | **Attitude toward the gospel** |
| **Presumptive:** | **Evaluation of the gospel** |
| **Volitional:** | **Decisions about the gospel** |

## THE BARRIERS

Understanding cultural, sociological, historical, political, and economic concerns are of primary importance in our approach to Muslims. What are their deepest issues and felt needs? Once we understand Muslims' cultural contexts and the historical obstacles between us, we can address these barriers. Then we may find significant opportunities to share our faith with Muslims. But, if we fail to address sociological issues in our relationships with Muslims, they may reject our words and actions before ever really hearing or seeing the beauty of the gospel. Providentially, as yet, humankind has not developed an effective defense against love, humility, vulnerability, and authenticity lived out in relationships. This was Christ's method and Paul's.

Many times Muslims react against our culture and are unable to focus on the gospel message we intend to proclaim. Islam was founded partially in reaction to the "Greek-ness" of Christianity. This lesson asks: How can we communicate the gospel message more clearly with less cultural baggage? How can we affirm the positive aspects of Muslim society, use these as bridges to build a biblical understanding and worldview, and call on the Holy Spirit to redeem and correct our methods of sharing our faith?

Muslims react strongly against so-called Christian behaviors: immodest dress, offensive diets, drunkenness, drug use, dysfunctional families, abortion, homosexuality, and other immorality demonstrated in television, movies, and pornography exported to Muslim communities. We cannot just write these off as negative byproducts of western culture, and not a picture of true Christianity. Many Muslims have yet to meet Christians who abhor these practices and effectively articulate that opinion, Christians who are honestly critiquing their own culture.

Imagine yourself a Muslim visiting a church service: the sexes mix freely; wor-

## BARBED WIRE

A great barbed-wire barrier of peripheral offense has often been erected by well-intentioned missionaries. The biblical message has become interwoven with western economics, politics, and a very western approach to religion.

Phil Parshall, *Muslim Evangelism* (Waynesboro, Ga.: Authentic Media, 2003), p. 85.

shipers wear shoes and sit on pews in the presence of God; people talk even as the service starts, to rock music, with worship dance performed by immodestly dressed women; and wine is served at communion! Might not that Muslim exclaim, "God, please rescue me from this discothèque!"? How we dress, what we eat, how long we live among Muslims, what our attitudes are toward their culture, how we use our money, how we raise our children, even what kind of house we live in all affect Muslims' impression of Christ.

In 1 Corinthians 9, Paul declares that we endure all things so that we will cause no hindrance to the gospel of Christ. The only acceptable stumbling block can be Christ, not our cultural behavior. Therefore, Paul became a Jew culturally to win the Jews, and a Greek culturally to win the Greeks. Surely, we can do the same for Muslims. In Galatians and elsewhere, Paul strongly argues that the Greeks did not need to adopt Jewish practices in order to become Christians. Surely, we can allow Muslims to stay in

## Cultural and Social Barriers That Turn Away Inquirers

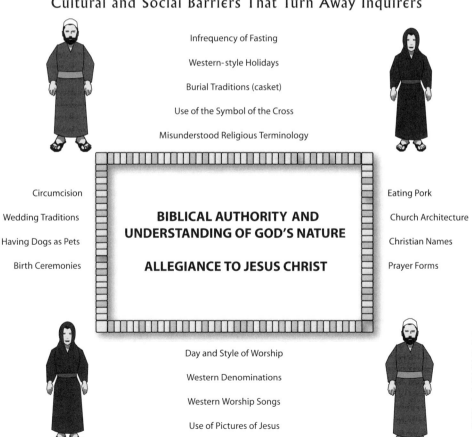

Infrequency of Fasting

Western-style Holidays

Burial Traditions (casket)

Use of the Symbol of the Cross

Misunderstood Religious Terminology

Circumcision

Wedding Traditions

Having Dogs as Pets

Birth Ceremonies

**BIBLICAL AUTHORITY AND UNDERSTANDING OF GOD'S NATURE**

**ALLEGIANCE TO JESUS CHRIST**

Eating Pork

Church Architecture

Christian Names

Prayer Forms

Day and Style of Worship

Western Denominations

Western Worship Songs

Use of Pictures of Jesus

Style of Dress

Source: Phil Parshall, © Caleb Project

their cultural context while they are being transformed by Christ.

Historical barriers also influence how Muslims feel about Christianity. For us, the Crusades and colonialism may be distant history, but these memories are echoed in Muslims' present-day thinking as they interpret current events in Israel, Bosnia, Kosovo, and Iraq. Can we be nationalists first and biblical Christians second? What does the Bible say about justice for the poor and the politically oppressed? Do we react only when Christians are persecuted, while ten times as many Muslims are abused by "Muslim" dictators? Many Christian humanitarian organizations have excellent records of offering assistance to all those in need, regardless of religious background. Could Christians go further by seeking reconciliation, asking for forgiveness, and pressuring governments to address long-standing conflicts affecting Muslims?

Typically, we view questions of economics and politics as non-religious topics. How Muslims feel mistreated by western countries, unfairly judged for their human rights record, and inundated by western pop culture and products: these sensitivities may not have registered with us as factors in how we represent Christ to Muslims. We may try to quickly distance ourselves from "Christian" government policies, and we may disagree with western "Christian" figures in the news, but should we speak out more adamantly against these things? "What would Jesus do?" does not merely apply to children obeying their parents. Christian values have economic and political consequences, whether the issue is exploitation of Jews, or of Palestinian Christians and Muslims, or of ourselves.

## GREATEST FELT NEED, GREATEST POWER

In addition, the western cultural value of individualism often causes friction in societies where conformity and the group are valued more highly than the individual. Muslims often perceive Christians of the West as relationally insincere and aloof. Often we tend to make friends and encourage a response to the gospel among already independent, non-conformist or culturally rebellious individuals, thus cutting off the potential strength of community in the life of the Muslim-background-believing church. Moreover, when Muslims become Christians, we often delay baptizing them until they have a proven track record. One consequence of this is that baptism becomes a rite of passage rather than a celebration of welcome into community. Yet, Muslim-background believers suffer an unusual sense of isolation western Christians do not comprehend. They hunger for community to fill the void left by what they have given up, especially if their families have rejected them because of their newfound faith.

In order to be good friends to Muslims, we need to understand their political and economic realities. We should encourage them to mentor us in learning about their cultures, languages, and values. Building trust takes time, as does finding those who are spiritually sensitive or seeking God. The early church struggled with community issues of unity, morality, rights, acceptable food, freedoms, standards,

propriety in worship, body life, and love. First and Second Corinthians are devoted to helping new believers wrestle with these dilemmas. One of the central solutions proffered for all of these complications is the energetic personal activity of the Spirit of Christ in the community of believers and evidence of his work in us. We desire to express our love of Christ and the biblical truths of salvation to our Muslim friends. However, we cannot do this solely through persuasive words.

> For Christ did not send me to baptize, but to preach the gospel—not with words of human wisdom, lest the Cross of Christ be emptied of its power. (1 Cor. 1:17)

> When I came to you, brothers, I did not come with eloquence or superior wisdom as I proclaimed to you the testimony about God. For I resolved to know nothing while I was with you except Jesus Christ and him crucified. I came to you in weakness and fear, and with much trembling. My message and my preaching were not with wise and persuasive words, but with a demonstration of the Spirit's power, so that your faith might not rest on men's wisdom, but on God's power. (1 Cor. 2:1–5)

*– K.S., Editor.*

## FOR FURTHER STUDY
Anne Cooper and Elsie Markwell, ed. *Ismael, My Brother: A Christian Introduction to Islam* (Grand Rapids: Monarch Books, 2003).

# THE VALLEY OF DECISION

*by Lyndi Parshall Thomas*

It was a beautiful, tropical sunny day. A chicken scurried across the road. Akbar Khan watched it as he walked toward the village market. He turned down the dusty street, and there stood the talk of the town. A large, bright yellow building stood majestically before him, practically shining in the blazing morning sun. He stood on the corner watching what was going on. People were walking through the gate, dressed in their best clothes.

Just yesterday, his father had laughed at the person everyone called a missionary. Akbar wasn't too sure what he thought about the man. He had observed him when the building they called a "church" was being built. The missionary always wore clean suits, and he seemed to have plenty of them. Of course, if he supplied the money to build the building, he must have a lot of money left over.

Just then, he saw Mohammed, the silversmith, go in the gate of the church. Akbar watched with curiosity. There was word going around that Mohammed had come to believe what the missionary was preaching. People said his attitude had changed and that he was a much nicer man now, with more patience.

Akbar's curiosity grew. What did this missionary have to say? Most of the people in his village spoke contemptuously of the white man. They were jealous of his money and wondered why he couldn't use it to help them instead of spending it on a silly building.

A young boy chasing a stray cow ran into Akbar, jolting him into remembering that he was supposed to be canvassing for the prices of lamps. The month of fasting would be coming up soon, and he wanted to have a good lamp by which to see when he ate in the early hours of the morning.

Akbar was tempted to go inside this foreign church and see for himself what was going on. His wife would probably get mad at him if he did. Slowly, he walked towards the gate, noticing the barbed wire running along the top of the high wall. It was placed there to keep out the beggar kids. Then he looked up at the cross standing tall on the top of the building. How awful! The cross! What a symbol of hatred that represented to Akbar. It reminded him of the grotesque stories he had learned in school about the Crusades—how his Muslim ancestors had been killed by cross-carrying Crusaders.

Akbar decided not to think about it but to go on in. He felt strange going to a place of worship on Sunday. Normally, he would have gone on a Friday. He followed the little brick walkway past the small cement house where the national evangelist lived

---

Lyndi Parshall Thomas is a missionary kid from Bangladesh and wrote this paper when she was a high school student at Faith Academy in Manila.

Adapted from Phil Parshall, ed., *The Last Great Frontier* (Philippines: Open Doors with Brother Andrew, 2001), pp. 185–188. Used by permission. *www.opendoors.org*

with his family. He looked in and saw a fan hanging from the ceiling. What luxury! Electricity! Why, even the Muslim holy man doesn't have a cement house. Only the banker and other high class people have electricity. He then made his way to the front door of the church.

Akbar reached down to unbuckle his sandals, but he noticed that there were hardly any shoes outside compared to the number of people inside. How repulsive! In a mosque, no one is allowed to wear shoes. He pulled off his sandals, added them to the small pile, and walked in the door. He looked up towards the front of the room and saw an elevated stand that held some books on it. He saw another cross behind the pulpit.

His eyes swept the room. It was full of chairs—new ones. Where did the white man get all his money? "How different from the mosque where you sit on the floor," he thought. He noticed that men were on one side and women on the other. That was good, but even that was unique because women usually would not go to a mosque.

On the front row, sitting all together, was the missionary's family—husband, wife, and two daughters. Akbar was amazed to see them all together on the women's side. He hoped no one else would be offended like he was.

His eyes fell on a picture on the wall. It was of a man who looked nice enough, with long hair and a beard. But then,

How does our behavior affect our impressions on Muslims?

slowly Akbar read the words under the picture: "Jesus Christ." He couldn't believe it! No Muslim would have a picture of a prophet hanging on a wall! It was totally forbidden. His thoughts were interrupted when a little boy ran by him. He turned around and looked for a place to wash his face, hands, and feet. Surely, they would have a washing place like the mosque did. But, no, there was none. He walked down the center aisle looking for someone he knew. He saw a few familiar faces, but he decided to sit by himself so he could silently analyze the service. He found a seat and sat down. Picking up one of the books, he saw that it was thick and nicely bound. He opened it and tried to read it, but he couldn't really understand the words. One word he saw was "Bible." This was the Christian's Holy Book! Did they just let it lay around where it could get messed up? Didn't they care if someone dropped it or touched it with dirty hands?

He looked up and saw the missionary's children running around. In a mosque, children wouldn't be allowed to be a nuisance. The children were playing with the same type of book he had in his hands—the Bible. Didn't the missionaries care if their children showed disrespect to a Holy Book?

Akbar saw flowers by the pump organ and wondered if they were for decoration, or if they were an offering to the Jesus man. He caught sight of a paper lying on the floor that a child had dropped. There was a picture on the paper of a small fenced area with some animals in it. He saw a cow, a horse, and a pig. A PIG!! How terrible. Oh, that's right. The missionary didn't think pork was bad. Now that he thought about it, Akbar remembered that someone

had told him the missionaries buy pork from the Christian butcher. They actually eat the vile meat!

He looked up towards the white man and his family again. What beautiful clothes they wore. How that watch shone in the sun. Looking at the missionary's wife, he saw that she wore a sleeveless long dress. Even the high class women in the town didn't wear sleeveless blouses with their saris. It was indecent! He noticed that she didn't have any way to cover her head when she prayed.

Just then, the evangelist stood up in the front and began to talk. He welcomed everyone, and then gave some announcements. Then he told them to turn to page thirty in a songbook. Were they going to

## EVANGELISM AS A PROCESS

Isn't "So how many were saved on your last mission trip?" the usual question? Or, "How many were baptized?" "How many attend your church?" Why this focus on numbers? Too often our goal-oriented culture binds us, fooling us into thinking figures and events tell the story and measure the task. Are we are satisfied if someone keeps us accountable to such goals?

Evangelism is a process—of befriending, supporting, and loving, and our progress should be measured against the goal of becoming more like Christ. I am encouraged by God from his Word, specifically, his servant Paul's testimony: "I planted the seed, Apollos watered it, but God made it grow" (1 Cor. 3:6). We all have our "assigned tasks" in God's field, but God is the one who grows the seed and gives salvation in his time. Ministry among Muslims can take a long time, sometimes years, before the first fruits are seen. As God is the One responsible for the outcome, we should enjoy the friendships and the process!

On my overseas assignment, my coworker Peter befriended a Muslim named Mahmud. After seven years, Peter expressed frustration, questioning whether he was wasting his time in this relationship. Even though Peter had helped Mahmud many times (he had found him a job), Mahmud seldom expressed any spiritual interest. Our team prayed for them both, encouraging Peter to press on. At the next meeting, Peter had exciting news. Mahmud had told him, "I've known you for seven years, and often wondered if you were really my friend, or if I was just another potential convert to Christianity. I've decided that you really have been a caring friend, and now I want to be baptized."

Source: Annee W. Rose, *www.frontiers.org*.

sing? Sure enough, a man got up, went to the pump organ, and began to play. It was very strange to Akbar as Muslims only chant their songs.

Akbar reached for the only other book he saw and found the page. He couldn't read well enough to follow along too well, so he just listened. The tunes sounded totally foreign. He could tell everyone was having trouble singing the song. He liked chanting much better.

The foreigner then stood up and read a passage out of the Bible. My, what an accent! After ten years in this country, couldn't he speak more like we do? Akbar noticed that most of the national women covered their heads, but the white woman did not. When the foreigner was finished reading, he sat down and the service went on. They then said they would take an offering. Some men got up and passed around a plate so that people could drop their money into it. In a mosque this would not be done in such a manner. The church system seemed like begging to him. He wondered what the money was used for. Surely the white man had plenty already!

Again, the missionary got up and began to speak. Akbar listened for awhile, but at the word "Jesus," he could no longer listen. As a Muslim, he only saw Jesus as a good prophet that lived long ago—not as the "Son of God." How repulsive to think of God having relations with Mary and having a son whom they named Jesus.

The missionary stopped talking and began to pray. Akbar noticed the people all closed their eyes, but they didn't change positions. None prostrated themselves. They just sat in their chairs. How different was this religion!

The service ended and people began to file out. Akbar got up and, as he walked out the door, the missionary shook his hand and mumbled something he couldn't understand.

He put on his sandals and went out into the road. He heard someone call out to remind everyone to come again that night. Akbar went out the gate and toward the lamp shop, thinking about what he had seen and heard.

That night, he went out to stand in front of the well-lit church. Akbar watched the people going in. He stood and pondered the events of the morning. Looking to his right, he saw his mosque in the distance, lit with small flickering candles. He looked back at the church once—then turned and began to slowly walk down the dusty road towards the mosque.

# TEN STUMBLING BLOCKS TO REACHING MUSLIMS

*by Waleed Nassar*

Since the fall of communism, and the opening of Eastern Europe and the former Soviet Union to the gospel, many in the western church have now turned their attention to reaching Muslims.

Many books have been written on this subject in recent years. Some offer a narrow, "prophetic," Armageddon-type perspective on the Middle East and Muslims. Others approach the subject more positively, emphasizing spiritual warfare and mission strategies. My concern is that many of our efforts are likely to prevent the western church from reaching Muslims, unless we make some drastic changes in our attitudes and conduct. Speaking as a Middle Easterner and as one who has had the privilege of discipling Muslim converts here in the West, I see ten major hindrances to reaching Muslims:

## 1. The church's political bias toward Israel.

The western church often fails to see the Middle East conflict as more than an Arab-Israeli conflict. In reality, it is a Muslim-Jewish conflict that dates back to the friction between Muhammad and the Jews of Arabia in the seventh century.

If the church wants to reach Muslims, it must refrain from taking sides. It must leave the politics to God and concentrate on sharing the gospel with Muslims in a loving and unbiased way.

## 2. Insensitive teaching of prophecy.

This is the kind of teaching that sees the Muslims as "wood for Armageddon." Bible teachers who see Arabic countries as enemies of Israel and Muslims as the people of the Jihad, or "Holy War," do more harm than good. We cannot insult Muslims in our interpretation of the Bible and still expect them to respond to our message.

## 3. Extreme nationalism.

The nationalistic pride of American believers often supersedes their Christian humility. If we are to boast, we must boast only about the Lord (1 Cor. 1:31). This kind of narrow, zealous "patriotism" is way out of biblical proportions. It is offensive to all non-Americans and particularly to Muslims, who consider western policies unfair toward them.

## 4. Loose morals.

Nothing offends a Muslim more than "talking the talk" while not "walking the walk." Their religion is a legalistic one with heavy emphasis on punishing moral offenses.

---

Waleed Nassar is an international evangelist teacher and missions speaker based in Dearborn, Michigan. He has written tracts for Muslims and is currently completing a manual on reaching them with the gospel.

Reprinted with permission from *Ministries Today*, July–August, 1994, p. 80. © Strang Communications Co., U.S. All rights reserved. *www.ministriestoday.com*

For many Muslims, the blatant, open sin among some Christians is a great stumbling block. We must remember—and demonstrate—that while there is freedom in Christ, it is not freedom to sin.

### 5. Immodest lifestyles.

Other stumbling blocks include the unbalanced "prosperity" teachings and materialistic lifestyles of many western Christians. Another is immodest dress, particularly among Christian women. All the Muslims I have discipled have been uneasy with this at best—and disgusted at worst. These are people who have lived in the West for many years, so the issue is not merely one of cultural adjustment. They simply expect the values of the church to be higher than those of society at large (see Rom. 2:24).

### 6. Low degree of reverence.

In the eyes of Muslims, the way we talk to and about God reflects our reverence for him—or our lack thereof.

Americans are virtually addicted to entertainment, and, unfortunately, this has invaded the church both practically and theologically. Muslims are turned off by this lack of reverence. Even excessive humor from the pulpit offends them. After their conversion, former Muslims would like to keep revering God while enjoying him as Father (see Mal. 1:6).

## WHY DO MUSLIMS SAY, "INSHA ALLAH"?

Muslims believe everything in life is planned by God. Nothing happens unless God wills it. Therefore, throughout the Muslim world, you will hear the Arabic phrase, *Insha Allah,* "if God wills," on a daily basis for every situation of life. Sometimes it is used as polite way to say no. Many criticize this view as too fatalistic, leading to pessimism, complacency, and passivity; from this frame of reference, because God is sovereign, the faithful have no leverage to change future events. "Those whom God (in his plan) willeth to guide, he openeth their breast to Islam; those whom he willeth to leave straying, he maketh their breast close and constricted, as if they had to climb up to the skies: thus doth God (heap) the penalty on those who refuse to believe" (Sura 6:125, YUSUF ALI).

Yusuf Ali's footnotes on Sura 76:30–31 explain: "Man in himself is weak; he must seek God's Grace; without it he can do nothing; with it he can do all. For God knows all things, and his wisdom comprehends the good of all. That is according to his just and wise plan. If the will is right, it obtains God's Grace and Mercy. If the will of man rejects God, man must suffer the penalty."[1] The verses referred to state: "But ye will not, except as God wills; for God is full of knowledge and wisdom. He will admit to his mercy whom he will; but the wrongdoers, for them has he prepared a grievous penalty" (Sura 76:30–31, YUSUF ALI).

In contrast many Christians do not seek daily God's guidance for tomorrow: "Instead, you ought to say, 'If it is the Lord's will, we will live and do this or that'" (James 4:15).

1. Yusuf Ali, *The Holy Qur'an,* footnotes 5861 and 5862.

Source: Annee W. Rose, *www.frontiers.org.*

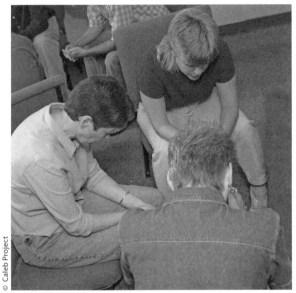

© Caleb Project

Do we regularly pray for the needs of Muslims?

show our apathy and careless-ness. This lack of sensitivity or concern for their souls must be transformed by the Spirit of God if we are ever going to reach Muslims.

### 9. Lack of prayer and outreach.

Sadly, the western church is too often a prayerless church. Life in the West is so fast-paced and hectic that people do not know how to make time to pray. Added to the hindrances above, one can understand why outreach to Muslims is the weakest of all missionary efforts.

### 7. Ignorance of Islam.

Most western Christians know very little, if anything, about Islam or its history, beliefs, and practices. As a result of this ignorance, people unfairly project the media images of Khomeini, Saddam Hussein, and Islamic Fundamentalism upon all Muslims.

This lack of understanding is reflected in the pulpit as well. I have seen preachers receive standing ovations as they shouted, "Allah is not God! Jesus Christ is!"—not realizing that "Allah" is the only word for God in the Arabic language.

### 8. Lack of compassion.

Most Christians have as much compassion for Muslims today as first-century Jews had for the Samaritans. At best we

### 10. Disdain for Muslims' culture.

I once heard a pastor say to his congregation, "I'm glad I was not born in Iran or one of those other countries." In a sense, I understand his feeling, but I do not believe it is an appropriate Christian attitude—certainly not one to be expressed from the pulpit. What if an Iranian were there that day?

The western church has a tendency to look down on all non-western cultures. We need to begin appreciating the positive aspects of Muslim tradition—close relationships and hospitality, for example.

Ultimately, our call is not to present a westernized adaptation of Christianity to our Muslim friends. We must show them Christ. They will respond to him.

# THE RECONCILIATION WALK

*by SOON Online Magazine*

On Easter Sunday morning in 1996, the Reconciliation Walk started from Cologne in Germany. Nine hundred years before, the first Crusade started off from that very place. A large group of Christians began to march along the highways taken by the Crusade soldiers so many years before. They traveled along different routes, through former Yugoslavia, to reach Istanbul, Turkey, in the autumn. The Crusaders committed many atrocities against Arabs, and also Jews, over a period of two hundred years. Worse yet, they did these things in the name of the so-called Christian religion, and these things have never been forgotten.

As the Christians (of 1996) walked along the same ancient route, they prayed at different places and asked for forgiveness from Muslims they met for the actions of the soldiers in the Crusades nine hundred years earlier.

Lynn Green, the leader of the march, reported: "As we walked, the highlight of the day was a visit to a Turkish mosque and teaching center in Cologne. The previous day, a local Christian had contacted the imam, giving him a printed message of apology, and asking if we could visit the mosque.

"We were ushered into a spacious room of prayer where about two hundred men and boys gathered. The women and girls stayed in an adjoining room, but the imam instructed them to read the message, too.

"When everyone was settled on the carpet, the imam welcomed us. Then I explained that we had come to apologize for the atrocities committed in the name of Christ during the Crusades. The reading of the message of apology (see p. 240) in German, Turkish, and English was greeted with loud sustained clapping.

"Then the imam, who can speak all three languages, said: *'When I heard the nature of your message, I was astonished and filled with hope. I thought to myself, "Whoever had this idea must have had an epiphany, a visit from God himself." It is my wish that this project should become a very great success.'*

"Then he told me privately that many Muslims were beginning to examine their own sins against Christians and Jews. He said that our example would show them how to act about the sins of the past. He promised to send the message out to 250 mosques in Europe.

"At the time of the Crusades, the people of Cologne rose up and destroyed all the Jewish population. So later in the day, we paused near the synagogue and prayed for blessing and healing."

---

Adapted from *SOON Online Magazine.* "The Reconciliation Walk" (6 May 2003). *www.soon.org.uk/page15.htm* (cited 10 December 2004). Used by permission.

## The Text of the Apology

Nine hundred years ago, our forefathers carried the name of Jesus Christ in battle across the Middle East. Fuelled by fear, greed, and hatred, they betrayed the name of Christ by conducting themselves in a manner contrary to his wishes and character. The Crusaders lifted the banner of the cross above your people. By this act, they corrupted its true meaning of reconciliation, forgiveness, and selfless love.

On the anniversary of the first Crusade, we also carry the name of Christ. We wish to retrace the footsteps of the Crusaders in apology for their deeds and in demonstration of the true meaning of the cross. We deeply regret the atrocities committed in the name of Christ by our predecessors. We renounce greed, hatred, and fear, and condemn all violence done in the name of Jesus Christ.

Where they were motivated by hatred and prejudice, we offer love and brotherhood. Jesus the Messiah came to give life. Forgive us for allowing his name to be associated with death. Please accept again the true meaning of the Messiah's words: "The Spirit of the Lord is upon me, because he has anointed me to bring good news to the poor. He has sent me to proclaim release to the captives and recovery of sight to the blind, to let the oppressed go free, to proclaim the year of the Lord's favor'" (Luke 4:18–19, NRSV).

As we go, we bless you in the name of the Lord Jesus Christ.

FOR FURTHER STUDY

Christine A. Mallouhi, *Waging Peace on Islam* (London: Monarch Books, 2000).

# SELECTIONS ON CONVERSION

## EDITOR'S NOTE

Our understanding of the nature of conversion affects how we interact with our Muslim friends. These comments on the subject from several with experiences in widely different Muslim cultures will help us to develop a more useful understanding of conversion.

 ## FORMS OF CHANGE

*by David W. Shenk*

What forms of social and theological change take place in conversion? Is the worldview touched in the conversion process, or does the change of orientation take place at the value level of culture and psyche? In many so-called Christianized societies, the church has achieved a fairly comfortable rapprochement with the mainstream culture. Is it right to expect Muslims to undergo a much more radical break with their culture than is true of Christians in so-called Christianized cultures, even though in many respects the Islamic culture may be more attuned to biblical themes than is true of secular Christianized cultures?

While these questions are urgent and significant, we perceive that the center point of conversion is a reorientation of life to a focused commitment to Jesus Christ as Lord and Savior, and the amazing discovery that God is our loving heavenly Father. Sometimes conversion is an event. More often conversion for Muslims seems to be a process. Many in our own group [culture in which Shenk worked] have suffered much persecution after conversion. Yet, the precious prize of knowing Jesus as Lord and Savior, and God as Father, was a gift worth suffering for. The outworkings of that commitment are varied and fascinating; they operate at many different levels of the psyche and the culture. Yet, in every culture and within every person, the center point of conversion is the confession that Jesus Christ is Lord and Savior, and that God is our loving Father. It is the Holy Spirit who reveals that Jesus is Lord and brings to pass a new creation that is the fruit of repentance and commitment to Christ.

We are sobered, however, to learn that in some situations individual Muslims who confess faith in Christ do not become fully part of a believing community, and some therefore return to the Muslim community. Oftentimes believers also face pressure from family and the umma. They may be ostracized from the economic structures of the Islamic community and become impoverished. The church must therefore

Dr. David W. Shenk is global missions consultant with Eastern Mennonite Missions in Salunga, Pennsylvania. He was born into a missionary family in Tanzania and has worked in Somalia, Kenya, and the United States, and taught in Lithuania. He has authored more than a dozen books related to missions and the relationship of the gospel to other religions.

Adapted from David W. Shenk, "Conversations Along the Way," in J. Dudley Woodberry, ed., *Muslims and Christians on the Emmaus Road* (Monrovia, Calif.: MARC Publications, 1989), pp. 8–9. Used by permission of the Zwemer Institute of Muslim Studies.

become not only an evangelizing and nurturing community but also a new and supporting family for the new believer. Conversion is not only to Christ, but also to the church, which must be ready to receive and encourage the new disciple.

We also believe that the church has a mission within Islam, in addition to inviting individuals to faith in the Messiah. This is a witness to Islam itself, calling for a conversion within the spirit of Islam. This call is to consider the Spirit of Jesus in matters such as attitudes towards women and family, human rights, or ecology. It is a call to recognize the legitimacy of the witnessing church in their midst. The presence of the church should be an invitation to the umma as a whole to a fuller quality of life. Prayer for the peace of the community is also a most significant ministry.

## Discreet Witness

*by Phil Parshall*

Often, there is too little consideration given regarding sociological issues involved in the conversion process. Tim Matheny explains:

> In Arab society the initial approach may be made to a younger person, but the challenge for a decision to change should be made to the head of the nuclear family or extended family. Allowing sufficient time for the making of decisions is indispensable in the group-oriented Arab society. The evangelist's tendency, to encourage some especially responsive person to step out and make an individual decision, may often cause the people as a whole to reject the message. Until a people are able to make what seems to them a valid decision, any pulling out [isolation of] group members immediately raises the fear of the loss of solidarity.[1]

In our evangelistic outreach, we have consistently urged the solitary convert to go back among his friends and family and discreetly share his faith. This is not to be done in a way that will stimulate social opposition. If necessary, we counsel the new believer to say nothing about his conversion until others notice a qualitative change in his life, and this then opens the door for a quiet word of witness. We are extremely honest from the start with the convert; he is told he must remain within the Islamic community.

Our goal is to see a small cluster of believers within a given geographical area. When the ideal of sociological strength, plus maturity on the part of the believers, is reached, it becomes possible to consider baptism. Premature baptism has often sparked off intense persecution from the Islamic community.

Phil Parshall is one of today's leading authorities on ministry to Muslims. He and his wife, Julie, have lived among Muslims since 1962 in Bangladesh and the Philippines. He is the author of nine books on Christian ministry among Muslims.

Adapted from Phil Parshall, *Beyond the Mosque* (Grand Rapids: Baker, 1985), pp. 186–187. Used by permission. *www.bakerbooks.com*

## PERSONAL RELATIONSHIP WITH CHRIST

*by Harvie Conn*

Under the cultural impact of pietism [personal devotion and purity], missionaries have understood conversion as leading "a single soul belonging to a heathen people to God."[2] Though modified by a concern for man's social needs,[3] this narrow individualism, reinforced by Puritan moralism [scrupulous moral rigor] and Protestant scholasticism [scholarly conservatism], reduced conversion to a mere act of repentance and faith, distinct from other isolatable categories such as sanctification, adoption, and so forth. The end result has been to downplay, or lose altogether, a sense of conversion as a comprehensive designation for the entire renewal of man (Calvin's view), and conversion as a sign of Christ's kingdom, into which we are daily engrafted. Conversion as the process of change of vesture (Eph. 4:24, Col. 3:9–10), and conversion as metamorphosis over time (Rom. 12:1–2) has been narrowed down to a deed of transferal, turning from idols and turning to God in Christ (1 Thess. 1:9). In so doing, Paul's perspective on conversion as an ongoing event—begun with Christ's power encounter with the sinner, but not consummated until the coming of God's Son from heaven (1 Thess. 1:10)—has been isolated from glorification, and narrowed to conversion as initiation. The strong focus on individualism and one-step decisionism as a feature of a conversion was a cultural bias, theologized by the Pietists, against a European background where there were huge numbers of nominal Christians. It can easily be repeated in the face of the nominalism also present in Christian communities in the Muslim world. Therefore, we must continue to stress the necessity for a personal relationship to Christ as an essential part of conversion. But we must also recognize that in the world's cultures, such personal relationships are entered into, not always by isolated "individual" decisions in abstraction from the group, but, more frequently, in multi-personal, infra-group judgments. "Personal" cannot be equated with "individual."

## SYMBOLS OF CONVERSION

*by Dean Gilliland*

My African students at the Christian seminary had been taught that Muslim forms were absolute, unchanging, and loaded with negative messages, so that for them the forms carried an emotional, negative message. Hamidu was a convert for whom

Harvie Conn was professor of missions at Westminster Theological Seminary in Philadelphia, Pennsylvania, until his death in 1999. He served in Korea as an itinerant preacher and evangelist in inner Seoul. He was a pioneer in modern urban evangelism.

Adapted from Harvie Conn, "A Muslim Convert and His Culture," in Don McCurry, ed., *The Gospel and Islam: A Compendium* (Monrovia, Calif.: MARC Publications, 1979), pp. 97–111. Public domain.

Dean Gilliland spent twenty-two years as missionary in Nigeria where he worked in theological education and co-founded the West African Association of Theological Institutes.

Adapted from Dean S. Gilliland, "Modeling the Incarnation for Muslim People: A Response to Sam Schlorff" in *Missiology: An International Review*, 28, no. 3. (Scottdale, Pa.: America Society of Missiology, 2000), pp. 332–33. Used by permission. *www.asmweb.org*

© Caleb Project

Railway dividing Muslims and Hindus in North India

denominations. The students were impressed with Hamidu's conversion story. While he was performing the salat, he had heard a voice telling him to end his Muslim prayers in the name of Isa al-Masih. This was all he had with which to begin his journey toward Jesus. What an aggressive believer he turned out to be! When I asked him to read the Bible in the seminary chapel, he agreed. First, he read passages in Arabic dealing with Isa from the Injil. He then read relevant verses from the gospels dealing with Jesus' birth. Even more controversial was that he stood at the pulpit in full Muslim dress including the *taqiyya* (skullcap). He had not asked me if he could do this, and I was in a quandary

Muslim dress was inconsequential as a symbol of his identity as a Muslim. His Qur'an was a Holy Book that he carried around with his new Bible. Yet the meaning of these Islamic forms was anathema to my Christian students. Hamidu arrived at the Theological College of Northern Nigeria in 1972 when I was the principal. He was sent by one of the supporting U.S.

## WHO CAN REACH NORTH INDIA?

Steven is an Indian believer from a family that has followed Jesus for generations. Now he is a missionary to the Muslims of a North Indian city. "You know, there has been a trend, Indians saying, 'Foreigners should go home. We can do it better,'" explains Steven. "Now I hear people say, 'South Indians should go home. We Northerners can do it better than you.' It's true that anyone from the outside is going to make some mess; people cannot help bringing their culture with them. So we are working to mobilize local people.

"Our city is divided diagonally by a railway, Muslims on one side and Hindus on the other. The Christians, churches, and Christian activity are all on the Hindu side! There are three bridges between the two, a footbridge and two larger bridges. The Christians and the gospel should cross these bridges. We are praying for a city-wide movement to Christ.

"My wife is part of a Friday fellowship with Muslim women now. They read from the Qur'an and Hadith, but they don't understand it. My wife is learning Urdu and waiting for an opportunity to talk to them about the Bible. You see a lot of openness among Muslim women now. They tell us, 'We want to be free to explore the world and be like you.' They think they need education, but what they really need is to find freedom in Christ.

"Men can do a lot of the work of the ministry here, but we need more women. The main obstacle? Husbands. We need Christian men who are able to see the urgent need, who will come, bring their families, and allow their wives to be involved in ministering to these Muslim women."

Source: Marti Smith, *calebproject.org*

about how to respond. When Hamidu finished, there was consternation. The students had a meeting and demanded that he leave the campus. As principal, I had to explain. I attempted to justify what he had done to the board of directors (western missionaries) and Nigerian church leaders. It was all a matter of form and meaning. Hamidu was completely naïve about the environment in which Christians had learned to reject Muslim forms instantly. The result was that, when he resisted their demand to separate himself completely and immediately from the habits of his culture, they told him to leave the school. I participated in this and I regret, more than I can say, that I allowed the "form equals meaning" idea to prevail. I lost my chance to lead in how to disciple a precious new believer and to model what those seminary students needed to know.

I am making the point that forms and meanings can be controlled by the person. Cases differ, obviously. I have seen that meanings are, shall we say, "bendable" at certain levels by the individual who makes the choice to do so. Meanings attached to forms do not dictate in absolute ways what an individual in a particular place can or cannot do. There is a most important point that I want to make. It is this: We must trust the Holy Spirit with the *metanoia* [Greek, repentance] that leads a Muslim to follow Jesus, regardless of his or her circumstances. The way the metanoia is manifested always depends upon the particular situation. The big thing is to help the Muslim believer to make Jesus the Lord and the new center of life.

## ENDNOTES

1. Tim Matheny, *Reaching the Arabs: A Felt Need Approach* (Pasadena, Calif.: William Carey Library, 1981), p. 63; cited by Phil Parshall, *Beyond the Mosque* (Grand Rapids: Baker, 1985), pp. 186–187.
2. Christensen, Jens, *The Practical Approach to Muslims* (Upper Darby, Pa.: North Africa Mission, 1977), p. 118.
3. Verkuyl, J., *Contemporary Missiology* (Grand Rapids: Eerdmans, 1978), pp. 176–181; cited by Conn, "Muslim Convert", pp. 97–111.

# GOD'S MESSENGER

*by Phil Parshall*

## GOD'S COMMUNICATOR

It is a great calling and privilege to be a missionary. It is my joy to have rubbed shoulders with hundreds of foreign missionaries over the past decades. By and large, they impress me very positively.

The missionary calling has unique features. The missionary must be reasonably well-educated, cross geographical boundaries, leave loved ones behind, sacrifice financially (though not always), adjust to another language and culture, and work on a close-knit team. At the same time, missionaries must open themselves to criticism, from both friend and foe. They must be willing to reevaluate sacrosanct methodology.

Dr. Saeed Khan Kurdistani was an outstanding Iranian Christian who died in 1942. In 1960, a man went to the area where Dr. Saeed had lived and ministered. An aged man of the community was asked by the visitor if he had known Dr. Saeed. The elderly man caught his breath and whispered, "Dr. Saeed was Christ himself!" Reverently, it can be said that this is our goal. But as we head into a new millennium we need to take a hard look at practical matters such as missionary finances, housing, intellectual life, and ministry with churches.

## FINANCES

There is an overwhelming difference of opinion on this subject. Some feel it is imperative to "go native," and to denounce all who do not meet their standard. Others feel strongly that they must live on a western standard for the sake of their family's mental and physical health. They defend their position by saying the nationals will understand their needs. Between these two extremes we find every conceivable view.

Many Third World countries are economically depressed. This fact sets the stage for the conflict between the living standard of the western missionary and the national. Chaeok Chun, a Korean missionary in Pakistan, comments on this tension: "I think it is significant that today's image of the Christian missionary endeavor, from the Asian receptor's point of view, is an image of comfort and privilege. Hence, Asians tend to reject the missionary and misunderstand his message."[1]

The Irish monks of the seventh and eighth centuries were well-known for their asceticism. Their entire outfit consisted of a pilgrim's staff, a wallet, a leather water bottle, and some relics. When they received money from the wealthy, they quickly gave it away to the needy.[2]

Phil Parshall is one of today's leading authorities on ministry to Muslims. He and his wife, Julie, have lived among Muslims since 1962 in Bangladesh and the Philippines. He is the author of nine books on Christian ministry among Muslims.

Adapted from Phil Parshall, "God's Communicator in the '80s," *Evangelical Missions Quarterly* 15, no. 4 (Wheaton, Ill.: Evangelical Missions Information Service, October 1979), pp. 215–221. Used by permission.

Is this a proper model for the contemporary missionary? In this vein, Dr. Donald McGavran suggested that "the missionary from an affluent country lives on a standard far higher than he needs to. What is called for—if we are to meet this problem head on—is an order of missionaries, celibate or married without children, who live in Bangladesh on three hundred rupees (ten dollars) a month. But any such move is at present unthinkable, alas."[3]

Many Muslims around the world live in poverty

At the risk of being controversial, I would like to pull some thoughts together on this very important issue.

1. It does matter what nationals think about the financial profile of the missionary community. Generally, they are appalled at the gap between their living standard and the western missionary's. If we turn away from this concern with indifference, we are in danger of being insensitive to Paul's clear teaching about being a stumbling block to others.

2. Singles and couples without children can more easily make the adjustment to a simple lifestyle. This should be encouraged but not legislated.

3. Experimentation should be allowed. One couple with a newborn infant is living in a bamboo hut with a mud floor in a Muslim rural village. They should be supported, but at the same time, not made to feel embarrassment when, at any time, they feel withdrawal is advisable.

4. Each family should be open before the Lord on this subject. They should prayerfully evaluate their own physical and emotional needs. The goal is to live as closely as possible to the lifestyle of their target people without adverse results to anyone in the family. Balance is a key word.

5. Often the missionary can reside in stark simplicity in a rural area and then take an occasional weekend trip to a nearby city for relaxation and necessary shopping. This accommodation to our cultural backgrounds is not, in my view, an act of hypocrisy. We must be realistic concerning our needs and various levels of capacity to endure deprivation within a foreign culture.

6. It is permissible to consider this a moot issue with missionaries, but idle criticism, a judgmental attitude, and self-righteousness must be studiously avoided. Often, missionaries living in extreme poverty or those living in great affluence are the most opinionated and self-defensive. For the sake of unity in

the body, it may be wise to avoid entering into heavy discussions with these particular missionaries on this subject.

## HOUSING

The day of the "mission compound" is by no means over. These western enclaves are still found throughout the developing world. They are often misunderstood and, in some cases, despised by the nationals. A convert questioned their existence by asking, "Am I wrong if I say that mission bungalows are often a partition wall between the hearts of the people and the missionaries?"[4]

It is my personal conviction that remaining mission compounds should be dismantled. This would free the missionary to move into the community and share his incarnational testimony among people rather than being shut off in a large plot of land that has a very negative appraisal in the minds of the community. It is preferable for the Christians to scatter out among their non-Christian townspeople rather than live in a sealed-off community. Light must be diffused to be of any benefit.

Our first five-year term living in a small town in Bangladesh was a great learning and sharing experience. Just outside the bedroom window of our rented home lived a Muslim lady who was separated from her husband. Her two young daughters lived with her. Quickly we became very intimate friends. The girls were always coming over to borrow a spice or an egg. We felt free to do the same. When the youngest daughter had a raging fever, we brought her over and nursed her. From our bedroom window we learned more about Muslim culture than scores of books could ever have taught us. A mission

## TIPS FOR SHARING WITH A MUSLIM

1. Take time to build a real relationship—which Muslims value highly—to let your friend see Christ in your actions, attitudes, and daily struggles.
2. Practice hospitality—also prized. Spend time over coffee or a meal.
3. Listen. A good listener focuses on the friend's concerns and needs. Look for bridges between his or her understanding and biblical truths.
4. Use creative questions to reveal truth and assist your friend in critical thinking, in recognizing his or her need for a savior.
5. Keep communication open by discussing issues you have in common, not those that divide. Agree whenever possible, especially with anything consistent with the Bible.
6. Share your testimony of how God transformed your life through the power of the gospel.
7. Pray regularly for your friend, that God will reveal his or her needs to you, and that the Holy Spirit will intervene supernaturally in this life. Your words are just one part of God's intervention.
8. Be a good, loving friend. Your unconditional love will attract him or her to our best friend, Jesus Christ, in whose hands are the results.
9. Be patient, a fruit of the indwelling Holy Spirit, who will create in this Muslim woman or man the desire to know more about Jesus.

Source: Fouad Masri, *www.crescentproject.org.*

compound experience would not have made such a lifestyle and involvement in the community possible.

There needs to be some latitude regarding city, town, or village life. The main concern is to relate to the group with whom one is working. Student work in a university area would demand facilities quite different from a rural village setting.

## INTELLECTUAL LIFE

Missionary work has undergone a radical transformation since the end of the colonial era. New approaches and attitudes have been demanded. Pioneers like Dr. Donald McGavran have popularized the science of missiology. Hundreds of case studies and textbooks are now on the market that can be utilized as resource material. Many outstanding graduate schools offer mission studies, and some offer extension study for the missionary on the field. Journals like *Evangelical Missions Quarterly, International Journal of Frontier Mission,* and *Missiology* keep the missionary abreast of fast-breaking concepts and practical outreaches around the world.

Joseph A. McCoy's relevant bit of advice to missionaries is that they should "keep an open mind, realizing that times change and one must make adjustments. Tactics of ten years ago will not work and even those of five years ago are outdated."[5] It is always sad to see missionaries become rutted and inflexible. The orientation and allegiance of some missionaries (both older and younger) to traditional methodology can cause them to think that a careful move into new areas of sensitive experimentation is almost a denial of truth.

Younger missionaries arriving on the field with a more venturesome approach become frustrated. Their ideas and zeal are often lost, smothered under a patronizing "Keep it under your hat for a few years. Experience will mellow you and mature your input." A fresh and non-threatening relationship between the senior and junior missionary must develop. One adds experience and the other brings the latest in theory and enthusiasm. United, they are almost unbeatable. Divided, they are a catastrophe, not only to the inner team of missionaries, but also to the perceptive, onlooking national community.

Our commitment to Jesus Christ means that we want to be the best servants possible for his glory. It means stretching, not only in spirit, but also in intellect. True academic excellence leads to greater effectiveness, not to pride or snobbery. We must beware of vegetating on the mission field. Both our hearts and our minds must stay alive and alert.

Still fresh in my mind are the words of Harold Cook, for many years professor of missions of Moody Bible Institute, who told his missions class in 1959: "Students, the single most important area of your life and ministry will be in the realm of attitudes. It is here you will either succeed or fail as a missionary. Attitudes touch every nerve end of life. Your relationship to Christ, fellow missionary, national believer, and non-Christian will be deeply affected by proper or improper attitudes."

There are a number of ingredients to a positive attitude toward nationals. One is empathy. Let me illustrate. Each morning at sunrise, a Hindu neighbor in our village would rise up, wash, and go out and stand near his cow. He would then look up at the sun, fold his hands and go through a ceremony which involved worship of both the sun and the cow. I watched our Hindu friend perform this ritual scores of times. One day the cow became ill and died suddenly. Grief struck the Hindu household. It was indeed a tragic loss to them. Personally, I disagreed with worshiping a cow, but I had somehow entered into the worldview of that Hindu. He hurt and I hurt. Quickly I learned a few appropriate phrases (as we were new in the country) and went along to his shop. I stuttered out a few incorrectly pronounced words about being sorry that his cow had died. My Hindu friend was deeply touched. We were worlds apart in culture and religion, yet I cared. I had, for a brief moment, stepped into his life.

There is an old adage that contains a great deal of truth. "The gift without the giver is bare." Missionaries are giving people. Their job demands that role. They may be engaged in relief, teaching, medical work, or some other ministry that necessitates the act of sharing. But the act of giving is inadequate in itself. What is the force behind the action? Is there love? Is there a deep concern for the other person? Has giving become a professional obligation? Have the poor or the unreached become a product to sell? These are heavy questions.

## MINISTRY

It is time now to consider the ministerial focus of the missionary. When we turn to New Testament missions, we find that Paul's involvement was exceedingly temporary. He came, stayed a few weeks or months, or at most a few years, and left to go into new areas. The churches he planted did not remain in his control. Even if a heretical influence came into the churches, Paul could only exhort the Christians to walk in truth. He had no funds to cut off. The believers were totally free. Certainly the contemporary picture of missions is different from Paul's day.

## ISSUES WHICH AFFECT MUSLIM PERCEPTIONS

1. Israeli-Palestinian conflict.
2. American invasion of Iraq.
3. American military presence in places like Saudi Arabia, Afghanistan, and Iraq.
4. United Nations' sanctions against Muslim nations.
5. International Monetary Fund and World Bank restrictions on Muslim economies.
6. Qur'anic stereotypes of non-Muslims.
7. Legacy of Crusades and colonialism.
8. Effect of the global economy.
9. Phobia of the West in Muslim media.
10. Conspiracy theories.

### FOR FURTHER STUDY
Updated and adapted from: Peter G. Riddell and Peter Cotterell, *Islam in Context: Past, Present, and Future* (Grand Rapids: Baker Academic, 2003), pp. 153–163. *www.bakeracademic.com*

Lesslie Newbigin writes about Paul totally entrusting leadership into local hands. He pungently comments that Paul did not do what modern missionaries have done: "He does not build a bungalow."[6] George W. Peters maintains that Paul could have rightfully said, "Here is enough work for me to do. This is where I am." Paul resisted the temptation and kept on the move.[7] Roland Allen points out that Paul did not neglect the churches. He continued to visit and correspond with them. But the basic leadership responsibility was all put in local hands.[8]

The missionary must move on as soon as possible after worshiping groups have been established. Converts must not transfer their dependence onto the missionary and away from the Lord.

Having travailed, given birth, and cared for young churches, the missionaries (whether Tamil or Naga or American or Australian) should turn authority over to indigenous leaders. Travail must not go on too long. It must be followed by weaning and pushing out of the nest. Then the missionary goes on and repeats the process.[9] He must keep before him constantly the imperative of pressing out to new frontiers.

## CONCLUSION

A beautiful picture of a ship on an ocean in the midst of a storm graces my bedroom door. The inscription reads, "A ship in a harbor is safe, but that is not what ships are built for." The frontline of a battle is risky, but no victory has ever been registered in the annals of history as having been won solely by those supportive people who linger far behind the range of enemy gunfire. Our task calls for reflection, decision, and engagement.

**End of Key Readings for Lesson 7. See** RECOMMENDED READINGS & ACTIVITIES **on pp. 265.**

## ENDNOTES

1. "An Exploration of the Community Model for Muslim Missionary Outreach by Asian Women," an unpublished D. Miss. dissertation. Fuller Theological Seminary, Pasadena, 1977.
2. Sister Mary Just, *Digest of Catholic Mission History* (Maryknoll, N.Y.: Maryknoll Publications, 1957), p. 22.
3. Letter to the author, March, 1979.
4. D. A. Chowdhury, "The Bengal Church and the Convert," *The Moslem World* no. 29 (1939), p. 347.
5. *Advice From the Field* (Baltimore, Md.: Helicon Press, 1962), p. 144.
6. *The Open Secret* (London: SPCK, 1978), p. 144.
7. "Issues Confronting Evangelical Missions," *Evangelical Missions Tomorrow* (Pasadena, Calif.: William Carey Library, 1977), p. 162.
8. *Missionary Methods: St. Paul's or Ours?* (Grand Rapids: Eerdmans, 1962), p. 151.
9. Donald McGavran, *Ethnic Realities and the Church* (Pasadena, Calif.: William Carey Library, 1979), p. 130.

# ISRAEL OR PALESTINE?

*by Chawkat Moucarry*

As a Christian Arab, the Arab-Israeli conflict and the rights of the Palestinian people have been on my agenda ever since I came to Europe. I am convinced that this issue, along with the situation faced by Muslim immigrants in Europe, both impact Christian-Muslim relations.

The majority of immigrants living in Europe are Muslims, yet for centuries Europe has been closely associated with Christianity. So what is the place of Muslims in any non-Muslim country? How should they be treated? How do the Torah and the gospel call us to respond?

Most European countries gave unconditional support to the establishment of the state of Israel in 1948. Many Christians too, and especially evangelicals, continue to give it their backing, claiming that it fulfils biblical prophecies.[1] But is such an endorsement necessarily the right attitude? Is it consistent with God's purpose for the land? And is it compatible with God's justice? Christians cannot escape the questions presented to them by the conflict in the Middle East.[2]

## THE PROMISE OF A LAND

The theological debate about the land of Israel begins with the promise God made to Abraham: "'Leave your country, your people and your father's household and go to the land I will show you. I will make you into a great nation and I will bless you; I will make your name great, and you will be a blessing. I will bless those who bless you, and whoever curses you I will curse; and all peoples on earth will be blessed through you'" (Gen. 12:1-3).

This promise is seen by many Zionist Jews and a number of evangelical Christians as the biblical foundation for the eternal right of the Jewish people to have a nation in Palestine. But this is not the only way to understand this promise and its fulfillment. We must remember that the gospel teaches that Jesus of Nazareth is the Messiah of Israel, and that in him God's promises to his people are fulfilled.

First of all, the gift of the land of Canaan to the people of Israel was temporary. The coming of the Messiah made obsolete the very concept of a promised land. Speaking about the radical changes that the coming of the Messiah would bring about, the prophet Ezekiel announced that the land of Israel would no longer be the exclusive property of the Jews:

> "You are to distribute this land among yourselves according to the

---

Chawkat Moucarry is Syrian and has lived in both Muslim and Christian communities. He earned his doctorate in Islamic studies from the University of Sorbonne (Paris) and tutors and lectures in Islamic studies at All Nations Christian College in England.

Adapted from Chawkat Moucarry *The Prophet and the Messiah: An Arab Christian's Perspective on Islam and Christianity* (Downers Grove, Ill.; InterVarsity Press, 2001), pp. 275-282. Used by permission. *www.ivpress.com*

tribes of Israel. You are to allot it as an inheritance for yourselves and for the aliens [non-Israelites] who have settled among you and who have children. You are to consider them as native-born Israelites; along with you they are to be allotted an inheritance among the tribes of Israel. In whatever tribe the alien [non-Israelite] settles, there you are to give him his inheritance," declares the Sovereign LORD (Ezek. 47:21–23).

This command to share the land with non-Jews on an equal footing with the Jews is highly significant: it symbolizes that the coming of the Messiah marks a new order. God's promises to Israel would be enjoyed by all peoples, for there would be no more discrimination between Israel and the nations.

If this prophecy is taken literally, it demonstrates the irony of the present situation: the state of Israel was established mainly by European Jews at the expense of native Palestinians, many of whom have been dispossessed of their own lands and made refugees in neighboring countries!

Secondly, the land of Israel stood for the kingdom of God. The gospel is all about the kingdom of God Jesus came to establish (Matt. 4:17; Luke 17:21). The only time Jesus alluded to the Promised Land was in the Beatitudes: "Blessed are the meek, for they will inherit the earth [or the land]" (Matt. 5:5).

Jesus' disciples were convinced that all the promises made to Israel, including the restoration of David's kingdom, had been fulfilled by Jesus, "the son of David" (see Acts 15:12–18). After all, Abraham himself, to whom the promise was initially made, "was looking forward to the city with foundations, whose architect and builder is God" (Heb. 11:10). This city is Jerusalem, not the city in the land of Canaan, but "the heavenly Jerusalem" (Gal. 4:26; Heb. 12:22). If my interpretation amounts to spiritualizing God's promise to Israel, it has the merit of being based on how Jesus and his disciples interpreted it.

Finally, God's promise to Abraham was conditional. In other words, it stipulated that the Israelites would inhabit the land only as long as they obeyed God's laws. Otherwise God would punish them, just as he did with the Canaanites, the former inhabitants of the land (Gen. 15:16; Deut. 18:12). Moses clearly warned his people, and spoke of the judgment they would face if they turned away in disobedience: "Just as it pleased the Lord to make you prosper and increase in number, so it will please him to ruin and destroy you. You will be uprooted from the land you are entering to possess. Then the Lord will scatter you among all nations, from one end of the earth to the other" (Deut. 28:63–64). This warning became reality twice in the history of Israel. In 586 B.C., Nebuchadnezzar, king of Babylon, invaded Jerusalem, destroyed its temple and deported its people. In A.D. 70, the Roman army besieged Jerusalem and expelled its inhabitants.

Jesus knew what was going to happen to Jerusalem and wept over the future judgment of the city. Nevertheless, he presented this tragic event as the direct consequence of the people's rejection of him:

## United Nations Partition Plan of Palestine (1947)

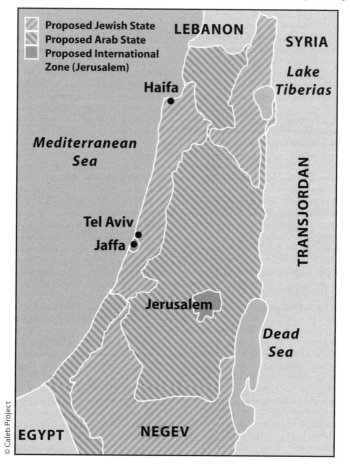

As he approached Jerusalem and saw the city, he wept over it and said, "If you, even you, had only known on this day what would bring you peace—but now it is hidden from your eyes. The days will come upon you when your enemies will build an embankment against you and encircle you and hem you in on every side. They will dash you to the ground, you and the children within your walls. They will not leave one stone on another, because you did not recognize the time of God's coming to you" (Luke 19:41–44, emphasis added).

Unlike the prophets who foretold that the Israelites would return from Babylon, Jesus did not promise his people that their nation would be restored (Luke 21:20–24). The present-day state of Israel, therefore, has no theological significance. If anything, Israel is no better or worse than any other nation. Its recent history

## Current Situation in Palestine (2004)

© Caleb Project

*Israeli-occupied, with current status subject to the Israeli-Palestinian Interim Agreement.

**Syrian Territory occupied by Israel since 1967.

demonstrates that it is far from God's moral standards.

## THE ONGOING CONFLICT

The establishment of Israel on Arab land was an immense injustice. It was bound to create human tragedy for the historical inhabitants of the land. Indeed, it deprived the Palestinian people of their homeland and forced many into refugee camps. This sense of injustice was deeply felt by Arab peoples throughout the world. Many Palestinians were plunged into despair, especially after Arab governments failed to achieve what they had promised them:

to bring them back to their homeland. Palestinian refugees decided to take their destiny into their own hands: the Palestine Liberation Organization (PLO) was born. Although some resorted to terrorism when the world seemed indifferent to their plight, Israel seemed invincible. In June 1967 it conquered new Arab territories, and, as a result, the problems faced by an Arab population living under Israeli occupation increased.

The 1980s witnessed the *intifada* (uprising) of the Palestinian youth in the occupied territories of the West Bank and Gaza Strip. There were demonstrations and stone-throwing attacks on Israeli soldiers and civilians. The government reaction was harsh. This "stone revolution," well-covered by the media, had a dual impact: it showed the world that the Palestinians had not given up their hope for independence and forced many Israelis to ask soul-searching questions about their own identity. Those who for years had considered themselves to be the oppressed were becoming the oppressors. The policy of the Israeli government resulted in an increasing number of Palestinians being imprisoned, deported, and tortured. Palestinian lands were confiscated and new Jewish settlements were established. Israel was becoming a country of apartheid.

In the early 1990s both parties came to realize that the only way out was to acknowledge each other's right to exist. In September 1993, Israeli and Palestinian leaders signed the Oslo Agreement—the first step towards peace. Nevertheless, people opposed to the peace process remained active on both sides. In November 1995, Israeli society was shaken when Prime Minister Yitzhak Rabin was assassinated: a Jew murdered, not by an Arab, but by another Jew.

In the summer of 2000, the peace process reached a critical stage. The sensitive issue of Jerusalem, which had been left deliberately until this point, was now the focus of the talks. Ever since the Israeli army conquered East Jerusalem in June 1967, all the Israeli leaders had been claiming that "Jerusalem is the eternal and indivisible capital of Israel." Thus Israeli negotiators were not prepared to make a serious compromise over Jerusalem. They refused to accept the return of East Jerusalem under Arab sovereignty. As a result, the Palestinians felt that the Israeli government wanted to have peace with them without acknowledging their equal rights to the land, and, more specifically, their equal rights to Jerusalem, which is cherished not only by Jews but by all the native people of the land. Israel's intransigence, combined with its ongoing policy of establishing new Jewish settlements in Palestinian territories, inflamed the Palestinian people with rage and despair. The response to the failure of this decisive round of the peace talks was the second intifada. This uprising, which started in September 2000, claimed the lives of over eight hundred people, mostly Palestinians, in less than twelve months. A United Nations resolution blamed the Israeli government for its use of excessive force against Palestinians.

## APPLYING THE TEACHING OF SCRIPTURE

A few observations need to be made about this conflict, which has placed Israel in opposition to Arabs, Christians, and Muslims alike.

First, the Jewish, Christian, and Muslim Scriptures teach that the earth is the Lord's. He is the ultimate owner of the land. Arabs and Jews both claim ownership of the disputed land, yet it is by no means inherently theirs; it belongs to God (Sura 7:128, YUSUF ALI; Ps. 24:1; 1 Cor. 10:26).

Jesus warned his disciples against putting all their hope and energy into gaining this world in a way that would endanger their eternal lives: "Will a person gain anything if he wins the whole world but loses his life? Of course not! There is nothing he can give to regain his life" (Matt. 16:26, GNB). It is extremely sad that many Jews and Arabs have literally lost their lives in the successive wars against each other. Yet there are even more people who have jeopardized their eternal lives by putting their political commitment first on their agenda. This conflict between Arabs and Jews has exposed the sinfulness of all. No one can claim to have clean hands. So far, the only victor in this conflict is evil, inflicting so much suffering on both communities.

Secondly, the Bible teaches that God is a merciful God. He calls people to repent and to receive his forgiveness. God not only forgives but exhorts his people to do likewise. The "Holy Land" has been, in a sense, one of the most unholy places in the world, because of all the wars that have taken place there, wars waged by people who supposedly worshipped a merciful God. Arabs and Jews need to go back to their Scriptures and to seek God's mercy and help to enable them to be merciful to each other.

For Christians, God's mercy has been demonstrated in history through the Suffering Servant, Jesus Christ. Jesus' love led him to suffer to bring us reconciliation with God. Looking to him as the Suffering Servant can help us make sense of our own suffering.

Thirdly, the God of peace is also the God of justice. The initial injustice suffered by Arabs, and especially the Palestinians, needs to be acknowledged and redressed by the international community. In political terms, this means that Israel and the Arab nations should no longer be treated with double standards. Will Israel ever be forced to end its occupation of Arab lands and to comply with the United Nations resolutions, as Iraq was forced to withdraw from Kuwait, Indonesia from East Timor, and Serbia from Kosovo? Israel seems to be the only country in the world to defy U.N. resolutions without having to face international sanctions.

The cry for "justice, only justice" of the Palestinian people must he heard.[3] This means recognizing their right to have a credible state in which to recover their dignity and national identity. It means accepting East Jerusalem as their capital, and removing the Jewish settlements in Gaza and the West Bank. Otherwise, in the words of one Israeli, this state would be nothing more than a "trussed chicken." The Gaza Strip, for instance, is one of the most densely populated places in the world. This autonomous Palestinian territory, which measures 140 square miles, is inhabited by one and a half million people. The Palestinian population lives on 65 percent of the territory. The remaining 35 percent is occupied by

Jewish colonies owned by just six thousand Jewish settlers.

Fourthly, the concept of a Jewish state is in itself problematic. History and many contemporary situations indicate that whenever a country is closely associated with one religion or ethnic group, religious and ethnic minorities are likely to be at best discriminated against, and at worst persecuted. A secular, plural, and democratic state is more in line with Jesus' teaching than a religious state, be it Christian, Islamic, or Jewish (Matt. 22:21).

How would we react, for example, if the United Kingdom were designed for white Christians only? Few would advocate such a thing, yet the state of Israel was conceived by Zionist ideology as the homeland for the Jews, Jewishness being defined by racial and religious criteria.[4] This ideology is challenged not only by the Arab population living in Israel, but also by "Messianic" Jews. Are Messianic (Christian) Jews still Jews? While the answer is a definite yes for them, their very existence, especially in Israel, let alone their missionary activity, is seen as a threat to Jewish identity. In no state will the protection of human rights be guaranteed unless its citizens are seen for who they are: human beings, regardless of their ethnic and religious background.

The Middle East conflict therefore raises some fundamental issues: Is it possible for a state to be closely associated with one particular religion or ethnic group without residents from other backgrounds

## SUB-SAHARAN PEOPLES

The 160 million people of sub-Saharan Africa—the region just south of Arabic-speaking North Africa—adhere to a wide range of beliefs, including Christianity and animism. Recent Muslim missionary efforts have extended into each of the seventeen non-Arab African countries where Islam is the predominant religion.

Although the non-Arab population of southern Sudan is estimated to be 75 percent Christian, Sudan is 65 percent Muslim. Some 65 percent of Ethiopians and almost 50 percent of Eritreans are Christian; but the other nations in the Horn of Africa, Djibouti, and Somalia are more than 95 percent Muslim. Christian-Muslim conflict rages along these dividing lines, with atrocities committed on both sides.

The Fulani tribes live all across the sub-Sahara, stretching from Mauritania and Senegal to Sudan, and form a minority in nineteen countries. Their numbers are estimated to be anywhere between 16 and 35 million. The Fulani have a long history as nomadic cattle herdsmen. As one of the first African tribes to follow Islam seven centuries ago, their nomadic lifestyle helped to spread the religion across much of West Africa. Although they are the largest nomadic-culture people in the world, more than half of the Fulani now live settled lifestyles. Many noted Islamic scholars and teachers are among the educated Fulani, and the urbanized and more affluent tend to be the most orthodox in their beliefs. The majority of Fulani, however, observe a mix of traditional and Islamic beliefs and practices.

Sources: *Operation World, 30-Days Muslim Prayer Focus, www.joshuaproject.net.*

Children from Sub-Saharan Africa

© Dave Richards

becoming second-class citizens? How will a relatively small land accommodate the claims of both the Jewish and Palestinian peoples? Will they ever really accept each other and not merely tolerate each other? Of course, these questions are relevant not only to Israel, but to the other states in the region too. The solution of one secular and democratic state for all, regardless of religious and ethnic identity, may seem idealistic today, but in the long run this option will guarantee peace because it does justice to both Jews and Palestinians, to people with one faith and to those of no faith at all. Unless the structural discrimination of the state of Israel is adequately addressed, it is wishful thinking to believe that Israelis and Palestinians can live alongside each other (Jer. 6:13–15). It is high time for Israel to realize that military power and nuclear weapons represent no guarantee for peace with the Palestinian people. Critical and courageous decisions, including the repudiation of Zionist ideology, need to be made. Only then will justice, peace, and reconciliation be given a serious chance to become a meaningful reality in the Middle East.

## DO NOT SHOW PARTIALITY

Many Christians in the West naturally sympathize with Israel as God's chosen people and as the victims of the Holocaust. However, the undue and damaging result of this attitude is often a pro-Israeli bias. Combined with prejudice against Arabs and Muslims, this bias has meant that Christians have been unable to make a positive contribution to implementing justice and peace in the Middle East. It also explains, to some degree, why

## Percentage of Muslim Population in Sub-Saharan Africa

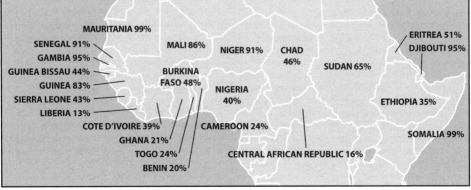

MAURITANIA 99%
SENEGAL 91%
GAMBIA 95%
GUINEA BISSAU 44%
GUINEA 83%
SIERRA LEONE 43%
LIBERIA 13%
COTE D'IVOIRE 39%
GHANA 21%
TOGO 24%
BENIN 20%
MALI 86%
BURKINA FASO 48%
NIGER 91%
NIGERIA 40%
CAMEROON 24%
CENTRAL AFRICAN REPUBLIC 16%
CHAD 46%
SUDAN 65%
ERITREA 51%
DJIBOUTI 95%
ETHIOPIA 35%
SOMALIA 99%

© Caleb Project

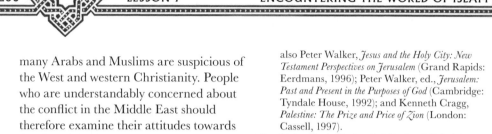
many Arabs and Muslims are suspicious of the West and western Christianity. People who are understandably concerned about the conflict in the Middle East should therefore examine their attitudes towards Israel and the Arabs, to ensure that they are not showing favoritism to one party to the detriment of the other. "Do not show partiality in judging; hear both small and great alike. Do not be afraid of any man, for judgment belongs to God" (Deut. 1:17).

## ENDNOTES

1. See T. Weber, "How Evangelicals Became the Best Friends of Israel," *Christianity Today* 42, no. 11 (5 Oct. 1998), pp. 38–49; P. Bennis and K. Mansour, "'Praise God and Pass the Ammunition!' The Changing Nature of Israel's U.S. Backers," *Middle East Report*, no. 208 (fall 1998), pp. 16–18, 43. See also periodicals such as *Israel and Christians Today*, and the so-called Christian Embassy in Jerusalem.

2. One of the outstanding books written on the issue is by Colin Chapman, *Whose Promised Land? Israel or Palestine?* (Oxford: Lion, 1983). See also Peter Walker, *Jesus and the Holy City: New Testament Perspectives on Jerusalem* (Grand Rapids: Eerdmans, 1996); Peter Walker, ed., *Jerusalem: Past and Present in the Purposes of God* (Cambridge: Tyndale House, 1992); and Kenneth Cragg, *Palestine: The Prize and Price of Zion* (London: Cassell, 1997).

3. Naim Ateek, *Justice, Only Justice: A Palestinian Theology of Liberation* (Maryknoll, N.Y.: Orbis, 1989). See also Riah Abu El-Assal, *Caught in Between: The Story of an Arab Palestinian Christian Israeli* (London: SPCK, 1999); Elias Chacour, *Blood Brothers* (Eastbourne, UK: Kingsway, 1984); and Audeh Rantisi, *Blessed Are the Peacemakers: The Story of a Palestinian Christian* (Guildford, UK: Eagle Publishing, 1990).

4. As soon as the state of Israel was created in 1948, its government sought to rid the land of the remaining Arab population. This policy is evidenced by a well-documented case in which the Israeli government devised a secret transfer scheme designed to encourage the Palestinian population in Galilee to leave the country and settle in Argentina and Brazil. See Nur Masaiha, "A Galilee without Christians? Yosef Weitz and 'Operation Yohanan' 1949–1954," in Anthony O'Mahony, ed., *Palestinian Christians: Religion, Politics, and Society in the Holy Land* (London: Melisende, 1999), pp. 190–222.

# LIVING AS THE FAMILY OF GOD

*by Christine Mallouhi*

Worshipping God does not need to be a "religious activity" where we go through a ritual. St. Paul tells us, "In him we live, and move, and have our being" (Acts 17:28, KJV), but we often act as if we are only truly with God in formal worship times, in a room where we are engaged in a certain ritual. What is the purpose of a Christian fellowship? Is it not for building each other up in the faith and worshipping God? There are many other ways that we can accomplish this without always sitting in a room in a formal meeting.

I have rich memories from my years of living in the Arab world of some of the most wonderful times of worship we had in the great outdoors. Our group set up tents for the weekend and had barbecues by a lake, with prayer, fellowship, and Bible studies. Baptisms were usually a weekend camp-fellowship. Large boats were hired for four-hour parties on the river. Nobody wanted to miss these fun times of fellowship. As we glided down the river, we partied on the feasts we brought. People who had not seen each other recently went into a corner and shared their lives.

We sang choruses, read the Word, prayed over those needing special ministry, and gave messages as different ones were led. The same pattern was followed for home meetings. Food and fun first, and from this shared experience, fellowship flowed, and from there worship developed. How many times have we sat in a church meeting and felt isolated, untouched, or unwarmed in our hearts? Sometimes the formality of a meeting prevents people from being natural or cuts across direct communication with each other. Unless we have a particularly caring group, a person could take part in corporate worship feeling starkly alone. Then, at the end of the meeting, everyone relaxes and the real fellowship begins when people begin talking intimately together and giving each other advice or personal prayer.

The sense of family is often what is missing in these sterile worship experiences. It is especially difficult for people to be open with others if they have nothing in common except faith, and the only shared experience is the formal meeting time. The Christian family needs shared family experiences together. A well-liked minister in an Arab country retired and was replaced by another veteran worker. A church member telephoned the new minister for mutual encouragement. The minister returned his greeting and then asked, "What can

Christine Mallouhi is an Australian who has lived thirty years among Muslims in the Arab world. She is married to an Arab follower of Christ from a Muslim family and together they direct an association publishing Arabic books bridging Christ to Muslims. Christine has published numerous articles on Muslim-Christian relations and is the author of *Waging Peace on Islam* (Downers Grove, Ill.: InterVarsity Press, 2000).

Adapted from Christine A. Mallouhi, *Miniskirts, Mothers and Muslims* (Carlisle, UK; Spear Publications, 1997) pp. 93–95. Used by permission of Christine Mallouhi. This material appears in part in the newly revised book, *Miniskirts, Mothers and Muslims* (Grand Rapids: Monarch Books, 2004). *www.lionhudson.com*

I do for you?" The local quickly hung up and crossed the minister's name out of his phone book. He interpreted the response to imply that the minister was not interested in friendship. The minister was not part of the church member's family and only expected phone calls for a specific reason. The local had no other reason to call other than to say "I care for you." The local felt rejected and offended.

Our family in Syria calls each other numerous times during the day just keeping in touch. In Egypt, my husband Mazhar telephoned about twelve people daily even though he saw all of these people weekly. The calls were just a friendly touch until the next get-together. How often do we begin a call or visit by apologizing for intruding on the person's time and stating our reason for calling? This implies we wouldn't bother with this person if it was not for business we need to accomplish with them.

In North Africa we took a day to be with one of the Christian couples from another city. We walked through parks and gardens, ate at a special restaurant, and took the children to an amusement park. And while we had fun, we talked. We talked about marriage, about the difficulties of raising children for Christ in a totally Muslim society, and about what the church should look like according to locals. An old, deep hurt surfaced, and the steps towards healing and putting it right were taken right there in the main street. They told us

## THROUGH HER EYES

Seeing the world through a Muslim woman's eyes may be more helpful than listening to others describe what they think Muslim women feel. It is possible to glean thoughtful insight from Muslim magazines and other on-line resources: What do they think? What topics are on their hearts? What are their concerns? How do they feel? By simply reviewing article titles, one begins to "see" issues and topics of concern for Muslim women. The reader of a recent issue of *Azizah*[1] could infer the following:

- I am concerned about modesty and harassment: "Why I Veil."
- I want to follow my religion well: "Is It Halal?", "Devout Deeds and Worthy Works."
- I am proud of my Islamic heritage: "Celebrating Style. Exquisite Clothes from Seven Talented Designers," "How Much Does Your Masjid Reflect the Ethnic Diversity of Islam?", "Décor: Faith in Every Moment of Existence, A Look at Geometry in Persian Art and Tradition."
- I am concerned about the place of Islam in geopolitical relations these days: "Waging Peace."
- I am very much like other North American women: "Well-being: Ask Your Doctor," "Celebrating Style: Exquisite Clothes from Seven Talented Designers," "Stolen Names, Stolen Lives: Having your personal information stolen can turn into a nightmare."

If we open our eyes to the current affairs of the Muslim communities around us, we may see more than we did at first glance!

1. See *www.azizahmagazine.com* (vol. 1, issue 1).

Source: *www.frontiers.org*

with tears in their eyes that they had never had such a special time before. "Christians usually have meetings. They don't have fun and social times." This casual day of fellowship had a special spiritual significance in their lives and ours.

Families need to have fun together and shared experiences and memories. This type of fellowship should be a regular part of our lives. It is a good opportunity for mutual encouragement. In Egypt, our boys were the eldest among the group's children. A long boat ride did not hold the same pleasure for them as for the younger ones who would bring their toys, but the single Egyptian men spent time with them playing chess. This helped them bond in a way that would not have happened in a house meeting because the children would not be so involved.

This type of fellowship has helped bond the church because it combines two of the most important aspects of eastern culture: hospitality (the meetings are centered around sharing food) and family. The Christian family needs time together in normal life activities to reinforce their new values as any family would. Family has a double bind on Muslims. They are members of their natal families and the umma, the family of Islam. Individuals are expected to waive their rights in the interests of both, and have been trained to do so since birth. New believers often have the burden of bringing shame on their families by their faith and it is very difficult for them to stand alone against both their families and society. Authors Ibrahim Muhawi and Sharif Kanaana explain this well: "Through respect for tradition and deference to age, individuals are socialized from childhood to harmonize their will with that of the family. They are encouraged to perceive themselves as others see them, and to validate their experience in terms of the approval of others. Standing out, doing things differently, or disobeying authority brings punishments ranging from the physical to the psychological, such as the show of displeasure, reproach, public censure, or social ostracism."[1]

As we spend time growing closer to each other, caring for each other and supporting each other, we become the church in action before we master all the biblical facts about what the church should look like. Then when we read about meeting together and the brotherhood of believers, we understand the importance of these principles because it was already part of our lives and hearts.

These family-type fun activities are also helpful for western churches. When we first lived in the United States we invited ten couples from church for an evening of fellowship at home. After dinner they sat formally around the living room waiting for the meeting to begin. They were expecting prayer and Bible study and were surprised when we announced there was no agenda other than enjoying ourselves. We shared a lot of mirthful stories of how we met our spouses (which often included how we had come to Christian commitment) and discovered a new understanding of each other. The next day we received a number of phone calls expressing not only delight in such a fun night, but appreciation for the deeper bonds experienced with others of the group after knowing each other for years. It was a family sharing time. These ten

couples now had a deeper bond when they worshipped together.

**End of Basic Readings for Lesson 7. See** RECOMMENDED READINGS & ACTIVITIES **on pp. 265.**

**Go to:**
*www.encounteringislam.org/ readings* **to find the Full Readings for Lesson 7.**

## ENDNOTE

1.  *Speak Bird, Speak Again: Palestinian Arab Folktale* (Berkeley: University of California Press, 1989), p. 31.

# DISCUSSION QUESTIONS

1.  A key theme of this lesson is the role that culture and cultural misunderstandings play in Muslim-Christian relationships and in Muslims embracing Christ. Read Colossians 4:2–6. What does Paul desire for himself? What instructions has he for us?

2.  Klein, Hubbard, and Blomberg say, "Contextualizing biblical truth requires interpretive bifocals. First, we need a lens to look back into the background of the biblical world to learn the intended meaning. Then, we need another lens to see the foreground to determine how to best express—contextualize—that truth for today's world."[1] What does it mean to contextualize our message for Muslims? What culture(s) do we need to understand in order to do so?

1. William W. Klein, Robert L. Hubbard Jr., and Craig L. Blomberg, *Introduction to Biblical Interpretation* (Nashville, Tenn.: Nelson Reference, 1993), p. 174.

# RECOMMENDED READINGS & ACTIVITIES*

Read: Phil Parshall, *Muslim Evangelism*, rev. ed. (Waynesboro, Ga.: Gabriel Publishing, 2003).

Badru D. Kateregga and David W. Shenk, *A Muslim and a Christian in Dialogue* (Scottdale, Pa.: Herald Press, 1997).

Watch: Watch a television program and take notes: Which elements might cause Muslims offense? How do the television shows you watch portray western or non-Muslim culture?

Pray: Fast from first light to sunset for a day, as Muslims do during Ramadan. Use your hunger to fuel your prayer for Muslims.

Journal: For one day, keep a journal of all the foods and beverages you consume. How many of those items would be considered halal by Muslims? For a second day, eat and drink only those items that are halal. See "What Is Permitted?" on page 84.

Surf: Discover related web sites at *www.encounteringislam.org/lessonlinks*.

* For expanded details on these Recommended Readings & Activities, visit *www.encounteringislam.org/lessonlinks*.

# LESSON 8
## THEOLOGICAL ISSUES

## PONDER THIS

- How should we respond to those who oppose our faith?

- What are the most helpful ways we can communicate the gospel to Muslim friends?

- How do we incarnate the gospel among Muslims?

- How do you live out your "theology"?

# LESSON OBJECTIVE

Describe the theological misconceptions Muslims typically have of Christianity and how Christians can respond to these inaccurate impressions.

1. The most significant areas of erroneous understanding are: Jesus, his divinity and titles (Son of God and prophet); original sin; and the oneness of God with the existence of the Trinity.

2. Other areas of importance are: the Crucifixion and the Resurrection (Why would God let Christ suffer?); revelation, and the accusation that Scriptures have been changed; heaven or paradise, and hell.

3. Responding to people who see our faith as foolish: How did Paul respond to the Greeks (1 Cor. 1:18–31, 9:19–27)? What did Peter advise (1 Peter 3:15)?

4. Building blocks of the gospel for Muslims: God's redemptive nature and his great love for his creation; man's innately sinful nature; the deadly, destructive character of sin.

5. Communication and incarnation of the gospel: Communicate not merely propositional truth but love and sacrifice as well. Does the gospel change our lives? If so, can others see that?

# LESSON READINGS

# INTRODUCTION

Muslims have many mistaken assumptions about our Christian faith. Some of these come from Islamic teachings and others from popular hearsay on the Muslim street. For example, we treasure the Bible and would never allow anyone to change it; yet, Muslims have often been told that the Bible has been changed. In responding to this and other misconceptions, we do not

Encourage Muslims to read the Bible

need to convince our Muslim friends that we are right. We may need to gently assure them that we honor God's Word, but we must not let initial disagreements distract us from our friendship. We believe in the power of God's Word, and we can trust Christ to reveal truth when we put the Bible directly into our friends' hands, encouraging them to read it for themselves.

Similarly, our friends may have great difficulty understanding the Trinity, thinking we worship three gods. Rather than becoming mired in a vain argument, we can assure them that we believe God is one, and continue to pray that, over time, God will help them discern this concept. Indeed, the doctrine of the Trinity is difficult even for Christians to understand, so we certainly do not want to make that a condition for friendship with Muslims.

The necessity of Christ's death on the cross; his payment for our sins by his blood and righteousness; and the power over death, sin, shame, and fear that is available only through his resurrection are all essential to comprehending Christianity. However, before grappling with the end of the story redemption,

Muslims may need an introduction to the rest of God's revelation.

## GOD'S TRUE NATURE

While Muslims believe in God, worship him, and ascribe to him many of the same characteristics that the Bible does, they may not fully understand God's redemptive nature. In the Old Testament, we are convinced of the need for a perfect sacrifice for sin. The clear foreshadowing of Christ's coming and mission is revealed, and examples of the many times God consistently rescued and provided for his people are recorded. If we study these stories with our friends, they may find it easier to accept that God could become fully human, without giving up his divinity, and to comprehend why he would allow himself to be sacrificed in our place. If we can help our Muslim friends grasp a fuller picture of God's nature, they may be able to accept his ability and desire to send Christ to die for us.

Muslims also require a correct interpretation of how our holy God views sin and of how completely all of us fail to follow his standards. Until we realistically face our predilection for sin, as illustrated in the life of God's people, we will not conclude that we need God's provision of a savior. How can we expect our Muslim friends to accept God's unusual step of redeeming us through Christ unless they first view God as redemptive and understand the deadly nature of sin?

As evangelicals, we are tempted to focus on theological facts we think not-yet-believers need to know in order to believe in Jesus Christ. In fact, many people actually put their trust in Jesus before understanding much of the gospel's content. When we overemphasize the cognitive, we may communicate in ways that distance us from relationships and separate us from demonstrating love to our neighbors. Are we not overlooking the very means God uses to bring people to himself?

## RELATIONAL WITNESS

If we are focusing on knowledge, we will be living from our heads rather than living from our hearts. Our interaction becomes abstract and avoids real relational connection. It is true, we may prefer this avoidance so as to maintain personal space, or keep secret our weaknesses, the areas in which we fail to live by the biblical design. Talking about what the Bible means,

instead of about our struggles to apply it daily, seems easier. We may not even be intimate with our spouses, ourselves, or God, let alone a new friend from a different culture or religion. We are strongly tempted to stay hidden behind what we know, instead of revealing the imperfect reality of who we are. In *The Pursuit of God*, A. W. Tozer says, "We Christians are in real danger of losing God amid the wonders of his Word."[1]

Islam's teachings about Christianity are largely based on the early interaction of Muslims with Jews and aberrant Christians. In addition, the issue of the atoning sacrifice of Christ on the cross for our sins is greatly misunderstood. The Jews understood the basic biblical concepts—God's redemptive nature, his great love for us, humankind's innately sinful condition, and the fatal results of our sin—through God's revelation, their history, and many aspects of their culture and rituals. Even so, the Jews find the idea of Christ's crucifixion (and resurrection) offensive, a stumbling block. "Christ crucified" was foolishness to the Greeks as well (1 Cor. 1:17–25).

Muslims respond in much the same way: like the Greeks, Muslims have little biblical understanding; they do not see the logic or dignity in Christ's sacrifice on the cross. They do not believe that there is a significant need for a savior, so they often deny the Crucifixion or explain it away. They reject the idea mentally before it ever confronts their hearts. How can we direct them to the deep joy of knowing that God has graciously provided us with his righteousness, love, forgiveness, and adoption?

## ATTRACTIVE WITNESS

The question for the Greeks was why God would do such an unlikely and illogical thing as to become a man, and live a sinless life, only to die an unjust death? As they have a similar problem, Muslims may benefit from a slower-paced approach. This will permit us to carefully fill in the missing biblical background of the gospel message, while demonstrating it so our Muslim friends may observe our lifestyle. In turn, this will be a more tangible, more attractive witness than that provided in a "drive-by shooting" of logical-truth arguments that do not correspond with what Muslims observe in the "Christian" world. Most Muslims come to true appreciation of the gospel and desire for our Lord by seeing our faith lived out in the daily struggles of real Christians, serving openly, humbly, faithfully, by their sides in their communities.

*– K.S., Editor*

## ENDNOTE

1. Tozer, *Pursuit of God* (Camp Hill, Pa.: Christian Publications, 1993), p. 13.

# WHY DO WE SHARE THE GOOD NEWS ABOUT JESUS WITH ALL PEOPLES, INCLUDING MUSLIMS?

Why do some Christians risk their freedom and their lives to talk about Jesus Christ in seemingly inhospitable environments, such as some Muslim countries? Is it right for them to do so? How do they go about it, even in countries that refuse to allow their citizens to exercise the internationally recognized right of religious freedom?

The undersigned leaders of fifty-five Christian organizations from nineteen countries explain our motives and methods in the following statement. Our job is not to represent any government or civilization, but to obey and follow Jesus.

## UNIVERSAL DECLARATION OF HUMAN RIGHTS

First of all, it is important to realize that everyone has an internationally recognized right to discuss his or her faith with others, no matter where we live or visit. The international community agrees: 151 nations have ratified the UN's International Covenant on Civil and Political Rights, which affirms: "Everyone shall have the right to freedom of thought, conscience, and religion. This right shall include freedom to have or to adopt a religion or belief of his choice, and freedom, either individually or in community with others, and in public or private, to manifest his religion or belief in worship, observance, practice, and teaching. No one shall be subject to coercion which would impair his freedom to have or to adopt a religion or belief of his choice."[1]

There should be no double standards. Muslims who live in the West are free to respectfully express and share their faith. Followers of Jesus who live in the Muslim world should be equally free to respectfully express and share their faith.

**But *why* and *how* do we share about Jesus with Muslims?**

1. We are followers of Jesus, called Isa al-Masih by Muslims. This means that he holds supreme importance for us. We seek to center our lives on Jesus and the Good News about him.[2]

2. What is this Good News? We have experienced peace with God, the forgiveness of our sins, and the hope of eternal life through the death and resurrection of Jesus Christ.[3]

3. It is our delight to share this Good News with others.[4] It is also our duty to share the Good News with all the peoples of the world because Jesus instructed us to do so.[5]

4. Therefore, we seek to live in the world as peacemakers, inviting men and women everywhere to be reconciled to God and to one another.[6]

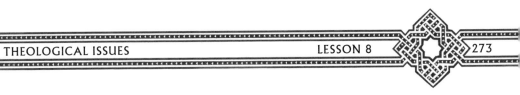
5. We, who come from many cultures, countries, and backgrounds, offer this message of peace to all people, in love, with respect and cultural sensitivity, without coercion or material inducement.[7]

6. We believe that only God can convert people. Christianity and Islam agree on this point.[8] For many, the titles "Muslim" and "Christian" define an external, cultural identity. Instead of focusing on external labels, we invite all people, including Muslims, to an inward change through Jesus.[9]

7. We rejoice that when the gospel brings inward change to believers who embrace it, they then bring positive transformation to the communities where they live.[10]

8. As followers of Jesus, we are motivated to do good deeds. In this way, we imitate Jesus, honor God, and seek to heal a hurting world.[11]

9. For us, all of life is devoted to Jesus. Therefore, wherever we live and whatever our occupation, our work is witness and we witness at work.[12]

10. Jesus and the Good News about him are so precious to us that we are willing to sacrifice and suffer in order to give people an opportunity to know the Good News about him.[13]

## THIS STATEMENT WAS AFFIRMED IN MARCH 2004 BY:

**Australia**
Rev. Dr. Stuart Robinson
Senior Pastor
Crossway Baptist Church

**Brazil**
Dr. Barbara Helen Burns
Educational Coordinator
Centro Nordestino de Missões

**Canada**
Rev. Geoff Tunicliffe
Director, Global Initiatives
Evangelical Fellowship of
    Canada

Dr. Jon Ohlhauser
President
Prairie Bible Institute

**Cote d'Ivoire**
Mr. Younoussa Djao
Partnering Advisor
Interdev Partnerhip Associates

**Ghana**
Rev. Johnson Asare
Director
Markaz Al Bishara

**India**
Dr. K. Rajendran
General Secretary
India Missions Association

Dr. Daniel Sathiaraj
Founder
Prayer Fellowship International

**Jamaica**
Mrs. Paula Wong
Executive Director
NEST (The Networking
    Equipping Sending Team
    for World Evangelization)

**Jordan**
Dr. Imad Shehadeh
President
Jordan Evangelical Theological
    Seminary

**Kenya**
Rev. Canon 'Bayo Famonure
Executive Secretary
Evangelism and Missions
    Commission of Association
    of Evangelicals in Africa

**Korea**
Dr. David Tai Woong Lee
Director
Global Missionary Training
    Center

**Netherlands**
Mr. Trev Gregory
International Director
TEMA-MISSION

Mr. Drs. Marco Vermin
Director
Gave (church work among
    refugees)

**Nigeria**
Rev. Nahor Samaila
Director
Evangelical Missionary Society

**Portugal**
Rev. Paulo Carlos Noivo Pascoal
Missions Commission Director
Portuguese Evangelical Alliance

**South Africa**
Rev. William F. Crew
International Director
World Mission Centre

**Spain**
Rev. Marcos Amado
President
Pueblos Musulmanes
   Internacional

**Switzerland**
Mr. Marcel Durst
International Team Leader
Latin Link

Rev. Martin Voegelin
Executive Secretary
Association of Evangelical
   Missions

**United Kingdom**
Rev. Dr. David Lundy
International Director
Arab World Ministries

Dr. Rick Love
International Director
Frontiers

Mr. Clive James Pritchard
International Director
People International

Rev. Evan Davies
International Director
WEC International

Mr. Patrick Johnstone
Author, *Operation World*
WEC International

**United States**
Rev. Jim Killgore
President/CEO
ACMC

Dr. Gregory E. Fritz
President
Caleb Project

Dr. Hans Finzel
President
CBInternational

Dr. Steve Hoke
VP People Development
Church Resource Ministries

Dr. Patrick Cate
President
Christar

Dr. Warren F. Larson
Director, Zwemer Center for
   Muslim Studies
Columbia International
   University

Dr. Paul McKaughan
President
Evangelical Fellowship of
   Mission Agencies

Dr. A. Scott Moreau
Chair, Missions and
   Intercultural Studies,
   Wheaton College
Editor, *Evangelical Missions
   Quarterly*

Dr. J. Dudley Woodberry
Professor of Islamic Studies and
   Dean Emeritus
School of Intercultural Studies
Fuller Theological Seminary

Dr. John H. Orme
Executive Director
Interdenominational Foreign
   Mission Association

Dr. David Pollock
Executive Director
Interaction International Inc.

Dr. David W. Stoner
Lead Global Outreach Pastor
Mars Hill Church

Mr. Lloyd A. Cooke
Jamaica Co-ordinator
Ministries-In-Action

Dr. Paul D. Kooistra
Coordinator
Mission to the World

Rev. John E. Fletcher
International Director
Pioneers

Dr. J. B. Crouse Jr.
President
OMS International, Inc.

Dr. W. Ward Gasque
President
Pacific Association for
   Theological Studies

Dr. Steve Strauss
Director
SIM

Dr. Miriam Adeney
Associate Professor of World
   Christian Studies
Seattle Pacific University

Dr. Charles A. Davis
Executive Director
TEAM

Mr. Kenneth O. Smith
TIE International Coordinator
TIE Tentmakers

Dr. D. Jim O'Neill
President
UFM International

Rev. Tom Correll
Pastor, Wooddale Worldwide
Wooddale Church

Rev. Gary Edmonds
Secretary General
World Evangelical Alliance

Dr. William David Taylor
Executive Director
World Evangelical Alliance
   Missions Commission

Rev. Albert Ehmann
Executive Director
World Team (Global Ministries)

Rev. H. Allan Graham Jr.
President
World Thrust North America

Mr. Min-Young Jung
International Coordinator,
 Asian Diaspora Initiative
Wycliffe Bible Translators
 International USA, Korea

Rev. Steve Cochrane
Director
Youth With A Mission
 Neighbours

**West Indies**
Mr. David Harper
Director
Youth With A Mission Barbados

## ENDNOTES

1. Source: *www.unhchr.ch/html/menu3/b/a_ccpr.htm*.
 The UN's Universal Declaration of Human
 Rights uses even stronger language, asserting
 that: "Everyone has the right to freedom of
 thought, conscience, and religion; this right
 includes freedom to change his religion or
 belief, and freedom, either alone or in community with others, and in public or private,
 to manifest his religion or belief in teaching,
 practice, worship, and observance." Source:
 *www.un.org/overview/rights.html*.

2. Phil. 1:21; Gal. 6:14.

3. Acts 10:43; Rom. 5:1, 6:23; 1 Cor. 15:1–4.

4. 2 Cor. 5:14; Eph. 5:2.

5. Matt. 28:18–20.

6. Matt. 5:9; 2 Cor. 5:18.

7. Rom. 12:17–18; 1 Cor. 16:14; 2 Cor. 8:2; 1 Peter
 3:15.

8. Jesus pointed out: "No one can come to me,
 unless the Father who sent me makes them want
 to come" (John 6:44, CEV). The Qur'an agrees,
 saying, "God converts whom he will" (Sura
 24:46; 35:8). In fact, both are missionary

religions, with a message for all people (Sura
 3:20; 25:1; 38:87; John 3:16). Both faiths claim
 the final messenger (Sura 33:40 [Seal of the
 Prophets; *Rasul-Ullah*, Messenger of Allah];
 Heb. 1:1–2). Both groups are called to be
 witnesses (Sura 2:143; Matt. 28:19–20). Both
 Scriptures make exclusive claims for their message (Sura 3:85; John 14:6; Acts 4:12). Yet both
 are called to witness in a gracious manner (Sura
 16:125; 29:46; 1 Peter 3:15).

9. Ezek. 36:26–27; John 3:3–7; 2 Cor. 5:17–20.

10. Historically, religious voluntary organizations
 have had a very large positive impact on international development in non-western countries.
 It has been estimated that such organizations
 are responsible for roughly 70 percent of the
 work of international development, having
 founded, for example, more than half of the
 colleges and hospitals of Africa and Asia.
 (Source: Dr. Ralph D. Winter, William Carey
 International University).

11. Matt. 5:16; Acts 10:38; Titus 2:7–8, 14, 3:14.

12. 1 Cor. 10:31; Col. 3:17, 23.

13. Acts 5:41; Phil. 1:29.

# THEOLOGICAL DIVERGENCE

*by Bruce McDowell and Anees Zaka*

While Muslims and Christians can affirm and give thanks for those things that unite them, both must confess that there are some important differences between them. The Muslim testifies that the Qur'an is God's final and definitive revelation of his perfect will to mankind. The Christian testifies that Jesus Christ is the living Word of God in human form. For the Muslim, the Qur'an is the criterion of truth, while for the Christian, the total biblical witness, culminating in Jesus the Messiah, is the criterion of truth. These commitments determine what the Muslim and the Christian believe about God, man, salvation, guidance, righteousness, revelation, and judgment.[1]

For the Muslim, man's success and salvation lie in accepting God as his God, as *Ma'bud* (the object of worship, reverence, loyalty, and obedience). Just as the revelation of Christ is the redemptive act of God for Christians, so Islam believes that the revelation of Muhammad is the redemptive act of God. As the revelation of Christ redeemed man from bondage to sin, so the revelation of Muhammad redeemed man from bondage to shirk (associating partners with Allah) and *kufr* (ungodliness or no faith).[2]

Both Islam and Christianity agree that God is merciful and that he loves. The question is, how closely does God choose to identify with our human situation? How does God express his love and mercy? God's mercy is expressed in Islam supremely through the revelation of a perfect law. God's love is supremely expressed in Christianity in the suffering, redemptive love that was revealed in the life, crucifixion, and resurrection of Jesus the Messiah. These differences are very significant.[3]

From the Christian perspective, the holiness of God and the sinfulness of men are two vital omissions in the Qur'anic revelation. These two truths are inseparable and together pose the problem that required as its solution the vicarious sacrifice of the Righteous One in the place of the sinner, in order that salvation might be provided. If either the holiness of God or the sinfulness of man is reduced or overlooked, the need for salvation by grace disappears, and a religion of human good works becomes plausible. This is just what is found in Islam.

Both Muslim and Christian can agree on this: Truth is the authoritative revelation from God. But this starting point is also the point of divergence. Is the word of revelation preeminently a book that descended

Bruce A. McDowell studied Islam at Temple University and has experience in Muslim ministry in the United States and countries around the world.

Anees Zaka is the founder and director of Church Without Walls and founder and president of Biblical Institute for Islamic Studies.

Adapted from Bruce A. McDowell and Anees Zaka, *Muslims and Christians at the Table* (Phillipsburg, N.J.: P & R Publishing, 1999), pp. 149–150. Used by permission. *www.prpbooks.com*

from heaven with Allah's revealed will, or is it supremely evident in the person of Christ, who is revealed to us through understanding the Bible that was inspired by the Holy Spirit? For the Muslim, the Qur'an is revered as an eternal, uncreated book preserved in heaven and almost worshiped. The Bible-believing Christian trusts in the Bible as God's authoritative, inerrant word, which reveals God supremely in Christ for our salvation.

### ENDNOTES

1. Badru D. Kateregga and David W. Shenk, *Islam and Christianity: A Muslim and a Christian in Dialogue* (Grand Rapids: Eerdmans, 1981), p. 170.

2. Isma'il Ragi al-Faruqi, *Christian Ethics* (Montreal: McGill University Press, 1967), p. 225.

3. Kateregga and Shenk, *Islam and Christianity*, pp. 169–70.

# THE PRESSURES OF MARRIAGE

Gulzar became a believer in Christ while she was a university student and grew quickly in her faith. She understood God's standard of not being "unequally yoked" (2 Cor. 6:14), and told her boyfriend, Rustam, they could not marry unless he became a believer. Rustam saw the difference in Gulzar and began searching for the truth. Eventually, he came to Christ, was baptized, and married Gulzar.

Family pressures for them to divorce mounted immediately. Rustam's parents were opposed to Gulzar, blaming her for leading Rustam away from their Islamic traditions. His friends enticed him to begin drinking again, and he stopped associating with other believers. When drunk, Rustam verbally abuses his wife, but has not hit her. Gulzar loves Rustam and believes he knows Jesus, but he is weak and has not joined her as she stands against sin.

In this couple's society, marriage is considered so important that it is thought better to marry and divorce than never to marry at all. For many, this is a huge barrier to their decision to accept Christ. Becoming a Christian can mean a person may never marry.

Source: *The Uyghurs of Central Asia*, Caleb Project

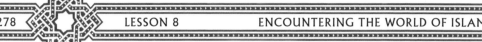

# EMERGENCY APOLOGETICS: ANSWERING COMMON OBJECTIONS

*by Edward J. Hoskins*

When a Muslim meets a Christian for the first time, invariably he asks questions and raises objections to the Christian faith. His forthright manner may seem rude to a Westerner not used to this style of relating. The Christian may feel threatened and uncomfortable, and usually responds by attempting to present a thorough and logical defense of the gospel. Either a strident exchange ensues and offends both people, or the Christian, frustrated at not being able to finish his argument, becomes subdued. The Muslim then wonders about the Christian's passivity and lack of courage. This does not bode well for a budding friendship!

There is another option. I have developed some concise responses to a Muslim's common questions about Christianity. They can all be said with a smile and will satisfy most inquirers. Listen carefully to the Muslim's reply. It will tell you a lot about his level of spiritual interest. A Muslim's questions may not be what they appear.

He may be searching for more than just your beliefs; he maybe probing to find out if you respect him and the views he holds.

The responses that follow are not intended to be exhaustive apologetics. Rather, they are a way to show that you care about the person and his or her religion and that you are interested in future dialogue.

## "WHAT DO YOU THINK ABOUT MUHAMMAD?"

To a Muslim, Muhammad is the most precious person in the world. How you respond to this question will set the tone for any future relationship. Be honest, but refer to Muhammad with respect, just as you would want your Muslim friend to be respectful of Jesus.

Response: "You know that Muhammad is not my prophet; he is yours. Although I do not believe exactly what you believe about him, I do respect him. Politically, he was a reformer, a statesman, and a national leader. Religiously, he called idolatrous people back to worship the One True God. He also said many positive things about my Lord Jesus. I believe each of these reasons makes him worthy of my respect."

---

Dr. Hoskins is a physician at a major midwestern university and has been involved with Muslims for more than two decades. He and his family lived in Beirut, Lebanon in the early 1980s. *A Muslim's Heart* is published by Dawson Media, a ministry of Navigators.

Adapted from Edward J. Hoskins, *A Muslim's Heart: What Every Christian Needs to Know to Share Christ with Muslims* (Colorado Springs: Dawson Media, 2003), pp. 35–38. Used by permission. *www.dawsonmedia.com*

## "What Do You Think about the Qur'an?"

Response: "Since I am a Christian, you know that the Qur'an is not my book; it is yours. Although I don't believe exactly what you believe about the Qur'an, I do read it. I appreciate it because of the many wonderful and beautiful things it says about my Lord Messiah Jesus.

## "Why Haven't You Become a Muslim?"

Response: "You know that I'm a Christian, which means I'm not a follower of your religion, your prophet, or your book. However, if you are using the word 'Muslim' (surrendered) in its truest sense—as one who is surrendered to God—then I am already that. I have surrendered my life to God and have been made completely clean through his mighty blood sacrifice of Messiah Jesus."

The cross: God's initiative

## "Was Muhammad Prophesied in the Bible?"

Muslims believe the Bible prophesies the coming of Muhammad, beginning with the call of Abraham (Gen. 12:1–3): "The Lord had said to Abram, 'Leave your country, your people, and your father's household and go to the land I will show you. I will make you into a great nation and I will bless you; I will make your name great, and you will be a blessing. I will bless those who bless you, and whoever curses you I will curse; and all peoples on earth will be blessed through you.'"

Muslims believe this worldwide blessing is the arrival of Islam. They interpret this to

## " " Who Is Responsible for Man's Salvation?

In Islam, man's salvation rests on his own shoulders and his obedience to the law, while in Christianity, it rests purely and solely on the grace of God…. Islam tells man what to do to earn salvation; Christianity tells man what God has done to give him salvation…. Islam is a call to obedience; Christianity is a proclamation of God's initiative.

James P. Dretke, *A Christian Approach to Muslims* (Pasadena, Calif.: William Carey Library, 1979), p. 38.

mean that God will make a great nation through Hagar and her son Ishmael (see Gen. 17:20).

They also believe Moses prophesied about Muhammad in Deuteronomy 18:18 when God said to Moses: "I will raise up for them a prophet like you from among their brothers; I will put my words in his mouth, and he will tell them everything I command him."

Response: "I do believe that God, in the Bible, prophesied about a very special prophet who would come in the future. A few of the prophecies could be confused with Muhammad. However, there are more than three hundred prophecies, which are very specific. As I have studied them, I believe there is only one person who could (and did) fulfill each of them—the Messiah Jesus, Son of Mary. Sometime, would you like to look at a few of these prophecies?" Gently, and with a smile, point the way back to Jesus and the Scriptures.

Without compromising the truth, respond to these common objections and others like them with short, concise, and respectful answers. Our goal is not to win an argument but to gain a friend and a hearing for the gospel.

# GOSPEL COMMUNICATION FROM WITHIN

*by Patrick O. Cate*

Historic walls separate one billion Muslims from a personal relationship with God through faith in Jesus Christ. This article deals with some of the historical theological walls, besides the cultural, social, familial, political, and linguistic barriers that are present. We need to continually keep in mind that there is no substitute for prayer, love, and a personal relationship for bringing Muslims into the light of our Savior. These require time, energy, and high rank in our priorities.

## WITHIN THE MUSLIM MIND

To begin outside of the Muslim mind, driving home points which Muslims categorically and antagonistically reject, is similar to banging our heads against a wall. If we are to specialize in opening windows and doors in Muslim walls, we have to begin where the Muslim mind is, with what he accepts, not what he rejects. We do not begin where we want him to arrive.

Throughout the fourteen centuries in which Muslims and Christians have

been dealing with each other, the same arguments have continued to emerge: the deity of Christ, the triune God, the sonship of Christ, and the trustworthiness of the Bible. We could profit by reading John of Damascus (A.D. 740) and many others who debated with Muslims in the first centuries.

Exchanges with Muslims can frequently become logical debates, building on premises which Muslims already reject, resulting in apparent attacks on Islam. Sometimes, in the discussion, Muslims are permitted to state the nature of the trial—the accusations—and be both the judge and the jury, leaving Christians on the defensive. In communicating the love of Jesus Christ to Muslims, we need to prayerfully understand the Muslim mind, and to share God's sincere love for Muslims, beginning from within their minds, hearts, and frame of thinking. It is crucial to begin **where they are**, with what Muslims accept and value, and not start with presuppositions they reject. Opening with what they accept, we need to gradually help them overcome their preconceived notions for rejecting the gospel so that they can come to know God in a personal way through faith in Jesus Christ. We offer the following practical, step-by-step approach to gospel witness to Muslims, disarming them in key areas and lowering barriers to the gospel.

Dr. Patrick O. Cate is president of Christar, formerly International Missions, Inc. (IMI). Christar has been working with Muslim peoples in twenty countries for more than seventy years. *www.christar.org*

Adapted from Patrick O. Cate, "Gospel Communication from Within," *International Journal of Frontier Missions* 11, no. 2 (April 1994), pp. 93–97. Used by permission. *www.ijfm.org*

## THE DEITY OF CHRIST

Muslims have been taught to reject the idea of the deity of Christ. However, it is possible to lead some to become open to this concept, and to even accept it, without quoting the Qur'an or the Bible, and without using the precise words "deity of Christ."

After establishing rapport, I turn the conversation to spiritual things, especially towards Christ. I like to ask my Muslim friends if they believe that Christ had a virgin birth. They respond in the affirmative. Then I say, "So he had no father and, therefore, his birth was unique and supernatural, wasn't it?" Sometimes Muslims will point out that Adam did not have a human father or mother, to which I also agree. But I come back to Christ and point out, "But he did not have a father like the rest of us, did he? So his birth was unique and it was supernatural, wasn't it?" Although this is clearly mentioned in the Bible (Matt. 1:23), as well as in the Qur'an (Sura 3:45–47), I usually do not quote either of them at this stage.

## TURKIC PEOPLES

The Turkic peoples comprise 86 people groups, number more than 160 million people, and spread across China, Russia, Turkey, and Central Asia—mostly in the countries of Iran, Iraq, Afghanistan, Azerbaijan, Kazakhstan, Kyrgyzstan, Tajikistan, Turkmenistan, and Uzbekistan. Significant numbers of Turkic peoples have also formed communities in European countries, including France, Germany (where more than 2 million Turks now live), and the United Kingdom.

Because the former USSR once ruled a number of the countries that are home to Turkic peoples, the populace in these regions has seen incredible changes since their nations gained autonomy in the last two decades of the twentieth century.

One such country, Azerbaijan, earned independence from Russia in 1990. Azerbaijanis in the nation of Azerbaijan number nearly 7 million. Even more, 15 million, live in Iran. Nearly 90 percent of Azerbaijanis are Muslim.

Baku, the capital city of Azerbaijan, is a developed urban center. Its residents experience significant western influence because of the city's international oil trade. Rural villages, however, tend to retain traditional Azerbaijani lifestyle and customs. The widening cultural gap has become apparent in Baku, since Azerbaijan's war with neighboring Armenia in the early 1990s sent an influx of rural Azerbaijani refugees from Armenian-occupied areas to the city. Baku also draws many rural students to study at its universities.

Azerbaijani people are proud of their extensive heritage of poetry and music. Some Baku streets are named after famous Azerbaijani poets and feature a number of gigantic statues paying tribute to famous writers.

Many Azerbaijanis mix their Islamic practices with an ancient form of fire worship, which emerged because the region's abundant, natural gas reserves sometimes cause fires to burn spontaneously from the earth.

Sources: *Hope and a Future for Azerbaijan: A Prayer Guide* (Littleton, Colo.: Caleb Project, 1999); *Operation World; www.joshuaproject.net.*

## The Turkic World

© Caleb Project

Then I point out that Christ performed many miracles of love, kindness, and compassion. He healed people who were blind from birth and they could see; he healed people who were lame from birth and they were able to jump with joy; he healed those with leprosy and even raised the dead (Sura 3:49; 5:110). Therefore, Christ's life was unique and supernatural. Sometimes, Muslims will say, "Other people have performed miracles, and the Qur'an is a miracle of Muhammad." I respond, "The Bible does say that there were others who performed miracles. However, the miracles of Jesus Christ were supernatural and unique acts, weren't they?"

## THE GOSPEL WITNESS

Even though what I have shared up to this point is already believed by Muslims, and although I usually do not quote the Bible nor the Qur'an, nevertheless they generally accept what I share with them concerning Christ. This now sets the stage, and I briefly introduce something that they usually do not accept: "And the prophet Jesus died on the cross, for the forgiveness of our sins, and also arose from the grave, and conquered death." Sometimes, at that point, a Muslim will reject what I said, but I try not to answer

his contradiction. Muslims need to hear the gospel, and often I do not know how many times a particular Muslim will need to hear it before he or she believes. But since I want it to be one less gospel witness that he or she needs to hear, I try to state mine well. Also, it is possible that I will never see this person again, which is another reason for clearly sharing the gospel with him.

Then I introduce another point about Jesus which they already believe: "Then the prophet Jesus ascended to heaven." But I add, "And there is not a grave where you can go to worship at his dead bones. The end of his life was unique and supernatural, wasn't it?" (see Sura 3: 55, which deals with Jesus' ascension). I include the phrase, "So there is no grave where you can worship at his dead bones," to alert Muslims to the facts of their roots and tendencies toward animism. Not only in Medina, where they go to pray at the bones of Muhammad, but throughout the Muslim world, Muslims hold to animism or to a supernatural power, in this case, the dead bones of their dead saints, through which they believe their prayers can be answered. This is attributing a partnership to God, or shirk, the unforgivable sin. Although I do not go

into a detailed explanation of this point, it nevertheless serves as a gentle reminder.

Avoiding, at this point, the fact of the death and resurrection of Christ, I say, "So the end of Christ's life was unique and supernatural. The end of his life is not like the rest of our lives, where there is a grave and a dead body." I do not use the phrase "death of Christ." At each of the three points in the discussion on the life of Christ, I ask the question, "Wouldn't that make his birth, his life, and the end of his life unique and supernatural?" I keep asking this question until I get an affirmative answer from my Muslim friends.

## UNIQUE AND SUPERNATURAL BIRTH, LIFE, AND LIFE'S END

To introduce the crucial part in the development of this thought, I review: "So that would make Christ's birth, his life, and the end of his life unique and supernatural," which leads up to the fact that, "The prophet Jesus would be the only person who ever lived, who had all three: a unique and supernatural birth, a unique and supernatural life, and a unique and supernatural end to his life, wouldn't he?" Sometimes Muslims will point out exceptions of individual cases, and, of course, I point out, "Yes, there are other people who had a supernatural birth or performed miracles." Therefore, it is important to emphasize Jesus's singularity by using the words "only" and "all." Christ was the only one who was singular and unique in all three.

I keep asking these questions until I get an affirmative answer. I ask, "Since the prophet Jesus is the only one to have a

unique and supernatural birth, and life, and end to his life, that would make him the most unique and supernatural person who ever lived, wouldn't it?" Recently, when I came to that point with a Muslim, he answered, "Yes." He dropped his objections and immediately asked, "Could you get me a copy of the New Testament so I can read it?" So, without using the words "God," "deity," or "Son of God" throughout this discussion and progression of thought, it truly is possible in a first conversation to get a Muslim to agree that Christ is the most supernatural and unique person who ever lived, which comes very close to acknowledging the deity of Jesus Christ.

## REALIZATION OF CHRIST'S SIGNIFICANCE

Some time ago I was dialoguing with a number of Muslim friends on the floor of one of the major mosques in America, discussing these questions. There were some ten of us from a local seminary and about ten Muslims, and the conversation got rather heated. However, I kept asking my same question, "Wouldn't that make him the only person who ever lived who had a supernatural and unique birth, life, and end to his life?" I kept asking it until the resident scholar, a sheik, answered, "Yes." This then changed the conversation radically from attacking Christianity to praising Jesus. Obviously, that does not mean that they believed and were saved. But it helped to stop their attack and opened their minds to possibilities they had never thought of before.

One advantage of this type of approach and train of thought is that it proceeds

from within the Muslim mind, moving from the known to the unknown. The fact that they are ready in their minds to accept the virgin birth, the miracles, and the ascension of Christ can help them see that Christ is the most unique and supernatural person who ever lived, since he is the only one to have all three attributes. Muslims have never quite put it all together before, or realized the significance of such a life. I suggest that other lovers of Muslims try this approach also.

## THE SON OF GOD

In most conversations with Muslims, it is not the Christians who bring up the concept and discussion of the "Son of God," but Muslims who begin to address it with their absolute rejection of it. However, I have found that this is one of the easiest objections to answer. For starters, we need to ask, "What do you mean by 'Son of God'?" Usually they do not offer an answer, so I try to probe: "Do you mean that God, in a sense, got married to Mary or had sexual relations?" When they affirm or acknowledge this, then I say, with greater emotion than they have voiced, "*Haram, fosh*—blasphemy!", expressing a much stronger denial of this concept than they felt or expressed. It is important for them to hear and realize that what they reject, namely that God had sexual relations with Mary, is more blasphemous to us than it is to them.

But then what does "Son of God" mean? Again, I think it is crucial to begin within the Muslim mind and proceed step by step. A little research can be of considerable value. I encourage every Muslim evangelist to make a study of the

Muslim language he uses, to find as many metaphorical and kinship terms and illustrations as he can within that language for son, father, mother, daughter, and sister. I have a list of sixty kinship analogies in Arabic and five in Persian.

## USE OF KINSHIP ANALOGIES IN CORRECTING THEIR DEFINITION

Possibly the most common figure of speech using "son of" in Muslim languages is "*Ibn is sabil*," which literally means "son of the road." The meaning from Arabic would be "wayfarer, wanderer, passerby, or traveler." The reason that it could be the most universal concept is because it is found in the Qur'an five times (Suras 8:41; 9:60; 17:26; 30:38; 59:7). In the Qur'an, "son of God" is rejected as a title for Christ and "son of Mary" is accepted.

My method of using this with a Muslim is very simple. I simply ask, "'Ibn is sabil': What does this mean? Does it mean that the road got married and had a baby road who was a traveler? Does it mean that the road got married and had sexual relations that produced a son of the road?" The usual response is, "No, no, no!" So I say, "What do you mean?" The response usually is something like, "A wayfarer, a wanderer, a passerby, or a traveler." Then I respond, "So you do not mean it literally, or physically, or biologically, but you mean it in a spiritual way, or a metaphorical way. In the same way, when the Bible says that Christ is the Son of God, we do not mean that God got married to Mary and had sexual relations and produced a baby Jesus. We do not believe in a 'papa God' and a 'mama God' producing a 'baby God.' That is blasphemy!" I usually say,

© Caleb Project

What kind of witness will he receive?

you mean it in a spiritual and a metaphorical way. It is the same when we say, 'Christ is the Son of God.' The Bible doesn't mean it literally, physically, or biologically, that a 'papa God' got married to a 'mama God' and had a 'baby God.' We mean it spiritually and metaphorically."

Shiites often revere Ali more than Muhammad. So, in the Persian language, I go through the same analogies, as they speak of Ali as "the husband of widows, the father of orphans, the sword of God, and the hand of God." I ask questions like, "Did Ali father all the orphans of the world? That would not be right! Did Ali marry all of the widows of the world? That would not be right! Are not four marriages enough? Isn't it immoral to marry them all? So what does it mean? Do you mean it literally, physically, or biologically? In the same way that you do not mean it literally, physically, or biologically, we do not mean God got married and had sexual relations with Mary and produced a baby God when we say 'Christ is the Son of God.'"

"We don't mean it literally, biologically, or physically, but we mean it spiritually and metaphorically." I repeat this series of questions and responses concerning "Son of God" with each of the analogies I use in this approach.

A common Egyptian idiom is that the Sphinx is the *Abul houl*, which translates, "the father of terror." I ask what this means. Does this mean that the Sphinx got married and had baby Sphinxs who were terrors?" They respond, "No, the Sphinx guards the desert and the pyramids." So I reply, "So you don't mean it literally, physically, or biologically, but

These are just a few analogies from Persian and Arabic. Much of this is very cultural, and different idioms would be used in each of the various Muslim languages.

## PROVIDING THE CORRECT CHARACTERIZATION

It is important, not merely to help Muslims realize that their definition of Son of God is incorrect, but also to provide a positive definition. And we must not only ask ourselves what it means, but what must the concept communicate? Theologically, the phrase "Son of God" conveys several important ideas. One of those is that the Son reveals the Father. Hebrews 1:1–4 indicates this: God "has spoken to us by his Son," and "The Son is the radiance of God's glory and the exact representation of his being (nature)."

We need to deal with the concept of revelation. What does it mean "to reveal"? Sometimes I'll use a visual aid. Touching the curtains in a nearby window, I say, "If I had not been in this country before, and had arrived at night, when it was dark and these curtains were closed, in the morning they would be opened, and "the veil" would be removed. Revelation would occur and I could look out and see how beautiful the country is. We cannot see God face to face, but he has chosen to remove the veil to let us get to know him better through getting to know the prophet Jesus. In this world, a physical son reveals his father to us. When we see a son, we know something of his father, even if we have never met the father before." Muslims frequently think we are taking a good man, Jesus, a prophet, and making him into God. By beginning from within the Muslim mind, where he is and what he values, we can gradually lead him to the truth.

## GOD'S CHOICE: REVELATION OF HIMSELF IN JESUS

In Islamic history and theology there were two leading groups, the Asharites and Mutazalites. The Mutazalites, who held to man's free will and human responsibility, lost out to the Asharites, who held to the sovereign free will of God. This concept is made famous in the cry, "Allahu akbar" ("Allah is the Most Great!" or "the Greatest!"). "Allahu Akbar," *takbir*, is shouted from every minaret five times a day and mentioned during each time of prayer. Mobs shout it against their governments, dramatically asserting, "We are on God's side and you are not, and with his help, we will overthrow you!" It clarifies that God is completely sovereign and we are to submit to him. He can do whatever he wants to do. We, as puny beings, here today and gone tomorrow, cannot tell God what he can or cannot do. We cannot tell God that he cannot reveal himself in the form of the prophet Jesus for our salvation. It is not a case of man becoming God, but of God choosing to remove the veil and to reveal himself in the form of the prophet Jesus for our salvation.

## THE TRINITY

In addition to dealing with the concepts of the deity of Christ and the Son of God, there are a variety of approaches which contribute to communicating the idea of the Trinity. One which comes from within Islamic thinking leads back to Asharite theology, embraced by all Muslims. Asharites hold to two basic points of theology: the sovereign free will of God, and that the Qur'an is the uncreated speech of God, existing in the mind of God from eternity past.

Normally I do not broach this subject. However, when Muslims accuse Christians of having three gods, I ask them, "Do you believe the Qur'an is created or uncreated?" I keep asking them until they answer the question. When they assert that the Qur'an is uncreated, I say, "So the Qur'an is eternal and uncreated, and God is eternal and uncreated. You have two eternal and uncreated beings or things; you have two gods, right?" Of course, they strongly refute that. I go back to the same question again, and maybe even a third time. Finally, I say, "You are telling me that you have two eternal and uncreated things, but one God. You know, we also have two or three eternal and uncreated beings or things, but only one God" (see John 1:1).

## SIN PROPERLY EXPLAINED

It may seem easy to conclude that if we can prove the deity of Christ, the sonship of God, and the Trinity, and so forth, that Muslims would take the next step and become Christians. But too often this is not the case. Believing Christ is God and the Son of God, and believing in the Trinity, does not make a person a Christian. A person has to believe that he is a sinner, confess his sin, repent, and believe that Christ died on the cross for his sin. The root problem is not the smoke screens that Muslims raise, but the biblical definition and existence of sin that they want to deny. For most Muslims, sin is like a child cheating on a quiz in first or second grade. It is not a big issue. It is not a moral affront to a holy God. One of our main tasks as Muslim evangelists is to help them realize that they are sinners, and because God is holy, sin is no small matter.

But how can we convey the problem of sin? We need to know the deep issues involved. Muslims do not seriously consider themselves sinners who are an affront to a holy God. Therefore, they could care less about a Savior who delivers them from their sin.

## PERVASIVENESS OF SIN

One way to communicate the concept of sin is by a visual aid. I ask my Muslim friend, "Wouldn't it be great to have a cup of hot tea right now, or a Coke?" He replies, "Yes, that would be great!" But just before I give it to him, I say, "Wait, a minute!" At this point, I add a bit of poison or bug spray or Drano. When a bit of liquid Drano is added to Coke in a clear glass, it changes the Coke's color and makes the visual aid even more effective. Then I offer it to my friend to drink, saying, "Don't you want it?" As he refuses it, I point out, "But I only put a little bit of poison in it; most of it is very good tea or Coke; why don't you want to drink it?" Then I ask the question, "How many sins did Adam have to sin in order to get out of fellowship with God? God told Adam to till the ground. He tilled the ground. God told Adam to name the animals. He named the animals. He just sinned once. He took fruit from one tree, and, by that one sin, he lost fellowship with God." At this time, I point out that I have sinned far more than one sin, and so has he, and so has everyone else.

## THE PROBLEM OF GOD'S HOLINESS

God is holy and man is sinful. God is in heaven and there is no room for sin in heaven. "Who wants to go to heaven if, like this world, it is going to be filled with people who are adulterers or think adulterous thoughts, who steal and cheat people, who speak and think with profanity, who do not speak the truth? Heaven is filled with God. God is holy and pure. God is completely separated from sin, so we cannot go to heaven and take our sin with us. Our sin must be forgiven before we can go to heaven. Just as adding more tea (or Coke) will not get rid of the poison in the glass, adding more good works will not get rid of our sin. That is the wonderful thing about the prophet Jesus.

When he died, he died on the cross as the complete sacrifice for our sins, so we can be completely forgiven, so that we can go to heaven and not bring our sins with us."

Muslims are attracted to animism because they believe it gives them power over weak areas of their lives. But when they are honest, they readily acknowledge their lack of power over personal sin. More than anything else, Muslims need to know Christ has the power to forgive sins and to give personal victory over sin's power.

## INCARNATIONAL WITNESS

"The Word became flesh and made his dwelling among us" (John 1:14a).

Jesus adopted a servant's identity, becoming part of a community, with its cultural norms and mores, and we aspire to emulate his example. Paul modeled incarnational witness in the community (1 Cor. 9), and we aim to follow his pattern, modifying our lifestyles to be effective Christians. How can we become like Muslims—culturally, in our lifestyles—in order to win Muslims?

In Athens, although Paul was "distressed to see that the city was full of idols" (Acts 17:16b), he referred to a pagan altar and quoted a Greek poet in order to help the Athenians understand Jesus Christ (Acts 17:16–34). Peter encouraged wives to incarnate Christ in their home life: "Be submissive to your husbands so that, if any of them do not believe the Word, they may be won over without words by the behavior of their wives" (1 Peter 3:1). Similarly, Paul encouraged slaves, as their responsibility to God, to "remain in the situation God called [them] to" (1 Cor. 7:24). For us, presenting an incarnational witness among Muslims could start with appreciating their worldview and culture, and learning their language, but primarily we want them to understand who Christ is. Even after prayerful consideration, people's convictions differ on how to witness wisely; however, the outcome of our witness must be that Christ is plainly evident. This distinction may result in our persecution. Incarnational witness embraces this consequence: "We put up with anything rather than hinder the gospel of Christ" (1 Cor. 9:12).

> Your attitude should be the same as that of Christ Jesus: Who, being in very nature God, did not consider equality with God something to be grasped, but made himself nothing, taking the very nature of a servant, being made in human likeness. And being found in appearance as a man, he humbled himself and became obedient to death—even death on a cross! (Phil. 2:5–8)

Source: *Encountering the World of Islam*

## FOUR CHRIST-SHAPED VACUUMS

There are four things which Jesus Christ offers that Islam does not have. Islam does not emphasize a loving God, a personal God, the assurance of forgiveness of sins, or the assurance of eternal life. There are a variety of ways in which we can communicate that God is a loving, personal God. We should remember that "Love" is one of the *ninety-nine names of God* (See Appendix 1, p. 469). It is the forty-seventh name, *al-Wadud*. This is not a strong notion within Islam. Rather, the concepts of God's justice, sovereignty, greatness, and unity are central to Muslims. They really do not have an image of a loving God who cares for them, and they certainly do not have the thought of a personal God. For them, God is transcendent. He created the world, but is removed from it and them. When a Muslim wants something personal, he frequently prays to a dead saint, or uses a fortuneteller, or reverts to animistic rituals. When he prays to God, he uses memorized, recited prayers, but he does not enjoy a personal relationship with a loving personal God.

A wonderful way that the gospel can be communicated—and corrected—is by praying for our Muslim friend at the end of a conversation. In our discussion, we should have discerned where he is hurting and what some of his problems are. So I frequently ask, "May I pray for you? It's my custom to close my eyes and bow my head when I pray." Then I pray to God, to our loving Father, concerning the particular problems my friend has. This demonstrates a loving personal God who hears our prayers. About half the time, when I lift my head, I see tears in their eyes. Those who have been Muslim

adherents most of their lives have said, "You are the first person who ever prayed for me."

Of course, Muslims do not have the assurance of the forgiveness of sins or of eternal life. Yet this is a wonderful gift that Christ promises and the Word of God teaches. We need to be very careful to lovingly point out these four areas, because they are vacuums within the Muslim's heart which he does not know how to fill.

## GOAL: MUSLIMS STUDYING SCRIPTURE

In conversation with Muslims, one of our goals is to persuade them to read the Bible. It is obviously advantageous to have a copy of a Gospel (I prefer Luke) in their language to give to them and to ask them to read. Frequently, I will ask, "Don't you think it's wise if we read all of the books given by God?" Most Muslims will answer, "Yes." The truth is, most Muslims have never really read the Gospels. I tell them, "This is a biography of the Prophet Jesus." I ask that they promise to read it, saying, "This will not do you any good as a fetish to keep off the evil eye (as many Muslims might think), but it can help you to come to know the Prophet Jesus Christ. He can answer your prayers and can give power over sin and evil in your life."

This might be the time to suggest they watch the *Jesus* film on video in their language. An additional goal, toward which we should prayerfully direct our efforts, is to find those who would like to get together with us to read and study the Bible. In an ideal relationship, we would have an in-depth study of the person of Christ,

possibly through the Gospel of Luke; an in-depth study through the Old Testament prophets, which a Muslim accepts; or an in-depth, chronological study, beginning in Genesis. These types of studies provide an excellent foundation for faith. However, since Muslims normally reject the Bible as authoritative, it is usually advantageous to begin from within their own thinking, from where they are, and from within mutually-accepted theological concepts.

## CONCLUSION

I encourage others prayerfully to test and adopt some of the ideas and practical steps suggested here. Perhaps God would bless this approach to open the minds and hearts of many Muslims to the wonderful news of the Savior of the world, who loves them and died for them. However, no matter what we do or how we look at it, the sine qua non of introducing Muslims to our Savior and Lord is love and prayer—prayer that God would lead us to Muslims who are open to spiritual things. Indeed, may it be that God would redeem from all Muslim nations, tribes, and tongues a people for himself, for his glory.

**End of Key Readings for Lesson 8. See** RECOMMENDED READINGS & ACTIVITIES **on p. 308.**

# A QUESTION THAT MUST BE ANSWERED

*by Del Kingsriter*

As I travel worldwide, even into remote areas untouched by media, I find a wall—an incredible barrier between Muslims and Christians. For centuries, Muslims and Christians have stood on separate hills and shouted across the valley at each other, never daring to come close enough together to truly examine each other's beliefs and answer each other's questions, never truly listening to each other's heartbeat. It is a futile exercise to point the finger of blame at events of the past, or even those of the present. The fact is, there is a deep gulf that must be bridged by love and understanding.

Thank God, this is rapidly changing. Christians and Muslims are not only becoming interested in the differences in each other's belief systems. They are becoming interested in each other as individuals—individuals who are equally created by God. This is good and needs to be encouraged at every possible level.

## MANY MISUNDERSTANDINGS

In dialogue with Christians, I often find that there are many misunderstandings about Muslims. Many Christians are afraid of getting too close to Muslims; some even believe Muslims are all terror-ists or evil people. As a general rule, I have found Muslims to be very God-conscious.

Conversely, in my dialogue with Muslims, I find the same fear and suspicions. However, they are also asking some very fundamental questions, questions which need to be answered. One area my Muslim friends are sincerely concerned about is the supposed corruption of the Christians' Scriptures.

## HAS THE BIBLE BEEN CORRUPTED?

God's Holy Word is very important. Both Muslims and Christians believe that God has given instructions to humanity concerning how they should live and find the way to heaven.

Christians believe that God spoke through his Holy Spirit to men, and they wrote as the Holy Spirit breathed upon them (2 Peter 1:19–21). The apostle Paul said, "All Scripture is God-breathed and is useful for teaching, rebuking, correcting, and training in righteousness" (2 Tim. 3:16). The Bible itself explains that the Scriptures were given by God to holy men, who were submissive to the Holy Spirit, holy men who wrote as God's Spirit "breathed" upon them.

On the other hand, Muhammad said that the Qur'an was given to him by the angel Gabriel, and that it was given exactly as it is recorded in the "mother of books which

Del Kingsriter served as a missionary in Kenya and Tanzania through the Assemblies of God World Missions and was instrumental in founding the Center for Muslim Ministry.

Adapted from Del Kingsriter, *Questions Muslims Ask That Need to Be Answered* (Springfield, Mo.: Center for Ministry to Muslims, 1991), pp. 1–36. Used by permission. *www.cmmequip.org*

is on the throne of God." Muslims say that the Qur'an is the final revelation of God to humankind and supersedes all previous revelation. Christians hold that the Bible, which was given centuries before the Qur'an, is the complete Word of God and is the rule of faith and practice for all people. The Bible itself asserts that it is the final revelation of God to humanity (Rev. 22:18–19).

Interestingly, Muhammad firmly believed in the authenticity of the Bible as it existed in his day. There are many verses in the Qur'an which demonstrate his confidence in the Holy Books that came before him. "Say, 'O People of the Book! Ye have no ground to stand upon unless ye stand fast by the Law, the Gospel, and all the revelation that has come to you from your Lord'" (Sura 5:68, YUSUF ALI). "Before thee, also, the apostles [messengers] we sent were but men, to whom we granted inspiration. If ye realize this not, ask of those who possess the Message" (Sura 21:7, YUSUF ALI). Dr. Akbar Abdul-Haqq, in *Sharing Your Faith with a Muslim*, says:

> In view of the clear teaching of the Qur'an about the authenticity of the Bible and its freedom from corruption, it is no wonder that, not only the earliest doctors of Islam, but also many other Muslim scholars after them, have refused to entertain a belief contrary to that. Their position is further strengthened by a crucial verse in the Qur'an: "The words of the Lord are perfect in truth and justice; there is none who can change his words" (Sura 6:115, TRANS. UNKNOWN). Again: "No change can there be in the Words of

God. This is indeed the supreme felicity" (Sura 10:64, YUSUF ALI).[1]

Christians can say "amen" to that. Parenthetically, please note that this author's use of the Qur'an does not mean that followers of Christ accept it as authoritative for themselves. However, as Muslims consider it authoritative, Christians should accept the testimony of the Qur'an as it relates to the authenticity of the Bible or of Jesus Christ.

## WHEN DID CORRUPTION OCCUR?

With this in mind, a Christian should ask his Muslim friend: "If Muhammad believed in the authenticity of the Bible and if Muslim scholars did not question it, then when was the Bible corrupted?" Manuscripts of both the Old and New Testaments, dating back to several hundred years before Muhammad, were placed in museums and are intact today. These original manuscripts give credence to the content of the Bible. The Christian might want to phrase his question in this manner: "When was the Bible corrupted? Was it before or after Muhammad lived?"

If the Muslim replies "before," he is in a dilemma, because then he accuses Muhammad of being a false teacher, because, as has already been noted, the Qur'an—which Muslims say is the very Word of God—clearly refers to the Bible as God's Word, which was to be obeyed and followed. If, on the other hand, the Muslim says "after," he is also in a great dilemma, because the Bible had already been written in many languages and distributed widely in the world.

The Christian could then ask another series of valid questions. "Who changed it? When was it changed? How could this possibly happen? What did it say before it was changed? Does history record such an historic event, as it would certainly have been if all the leaders of the Christian and Jewish communities worldwide came together to rewrite the Bible?" Christians love their Scriptures and would never, at any time, agree to any attempt at changing them. In fact, the Bible itself promises the severest penalty against anyone who attempts to change them. The Jews love their Old Testament Books of the Law and would never collaborate with Christians or anyone in an attempt to change these Scriptures.

## MANUSCRIPTS ARE ANCIENT

In recent years, archeological discoveries have unearthed ancient manuscripts dating back more than two thousand years. These manuscripts include portions of every book in the Old Testament, with the exception of Esther. The entire book of Isaiah has been uncovered. All of these ancient manuscripts show no major differences from the Bible we have today.

But the most convincing answer to the question must come from God himself:

## BARRIERS TO THE GOSPEL

For Muslim women, illiteracy and Islamic views of female spirituality are two of the largest barriers to the gospel. In some countries, up to 93 percent of women are illiterate.[1] Most Muslim women also face entrenched cultural thinking that denigrates the value of a woman's soul and her ability to comprehend spiritual matters.

Since Muslim men are more apt to frequent public places where contact with Christians is possible, and because historically Christians have presented the gospel mainly in writing, more Muslim-background believers (MBBs) are educated men than women. Lamentably, this approach sidelines the less literate and many women. Of believing women, many lack maturity, having less teaching and discipleship.

In addition, when married Christian women focus mainly on caring for their children, we may reduce the access of Muslim women to the gospel. While men share their faith with brothers, uncles, nephews, and friends, little witness flows back to wives, mothers, sisters, aunts, and nieces. Perhaps because they think women are inferior and not worth the effort, male MBBs transfer their old assumptions into their Christianity.

However, change is coming with rising awareness of gaps in outreach to Muslim women. Oral methods are being used to teach Muslim women about Christ. Christians discipling MBB men are including more biblical teaching on women's equal value, ability, and access to God. MBB families are being encouraged to model Christ-like marriages among their Muslim friends. Reaching and teaching women are becoming more integral features of church planting and discipleship.

1. A. H., "Discipleship of Muslim Background Believers," *Ministry to Muslim Women: Longing to Call Them Sisters*, ed. Fran Love and Jeleta Eckheart (Pasadena, Calif.: William Carey Library, 2000), p. 151.

Source: Annee W. Rose, *www.frontiers.org*.

"Heaven and earth will pass away, but my words will never pass away" (Matt. 24:35). The sincere question concerning who corrupted the Bible must be answered with God's own words, "My words will never pass away." God's Word is eternal and he would never permit his Holy Word to be changed. It is so important that we read and obey the Bible and accept it as his pure Word, "which can save you" (James 1:21). "From infancy you have known the holy Scriptures, which are able to make you wise for salvation through faith in Christ Jesus" (2 Tim. 3:15).

## Do Different Translations Create Confusion?

The original Old Testament was written mainly in Hebrew, with some portions in Aramaic. The New Testament was written in Greek. Many manuscripts of the Bible still exist in these languages. As the message of the gospel of Jesus Christ spread into many countries, the Bible was translated into the languages of these countries. Some Muslims may be confused by the various translations of the Bible and an explanation is in order. For example, in English, the King James Version dates back to 1611 and is still widely used. However, as the language of the people has changed since then, revised versions have been printed to make the Bible more readable. Since these translations are made from the original documents, there is no difference in meaning.

The Christian may also point out that there are many versions of the Qur'an, translated by different scholars, which differ in many aspects. I have the Dawood, Yusuf Ali, Arberry, and Pickthall versions of the Qur'an in my library. Each translation differs, although each seeks to be true to the original meaning.

In conclusion, I appeal to my Christian and Muslim friends to listen to each other. What is really needed is for you to sit down to discuss these vital matters of disagreement and misunderstanding openly. Yes, dare to come close and truly examine each other's beliefs. Answer each other's questions in a spirit of love and understanding. I pray you will not only come to a better appreciation of each other, but will reach a deeper awareness of God and his plan for mankind.

### For Further Study
John Gilchrist, *Facing the Muslim Challenge* (Cape Town, South Africa: Life Challenge Africa, 2002).

### Endnote
1. Abdiyah Akbar Abdul-Haqq, *Sharing Your Faith with a Muslim* (Minneapolis: Bethany, 1980), no p. cited.

# ISLAM AND CHRISTIANITY ON THE FATHERHOOD OF GOD

*by R. C. Sproul and Abdul Saleeb*

## SALEEB'S PERSPECTIVE

One of the most important concepts in the Christian faith is the fatherhood of God. Jesus taught us in the Lord's Prayer to address God as "our Father in heaven" (Matt. 6:9). We Christians feel privileged to be able to talk to God in such intimate terms. And we believe that through faith in Christ we can become adopted children of God. When Christians talk about this to Muslims, they think that they are sharing Good News. Christians do not understand that to Muslim ears, that sounds like horrible news. To them it sounds blasphemous to think of God as our father and us as his children.

As Christians, again, we need to understand that, since both Islam and Christianity are monotheistic faiths, there are many things we do hold in common. Christians and Muslims believe that God is one, that God is just, that God is sovereign, that God rules, and that God forgives. God has sent prophets and has sent revelations. There are many areas of agreement, but we cannot ignore the fact that there are very fundamental differences also.

This is Sura 112 of the Qur'an, recited in prayer every day by millions of Muslims around the world. It is an essential part of the daily prayers of a Muslim: "Say: he is Allah, the one and only; Allah the eternal, absolute; he begetteth not, nor is he begotten; and there is none like unto him" (YUSUF ALI).

Islam heavily emphasizes the absolute sovereignty of God: "It is not befitting (to the majesty of) Allah that he should beget a son. Glory be to him! When he determines a matter, he only says to it, 'Be,' and it is" (Sura 19:35, YUSUF ALI). In a footnote to this verse, Abdullah Yusuf Ali, translator of the version of the Qur'an to which this article refers, writes: "Begetting a son is a physical act depending on the needs of men's animal nature. Allah Most High is independent of all needs, and it is derogatory to him to attribute such an act to him. It is merely a relic of pagan and anthropomorphic materialist superstitions."[1]

This belief goes back to the Qur'an itself—that to talk about God as our father implies sexual relations, and attributes something that is not right to God: "To him is due the primal origin of the heavens and the earth: How can he have a son when he hath no consort? He created all

---

R. C. Sproul is a noted author and visiting professor at several seminaries and hosts a radio program.

Abdul Saleeb was born and raised in a Muslim country and converted to Christianity while a student in Europe. He is a missionary to Muslims in the United States.

Adapted from R. C. Sproul and Abdul Saleeb, *The Dark Side of Islam* (Wheaton, Ill.: Crossway Books, 2003), pp. 25–33. Used by permission. *www.gnpcb.org*

things, and he hath full knowl-
edge of all things" (Sura 6:101,
YUSUF ALI).

Sura 2:116 reads: "They say,
'Allah has begotten a son': Glory
be to him—Nay, to him belongs
all that is in the heavens and
on earth: everything renders
worship to him." In his footnote
on this verse, Yusuf Ali says, "It
is a derogation from the glory

Kyrgyz men gather for the daily exchange of news

of Allah—in fact, it is blasphemy—to say
that Allah begets sons like a man or an
animal."[2] And of course, as Christians, we
say, "That's not what Christians believe.
We are not attributing a sexual act to God
when we talk about the fatherhood of God
or that we are sons of God."

But that is not how a Muslim understands
it. Yusuf Ali goes on to say, "The
Christian doctrine is here emphatically
repudiated. If words have any meaning, it
would mean an attribution to Allah of a
material nature, and of the lower animal
functions of sex."[3] Thus, to Muslims, it
sounds like blasphemy to call God, with
such intimacy, "our heavenly Father."

And I am just using the word "father,"
but there is a plethora of other images in
the Bible about God: as a shepherd who
carries the sheep in his arms, and as a
wounded husband who goes after his unfaithful wife, the nation of Israel. Christ is
viewed as the bridegroom coming for his
Church, the bride. We have many tender
images of God and his relationship to
humanity. But the dominant Qur'anic and
Islamic image of God is that of a master,
and our relationship with him is that of a
servant to a master. Islam does not allow

for any intimacy between humanity and
God, or for us to call God "our heavenly
Father." As Christians, we need to be
informed about the Muslim mindset and
what they hear when they hear phrases
like "heavenly Father" or "Son of God."

## R. C. SPROUL RESPONDS

First of all, as you have indicated,
orthodox Christianity would agree with
virtually every one of those texts, in terms
of a complete repudiation of any kind of
crass idea of divine physical propagation
of children, like we find in Greek and
Roman mythology. The idea of gods
sexually interacting with human beings is
as utterly foreign to Judeo-Christian tenets
as it would be to those of Islam.

Obviously, when Christianity speaks of the
fatherhood of God, the Son of God, and
the children of God, it does not mean to
communicate this idea of physical, biological propagation. Although that has arisen
in certain cults, it has been completely
rejected by virtually every Christian
denomination, liberal or conservative.

We need to look carefully at how the Old,
and particularly the New, Testaments

articulate their understanding of the fatherhood of God and the so-called brotherhood of man. An important twentieth-century scholar, Joachim Jeremias, studied the fatherhood of God. He looked through all of the literature—not only the Old Testament, but the Talmudic writings, the Rabbinic writings, and every extant Jewish text that survives to the twentieth century—to examine how, within Judaism, the title "Father" was attributed to God. Nowhere in the Old Testament, or in any of the Rabbinical writings, could he find a Jewish person addressing God in prayer directly as Father. This seems to parallel the absence of intimacy pointed to by Muslim scholars.

In fact, Jeremias concluded that the earliest example of a Jewish person addressing God directly as "Father" is in the tenth century A.D. (However, in every prayer of Jesus of Nazareth, recorded in the New Testament, with one exception, Jesus addressed God as Father.) Jeremias wrote that the Jewish people had a list of proscribed and acceptable titles, that could be used in worship and in private prayer, that would not be in any way denigrating to the glory and majesty of God. Conspicuously absent from that list was the title "Father." On rare occasions, God was referred to indirectly as the father of the human race, only insofar as he was its Creator, but not in the crass way to which the Muslims object, or in the way that Christians understand God's fatherhood.

Jeremias's thesis was that we in the Christian community today routinely address God as Father. The Lord's Prayer is an integral part of our corporate worship. And if you listen to a group of Christians praying, inevitably, the most common form of address you will hear from their lips as they pray is "Father." And yet, because it is so predominant in Christian culture, we often take this for granted. Jeremias was claiming that in Jesus' day, his calling God "Father" was a radical departure from Jewish tradition. The significance of this radical innovation was noted by his contemporaries. In fact, it infuriated his enemies—that he would have the audacity to suggest that he had this kind of intimate relationship with God.

Further, in the New Testament, that relationship is seen from the other perspective. God is heard speaking from heaven declaring, "This is my beloved Son in whom I am well pleased" (Matt. 17:5, NKJV). And Jesus bears the title "Son of God," although in a very carefully guarded way. When Christ is called the Son of God, he is called the *monogenesis*, Greek meaning "the only begotten" of the Father. The church understood very early that this did not mean he had a beginning in time. There was not any idea of the Father's procreating or siring a son.

When the Bible speaks in terms of sonship, it refers not only to biological generation: it also speaks regularly of sonship as a description of a relationship of obedience. When Jesus talked about setting people free, the Pharisees became upset, saying, "We are Abraham's descendants, and have never been in bondage to anyone" (John 8:33, NKJV). Jesus replied, "If you were Abraham's children, you would do the works of Abraham" (v. 39). To be called a child of God meant to be one who obeyed God. Sonship here was defined, not in biological terms, but in

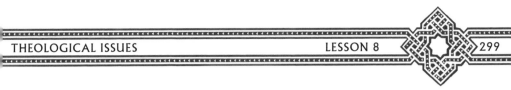
## Jesus in the Qur'an

While Muslims do not believe that Jesus is the Son of God or that he died on the cross for the sins of the world, the Qur'an (especially Suras 3 and 19) confirms his unique qualities. We recommend studying the passages listed below for yourself, and ask a Muslim friend what the Qur'anic passages mean.

| SUBJECT | QUR'ANIC REFERENCE | SIMILAR BIBLE REFERENCE |
|---|---|---|
| Word from God, the Gospel | 3:45; 5:46, 110; 57:27 | Mark 1:14–15; John 1:1–18 |
| Spirit from God | 4:171 | Rom. 8:9–17 |
| Messiah | 3:45; 4:171; 5:17, 72, 75 | John 4:25–42 |
| The image of Adam | 3:59 | 1 Cor. 15:22, 45 |
| Born of a virgin | 3:47; 19:20–22; 21:91; 66:12 | Matt. 1:18–25; Luke 1:26–38 |
| A sign | 3:49; 19:21; 21:91 | Luke 2:8–35; John 20:30–31; Acts 10:38 |
| Honored | 3:45 | Luke 1:32; Phil. 2:5–11 |
| Servant of God | 4:172; 19:30 | Isa. 42:1–4; 49:1–6; 50:4–9; 52:13–53:12; Mark 10:42–45 |
| Will gather all people to himself | 4:172 | Mark 13:26–27 |
| A Prophet or a Messenger of God | 3:49; 6:85; 19:30; 57:27 | John 5:30; 6:38; 7:29; 8:25–30, 42; 9:4; 10:36; 17:8, 21; 20:21 |
| Healed the sick | 3:49; 5:110 | Matt. 4:23–24; Luke 17:11–19; John 9:1–11 |
| Ascended to heaven | 3:55 | Mark 16:19–20; Luke 24:50–53; John 10:14–18; Phil. 2:8–11 |
| Performed miracles | 2:253; 5:112–115 | John 10:32 |
| Raised the dead | 3:49; 5:110 | Matt. 8:18–26; Luke 11:17–44; John 11:1–44 |
| Strengthened by the Holy Spirit | 2:253 | Matt. 3:13–17 |
| Given revelation from God | 3:48; 5:110; 19:30–34 | John 7:16–18 |
| Died | 3:55; 5:117; 19:33–34 | Matt. 27:32–54; John 19:1–37 |
| Was raised from the dead | 3:55; 19:33–34 | Acts 1:9; 2:24; Phil. 2:9–10 |
| Came with wisdom | 5:110; 43:63 | Eph. 1:2–14 |
| His return will signal the coming of judgment | 43:61 | Matt. 25:31–46 |
| Power to create | 5:110 | John 1:3; Col. 1:13–23; Heb. 1:1–14 |
| Intercedes for us | 6:70; 19:87; 43:86 | Rom. 8:34–39; 1 Tim. 2:1–6; Heb. 7:22–28 |
| Pure, sinless | 19:19 | Heb. 4:14–16 |

ethical terms. And in that sense, the New Testament speaks of Christ's unique relationship as the one who is perfectly obedient to the Father.

But Jesus then tells his disciples to pray, "Our Father in heaven" (Matt. 6:9). That was radical. That was astonishing, initially, to those who heard it. It does not surprise me at all that Muslims would be offended by that. Orthodox Jews would also be offended, because it was a serious departure from their tradition. In fact, from the Fall throughout the Old Testament, there is a history of the wall separating humankind from God because of sin. An angel with a flaming sword guarded the entrance to Paradise (Gen. 3:24) to prevent us from having an intimate relationship with God.

In Romans 8, Paul writes about the concept of our adoption by God the Father, by virtue of the work of the Holy Spirit, who gives us now, as we are adopted into the family of God, the right and the authority to say, "*Abba*, Father" (v. 15). We now have the right to address God as Father. The relationship of estrangement, that defined our connection prior to the work of Christ and the atonement, is now ended; the wall has been removed. God has been so gracious that he has not only forgiven us of our sins, but has invited us into the intimate fellowship of being family members. Even though we are not his children by nature, we are his children by adoption; by virtue of our relationship to Christ, we are now included in the family of God.

This relationship differs markedly from any found in Islam. This is one of the ways in which Islam is so profoundly impover-

ished; it does not have an avenue for us to be restored to that filial relationship, to that relationship of intimacy, for which we were created in the first place. This concept of adoption is vital to our whole understanding of redemption, something we must not take for granted. When John writes about this in 1 John, he introduces the statement with the word "behold." That is like a sign at a railroad crossing with a flashing red light: stop, look, and listen. Hold it right there, pay attention. Something important is coming. "Behold what manner of love the Father has bestowed on us, that we should be called children of God!" (1 John 3:1, NKJV). Even the apostles in the first century were overwhelmed with amazement that the status of a filial relationship to God would be accorded to us because of the work of Christ.

## SALEEB'S CHALLENGE

As we talk with Muslims about the fatherhood of God, it is important to know and emphasize the fact that we are not talking about physical procreation on the part of God. And an emphasis on the aspect of obedience, as a definition of sonship, is very important. We also need to understand that when Islam came on the scene, it was in the context of paganism. So, in fact, originally the Qur'an was denouncing the pagan views of the fatherhood of God and of humans being his children. Islam arose in that context, but later, Islamic theology simply took off from there, and never developed humankind's relationship with God in terms of intimacy and relationship.

Fuller Seminary recently conducted a survey of six hundred former Muslims

who had become Christians. One of the factors involved in the conversions of these former Muslims was the emphasis on the love of God and the intimacy that believers can have with God as their heavenly Father. This was an important influence in drawing these former Muslims to Christ. We need to present this truth to all Muslim people.

## FOR FURTHER STUDY

Timothy George, *Is the Father of Jesus the God of Muhammad?* (Grand Rapids: Zondervan, 2002). *www.zondervan.com*

## ENDNOTES

1. Abdullah Yusuf Ali, *The Meaning of the Holy Qur'an* (Beltsville, Md.: Amana Publications, 1989), p. 751.
2. Ibid., p. 49.
3. Ibid.

# SHARING OUR FAITH WITH MUSLIMS

*by Charles R. Marsh*

Some general principles should be used as guidelines in presenting the gospel to Muslims:

**1. We should avoid condemning Islam or speaking in a derogatory manner of the person of Muhammad.** Instead of criticizing Islam, we should try sympathetically to understand it, putting ourselves in the Muslim's place. It is wise never to allow oneself to be drawn into a discussion about the life or character of the man whom they honor as their prophet. Our aim should be to attract Muslims to the Lord Jesus, showing them that Christ is a living person, who is able to save and who can satisfy their hearts. The Lord gave an important principle of teaching in his rules to the disciples: "Men do not gather figs from thorns, nor do they pick grapes from a briar bush" (Luke 6:44, NASB). He inferred that the thorns and brambles of controversy repel, but that everyone is attracted by fruit.

Pointing out the deficiencies of Islam is to antagonize a Muslim. Some Christians tell a Muslim that Islam is a religion of works and that man can only be saved by the grace of God. They insist that the Muslim's form of prayer is not true prayer at all, for God seeks a humble and contrite heart and not the mere prostration of the body. They say that if Muhammad had been a true prophet, he would not have taken so many wives. The message of such Christians is negative and critical. The Muslim is repelled, pricked by the thorns. Our aim should be to present the true Vine in such a positive way that Muslims will desire to gather for themselves the fruit of the gospel. We do not want to provoke them to retaliatory argument.

**2. We must remember that a Muslim is a believer in the One True God and in his laws.** Muslims' ideas may be false, but a careful study of the ninety-nine names of God, recited with the help of prayer beads, shows that Muslims believe in and worship the One True God; many of these attributes are found in the Bible as well as in the Qur'an. Therefore, one can always speak about God, his existence, power, judgments, faithfulness, and holiness. Muslims know that God is omnipresent, omnipotent, and omniscient. They should never be treated as pagans, agnostics, or idolaters.

**3. In the heart of every true Muslim there is the fear of God.** This is the strongest point in our approach. Muslims not only believe in God theoretically, but they know in the innermost recesses

Charles Marsh was a pioneer missionary in Algeria for many years and also served as a missionary and translator in the Chad Republic. Since 1968, he has traveled in Algeria and Chad, training evangelists to reach Muslims.

Adapted from Charles R. Marsh, *Share Your Faith with a Muslim* (Chicago, Ill.: Moody Press, 1980), pp. 8–13. Used by permission. *www.moodypublishers.org*

of their hearts that they must meet with God's judgment. Muslims are aware of their own shortcomings and failures. They know that there is a hell and are afraid they might be cast there. Awareness of their awe is expressed when Muslims prostrate themselves in prayer and veneration, taking the attitude of slaves before their master. Though in direct contrast with the filial mindset of the believer in Christ, who knows God as heavenly Father, true fear or reverence of God is the basis for an appeal to the conscience. The awesome respect or fear of God, which is lacking in our own country today, is still found in many Muslim lands. Some may explain it as superstition, but it certainly exists, and every Christian worker among Muslims is aware of its potential merit.

## 4. Most Muslims have a definite sense of sin.

There is usually no deep conviction of sin, but Muslims are deeply aware of their failure to attain the standard required by God. Islam does appeal to some extent to the conscience and to the law of God which Muslims know they have transgressed. In their daily prayers, they ask for forgiveness, and they continually repeat this formula: "I ask forgiveness of God" (*astaghafr Allah*). Muslims know when they have done wrong, and they hope for forgiveness through the mercy of God. Yet, they are fully aware that their religion offers no assurance of forgiveness or pardon for sins. They can only hope. But the desire for forgiveness for sins exists deep in their hearts, and we can make use of this.

Muslims have little difficulty in understanding man's evil nature, which the Bible refers to as "the flesh" or "sin." Different people will express this in various ways, using different words, but in every devout Muslim, there is the acute awareness of evil within. Muslims know their nature is evil. They desire to do good, but are unable to do so. They have sincerely tried to follow their moral code, and failed. They know that this is because of their own evil hearts. Christ alone is the answer to the deep needs of the soul.

## 5. For the foregoing reasons, we must try to put aside their religious identity and remember that Muslims are human beings—like ourselves—and sinners.

Sinners need a Savior, and we have the message that can meet this need. Muslims will try to discuss their religion, appealing to the differences between Christianity and Islam. Trying to avoid such discussion, we must bring them back continually to the realization of their need for a Savior, appealing primarily to their consciences, rather than to their intellects. We must show them that our faith is logical. The whole person must be reached, and theological problems must be dealt with, but the primary appeal must be to the heart and conscience.

One characteristic of Muslims is that they are never ashamed to tell what they believe. They will always state their convictions quite plainly. Muslims will not hesitate to try to get us to repeat the witness (Shahada) to Muhammad and to convert us to Islam. They admire such zeal and frankness—this open confession of faith—in others. No attempt should be made to hide the truths of the Bible, to tone them down, or to make them fit in with Muslim beliefs. Islam and

Christianity are diametrically opposed, and it is impossible to seek a common faith by adapting the Christian message to Muslim thought. The Muslim has a keen, perceptive mind and quickly detects any effort to mask the truth or to compromise. Dr. Samuel Zwemer once said that one can say anything to a Muslim, provided it is said in love and with a smile. They respect the person who, alone in the midst of a crowd of Muslim opponents, has the courage of his convictions and does not hesitate to speak the whole truth. However, it is of the utmost gravity that this outspoken conviction be backed up by a consistent life.

**6. The message we bring is judged by the character of the messenger.** Indeed, at the first approach, the messenger is as important as the message, because, in the past, the messenger has so often been un-Christlike, with the result that Muslims and others have not wanted to listen to the message. "The fruit of the Spirit is love, joy, peace, patience, kindness, goodness, faithfulness, gentleness, and self-control" (Gal. 5:22). These virtues together constitute a Christlike character, and they can only be reproduced in us by the Holy Spirit.

The Bible consistently teaches that it is the character of the servant that counts. The character that counts and is respected has

## MORE TIPS FOR SHARING WITH A MUSLIM

1. Interact only in same-sex company. Genders are usually separated in Islam, and piety and purity respected (as they are in Christianity). Women, always dress modestly and do not enter a gathering of all men. Men, do not enter a home where no men are present.
2. Side step debate or argument. Let winning your friend be your goal, not winning the argument. Our message is not about religion and its regimen of rituals, or a philosophical system; it is about a relationship with God through Christ. Express your gratitude for, and share, what he has done for you.
3. Avoid insulting the Qur'an, Muhammad, or Islam. Humiliation is alienating, but our description of Jesus and his work is appealing and will draw our friend closer to faith.
4. Be sensitive to your Muslim friend's customs: how she sits or eats; how he enters a house. Our cultural habits may be an affront to their sensibilities.
5. Be aware of Islamic practice. We risk offense by placing Bibles on the floor, putting other objects over them, or marking passages in them.
6. Christians should not denigrate one another. Refrain from criticizing other Christians or ministries.
7. Uphold the simplicity of the gospel and of believing in it.
8. Maintain a consistent lifestyle, one that reflects that the gospel of Christ is power from God for salvation from sin and deliverance from sin's power.
9. On the issue of salvation, pray for a genuine work of the Holy Spirit, the one who seeks and secures followers for Jesus. The issue is not a person's decision, but are you letting God use you?

Source: Fouad Masri, *www.crescentproject.org.*

the following qualities: the love that goes on loving in spite of Muslims' hatred and bitterness, that suffers long and is kind, bears all, believes all, hopes all things, and endures all things; the joy in the Lord that rebounds in spite of opposition and persecution; the peace of God that Muslims so earnestly covet; the plodding patience that continues to go on; the practical goodness that Muslims cannot refute by argument; the faithfulness to

Our behavior is as important as the message

one's pledged word, on which one's Muslim friend may fully rely; the gentle meekness that persists when confronted with arrogance; and the self-control to remain even-tempered, when tempted to vent one's anger over senseless arguments. To this exemplary character must be added a spirit of reverence and sobriety. Muslims cannot understand the lighthearted emotion that characterizes some Christians. A man of God is joyful, yet he must be sober and reverent, especially when he is speaking of the truths of God, of his living faith in God and his message.

Having stated all this, we can now affirm the most important principle in our approach and our teaching.

### 7. We need to make use of the truth that Muslims know to lead them on to accept the whole truth of the Word of God. We will be able to find many points of contact as we explore what Muslims believe and already know. They know that God is light and that in him is no darkness at all. They know that Christ is the son of Mary. They are aware that one of his titles in the Qur'an is the Word

of God (*Kalimat Allah*). They know that the Lord Jesus Christ will soon return to reign. They know that people must be pure to approach God in prayer. In this and in many other ways, Muslims have a glimmer of truth. We can thank God for this, and we can congratulate Muslims on what they know and believe, and proceed to try to lead them into deeper truth. They may not accept it at first, but they will reflect.

In conclusion, two more ancillary principles should guide us:

### 8. The Muslim responds to love. Muslims must feel that we really care for them as persons, that we love them and have a genuine concern for them (not merely for their souls). In nearly every case of the conversion of a Muslim, that man or woman was first influenced by Christian love.

Si Mebarek was a young Qur'anic student who taught the boys in the mosque to recite their holy book. For many years he had attended Sunday school classes, but the teaching had left no impression on

him. He hardened his heart to the gospel and mocked his teachers. When he was eighteen and very proud of his knowledge of Islam, he went to the home of a woman missionary and asked for a gospel in Arabic, saying he would very much like to read it again. The servant of God was thrilled. Here was an answer to her prayers: a young man seeking the Lord. Si Mebarek took the gospel in his hand, glanced at it, and then, with a look of defiance, tore it to shreds and threw it on the ground, trampling on the pieces. He quite expected to receive a sharp reproof for having treated the Word of God thus. Instead he saw tears come into the eyes of the servant of God. With a look of inexpressible sadness, but of genuine love, she turned away without a word, going into the house to pray for him.

Si Mebarek headed for home, but that expression of the patient love of Christ, of his meekness and gentleness, really reached his heart. Within an hour, he was back again, now a convicted sinner seeking salvation. That simple expression of the love of the One who wept over Jerusalem achieved what the years of teaching had failed to accomplish. The loving messenger is as important as the message.

This is where Christians have failed down through the ages, especially from the time of the Crusades until now. Some missionaries still continue to battle against Islam with argument, abuse, and ridicule. It is so important to show genuine love in practical ways, gradually breaking down barriers. Never fail to greet your Muslim friends with a smile, even in times

of political tension. Show sympathy in times of illness or bereavement. Perform little acts of service. Invite them to your house and accept invitations to theirs. Be scrupulously honest in all business dealings. Show that you are a Christian in the smallest details of life. If a Muslim shopkeeper has given you the wrong change, be sure to point this out to him or her. Be respectful and show honor where honor is due.

Demonstrate that you love Muslims by trying to understand their point of view. Be a good listener. If there is one thing that God has taught me in old age, it is the wisdom of patiently listening to other people, no matter if they are English teenagers or bigoted Muslims. If we can affirm something that they say, by all means, we need to do so, but we must be transparently sincere. Muslims can read us like a book, and the nicknames they often give various missionaries and others are always very apt. Remember that true love does not mask the truth, and we have a message of life to communicate. But before Muslims can accept it and love our Lord, they must learn to love us. Before they trust our Lord, they must know that they can trust us. Love is God's way.

**9. Finally, our overall reliance must be on the work of the Holy Spirit.** We must depend wholly on him to teach us what to say, to bring conviction of sin and faith in Christ, to create new life, and to give assurance of peace. Apart from his working, all our efforts in this enterprise of sharing our faith with Muslims will be utterly futile (see John 16:8–14).

 **End of Basic Readings for Lesson 8.** See RECOMMENDED READINGS & ACTIVITIES **on p. 308.**

 Go to: *www.encounteringislam.org/readings* to find the Full Readings for Lesson 8.

# DISCUSSION QUESTIONS

1. What are some terms or concepts found in both Islam and Christianity which carry very different meanings, implications, or assumptions?

2. Banks train employees to recognize counterfeit currency by having them study genuine bills. What is "genuine" Christianity? Read Romans 5:1–11.

   • List the verbs that describe our actions.

   • List the verbs that describe God's actions.

   • Contrast the condition of our lives before Christ saved us and after.

   • What new insights have you found through studying this passage?

   • Meditate on this passage this week and let God convince you of his truth in a deeper way. Let his love pour into you and seep through you to others.

# RECOMMENDED READINGS & ACTIVITIES*

Read:   Norman L. Geisler and Abdul Saleeb, *Answering Islam*, 2d ed. (Grand Rapids: Baker Books, 2002).

Abdiyah Akbar Abdul-Haqq, *Sharing Your Faith with a Muslim* (Minneapolis: Bethany House, 1980).

Fouad Elias Accad, *Building Bridges: Christianity and Islam* (Colorado Springs, Colo.: NavPress, 1997).

Chawkat Moucarry, *The Prophet and the Messiah* (Downers Grove, Ill.: InterVarsity Press, 2001).

Watch: Watch a film that presents Islam from a Christian perspective.

Pray:   For at least one day, pray for Muslims at the five prescribed prayer times. Several web sites list these times according to where you live.

Meet:   Begin to build a relationship by starting a friendly conversation with a Muslim. Invite him or her to join you for lunch or tea.

Surf:   Discover related web sites at *www.encounteringislam.org/lessonlinks.*

---

\* For expanded details on these Recommended Readings & Activities, visit *www.encounteringislam.org/lessonlinks.*

# LESSON 9
## PAST APPROACHES TO OUTREACH

## PONDER THIS

- How has the church reached out to Muslims over the centuries, and with what results?

- How should we work with existing Christian churches in Muslim-majority countries?

- Why do Muslims get upset when other Muslims turn to Christ?

# LESSON OBJECTIVE

Describe and illustrate Christian ministry efforts among Muslims, including:

1. The church's general lack of effort to reach out to Muslims.

2. Results of outreach in the past: examples of significant responses to the gospel by Muslims in the past, reactions of Muslims and their society to converts and conversion, and human rights issues and persecution of Muslim-background believers.

3. Past ministry approaches, their effects and implications, including: over-reliance on debates and argumentative use of apologetics, extraction of converts from their communities to avoid persecution, and attempts to work with the historical Christian minorities within Islamic states.

# LESSON READINGS

# INTRODUCTION

What is the church's record of witnesses in the Muslim world? How should we respond to that record? As we reach out to Muslims today, the church's past efforts have provided us with many benefits. Yet we must not be slow to admit, and remediate, our failures and mistakes.

Growing up as a Muslim

© Caleb Project

It is disgraceful how little Christian effort has actually been expended in outreach to Muslims since Muhammad's time. Regrettably, even where we have witnessed, Muslims have frequently connected our work with the baggage of territorial expansion, imperialism, and war. They have accused the church of using financial aid and employment to "buy" converts from among the poor.

In fact, Christian outreach has often sprung from mixed motives. Long after the Crusades ended, politics and commerce continued to shape mission strategy. Even today, Muslims link many well-intentioned, evangelistic endeavors to colonialism and western cultural dominance. Attitudes of cultural superiority have undermined our good works: As "proof," Muslims claim the noisy actions of western militaries which often drown out the quiet endeavors of Christ's servants. Yet more evangelical work is being done among Muslims today than just thirty years ago, and that witness is striving to change these misperceptions. Therefore, we have great hope.

In the past, most evangelism tended to be non-relational. Workers gave out literature but did not actually live among Muslims, welcome them into their homes as guests, or rely on them for help. Missionaries often mounted polemic attacks on Islam as a heretical ideology, trying to convince Muslims of Islam's errors and inferiority, rather than emphasizing the uniqueness of Jesus Christ. Yet some who verbally attacked Islam early in their careers later became advocates of incarnational witness (most notably Samuel Zwemer) as they came to understand and appreciate Muslims as their friends.

Of the courageous few missionaries to Muslim communities in the past, many focused on minority Christians and other non-Muslim groups, such the Armenians in Turkey. Workers expected to mobilize these local Christians to reach the Muslims around them, an approach that was useful in a few cases, but not generally effective. The minority churches faced various barriers: persecution, racism (their own and Muslims'), fear of martyrdom, and the human tendency to produce converts in one's own cultural image. Although traditional Christians lived culturally and geographically close to Muslims, they maintained separate communities; in many cases, they carefully avoided relating to Muslims. As a result, most missionaries had little impact on either these churches or their nearby Muslim communities. In planning today's outreach strategies, we cannot ignore existing churches, but we also cannot assume that our efforts to build them up will result in reaching their Muslim neighbors.

## JESUS' DEATH

The generally accepted Muslim view is that Jesus did not die a human death, but lives in a body in heaven.[1] The most popular theory is that Jesus did not die on the cross but rather that someone else took his place. Others theorize that Jesus was crucified but did not die (swooned), or that the crucifixion is a legend. (For further study, see Lesson 8 Full Reading "Jesus' Crucifixion," *www.encounteringislam.org/readings*).

> That they said (in boast), "We killed Christ Jesus the son of Mary, the Messenger of Allah." But they killed him not, nor crucified him, but so it was made to appear to them, and those who differ therein are full of doubts, with no (certain) knowledge, but only conjecture to follow, for of a surety they killed him not. Nay, Allah raised him up unto himself; and Allah is Exalted in Power, Wise. (Sura 4:157–158, YUSUF ALI)

In the context, "they" refers to the Jews; the Qur'an is refuting the Jewish claim that they themselves killed Jesus. Other verses in the Qur'an seem to imply that Jesus died.

> I [Jesus] did not say to them aught save what thou didst enjoin me with: "That serve Allah, my Lord and your Lord," and I was a witness of them so long as I was among them, but when thou didst cause me to die, thou wert the watcher over them, and thou art witness of all things. (Sura 5:117, SHAKIR)

> When Allah said, "O Jesus, I will cause thee to die[2] and exalt thee in my presence, and clear thee of those who disbelieve, and make those who follow thee above those who disbelieve to the day of Resurrection. Then to me is your return, so I shall decide between you concerning that wherein you differ." (Sura 3:55, MAULANA)

1. See commentary footnote no. 664, Abdullah Yusuf Ali, *The Meaning of the Holy Qur'an* (Beltsville, Md.: Amana Publication, 1989), p. 236.
2. Most other translators avoid translating the Arabic verb "maut", literally, to die, to perish.

Source: Annee W. Rose, *www.frontiers.org*.

Several rare examples exist of Christians who worked productively among Muslims during the first fourteen centuries of Islam. The institutional approach, once a mainstay of Christian missions in Muslim lands, established the first modern universities and hospitals in many Muslim countries. However, the faithful lifelong presence of these institutions in the community did not always translate into relevant witnessing relationships. During this period, the few Muslims who did come to know Christ when persecuted were encouraged to leave their families and change their names. Some were even asked to curse Muhammad and stand on the Qur'an as preconditions for baptism. Even today, the stumbling block to the gospel for Muslims is often not Jesus or the cross, but the perception that believers must turn their backs on their home culture and become foreigners in their own communities. Conversion is seen as a rejection of family and local allegiances, more a rebellious breach of community than an inward transformation through Christ.

Yet many historical methods of witness among Muslims continue to be viable today. Though mission schools, hospitals, and orphanages may no longer be a strategic focus, Muslims still need to have God's Word in their vernacular languages. Roundtable conversations and long-term relationships with Muslim men of peace (see Luke 10:5–9) hold promise for generating Muslim-background communities of believers in Jesus Christ. Christian missionaries in the past often led the world's advocacy for the improvement of human conditions, human rights, and religious freedom. Their examples should be assimilated and improved upon by Christians today.

After the Six Day Arab-Israeli War in 1967, the OPEC-led oil crisis in 1973, and the Iranian revolution in 1979, Islam landed on the world stage. Also, during the 1970s, several events marked a change in Christian witness among Muslims: the Lausanne Conference on World Evangelization (1974), the Glen Eyrie Consultation on Muslim Evangelization (1978), the founding of the Zwemer Institute of Muslim Studies (1979), and the formation of several new mission agencies, including Pioneers (1979) and Frontiers (1982). Since these events, Christian outreach to Muslims has become more extensive and constructive. While it is still rare, Muslims are more likely to encounter a relevant witness of Jesus today than at any other time in history.

Let us be quick to say that we honor the example and legacy of earlier missionaries among Muslims. Their courage and faithfulness continue to inspire us, and present-day fruitfulness grows directly out of their willingness to bear Christ's afflictions: they served, they suffered, they even died for Christ (see Col. 1:24). Their blood has been spilled, as was Christ's, to see Muslims believe. At the same time, God calls us to evaluate the mistakes of our forebears (as one day our children will ours). We should model their faith, learn from their work, and closely examine their presuppositions so that we can avoid their pitfalls and serve with culturally and biblically appropriate methods.

– *K.S., Editor.*

## FOR FURTHER STUDY

Colin Chapman, *Islam and the West: Conflict, Coexistence, or Conversion* (Carlisle, UK: Paternoster, 1998).

# APPROACHES TO THE EVANGELIZATION OF MUSLIMS

*by John Mark Terry*

Christianity has encountered Islam since the time of Muhammad. The strategies utilized in fulfilling Christ's command to spread the gospel have varied, from harsh to benign, from failed to prosperous, with equally varied outcomes. This article is a brief historical overview of the five major categories into which the many different methods or approaches to Muslim evangelism fall. Of the models tried, contextualization seems best. However, the propitious approach probably is choosing the most appropriate elements from each model for each situation.

## 1. Confrontational Approach. In

the eighteenth and nineteenth centuries, some missionaries—Henry Martyn, Karl Pfander, and St. Clair Tidall, for example—tried to win Muslims by public debate. They also preached in the bazaars and produced apologetic and polemical literature in English and the vernacular. Their method was never very successful in terms of converts, and it often aroused increased Muslim antipathy toward Christianity.

This model is not widely used these days. Its earlier proponents often worked under the protection of colonial governments. Today, it is not condoned by most Muslim countries. Though occasionally a Muslim intellectual is convinced, or the Christian speaker is subsequently more respected because of his spirited presentation, such debates do not move the masses. Debate as an evangelism technique is quite different from dialogue (discussed below), as a means of building relationships.

## 2. Traditional Evangelical Model.

Samuel Zwemer (1867–1952), the "apostle to the Muslims," was the pioneer of this method. During his early years (1890–1916), he tended toward confrontation. In his books, *The Disintegration of Islam* (1915), and *Mohammed or Christ* (1916), he called for "radical displacement," a complete rejection of Islam by its adherents. However, later Zwemer took up a more anthropological and Christocentric approach, writing empathically of Muslims as seekers after God, while still maintaining that only Jesus could satisfy their needs.[1]

Zwemer believed that evangelism must emphasize the incarnation, atonement, and mediation of Christ. The evangelist must call Muslims to repentance, to submission to Christ, and to involvement in the church. In later years, Zwemer advocated witnessing to individuals and

Dr. John Mark Terry is the A. P. Stone Professor of Missions and Evangelism at the Southern Baptist Theological Seminary. He previously served as a missionary in the Philippines from 1976 to 1989.

Adapted from John Mark Terry, "Approaches to the Evangelization of Muslims," *Evangelical Missions Quarterly* 32, no. 2 (Wheaton, Ill.: Evangelical Missions Information Service, April 1996), pp. 168–73. Used by permission. *www.billygrahamcenter.org/emis*

small groups, advising his students to engage in friendship evangelism. He believed the human personality was the best bridge for conveying the gospel.[2] That Zwemer was a prolific writer is an example evangelicals have followed, producing innumerable books and tracts. They have distributed the Bible as widely as possible, and propagated the gospel by means of radio and Bible correspondence courses.

The traditional model has resulted in western-style churches. Missionaries have told converts to break with Islam and publicly identify with a church. Zwemer rejected the idea of the convert's remaining in Islam as long as possible so as to influence other Muslims.[3] The main criticisms of this approach are that it has not been very effective, and it is too western. But defenders say the model is biblically sound, and faithfully and hopefully continue to sow seed they expect will bear fruit in time. They attribute meager

results to political, historical, and social barriers beyond their control.

**3. Institutional model.** This model is used by several denominational missions: Presbyterians and Congregationalists sought to win Muslims through hospitals, schools, and orphanages; the Foreign Mission Board of the Southern Baptist Convention has operated three hospitals in Arab countries, as well as schools and orphanages in Lebanon, Jordan, and Israel (for Palestinians). The assumption is that demonstrations of love, compassion, and humility will break down walls of prejudice. Some missiologists hold we should send more teachers, doctors, nurses, and agriculturists, because their deeds will speak louder than their words.[4]

The institutional method continues to be valid, since institutions are a good way to overcome prejudice and win a hearing for the gospel, and, in some countries—Yemen,

## THE STEADY LOSS OF WITNESS

Reasons for 95 percent attrition of Muslim-background believers (MBBs) over ten years:

- Emigrating to flee persecution, for employment, or hatred of one's father and culture.
- Leaving home or choosing to remain single rather than marry a non-believer.
- Marrying a foreigner and emigrating.
- Extraction by expatriate workers (for employment, education).
- Family-arranged marriage to a Muslim, who will raise the children as Muslims or removal of children by family or government.
- Silenced or denial of faith out of fear of martyrdom and persecution.
- Martyrdom for reasons other than witness.

In all, 50 to 70 percent are extracted, up to 80 percent are educated outside the country, and as many as 60 percent marry foreigners, leaving only 5 percent of MBBs to witness in their cultures, disciple the next generation of believers, and form believing families with children.

Source: Nik Ripken. Nik has served with his family in Africa since 1984. Nik currently serves as a strategy consultant among the peoples of North Africa and the Middle East.

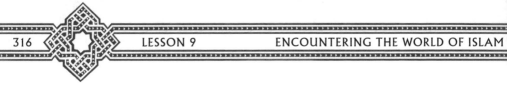
for example—are the only Christian presence allowed. However, institutions face difficult times: inflation makes maintenance difficult, and governments are taking over many of their services.

**4. Dialogical model.** An approach pioneered by Temple Gairdner (1873–1928) and developed more fully by Kenneth Cragg, dialogue is motivated by a sincere love that seeks to reconcile Muslims and Christians. It has four purposes: to learn what Muslims believe, and to appreciate their beliefs in relation to their culture; to establish both contact and rapport on the basis of sincere, honest friendship; to learn how to witness to Muslims; and to bring them ultimately to salvation in Christ.[5]

This approach must not be confused with the syncretistic, universalistic dialogues sponsored by some ecumenical groups. Missionaries do not surrender their convictions: they affirm them, using a method that permits concomitant growth in understanding of Muslims.

**5. Contextualization model.** In this approach, missionaries adopt culturally relevant methods of presenting the gospel in religious and cultural forms with which Muslims can identify. This method bears in mind the "offense of the cross," but tries to avoid objectionable irritants.[6] It requires changes in missionary lifestyles, worship forms, theological terms, and strategy.

Proponents of contextualization argue that this model for Muslim evangelism would include consideration of the following tactics:

- Initial, befriending contact should be with Muslim leaders, to reduce the possibility of overt opposition.
- Opinion leaders of the community, not those on the fringes of society, should be the focus of witness.
- Families, relatives, and groups of friends, not the individual, should be the initial conversion focus.
- Only basic theological concepts should be presented at first.
- Adequate time for change to take place must be allowed.[7]
- Encouraging new converts to repudiate Islam is not preferred. Better that "each one should remain in the situation in which he was in when God called him" (1 Cor. 7:20) to influence his or her peers.
- In many cases, baptism should be postponed so converts will have a greater opportunity to win other Muslims. Confession of faith should be open, but baptism is seen as a political act in some countries.

## FOLLOWING THE LAMB

Can we learn to trust God that matching our methods to the gospel's peaceable content will be the best way to proceed in witness among Muslims? The nature of the gospel itself points us in the direction of vulnerability and sacrifice. Can we 'follow the Lamb wherever he goes?' (Rev. 14:4).

Gordon D. Nickel, *Peaceable Witness among Muslims* (Scottdale, Pa.: Herald Press, 1999), p. 106. *www.mph.org/hp*

- Animistic practices should be reviewed to discover areas of felt need and provide useful points of evangelistic contact.[8]

In summary, the institutional model is needed in Arab countries where no other ministry is permitted. The dialogical method provides an approach to Muslims in different settings. The church-oriented emphasis of the traditional model is biblical and should be stressed. The contextualization approach, based on the insights of anthropology, offers necessary reforms that will lead to truly indigenous churches.

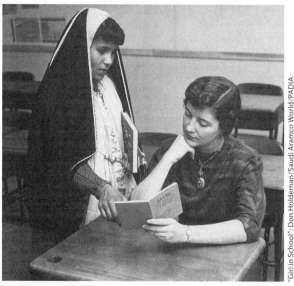

Teaching in Dhahran, Saudi Arabia in 1952

"Girl in School": Don Holdeman/Saudi Aramco World/PADIA

## CHARACTERISTICS OF A GOOD STRATEGY

In describing a useful model, and bearing in mind that Muslims vary culturally from place to place, I have incorporated elements from each. One strategy does not fit all situations. Some general rules that should characterize a strategy to evangelize Muslims are:

### 1. Church

Any model must be church-oriented. As Kenneth Cragg said, "No man comes into a churchless Christ."[9] However, the church must be contextualized. The model that does not bring new converts into a nurturing church will fail.

### 2. Worship

The successful model will emphasize worship designed to meet the needs of the people. The forms will be different, say, in Africa and Asia, contextualization remaining the key.

### 3. Qur'an

Missionaries should use certain passages from the Qur'an as a springboard for explaining the gospel, freely utilizing the names Allah and Isa.

### 4. Lifestyle

Missionaries in Muslim countries will have to adjust their lifestyles for the sake of the gospel. Mission agencies should test candidates for psychological fitness for such service.

### 5. Islam

New missionaries should be given several years to study Islam itself and the language and culture of their assigned country. Intensive preparation and reasonable expectations will reduce missionary dropouts and enhance productivity.

### 6. Storytelling

Missionaries need to adapt their teaching to the culture of their people. Storytelling may well be more effective than sermons.

### 7. Media

The media—radio, television, and literature—should be employed more fully. Programming and writing must be contextualized. Drama will be more effective than the traditional hymn and sermon format.

### 8. Pray

Above all, whatever the model, it must be characterized by love and prayer for Muslims, as confirmed by a Muslim convert: "It is stimulating to think that cases of conversion through sheer reasoning between dogmas of two religions are very rare, perhaps nonexistent. In cases of conversion where prosperity, social status, security, vengeance against native society, emotional experimentation, and the like are not the motives, the change of faith is motivated perhaps more frequently by love for charming virtues of a magnetic person, or love for a group of lovable associates, than by cold religious arithmetic."[10]

### ENDNOTES

1. Lyle VanderWerff, "Our Muslim Neighbors: The Contribution of Samuel Zwemer to

## COMPLETE IN CHRIST

Omar's early life was among a Bedouin community where he spent most of his days watching the goats and camels. When his father realized there was little future in desert life, he moved his family to the city so his sons could receive a formal education. Omar was first in his tribe to ever attend university. As a devout Muslim he quickly became the leader of the youth Islamic party. During these years he received the loving and persistent witness of a Christian who kept on caring even after Omar nearly beat him to death. Omar came to know Christ after he accepted the challenge to read the Bible.

After his transformation, he was persecuted by his family, sentenced to death and imprisoned. After a miraculous release, he was invited to seek refuge in a new country and offered a scholarship at a Bible school where he received his degree and was later ordained. He is currently the pastor of two Arabic-speaking churches.

Initially bitter toward Muslims, God began to challenge Omar to love his Muslim family and friends. At first he struggled to forgive those whom he felt had deceived him. Because of his obedience, God poured into Omar an overwhelming love for Muslims everywhere. Since then, he has traveled extensively to teach and disciple hundreds of Muslim-background believers in a variety of countries. He admonishes and trains them to forgive and to witness to Muslims out of gratitude for what Christ has done for them. Omar has come full circle and exemplifies maturity. "We proclaim him, admonishing every man and teaching every man with all wisdom, so that we may present every man complete in Christ" (Col. 1:28, NASB).

"Consider it pure joy, my brothers, whenever you face trials of many kinds, because you know that the testing of your faith develops perseverance. Perseverance must finish its work so that you may be mature and complete, not lacking anything" (James 1: 2–4).

Source: Annee W. Rose, *www.frontiers.org*.

Christian Mission," *Missiology* 10 (April 1982), p. 191.

2. Ibid., p. 195.

3. Samuel M. Zwemer, *The Cross Above the Crescent* (Grand Rapids: Zondervan, 1941), p. 261.

4. C. George Fry and James R. King, *Islam: A Survey of the Muslim Faith* (Grand Rapids: Baker, 1980), p. 133.

5. Ray G. Register Jr., *Dialogue and Interfaith Witness with Muslims* (Fort Washington, Pa.: Worldwide Evangelization Crusade, 1979), pp. 11–12.

6. Bashir Abdol Massih, "Incarnational Witness to Muslims: The Models of Jesus, Paul, and the Early Church," *World Pulse* (12 September 1982), pp. 1–8.

7. Phil Parshall, *Muslim Evangelism* (Waynesboro, Ga.: Authentic Media, 2003), p. 112.

8. John D. C. Anderson, "The Missionary Approach to Islam: Christian or Cultic?" *Missiology* 4 (July 1976), pp. 295–99.

9. Kenneth Cragg, *Sandals at the Mosque* (New York: Oxford University Press, 1959), p. 143.

10. Frank Khair-Ullah, "Evangelism Among Muslims" in *Let the World Hear His Voice*, ed. J. D. Douglas (Minneapolis: World Wide Publications, 1975), p. 824.

# SAMUEL ZWEMER

*by Ruth A. Tucker*

The intensity that so character-ized the educated young student volunteers who spread out over the world, beginning in the late nineteenth century, was a quality that spurred on the missionary effort in the Islamic world, where resistance to Christianity was fierce. The first significant Christian mission to the Muslims had been conducted by *Raymond Lull* in the thirteenth century. He was almost alone among Christians in his concern to evangelize the Muslims rather than fight them. And in the centuries following, according to Stephen Neill, the "Muslim lands" were "neglected by Christian missions in comparison to more productive fields."[1] That changed in the late nineteenth century, a period "marked by the beginning of a real encounter between the faith of Jesus Christ and the faith of Muhammad."[2] Anglicans entered the area in the 1860s, and other denominations hesitantly followed; but it was *Samuel Zwemer,* a student volunteer initially without denominational support, who coordinated Muslim missionary efforts and focused the attention of the world on the Muslim population and its need for Christ. Many other student volunteers, including W. H. Temple Gairdner, Dr. Paul Harrison, and William Borden, also gave their lives in this most difficult and unrewarding missionary endeavor.

Samuel Zwemer, the "Apostle to Islam," was born near Holland, Michigan, in 1867, the thirteenth of fifteen children. His father was a Reformed Church pastor, and it seemed natural for Samuel, as he was growing up, that he should enter Christian service. Four of his five surviving brothers entered the ministry, and his sister, Nellie Zwemer, spent forty years as a missionary to China. It was while attending Hope College that Zwemer sensed the urgency of foreign missions. During his senior year, under the persuasive preaching of Robert Wilder (the same missionary enthusiast who had stirred John R. Mott and the Mount Hermon Hundred), he and five of his seven classmates volunteered for foreign missionary service.

## LACK OF DENOMINATIONAL SUPPORT AND SLOW PROGRESS

After seminary studies and medical training, Zwemer and a fellow seminarian, James Cantine, offered themselves to the Reformed Board to serve in the Arab world; but they were turned down because of the prevalent belief that such a mission would be "impractical." Undaunted, the enthusiastic pair formed their own mission, the American Arabian Mission, and began raising support. Zwemer traveled some four thousand miles and visited "nearly every church in our denomination west of Ohio," while Cantine traveled in the East. Their method of deputation was unique. Instead of appealing for

---

Ruth Tucker is a missiological historian who teaches at Calvin Theological Seminary and is the author of more than thirteen books.

Adapted from Ruth A. Tucker, *From Jerusalem to Irian Jaya: A Biographical History of Christian Missions* (Grand Rapids: Zondervan, 1983), pp. 276–80. Used by permission. *www.zondervan.com*

funds for themselves, "Zwemer pled for Cantine's support and Cantine pled for Zwemer's. 'Lethargy of the pastors,' wrote Zwemer, 'is the great drawback,' but there were petty annoyances, too: 'Last Sabbath I preached in the afternoon on missions—although I was not allowed to hang up my chart because it was Sunday! That same congregation had a singing school for its youth after the service—"O consistency, thou art a jewel"—but by God's help I can speak without a chart, and I did.'"[3]

By 1889 Cantine's tour was over and he sailed for Arabia, with Zwemer following in 1890. Their determination and dedication did not go unnoticed by their church leaders, for in 1894 the mission was invited to become incorporated into the Reformed Church in America. The slow progress and opposition Zwemer faced during the early years of his ministry in the Persian Gulf region did not discourage him, but only verified what he had anticipated. Initially, he and Cantine lived with Anglican missionaries, but when the Anglican couple was relocated, they were on their own, except for a young Syrian convert who had come to work with them. His untimely death, less than six months after he arrived, was a painful setback to the work.

## "Purchase" of a Wife

In 1895, after five lonely years as a single missionary, Zwemer fell in love with Amy Wilkes, a missionary nurse from England, sponsored by the Church Missionary Society of the Anglican Church. But just as with his evangelistic work, Zwemer's courtship and marriage were not without

obstacles. Sidestepping the Church Missionary Society's "very strict rules about their young lady missionaries having gentlemen friends" was an ordeal in itself, but marriage faced even greater roadblocks, especially for a young missionary with limited finances. "True it is," writes Zwemer's biographer, "that the Church Missionary Society did not surrender their prize without something of a struggle. As is the custom with most Societies, a portion of transportation cost must be refunded if a new person does not remain a certain time on the field. It was necessary to meet this rule, so Samuel Zwemer purchased his wife in true oriental fashion."[4]

## Persevering in Hardships

After sailing to the United States for furlough in 1897, the Zwemers returned to the Persian Gulf to work among the Muslims on the island of Bahrain. They passed out literature and conducted evangelism in public thoroughfares and in private homes, but rarely did they experience any positive response. Living conditions further complicated efforts for a successful ministry. In an age before air conditioning, the heat was almost unbearable—"107 in the coolest part of the veranda." Personal tragedy also interfered with the work. In July 1904, the Zwemers' two little daughters, ages four and seven, both died within eight days of each other. Despite the pain and hardship, Zwemer was content in his ministry, and he could look back on this period some fifty years later and say, "The sheer joy of it all comes back. Gladly would I do it all over again."[5]

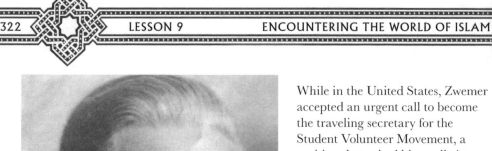

Source: Zwemer Institute of Muslim Studies

Samuel Zwemer (1867–1952)

By 1905, Zwemer's Arab mission had established four stations, and, though they were few in number, the converts showed unusual courage in professing their new-found faith.

## TRAVELING AND RECRUITING FOR MISSIONS TO MUSLIMS

Returning to the United States in 1905, Zwemer traveled and spoke out in behalf of missions to the Muslims. He aggressively raised funds, shunning any form of Hudson Taylor's philosophy of not letting the financial needs be known. Then, in 1906, he served as chairman of the first general missionary conference on Islam that convened in Cairo.

While in the United States, Zwemer accepted an urgent call to become the traveling secretary for the Student Volunteer Movement, a position that suited him well. At the same time, he served as field secretary for the Reformed Board of Foreign Missions, so that his time was taken up in traveling and speaking. Unlike his work with the Muslims, this work elicited an enthusiastic response, and many students answered the call to foreign missions. Nevertheless, Zwemer was anxious to go back to his post in Arabia; and in 1910, following the great Edinburgh Missionary Conference and a return trip to America, he sailed for Bahrain to continue his work.

Zwemer's wife and two youngest children accompanied him back to the Gulf region, but not to remain long. Living arrangements for the two older children back home had not been satisfactory, nor had the education of the two younger children on the field. Thus, Amy returned to the United States to oversee the family matters, a situation that placed the family, as Zwemer described, on "three horns of a dilemma"—a problem with no real solution. "If the wife went home with the children, some would remark that the missionary did not love his wife to let her go like that. If the children were left in the homeland, they were thought to be neglected by their parents. If husband and wife both spent more than usual furlough time at home, they would be accused of neglecting the work on the field."[6]

Back on the field, Zwemer found it difficult to reestablish himself in the work. His leadership abilities were in great demand, and conference planning and speaking engagements frequently called him away from his post. Then in 1912, he received a call from the United Presbyterian Mission in Egypt, that was seconded by the Church Missionary Society, also located there, requesting that he relocate in Cairo and coordinate the missionary work to the entire Islamic world. The Nile Mission Press, known for its literature distribution to Muslims, also joined in the call, and so did the YMCA and the American University of Cairo, leaving Zwemer with little choice but to respond in the affirmative.

## SERVING IN CAIRO

In Cairo, Zwemer found a far more open society, where educated young adults were eager to listen to the impressive missionary intellectual from the West. He spent hours each week on university campuses and, according to Sherwood Eddy, even "gained access to the leaders of the proud and influential al-Azhar Muslim University."[7] Sometimes he conducted meetings with as many as two thousand Muslims present, but actual conversions were rare, and opposition remained intense.

On one occasion he was forced to leave Cairo on the grounds that he had illegally distributed tracts among university students, but the incident contributed to the conversion of one of those students. In front of his class, an infuriated professor tore to bits one of Zwemer's tracts, and a student, curious as to why a small leaflet should create such an outrage, later picked up the fragments, pieced them together, and subsequently was converted to Christianity.

During his first year in Cairo, Zwemer was joined by William Borden, a young

## HIGH COST OF BELIEVING

Ali got involved with a rebel group in Ethiopia, was arrested, and still bears scars from bullet wounds suffered during his escape. He fled to another country, where he met some SIM missionaries. He became fascinated with the *Jesus* film in English, and after finding it in his native language, began to invite more and more friends to view it with him. At last, he declared himself a believer.

That is when Ali's troubles began. His Muslim neighbors took all his possessions and burned them in a bonfire. They evicted him from his home, and he and his family took refuge in a cardboard shelter behind a mud wall. Eventually, his persecutors found him, tied a rope around his neck, and dragged him to an open spot where they kicked, beat, and clubbed him until he was nearly unconscious. Then they dropped a huge rock on his back and left him lying in the middle of the road. Passersby took him to the police, who learned he was a Christian convert from Islam and refused to help him. Finally, some friends carried him to the missionaries' home.

Mohammed, a Muslim who has become convinced that the gospel is the truth, has heard Ali's story. He wonders, should he become a Christian and face suffering like Ali?

Source: Howard Brant, *www.sim.org.*

student volunteer from Yale who had signed the "Princeton Pledge" as a result of Zwemer's own preaching. Borden's humility and eagerness to pass out tracts as he rode through the steaming Cairo streets on his bicycle belied the fact that he had been born into wealth and was an heir to the vast Borden fortune. Before venturing to the mission field, he had given hundreds of thousands of dollars to various Christian organizations, while, at the same time, refusing to succumb to the temptation of buying himself a car—"an unjustifiable luxury." His single-minded goal was to serve out his life as a missionary. That he did, though his term was short. After four months in Cairo, he died following an attack of spinal meningitis.

For seventeen years Zwemer made Cairo his headquarters. From there he traveled all over the world, participating in conferences, raising funds, and establishing work among Muslims in India, China, Indochina, and South Africa. Zwemer's evangelistic methods were a combination of traditional evangelism and the more contemporary concept of "sharing" that was characteristic of the student volunteers. He dealt with Muslims on a plane of equality—sharing his own faith (a very conservative theology) as he sought to learn more about theirs, always show-

ing them the utmost respect. Although his converts were few—probably fewer than a dozen during his nearly forty years of service—he made great strides in awakening Christians to the need for evangelism among the Islamic peoples.

## DECLARING THE NEED

In 1918 Zwemer received a tempting offer to join the faculty at Princeton Theological Seminary, but the urgency for him to continue the work in Cairo was too great, and he rejected the call. In 1929 his work was well established, and when a call again came from Princeton, he was able to leave with good conscience, and to begin a new career as chairman of History of Religion and Christian Missions.

Besides his teaching, the remainder of Zwemer's life was filled with speaking and writing. For forty years he edited the *Moslem World* ("the most prestigious journal of its kind in the English-speaking world," according to J. Herbert Kane[8]), and he wrote hundreds of tracts and nearly fifty books.

To the very end, Zwemer was filled with nervous energy and incessant mental activity. A traveling companion once grudgingly recounted his overnight stay

## " HOW CAN I KEEP WITNESSING?

A young Muslim-background believer sat in our home near Beirut and said to me, "Brother David, how can I keep witnessing for my Lord Jesus? I have won three of my friends to Jesus, but each one has been killed by his family. My own family has tried three times to kill me, but the Lord allowed me to escape each time." I could only weep with him and encourage him to follow the Lord's direction, be obedient to his word, and let the Holy Spirit guide him.

Source: David King, International Mission Board of the Southern Baptist Convention, *www.imb.org*.

with Zwemer: "He could not stay in bed for more than half an hour at a time. For then, on would go the light; Zwemer would get out of bed, get some paper and a pencil, write a few sentences, and then again to bed. When my eyelids would get heavy again, up would come Zwemer, on again the light, and another few notes. Then off to bed again."[9]

Throughout his life, Zwemer faced tragedy and hardship. He mourned the deaths of his little daughters, of close associates, and of two wives (his first in 1937 and his second in 1950). Yet, he remained remarkably happy and optimistic, and he always had time for fun and joking. On one occasion, his fun became so "hilarious and riotous" in a restaurant in Grand Rapids, Michigan, that the headwaiter had to step in and restore order. He had a lively appreciation for the lighter side of life, and, in many ways, his personality was uniquely suited to his years of toil in the hard ground of the Islamic world.

### ENDNOTES

1. Stephen Neill, *A History of Christian Missions* (New York: Penguin, 1964), p. 366.
2. Ibid.
3. J. Christy Wilson Jr., *The Apostle to Islam: A Biography of Samuel M. Zwemer* (Grand Rapids: Baker, 1952), p. 23.
4. Ibid., p. 47.
5. Ibid., p. 43.
6. Ibid., p. 234.
7. [Author did not cite source.]
8. [Author did not cite source.]
9. Ibid., p. 81.

# WHY SO LITTLE FRUIT?

*by Greg Livingstone*

Why has pioneer church planting among Muslims only recently reached the agenda of God's church?

- Mission agencies thought it more important to revive the ancient churches in Muslim countries: their intention was that the resulting national believers would, in turn, proclaim the gospel to the Muslims. They not only failed to plant new churches, but, tragically, the western missionaries underestimated the fact that centuries of the indigenous churches' embitterment toward the Muslims could not be overcome simply by teaching or exhortation.

- The colonial rulers, who took over all aspects of life in these Muslim countries, decided to prevent missionary work focused on Muslims so as not to upset the Muslim populations. Therefore, church planters went instead to the Chinese, Indians, and tribal peoples in the colonies.

- Traditionally, mission agencies have only sent workers to countries that provided "missionary visas." Muslim governments do not offer these visas!

But why has the work among Muslims that *has* been done borne so little fruit?

- Because the Bible teaches that all God's children belong to his one family, non-Muslim churches have extracted any Muslim-background believers out of their cultures, thereby arresting witness to those Muslims.

- Historically, Christians have demanded that Muslims deny their cultures, causing them to dishonor their parents and families by not participating in Muslim observances and traditional family gatherings. Muslims have been less open to switch allegiance to a seemingly foreign Christ who rejects their culture and customs.

- Until recently, the Bible was not translated into many of the languages used by Muslims because: it was illegal to own a Bible, people did not have the resources to buy Bibles in their own languages, or not enough workers willing to give Bible translation high priority came forward.

- Over the centuries, most of the so-called witness to Muslims was no more than theological debate over the nature of Jesus, the Trinity, and the genuineness of Muhammad's prophethood. Any questioning of Muhammad's person or significance destroyed Muslims' ability to hear objectively.

---

Dr. Greg Livingstone founded Frontiers, a mission agency devoted to glorifying God by planting churches among all unreached Muslim peoples. He served fourteen years with Operation Mobilization in India, the Middle East, and Europe, and six years as a director of Arab World Ministries.

- Before Henry Martyn (d. 1812), most efforts to persuade Muslims to convert were chiefly politically motivated, and *not* primarily driven by concern for their present condition or burden for their eternal destination. Still today, Muslims interpret our preaching as western propaganda.

- Rare is that Muslim who has had a Christian friend who speaks his or her heart language, reflects a charming and disarming love of God, and a genuine love for that friend, as well as concern for his or her felt needs and soul.

- Over time, examples of Christians, integrating into local Muslim communities, with Muslims as best friends, or even with relationships of mutual trust with Muslims, appear to be rare.

- On the other hand, in fact, the Qur'an warns Muslims not to become close friends with Christians lest they stray from the True Path of Islam.

- Of the few Christians seeking to persuade Muslims of the truth of the Bible, the majority have not known the Muslim languages well enough to teach the Bible.

- For the most part, in Muslim-majority countries, the Christian worship services are usually not in Muslim languages, are not culturally appropriate, and can even be shockingly irreverent to the Muslim seeker.

- Many workers among Muslims have been gifted as scholars and teachers, not as evangelists. Servants with the gift of

## SHARING WHAT GOD HAS DONE FOR YOU

I was distributing New Testaments in a European country when a young man named Khaled started arguing with me about the validity of the New Testament and the superiority of Islam. I started to explain how God is more powerful than any man. "God sent both his message, the Injil, and his messenger, Isa. How could anyone change God's Word without his permission?"

As Khaled continued to argue, I silently prayed for wisdom and asked if he would join me for a Coke. As we enjoyed our soft drinks, he said he was reading the Qur'an for the second time. I described my experience with Jesus: how I had hated both Palestinians and Israelis, but Christ melted my hate, creating in me a heart for prayer, making me into a peacemaker. Then I shared how I came to ask Christ to be my Savior and how he redeemed me from my sin.

"I have been reading the Qur'an but I have not found any cure for sin," Khaled confessed. "That is because Jesus is the cure," I explained. "Christ's redemptive work on the cross is the only remedy for the sinful nature, the only cure for the penalty of sin." Khalid looked at me and asked, "Can I have this copy of the Injil?"

What if I had continued arguing instead of buying him a Coke and switching our conversation to a natural, personal testimony? When sharing your faith with a Muslim, ask the Lord to bring something to mind that he has done for you: an answered prayer, a comforting verse, or compassionate guidance in time of failure. Let that be your testimony.

Source: Fouad Masri, *www.crescentproject.org*.

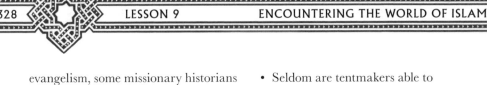

evangelism, some missionary historians think, went to places where they were free to preach openly, like South America or the Philippines.

- Living among poor, more spiritually open Muslims has been and is difficult for well-educated missionaries from rich countries to handle.

- Emphasis on quick evangelism, medical assistance, and education, has left only a precious few workers available for extensive, time-consuming, face-to-face disciple-making.

- Seldom are tentmakers able to hold down full-time jobs, learn the languages well, raise families, and **still** control enough of their time for making Muslims strong disciples.

- The intimidation of the Muslim culture—and their outright fear of it—still provokes in most workers an unwillingness to live among Muslims.

**End of Key Readings for Lesson 9. See** RECOMMENDED READINGS & ACTIVITIES **on p. 347.**

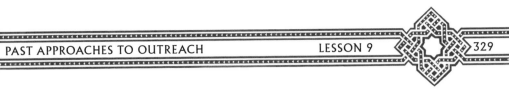
# MISSION LESSONS FROM HISTORY

*by Lyle VanderWerff*

The history of Christian-Muslim relationships provides a laboratory from which can be drawn many lessons for those committed to fulfillment of the Great Commission. The church would do well to research the record of the centuries since A.D. 622. Where in the past has the Church been effective in its witness amidst Islam, and where has it failed in its work of reconciling men and women to God in Christ's name? It is a bittersweet record with insights both negative and positive. In this brief study we will highlight several of these lessons.

## ISLAM'S FORMATIVE PERIOD

One of the factors prompting the rise of Islam was that the church had "Neglected Arabia" (title of a Reformed Church in America publication distributed in the time of Samuel Zwemer and James Cantine). The deserts and cities of Arabia had been passed over by churches that failed to realize the spiritual hunger of the predecessors and contemporaries of Muhammad. There were Christian communities, such as the Arab tribe of the Ghassanids and the Persian tribe of the Lakhmids, but these were barrier-builders rather than bridges for the gospel. Likewise, there was little evidence of reaching out to the Arabs by the churches in Bahrain, Yemen, and Ethiopia, although it is known that some of Muhammad's earliest disciples embraced Christianity after fleeing to Ethiopia. However, the heartlands of Arabia received only the heretical, fringe expressions of that faith, leaving Muhammad still seeking.

Because of the rapid expansion of Islam during its first century (622 to 722), Muslims openly borrowed from many cultures, incorporating much into Dar al-Islam (House of Islam). Islam continued to draw from the religious and cultural heritages of Syria, Egypt, North Africa, Spain, Eastern Turkey, Armenia, Mesopotamia, Persia, northern India, and other Asian contacts.

Although Muslim caliphs and army generals were power brokers who insisted upon surrender or death, they soon harnessed the dhimmi (subject and protected peoples) who paid the annual tribute tax, according to the Covenant of Umar. These terms of subjection severely handicapped Christian influence, but it was still amazing that so much knowledge, religious discussion, and technology was transferred into the House of Islam.

## MUTUAL MISUNDERSTANDING

Mutual misunderstanding was generated between Muslims and Christians from the beginning of Islam. Originally

Dr. Lyle VanderWerff served in Kuwait and is currently professor of religion and director for international students at Northwestern College in Iowa.

Adapted from Lyle VanderWerff, "Mission Lessons from History: A Laboratory of Missiological Insights Gained from Christian-Muslim Relationships," *International Journal of Frontier Missions* 11, no. 2 (April 1994), pp. 75–79. Used by permission. *www.ijfm.org*

Muhammad saw all monotheists as being co-religionists, but in his quarrels with the Jews at Medina there developed an animosity which influenced outside contacts. As he considered himself to be standing in the succession of Abraham, Moses, and the prophets, Muhammad made a direct appeal to the Jews of Medina. Hostility increased as they rebuffed his overtures, and he reciprocated by expelling them or killing their male leadership (Banu Qurayza was one of the tribes). He charged Jews with corrupting the Scriptures where they differed with his revelations. Although Muhammad's attitude towards the Jews soured, he solicited a more reconciliatory stance toward Christians and other "peoples of the Book." Early on, he urged his followers to count Christians as friends (Sura 5:82).

At first he sought to protect Christian leaders and places of worship. But, as the forces of Islam expanded politically, these freedoms were curtailed. The military conquests under the first four caliphs further eroded Christian-Muslim relations. Religion was used to sanction this expansion, and warfare has a way of obscuring the best of intentions. Records of theological discussions are limited. Political, economic, and military issues stole the limelight. Muslim Arab rulers discouraged fraternization, keeping their troops stationed in garrison towns nearby.

There were some rays of light. Positive Christian-Muslim communication is reported in the accounts of John I, Patriarch of Antioch, Nestorian Patriarch Isho Yahb III, and Rector John of Nikiu who was over the Coptic bishops. Christians were often courted by the ruling caliph as their help was needed in ruling this expanding dynasty. Syrian Christians had much to offer. Tribal desert Arabs had yet to learn to manage a rich cultural heritage, a heterogeneous empire. The Umayyads appropriated many Byzantine policies and practices in Damascus. There was a steady flow of Christian contributions, helping Muslims to shape their dream of a better society.

Trade and correspondence benefited all parties. Emperor Leo III wrote to clarify some Muslim misunderstandings about the Christian faith. He urged Muslims to read the whole of Scripture and answered the charge of corruption. He discussed the nature and work of Christ, the Judgment and Resurrection, afterlife, and the work of the Holy Spirit. Leo's letter had a positive impact on Umar. As a reformer, Umar also conversed with Pope Gregory and John of Damascus. In the persons of Umar and Gregory, one can observe the benefits resulting from sincere and cordial conversation. Unfortunately, some Muslims, jealous of the high offices held by Christians, pressured Umar to restrict those who were not politically correct. Properties, positions, and pressure tempted many to convert to Islam.

## THE UMMAYAD PERIOD

John of Damascus (c. 665–750) exhibits some of the qualities needed in effective witnesses amidst Islam. This Christian held high office and served as a personal counselor to the caliph. His writings demonstrate a knowledge of the Qur'an and Islamic beliefs, and a dialectical style influenced by Aristotle. In his book on heresies, he classifies Islam as a

Judeo-Christian offshoot. Sadly, he moves from sympathetic scholarship to verbal attack. It is hard to say where dialogue leaves off and debate begins. In his work on disputations, he describes a technique whereby Christians should answer Muslim questions. Such argumentation would have crippled a sensitive quest for the gospel. This reactionary style would influence Christian-Muslim communication for centuries. It would take great patience to move beyond the controversial format which Christians and Muslims borrowed from Greek philosophers. A thousand years and more would pass before Christian apologetics would take a more conversational tone.

## THE ABBASID PERIOD

Many Christian leaders continued to serve as physicians, financial administrators, political advisors, and so forth. In turn, Muslim rulers settled disputes between *Jacobites*, *Marionites*, and Nestorians. Christian professors served in the universities at Alexandria, Baghdad, Damascus, and Jerusalem. There was a hunger for physics, astronomy, philosophy, and literature. Classical works were translated from Greek and Latin into Arabic and Syriac by men like Theodore of Edessa (d. 785). It was a season of theological ferment.

Under the Abbasids 750–1258, Islam and Christianity were affected by rationalism and suffered a "hardening of the arteries." The scholastic theology of Al-Ashari (d. 935) represents an institutionalized religion. Al-Ghazali (d. 1111) attempted to recover an experiential faith by drawing from Sufism, which has drawn on the wellsprings of Christianity, but still much was to be desired. Islam and the West

## KIND AND DEVOUT

As Yenni was growing up in a small Sumatran city, the only Christians she knew were Chinese. As a young adult, she noticed that the Christians were different from many of the people she knew: They did not smoke, drink alcohol, or use drugs. Yenni herself had been involved in all three of these activities. She was particularly struck with the loving way Christians treated each other. She never considered learning about the God of the Christians, however: Yenni's people are Muslim.

When three Christians from Indonesia needed a place to stay, Yenni's family rented them rooms in their house. The outsiders ended up staying two months. Yenni saw something different about them, something she found very attractive. "They were very devout, very kind," she explains. Even though all three were from different ethnic backgrounds, they cared for each other and treated others in a loving way. None of them smoked, drank alcohol, or used drugs, and this challenged Yenni to examine her own life.

Before these men left town, they asked Yenni to pray with them to accept Jesus as her Lord. Although she did not understand much of what she had just prayed, she asked God to reveal the truth to her. After several days of prayer, God gave Yenni the conviction that Jesus Christ is the truth. "Now I too am a follower of Isa Al-Masih, Jesus the Messiah."

Source: Conversation of a Sumatran believer with a Caleb Project research team

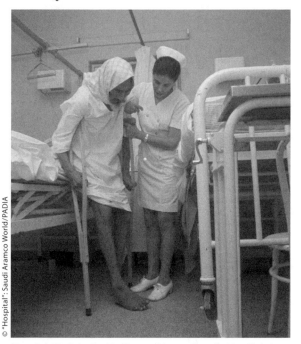

© "Hospital": Saudi Aramco World/PADIA

Many hospitals in the Muslim world were founded by Christians

Caliph commended Timothy for his meaningful theology but lamented his failure to accept Muhammad as a prophet. They differed too in their discussion of the unity and trinity of God. For Timothy, the Qur'an and Muhammad lacked the confirmation by miracles, an authenticating seal dear to Nestorians. Other Christians like Al-Kindi (c. 830) were not so gracious in their dialogue, and appeared more concerned with scoring points against Muhammad than sharing the grace of God. Aristotelian logic became a substitute for the gospel. Where discussions retained a biblical basis, Christian-Muslim dialogue was more productive. The Word of God remains a trysting place, an encounter in truth.

became isolated from each other. Nearly a millennium would pass before exchange in the public square would allow discussion as to the nature of God's redemptive rule in Christ. Christians, as dhimmis, were protected, yet, under the millet system,[1] they struggled to survive by turning to science and technology (much as did Christians in China under the cultural revolution, 1966–76). The surprise is not that many Christians became Muslim to escape the poll-tax and political pressure, but that millions of Christians stood their ground sacrificially.

Nestorian Patriarch Timothy, in his extensive correspondence (780–823), reveals a commitment to mission regardless of the cost. He spent two days at the court of Abbasid Caliph al-Mahdi in 781, giving expression to an orthodox faith. The

Herein is a lesson not to be lost. Both Christianity and Islam purport to be grounded in revelation. Islam acknowledges the authority of the Scriptures, in spite of the sometime charge of "corruption." Of necessity, Muslims are committed to the fact that God reveals himself and that he preserves what he reveals.

We do well to begin our conversations with the Old Testament. Christian-Muslim dialogue must be founded on what God has done. It is well to start with the basic biblical truths: creation, fall, redemption, covenant, and kingdom. Ask the basic question of Abrahamic faith: How did Abraham experience righteousness in the sight of God (Gen. 15:6)?

Muslims as well as our Jewish neighbors need to address such foundational issues. It will be amazing how much common ground we share. Today Christians in Europe and the United States are in a comparable position with an influx of peoples of Muslim background. There are new opportunities for dialogue, for fulfillment of Christ's call to bear witness, and for reaping a rich intercultural harvest of great blessing.

## EARLY AND REFORMATION MISSION MODELS

Initially, Europe responded to Islam out of fear. Muslim expansion threatened her existence. It is no wonder that the literature of the West was filled with harsh caricature and stereotype. Muhammad and Muslims in general were given bad press in Medieval Europe.

Fortunately, more accurate information began to circulate and more positive models of Christian witness began to emerge, such as: Peter the Venerable, Abbot of Cluny (1092–1156); Peter of Lombard (d. 1164), author of *Sentences*; Francis of Assisi (1181–1226), founder of the Franciscans; Raymond of Penaforte (d. 1275), who won many Muslims to Christ in North Africa and in Spain; Thomas Aquinas (d. 1272), whose *Summa* was concerned for witness to peoples of other religions: and Roger Bacon (d. 1292), who sought to view others free of prejudice. The last part of the thirteenth century could be called, "the hopeful decades."

One of the most outstanding figures in the Medieval period was Raymond Lull (1232–1315). Convinced of the futility

of violence (that is, the Crusades), and undergoing a drastic conversion at about age thirty, he made a covenant with God to serve the Muslim world in the Spirit of Christ. For over fifty years he devoted himself to three things necessary for effective witness.

First of all, Lull sought an accurate and comprehensive knowledge of the languages of the people. After painful grappling with Arabic for nine years, he established a college at his hometown, Marjorca, to train Franciscans. He urged the Pope at the Council of Vienna (1312) to form five more colleges for languages, geography, and culture. These colleges were located at Rome, Bologna, Paris, Oxford, and Salamca. Teaching himself, in biblical and mission studies at Paris, he appealed to popes and kings to reach out to Muslims in love.

Secondly, Lull's prodigious literary output resulted in several hundred pieces. His autobiography and mystical work, *Book of the Lover and the Beloved*, was as popular as his *One Hundred Names of God* was practical.Witnessing to Muslims at Tunis, North Africa, he made the case for "the law of Christ." He revealed a faith that was experiential as well as rational.

In the third place, Lull proved to be a man of action as well as words. He would witness to Christ and gathered converts in Tunis even though he knew it was prohibited on pain of death. He sought an open forum, a parliament of religions. He discussed with the leaders Islam's weaknesses: namely, the lack of love in its concept of God, and the lack of harmony in its attributes of God. Martyred when

past age eighty (June 30, 1315), Lull remains known for his exemplary life. That life was shaped by the motto, "The soul that loves not, lives not."

Space does not allow for a thorough treatment of the Roman Catholic and pre-Reformers who contributed to a healthier attitude towards Muslims, and fuller knowledge of and compassion for the Saracens. Protestants are often distressed to learn that reformers, Martin Luther (1483–1546) and John Calvin (1509–1564) were so slow in developing a clear concept of missions. Yet Luther was preoccupied with renewing congregations and supplying pastors who always were in short supply. He had a "sending" heart but inadequate resources. He did argue that the Pope should send evangelists to the Turks rather than troops.

Scholarly John Calvin was also convinced that only a reformed church could convey the gospel to all nations. He corresponded with three hundred Swiss-French Calvinists who settled in Brazil and took the challenge to evangelize the Indian peoples there, but unfortunately, these letters have been lost. However, Calvin's global vision of a sovereign God and a sinful world would later form the impetus for the modern mission movement.

## LIGHT ON MISSION METHODS

From 1800 to the present, Christian witnesses in India (including Pakistan and Bangladesh), have provided many insights as to effective communication with Muslims. William Carey, Henry Martyn, and the evangelical chaplains, Thomas Valpy French, Robert Clark, and others,

learned to encounter Islam without the sharp clash of the controversial method. Alexander Duff, J. N. Farquhar, and A. G. Hogg, among others, learned that education could become a vehicle for preparing the way of the gospel, as well as equipping future leadership in the land. Medical missions and other social services in India demonstrated the reality of God's love in Christ and gave the national churches a place in the sun.

Mission work in the Near East posed a complex set of concerns. Anglican and Reformed churches soon recognized that the weakened presence of the Orthodox Churches, which had long suffered under the millet system, needed revival if Christianity was to recover its larger mission. Presbyterians, the CMS, and others combined encouragement to these Eastern brethren, as well as limited evangelization of Muslims. Pioneer missions by the Arabian Mission, begun by Samuel Zwemer and James Cantine, stretched from the Mesopotamia valley to Kuwait, Bahrain, and Oman.

High points in the twentieth century are seen in the lives and labors of Temple Gairdner, a CMS missionary to Egypt, and of Samuel Zwemer, a Reformed Church in America missionary. The latter's tireless efforts founded the work and churches in the Arabian Gulf, before building an ecumenical network from Indonesia, to Egypt, to Europe, to Princeton. Zwemer's reforming theme of "proclamation" would influence a generation of missionaries following the Madras International Missionary Council conference in 1938. Gairdner was sensitive to culture and the crucial needs of

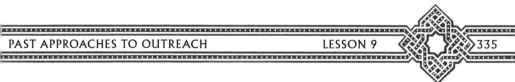
the national church. A respected scholar of Islam and committed to evangelism, he became an advocate of a "Christian presence amid Islam," an approach which matured under the superb leadership of Kenneth Cragg. In Zwemer and Gairdner one finds a balance which can still serve evangelical-ecumenical servants of Christ amid Islam.

## RESPECT FOR ANCIENT ORTHODOX AND NATIONAL EVANGELICAL CHURCHES

A careful reading of history should heighten appreciation for the Orthodox and Roman Catholic churches in lands with a Muslim majority. Those who have survived Islam's severe domination over fourteen centuries, and yet have retained a vibrant faith and a caring ministry,

## ISLAMIC HUMAN RIGHTS

The International Covenant on Civil and Political Rights became international law in March 1976 and has been ratified by 151 nations (see "Why Do We Share the Good News about Jesus with All Peoples, Including Muslims?" on p. 272). The Universal Declaration of Human Rights, part of the United Nations charter of December 1948, also strongly endorses religious freedom in Article 18:

> Everyone has the right to freedom of thought, conscience, and religion; this right includes freedom to change his religion or belief, and freedom, either alone or in community with others and in public or private, to manifest his religion or belief in teaching, practice, worship, and observance.

In addition to these international promises of religious freedom, a Universal Islamic Declaration of Human Rights has been published by the Islamic Council (London). It states:

### Article 12 Right to Freedom of Belief, Thought, and Speech
a. Every person has the right to express his thoughts and beliefs so long as he remains within the limits prescribed by the law. No one, however, is entitled to disseminate falsehood or to circulate reports which may outrage public decency, or to indulge in slander, innuendo, or to cast defamatory aspersions on other persons.
b. Pursuit of knowledge and search after truth is not only a right but a duty of every Muslim.
c. It is the right and duty of every Muslim to protest and strive (within the limits set out by the law) against oppression, even if it involves challenging the highest authority in the state.
d. There shall be no bar on the dissemination of information provided it does not endanger the security of the society or the state and is confined within the limits imposed by the law.
e. No one shall hold in contempt or ridicule the religious beliefs of others or incite public hostility against them; respect for the religious feelings of others is obligatory on all Muslims.

### Article 13 Right to Freedom of Religion
Every person has the right to freedom of conscience and worship in accordance with his religious beliefs.

Sources: *www.ispi-usa.org, www.un.org.*

deserve close examination. How did the Syrian, Armenian, Assyrian, Greek, Nestorian, Coptic, and other Orthodox churches sustain their faith? In the presence of Islam they still maintain body life in Christ's name for millions. Before we launch into creative, pioneer efforts in new locations, we are obliged to learn all we can from these "living saints" and form a partnership with them in the gospel.

When the first Protestant missionaries of Reformed and Anglican churches arrived in the Middle East in the nineteenth century, they were shocked by the conditions of the Eastern churches. They debated whether or not the Eastern churches could witness without first undergoing a revival. Yet it must be said that, even though sorely tried, they were still bearing witness to Christ as persecuted minorities. Since then, Eastern Christians have gained much deserved attention from Protestant and Roman Catholic brethren.

In the last two centuries, national evangelical churches have emerged. They represent the fruit of the modern missionary movement, mainly the result of Reformed Presbyterian and Anglican workers. Such evangelicals in Egypt, Palestine, Israel, Lebanon, Syria, Iran, Iraq, Kuwait, and the Gulf states deserve credit for providing a church home for both nationals and thousands of expatriate laborers and professionals. For example, in Kuwait the former Arabian Mission (begun in 1914) has blossomed into the National Evangelical Church. There a vibrant Arab congregation serves host to other ethnic congregations, including an International English Congregation (organized in 1962), which represents peoples from around the globe. Every day and night of the week, groups gather for study of the Word, prayer, stewardship, and fellowship. Truly this is the Church of Christ, united as one, the holy, catholic, and apostolic household of faith. It is the church, evangelical and ecumenical. In addition to the churches of the Reformation, there are Roman Catholics and Eastern Orthodox by the thousands. In the shadow of Islam, all often know they are joined by the Spirit for worship and witness.

There is no way that those who would be itinerant evangelists or pioneering witnesses can be effective apart from partnership with these indigenous bodies of Christ. It is scandalous when a touring Protestant evangelist visits an isolated house church in Kuwait or Bahrain, and reports that there are only a "dozen" Christians in the land, while ignoring the tens of thousands who are there living out their faith with courage. We must not underestimate the breadth and depth of God's work in our time. Likewise, in our talks with Muslims about the form God's covenant community should take, we must bear witness to the kingdom of God in Christ, which transcends the present form of the church.

## THE QUESTION OF RELIGIOUS FREEDOM

Muslims have yet to experience the major surgery which the church experienced in the Reformation, when it gradually divested itself of political "principalities and powers" and had to learn to live as a community of faith in a pluralistic world. Because Islam has long visualized itself as a totalitarian system, it has been frustrated

whenever it loses control. Even now, Muslim lands are struggling with the question of religious freedom, espoused in the United Nations Charter. While there have been recent waves of fundamental reaction, the rising tide of modernity will spare neither Muslims nor Christians. Diversity, plurality, and modernity are often viewed with suspicion by evangelicals, but they can also serve as allies. The same forces that disrupt traditions and shallow religiosity can also prepare the way for a fresh encounter with the living God. Religion, rather than secularism, will prevail, but it will be a reformed faith. Christians and Muslims and Jews alike will be humbled by the testing of history. Christians will do well to always remain advocates of religious freedom, giving all persons and peoples space in which to respond to the overtures and visitations of God.

To the degree that the church is able to become the embodiment of the kingdom of God, she will become in Christ the bridge for reconciling all peoples to the living God. To the degree that Muslims and Jews and others draw close to God's rule in Christ, they can be drawn into the circle of the Messianic community. If the church is to be both recipient and agency of the coming kingdom it is being called to transformation.

## For Further Study

Ergun Mehmet Caner and Emir Fethi Caner, *Christian Jihad* (Grand Rapids: Kregel Publications, 2004). *www.kregel.com*

## Endnote

1.  Millet, a separate, non-Muslim, religious group; a community of people with a particular religion, under Muslim control, which had the legal right to use its own language; develop its own religious, cultural, and educational institutions; collect and pay taxes to the Muslim government; and maintain courts for trying its own members. Each millet had a leader who was responsible to the Muslim government for the millet's taxes and for the good behavior and loyalty of the members of his community.

# WORLD WATCH LIST

*by Open Doors*

The World Watch List (WWL) of the top fifty countries is based on consideration of aspects of religious freedom, differentiating between the legal status of Christians and the actual situation faced by them. Attention is paid to the role of the church in society and to those factors that may obstruct the freedom of religion in a country. Of the top fifteen countries, nine are Muslim (indicated in bold).

## TOP 15 COUNTRIES

1. North Korea
2. **Saudi Arabia**
3. Laos
4. Vietnam (Highlands)
5. **Iran**
6. **Turkmenistan**
7. **Maldives**
8. Bhutan
9. Myanmar (Burma)
10. China
11. **Somalia**
12. **Pakistan**
13. **Afghanistan**
14. **Comoros**
15. **Sudan**

## OTHER COUNTRIES

Of the remaining thirty-five countries listed, twenty-seven are Muslim: Uzbekistan, Yemen, Eritrea, Egypt, Azerbaijan, Nigeria (North), Libya, Morocco, Qatar, Tunisia, Russian Federation (Chechnya, Kabardino Balkarya, Dagestan, and Tatarstan), Tajikistan, Iraq, Djibouti, Indonesia, Algeria, Turkey, Mauritania, United Arab Emirates, Kurdistan, Oman, Kuwait, Jordan, Bangladesh, Syria, Bahrain, and Malaysia.

## WITHIN THE TOP 10

There is almost no religious freedom in the strict Islamic Kingdom of Saudi Arabia. Christians and other non-Muslims are not allowed to meet for public worship. In 2003, several foreign Christians were jailed, and some were subsequently deported because of their connection with Christian activities such as involvement in house churches. No Christian is allowed to hold a position of authority over a Muslim, so the fact that one of the men had become a manager at his workplace could have played a role in his detention. However, the total number of imprisoned Christians prisoners was lower than in 2002.

The government of the Islamic Republic of Iran continued to restrict freedom of religion during 2003. Religious minorities in the country are regularly harassed, intimidated, and discriminated against because of their faith. In the newest WWL, Iran rose from number 10 to number 5, indicating a clear increase in the extent of persecution. During the past year, a considerable increase has occurred in the number of Christians arrested for their

Founded by Brother Andrew (*God's Smuggler*), Open Doors strengthens and equips the Christians living under or facing restriction and persecution because of their faith in Jesus Christ.

Adapted from *World Watch List* (Open Doors, January 2004). Used by Permission. *www.opendoors.org*

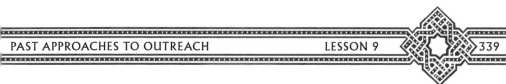

religious beliefs and held without trial. Many Christians of Islamic background were also physically harmed in connection with their newfound faith.

Religious liberty has been severely restricted in the country of Turkmenistan. As a result of the assassination attempt on President Niyazov at the end of 2002, and the ensuing increase in government control, the situation tightened for Christians. During 2003, believers have been harassed, threatened, fined, and detained because of their faith. Turkmenistan increased its pressure on believers by adopting a new religion law which outlaws all unregistered religious activity, a clear violation of the international human rights agreement it has signed. Members of minority faiths are now vulnerable to criminal charges, and penalties for breaking the law range up to a year of "corrective labor."

There was no change in the lack of religious freedom in the archipelago of the Maldives. Islam is the official state religion and religious liberty is severely restricted. The government requires that all citizens be Muslims, and the public practice of any other religion is prohibited. Non-Muslim foreigners are allowed to practice their religions in private, but may not invite citizens to join. No churches are allowed in the country, and the importation of non-Muslim religious materials is forbidden, apart from those for personal use by non-citizens. The few indigenous Christians live their faith in secrecy and extreme isolation. If discovered, they risk losing their citizenship.

## MUSLIM COUNTRIES WHERE THE SITUATION DETERIORATED

In Eritrea, more than 300 evangelical Christians are currently imprisoned for their faith, since Eritrean authorities extensively applied a law which prohibits the practice of "new religion." Mainly Pentecostal believers are victimized by this law. Several were beaten, and more than 60 teenage Christians were locked in metal shipping containers and pressured to renounce their faith in exchange for freedom. Meanwhile, the Eritrean government continues to deny that religious persecution exists in that country.

The murder of a Christian evangelist after he showed a Christian film underscores growing violence against Christians in Bangladesh this past year. An observable surge in Islamic nationalism has been observed since the election of a fundamentalist Islamic government in October 2001.

## MUSLIM COUNTRIES WHERE THE SITUATION IMPROVED

In Pakistan, 2003 saw an absence of the large attacks on churches or Christian institutions of 2002, when Christians were injured or killed. This does not mean the situation for Christians has improved substantially, for it is still constricted, with Islamist sentiments rising, especially since the U.S.-led war in Iraq. A Catholic priest was murdered, possibly since the government decided to return ownership of a former church school to the priest's parish. Blasphemy charges against three Christians were lifted, but life sentences were upheld for two other Christians

accused of burning the Qur'an, and for another sentenced on blasphemy charges.

In comparison to previous years, the absence of major attacks against Christians and massive killings also led to a slight improvement for Nigeria. But tensions between Muslims and Christians, especially in the northern Shari'a (Islamic law) states, did not diminish. Several Christian schools were attacked by Muslim extremists, who required female students to wear the Muslim head covering. Hundreds of students and teachers were injured in the attacks. In Kano state, all schoolgirls in state government-run schools are now obliged to wear the scarf. The enforcement of Shari'a, which should only affect Muslims, is now trampling on the rights of non-Muslims, as Christians are being convicted by Shari'a courts in several states. Although the overall conditions during the past year improved, Christians were still being killed for their faith and churches attacked or demolished.

With the fall of Saddam Hussein's regime in 2003, coercion of Christians by the government in Iraq and its northern region of Kurdistan has disappeared. At the grassroots level, however, pressure still exists. Religious minorities are the main victims of postwar lawlessness and unrest in the country. A Kurdish convert was killed when he refused to return to Islam. The general insecurity provides the ideal conditions for crimes—such as killings, rapes, and property confiscations—to slip past unpunished. Christians face overt discrimination from Islamist elements. Two were murdered because their shops sold alcohol, jobs forbidden for Muslims but permitted for Christians under Hussein's rule.

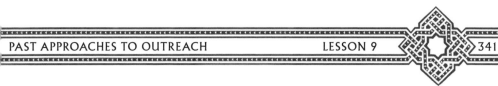
# DECLARATIONS ON CHRISTIAN ATTITUDES TOWARDS MUSLIMS

*by Accelerating International Mission Strategies*

Current statistics describe western contributions to Christian work among Muslims as less than two percent of total western mission resources. This uneven distribution appears to be the result of general misconceptions about the Muslim world. These misconceptions are particularly intensified in western countries due to the Gulf War of 1990–1991, hostage crises, and terrorist attacks. Popular imagery within both national media and religious circles can lead to conclusions suggesting Muslims to be enemies and people unable to receive the gospel of Jesus Christ.

We are commanded by Scripture to love all people, including Muslims. As followers of Jesus Christ, we are obligated by the Great Commission mandate in Matthew 28:18–20 to effectively communicate the gospel of Christ to all peoples, without exception or criteria.

Regardless of how much effort we have contributed to world mission, we have failed to provide the necessary resources to adequately communicate the gospel of Jesus Christ to the Muslim world. In the future, we will endeavor to assure that our view of the Muslim world demonstrates the same love Jesus Christ displayed for all humanity on the cross of Calvary.

We who are followers of Jesus Christ, believing that it is our primary responsibility to share the Good News of Jesus Christ with all the peoples of the world, confess that:

1. We have failed to understand the significance of the many emotional issues of Muslim peoples, especially in regard to the nation of Israel.

2. We have allowed our false perceptions and lack of understanding to result in wrong attitudes and a lack of compassion for Muslim peoples, and, therefore, have not sought to alleviate suffering among them.

3. We are guilty of believing and perpetuating misconceptions, prejudice, and, in some instances, hostility and outright hatred toward Muslim peoples.

4. We have not recognized the timing of the Lord when the Holy Spirit has moved on the hearts of Muslims and given these nations a hunger for an understanding of true Christianity. In spite of our attitudes, the Holy Spirit is working among Muslim peoples through Christian witness and direct revelation.

We repent of attitudes of apathy and hostility we have borne toward Muslims. Repentance is a decision that results

Drafted by Accelerating International Mission Strategies (AIMS), in cooperation with AIMS member agencies focusing on the Islamic world. *www.aims.org*

Adapted from Accelerating International Mission Strategies, "Declaration on Christian Attitudes Towards Muslims," *International Journal of Frontier Missions*, 13, no. 3 (July-September 1996), p. 117. Used by permission. *www.ijfm.org*

in a change of mind, which, in turn, leads to a change of purpose and action. Reconciliation is the goal of our repentance. In an effort toward reconciliation, we pledge to:

1. Earnestly pray on a committed basis for the acceptance of the gospel of Jesus Christ by all Muslim peoples.

2. Earnestly pray on a committed basis for followers of Jesus Christ to develop attitudes of compassion, love, and forgiveness toward Muslims.

3. Act within our individual spheres of influence to rebuke sinful attitudes that we encounter within the Christian community.

4. Earnestly advocate prayer and relief and development assistance for Muslim peoples, some of whom are the poorest, least educated, least medically provided for, and most victimized by violence.

5. Support on a committed basis our brothers and sisters already working in the Muslim world through prayer and financial support.

6. Earnestly pray and seek God's will to determine our individual roles in ensuring that all Muslims have an opportunity to understand and respond to the Good News of Jesus Christ. One clear way is by developing relationships and sharing our faith with Muslims who live in our communities and around the world.

## THE MUSLIMS OF CHINA

Although Muslims make up only 2 percent of China's population, they number more than 25 million people, from a variety of ethnic groups, including the Uygur, Kazak, Uzbek, Kyrgyz, Tajik, Tatar, Salar, Dongxiang, and Hui peoples. Despite this large number, Chinese Muslims are a minority in their country, much like the Muslims of India.

The Hui are the largest Muslim ethnic group in China, numbering more than 10 million people. Members of this group live in all provinces of China, with higher concentrations in some provinces. The Hui make up 33 percent of the population of the Ningxia Hui Autonomous Region, along the Yellow River in north China. In this region, 34 percent of the people follow Islam, the majority religion.

The Hui are descendants of Mongolian and Chinese Muslim traders. They speak Mandarin, the national language, yet many maintain their own culture within clustered communities in urban centers. In rural areas, the Hui raise livestock and make a living as farmers and traveling merchants. The Hui population has increased through migration, intermarriage, and even adoption. Hui families adopt the children of the Han (the majority people of China) and raise them as Hui.

As an ethnic minority population the Hui may face social discrimination. However, they also enjoy several government entitlements, privileges such as subsidies for beef and lamb, and for the reconstruction of mosques, and permission to publish and sell Islamic literature.

Sources: *Operation World, www.chinasource.org, www.tconline.org.*

# WHAT DRAWS MUSLIM WOMEN TO CHRIST?

*by Miriam Adeney*

No disrespect for Islam is intended when we write about Muslim women coming to Christ. Spending time with Muslims, I have been blessed by their high concept of the nature of God; their prayerful lives; their emphasis on community; their insistence that faith must be expressed in the public sector; and their concern for ethics in society. Again and again, Islam points us to our Creator.

Yet, if a faith does not lead to God in Christ, it misses the core. In Christ, God visited this planet in human form. In Christ's death, God experienced the depths of human pain. In Christ's resurrection, God generated the power for new beginnings, for transformation of life. Muslims continually refer to God as "the Merciful and Compassionate." It is in Christ that God most fully demonstrates these qualities. This is why Muslim women come to Christ. Through Christ, the God whom they knew far off and incompletely becomes their personal Father.

There are all sorts of specific paths by which Muslim women come to the Lord Jesus Christ. Some come when they read the gospel story. Others come because they see Jesus in visions or dreams. Others, during a struggle with demons or spirits, find that the name of Jesus brings liberation and help.

Some have been abused in dysfunctional relationships and find Jesus offering them healing and dignity. Others have been schooled in the ideals of righteousness and long for justice in their society. They find the power for this in the Lord Jesus. Some come because of Christ's affirmation of women. Some who have lived promiscuously cry out for a moral foundation for their own lives. Others fear death and long for an assurance of Paradise. Two women I interviewed hungered for God almost single-mindedly from their earliest childhoods. Many come because their family has decided jointly to follow Christ.

Muslim women are human beings, and their motives are complex. However, several milestones recur on these journeys again and again: Scripture, spiritual power encounters, the love of Christians, sex and beauty matters, and social justice issues.

## MYTHS ABOUT MINISTRY WITH MUSLIM WOMEN

In the popular mind and in anthropological studies, missionaries often have been labeled paternalistic, judgmental, condescending, and colonialist. In his book, *Orientalism*, for example, Edward Said argues that missionaries and other expatriates during the Age of Empire

---

Dr. Miriam Adeney, whose Ph.D. is in anthropology, is associate professor of global and urban ministries at Seattle Pacific University.

Adapted from Miriam Adeney, *Daughters of Islam: Building Bridges with Muslim Women* (Downers Grove, Ill.: InterVarsity Press, 2002), pp. 18–21. Used by permission. *www.ivpress.com*

© Arab World Ministries

Conversing together

viewed Muslim history, culture, and ethics through western lenses. Therefore, their reports were faulty.[1]

There is some truth to this. An article in the magazine of the premier American women's mission agency observed in 1866: "The degradation of the female sex in many parts of the East is not sufficiently considered in Christian lands. They are utterly destitute of nearly all those blessings which distinguish us, as rational and religious beings, and without which we should deem life insupportable."[2] The "deplorable state of heathen women," "utterly benighted," "less-favored sisters," "pathetic, pitiable, downtrodden"—such phrases were common during the nineteenth century, the "Great Century" for missions in general and for women's missions in particular. Certainly there were abused women in Muslim countries, as elsewhere. Even in loving Muslim families today, there are millions of women who need schooling, health care, income-generating skills, and, above all, the words of the gospel.

Yet, when we focus on the weaknesses of another culture, we miss its strengths and beauties. We also miss the sins in our own culture. For example, Muslims are appalled at western family life when they hear about abortions, promiscuity, disrespect for parents, and neglect of the elderly. In any case, even at the height of the Age of Empire, women missionaries often lived and worked closely with local women. Women's ministry never has been merely cerebral. It always has been holistic, involving body, mind, and spirit. And, as women have worked together, rested together, laughed together, and cried together, *de facto* empathy has grown. Sisterhood has bonded women across cultures, whatever the missionary's ideology.[3]

And some early women missionaries did see the difference between their culture and the gospel. In Iran in 1903, Dr. Winifred Westlake wrote, "We don't want to Anglicize the Persian women, do we? No, if we may be used to set them free from the trammels of Islam, placing them in the light of the gospel of Christ, they will develop as God wills, and who can tell what they may do in his honor and glory?"[4]

Today there are new assumptions, new "myths" about ministry with Muslim women. Some focus on ministry strategy. Such myths can mislead us:

### Myth 1

Muslim women are passive and submissive. They rarely think for themselves or exert much leadership.

### Myth 2

Muslim women usually cannot come to Christ and grow in Christ unless their husbands become believers too.

### Myth 3

A Muslim family will feel more threatened if a daughter or wife believes in Christ than if a son or husband does.

### Myth 4

Muslim women and men can be evangelized and discipled together effectively, using the same strategies and the same Scripture texts.

### Myth 5

Muslim women ought not to be evangelized until there is a Christian man available to evangelize the men. To do otherwise would be poor stewardship of personnel, since women will not lead a lasting fellowship.

## WOMEN'S RIGHTS

Women's rights in Islam are shaped by the Qur'an, the Hadith, Shari'a law, and local custom. On the issue of a woman's right to divorce, the Qur'an and hadith allow for it under certain conditions. But various schools of law interpret those conditions differently, and they are either enforced or reformed, from country to country, depending on the nation's traditions. The Qur'an does not sanction female circumcision, but a few hadith refer to it; in Shar'ia law it is not obligatory, but neither is it prohibited. In Africa, female circumcision, a practice that predates Islam, persists today for cultural reasons.

Islamist groups may enforce strict interpretations, refusing to grant women rights to education and employment based on local observance and narrow readings of Islamic law. Islamic feminists and moderates reject these rigid views, believing they are based less on the Qur'an and more on weak hadith and cultural traditions. They are pushing a movement "back to the Qur'an," which they believe projects a tolerant view of women. They admire and revere Muhammad as an emancipator of women who forbade the killing of female infants and gave women prerogatives unheard of in pre-Islamic Arabia.

These rights include a woman's ability to own property, acquire education, earn and manage her own money, negotiate the marriage terms, be provided for by her husband and treated equally among all his wives, receive sexual satisfaction from her husband, and divorce.

Not surprisingly, discrepancies occur between Qur'anic teaching and how societies apply it. In the name of Islam, abuses of women's rights exist in the areas of marriage, family, and personal freedoms. In Saudi Arabia the segregation of men and women has reached the extreme: women are not allowed to drive because they would have to unveil for license photos, or might be in contact with male traffic police if involved in accidents, or unsupervised by male chaperones.

Many Muslim nations are trying a new posture: abiding by Islamic law while concurrently dealing more sensitively with the social problems resulting from inequities in how the law is applied.

Source: Fran Love, *www.frontiers.org*.

Consider myths 4 and 5. Can women be evangelized and discipled just like men? Should women's evangelism be subsumed under men's? The short answer is, "Sometimes." How beautiful it is when a household follows Jesus together. How natural it is in places where most important decisions are made corporately. Unfortunately, Islam so resists the lordship of Jesus that even if a kingroup initially hears the gospel together, members may hold each other back from moving closer. Then individual seekers have to pursue truth privately. Sometimes the opportunities to speak to women arise before there are opportunities to speak to men. Sometimes Christian women are available to reach out before there are Christian men to do the same. Sometimes the abuses women have suffered or, alternatively, the richness of women's worlds calls for a gendered approach.

Hagar surely would have resonated with this. Fiercely nurturing, desert-competent, spiritually alive, and quiveringly vulnerable, Hagar went on to network a future for her boy. After they drank from God's well in the wilderness, they revived. The boy grew and became a strong hunter. In time, Hagar got him a wife from Egypt, and he had sons and daughters. Some of those sons appear when the prophet Isaiah envisions a grand procession around the throne of God at the end of time. Descendants of Nabaioth, Hagar's first grandson, and Kedar, another grandson, march in that train. No longer are they outsiders. God accepts their offerings (Isa. 60:7).

Hagar's daughters will be there too.

 **End of Basic Readings for Lesson 9. See** RECOMMENDED READINGS & ACTIVITIES **on p. 347.**

 **Go to:** *www.encounteringislam.org/readings* **to find the Full Readings for Lesson 9.**

## ENDNOTES

1. Edward Said, *Orientalism: Western Conceptions of the Orient* (London: Penguin, 1995).
2. Judith MacLeod, *Woman's Union Missionary Society: The Story of a Continuing Mission* (Upper Darby, Pa.: Interserve, 1999), p. 12.
3. See Erik Freas, "Muslim Women in the Missionary World," *The Muslim World* (April 1998), pp. 141–64; and Guli Francis-Dehqani, "CMS Women Missionaries in Persia: Perceptions of Muslim Women and Islam, 1884–1934," in *The Church Mission Society and World Christianity 1799–1999*, ed. Kevin Ward and Brian Stanley (Grand Rapids: Eerdmans, 1999), pp. 91–119.
4. Francis-Dehqani, "CMS Women Missionaries," p. 118. [Dr. Westlake is quoted as having used (in 1903) the now not-preferred term, "Mohammedanism"; changed here to "Islam."]

# DISCUSSION QUESTIONS

1. What principles have you learned from past approaches to Muslim ministry?

2. Based on an evaluation of historical efforts to reach out to Muslims, which examples do you think we should continue to follow? What would you want to do differently?

3. Most Muslim-background believers in Christ suffer for their faith, and some have given their lives. What does "suffering for Christ" mean to you and your community?

# RECOMMENDED READINGS & ACTIVITIES*

Read: Thomas L. Friedman, *From Beirut to Jerusalem* (New York: Anchor Books, 1989). *www.anchorbooks.com*

William Miller, *My Persian Pilgrimage*, 2nd ed. (Pasadena, Calif.: William Carey Library, 1995). *www.wclbooks.com*

Watch: A Hollywood portrayal of the Muslim world, such as *Hidalgo*, starring Viggo Mortensen (2004); *Not Without My Daughter*, starring Sally Field (1991); *Lion of the Desert*, starring Anthony Quinn (1980); or *The Wind and the Lion*, starring Sean Connery (1975). In light of what you have learned during this course, what thoughts do you have about the way these movies present Muslims?

Pray: Gather a group of Christian friends to pray for Muslims at noon on Fridays.

Order: Learn more about the Muslim world by ordering a free subscription to *Saudi Aramco World* magazine through *www.saudiaramcoworld.com*.

Surf: Discover related web sites at *www.encounteringislam.org/lessonlinks*.

---

\* For expanded details on these Recommended Readings & Activities, visit *www.encounteringislam.org/lessonlinks*.

# OUR RESPONSE
# TO ISLAM

# LESSON 10
## CHURCH PLANTING AND CONTEXTUALIZATION

## PONDER THIS

- How can we become "all things to all" Muslims (1 Cor. 9:19–23)?

- What would it take for Muslims to follow Christ in large numbers?

- What traditions does your home church practice? Describe those that are biblically mandated.

# LESSON OBJECTIVES

Describe current redemptive efforts toward Muslims. Include:

1. Ministry approaches employed today (which are different from those of the past): contextualization, tentmaking, development, and media. Also address our continuing procedure of allocating meager effort and minimum resources to the Muslim world.

2. Give a detailed justification of the necessity for a long-term church-planting strategy.

3. Illustrate successful church planting with models and stories.

# LESSON READINGS

# INTRODUCTION

What will it take for Muslims to understand that Jesus Christ came for them? If we want to see Muslims reached with the gospel, then the planting of strong, indigenous, re-producing, self-supporting churches among each Muslim people group is of primary importance. This requires a long-term team effort that begins with per-sonal incarnation and a deep love for Muslims, the basic building blocks of ministry.

While many Muslim countries do not permit Christians to come and live as missionaries, we are still welcomed as engineers, teachers, medical workers, and other professionals. We enter communities as professionals (tentmakers), not to deceive and obscure our purpose, but to clearly demonstrate our Christian intention to abide by their laws, respect their cultures, and deliver tangible benefits. Responding to the dire needs of Muslims gripped by poverty, natural disasters, or social or political calamities with long-term Christian community and economic development is far more than a mere entry strategy. It is a holistic approach to people that communicates and validates the character of Christ and his church.

Dungan woman of China

© Caleb Project

To create a witnessing presence within a community, we need to live in it, and to learn the local language, including idioms, proverbs, and figures of speech. We ought to know the language of the home and family, not just that of the marketplace. In proclamation, no substitute exists for personal evangelism and discipleship, and that discipleship must be life-on-life, through all the vagaries of daily existence, enduring for years. In one church-planting movement, the expatriate worker never entered the home territory of the people group being reached. Yet thousands came to Christ and dozens of churches were planted in just a short time—after he had concentrated for years on a small circle of men (from this people group), teaching them everything he knew about Jesus.

## Phases of Church Planting

| | |
|---|---|
| 1. Presence | 4. Planting |
| 2. Proclamation | 5. Propagation |
| 3. Persuasion | 6. Partnership |

Stories often bridge literacy and cultural barriers better than other teaching methods. Drama and storytelling adapt to mass media through television and radio. Stories penetrate real life immediately. In fact, most of the Bible is narrative. One of my first experiences with Muslims was in the disheveled huts of a slum outside Mombasa, Kenya, listening as a veteran worker read and discuss a Bible story with a Somali refugee leader. With gentle patience, the Christian honored this Somali man, spending time as his guest each week, as they slowly worked their way through the Bible from Genesis to Christ. As you will see in this lesson, storytelling is a respected way to declare the Good News in many Muslim cultures.

To proclaim Christ, we must understand the local cultural context from which to develop a specific approach for communicating the whole gospel to the hearts and minds of that Muslim community. It is not our goal to see Muslims secretly believe in Jesus (what authors here refer to as C6; see p. 379). Nor is it to see Muslims rebelling against their communities, attending western-model churches that fail to use local languages (C1). Lamentably, C1 and C6 have been the default models in the

past. Those who serve among Muslims today work to build churches that use local languages and indigenous forms of music, diet, and dress (C2). Most workers, in good conscience, also want the local church to include biblically acceptable Islamic language and practices (C3).

How far beyond these obvious, "safe" steps we may go in contextualizing the gospel for Muslims is a matter of debate. But the goal of contextualization is not open for discussion. We want to see Christ-transformed communities, publicly worshiping Jesus Christ as Lord and Savior, growing in Christ through Bible instruction, and effectively witnessing in their neighborhoods. Only when Muslims are persuaded to follow Christ is our proclamation of the gospel effective.

As the church emerges, believers have to be guided and encouraged by the Holy Spirit in their response to the tensions of contextualization and persecution, for it is they who must remain planted in the local context. Eventually, the indigenous church has to be able to support and govern itself and witness independently. Too often foreign money and influence have molded the church into an alien image. For example, local forms of music and worship, although strange to us, must be encouraged by avoiding the lazy copying of our favorite tunes into the new church. I once attended a multi-ethnic meeting in London. The usual mix of hymns and praise choruses were sung. But then the Westerners left and just the Punjabi believers remained: out came the harmonium, a popular South Asian instrument. The place rocked with a power

and passion in worship unlike anything I have ever seen.

Moreover, it is not enough to position one small congregation of Muslim-background believers within a people group of thousands or millions. Surely, God has a plan to reach all Muslim peoples with the Good News and will provide his guidance as we search for new methods of outreach. As Jesus' fishers of men, do we envision "casting the net," asking for whole families, entire communities, even thousands to be saved at one time? This demands bold faith, starting with prayer, to believe God loves Muslims and calls for their salvation. We press on to see God glorified by mass movements of Muslims to Christ, which propagate the church throughout whole societies, as has happened in parts of Indonesia, North Africa, and Bangladesh. By God's grace, let us labor so that this comes to pass.

It is God's prerogative to change hearts. It is our responsibility to carry the gospel, by word and deed, to Muslim communities; to make sure the gospel, once rooted, prospers; and then to welcome and trust Muslim-background believers as our

## UNITY, SUBMISSION, AND COMMUNITY

"And let us consider how to stimulate one another to love and good deeds, not forsaking our own assembling together, as is the habit of some, but encouraging one another; and all the more as you see the day drawing near" (Heb. 10:24–25, NASB).

Long before Islam emphasized unity (tawhid), submission (abd) to God, and community (umma), God established the church to exemplify unity, submission, and community as its hallmarks.

Christ prayed for our unity so that the world would know that God had sent him: "And the glory which you gave me, I have given them, that they may be one, just as we are one: I in them, and you in me; that they may be made perfect in one, and that the world may know that you have sent me, and have loved them as you have loved me" (John 17:22–23, NKJV).

Our submission to God, to other Christians, and to human authorities gives testimony to Christ: "God opposes the proud but gives grace to the humble. Submit yourselves, then, to God" (James 4:6b–7a). "Submit to one another out of reverence for Christ" (Eph. 5:21). "Submit yourselves for the Lord's sake to every authority instituted among men" (1 Peter 2:13a).

There is nothing as joyful as coming together with people who love one another. We worship God through this Christian community. We serve one another in fellowship with one another as Christ called us to do. The ideal toward which we strive was demonstrated in the early church:

> They devoted themselves to the apostles' teaching and to the fellowship, to the breaking of bread and to prayer. Everyone was filled with awe, and many wonders and miraculous signs were done by the apostles. All the believers were together and had everything in common. Selling their possessions and goods, they gave to anyone as he had need. Every day they continued to meet together in the temple courts. They broke bread in their homes and ate together with glad and sincere hearts, praising God and enjoying the favor of all the people. And the Lord added to their number daily those who were being saved. (Acts 2:42–47)

Source: *Encountering the World of Islam*

partners, joined in the global community of those who claim Jesus Christ as Lord.

*– K.S., Editor*

## For Further Study

*The International Journal of Frontier Mission* has ten issues which focused on Islam, Tentmaking, and Contextualization. On-line archives are available at *www.ijfm.org*. *Evangelical Muslims Quarterly* has had more than twenty articles on Muslims; on-line archives are available at *www.billygrahamcenter.org/emis*.

## The Muslims around Us

"There are no Muslims in our community. It's not that diverse." Sadly, we Christians often cannot see the immigrants, students, and Muslim converts all around us. How can we recognize and reach out to these Muslims?

- Set a regular time to pray for Muslims. (Perhaps noon on Fridays?)
- Prayer walk in your neighborhood. Welcome newly found Muslim neighbors to your community; befriend them and expose them to your faith.
- Frequent local, Muslim-owned restaurants and businesses. Search for Muslim names in the Yellow Pages or on the Internet to discover the wonderful cultural experiences available nearby.
- In grocery stores and markets that cater to Muslims, ask how to cook favorite dishes from Muslim lands. This may open discussions, build friendships, and lead to tasty food!
- Visit religious web sites and chat rooms. Many Muslims are uninformed and need to learn from understanding Christians who display love, compassion, and tact.
- Help the hurting. Many Muslims are refugees fleeing their homelands' wars and turmoil. Local agencies and non-profit organizations need volunteers to assist them.
- Befriend the lonely. Many Muslims are international students, as was I. Holidays can be the loneliest time, a great opportunity to invite them over!
- Befriend people who have converted to Islam from Christianity. We can learn from why they converted. Your friendship can counteract inaccurate biblical understanding or a negative opinion of Christians.

Source: Fouad Masri, *www.crescentproject.org*.

# IS PLANTING CHURCHES IN THE MUSLIM WORLD "MISSION IMPOSSIBLE"?

*by Jim Rockford*

Two half-truths: church planting among Muslims is an impossible task, and God must intervene in a special way to reveal how to do it. First of all, in a sense it is impossible. When we consider all that is stacked up against seeing a movement of Muslims coming into the kingdom, the possibility seems almost ludicrous. Second, who can debate that without the miraculous work of the Holy Spirit in a person's heart no one's eyes are opened? Yet in our brief experience, Frontiers's ninety-one teams across North Africa, the Middle East, Central Asia, South Asia, and Southeast Asia are seeing churches planted. God is forming his church out of Muslim-background believers (MBBs) in nearly every country. It is not impossible!

## A BIBLICAL PLAN

God does not expect us to make this up from scratch. Sure, we depend on him to lead in specific ways and to provide the keys that will unlock the doors in each lo-

cation. But now we see that he has already revealed in the Bible most of what we need to know about getting the job done. Much of it comes down to a steady aim.

In Frontiers, we see a strong correlation between the narrowness of a team's objectives and its eventual effectiveness. When a team goes into an unreached place with the singular aim of planting a church among the Muslim majority—and is committed to doing nothing else except what will lead to that goal, with some clearly understood stages in mind—then usually MBB fellowships emerge.

Where teams go in with broad multiple goals—having only a vague notion of how to get there and conflicting views on strategy within the team—then usually there are little or no results. When a church appears among an unreached people group, it is like finding a turtle atop a fence post: clear intentionality from an outside party was involved.

## THE SEVEN PHASES MODEL

Frontiers' "Seven Phases of Church Planting" model (see "Seven Phases of Church Planting: Phase and Activity List" on p. 361) has grown out of such experience. While some may object that there is no magic plan in the New Testament for church planting, we believe that, in fact, definitive stages are indicated. Common sense tells us that before we can have a

Jim Rockford serves as field director in the international headquarters of Frontiers in England. Previously he was a church planter for eleven years in the Middle East.

Adapted from Jim Rockford, "Is Planting Churches in the Muslim World 'Mission Impossible'?" *Evangelical Missions Quarterly* 33, no. 2 (Wheaton, Ill.: Evangelical Missions Information Service, April 1997), pp. 156–65. Used by permission. *www.billygrahamcenter.org/emis*

church, no doubt first there will form a gathering of believers that may not yet have the minimum New Testament characteristics of "church." Before that, at least one from the target group came to Christ, and we are discipling him or her. And that presumes we have been evangelizing. So it is no surprise that these basic stages (with some variation) appear in each of Paul's church-planting situations.

Multistage church-planting models are not new (for example, David Hesselgrave's "*The Pauline Cycle*"). Other models have certainly influenced our seven phases, which have been contextualized to our Muslim church-planting teams and agency ethos.

## RESULTING ADVANTAGES

Promoting and using the seven phases widely in our organization has proved invaluable. Some positive results are:

• When a new team is formed in Frontiers, it is linked with ninety-plus other teams working at the various phases, 1 through 7—a great milieu for peer-to-peer coaching. The new team is energized by the assurance that, by God's grace, it too will eventually be at Phase 5, 6, or 7.

• When a team has a clear picture of the next one or two steps, it is able to work with greater confidence and intentionality (for instance, on language learning). Much time is saved by not needing to figure out the next step.

• The model deals with a major cause of team conflict and ineffectiveness,

mismatched ideas about crucial goals, strategy, methods, time allocation to specific tasks, and so forth. It provides, as a planning tool, a shared vehicle that reduces conflicting expectations. Individual members can identify their places in the bigger picture.

• The seven phases give us a common language to identify progress levels, strategy, and activities across the whole organization.

## WHAT CHURCH PLANTING PHASES ARE NOT

This model is not a precise recipe or road map. Establishing communities of believers in some of the most hostile, dangerous places of the world is not simple or automatic. Of course, there are spiritual battles, persecution, ingrained sin, false conceptions of God, falling away, betrayals, and departures from our expectations. Our fielded teams still require both help—course corrections from leaders and coaches—and their own creativity and Spirit-led ingenuity, this being art, not a science.

Frontiers comprises wide diversity in evangelical theology, philosophy of ministry, and ideas about "church." The seven phases model, to be functional, is intended to encompass a variety of church-planting patterns. For example, one team intends to plant house churches. Another a cell church. Another team will plant a large traditional or normative-type church. Specific philosophies of ministry have been kept to a minimum for the sake of broad applicability.

## ACTUAL FIELD EXAMPLES

We have a team of three families in a large Indonesian city. Having started a growing MBB fellowship, they are in Phase 5. The fellowship has around twenty adult believers, plus children. A spiritually mature, middle-aged MBB couple provides the group's primary leadership. The expatriate team leader and his wife are very close to this couple and are disciplining them, now focusing largely on ministry and church matters, a fine example of 2 Timothy 2:2.

What will open the doors of the Church to Muslims?

But the situation is far from being one-dimensional. Various team members must work hard at discipling MBBs, training other leaders, learning the language further (especially for newer members), and carrying out the necessary governmental work related to projects and other logistics. Also, some of the team members are not highly involved in the MBB group, as the cultural dynamics do not allow too much of an expatriate presence. So they focus mainly on evangelism and training some Christian-background believers in Muslim evangelism.

All the while, the team must pay attention to its own life and growth. So, under the Phase 5 umbrella, they still remain active in many facets of previous phases (language learning, evangelism, discipling, and the like). Nonetheless, this team needs to move on toward Phase 6 (later aspects of the work just prior to full "churchship," such as focusing on leadership development), and also keep an eye on the approach of Phase 7 (appointing elders, ensuring a mode of reproduction, and

exiting). Keeping these two later phases in view prevents the team from straying into cul-de-sacs or attractive ministries that do not contribute to the main thing: church planting.

A very large team in Kazakhstan has planted a large MBB church and some satellite groups in other cities. As in the previous example, quite a variety of work remains, opportunities for team members to exercise their gifts, whether teaching the Bible, discipling, evangelizing, serving, counseling, leading, music, youth work, administration, or the like. Since it is at Phase 7, the work concentrates on multiplication—starting new fellowships and churches.

Another team has worked for years in a major Arab capital. After experiencing many setbacks and waves of opposition from the government, the MBB fellowship they started has grown in size and maturity. This church is composed of around twenty adults, plus children, and two MBB men have been recognized as elders through their active leading and teaching. However, one of these elders, highly gifted as a church planter, is yearning to move

his family to a new city and start afresh. So this ministry must focus on both Phase 6 and Phase 7 priorities.

## AVOIDING DIVERSIONS

In Phases 2 and 3, in particular, it is difficult to persevere. There is usually a strong temptation to give up. More commonly, there is the danger of being diverted into other good things: heavy tentmaking involvement, working with ethnic Christians, creating media, computer work, frequent team activities, or enjoying time with Muslim friends (without challenging them to a decision point for Christ). All these may be worthwhile pursuits, but they may not be really leading toward planting a church. Therefore, the seven phases are a constant reminder and discipline for pulling the team back to the main goal. The phase model provides specific guidance on objectives the team should be pursuing in Phases 2 and 3.

Finally, Frontiers has several teams at Phase 5; that is, they are giving leadership to MBB fellowships started in their target cities. But some might be tempted to conclude they are finished. Our model calls for more effort before completion so their groups are brought to the same ecclesiastical condition as those Paul and Titus left in Crete, real churches, each under a plurality of qualified elders.

## THREE SIGNS OF A CHURCH

The issue of "What is a New Testament church, and how do we know when we have planted one?" is beyond our scope here. However, from New Testament examples and criteria, three things must be true:

1. There must be some "critical mass," some minimal size and social makeup. A group of three single men is not a church. A fellowship of fifteen adults, plus children, may be. The New Testament does not give us a number, probably because what is minimal critical mass will vary.

2. There must be two or more men meeting the qualifications for eldership willing to serve as such. The New Testament teaches a plurality of elders in a given church. Though no number is given, three or more is usually superior to two.

3. These elders must be installed and assuming the leadership authority and responsibility. If the believers are still looking to the planters for this, the church planting is not yet concluded.

Here, at the mark of two millennia of the church's efforts in obeying the Great Commission, clearly the task is unfinished. Yet the signs are that God is pouring out his mercy on more and more unreached people groups, and pioneer church-planting teams are reporting results that, in many cases, are unprecedented. We believe that the main thrust of the church's work to extend the gospel to "those who were not told about him, and those who have not heard," should be church planting. Tools such as the "Seven Phases of Church Planting" can aid in this task.

# SEVEN PHASES OF CHURCH PLANTING: PHASE AND ACTIVITY LIST

*by Dick Scoggins and Jim Rockford*

## PHASE 1: LAUNCHING THE TEAM

**Definition**
Preparing the team. Initial church planting plans and strategies.

**When Begun**
The aspiring team coordinator has been officially selected by the general director to become the designated team coordinator.

1. Research best information available on language, history, and culture of country and target group.
2. Prepare a vision statement.
3. Develop memorandum of understanding.
4. Recruit a team.
5. Acquire church approval and support for each team member.
6. Prepare a strategy paper.
7. Each team member secures adequate prayer and financial support.
8. Obtain team ownership of the vision and strategy for church planting.

## PHASE 2: PREPARING TO SOW

**Definition**
Learning the language, adjusting to the culture, becoming "belongers" in the society.

**When Begun**
Most of the team is on-site, and, usually, engaged in aggressive language learning.

**Activities**
1. Members arrive and secure suitable housing. Arrange for team's initial entry strategy.
2. Resolve conflicts arising in team families.
3. Address team conflicts.
4. Develop a team life which sustains members spiritually.
5. Plan and goal-set for the team.

**Language and Culture Adjustment:**
6. Team members work hard at learning the target language.
7. Set up language-learning program and accountability method.
8. Learn how to survive in area chosen, feel comfortable, and enjoy life in the country.
9. Enable each team family to do the same.
10. Start residency procedure on basis of strategy.
11. Develop multiple relationships of varying depth with target persons.

Dick Scoggins has trained church-planting teams in the Muslim world with Frontiers and other agencies. Jim Rockford serves as field director in the international headquarters of Frontiers in England. Previously he was a church planter for eleven years in the Middle East.

Adapted from Jim Rockford, "Is Planting Churches in the Muslim World 'Mission Impossible'?"; and Dick Scoggins, "Seven Phases at Church Planting: Phase and Activity List," *Evangelical Missions Quarterly* 33, no. 2 (Wheaton, Ill.: Evangelical Missions Information Service, April 1997), pp. 156–65. Used by permission. *www.billygrahamcenter.org/emis*

12. Help family members (wives and children) to develop relationships with target persons.
13. Introduce redemptive elements into such relationships.
14. Grow character through the stress of adapting to culture personally, as a family, and as a team.
15. Discover and collect any evangelistic tools available in the target language.

## PHASE 3: SOWING

**Definition**
The noble work of evangelism.

**When Begun**
Most members of the team are spending most of their ministry time on evangelism, as opposed to language learning.

**Activities**
1. Memorize parts of the Bible (parables or miracles, and the like) in the target language.
2. Learn to share biblical truths in the language.

3. Develop a sympathy for the gospel in friends.
4. Develop a strategy for reaching receptive people and their closest relationships (family or friends) as a group.
5. Begin evangelistic Bible studies.
6. Encourage contacts to bring some interested relatives.
7. Prayerfully evaluate relationships for a prospective man of peace, a man of influence in his extended family or community: Could he bring others with him?
8. Prayerfully identify one or more friends as potential men or women of peace. (Women may be more readily identified, especially if they are responding but men are not.)
9. Lead someone to commit to follow Jesus.

## PHASE 4: DISCIPLING BEGINS

**Definition**
Discipling one or more Muslim-background believers (MBBs) from the target group. Both parties should recog-

## A GOD NOT FAR AWAY

"I was a religious Muslim," says Ayse. "I read a book about hell and it scared me into becoming religious, but I found that the God of Islam is too far away." Then a friend gave Ayse an Injil and challenged her to read it. "I became a Christian after only four days of reading my Bible!" she says.

As she read, Ayse understood it was possible to know God for herself: "The God of the Bible is *not too far away.* We can reach him. I could see myself in the story of the Prodigal Son. God is my heavenly Father who welcomed me back."

Some say the single most effective way to persuade Muslims to turn to Christ is to place a Bible in their hands. "For the word of God is living and active. Sharper than any double-edged sword, it penetrates even to dividing soul and spirit, joints and marrow; it judges the thoughts and attitudes of the heart" (Heb. 4:12).

Source: *Turkey: A Time for Harvest,* (Littleon, Colo.: Caleb Project, 1997).

nize this as a process of maturing of the MBBs in character and service for Christ.

**When Begun**
Regular discipleship with a MBB begins, regardless of how he or she came to Christ.

1. Challenge one or more MBBs (man or woman of peace, if possible), to be discipled by a team member, so they may grow "unto the full measure of Christ" (see Eph. 4:13).
2. Model Christ's lifestyle before this person and his network.
3. Persuade this believer to include some of his or her family or friends in the discipling.

**Disciple the Believer(s) To:**
4. Instruct the believer as to one's new identity as a child of God, by faith, not works. Deal with any tendencies to return to the works mindset of Islam.
5. Teach him or her the purpose of baptism as an outward sign of the death of self and rebirth in Christ.
6. Introduce the believer to Bible stories that will influence daily life.
7. Disciple him or her to make a regular habit of turning to the Bible to deal with specific problems as they arise.
8. Show the believer how to recognize sin in one's personal life, and respond with repentance, confession, and developing new patterns.
9. Challenge him to live out Christ's life in the extended family (for example, Matt. 5–7).
10. Help believers to develop godly patterns of loving their spouses; resolving conflict, asking for forgiveness, achieving reconciliation.

11. Teach believers to develop godly patterns of child rearing and family leadership.
12. Demonstrate how to implement godly patterns of conflict resolution with others.
13. Lead believers to understand the place and function of suffering in believers' lives, and to apply this to their own.
14. Encourage them in practicing godly responses to those hostile to their faith (for instance, government, family, employer, friends).
15. Teach them the biblical perspective on local occult practices and godly alternatives and responses.
16. Train the believer to be ready to give a reason for his faith; the presentation chosen should be prepared, and assertive, but not fearful or combative.
17. Support him or her in sharing the Good News with his or her family and friends.
18. Challenge him to begin identifying his gifts and calling.
19. See that he or she becomes familiar with God's plan for the extension of his kingdom in the book of Acts.
20. Team women: Begin discipling women in Titus 2:3–5 skills and submission to husbands.

## PHASE 5: BEGINNING THE CHURCH

**Definition**
The ministry of gathering MBBs together and leading that fellowship toward maturity. Growing the fellowship into a church or conducting such work with more than one group. During this phase, the church

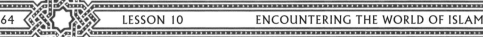
planters exert significant influence in the community.

## Criteria for When Begun

**Group Commitment:** To meet together regularly for the purposes of fellowship in Christ, teaching, prayer, and the like.

**Size:** Three or more MBBs (with at least two being of the target group).

**Breadth:** Not specified.

**Leadership:** Not specified; presumably the church planter is doing all or mostly all the leading and teaching at first.

**Strength:** Not specified; usually pretty fragile at first.

## Goal

Numerical growth and maturing of the group, with the MBBs committed to one another as an expression of the Body of Christ. (Note: the Phase 5 Goal is the Phase 6 Criteria for When Begun.)

## Activities

1. Family and friends begin to explore the Good News together.
2. Three or more believers agree to follow Christ in a committed community.
3. Church planters share God's plan for forming kingdom communities among family and friends.
4. Believers embrace God's plan for forming kingdom communities and, together with church planters, decide on a culturally meaningful pattern for regular gatherings.
5. Believers learn to recognize and maximize spiritual gifts in the emerging community of believers.
6. The older believers demonstrate an understanding of the "one another"

verses of the Bible and how they define Christian community.

7. Older believers have settled on an appropriate way to regulate the fellowship in their community (for instance, a covenant).
8. The community has become identifiable (again, via its covenant).
9. The community celebrates the Lord's table.
10. The community meets together regularly for meaningful worship, instruction, and prayer.
11. The believers do the work of evangelism.
12. Community gatherings are culturally relevant.

## Church Planters Begin to Phase Out:

13. Responsibilities of church planters and MBB leaders are each defined.
14. Withdrawal of most church planters from meetings.
15. Withdrawn church planters focus on starting new communities of believers (Phase 4).
16. Remaining church planters take lower profiles in meetings.

# PHASE 6: TRAINING LEADERS

## Definition

Preparing the fellowship for being on their own as a church. Developing a plurality of men who can soon assume eldership. Main focus of church planter(s) is developing multiple leaders (2 Tim. 2:2), rather than ministering to the fellowship.

## Criteria for When Begun

**Group Commitment:** The MBBs have covenanted (or otherwise expressed

their commitment) to one another, and see their assembling
together as an expression of
being a local church.

**Size:** Ten or more MBBs
regularly involved (including
believing children). This does
not necessarily mean that
meetings average ten or more,
just that there is some sort of
regular involvement (of MBBs,
not just seekers).

**Breadth:** Three or more
married male MBBs
regularly involved.

Peers, coworkers, and brothers

**Leadership:** At least one key MBB
man, who clearly seems to be an "elder
in the making," and is seen by others
as a leader, is assuming more and more
leadership and teaching responsibilities.

**Strength:** MBBs are not all hidden
believers with hidden faith. Some MBBs
are baptized and have already faced
persecution or serious threats and come
out well, maintaining their faith and
their confession of Christ before men.
(See Matt.10:32.)

### Goal

Appointing two or more elders (preferably
three or more). See Phase 7, When Begun.

### Activities

#### Leaders Emerge:

1. Older believers have baptized
   new believers.
2. Older believers are discipling
   new believers.
3. Older women teach newer women
   believers Titus 2 skills.
4. Older, more mature men are
   trained to take leadership of
   community gatherings.

5. Believers take responsibility for
   biblical instruction.
6. Older believers preside at the
   Lord's table.
7. Initial leaders are emerging and
   functioning as shepherds.
8. Growth in godliness in believers'
   homes sets pattern for others.
9. Gifts are encouraged and developed
   for edification.

#### Peacemaking Skills Exercised by the Community:

10. The community is forbearing and
    forgiving of one another.
11. The fellowship is confronting, exhort-
    ing, and reproving erring members.
12. It is shunning, "disfellowshipping,"
    those persisting in sin.

#### Train and Recognize Leaders:

13. Character is being developed in the
    fellowship's marriages.
14. Team leadership concepts are being
    taught, implemented.
15. The will of the Lord is discerned by
    leaders, taught to the community,
    and practiced.

16. Leaders' place in conflict-resolving and peacemaking in the community is taught and practiced. See Phase 6, Peacemaking.
17. Emerging elders are recognized (provisional leadership).
18. Mature women also are recognized in ministry.
19. Conflicts about leadership appointments are dealt with.
20. Leaders begin shepherding and church discipline.
21. Leaders are looking for new men to develop as leaders.
22. Leaders begin discipling new leaders. (See Phase 4, Disciple the Believers and Phase 6, Leaders Emerge.)
23. Church planters are often absent from community meetings; leaders lead.
24. Church planters are often absent from leadership meetings.
25. Elders are formally ordained.

## PHASE 7: REPRODUCING AND EXITING

### Definition

Developing church reproduction, other new church-planting efforts, or assisting the new church for a temporary period. The church planters are not making a career out of working with the one church they have planted, but are working with national believers to plant more churches.

### When Begun

Plurality of biblically qualified elders recognized and installed in the first church, which is of sufficient "critical mass." Local authority and responsibility for shepherding that church rests solely in the hands of indigenous leaders.

### Criteria for When Begun

**Group Commitment:** Same as Phase 6.

**Size:** Same as Phase 6 and of sufficient "critical mass."

**Breadth:** Same as Phase 6 and of sufficient "critical mass."

**Leadership:** Plurality of (minimum of two) biblically qualified MBB elders recognized and installed in the first church. Local authority and responsibility for shepherding that church rests solely in the hands of indigenous leaders.

**Strength:** Same as Phase 6.

### Activities

#### Reproduction Begins:

1. Fellowship equipped with intense teaching on reproducing communities.
2. Community embraces goal of reproducing.
3. Members begin to look for new men of peace around whom to start another community.
4. New gathering (Bible study) started or ownership taken by the church (if started by other church planters).
5. Leaders begin to network with emerging leaders of new gathering, taking some responsibility for their training.
6. Leaders formally recognize newer emerging leaders (provisional elders).
7. Leaders of two communities start meeting regularly.
8. Elders take more responsibility to develop leaders in the new community.
9. A new community meeting is started.
10. Communities care for each other and resources are shared.
11. Peacemaking skills among leaders (of different communities) are practiced.

12. Elders (possibly with church planters) lay hands on new elders in the newer community.
13. Relationship between communities and leaders worked out, formalized (with a covenant).
14. Peacemaking skills between communities and leaders of different communities exercised.
15. Church planters commit the initial community to God, seldom visit community meetings.
16. Church planters redefine their relationship to leaders as coaches, attend leadership meetings only if invited.
17. New churches are started without non-indigenous church planters.

### Great Commission Vision:
18. The vision to plant churches beyond the local area is developed.
19. The vision includes recognizing, training, and sending national church planters to other cities and countries.
20. Leadership communicates its vision to the congregation.
21. Means of sending teams of nationals is devised.
22. Church planters sent out, either with a Frontiers team or other teams.
23. New clusters of communities are started.
24. National teams of church planters are sent out.

### FOR FURTHER STUDY
Greg Livingstone, *Planting Churches in Muslim Cities: A Team Approach* (Grand Rapids: Baker Books, 1994).

Trent Rowland and Vivian Rowland, *Pioneer Church Planting* (Littleton, Colo.: Caleb Project, 2001). *www.calebproject.org*

Tom A. Steffen, *Passing the Baton: Church Planting That Empowers* (La Habra, Calif.: Center for Organizational & Ministry Development, 1997). *www.comd.org*

# CHURCH PLANTING THAT INCLUDES MUSLIM WOMEN

*by Fran Love*

❖ By wisdom a house is built, and through understanding it is established; through knowledge its rooms are filled with rare and beautiful treasures. (Prov. 24:3–4)

When my husband and I were planting a church in Indonesia, I liked to think that it was built by wisdom and understanding, and that the rare and beautiful treasures of Proverbs 24:3–4 were Muslim women.

From my two decades' experience in missions to Muslims, and discussions with fellow workers, I have concluded that Muslim women are often not factored into church-planting strategy due to what I call a "gender-blind missiology." According to this theory, missionaries need to influence heads of households and leaders, who will then lead their families and those under their authority. While based on conventional wisdom, probably true in general, it represents an incomplete perspective, both for biblical and practical reasons.

First of all, there are the Lydias in the world who will be used of God as strategic bridges to reach others, contrary to typi-

cal, male-oriented, cultural conventions (see Acts 16). Second, experience in the Muslim world teaches that the gospel does not always follow along these male bridges to God. When applied to church planting among Muslims, this perspective is inadequate because it supports strategies focused almost exclusively on reaching men, not women, and thus the label, gender-blind missiology.

How marvelous when men give their lives to Jesus Christ, and then in their new joy and love, introduce Jesus to the women in their families. Sadly, this is not always the case in many countries. Workers among Muslims in Yemen, Bangladesh, China, Mauritania, and Turkey report that, while the men had become Christians, the women had not. They give several reasons.

## WHY FEW WOMEN CONVERT

First, in the opinion of many Muslim men, Muslim women are creatures neither worthy of, nor interested in, spiritual matters. Typically, when a Muslim convert is asked why he does not bring his wife to a Christian gathering, he will say, "She is a woman; she wouldn't understand." Sadly, our missionaries, especially women, reinforce this stereotype, complaining that Muslim women are not interested in talking about God. They say trying to bring God into their conversations is frustrating because Muslim women would rather talk about the price of vegetables at

---

Fran Love was born and raised in Indonesia. She and her husband returned to Indonesia later to live among Muslims, to learn from them, and to help them know and experience the love and power that Jesus has for them. She currently resides in England.

Adapted from Fran Love, "Church Planting that Includes Muslim Women," *International Journal of Frontier Missions* 13, no. 3 (July–September 1996), pp. 135–38. Used by permission. *www.ijfm.org*

the market, cooking, babies, and methods of birth control.

Second, the religious role assigned Muslim women stresses that being good Muslims means they are to be a good wives and daughters. While a man's religious practice—submission to God—ties him directly to God, a woman's ties her directly to the men in her life; her submission is to her father, husband, brother, and uncle. The value of a Muslim woman's life is measured by the degree to which she brings honor to her family.[1] This mindset characterizes even the new male convert. He sees little value in fostering an independent relationship between God and his wife or daughter. It is enough that they bring him honor.

Third, women are perceived as jeopardizing men's earnest attentiveness to God. Fatima Mernissi, in *Beyond the Veil*, says of the husband-wife relationship: "Such involvement constitutes a direct threat to man's allegiance to Allah, which requires the unconditional investment of all his energies, thoughts, and feelings in his God."[2] For this reason (in most Muslim countries), when it comes to religious matters, a strict separation between men and women prevails. Women rarely attend mosque, and when there sit behind partitions. Religious discussion is almost exclusively between men, seldom between women, and never between men and women.

The fourth reason is the personal fears of converted men. A male believer may be afraid his wife's family will pressure her to divorce him. He may also fear spiritual retaliation by the women in his family, not an unlikely possibility due to the high percentage of Muslim women deeply involved in animistic and occultic practices. Then he may apprehend that, as soon as his wife is converted, the family will be labeled Christian, with such painful consequences as ostracism, economic pressures, and limited educational opportunities for his children.

## NEEDED: AN INCLUSIVE STRATEGY

These four reasons alone have robbed many women, the hidden half of the unreached Muslim world, of opportunities to hear the gospel. My intent in this report is to supplement the strategies of church planters unaware of the ramifications of gender-blind missiology. While reaching males first can be the main paradigm, we need a comprehensive strategy that includes Muslim women.

Missionaries are becoming more aware of this injustice, deliberately correcting it in three ways: First, by teaching the Word and setting a personal example, male missionaries are able to challenge new male converts. Second, missionary wives devote personal attention and ministry to the women. Third, teams deliberately focus on strategies to reach Muslim women.

Since it is apparent that Muslim women will not automatically or eventually become believers even if their husbands or fathers do, we should discard the hope that the new male converts will do all the hard work for us. Our ministries to Muslims must be undergirded with wisdom, understanding, and knowledge (see Prov. 24:3). In my experience and opinion, the Seven Phases of Church

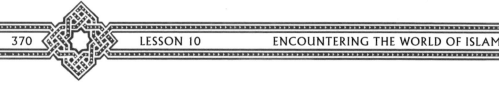

Planting program developed by Frontiers, a mission agency focused exclusively on planting churches among Muslims, directs missionaries to a wise plan for filling new churches with those rare and beautiful treasures, Muslim women.

The steps identified in Seven Phases of Church Planting: Phase and Activity List (see page 361) guide a team of church planters from the initial phases of ministry all the way to reproducing themselves and then exiting the field.[3] Acting as a measuring stick, it allows the mission organization to track teams in the church-planting process. Serving as a guidebook, it helps missionaries envision the next steps they need to take. I have highlighted each phase, illustrating with personal or other's examples the strategic thinking, attitudes, and activities (complementary to other ministries), that will assist missionaries ministering to Muslim women. My suggestions are intended to support women working alongside their male colleagues in establishing churches in which both Muslim men and women are included in the church.

## LAUNCHING THE TEAM

In this first phase, the most important activity is to pray for compassion. Muslim women can appear to be inaccessible, tucked away behind veils, in closed living circumstances. Apprehension about reaching them is dispelled by compassion and understanding of the hurts Islamic cultures have inflicted on women: inferior status, polygamy, easy divorce, female genital mutilation, forced veiling (in areas ruled by fundamentalists), imprisonment

and divorce for being raped, and even honor killings.

Jeremiah, the weeping prophet, draws us compellingly to this compassion: "My eyes will flow unceasingly, without relief, until the Lord looks down from heaven and sees. What I see is grief to my soul because of all the women of my city" (Lam. 3:49–51).

## PREPARING TO SOW

A missionary woman works hard during this second phase, balancing family and team demands while trying to make a home in her new culture. Her long list of activities can overwhelm her as she tries to survive, understand, and be understood. However, for women who work among Muslims, there is an even more crucial dimension to this second phase, a dimension, which, if not cultivated, will over time undermine any ministry they might have: the need to act as honorable women whom Muslim families, especially the men, can trust. The ways female workers conform to what the local society holds to be honorable and right will be keys to the effectiveness and longevity of their ministries with Muslim women. Among the best ways to develop and communicate trustworthiness are in the area of dress, public behavior, and modesty around men. Too often our cultural traditions, and sometimes even our supposed freedom in Christ, desensitize us to clear biblical teaching about modesty (1 Tim. 2:9–10; 1 Peter 3:3–4). We identify a Muslim woman's veil and dress, covering almost all her body, as Islamic, meaning nothing more, nor requiring emulation. Unfortunately, our lack of appreciation and respect for Islamic culture sends a message, not of freedom in Christ, but of freedom in sexuality.

An American worker told about inviting a Muslim woman to her home, not realizing she would bring her husband. The woman acted cold all evening, not even attempting to make eye contact or conversation. Puzzled, my acquaintance tried to guess why there was such a shift in her friend's attitude. Eventually she realized she had been wearing jeans, and had not changed into something more modest when the husband arrived. Her Muslim friend never returned.

Intentionally including women

When I was a new missionary in Asia, I wanted to treat my friends to trips into town to window-shop and eat together, American women's normal pastime. The Muslim wives finally found the courage to tell me their husbands were upset. Honorable women did not go out during the day when they should be doing housework or taking care of children. The husbands were suspicious of my intentions, believing that I was distracting their wives into frivolous, loose behavior.

## SOWING

Frequently, one hears from missionaries among Muslims that Muslim women do not want to talk about God: "How can we evangelize those who have no spiritual hunger?" A male colleague told me how sorry he was that the job of winning Muslim women was so much more difficult than evangelizing Muslim men, who love to debate about God

and religion. I replied that men might enjoy talking about God, but women enjoy talking about life. This is to our advantage because the Bible has so much to say about life. In this third phase, the most important task is to bring God into a Muslim woman's everyday life situations.

Missionary women have found numerous creative ways to share the gospel: classes where skills are taught, shared activities and community involvements, ministries of mercy, counseling, and praying out loud, and in their presence, for and with Muslim women. As urbanization increases, and with it the anonymity and independence of Muslim women (from traditional family values), our opportunities will expand, even look very modern, as we shelter abused women, counsel families in crisis (especially over children's drug abuse and sexual promiscuity), give career guidance, and aid women stressed with balancing job and family demands.[4]

Our ministries will be effective to the degree that God is introduced into their individual

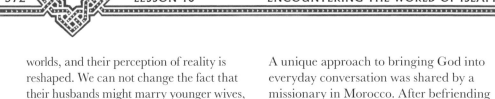

worlds, and their perception of reality is reshaped. We can not change the fact that their husbands might marry younger wives, but we can show them how God loves them and how he views marriage.

A unique approach to bringing God into everyday conversation was shared by a missionary in Morocco. After befriending several neighborhood women, she was asked what she thought about a certain topic. Wisely, from a cultural perspective,

## THE IDEAL WOMEN

The ideal women are faithful and chaste, like Pharaoh's wife and Mary, Jesus' mother.

> And Allah sets forth, as an example to those who believe, the wife of Pharaoh: Behold she said: "O my Lord! Build for me, in nearness to thee, a mansion in the garden, and save me from Pharaoh and his doings, and save me from those that do wrong"; and Mary the daughter of 'Imran, who guarded her chastity; and we breathed into (her body) of our spirit; and she testified to the truth of the words of her Lord and of his revelations, and was one of the devout (servants). (Sura 66:11–12, YUSUF ALI)

And women are to be obedient to God and to their husbands, unlike the wives of Noah and Lot.

> Allah sets forth, for an example to the unbelievers, the wife of Noah and the wife of Lot: they were (respectively) under two of our righteous servants, but they were false to their (husbands), and they profited nothing before Allah on their account, but were told: "Enter ye the fire along with (others) that enter!" (Sura 66:10, YUSUF ALI)

They make it easy for their husbands to help them be good wives.

> Men are the maintainers of women because Allah has made some of them to excel others and because they spend out of their property; the good women are therefore obedient, guarding the unseen as Allah has guarded; and (as to) those on whose part you fear desertion, admonish them, and leave them alone in the sleeping-places and beat them; then if they obey you, do not seek a way against them; surely Allah is high, great. (Sura 4:34, SHAKIR)

But if they have a hard time with their husbands, they are to take their complaints to Allah.

> Allah has indeed heard (and accepted) the statement of the woman who pleads with thee concerning her husband and carries her complaint (in prayer) to Allah. And Allah (always) hears the arguments between both sides among you: for Allah hears and sees. (Sura 58:1, SHAKIR)

The ideal women are to emulate the Prophet's wives, who are called the *Mothers of the Believers*.

> The Prophet has a greater claim on the faithful than they have on themselves, and his wives are (as) their mothers. …O wives of the Prophet! If you will be on your guard, then be not soft in (your) speech, lest he in whose heart is a disease yearn. And speak a good word. And stay in your houses and do not display your finery like the displaying of the ignorance of yore. And keep up prayer, and pay the poor-rate, and obey Allah and his apostle. Allah only desires to keep away the uncleanness from you, O people of the house, and to purify you a (thorough) purifying, and to keep in mind what is recited in your houses of the communications of Allah and the wisdom. (Sura 33:6, 32–34, SHAKIR)

she replied, "I am just a woman. What I think is not important. But I know what my Prophet says about this." She paused. Intrigued, the women asked her to tell them what her Prophet had to say. After several such incidences, the women began to ask her what her Prophet had to say about very personal issues affecting all women, such as divorce, marriage relationships, and so on.

## Discipling and Beginning the Church

Discipling individual believers and gathering them into fellowship groups is the theme of the fourth phase, crucial for ensuring that discipleship groups become churches and that Muslim women participate. Time and again, the stories are similar: fellowship groups struggling to stay alive because they are made up mostly of single men, prayer requests from the field

(cont. from p. 372)

The ideal women are modest.

> And say to the believing women that they cast down their looks and guard their private parts and do not display their ornaments except what appears thereof. And let them wear their head-coverings over their bosoms and not display their ornaments except to their husbands or their fathers, or the fathers of their husbands, or their sons, or the sons of their husbands, or their brothers, or their brothers' sons, or their sisters' sons, or their women, or those whom their right hands possess, or the male servants not having need (of women), or the children who have not attained knowledge of what is hidden of women. And let them not strike their feet so that what they hide of their ornaments may be known. (Sura 24:31, SHAKIR)

The ideal women are pious, fulfilling all the laws of Allah and his Apostle, the Prophet Muhammad.

> Surely the men who submit and the women who submit, and the believing men and the believing women, and the obeying men and the obeying women, and the truthful men and the truthful women, and the patient men and the patient women, and the humble men and the humble women, and the almsgiving men and the almsgiving women, and the fasting men and the fasting women, and the men who guard their private parts and the women who guard, and the men who remember Allah much and the women who remember—Allah has prepared for them forgiveness and a mighty reward. (Sura 33:35, SHAKIR)

And their reward will be great in heaven.

> Allah has promised to the believing men and the believing women gardens, beneath which rivers flow, to abide in them, and goodly dwellings in gardens of perpetual abode. And best of all is Allah's goodly pleasure; that is the grand achievement. (Sura 9:72, SHAKIR)

But if they do not obey Allah nor his Apostle, they will burn in hell.

> The hypocritical men and the hypocritical women are all alike. They enjoin evil and forbid good and withhold their hands. They have forsaken Allah, so he has forsaken them. Surely the hypocrites are the transgressors. Allah has promised the hypocritical men and the hypocritical women and the unbelievers the fire of hell to abide therein. It is enough for them, and Allah has cursed them and they shall have lasting punishment. (Sura 9:67, SHAKIR)

Source: Fran Love, *www.frontiers.org.*

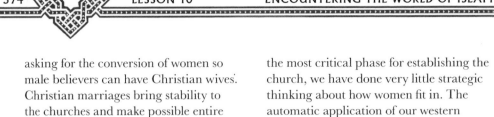
asking for the conversion of women so male believers can have Christian wives. Christian marriages bring stability to the churches and make possible entire families coming to Christ, transforming emerging, incomplete fellowship groups into established, complete churches.

In this phase, missionaries need to form ecclesiology which reflects the local cultural realities of male-female interaction, biblical exegesis of ministry roles women can have in the churches, and practical theology of ministries to women. My concern is that, although we call this

the most critical phase for establishing the church, we have done very little strategic thinking about how women fit in. The automatic application of our western ecclesiology of males only as elders and pastors might prove inadequate in cultures where women and men do not mix in religious gatherings.

The problems connected to having Muslim men and women mix in Christian groups came up when a worker in Sri Lanka asked me what to do about the older women who refused to be in the same room with men. Or women who

## MARRIAGE AND DIVORCE

The Qur'an specifically forbids marrying a Muslim woman against her will. When she marries, she passes from her father's to her husband's authority. In many societies, she also physically moves into her husband's family home. Often the wife is given a set financial sum or dowry, a term of the marriage contract, intended to provide money to survive in the event of divorce or widowhood.

Two passages in the Qur'an profoundly affect wives: a man may marry up to four women, but only if he treats them all fairly (Sura 4:3); and the husband may beat the wife in whom he sees impropriety (Sura 4:19, 34). Muhammad minimized the negative effect of these concessions: he insisted, since men cannot treat all wives fairly (Sura 4:129), they should at least fulfil their obligations to them, and that beating might occur only after other conflict-resolving methods failed. Nevertheless, these verses have freed men to indulge their own selfishness, causing many women sorrow and harm.

If a woman is caught in adultery, she is to be flogged one hundred times, and so is the man (Sura 24:2), but she is supposed to be protected by the requirement for four witnesses of her transgression before she can be punished (Sura 4:15). However, even if she was raped, any resulting pregnancy can act as "proof" of her infidelity.

When serious marriage problems arise, the wife and the husband are to appoint arbitrators from their families to help them reconcile (Sura 4:35). If they cannot reconcile, the husband is to return the wife's dowry. She can divorce him on certain conditions (lack of financial provision or desertion), but the husband must consent. Usually men initiate divorce proceedings.

Both Islam and Christianity set behavioral rules, but our sinful hearts do not respect them. Biblical marriage is modeled on Christ's love for the Church and his submission to the Father. His followers have available Holy Spirit power, enabling unconditional love and submission.

Source: Fran Love, *www.frontiers.org*.

refused to become Christians because they heard that they would have to be baptized by men. Or women uncomfortable mixing with men or having evening meetings, asking to meet with women only, during a noon hour.

Because of these needs, we should look at the church-planting process as a continuum from the emerging church to the established church, and provide for an all-women's group on that continuum. Such a group would be nurtured and developed just like any church, and carefully allowed to assimilate naturally into the larger body of men and women.

In exegeting passages, close attention should be paid to the lives of women in the Bible: What kinds of ministries did women have in Israel's religious system, and later on in Paul's church-planting ministry in the early churches? The cultural view of women then is strikingly similar to what we see today in Islamic cultures. If godly women could accomplish what they did back then, we should expect no less for women converts today, by praying for women like Lydia, Priscilla, Phoebe, Junias, Eunice, Lois, Dorcas, and others (Acts 9, 16, 18; Rom. 16; 2 Tim. 1).

As the result of addressing their felt needs the most important activity in the fourth phase is that a practical theology of ministry to Muslim women must be developed. This covers more than applying the Bible to their lives. It means creating a church system, and ministries within that system, in which they will feel safe and comfortable, and can grow in their gifts and walk with the Lord. This environment is best facilitated in house churches, the norm

in most Muslim contexts, but which, sad to say, many fielded missionaries have no experience in planting. They try to, or do, reproduce the ministries of a traditional church structure, inadvertently losing many opportunities afforded by the house church model for more rapid, deeper spiritual growth, especially for women.

The house church structure offers Muslim women numerous advantages. They usually form around family networks and are where women are most comfortable. They feel safe in familiar surroundings and with people they know. Because the house church depends less on one teacher and more on participatory discussion, it is an atmosphere which encourages women to ask questions and share insights. House churches focus less on conducting church services and more on the transformational ministries of changing lives. In this context, a Muslim woman can ask for and obtain help in any area of her life, knowing that her husband and children or other family members will receive the same attention and aid. The single, most important advantage is the natural environment a house church offers for women to develop their gifts and leadership, necessary to church reproduction.

One practical method we used to disciple and develop women was a children's ministry, a natural, unintimidating, and essential aspect of a house church. The women, especially the mothers, assumed responsibility for the children's spiritual education. Their inherent love for the children drew them into learning how to pray, teach Bible stories, and memorize Bible passages along with them.

## TRAINING LEADERS AND EXITING

This phase includes completing the church by developing, training, and appointing leaders. Many say that completion of the church occurs when male elders are released into leadership. Male eldership is important but is not the only leadership needed in a self-sustaining, growing church among Muslims. Older women training younger women must also be in place (Titus 2:3–5). Definition of their leadership roles and responsibilities—as elders, pastors, senior shepherds, over-seers—will be shaped by the theological convictions of the missionaries. My plea is for moving beyond titles and offices to a concept of church leadership best for Muslim women: women leading women, in cooperation and partnership with men.

When the pastor of the church we planted in Indonesia was ordained, his wife was ordained with him. Clearly, from the beginning, they were a team, and both were being commissioned into the ministry. Several years earlier, as they were contemplating this step, they studied, then adopted, the Priscilla and Aquila model in the New Testament,

even naming a son Aquila, signifying their teamwork in leadership.

In summary, the problem of integrating Muslim women into emerging churches may be solved through specific attitudes and activities suggested for each of the seven phases of church planting: praying for compassion for Muslim women; building trust by behaving as honorable women; bringing God into their everyday lives; developing a relevant and helpful ecclesiology, practical theology of ministry, and biblical models for discipleship; and developing and appointing women leaders.

 **End of Key Readings for Lesson 10. See** RECOMMENDED READINGS & ACTIVITIES **on p. 398.**

### ENDNOTES

1. Christine Mallouhi, *Miniskirts, Mothers, and Muslims: Modeling Spiritual Values in Muslim Culture* (UK: Spear Publications, 1994).
2. *Beyond the Veil: Male-Female Dynamics in Modern Muslim Society*, rev. ed. (Indianapolis: Indiana University Press, 1987), p. 8.
3. In Dick Scoggins and Jim Rockford, "Is Planting Churches in the Muslim World 'Mission Impossible'?" *Evangelical Missions Quarterly* 33, no. 2 (April 1997), pp. 156–65.
4. Bob Hitching, *McDonalds, Minarets, and Modernity* (UK: Spear Publications, 1996).

# THE C1 TO C6 SPECTRUM

*by John Travis*

The C1 to C6 Spectrum compares and contrasts types of "Christ-centered communities" (C, or groups of believers in Christ) found in the Muslim world. The six types in the spectrum are differentiated by language, culture, worship forms, degree of freedom to worship with others, and religious identity. All worship Jesus as Lord, and core elements of the gospel are the same from group to group. The spectrum attempts to address the enormous diversity which exists throughout the Muslim world in terms of ethnicity, history, traditions, language, culture, and, in some cases, theology.

This diversity indicates that myriad approaches are needed to successfully share the gospel and plant Christ-centered communities among the world's over one billion followers of Islam. The purpose of the spectrum is to assist church planters and Muslim-background believers in ascertaining which type of Christ-centered communities may draw the most people from the target group to Christ, and best fit in a given context. All of these six types are presently found in some part of the Muslim world.

Note: *Insider* refers to the local Muslim population; *outsider* refers to the local non-Muslim population.

## C1
### Traditional Churches Using Outsider Language
May be Orthodox, Catholic, or Protestant. Some predate Islam. Thousands of C1 churches are found in Muslim lands today. Many reflect western culture. A huge cultural chasm often exists between the church and the surrounding Muslim community. Some Muslim-background believers may be found in C1 churches. C1 believers call themselves Christians.

## C2
### Traditional Churches Using Insider Language
Essentially the same as C1 except for language. Though insider language is used, religious vocabulary is probably non-Islamic (distinctively Christian). The cultural gap between Muslims and C2 is still large. Often more Muslim-background believers are found in C2 than C1. The majority of churches located in the Muslim world today are C1 or C2. C2 believers call themselves Christians.

John Travis has been involved in planting congregations among Muslims in Asia for the past eighteen years.

Adapted from John Travis, "The C1 to C6 Spectrum." *Evangelical Missions Quarterly* (Wheaton, Ill.: Evangelical Missions Information Service, July 1996), pp. 304–10. Used by permission. *www.billygrahamcenter.org/emis*

## C3

### Contextualized Christ-Centered Communities Using Insider Language and Religiously Neutral, Insider Cultural Forms

Religiously neutral forms may include folk music, ethnic dress, artwork, and the like. Islamic elements (where present) are filtered out so as to use purely cultural forms. The aim is to reduce the foreign-ness of the gospel and the church by contextualizing to biblically permissible cultural forms. May meet in a church building or more religiously neutral loca-tion. C3 congregations are comprised of a majority of Muslim-background believers. C3 believers call themselves Christians.

## C4

### Contextualized Christ-Centered Communities Using Insider Language and Biblically Permissible Cultural and Islamic Forms

Similar to C3, however, biblically permis-sible Islamic forms and practices are also utilized (for instance, praying with raised hands; keeping the fast; avoiding pork, alcohol, and dogs as pets; using Islamic terms, dress, and so forth). C1 and C2 forms avoided. Meetings not held in church buildings. C4 communities are comprised almost entirely of Muslim-background believers. C4 believers, though highly contextualized, are usually not seen as Muslim by the Muslim com-munity. C4 believers identify themselves as "followers of Isa the Messiah" (or something similar).

## C5

### Christ-Centered Communities of "Messianic Muslims" Who Have Accepted Jesus as Lord and Savior

C5 believers remain legally and socially within the community of Islam. Somewhat similar to the Messianic Jewish movement, aspects of Islamic theology which are incompatible with the Bible are rejected, or reinterpreted, if possible. Participation in corporate Islamic worship varies from person to person and group to group. C5 believers meet regularly with other C5 believers and share their faith with unsaved Muslims. Unsaved Muslims may see C5 believers as theologically deviant and may eventually expel them from the community of Islam. Where entire villages accept Christ, C5 may result in "Messianic mosques." C5 believ-ers are viewed as Muslims by the Muslim community, and refer to themselves as Muslims who follow Isa the Messiah.

## C6

### Small Christ-Centered Communities of Secret or Underground Believers

Similar to persecuted believers suffering under totalitarian regimes. Due to fear, isolation, or threat of extreme govern-mental or community legal action or retaliation (including capital punishment), C6 believers worship Christ secretly (individually, or perhaps infrequently in small clusters). Many come to Christ through dreams, visions, miracles, radio broadcasts, tracts, Christian witness while abroad, or reading the Bible on their own initiative. C6 (as opposed to C5) believers are usually silent about their faith. C6

## The Church Contextualization Spectrum

| | CHRIST-CENTERED COMMUNITY DESCRIPTION | SELF-IDENTITY | MUSLIM PERCEPTION |
|---|---|---|---|
| C1 | A church foreign to the Muslim community, both in culture and language | "Christian" | Christian |
| C2 | Like C1, but speaking the language used by Muslims, though their religious terminology is distinctly non-Muslim | "Christian" | Christian |
| C3 | Like C2, but using non-Islamic cultural elements (dress, music, diet, and arts) | "Christian" | Christian |
| C4 | Like C3, but with some biblically acceptable Islamic practices<br><br>Not a church | "Follower of Isa" | A kind of Christian |
| C5 | Gathering of Muslims within the Muslim community, centered on Christ<br><br>Not a church | "Muslim follower of Isa"<br><br>Not a Christian | A strange kind of Muslim |
| C6 | Secret believers, may or may not be active in the religious life of the Muslim community<br><br>May be an underground church | Privately "follower of Isa," or "Muslim follower of Isa," or Christian | Muslim |

Adapted from *Evangelical Missions Quarterly*, 35, no. 2 (Wheaton, Ill.: Evangelical Missions Information Service, April 1999), p. 190.
www.billygrahamcenter.org/emis

is not ideal; God desires his people to witness and have regular fellowship (Heb. 10:25). Nonetheless, C6 believers are part of our family in Christ. Though God may call some to a life of suffering, imprison-ment, or martyrdom, he may be pleased to have some worship him in secret, at least for a time. C6 believers are perceived as Muslims by the Muslim community and identify themselves as Muslims.

## EUROPEAN IMMIGRANTS

Many of Europe's great cities—Rome, Paris, London, Amsterdam—have become home to a multitude of cultures and languages as immigrants and refugees have flooded the continent. Some, from now-independent European colonies, sought opportunity and education. Millions immigrated after World War II, guest workers helping rebuild Europe, eventually bringing their families, and settling in the cities. Many refugees still arrive, fleeing war, famine, economic deprivation, and other circumstances.[1]

Nearly 30 million people have emigrated from other continents to Europe since 1945, and almost 500,000 apply for asylum yearly. Among these newcomers are many Muslims, largely from the Middle East, North and Sub-Saharan Africa, and southwest Europe (mostly Bosnians, Albanians, and Turks). In Europe, Islam continues to grow, through a high birthrate, as well as immigration: Islam is now Europe's second largest religion.[2]

Many native Europeans view the newcomers as outsiders, and they are often disproportion-ately blamed for urban problems. Columnist Thomas Friedman charges that Europe has not been successful in "integrating and employing its growing Muslim minorities, many of whom have a deep feeling of alienation."[3]

A young Algerian Muslim man living in Brussels expressed the tension many immigrants feel: "I don't belong anywhere. We go to North Africa on holiday and are laughed at because of our poor Arabic.… Then we…come back home to Europe, where we're the 'dirty Arabs.'"[4]

1. *Immigrants and Refugees: The New Faces of Europe* (Littleton, Colo.: Caleb Project, 2003), p. 2.
2. Patrick Johnstone and Jason Mandryk, *Operation World, 21st Century Edition* (Waynesboro, Ga.: Paternoster USA, 2001), p. 54.
3. Thomas Friedman, "War of Ideas, Part 6," *New York Times* (25 January 2004), p. 15.
4. *Immigrants and Refugees*, p. 5.

Source: *Encountering the World of Islam*

# HOW FAR IS TOO FAR?

*by David Racey*

In a bold effort to contextualize the gospel, five Christians in Cairo—three Americans, one New Zealander, and one Egyptian—attempt to remove stumbling blocks to the gospel. The Westerners grow beards like the Muslims around them, and their wives wear the veil. They call themselves "Muslims who follow Christ." The Americans are employees of a western tentmaking agency. Muslim neighbors begin to hear about Jesus, and some of them decide to follow him. Those who follow are taught to retain all Islamic forms but to change some of the memorized phrases. All goes well, for a while.

But one night, the authorities pound on their doors and arrest them on charges of "exploiting religion to debase Islam and to foment sectarian rebellion." Large amounts of incriminating Christian literature are found. All five are interrogated, then thrown into prison. Their families are harassed, then evicted from their homes. The Egyptian is separated from his western friends and strapped to a bed in a psychiatric prison. Wild cats are thrown on his chest. Finally, following forty-five days of incarceration and sustained pressure from western govern-

ments, the four are released and kicked out of Egypt.

However, one way or another, contextualization is here to stay. Cross-cultural workers may try to avoid it—either because of changes it demands in their lifestyles, or because they are afraid of compromise and syncretism—but there is no place to hide from it on the field. If we do not contextualize, our gospel appears irrelevant to our hearers. However, we must be sure that our contextualization is both sensitive to local culture and true to God's Word.

## BROAD AND NARROW CONTEXTUALIZATION

The broad definition of contextualization is "any action that puts the gospel into a more understandable, culturally relevant form by including elements from a target culture's customs, language, and traditions."[1] The narrow (strict) definition followed by many Christian workers in the Middle East might better be called Islamization, an attempt to look and act as Islamic as possible, while maintaining allegiance to Christ. It means adopting Islamic names and clothing, and following as many of the five pillars of Islam as one's conscience allows.

Practitioners of the narrow definition say they want to appear as cultural insiders, so Muslims will not reject the gospel for

---

David Racey is a worker with Christar, formerly International Missions, Inc. (IMI), who has lived nine years in the Middle East.

Adapted from David Racey, "Contextualization: How Far Is Too Far?" *Evangelical Missions Quarterly* 32, no. 3 (Wheaton, Ill.: Evangelical Missions Information Service, July 1996), pp. 304–9. Used by permission. *www.billygrahamcenter.org/emis*

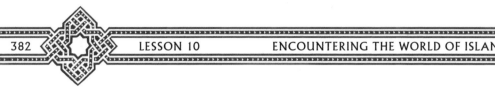

the wrong reasons. They also desire to provide a model for inquirers to observe and new believers to follow, and to show that a Muslim can become a true Christian believer, while not becoming a "cultural traitor." The broad definition of contextualization becomes difficult to practice in Islamic countries, because culture is so closely intertwined with religion. The closer one comes to identifying with Islamic culture, the closer one comes to practicing Islam. Therefore, we have to think carefully about applying the narrow definition.

For example, we cannot oppose such things as eating local food and following local customs, or even removing church pews for the sake of converted Muslims, and taking off our shoes for worship. But is it permissible to use the Qur'an when witnessing? To use the term Allah in reference to almighty God? To fast during Ramadan? To pray and give to the poor publicly? To use ritualized forms of prayer? To dress in a distinctly Muslim fashion? To call oneself a Muslim? To pray at a mosque in a line with Muslims,

facing Mecca? To travel to Mecca itself? To recite the Islamic Creed?

We require some answers. We need to know where to draw the line, and when contextualization has gone too far and our faith has been compromised. The following are some principles I recommend as guidelines.

## INDIVIDUAL CONSCIENCE

One's conscience helps each of us stay in line with what we know of God's will. When we violate our moral principles, we sin (Rom. 14:14, 22–23). In contextualization, if a person has any doubts about practicing an Islamic custom, then it is wrong.

Understanding on what basis a person decides what is appropriate behavior, according to his conscience, is difficult. Further, we all have an amazing ability to justify our desires. For example, we can convince ourselves that calling ourselves Muslims is not deceptive. We can rationalize that

## WHAT IS A CHURCH?

A local church is a grouping of members of the universal church, with sufficient structure to demonstrate its corporate identity, within its given social and cultural context, and to carry out its corporate functions of worship, edification, and outreach.

We have defined what we believe to be the essential elements of an autonomous functioning local church as:

- Baptized believers.
- Christian families.
- Scripturally qualified and locally recognized leaders.
- Meeting place(s) independent of the expatriate church planter.
- Assumption of responsibility for finances and ministry by the local group.

Wendell Evans, *Church Planting in the Arab-Muslim World* (Upper Darby, Pa.: Arab World Ministries, 1986), p. 2.

since the definition of a Muslim is "one who submits to God," it is acceptable for Christians to say they are Muslims. This may make us uncomfortable at first, but the more we do it, the less our consciences object.

Conscience is often cited as the sole measure for Islamicizing our witness. If my conscience does not bother me, then the practice must be legitimate. However, other considerations come into play. Team unity is one. Sharing goals makes working together possible. This requires both cooperation and coordination in our witness (Amos 3:3; Matt. 12:25; Eph. 4:2–3).

Christian work in Muslim lands is difficult enough without divisions in the ranks. Unity is a basic requirement for any team. If one member's approach to contextualization goes against the views of other team members, team unity is broken and the team becomes ineffective. Sometimes mature teams develop two opposing views on a very important subject. In that case, a friendly separation may be in order, but not until the issue has been thoroughly discussed and serious attempts at reconciliation have been made.

What will a Muslim-background believer fellowship look like?

© Arab World Ministries

## TARGET CULTURE'S CONSCIENCE

Robert Priest has argued that our approaches to a new culture should not be determined primarily by our own standards, but by the scruples of the people we have come to serve.[2] In other words,

to be clean vessels for our Master's use, we need to be seen as holy in the eyes of those we are attempting to reach (2 Cor. 4:2). The principle is that we must live in such a way that our behavior is commended, or approved, by those to whom we minister. If we are seen as unholy, then our message will be rejected as contaminated.

For example, some workers in Japan take pride in their commitment to truth. They believe by directly telling the truth, no matter what the consequences might be, they are projecting a testimony of godly lives. However, the Japanese only see the workers' insensitivity to the feelings of others.[3] I violated such sensitivities when I had an upper-class Iraqi lady sit next to a lower-class garbage collector. I thought I was demonstrating the egalitarian nature of the gospel. All she saw was my disrespect.

In Islamic areas, we are disregarding this principle of conforming our behavior to the target's cultures definition of what is expected when we refuse to pray in public. Jesus exhorted private prayer (Matt. 6:5–6), but he also prayed publicly for others (John 11:42–43). If we pray only when we are out of sight of our maids and friends, they assume we never pray and consider us unholy. We have to recognize that our scruples of conscience vary considerably from the scruples of conscience of the culture we are trying to adapt to and reach.

## DOUBLE STANDARDS

Changing our behavior to match local customs, while not attempting to understand what our friends think of our behavior, may merely defy moral sensitivities important to them. Just because something does not offend our consciences does not mean it will not offend the local conscience. Honoring what is acceptable to our target group is critical when we present truth to a new culture. So as not to be perceived as deceptive (Eph. 4:25), we must learn what constitutes deception in the local culture, especially with regard to religion, and then avoid all appearances of duplicity.

Admittedly, it is difficult to determine where being considerate or clever ends and deceit begins. Various cultures draw the line at different places. Ask Americans how they feel, and they will always say, "Fine," no matter how they feel. Arab Muslims tolerate deception in business and sex far more than do Americans. Arab Muslims lie rather than offend. They think it is better to say they have no money than to refuse a request for a loan. Lying to achieve good is expected and does not bother conscience or affect reputation.

However, Arab Muslims judge religious matters in a different light, and evaluate foreigners by a different standard. Double standards may seem wrong to us, but they are respected in many cultures. Muslims may swear on the Qur'an and then break their oaths without remorse, as long as the reasons are important. They may twist our Scripture to prove a point, or endorse a forged document like the Gospel of Barnabas, but if they think we are doing such things, they cry foul.

In cultures that are not strongly Islamic, praying in a mosque and calling oneself a Muslim may be regarded as nothing more than the mark of a religious person. People may even call the Christian worker a Muslim because they see him as righteous, even though he attends church and conducts other Christian activities. In such cultures, the term "Islam" is used very broadly. It means everything good and wholesome, and even allows theological deviations from traditional Islam. However, in strict Islamic cultures, praying in a mosque, calling oneself a Muslim, and adopting certain Islamic behaviors sends an entirely different signal. If this person does not renounce allegiance to Christ, adopt the Muslim Creed, and make Muhammad central, then he is judged deceptive.

Again, locals are evaluated by a looser standard than foreigners. Therefore, a national Muslim who trusts Christ may get by with continuing to call himself a Muslim and not be considered duplicitous. In the eyes of most, one born Muslim is always a Muslim, no matter what he believes. However, foreigners who call themselves Muslims are measured by an entirely different standard. By adopting Islamic titles and customs, they are saying that they are just like the locals. Afterwards, when people get to know them and find out this is not true, they accuse them of deception. Once that happens, the foreigners' testimonies are discredited.

### EDITOR'S NOTE

Up to this stage, the author has been quite articulate in his analysis. In contrast, Racey's concluding points—grace and Christ-centered witness, which we all would affirm—have a decidedly different tone and seem terse. One wishes he had more fully explained his strong convictions against some expressions of contextualization in connection with these last points.

We also wish we had the space to include an article written by one of the wives of the men who were imprisoned in Cairo. We have posted the article on our web site at *www.encountering islam.org/readings.*

### GRACE

We have been saved by grace and are to continue living by grace (Gal. 2:14–16; 3:3). We can temporarily live under law to win people who are under law (1 Cor. 9:20), but our lives must not become law-centered. Our goal is to educate and liberate people under law, not to subject ourselves and them to it (Col. 3:20). We are to become examples of grace, demonstrating liberation from the slavery of legalism (Gal. 4:9–10; 5:1).

Therefore, in our zeal to fit in with Islamic culture, we must be sure that we do not cause those who know God's grace to stumble. Do we really want our converts to follow our example, and continue practicing the same legalistic rituals that

## HEALING FOR BODY AND SOUL

Ibrahim, a desperately sick man, came to Galmi Hospital in Niger four years ago. As he treated his disease, a missionary doctor shared the Good News about Jesus with him, and loaned him a Hausa Bible. Nigerian staff and missionaries had recently produced a dramatic audio-cassette answering Muslims' common questions from a biblical perspective. Ibrahim heard it again and again, and when he was well, he asked to take the Bible and the cassette tape home with him.

Four years later, hearing that his missionary friend had returned, Ibrahim came back. In a rare private moment, he told the doctor that his repeated use had worn out the tape, but had convinced him that Jesus is the true Way. He asked the missionary to explain how he could become a follower of Jesus. Soon Ibrahim bowed his head and yielded his life to Christ. A short time later he returned to his village—taking with him a new copy of the cassette tape to play for his neighbors.

Source: *www.sim.org*

What Muslim forms are biblical?

could never bring them eternal life? To practice Islamic rituals in the name of contextualization, and preach the gospel of grace, is a contradiction. As William Saal has put it, "It is naïve to suppose that these rituals can be performed as prescribed by Islamic law and made to mean anything other than what they have always meant to Muslims. What you may hope to convey by your participation is irrelevant."[4]

Denis Green explains: "The identification of all of these items (Islamic forms of prayer, fasting, observing dietary regulations, and ceremonial purity) with the works necessary for favor with God in Islam could easily lead to a continued reliance upon them for salvation, rather than on faith alone."[5] Also, is it not naïve to ignore the spiritual forces that have operated for centuries through these rituals to keep people in bondage to evil spirits?

## CHRIST-CENTERED WITNESS

Contextualization is just a means to an end. A Christ-centered witness must be

our goal (Acts 4:12). Rather than see how close to the host culture we can come, we need to see how close to Christ we can come. Christ must be honored and glorified in all we say and do.

We disobey this doctrine if we allow Muhammad, or any religious figure, to be central in any part of our lives. It is a mistake to think that we can say the Creed of Islam, "There is no god but God, and Muhammad is his Prophet," without removing Christ from the center.

Practicing most of the five pillars of Islam, especially the Hajj (pilgrimage to Mecca) and the rakat (ritual prayers in the mosque), comes close to partaking of the table of demons (see 1 Cor. 10:21). To practice these rituals is, in Saal's words, to "declare the worshiper's submission to God in the way Muhammad prescribed," and to elevate false worship over proper worship of the person of Christ.[6]

Other principles could be added. For example, edification—does it build up Christ's body? Profitability—does it add to the fullness of life in Christ? Ecclesiastical propriety—does it give offense to local members of the body of Christ? However, the guidelines suggested here should be sufficient.

# WHAT I LEARNED BY KEEPING THE FAST

*by Erik Nubthar*

The toughest part of Ramadan for me was not the fasting (I got used to that), but the lack of sleep. I tried to get a normal amount of sleep, but many Moroccans would stay up until 1 or 2 A.M. (3 A.M. on weekends) to eat their big meal.

Days and nights became reversed, and nights were times of celebration, feasting, fun, socializing, and a month of special TV programming. I could feel the electric atmosphere and understood why one of my Moroccan friends in France always loved to go home to Morocco for Ramadan.

On the spiritual side, a mosque banner quoted one of the hadith (traditions of Muhammad): "He who keeps the fast of Ramadan faithfully and truly will come out from under his sins as on the day his mother bore him." People told me that fasting during Ramadan earned them a lot of merit before God and could make up for a lot of disobedience.

This is the overwhelming legalism that outsiders to Islam rarely see: always one more thing, one more rung, one more step. There is always more to do and always people willing to do more to establish their own righteousness. These statements about spiritual merit led to

excellent discussions with people about sin, judgment, and the need for a savior. Although people told me before I went to Morocco that Ramadan is a very difficult time for missionaries, I had all sorts of opportunities to talk about Christ and true fasting. I carried some photocopies of Bible verses which spoke about fasting in Arabic and showed them to people.

Some missionaries would disapprove of my keeping the fast, saying that it would convey to Muslims that I was interested in becoming a Muslim. However, no Muslim ever suggested out loud that I was trying to become a Muslim by keeping this fast. I always made it clear that I was a Christian, that Christians fast at times, and that we fast, not to earn merit before God, but for other reasons. Often a good spiritual discussion followed.

Thus, my fasting, far from communicating an interest in Islam, communicated, "This is a good man—and a Christian nonetheless—who speaks true and good words about the worship of God, yet very different words from what I'm used to hearing." My hope is that Muslims will continue with the thought: "I'd like to hear more about this."

My fasting helped my relationships with people (one less cultural barrier between them and me—and fasting in Morocco definitely has not just a religious, but also a cultural, aspect to it). The following year I did not keep the fast, but still got into all

---

Erik Nubthar is a Mission to the World missionary who works with Arab World Ministries.

Adapted from Erik Nubthar, "Contextualization: How Far Is Too Far?" *Evangelical Missions Quarterly* 32, no. 3 (Wheaton, Ill.: Evangelical Missions Information Service, July 1996), pp. 309–10. Used by permission. *www.billygrahamcenter.org/emis*

the same types of discussions and witnessing opportunities, and it did not appear that my not fasting during Ramadan hindered any relationships.

Overall, I was very glad that I kept the fast, and I would recommend that anyone ministering among Muslims do it at least once. It was important to feel what Muslims feel and to enter into their worldview a little bit. It also had a positive effect on my relationships with Moroccans. But I probably will not keep the fast again. The benefits did not seem to be so significant as to warrant doing this every year—and the fast was quite difficult. The hardest part was shaking up our family schedule

and my sleep patterns. I could do without eating, but setting that alarm for 4:30 every morning got old quickly.

## ENDNOTES

1. Adapted from David Hesselgrave and Edward Rommen, *Contextualization: Meanings, Methods, and Models* (Grand Rapids: Baker, 1989), pp. 1–2.
2. Robert J. Priest, "Missionary Elenctics: Conscience and Culture," *Missiology* 22, no. 3 (July 1994).
3. Ibid.
4. William Saal, *Reaching Muslims for Christ* (Chicago: Moody Press, 1993), p. 158.
5. Denis Green, "Guidelines from Hebrews for Contextualization," in *Muslims and Christians on the Emmaus Road* (Monrovia, Calif.: MARC, 1989), p. 247.
6. Saal, *Reaching Muslims*, p. 147.

## RESPONDING TO ILLITERACY AND POVERTY

In Bangladesh, illiteracy and extreme poverty go hand in hand. The Community Development Project Kushtia (CDPK) provides a way out. Twenty-five people at a time study literacy and math six days a week for six months. At the end of the training, they form a savings cooperative. Villagers in the cooperative contribute funds in order to provide small loans to other members. They, in turn, invest the borrowed money in innovative, income-producing tools: rickshaws, sewing machines, a sugarcane press, or commodities to set up a small store. Women make up most of the clubs, and their new sources of income are making a dramatic change in the lives of their families. There are eighty-nine such groups, benefiting more than five thousand people. Ten groups have already "graduated" from needing supervision by CDPK. Some of these groups are now passing on what they have learned to new groups. The required literacy and financial management training helps ensure success; loan defaults are very rare. Imagine!

Source: *www.sim.org.*

# LIFTING THE FATWA

*by Phil Parshall*

 *Fatwa*: An edict of a religious nature, pronounced by an Islamic authority.

I was somewhat shocked to read the following statement by a respected Christian leader involved in a controversial approach to Muslim evangelism: "I am praying Phil Parshall will lift his fatwa against our ministry among the followers of Ishmael."

The October 1998 issue of the journal *Evangelical Missions Quarterly* kicked off public debate on how far contextualization has gone, is going, and probably will continue to go. My lead article expressed concern that a legitimate strategy could tumble over into syncretism if great care is not exercised.[1]

And so, where are we now, five years later? It is appropriate, I think, to say that the focal points are in seven major areas: 1) using the C1 to C6 spectrum, as conceptualized by "John Travis;"[2] 2) employing certain Bible passages to validate one's position; 3) encouraging the Muslim-background believer (MBB) to continue calling himself or herself a "Muslim" without qualifier; 4) allowing the MBB to remain in the mosque permanently, as a strategy to win Muslims to Christ; 5) explicitly or implicitly affirming the Islamic Creed (Shahada), "There is no god but Allah, and Muhammad is his Prophet;" 6) inserting "Isa al-Masih" ("Jesus the Messiah") for "Son of God" in Bible translations; and 7) delineating an appropriate response toward those who disagree with one's position on some or all of the above.

My purpose here is to briefly explore these seven areas. Sadly, space restrictions will inevitably elicit the criticism that I have dealt superficially with some or all of these issues. But, at least, these thoughts should move us away from the in-house monologue currently quite pervasive among concerned churches, mission boards, missionaries, and MBBs, and more toward a dialogue.

## 1. USAGE OF THE C1 TO C6 CONTINUUM

All of us are indebted to Travis for his abbreviated identification system of evangelistic strategy. It is much more convenient to say, "I practice C4,"than to give an accurate but lengthy description that loses the audience. But, regrettably, a heavy fog has resulted, producing more confusion than clarity. Numerous times I have heard people who profess to be C5 vehemently deny that they believe in some important strategy point that another self-declared C5er holds.

Phil Parshall is one of today's leading authorities on ministry to Muslims. He and his wife, Julie, have lived among Muslims since 1962 in Bangladesh and the Philippines. He is the author of nine books on Christian ministry among Muslims.

Adapted from Phil Parshall, "Lifting the Fatwa," *Evangelical Missions Quarterly* 40, no. 3 (Wheaton, Ill.: Evangelical Missions Information Service, July 2004), pp. 288–293. Used by permission. *www.billygrahamcenter.org/emis*

Let me illustrate. Some of us naively thought that comprehensive, contextualized, Muslim evangelism outreach originated in the mid-1970s in a certain South Asian country. But what about Sadrach?[3] This Indonesian was born in 1835, and died in 1928, at age ninety-three. Until he was thirty-two, Sadrach was a devout Muslim. Following his conversion, he worked tirelessly to create a church. At the time of his death, there were 7,500 MBBs on the island of Java as the result of his work. Some characteristics of Sadrach's contextualized ministry were:

- Leaders were called imams.
- Festivals similar to those of Islam were observed.
- Zakat (offerings) were collected.
- Church buildings were called mosques. No crosses were displayed.

## WHAT IS A CHURCH-PLANTING MOVEMENT?

"A church-planting movement is a rapid multiplication of indigenous churches planting churches that sweeps through a people group or population segment."

### Universal Elements of Church-Planting Movements

1. Extraordinary prayer.
2. Abundant evangelism.
3. Intentional planting of churches that will reproduce.
4. Scriptural authority of the Bible (either oral or written in the heart language).
5. Local leadership.
6. Lay leadership.
7. Cell or house churches.
8. Churches planting churches.
9. Rapid reproduction.
10. Healthy churches.

### Other Common Factors in Church-Planting Movements

1. A social climate of uncertainty.
2. Insulation from outsiders.
3. High cost for following Christ.
4. Bold fearless faith.
5. Family-based conversion patterns.
6. Rapid incorporation of new believers into ministry.
7. Worship in the heart language.
8. Divine signs and wonders.
9. On-the-job leadership training.
10. Missionaries suffering affliction.

### FOR FURTHER STUDY

Adapted from: David Garrison, *Church Planting Movements: How God Is Redeeming a Lost World* (Midlothian, Va.: WIGTake Resources, 2004).

- Like the Muslims, they used a drum to call people to worship.
- Before they were slaughtered, cows were prayed over, in Islamic fashion.
- The following creed was recited in their churches: "I believe that God is one. There is no God but God. Jesus Christ is the Spirit of God, whose power is over everything. There is no God

Outside a mosque in Damascus

but God. Jesus Christ is the Spirit of God." This was chanted in a dhikr (recitation) style, with intense emotion, which was purported to lead to some sort of mystical union between God and devotee.
- Believers called themselves "Christians." They did not affirm Muhammad in any manner, but rather spoke very openly of the superiority of Jesus over Muhammad.

So, do we have C1, C2, C3, C4, C5, or an amalgam of all five? Without seeking to annihilate the C categories, I only press the need for clarity when using such an identification of strategy.

## 2. HERMENEUTICAL INTEGRITY OR CARELESSNESS?

The answer to this question depends somewhat on where you have come from and where you want to go. Contextualists have always relied heavily on 1 Corinthians 9:19–22. In the present controversy, "becoming a Muslim in order to win Muslims" has a very different meaning for C4 and C5 groups. Each insists that

their own exegesis of these verses is proof positive of their position's validity.

But the new hermeneutic in the discussion centers on 1 Corinthians 7. In verse 20, "Each one should remain in the situation which he was in when God called him," certain contextualists see an exhortation for MBBs to remain maximally Muslim.

Scott Woods, an experienced missionary among Muslims in Indonesia, comments:

The context in 1 Corinthians 7 is addressing the issues of marriage and singleness, believers married to unbelievers; circumcision and uncircumcision; and, finally, slaves and free. This passage has nothing to do with dictating that people from a false religion should remain in their false religion so as not to disturb the situation. C5 proponents could be accused of "isogesis" (reading meaning into the text) here. This passage makes provision for believers remaining in their familial and social status where they were prior to knowing Christ, but it is

not giving an allowance for believers to continue in their former religion.[4]

As each strategist carves out his or her theological apologetic, it is important to grapple with biblical teaching and its implications. Admittedly, church history has proved repeatedly through the centuries that the one absolute certainty in this process is that true, God-fearing believers will frequently differ with one another in their conclusions. Some say, "Just give the Bible to the MBB, and let him come to his own conclusion." But we must remember the scriptural mandate to teach the new believers.

## 3. IDENTITY ISSUES

Does the MBB continue to bear the name Muslim without any qualifier? Ramsay Harris, a long-term missionary among Arabs, shares his view: "Most of those I have led to Christ do not identify themselves as Muslims anymore, but some do. I do not push them either way. For most people, the word Muslim means "an adherent of the religion of Muhammad." But there is one principle which must be universal: One must always identify oneself with the person of Jesus Christ (Matt. 10:33; 1 Peter 4:16)."[5]

Harris's latter point underscores the controversy. "I am a Muslim follower of Isa al-Masih" is much more readily accepted by certain missionaries than just the designation "Muslim." The word "Muslim" is defined as one who is submitted to God. In practice, however, every Muslim worldwide thinks of this term as referring to those who adhere to Islam's theological tenets.

At this point, the charge of deceit arises. Are we purposefully misleading? Is integrity at stake? The answer for some is, "definitely not." One, they say, must look at "Muslim" in its broadest cultural and societal context, as we do with the word "Christian." How many people who call themselves Christians are really practitioners of the faith? Are they then deceivers, or just going with the flow of society? The rebuttal will be, "Yes, but these people are not seeking to use this term as a strategy to win others to their faith." And so, the arguments and counter-arguments continue.

## 4. STAYING IN THE MOSQUE?

The pro camp points to early Christians continuing to worship in the synagogue. Woods postulates:

> Paul came to preach Jesus to the synagogue members. Most C5ers come into the mosque and line up in the salat line. They are perceived as Muslims. They have no distinguishing mark that says they are followers of Isa. Even if they pray to Isa, the perception is that they are Muslims. Paul was clearly received (at times) within the Jewish setting, but acknowledged as a follower of the risen Messiah. Is this the same with our C5 MBBs?[6]

All would probably agree that there is validity in the policy of MBBs remaining in the mosque for a brief time following conversion. Otherwise, there would be a serious societal dislocation. The disagreement is over whether they should remain permanently within the context of false religious teaching.

The pro-mosque position emphasizes that the MBBs will be giving discrete testimony of their faith to the Muslims in the mosque. Therefore, it would be up to the imams to excommunicate the MBB. He is free to stay as long as they will have him. Harris believes MBBs could continue to pray in the mosque with these conditions: "It does not violate the MBB's own conscience; it is not done for purposes of deceit or denial of Christ; the MBB does not speak, in prayer, words which he does not believe. For me personally, this includes the Shahada. All of the MBBs I have led to Christ simply find the mosque boring and depressing after they have come to know the spiritual riches of Jesus Christ."[7]

## 5. RECITATION OF ISLAMIC CREED?

This issue flows from one's identification as a Muslim and continued mosque attendance. The Creed is the central foundation upon which all of Islam rests, the first Pillar. It not only affirms the oneness of Allah, but the centrality of Muhammad, as a prophet or messenger of God. To be a true Muslim is impossible without affirming this Creed.

## STORYING IN TEN STEPS

*by Avery Willis*

1. Select an essential, but simple and clear, biblical principle, that should be taught.
2. Define the worldview concerns of the chosen people group that will determine story selection and storytelling methodology.
3. Identify pertinent gaps, barriers, and bridges in the people group's worldview: this process will confirm how to deal with these.
4. Select the biblical story or stories appropriate for communicating the specific biblical principle or concept to the people group.
5. Craft the story within the suitable narrative method. Plan the follow-up dialogue to assist the listeners in learning how this biblical story addresses their critical worldview issues.
6. Tell the story in a culturally appropriate way (including narrative, dance, song, or object lessons).
7. Facilitate the follow-up dialogue, usually by asking questions that will help the listeners discover the story's truths and their applications.
8. Guide the listeners in discussing choices for applying the story's biblical principle, for obediently living it out in practical ways.
9. Establish accountability responsibility in the listening group so they are helping each other obey the biblical principle.
10. Encourage the listeners to be reproducers by modeling the principle in their own lives and retelling the stories to others.

See Full Reading on Storying, "Telling Stories that Grip the Heart," by Trudie Crawford, for more information.

Dr. Avery T. Willis Jr. is the senior vice president for Overseas Operations at the International Mission Board of the Southern Baptist Convention in Richmond, Virginia. In the past, he spent fourteen years as a missionary in Indonesia.

Provided courtesy Dr. Avery T. Willis, *Following Jesus* series (2003). www.fjseries.org/low/storying.html (cited 10 December 2004). Used by permission of the International Mission Board (IMB). www.imb.org

## Process of Contextualization

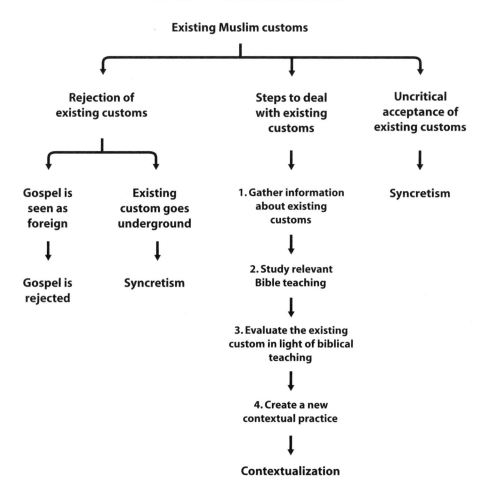

Source: Paul G. Hiebert, *Anthropological Insights for Missionaries* (Grand Rapids: Baker, 1985), p. 188.

Brian Armstrong, who served many years in the Middle East, was an early theoretician and practitioner of the C5 movement. He told me this concerning the Creed:

> I believe that an MBB can repeat the Creed with conviction and integrity, without compromising or syncretizing

his faith in Jesus. The recognition of Muhammad would be in his prophetic mission as a messenger proclaiming one god, and submission to his will in the context of idolatrous seventh-century Arabia, or, in the pagan, pre-Islamic setting of any given people who have subsequently accepted Islam. Although Muhammad's mission was chronologically A.D., we should not allow this to cloud the fact that the spiritual milieu to which he spoke was substantially B.C. In a Jesus movement in Islam, Muhammad would be understood as an Old Testament-style messenger. For those Christians who may stumble at certain aspects of Muhammad's lifestyle, I urge them to study more objectively the lives of the Old Testament prophets, where both holy war, in a form more violent than Islam calls for (genocide in the book of Joshua), and polygamy were quite common.[8]

Yes, but if one is to affirm the "prophet" of the Creed, does it not follow that one must therefore believe his prophecy? And that prophecy, being the Qur'an, presents us with a major problem. It is not my place here to exegete the varying views of Qur'anic teaching, but my conclusion is that I cannot affirm the Qur'an as the Word of God.

In my opinion, articulating the Creed automatically defines me theologically. However I may reinterpret the words, onlooking Muslims would accept me as one of theirs, in every sense of the word.

## 6. ISA AL-MASIH FOR "SON OF GOD"

The words "Son of God" have always been repugnant to Muslims. They can only understand this term in a biological framework. For them, for God to have offspring is pure blasphemy. So how can we overcome our Muslim friends' error in comprehension? Some current contextual-

ists have opted for radical surgery, followed by a linguistic transplant: just remove "Son of God," and insert Isa al-Masih.

This new translation is being promoted in a number of languages throughout the Islamic world. Early feedback from Muslims and MBBs is positive. The offense of the word "son" is gone. Jesus as Messiah is retained and highlighted. The meaning of "Messiah" can then be explained.

A defense of this approach is that certain New Testament passages place "Son of God" and "Messiah" together, thus proving the terms' interchangeability (Matt. 16:16, 20; 26:63–64; Luke 4:41).

Rick Brown is an international translation consultant. He has these insights: "The fact is, although Jews had different concepts for the awaited Messiah, they used most titles interchangeably, and both 'Christ' and 'Son of God' were fairly equivalent. But, because these were favored by nationalistic zealots, Jesus generally avoided them both, preferring the inclusivist, heavenly savior title, 'the Son of Man' or the shortened form, 'the Son,' and sometimes, 'the Lord.'"[9]

In personal correspondence, I asked Brown his view of replacing "Son of God" with "Isa al-Masih" in Bible passages where they do not appear together. He responded: "Although the title 'Son of God' evoked the same concept as 'Masih,' it also evokes the concept of God, and this will be lost if one says only 'Isa al-Masih.' So I would suggest, 'the Masih whom God has sent.' In general, for our audience, it is best to put 'Son of God' in the footnote or introduction."[10] I leave it to linguistic

experts to grapple with this, the newest contextual controversy to present itself.

## 7. OUR RESPONSE?

Adherents to some or all of the C5 position are growing. The country where C5 was birthed now lays claim to tens of thousands of MBBs of the C5 variety. Thousands of C4 MBBs are found there as well. Scores of missionaries and several evangelical mission boards are practicing and promoting C5 in a significant number of Muslim countries. I personally have known many of these missionaries, some for twenty years. There is no doubt that they are sincere and long with all their hearts to see Muslims come to Christ. In one instance, a highly respected evangelical Islamist investigated a large C5 movement and declared it to be a wonderful work of God. Armstrong comments: "Those that will be involved in encouraging a movement for Jesus in Islam cannot be heresy-hunters or suspicious types, always ready to pounce on every manifestation of Christ that does not immediately match what they have been used to before. They cannot be the kind of people that can only see 'black and white,' for the world they will be laboring in will be full of shades of gray. If we are, regrettably, the mission that plants a heresy, are those that adhere to it any worse off than before?"[11] Armstrong's view is that such a "heresy" could be a future steppingstone for those Muslims to come to full-blown faith in Christ.

I struggle to form a personal position on such an important issue. The Lord has been speaking to me as I have been seeking to process the macro picture. These are the Bible verses on which I have been meditating:

- Romans 14:10: "Why do you judge your brother? Or why do you look down on your brother?"
- Romans 14:13: "Let us stop passing judgment on one another."
- Romans 15:2: "Each of us should please his neighbor for his good, to build him up."
- Romans 15:7: "Accept one another, then, just as Christ accepted you."

I am quite aware of other New Testament passages that call theological aberrants "dogs," call down a curse on them, and designate them as antichrists. In church history, we find the same theme in the Inquisition. Even the Reformers had hard words for those who dared disagree with their interpretation of the Bible.

And so, where do we end up? Consider the fatwa—which was never decreed!—lifted. I do not want to end my life, now sixty-five years along, known as a heresy hunter. Yes, I will continue—with greater sensitivity, I trust—to voice my concerns. But if I am to err toward imbalance, I want it to be on the side of love, affirmation, and lifting up my colleagues as better than myself. I lay no claim to personal infallibility. As to who is right or wrong, and to what degree, let us lean heavily on the ultimate Judge of our hearts' intents.

### FOR FURTHER STUDY
Phil Parshall, *Muslim Evangelism: Contemporary Approaches to Contextualization* (Waynesboro, Ga.: Authentic Media, 2003). *www.authenticbooks.com*

**End of Basic Readings for Lesson 10.** See RECOMMENDED READINGS & ACTIVITIES **on p. 398.**

**Go to:**
***www.encounteringislam.org/readings* to find the Full Readings for Lesson 10.**

## ENDNOTES

1. Phil Parshall, "Danger! New Directions in Contextualization," *Evangelical Missions Quarterly* 34, no. 4 (October 1998), pp. 404–10.

2. John Travis, "The C1 to C6 Spectrum," *Evangelical Missions Quarterly* 34, no. 4 (October 1998), pp. 405–08.

3. Sutarman Soedeman Partonadi, *Sadrach's Community and Its Contextual Roots* (Amsterdam: Rodopi, 1988).

4. Scott Woods, "A Biblical Look at C5 Muslim Evangelism," *Evangelical Missions Quarterly* 39, no. 2 (April 2003), p. 190.

5. Ramsey Harris, personal correspondence with author, 2002.

6. Woods, "A Biblical Look," pp. 193–94.

7. Harris, personal correspondence with author, 2002.

8. Brian Armstrong, personal correspondence with author, 2002.

9. Rick Brown, "The 'Son of God': Understanding the Messianic Title of Jesus," *International Journal of Frontier Missions* 17, no. 1 (Spring 2000), p. 48.

10. Rick Brown, personal correspondence with author, 2003.

11. Armstrong, personal correspondence with author, 2002.

# DISCUSSION QUESTIONS

1.     Consider some of the issues a new Muslim-background congregation might face. What advice would you give in these situations: When a man with several wives becomes a Christian, should he divorce all but one? See 1 Corinthians 7:17–24. What other principles should apply? In many parts of the world, alcoholism is rampant among men, and whole families suffer. What should a believing woman do if her husband is an alcoholic?

2.     What other challenges might a believer or group of believers be likely to encounter?

# RECOMMENDED READINGS & ACTIVITIES*

Read:     Greg Livingstone, *Planting Churches in Muslim Cities* (Grand Rapids: Baker Book House, 1993).

Bruce A. McDowell and Anees Zaka, *Muslims and Christians at the Table* (Phillipsburg, N.J.: P&R Publishing, 1999).

Yehia Sa'a, *All the Prophets Have Spoken* (Durham, Canada: Good Seed International, 2001).

Watch:     CNN or a local newscast, paying attention to items relating to Muslims. Can you detect any bias in the way these stories are presented?

Pray:     Subscribe to Global Prayer Digest and receive daily prayer requests by e-mail.

Give:     Extend a gesture of friendship by giving a gift to a Muslim individual or family, to celebrate either a Muslim or Christian holiday.

Surf:     Discover related web sites at *www.encounteringislam.org/lessonlinks.*

---

\* For expanded details on these Recommended Readings & Activities, visit *www.encounteringislam.org/lessonlinks.*

# LESSON 11
## OUR RESPONSE TO ISLAM

## PONDER THIS

- Which is more significant, obeying the Great Commission—making disciples—or the Great Commandment—loving God and your neighbor?

- At what point in a relationship with a Muslim friend is it appropriate to offer them the gift of life in Jesus?

- When you share your faith, with Muslims or others, what aspects of your faith seem to connect with and appeal to them?

# LESSON OBJECTIVE

Identify ways of developing friendships with Muslims and ways we can respond to Muslims.

1. Hear the stories of ordinary people who have reached out to Muslims.

2. Share with fellow students ideas and personal plans for Muslim outreach, mutual encouragement, and accountability.

3. Identify specific incidents or conversation openers that sparked the interest of your Muslim friends and explain how you responded to them.

4. Share prayer requests about the needs of your Muslim friends.

# LESSON READINGS

# INTRODUCTION

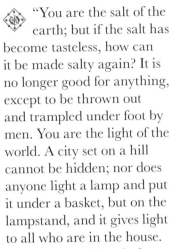

"You are the salt of the earth; but if the salt has become tasteless, how can it be made salty again? It is no longer good for anything, except to be thrown out and trampled under foot by men. You are the light of the world. A city set on a hill cannot be hidden; nor does anyone light a lamp and put it under a basket, but on the lampstand, and it gives light to all who are in the house.

127 million Muslims live in India

© Caleb Project

Let your light shine before men in such a way that they may see your good works, and glorify your Father who is in heaven" (Matt. 5:13–16, NASB).

Could it be that few Muslims have come to know Christ because few have ever known a true follower of Christ? Muslims, like most, respond positively to friendship, if our words and actions are genuine. This course has been designed to motivate us to be strong in theory *and* effective in practice, to help us answer our calling to be salt and light. Now is the time to ask, what is our plan for reaching out? In light of all we have learned, what response is justified and suitable?

A simple but elegant fact about humankind is that if we avoid taking risks, we do not learn. By building relationships with Muslims here in our present communities, we can apply our new understanding and flesh it out. Some of us hope to one day to have the privilege of living in Muslim communities. But, if we have not yet integrated comfortable, natural engagement with unbelievers into our lifestyles, how do we expect to be able to do so later, in unfamiliar places?

Start with what you have today! Anything will work, and everything is needed.

Need to do laundry? Go with a newfound friend. Attending your child's soccer practice? Take an international student along. Some Christian women, wanting to lose weight and get in shape without male spectators, have started all-female workout groups. What a great idea, and how appealing to Muslim women!

Alumni of this course in Houston, Texas, started reaching out to refugees. Now several of them have moved into an apartment complex where refugees are first resettled. Now that sounds like something Jesus would do! Living in this

neighborhood has resulted in their cars being defaced and personal property being stolen, but the church is being established, and the fragrance of eternal purpose emanates from their lives. And they eat the best foods and laugh with true friends until all hours of the night! Sound attractive?

Being like Christ takes boldness, not just in speech, but in attempting those efforts others are not willing to undertake. Choices that harm careers or choices to live in neighborhoods where needs are so obvious that it is awkward not to reach out—these are not popular routes in Churchianity. Another alumnus of this course befriended a local, Muslim pizza shop owner, and started praying and worshipping with Christians from Pakistan and India. They taught him to play an Asian instrument and invited him to join the worship team. Sadly, his behavior was too radical for most in his church. Our main obstacle may be our own Christian community's misunderstanding.

Do not be deterred. In fact, take other believers with you. Their desire to reach out may not be lit until they taste the sweetness of spending time with Muslims. C. S. Lewis, in his essay "The Weight of Glory," describes such people as urban children who have never experienced a vacation at the beach. Offered the chance, they would rather continue making mud pies on a hot city street. They have no image of ocean breeze![1] We cannot afford to allow our friends—or ourselves—to cling to limited imaginations, when all God's "incomparably great power for us who believe" (Eph. 1:19a) is at our disposal for ministering to people who need an encounter with Jesus.

Early in the 1900s, William Borden, heir to the Borden family's dairy fortune and a graduate of Yale University, went as a missionary to Muslims. He turned down a place in the family business and other prestigious job offers only to die of spinal meningitis during language studies. His shocked classmates may have felt that this sacrifice was a waste, but in his Bible, Borden had written: "No Reserves, No Retreats, No Regrets."[2]

Too many of Jesus' followers live half alive, on the treadmill of life, rolling the same boulder up the same hill again and again. This is Greek mythology's image of hell! Contrast that with a young Irish minister with untreated asthma whom I met. He was living in self-imposed poverty in a Bengali neighborhood of London. Previously, he had been beaten up by Muslims and hospitalized after a false rumor had been spread that he insulted Muhammad, but as we walked around this community, he was frequently greeted and warmly received. He said, "My friends from seminary suggest, 'Why don't you take a parish in a quiet town where you'll have your mornings free to study?'" Repulsed, he replied, "What? I'd rather see some people come to know Jesus!"

Are we too busy? Are we held back by family obligations? Financial debt? Do we lack gifting? All these concerns may be brought to our loving God. Many legitimate excuses are really rooted in our hearts' reluctance to trust Christ. We shy from witness, not because we lack the Spirit's empowerment, but because we have allowed our fear and lack of experience to absolve us of being involved. I understand: I too have been embarrassed

when—though the Muslims with me sensed Christ in me—I have not sensed his presence within me. If we have been freed from sin, shame, and fear, why are we mute?

All people everywhere—us included—are harassed and helpless, like sheep without a shepherd (see Matt. 9:37). Being called a sheep is not a compliment, because sheep are not intelligent creatures. If they roll over on their backs, they will starve to death, because they cannot even right themselves to stand up. We Christians are not "super smart sheep." The thing is, we have a Shepherd, and that is our job—to follow the Good Shepherd. When we do, other sheep will join us! Following the Shepherd does not take intellect, or gifts, or experience. It is not our job to watch out for lions, the narrowness of the path, or the depth of the ravine: we just follow the Shepherd. And following the Shepherd is always better than we expect—even comforting, like a cool drink from a stream near a green pasture.

Alumni becoming integrated into their communities, finding simple ways to alleviate the economic needs of their neighbors, or seeking reconciliation and justice for the oppressed: their stories excite me! I am also pleased to hear the testimonies of those who say, "I'm not there yet. I'm still struggling to love Muslims, but I'm beginning to see God's love for them; and I'm praying that God will change my heart to more perfectly reflect his. Will you pray for me?" This is an honest and admirable response too.

We can do this! We can know the joy of hearing our Savior say, "Well done, my good and faithful servant," and of having Muslim-background believers welcome us into heaven. We can take the time to build loving friendships with our neighbors. Jesus' greatest imperative for us is: "'Love the Lord your God with all your heart and with all your soul and with all your mind.' This is the first and greatest commandment. And the second is like it: 'Love your neighbor as yourself.' All the Law and the Prophets hang on these two commandments" (Matt. 22:37–40).

Christians believe that loving and caring for people is synonymous with reaching out to them with the gospel. If we say we love people and do not act on it, do we love them? Muslims will know whether we have developed friendships with them simply as a "project," or whether we truly care for them as friends. When Muslims see that we really do love them, they will also see God's love demonstrated. That alone may open their hearts to receive his love and salvation through Jesus Christ.

## OUR PERSONAL PATH TO MUSLIM HEARTS

The nearest way to the Muslim heart can often be found better by subjective than objective study. The barrier may be in the heart of the missionary as well as [in] the heart of the Muslim. [The missionary] should cultivate sympathy to the highest degree, and an appreciation of all the great fundamental truths which we hold in common with Muslims.

Samuel Zwemer, *The Muslim Christ* (London: Oliphant, Anderson, and Ferrier, 1912), p. 183.

"From everyone who has been given much, much will be required." (Luke 12:48b, NASB)

*–K.S., Editor*

## FOR FURTHER STUDY

Shirin Taber, *Muslims Next Door: Uncovering Myths and Creating Friendships* (Grand Rapids: Zondervan, 2004). *www.zondervan.com*

Tony Payne, *Islam In Our Backyard* (Kingsford, Australia: Matthais Media, 2002).

## ENDNOTES

1. C. S. Lewis, *The Weight of Glory and Other Addresses* (New York: Touchstone, 1996), p. 26.
2. Mrs. Howard Taylor, *Borden of Yale* (Minneapolis: Bethany House, 1988).

## CONDITIONAL LOVE

While Muslims view God as loving, gracious, merciful, and compassionate, most Muslims do not perceive God as being close or personal. His love is experienced through conditional blessings. The Qur'an does speak of God's love:

> On the day when every soul will be confronted with all the good it has done, and all the evil it has done, it will wish there were a great distance between it and its evil. But Allah cautions you (to remember) himself, and Allah is full of kindness to those that serve him. Say: "If ye do love Allah, follow me: Allah will love you and forgive you your sins; for Allah is oft-forgiving, most merciful." Say: "Obey Allah and his Messenger." But if they turn back, Allah loveth not those who reject faith. (Sura 3:30–32, YUSUF ALI)

Other Qur'anic verses also illustrate God's conditional love:

> But seek, with the (wealth) which Allah has bestowed on thee, the home of the hereafter, nor forget thy portion in this world: but do thou good, as Allah has been good to thee, and seek not (occasions for) mischief in the land; for Allah loves not those who do mischief. (Sura 28:77, YUSUF ALI)

> Those who reject faith will suffer from that rejection; and those who work righteousness will spread their couch (of repose) for themselves (in heaven): that he may reward those who believe and work righteous deeds, out of his bounty. For he loves not those who reject faith. (Sura 30:44–45, YUSUF ALI)

> Ye may not despair over matters that pass you by, nor exult over favors bestowed upon you. For Allah loveth not any vainglorious boaster. (Sura 57:23, YUSUF ALI)

The Bible also warns against pride, mischief, and faithlessness: "But God demonstrates his own love for us in this: While we were still sinners, Christ died for us" (Rom. 5:8). "If we are faithless, he will remain faithful, for he cannot disown himself." (2 Tim. 2:13)

Source: Annee W. Rose, *www.frontiers.org*.

# ANN CROFT AND THE FULANI

*by Fatima Mahoumet*

Ann Croft's father had planted many churches in the midwestern United States during her childhood, but she was not thinking of herself as a missionary when she went to Nigeria. She was simply a teacher of English as a second language. She was able to get to know some of her Nigerian students better, joining them for some meals, and eventually reading and discussing stories from the Bible. One student expressed an extraordinary interest in the Bible.

## ACCESS TO THE COMMUNITY

As their friendship grew, this student opened doors for her into the labyrinth of extended family life among the Fulani people in her area. He had many sisters who had married into a number of families. When her student visited them, Ann accompanied him and met each family member.

As a teacher, Ann was respected by the male leaders of the community. At their request, she spent many hours answering their questions about the Bible, helping them understand more fully the biblical events and characters, including Jesus, whom they had encountered in the Qur'an. In preparation, she had made a comparative study of the Qur'an and the Bible, noting their uniqueness, differences, and similarities. She used their folk tales as bridges for discussing the Bible.

Soon, Ann had access to every part of the Muslim community. As a woman, she was able to meet the women related to all of her male contacts, even those in the strictest *purdah* (seclusion) who would otherwise be well beyond the sphere of married, let alone single, Christian men. One of the women was especially drawn to Ann. She took her to all the special ceremonies: naming ceremonies, weddings, and funerals. She helped her with the language and provided many needed bridges of communication and explanations as Ann continued to learn about the Muslim way of life. Ann also learned the traditional stories of her new people and grew to deeply love and appreciate the rich fabric of their lives.

She discovered that being a single woman had its advantages. In response to questions as to why she was not married, Ann referred to 1 Corinthians 7 and a comparable passage in the Qur'an about single women being able to be totally involved in the work of the Lord. She added that the Bible, unlike the Qur'an, allowed her to do so well past her twentieth birthday. Besides, she remarked, how could she otherwise teach their children and always be available to them any time they were having trouble, day or night? She was not subject to the demands of marriage or the constraints of purdah. She was always free to help.

Adapted from *The Zwemer Institute Newsletter*, (Spring 1981). Used by permission of the Zwemer Institute of Muslim Studies, Colombia, South Carolina.

## ACCESS TO THEIR HEARTS

Ann began to focus her efforts among the Fulani people of Northern Nigeria. The Fulani are a largely nomadic people whose search for good pasture for their cattle has scattered them throughout sub-Saharan West Africa. Strong clan fidelity and six centuries of Muslim evangelism have made them the most effective champions of Islam in West Africa. Of 6.7 million Fulani, only four hundred are known Christians.

As Ann studied more about the people to whom God had sent her, she discovered ways of showing the Fulani cattle herders that they are very special to God. She found numerous references in the Bible to nomadic cattle-herding peoples who played special roles in biblical history.

Knowing the great importance of cattle to them, Ann began to help upgrade the health of the cattle with veterinary medicine, which assisted the Fulani in starting to cope with some of the economic problems they faced from the growing pressure of urbanization.

Caring for cattle was the way to the Fulani heart. On one occasion she helped a Fulani elder get tuberculosis medicine for his son and worm medicine for himself. But it was not until she gave him medicine

## REACHING OUT

After thirty-eight years of ministry to Muslims, an experienced missionary said she found that many Muslim women need to hear the gospel 150 times before they understand it. Building a bridge of friendship, strong enough for the gospel to be carried across, takes time and commitment. Consider these practical means of building a sturdy friendship bridge for reaching a Muslim woman:

- Be a learner—be a listener. Learn about her family, culture, language, even how to cook her favorite foods. This will bless both of you.
- Recognize that she may learn differently. Many Muslim women cannot read or write. Even if they do, they may not value or enjoy reading, or relate to forms of teaching based on reading. Many live in an oral world, and learn by hearing.
- Identify yourself as a one who follows the teaching of Jesus. Identify beliefs you have in common, and share how God is at work in your life, how he answers your prayers, and meets your needs.
- Tell stories. "Chronological Bible storying" is a very effective way of presenting the gospel.[1] Express your artistic imagination through poems, songs, and drama.
- Lend a hand to meet your friend's practical needs and in times of crisis. Be available to drive her to the doctor, cook a meal when she is ill, run errands, or help with language learning or her children's school work.
- Pray with her. Find out her specific needs and lift them aloud to God together. Ask for signs and wonders, believing God will reveal himself through dreams, visions, and healings.

1. A. H., "Discipleship of Muslim Background Believers," *Ministry to Muslim Women: Longing to Call Them Sisters,* ed. Fran Love and Jeleta Eckheart (Pasadena, Calif.: William Carey Library, 2000), p. 146.

Source: Annee W. Rose, *www.frontiers.org.*

for his cows that he said, "Now I know you *really* love us!"

Ann was able to join forces with another mission agency in a distant city that was planning an three-day evangelistic conference especially for Fulani. Fulani people were told that it would be a religious conference studying one of the prophets, Abraham, a superherdsman who had cows and sheep and donkeys and goats and camels. This was a big event for the Fulani, not accustomed to special events just for their people.

Fulani herdsman in Burkina Faso

At the end of the evangelistic conference, the chief of the area said to Ann that he wanted his people to become part of the Christian community. He had seen that Christians and their Holy Book cared about the needs of his people. Some of the greatest prophets, after all, like Abraham, were cattle herders too! He also told her that to get a lot of people interested in the Christian faith, one of the best things she could do would be to continue to show a real, genuine interest in every aspect of their culture.

Gathering new believers into viable fellowships is proving to be a tremendous challenge. It is hard enough for some Fulani youth to settle down for Bible school. A permanent location for a tribe might unravel nomadic life. Perhaps now is God's time for the Fulani people, as they move towards a future that is economically, politically, and socially uncertain.

# FILLING THE GAP: YOUNG NEWLYWEDS ANSWER GOD'S CALL TO SERVE MUSLIMS

*by Frontiers*

"Will and Jamie Jordan" had only been married nine months when they joined the Phoenix-based Livingstone Internship. They believed this year of training with career Frontiers workers would help them reach their long-term goal—serving overseas as a witness to Jesus among unreached Muslim people.

The Jordans found a small apartment in a complex full of refugees. Seeking genuine relationships and understanding of their Muslim neighbors, Will and Jamie were soon welcoming their new friends into their home for tea and dinner. In every case, their guests returned the favor. The couple took secular jobs to fund their year of ministry—Will hoisted luggage and Jamie worked at a children's daycare.

Each week, the Jordans and other interns met with Frontiers coaches: worshipping and praying together. Will and Jamie were held accountable for writing research papers, meeting with Muslims weekly, and doing Bible studies. As character issues arose and bad habits surfaced, Frontiers leaders graciously challenged them to set goals for growth in these areas. By September 2001, the couple had successfully completed their internship and began actively looking for an overseas ministry field. They wrote to their friends: "The time has come to experience Middle Eastern culture without an American accent."

Will and Jamie didn't have to wait long as the events of September 11 and the aftermath brought significant changes to a Central Asian country resulting in great needs. After the majority of fighting ceased, the Jordans led a "Gap Team" consisting of several singles and two couples committed to at least six months of humanitarian aid that would meet immediate needs of the people in this predominantly Muslim country.

Describing their "call" to this nation, Will and Jamie later wrote in a newsletter, "What had we spent a year preparing for, if not for this? How could we hear the plea for workers to bring food to a starving nation and not respond?"

## JULY – "LOVING EVERY MINUTE OF IT!"

After the Jordans and their team arrived in country, they quickly linked with long-term workers to find their place in the development ministries that had begun already. Will and Jamie spent four hours daily learning their new roles and finding their way in the city; another four hours was spent in an intensive language

Frontiers' passion is to glorify God by planting churches among all unreached Muslim peoples. "Filling the Gap: One Couple's Diary During Six Months in Central Asia," *Frontiers Frontlines* 4, no. 3 (September–October 2003), pp. 1, 3–6. Used by permission. *www.frontiers.org*

study course. The team was careful to always stay dressed in typically modest garb, which, for Jamie, meant she wore a headscarf to cover her hair at all times.

The team was blessed to have some local household help, including a cook, "Tabitha," who embraced Jamie and said, "Because you are far away from your mother, I will be your mother here, and you will be my daughter." Their driver, "Ahmed," was also a great source of help, bartering for good prices on food on the teams' behalf and assisting in countless other ways.

After the first few days, Will e-mailed home: "A fourteen-year old boy taught me how to put on my pants yesterday. Basically we are the cultural equivalent of five-year olds, and we are loving every minute of it. The challenges of daily life are still adventures for us. I hope that never changes."

## AUGUST – SUFFERING LOSS

Shortly after arriving, Jamie's grandfather passed away in the U.S.—a loss punctuated by the fact that she could not come home for the funeral. Her team held a memorial service, so she could mourn. Around the same time, Jamie began experiencing morning nausea and soon realized she was pregnant. Will began supervising the construction of two schools for one thousand children, including girls; Jamie taught English to professors, who then used what they learned to teach others. Will also worked with the rest of the Gap Team to begin digging twenty wells for desperate villages.

## SEPTEMBER – COUNTING THE COST

Jamie wrote home:

"Father has been a true comfort, in a way I've never experienced, and has given me energy and joy that I know doesn't come from any external sources. Losing the baby has been so hard. It has also given me a way to better identify with the women here. In one village, I heard "Nancy" ask a local woman how many children she had. The woman replied that she had ten. Nancy asked, with the wisdom of one who has lived here for several years, how many children were still living. The woman said, 'I have one son still with me.' Nancy then asked if any of those had been miscarriages, and she said she'd given birth to ten children, as well as having some miscarriages. Nancy asked the doctor if it was because she had some medical condition that made it impossible for her to have healthy children. The doctor replied that no, she lost them in the usual way children die here: waterborne disease, malnutrition, and war."

## OCTOBER – PURIFYING WATER

Will wrote:

"I'm in the throes of designing and implementing a water system for a whole village (about fifteen hundred people). Currently, the villagers are drinking from irrigation ditches and open ponds when the water is running, and open shallow wells when it is

Sojourning with Madurese women

© Caleb Project

## DECEMBER – WALKING THE EXTRA MILE

When Muslims' thirty days of daylight fasting, called *Ramazan*, comes to an end, the biggest holiday of the year begins—*Eid*. Will wrote, "Eid has the popularity and spiritual importance of Christmas, but in my opinion is a lot more fun."

In keeping with tradition, the Jordans visited many homes during the three-day holiday, eating candy, drinking tea, and sharing what they appreciated most about their hosts. In this culture, people typically put on new clothes to represent a spiritual cleanliness they feel is gained by the previous month of fasting. The Jordans visited only nine families during the holiday, a scant figure for a local, but, Jamie wrote, "We felt like we couldn't eat another sugared almond by the end of each day. It was below freezing over the holiday and some of the windows didn't have glass. We were really glad for hot tea and warm clothing to fight off the chill. I think I had on five layers. Even in these extremely humble homes, we felt like honored guests. Hospitality is definitely a market this people group has cornered."

not. Both sources of water are heavily contaminated with sewage and other disease-causing agents. With the help of another agency, we are drilling a very deep well and setting it up with a pump and a water tower. From the tower, underground pipes will bring water to taps on the streets and one day into each house. Finding parts and tools has been a little like looking for auto parts in a hardware store, but I am enjoying the challenge."

## NOVEMBER – FEASTING WITH NEW FRIENDS

The Gap Team and their local friends celebrate Thanksgiving together—Muslim-style. The team cooked two turkeys and laid out many different dishes on carpets for their twenty-seven guests. One villager took the bowl of Italian dressing, put it to his lips, and began to drink, thinking it was soup. Grimacing slightly, he smiled politely and handed it off to the next person. Jamie wrote, "After the meal, a team worker made a speech about thanksgiving and then asked people to say what they were thankful for. Several of our local friends said how glad they were to be working for the development project, and that they thought of us like family."

## 2003

With their six-month commitment completed, the Jordans and several other Gap Team members decided to stay on until April 2003, in order to continue helping the long-term workers with village-aid projects. This summer, Will and Jamie were involved in a car accident that, miraculously, did not claim their lives, when they struck another vehicle (making an illegal U-turn) while traveling 55 miles

per hour. Paramedics were astonished that the Jordans escaped with only minor injuries, which included Jamie breaking her nose and Will cracking a rib. They wrote afterwards about the at-fault driver, "We had a chance to minister peace to him while we were in the hospital, peace that we can take no credit for. The peace of God was supernaturally present and a great comfort."

They would later describe their experience in Central Asia as the hardest time they have ever experienced, but also the best. God did wonderful work in them through all their circumstances: vibrant relationships and dull down times, strife and peace between team members, successful projects and failed plans. The Jordans' experience was transformational.

Will and Jamie and others are planning to return to Central Asia for years of church planting, along with further humanitarian aid, among the people whom they love. They realize that to make a significant impact among this people group will require time, effort, and long-term friendships. The Gap year helped open the Jordans' eyes to the harsh realities and heaven-sent possibilities of life and witness and service among a Muslim people in Central Asia. They are currently recruiting a team and working with the Frontiers U.S. office to sign up people for Gap Teams going into the Middle East.

### FOR FURTHER STUDY
Marti Smith, *Through Her Eyes: Perspectives on Life from Christian Women Serving in the Muslim World* (Waynesboro, Ga.: Authentic Media, 2005).

## BRINGING HOME NEW FAITH IN CHRIST

An underground Christian movement is growing in war-torn Afghanistan. Before the Taliban regime, Afghanistan was one of the least-reached countries in the world, with fewer than three thousand Afghan believers. Now a surprising two million refugees have come back, and some are bringing with them something they did not have when they left—faith in Christ.

"It is surprising how many people found the Lord while they were in Pakistan," one relief worker told *Charisma* magazine. "Many had supernatural dreams in which Jesus appeared to them and revealed himself to be the truth. Others were won to Christ through the network of Pakistani believers in remote, mountainous areas."

Information is difficult to obtain about the church in Afghanistan, and most foreign Christians working in the country are reluctant to give out information that might compromise their work and endanger Afghan believers, but evangelism continues.

"It is unnatural for Afghans not to talk about God," one Christian worker explained. "They are looking for something new, knowing that they cannot go forward with what they had in the past. I talk about Jesus every day because people ask me. It's that simple."

Source: *Charisma* Magazine (January 2004), *www.charismanow.com*.

# LETTER FROM A MUSLIM SEEKER

*by Philip Yancey*

*My deadline for writing this column came shortly after the terrorist attacks of September 11. A dozen different potential columns passed through my mind. In the end, I decided to devote this space to excerpts from a letter faxed to me on September 12, one day after the tragedy. It gives personal, individual focus to a conflict normally discussed in global terms—and poses an important challenge to the Church. For me, everything going on in the world took on a different slant because of this letter.*

Dear Mr. Yancey,
Considering the terrible tragedy that happened yesterday in this nation, I don't know whether this is the appropriate time to write about something personal. But perhaps because of what happened, I think I should write this letter, because I am convinced now that evil does exist in this world.

Growing up in Pakistan, I was a moderately religious Muslim. During the past few months, some of the events in my life caused me to think about God. A friend of mine had a brain tumor, and that caused me an immense amount of pain, and sent me searching for the answer to "Why?" I read some books about the prophet Muhammad and the Islamic faith by western scholars. I was shocked to learn a lot of things about my religion that I never knew. I felt—and still feel—betrayed and hurt. In a closed society like Pakistan, any sort of criticism of Islam is punishable by death, so one cannot have an unbiased view of the faith.

As I found out all these not-so-agreeable things about Islam, I found myself drawn toward the Christian faith. So I just called a local pastor in the United States. Over the past few months, I met with him regularly, and every time I asked him a lot of questions. Each time he would give me books to read.

For a Muslim person to be that interested in the Christian faith is unthinkable. My family and I have talked about issues like the concept of salvation in Islam (which is through deeds) and that of Christianity. They find it quite ridiculous—the concept of a Savior and one person dying for everyone's sins, and that all you have to do is to believe in him. To be honest, I find this concept a little strange too.

Islam does believe in the Virgin Birth of Jesus, but it says that he was a prophet of God and no more. It also says that he was lifted up by God and was not crucified; the Jews only thought that they crucified him. Islam even believes in the second coming of Jesus. I have found myself defending the Christian beliefs against my family, arguing that the crucifixion is a

Philip Yancey is editor at large for *Christianity Today* magazine and a Gold Medallion award-winning author. His books include *Where Is God When It Hurts?*, *Disappointment With God*, and *The Gift Nobody Wants*.

From Phillip Yancey, "The Back Page: Letter from a Muslim Seeker," *Christianity Today* 45, no. 15 (December 2001), p. 80. Used by permission. *www.christianitytoday.com*

historical fact and that someone who is so special as to be born of a virgin—and who would even come back to the world—can't be just a prophet of God.

But the most painful discovery for me about the Islamic faith has been its concept of militancy. I always used to think that these fanatics were just misguided people who give Islam a bad name. To be sure, Islam does not permit killing of innocent women and children, but as I have found out, its teachings are quite different from those of Jesus, who wants you to turn the other cheek. As I know now, violence does have a strong precedent in Islam.

## MUSLIMS IN NORTH AMERICA

The Muslim population of North America has grown dramatically since the 1960s. Although the U.S. Census Bureau does not collect data on religious background, most estimate that the United States is home to between four and six million Muslims. Some say there may be as many as seven million, outnumbering America's Jews.

Canada has between 500,000 and 750,000 Muslims, and Mexico has approximately 250,000. Canada's Muslim population is growing at 9 percent annually because of liberal immigration policies. Toronto, which claims to be the world's most racially diverse city, has an estimated Muslim population of 5 percent, one of the highest concentrations of Muslims in a North American city.[1]

In the United States, many Muslims are from Arab (25 percent) or South Asian (33 percent) descent. A large number are American-born or naturalized citizens. Not all Arab or South Asian immigrants are Muslims, however: a significant number of Arab-Americans are Christians, and many South Asian immigrants are Hindus and Sikhs. America is also home to two million Iranians, 500,000 of whom are in California. About 30 percent of the nearly 600,000 international students who come to the United States each year are Muslim, although, since September 11, 2001, the number of Middle-Eastern Muslim students has dropped significantly.

Not all of North America's Muslims are recent immigrants. The approximately 2.6 million African-American Muslims are a growing segment of American Islam. A study done in 2001 by the Hartford Institute for Religion Research found that U.S. converts to Islam are 64 percent African-American, 27 percent Caucasian, and 6 percent Hispanic. However, other studies have shown that many converts to Islam do not remain in Islam for long.

1. *www.torontomuslims.com.*

Sources: *Operation World, www.cair-net.org.*

### FOR FURTHER STUDY
Roy Oksnevad and Dotsey Welliver, *The Gospel for Islam: Reaching Muslims in North America* (Wheaton, Ill.: Evangelical Missions Information Service, 2001). *www.billygrahamcenter.org/emis*

Larry A. Poston with Carl F. Ellis Jr., *The Changing Face of Islam in America* (Camp Hill, Pa.: Horizon Books, 2000). *www.cpi-horizon.com*

© Caleb Project

Who will be your neighbors?

that his kingdom is not of this world but of the other world.

My mom is so distressed. She has been pleading with me not to abandon my Muslim faith. I love her so much. But how can I force my heart to believe in something that just doesn't seem right? I still have a lot of questions about Christian beliefs, but I know that if I decide to convert, I will be causing an immense amount of heartbreak. I would be ostracized by all my relatives. Also, my legal status in this country expires next year, and considering my views about Islam now—and my sympathetic and favorable view about the Christian faith—I can't imagine going back to Pakistan.

The terrible tragedy that happened yesterday in this country seems to be the logical outcome of teachings that tell you it's okay to reply in kind. I think that's what happens when you try to enforce God's will in this earthly world, rather than believing

Do you think I would find loving and open-minded friends in the church? Would it be fair to say some people would put their guards up and won't want anything to do with someone who belongs to some different Asian Indian race? Someone who has a different color of skin and speaks with an accent?

I really am so confused, so lost. Please tell me what to do. God bless you.

# INTO THE HUNGRY HEART OF ISLAM

*by Erich Bridges*

 Look into the shining face of "Esther," and glimpse part of the future of God's work in the Muslim world. Esther is a young Arab woman, born into one of the Middle East's traditional Christian minorities. Intelligent and well educated, she lives in one of the region's more prosperous countries. If she wanted, she could seek worldly success there, or anywhere.

But for Esther, proclaiming Christ is more than a faded historical heritage. She plans to move—on her own—to a nation notorious for persecuting Christians, especially if they dare to tell majority Muslims about Jesus Christ. There she will attend a university—and tell Muslims about Jesus Christ. Sound a little rash? "When you don't know anything, you trust God for everything," Esther explains with a laugh.

Actually, she does know something about the country where she is going. She made a trip there to scout locations for living and studying. She did not intend to tell anyone about her faith in Christ until she returned and settled there. However, she stayed in Muslim homes and behind closed doors people quietly asked her about Jesus. Even "men with beards" (conservative Muslims) inquired. "When you are hungry, you will ask for food," Esther says. "They are so hungry. They have Islam, but it doesn't stop their hunger."

Even so, she felt dark forces pressing to prevent her from sharing her spiritual food. "At night, I would be dead tired, and something would come and wake me up," she recalls. "I felt it was choking me. I couldn't even say the name of Jesus."

But people kept asking, and she found her voice. After she told them about God's passionate love for them through Christ, some of her listeners declared, "Now we understand!" as tears of joy and relief streamed down their cheeks.

Esther's spiritual adventure began several years ago, when she wondered why more Arab Christians do not reach out to the Muslims among whom they live. "I told God, 'I love Muslims,'" she says. "But he convicted me. He said to me, 'You don't love them. You don't even like them.' And we don't. If we did, more Arab believers would be sharing with Muslims. We don't love them. And we are afraid. Let's be honest: We are afraid of this giant called Islam."

She began an intensive study of Islam and traveled to Muslim strongholds in the Middle East, North Africa—even India. In one Arab country, she became friends with a Southern Baptist missionary who

Erich Bridges is a senior writer at the Southern Baptist International Mission Board. His column is distributed by Baptist Press.

Adapted from Erich Bridges, "Into the Hungry Heart of Islam," *TC Online* (International Mission Board, January–February 2003). *http://archives.tconline.org/trends/jan03t.html* (cited 10 December 2004). Used by permission. *www.imb.org*

has given many years of her life to loving and serving the people under difficult conditions. But it dawned upon Esther that, for all the missionary's dedication and effort, she would never understand the nation's language and people as well as Esther does. That realization sealed Esther's own call to be a missionary.

"We (Arab believers) know Arabic. We understand the culture. We understand Islam. We know the Qur'an," she says. "But we must take the next step." She believes the next step is action—loving Muslims and telling them about God's great salvation—despite cultural barriers, old suspicions and fears, and new threats of persecution.

That is what Esther is doing. And she is challenging other Arab Christians to go with her. She has no illusions about the difficulties that lie ahead, but after seeing the utter joy in the faces of Muslims she has led to Christ, she cannot turn back.

Some evangelical strategists believe the Christian minorities of the Arab world are too mired in tradition, too small, too marginalized, too fearful after long generations of persecution to make a significant impact for the gospel among Muslims. Some Arab Christians—by their words, actions, or inaction—seem to agree. Not Esther. She is following God into the heart of Islam. She hopes others go with her, but she is going whether anyone follows or not.

"When you make yourself available to God," she promises, "you will see miracles."

**End of Key Readings for Lesson 11. See** RECOMMENDED READINGS & ACTIVITIES **on p. 431.**

## " " SPEAK THE SCRIPTURES FROM MEMORY

From the very first days of my friendship with several Muslim women, I have had the joy of stirring Bible passages into our conversations. These friends came to expect wise counsel from me since it was apparent to them that I knew the Word of God and had applied it widely in my own daily life.

From Julia Colgate, *Invest Your Heart: A Call for Women to Evangelize Muslims* (Mesa, Ariz.: Frontiers, 1997), p. 29.

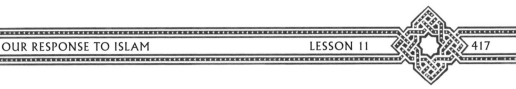
# HOMETOWN MINISTRY AS PREFIELD PREPARATION

*by Joshua Massey*

Today's missionary appointees have great opportunities for significant cross-cultural ministry experience before they go overseas. An ever-increasing number of Buddhist pagodas, Hindu temples, Sikh *gurudwaras,* and Muslim mosques are being built throughout North America. God has brought the nations to us. This mass immigration of the peoples is no longer confined to urban centers; the town where no immigrants reside is becoming rare. These trends provide tremendous opportunities for those God is preparing as his ambassadors to the nations.

In 1987, an elder at my church listened patiently as I described my vision to reach Muslims in South Asia. He then asked, "Tell me about your ministry to Muslims here."

"Well," I replied, somewhat befuddled, "I don't actually know many Muslims here. I do have a good Egyptian Muslim friend, but we don't see each other much these days. Besides, I am so swamped with work, school, and ministry at the church that I can't imagine I'd have much time to spend with Muslims locally even if I did know some."

Vern then gently asked, "What kind of ministry do you think will better prepare you for church planting among Muslims of South Asia: leading small group Bible studies (something I'd been doing for several years), or friendship evangelism among Muslims?" The answer was embarrassingly obvious.

Vern then encouraged me to pray that God would lead me to some South Asian Muslims right here, in my own hometown. I did. And within days, almost miraculously, I began seeing Muslims everywhere! I found Syed in my political science class—I never noticed him before. I saw one bearded student walking around my university campus and felt sure he must be a Muslim from South Asia. I met a young Muslim woman in my biology class the following semester and invited her and her husband to my home for dinner one night. Her husband was the bearded student I'd seen around campus! I began seeing South Asian Muslims at gas stations, mini-markets, and even in my own neighborhood. They were everywhere! God answered my prayer by opening my eyes. But one question still baffles me to this day: How could I have been so blind?

---

Joshua Massey is a cultural anthropologist, currently residing in the Middle East and coordinating the development of indigenous media to assist Muslim followers of Jesus, proclaiming God's kingdom, and making disciples.

From Joshua Massey, "Hometown Ministry as Prefield Preparation," *Evangelical Missions Quarterly* 38, no. 2 (Wheaton, Ill.: Evangelical Missions Information Service, April 2002), pp. 196–201. Used by permission. *www.billygrahamcenter.org/emis*

## ROOTS OF BLINDNESS

I believe my blindness to the incredible opportunities all around me was related to the erroneous idea that "missions" is something that occurs overseas, not in my hometown. Church and mission leaders all want to see some kind of "ministry experience" from missionary applicants before going overseas, but few expect significant prefield, local cross-cultural experience. Historically, of course, there are good reasons for this. Muslim, Hindu, Sikh, and Buddhist immigrants have not always been here in such significant numbers as they are today.

In the early 1900s, most foreign-born immigrants in North America came from Europe. European immigration steadily declined from 1910 to 1970, but the 1980s saw a clear turning point. According to current census reports, over half of all foreign-born immigrants in the United States arrived less than eighteen years ago. Just how many people in the United States today are foreign-born? Ten percent! One of every ten people in the United States was born elsewhere. And those foreign-born immigrants are now coming in increasing numbers from China, India, and Vietnam—centers for the greatest populations of Buddhist, Hindu, Muslim, and Sikh peoples.

What is God doing in our day? I believe he is trying to correct our erroneous ideas of what it means to "do missions." Missions is people, not geography. We need to abolish the idea that pioneer missions is only overseas. God has brought members of countless unreached people groups to live among us.

Ministry in the church prepares a missionary to minister primarily to believers, but the pioneer church planter must begin by ministering primarily to unbelievers. Add to that task the communicative challenges of language and culture, and it is no wonder many who go to unreached pioneer fields spend the bulk of their time ministering to believers in existing churches. Conversely, the new missionary with experience ministering cross-culturally to unreached Muslims, Hindus, Buddhists, or Sikhs in his or her own hometown is far more likely to weather the challenges necessary in pioneer church-planting contexts.

## DIVIDENDS OF BEGINNING NOW

When God began opening my eyes to see South Asian Muslims in my own hometown, I could never have imagined how he would use those relationships to prepare me for fruitful ministry abroad. I began learning not only language but also proper cultural etiquette from my newfound South Asian friends, elders, peers, and youth. I learned stories, anecdotes, and Islamic proverbs, which form a significant portion of being culturally literate in the eyes of these Muslims. I became increasingly comfortable with spicy food and South Asian music. South Asian films, humor, and pastimes taught me a great deal about their worldview, and helped me accumulate a wealth of trivia necessary to develop communicative illustrations rooted in their cultural traditions. As time neared for our departure to South Asia, one Muslim friend arranged for the head of an Islamic institute to meet us at the airport. He, in turn, introduced us to other Muslims who took us into their home until we found housing.

The warm reception we received from the Muslim community was all the more key, given that we were the first missionaries from our agency in the city, with no teammates upon whom we could have called for help. There were a few Americans in town, but my wife and I believed that the more we depended on Muslim friends for assistance, the more deeply we would grow in relationship with them, and the greater our circle of Muslim friends would grow. The fact that we knew their Muslim friends and relatives in the United States strengthened our bonds of friendship all the more.

Cultural advice from a Pakistani mentor

© Caleb Project

God used our time in the States to prepare a way for our entry into South Asia. Before we had even arrived, we already had a circle of Muslim friends just waiting to meet us. These friends introduced us to still others who opened their homes and hearts to me and my family. Throughout our first term, we had countless opportunities to share the gospel after trust had been established through friendship.

As we came to the end of our first term, a close Muslim friend insisted we stop by his home before going to the airport. To our surprise, his extended family (more than twenty-five people) had gathered from all corners of the city to say their goodbyes. We all sat on the floor to enjoy our last supper, and then they asked me to pray, as was my custom. As I asked for

God's blessing on the food and thanked him for leading us to such good friends, I marveled at what God had done in such a short time. We had only been there two and a half years! How did God develop such a large network of intimate Muslim friends with whom we could share his Good News? He did so by opening my eyes to see the amazing opportunities I had to get involved in Muslim friendships years before I even arrived in South Asia.

## TOO BUSY TO BE PREPARED?

As I travel to Bible colleges across the country, speaking to students about the opportunities to extend God's kingdom among Muslims, I find that the same blindness I suffered in the 1980s continues to plague God's people today. When I

share the encouragement God used to open my eyes, some reply, "But I'm working full time! How can I have a significant ministry to unreached peoples in my community now?" I ask, "Do you think it is going to be much different overseas? Tentmaking roles can be very demanding of your time. You need to think strategically here, even as you will there. Get started right here reaching internationals, even if it is only a few hours a week."

When a church-planting missionary candidate misses out on significant prefield preparation through intimate friendship evangelism with internationals of other religions, and instead merely engages in studying them through books, they often

## MEDIA REACHES RESTRICTED-ACCESS NATIONS

How do you share the gospel with people in restricted-access countries? Airwaves are one means to reach people where other means of communication are impossible, as Christian broadcasters well know. Radio broadcasts and Christian satellite television programming travel around the globe, into remote regions and into areas that are otherwise closed to the gospel message. These broadcasts are sharing the message of Christ's love, peace, and hope with millions of people.

In the country of Indonesia, one program in particular has been effectively ministering to the youth. *Key for Today* has been airing for many years, and countless numbers of Muslims have come to Christ as a result of these programs. *Key for Today* introduces subjects that are relevant to young people today. The gospel is presented in a careful, respectful manner. As a result, the follow-up phone lines are jammed for several hours after a program airs due to the number of callers who want to know more.

These programs are also the basis for follow-up events that are held in various locations. At these rallies, the radio speakers and Indonesian believers have wonderful opportunities to meet with listeners and more directly share the gospel. They establish relationships that lead to ongoing contacts for discipleship.

In China, the Uygur people—most of whom are Muslim—are being reached by radio programs that are being produced by Uygur believers who live outside the nation. As far as we know, this is the only Uygur-language broadcast that is being aired. Though it is difficult to do effective follow-up for these broadcasts, it is clear that God is using these programs to touch many hearts as they hear the gospel, many for the first time.

Broadcast media is also being used to reach Mindanao, a predominantly Muslim area of the Philippines. Over the years, many positive responses have been received and churches have been planted as a result of these broadcasts. There is no doubt that media works, and, in many "closed" nations of the world, it is opening doors and building relationships that are resulting in a kingdom harvest.

Psalm 104:4a says, "He makes winds his messengers." And truly, the winds that blow across the nations of this world are his messengers, broadcasting the gospel into the homes and hearts of men, women, and children from every race, tribe, and tongue.

Source: *Intercede, www.cmmequip.org.*

get to the field and wonder, "Now what do I do?"

Consider this example: A new missionary on the field is visiting a Muslim friend who excuses himself for prayer. The missionary contemplates, "What should I do? Should I go to the mosque and join him in prayer? Should I hang out here with the ladies and look like a Christian who doesn't pray? Should I wash up, ask for a prayer carpet, and prostrate in prayer toward Jerusalem? Maybe I should just go get a soda! What shall I do?" At a time when the new missionary could be beginning "upper division" course work in the ongoing learning process to reach his target people, it is as if he or she is just beginning with "lower division" work that could have been learned years before arrival.

A new missionary may have all kinds of theoretical ideas from books, but rather than test these ideas among Muslims at home before journeying overseas, he or she often begins experimenting on the frontlines, alongside the added complexities of learning language and culture. It is true that many lessons can only be learned on the field, but it is equally true that we could do a much better job of preparing for the field by developing genuine friendships with those to whom God has called us, by seeking them out wherever we are. God does not call us to geography; he calls us to people.

## THE NATURAL APPROACH

After recently serving as an interim missions pastor, I found it difficult to recommend to an agency any candidate who had not demonstrated at least some

faithfulness in the ministry that they were going overseas to do. While genuine humility, a servant's heart, and basic perseverance can go a long way, it seemed awkward to send candidates overseas to reach Muslims who had never taken the time to develop even one friendship with a Muslim during their years of preparation for missions service.

Consider how much easier it would be for a church to send a missionary to do pioneer church planting if that person had demonstrated their abilities in local outreach to unreached peoples. Commissioning such proven candidates would be natural for any sending church: "We have seen this person (or family) demonstrate faithfulness in ministry here. They have served poor Cambodian families, ministered to the Hindu community, cared for Bosnian immigrants, spent countless hours in loving dialogue with Muslims, or blessed numerous Vietnamese refugees. We now send them to Asia to continue the work for which God has obviously gifted them."

If you happen to live in one of those rare parts of the world where there truly are not any immigrants, you can still achieve experience by working among the poor, in "the bad" side of town, prisons, orphanages, drug rehabilitation centers, and shelters for battered wives and children. To be better prepared for the realities of church planting among the unreached, just about any uncomfortable place outside the secure walls of your church will suffice. There are real challenges in kingdom living all around us.

## PRACTICAL SUGGESTIONS FOR PREPARATION

God has brought millions of unreached peoples to our very own homelands, not only so that his church would have the privilege of partnering with him in drawing the nations to the Son, but also, I believe, to prepare us for works of service overseas where unreached peoples reside in greatest concentrations. If you are preparing for church planting among Muslims, Hindus, Buddhists, or Sikhs, consider logging at least one thousand hours in intimate friendship evangelism with such peoples before going. If you cannot see them around you now, pray for God to show them to you. Then lift up your eyes and look at the gas station attendants, workmates, schoolmates, and shopkeepers—especially in those parts of the city you do not often visit. They are all around you!

Do not worry if there are no Christian "programs" to position you among these people in your area. In fact, even if there are, you might consider focusing on more natural relationships with the coworkers, fellow students, restaurant owners, or shopkeepers you frequently see. Relationships that occur naturally are often much easier to maintain. Stay focused and be intentional.

Most of us will not have people knocking at our door to be our friends when we get overseas. We need to get used to the process of seeking out and making new friends. Nothing magical happens to us when we go to another country. We do not suddenly transform into some kind of super-missionary when we get off the plane. If God has called you to reach Muslims, Hindus, Buddhists, or Sikhs, get started now. Why wait?

# SOUTH ASIA: VEGETABLES, FISH, AND MESSIANIC MOSQUES

*by Shah Ali, with J. Dudley Woodberry*

My Muslim father tried to kill me with a sword when I became a follower of Jesus, after comparing the Qur'an and the Bible. He interpreted my decision as a rejection not only of my faith, but of my family and culture, as well. Historically, Christians were largely converts from the Hindu community and had incorporated Hindu words and western forms into their worship.

In trying to express my faith, I encountered two sets of problems. First, as indicated, Christianity seemed foreign. Secondly, attempts by Christians to meet the tremendous human need in the region had frequently led to the attraction of opportunistic shallow converts and the consequent resentment of the Muslim majority.

## CHRISTIAN FAITH IN MUSLIM DRESS

I was able to start dealing with the foreignness of Christianity when a missionary hired me to translate the New Testament, using Muslim rather than Hindu vocabulary, and calling it by its Muslim name, *the Injil Sharif* (Noble Gospel). Thousands of Injils were bought, mostly by Muslims, who now accepted this as the gospel of which the Qur'an spoke. This approach may be supported not only pragmatically by the amazing results, but, more importantly, theologically as well. Unlike the Hindu scriptures, the Qur'an shares a lot of material with the Bible. In fact, most Muslim theological terms were originally borrowed from Jews and Christians.[1]

Subsequently, a graduate of Fuller Seminary's School of World Mission asked me to train twenty-five couples to live in villages and do agricultural development. Only one couple was from a Muslim background. All the others had problems: Muslims would exchange visits with them but would not eat their food until they began to shower in the morning, thereby made ceremonially clean by Muslim law after sleeping with their spouses.

The Christian couples were called angels because they were so kind, honest, and self-sacrificing, and they prayed to God. However, they were not considered truly religious because they did not perform the Muslim ritual prayer five times a day. Thereafter, we only employed couples who followed Jesus from a Muslim background, and we developed a ritual prayer that

---

Shah Ali is a follower of Christ from a Muslim family in South Asia. His identity is concealed because of persecution of Christians in his country. He translated the New Testament into his national language using Muslim terms. J. Dudley Woodberry's love for Muslims and his knowledge of their beliefs and culture has long been acknowledged. He has served in Lebanon, Pakistan, Afghanistan, and Saudi Arabia.

Adapted from Shah Ali, with J. Dudley Woodberry, "South Asia: Vegetables, Fish, and Messianic Mosques," *Theology, News, and Notes* (Pasadena, Calif.: Fuller Theological Seminary, March 1992), pp. 12–13. Used by permission. *www.fuller.edu*

retained all the forms and content that Muslims and Christians share, but substituted Bible passages for Qur'anic ones. Little adaptation was necessary, because early Islam borrowed so heavily from Jewish and Christian practice in the formulation of the Pillars of religious observance (the confession of faith, ritual prayer, almsgiving, fasting, and pilgrimage).[2]

Our Muslim neighbors defined Christianity as "a foreign religion of infidels," so we often referred to ourselves as Muslims (literally, *submitters to God*). The necessity of submitting to God is certainly Christian (James 4:7), and Jesus' disciples call themselves Muslims according to the Qur'an (Sura 5:111).[3]

When villages have decided to follow Christ, the people continued to use the mosque for worship of God, but now through Christ. Where possible, the former leaders of mosque prayers (imams) are trained to continue their role as spiritual leaders.

## PERSUASION, POWER, AND GROUPS

God used other means as well as contextualization to bring Muslims to faith in Christ. On several occasions I have had public discussions with Muslim teachers (*malvis*) and have been able to show that, contrary to popular belief, the Qur'an does not name Muhammad as an intercessor. Rather, it states that on the Judgment Day, "intercession will not avail, except [that of] him to whom the Merciful will give permission, and of whose speech he approves" (Sura 5:109, Egyptian ed.; v. 108, Fluegel ed.). But the Injil (Gospel, which is from God, according to the Qur'an; Sura 5:47–48), not only states that God approves of Jesus (Matt. 3:17), but that he is the **only** intercessor (1 Tim. 2:5).

God has also shown his power through answered prayer; the recovery of a three-year-old girl who, the doctors said, would die in a few hours; the sending of rain and the stopping of flooding; and the appearance of an unknown man to stop a crowd bent on killing an imam who followed Christ.

A conscious effort has been made to foster the movement of groups rather than just individuals to Christ. People have only been baptized if the head of the family was baptized. Effort was made to see that leaders understood the message. A Muslim mystic (Sufi) sheikh, upon learning that the veil of the temple had been rent from top to bottom, threw down his Muslim cap, followed Christ, and brought his followers with him. Since illiteracy is high, the Bible and training materials are recorded on cassettes, and inexpensive cassette players are made available to the villagers.

There has been persecution. Our training center was closed down. A court case was made against me and three fellow workers. Likewise, there has been friction between the leaders and misunderstanding by other Christian groups. But the movement of people to Christ continues. Most new believers remain in independent Messianic mosques, but some contextualized congregations have joined the major denomination, while still other individuals are absorbed into the traditional, Hindu-background church.

## SELF-SUPPORT FOR THE INDIGENOUS CHURCH

Besides trying to express our faith in meaningful cultural forms, we have been trying to meet the tremendous human need around us. We want to proclaim the gospel and demonstrate its values. Trying to do both presents certain problems.

First, there is the problem of using human need for evangelistic purposes—of manipulating people and attracting the insincere. Consequently, we help all the villagers despite their religious affiliation and give no financial help to Jesus mosques or their imams. Second, the former colonizer-colonized dependency is easily transferred to donor-recipient dependency.

Third, even the distribution of donated food from abroad may only help in the city, because of the difficulty of distribution, while giving little incentive to the peasants to produce more because of the artificially reduced price. Fourth, the introduction of technology may only help those with the skills or the finances to make use of it, while the poorest can just watch the gap between the haves and have-nots widen.

To deal with these problems we have followed such common development

## PUTTING THE BIBLE IN THEIR HANDS

We believe in the power of God's Word. Many Muslim-background believers' testimonies include the point at which they began to read the Bible for themselves. So how do we give Muslims the gift of God's Word and help them discover its power?

- Pray, patiently expecting God to provide the right moment. Wait for the Spirit to prompt you to give your friend a Bible.
- Understanding that not everyone can read well, prepare to surmount this barrier. Help your friend learn to read, or find Bible recordings and videos.
- Be ready to give a Bible in your friend's language. Use the internet or other sources to find one. Imagine trying to read the Bible in a foreign language: even if you were fluent, it would never be the language of your heart.
- Guide your friend to the best place to start reading—Luke is often preferable. Show how to find a story or parable chosen from a Gospel.
- When sharing a story or looking up a verse, read together, sitting side by side. Give your friend the Bible to hold and read from out loud. Since your friend may feel uncomfortable reading, or even handling, a holy book, a gentle demonstration will help.
- Suggest your friend make a list of unfamiliar words from the Bible; then go over them together. Teach equivalent names like Ibrahim and *Ayyub*—more natural for most Muslims than Abraham or *Job*.
- Follow up by asking if your friend has read the passage you suggested. Everyone is busy and can forget.
- Keep praying that your friend will read. In many testimonies, people begin reading the Bible years after receiving one.

Source: *Encountering the World of Islam*

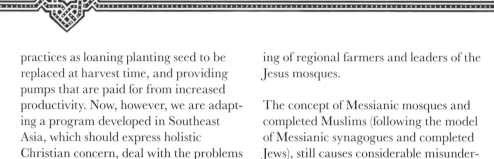

practices as loaning planting seed to be replaced at harvest time, and providing pumps that are paid for from increased productivity. Now, however, we are adapting a program developed in Southeast Asia, which should express holistic Christian concern, deal with the problems outlined, and ensure that the indigenous church remains self-supporting.

The program is training national workers in contextualized church planting and an integrated fish and vegetable cultivation system. The workers are, in turn, sent to needy districts where they are responsible for training local farmers in the easily transferable technology, so that they can become self-sufficient. Increased population means less land is available for cultivation, and a poor transportation infrastructure means food must be produced near its consumption.

The intensive food production system was developed elsewhere. In that system, fish ponds are dug and the excavated dirt used for raised vegetable plots. Excess stems and leaves from the vegetables are used to feed the fish, and the waste from the fish is used as fertilizer for the vegetables. These food production centers are within walking distance of regional urban centers for daily sales, and provide space for training of regional farmers and leaders of the Jesus mosques.

The concept of Messianic mosques and completed Muslims (following the model of Messianic synagogues and completed Jews), still causes considerable misunderstanding among other Christians. The combining of evangelism and humanitarian ministries by the same people also raises concerns among those who feel Christian agencies should only focus on one or the other. Nevertheless, the models we are developing have been used by God in raising up many new disciples and the expression of his concern for total persons with physical and spiritual needs. Likewise, the Messianic Muslim movement has spilled over into a neighboring country through the normal visiting of relatives; when colleagues and I visited a Southeast Asian country recently, a whole Muslim village began to follow Jesus.

## ENDNOTES

1. See Arthur Jeffery, *The Foreign Vocabulary of the Qur'an* (Oriental Institute, 1938).
2. For the details of this argument, see, J. Dudley Woodberry, "Contextualization among Muslims: Reusing Common Pillars," in *The Word among Us*, ed. Dean S. Gilliland (Waco, Tex.: Word, 1989), pp. 282–312.
3. In this context, however, they demonstrated their submission by believing in God and his apostle (apparently Muhammad, who had not yet been born).

# WHY AM I A MISSIONARY TO MUSLIMS?

*by E. J. Martin*

Four medical staff of Jibla Hospital in Yemen were gunned down in a morning meeting. Bonnie Witherall was shot on her way to a maternity clinic in Sidon, Lebanon. Heather Mercer and Dayna Curry were arrested in Afghanistan for showing a video on the life of Jesus. Martin Burnham was kidnapped and murdered in the Philippines. Four countries, five missionaries killed, and two detained for months. And this list includes only some of the North Americans who have recently made U.S. headlines.

Being a missionary among Muslims may seem suddenly to have become a dangerous business. Actually, it is nothing new. Nor is it a dangerous occupation only in Muslim countries. Yet, in light of these recent atrocities, it is reasonable to ask: Why do we missionaries to Muslims intend to carry on with our work?

First, there are several reasons we can rule out. I am not a missionary to Muslims for any political reason. Not all, but many Muslim nations are governed by repressive regimes that pay mere lip service to the notions of human rights. Of course,

I am particularly concerned about the basic human right of religious freedom. Under the UN's Universal Declaration of Human Rights, "Everyone has the right to freedom of thought, conscience, and religion; this right includes freedom to change his religion or belief, and freedom, either alone or in community with others and in public or private, to manifest his religion or belief in teaching, practice, worship, and observance." Those who oppose this are contradicting human rights and the most fundamental principles of freedom of belief and expression. In most Islamic countries, it seems that Christians have the freedom to become Muslims, but Muslims enjoy no such freedom to change their religion. Though appalled by this hypocrisy, bringing political change is not my aim.

I am not interested in ensuring that the West wins a so-called clash of civilizations, because I believe there could be no winners in such a clash. I am not a missionary because I wish to lure needy people into a soul-for-food trade. First, this accusation assumes the basest of motives on the part of Christians who leave the comforts of their own homes in order to provide compassionate humanitarian aid. Second, it presumes that such "conversions" would have any real meaning. Finally, such a ridiculous scenario insults the intelligence of Muslims. Inducements would not lead to genuine spiritual change, and everyone involved would

E. J. Martin holds a master's degree in education and worked for several years in a Muslim country where her husband was accused of distributing Christian literature and jailed for several months without being charged.

Adapted from E. J. Martin, "Why Am I a Missionary to Muslims?" *Mission Frontiers* (September–October 2003), pp. 12–13. Used by permission. *www.missionfrontiers.org*

A warm welcome to Niger

language and culture. Yet the fascination of adventure fades as quickly as most infatuations, and, I am thankful, deeper affections take root.

For example, I enjoy my life as a missionary to Muslims because I have made many Muslim friends. As they show me the world from their angle, they enrich me. I have discovered in them a common humanity. They love, hope, fear, and dream as I do. I have even found many things in Islam that we can affirm together as true about the holy God.

Through knowing each other, we break down the fallacious stereotypes that would pit our cultures against one another. I am eager for my friends to realize that, as a Christian, I join them in repudiating the moral degradation that the so-called Christian West represents for them. And they are eager for me to realize that not all Muslims are terrorists, though some of the atrocities dominating the news are committed by terrorists who claim the cause of Islam. But for every Islamic jihadist, my colleagues and I know many more peaceable, loving Muslims as our friends.

Still, this is an insufficient answer to the question of why my colleagues and I choose to be missionaries. Jesus Christ gave us the reason when he walked the earth: "Do to others as you would have them do to you" (Luke 6:31). If poor and living in Yemen or Jordan, would I want someone to help me deliver my babies safely? If desperately wanting to work, but without job skills or capital to start a small business, would I want someone to help me learn and loan me a little money

know this. This is a ruse by cynical on-lookers to distract and confuse.

I am not a missionary because I have a martyr complex. Though I realize there are dangers, I do not wish to pay the price my recently fallen colleagues have paid. We are not wild-eyed weirdos, recklessly throwing away our lives. While we take reasonable precautions to protect ourselves (as I have done in writing under a pseudonym), risk is inherent in what we do.

The lifestyle of the missionary does come with certain perks. We enjoy adventure and travel and experiencing new places and foods. Our children benefit from their multicultural exposure. We (mostly) enjoy the challenge of learning a new

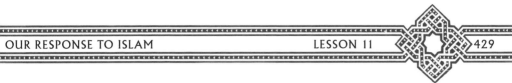
until I could get my feet on the ground? If without clean water to drink, would I hope for some help to drill a well near home?

Jesus also tells me, "From everyone who has been given much, much will be demanded" (Luke 12:48b). I grew up in a small town with loving parents, plenty of food on the table, very good education, enjoyable career, and entertainment. It was solid middle America. But when I compare my life to that of the rest of the world, I see how exceptionally wealthy I am, how much I have been given. "Do

to others." Can our society no longer understand the Golden Rule?

Have I "converted" Muslims? My Muslim friend tells me the Qur'an agrees with the Bible on this point: God converts whom he will (see Sura 42:13). I cannot convert people, but I am compelled to tell them the same message that reached through history and touched my heart. Intimate fellowship with the holy God is an exquisite banquet we cannot withhold. We will not eat and let others starve. So yes, I have told my friends about this exquisite banquet.

## FREE TO SUFFER

"Dear friends, do not be surprised at the painful trial you are suffering, as though something strange were happening to you. But rejoice that you participate in the sufferings of Christ, so that you may be overjoyed when his glory is revealed" (1 Peter 4:12–13). We need a biblical understanding of suffering: We hear that suffering is a normal part of the Christian life, but rarely do we welcome it as necessary for Christian witness. As a result, we fail to value the witness of the persecuted church in other parts of the world.

Why are only non-westerners suffering and dying for Jesus? Are westerners willing to walk through the fire as the non-western church has? Jesus said, "Go! I am sending you out like lambs among wolves" (Luke 10:3). When Muslims give their lives to Christ, they will almost certainly receive persecution. Jesus taught, "No servant is greater than his master. If they persecuted me, they will persecute you also" (John 15:20). As first-generation, Muslim-background believers are living, suffering, and dying for their faith in Christ, their sons and daughters must be discipled to be the next generation of believers. In China and the former Soviet republics, churches thrived under persecution as a result of second-generation believers carrying on their parents' faith. Research demonstrates that Christianity grows under persecution when believers are taught, as part of their discipleship, why they must suffer.

A veteran worker among Muslims, Nik, interviewed a Muslim-background believer who suffered years of imprisonment. The believer said, "I took great joy that I was suffering in prison in my country so that you could be free to share Christ in Kentucky." Nik began to weep: "That debt is too great and I can't accept it." The man replied with the tenderness of one who has suffered greatly: "That's the debt of the cross and the unity of God's people. When you are free to proclaim Christ freely, though I'm in prison, I too am free because I'm a part of the Church. And if I'm persecuted, you share in my persecution. There is no free or persecuted church; there is just the Church of Jesus Christ. Don't take away from me my joy. I was free to suffer so that you could be free to proclaim."

Source: Annee W. Rose, *www.frontiers.org.*

God's forgiveness available through Jesus the Messiah, an abundant life independent of outward circumstances, the promise of life in heaven with the creator who made me: I am grateful to the person who invited me to come. My life has been changed absolutely for the better. I have delighted in the privilege of seeing other's lives changed. And I have held the hands of Muslims who have endured rejection, prison, and torture because they found life with Jesus worth this price.

Will we missionaries to Muslims go home because of these recent brutal murders? This violent reaction to the message of Jesus is not new. Remember the fellow who was thrown into prison and warned by the local religious officials to be quiet about Jesus? The apostle Peter's response? "Judge for yourselves whether it is right in God's sight to obey you rather than God. For we cannot help speaking about what we have seen and heard" (Acts 4:19–20).

**End of Basic Readings for Lesson 11. See** RECOMMENDED READINGS & ACTIVITIES **on p. 431.**

**Go to:** *www.encounteringislam. org/readings* **to find the Full Readings for Lesson 11.**

# DISCUSSION QUESTIONS

Write down three actions you will take as a result of this class and tell them to others. Examples:

- Talk to my church leadership about what I have learned.
- Become an "advocate" for a Muslim group or help my church adopt one.
- Invite a Muslim student, family, or friend over for a meal.
- Participate in a short-term mission trip to a Muslim people group.
- Open correspondence with one or more mission agencies.
- Create a prayer group focused on Muslims.
- Join the mission committee at my church, or start one.
- Begin financial support of a missionary who is reaching Muslims.
- Keep in contact with other classmates, to encourage one another in seeing Muslims enter the kingdom.
- Start shopping at an international market owned by Muslims.
- Seek out Muslims in the service industries; for instance, go inside the gas station near my home to pay for gas, so I can build a relationship with the Muslims working there.

# RECOMMENDED READINGS & ACTIVITIES*

Read: Roland Muller, *Tools for Muslim Evangelism* (Belleville, Ontario, Canada: Essence Publishing, 2000).

Watch: *Born in the USA: Muslim Americans*, a documentary directed by Ahmed Soliman (2003).

Pray: Use the Internet or phone book to find mosques or Muslim-owned businesses and schools in your community. Stop by, introduce yourself, and ask if you could pray for them.

Visit: Telephone a local mosque or Islamic center; ask if they have a visiting time that is open to the public.

Surf: Discover related web sites at *www.encounteringislam.org/lessonlinks*.

* For expanded details on these Recommended Readings & Activities, visit *www.encounteringislam.org/lessonlinks*.

# LESSON 12
## PRAYER FOR
## THE MUSLIM WORLD

## PONDER THIS

- What will it take to see thousands of Muslims believe in Jesus Christ? Who can accomplish this?

- What are some specific felt needs of your Muslim friends? Who can meet these?

- Why is it difficult for us and for our churches to pray faithfully, and specifically, for Muslims and the Muslim world?

# LESSON OBJECTIVE

Respond to what you have been learning through a biblical, outward-focused, and guided time of prayer.

1. Hear and respond to the testimony of a Muslim-background believer.

2. Participate in a concert of prayer. Seek and respond to God's presence and power. Ask God to change our hearts and use us for his ends. Labor in prayer for Muslims out of the delight of being in God's presence and power.

# LESSON READINGS

# INTRODUCTION

"Do not be anxious about anything, but in everything, by prayer and petition, with thanksgiving, present your requests to God. And the peace of God, which transcends all understanding, will guard your hearts and your minds in Christ Jesus" (Phil. 4:6–7).

Pray for God to bless her future

Much of the time, our prayers are simplistic. We ask God to keep us and our friends safe and healthy, rarely asking specifically for the deep, the powerful, or the seemingly impossible. If we are to persevere in prayer for the Muslim world, we need to discover the thrill of entering God's presence, joining him in the working out of his will, and engaging in kingdom-focused praying. When we have experienced this kind of prayer, we will want to do so again!

This course has not focused heavily on the biblical imagery of spiritual warfare. At times in the past, these images have been used inappropriately to characterize Muslims as the enemy. But, in fact, we—just like Muslims—have been the victims of evil and oppression, blind to lies and deception. We all need the activity of God to overcome the darkness of this world and the battle against Satan, his forces, and our own sin which entangles us. Here, the imagery of war is valid.

Prayer may very well be the most-talked-about, seldom-practiced, spiritual discipline. We claim it as a priority, but an honest assessment of our busy lives reveals otherwise. Are we going through the expected, habitual motions of prayer, without vigorous belief in what we are doing? Have we lived as functional atheists until faced with personally desperate situations, prompting us to pray deeply only then? Or, is our praying weak and limited, and therefore boring and lifeless? Ever say to yourself, "Why pray? I can't

think of anything to ask," or "That's what I've asked for over and over"?

This is not what prayer should be! Real prayer is always vibrant. What is more, it is our precious prerogative! People invested in stocks or precious metals take an active interest in what happens to those investments in the exchange markets. Are we invested in God's kingdom? So what vital attention in our praying should follow?

We need to start by focusing on ourselves, praying that God will forgive us and change our hearts, penetrate past our raging distractions, and lead us to where we will wait in stillness. As hard as it seems, those initial minutes of naked dependence are very effective in focusing our attitudes and prayers. When we do not invite God to intercede through us, our prayers lack purpose and depth. If we do ask him to transform our unbelief, believing God is trustworthy—able and willing to answer—we can confidently present our bold requests.

Yes, many of us have not yet experienced praying like this. We are busy and impeded by bad habits which have discouraged our prayer lives. We neglect to give the Spirit control of our minds and hearts as we begin. A fresh experience will remind us of our ready access, of the joy of talking to our Father God, King of the universe, the all-powerful Creator! Gathering with other believers, to focus in worship and to pray afresh, will overcome our internal resistance and give momentum to our prayers.

Many of my own best encounters in prayer have been with ministry teams as we were taking risks and serving together. We were dependent on God and each other. What a delight to hear my teammates report, "So we prayed, and you'll never guess what happened!" Perhaps such service could be your goal as the best way to learn to pray boldly and see how God answers?

Muslims have had negative experiences with prayer also, and most Muslims do not follow the prescribed Islamic prayers. Even of those who do, many are very surprised when they first pray in the name of Jesus. "This actually works!" is the testimony of many Muslim-background believers. When someone prays for them in Jesus' name, or when they themselves pray and ask God to help them, heal them, speak to them, or prove himself to them, their prayers are answered with life-changing power and clarity.

## WHY PRAY FOR MUSLIMS?

All the knowledge about Islam, all our feeling for and understanding of the Muslim, even our intimate knowledge of the Bible, will not in the final analysis make us fit enough for outreach work. It is what God does through his available and loving servants that matters. When his power, love, and compassion operate in us, we are indeed his witnesses. What we are and say, however, is implanted when we live in his presence.

Gerhard Nehls, *Muslim Evangelism* (Cape Town, South Africa: Life Challenge Africa, 1991), p. 245.

I must confess that I am envious of, and confused by, some people's prayers, because God answers their audacious appeals for provision and miracles with such frequency! They have discovered the open secret to God's answering: focus on the kingdom. The Lord's Prayer is a simple but elegant model of kingdom prayer: "Thy kingdom come, thy will be done on earth as it is in heaven."

Remember, we are battling in the heavenly realms with a spiritual, divinely empowered weapon, pointed at the enemies of God (2 Cor. 10:3–5; see Lesson 6). God is sovereign. He is the rightful ruler, so he can exercise his authority and use his power (Eph. 1:18–20). He can answer our requests so that his name will be honored. When our hearts and minds are obediently centered on our Lord, he promises to wield this powerful weapon of our warfare through us.

*– K.S., Editor.*

### FOR FURTHER STUDY
Jean-Marie Gaudewl, *Called from Islam to Christ* (London: Monarch, 1999).

## PLURALISM AND DIVERSITY

In an age of political correctness, evangelicals may bristle at terms like tolerance, diversity, and pluralism. These words conjure up images of theological relativism and universalism. We fear that the insistence on tolerance and diversity, issuing from our post-Christian culture, will force us to accept values we deplore, or will silence our biblical voice in society.

Yet, at the same time, we believe in the global, universal church of Christ which one day will include members from every tribe, language, people, and nation. Even as churches disagree on baptism, spiritual gifts, styles of worship, forms of leadership, views of the end times, and other issues, we know that Christianity is inclusive. Can we rescue tolerance from the secular debate and embrace the biblical admonition to accept each other in love (Eph. 4:1–3)? Can we respect the plurality of approaches required to respond holistically to the needs of the world?

As we pray and work together for the coming of Christ's kingdom, we have a choice: Will we celebrate the diversity and pluralism of the church, or will we force our style of Christianity on others? In *The Gospel in a Pluralist Society*, Lesslie Newbigin calls on the church to be the vessel of Christian mission, even today.[1] Christians should not lose their confidence in boldly proclaiming the uniqueness and authority of Christ. However, rather than focusing on apologetics, Newbigin advocates open dialogue between Christians and people of other faiths. Our focus should be on developing open, trusting communication—in which Christians can lovingly proclaim the gospel.

1  Lesslie Newbigin, *The Gospel in a Pluralist Society* (Grand Rapids: Eerdmans, 1989).

Source: *Encountering the World of Islam*

# REACHING MUSLIMS THROUGH PRAYER

*by J. Christy Wilson Jr.*

"The opening of the Muslim world for the gospel," writes Patrick Johnstone, "cannot be organized by human effort or stratagems, but only by prayer. Our weapons are spiritual, not carnal. Pray for an army of intercessors to be raised up, that a breakthrough as decisive and sudden as that in China and the former USSR may also occur in the Muslim world."[1]

Of the approximately eleven thousand people groups in the world still to be evangelized, about four thousand are Islamic. Our Lord has promised, "This gospel of the kingdom will be preached in the whole world as a testimony to all nations (*ta ethne*, or all the peoples), and then the end will come" (Matt. 24:14). In that same passage, Christ said, "Heaven and earth will pass away, but my words will never pass away" (Matt. 24:35). Thus world evangelization is absolutely certain. But how are the Muslim people groups going to be reached? The answer is: foremostly through extraordinary prayer.

## PRAYER, FIRST LEVEL OF REVIVAL

Dr. J. Edwin Orr, in his books on the history of awakenings, has pointed out that there are four levels to every true revival.[2] This is true in the book of Acts and on down through church history. The first stage is prayer and reconciliation among Christians. The second is evangelism, as the lost are won to the Lord. The third is that of missions, with participation in world evangelization; and the fourth is our service for Christ in action, as we love our neighbors as ourselves and supply their needs physically, intellectually, socially, and spiritually.

Most of the revivals in the past have been localized because of the difficulty of transportation and communication. I believe that we are now on the verge of an awakening of worldwide proportions (see Joel 2:28–32). This will fulfill the prophecy of Joel, quoted by the apostle Peter:

> In the last days, God says, I will pour out my Spirit on all people. Your sons and daughters will prophesy, your young men will see visions, your old men will dream dreams. Even on my servants, both men and women, I will pour out my Spirit in those days, and they will prophesy. I will show wonders in the heaven above, and signs in the earth below…. And everyone who calls on the name of the Lord will be saved (Acts 2:17–19, 21).

This revival, I believe, will bring about the completion of Christ's commission of worldwide evangelization, and will be

Dr. J. Christy Wilson Jr., is Emeritus Professor of World Evangelization at Gordon-Conwell Seminary. He served as a missionary in Central Asia for twenty-three years.

Adapted from J. Christy Wilson Jr., "Undergirding the Effort with Prayer: Muslims Being Reached Foremostly through Extraordinary Prayer," *International Journal of Frontier Missions*, 11, no. 2 (April 1994), pp. 61–65. Used by permission. *www.ijfm.org*

the heart of reaching unreached Muslim groups for Christ.

## THOSE TOUCHED IN THE AWAKENINGS

We see this on a limited scale in the awakening of 1858 and following. It started with a convert of Charles Finney who was an urban missionary. Jeremiah Lanphier began the Fulton Street Wednesday noon prayer meeting in 1857 for workers and business people in New York City. Within six months, about ten thousand were gathering for prayer every noon. This revival resulted in over a million converts being added to the American churches in the next two years.

## MOVEMENTS OF MUSLIMS TOWARD CHRIST

More Muslims have become believers in Jesus Christ in the last fifty years than in the previous thirteen hundred years. Much of this shifting of belief has occurred amid social upheaval, as when two million Javanese Muslims became Christians in the 1960s, or when thousands of Iranians in diaspora have become Christians in the twenty-five years since the 1979 Islamic Revolution of Iran. Other movements have occurred, numbering from several hundred to several hundred thousand in Bangladesh, and among the Berbers of North Africa. The Balkans, Turkey, Central Asia, and many other places which did not have local fellowships of indigenous Muslim-background believers now do. House fellowships are also meeting in the heart of the Islamic world, at great personal risk.

Why is this occurring today? We believe this is God's timing. Other identifiable associated factors include:

- Near-global suffering of Muslims, from both economic privation and politically repressive regimes.
- Increasing awareness of unreached people groups in missions-minded churches since the Lausanne Conference on World Evangelization in 1974.
- Specific focus, by more mission agencies—such as Frontiers and Pioneers—on the needs of Muslims and other unreached people groups.
- Sending of missionaries to reach out to Muslims by African, Indian, Korean, Latin American, Egyptian, and other non-western churches.
- Widespread utilization of multi-media tools, such as the *Jesus* film.

Above all, prayer has increased, through the use of tools like the annual *30-Days Muslim World Prayer Guide*, for the needs of Muslims during the annual fast of Ramadan, or the discipline of lifting up the eternal needs of Muslims every Friday at noon, when Muslims gather for mosque services. This has certainly contributed to Muslims turning to Christ after they experience supernatural dreams, visions, miracles, and healings.

"And they sang a new song: 'You are worthy to take the scroll and to open its seals, because you were slain, and with your blood you purchased men for God from every tribe and language and people and nation'" (Rev. 5:9).

Sources: David Garrison, Greg Livingstone, and Don McCurry.

The most prominent leader of this awakening in the States, as well as in the British Isles, was D. L. Moody. One of his closest associates, Ruben A. Torrey, said that Moody was a far greater man of prayer than he was a preacher. Here again, we see the absolute necessity of intercession in great awakenings. Moody was not only involved in evangelism, as huge numbers came to Christ through his messages, but he also helped establish the YMCA in North America, started schools for girls and boys, established the Moody Bible Institute, and founded a Christian publishing house, now called Moody Press.

His involvement in missions, which is another stage of true revival, came through close friends like Arthur T. Pierson, who popularized the phrase, "The evangelization of the world in this generation." In reference to this, Moody said, "It can be done—it ought to be done—it must be done."[3] In the summer of 1886, Moody invited Pierson, along with Adoniram Judson Gordon, to speak to 251 student leaders who had been invited to his Mount Hermon School for Boys in Massachusetts. One of these was Robert Wilder, who had just completed his senior year at Princeton.

Wilder was born in India where his parents had been missionaries. He and his sister Grace prayed faithfully that one hundred of the students at the Mount Hermon Conference would give their lives for foreign missionary service. In answer to their intercession, exactly one hundred signed the pledge: "God helping me, I purpose to be a foreign missionary," and the Student Volunteer Movement was born.

## RESULTS OF PRAYER: MISSIONS TO MUSLIMS

The following academic year of 1886–87, Robert Wilder and John Foreman, a seminary student, spread the vision by visiting campuses across the United States and Canada. More than two thousand more signed the pledge to become missionaries. One of them was Samuel Zwemer, at Hope College in Holland, Michigan. He went on to become the greatest missionary to Muslim peoples in history.

Zwemer believed that God was calling him to the hardest mission field in the world, the Islamic peoples of Arabia. No mission board would send him. They said that he would be killed for sure and they did not want to be responsible for that. Therefore, he and Dr. James Cantine formed their own agency, the Arabia Mission. As Dr. Zwemer said, "If God calls you and the board won't send you, bore a hole through the board, and go anyway." After exploring around the whole Arabian Peninsula, they established mission stations in Muscat, Kuwait, Bahrain, and Basra.

After working in the Muslim world for twenty-five years, Zwemer was invited to speak at a Keswick Convention in England. He used as his text:

> Master, we have toiled all the night, and have taken nothing: nevertheless at thy word, I will let down the net. And when they had this done, they enclosed a great multitude of fishes: and their net broke. And they beckoned unto their partners, which were in the other ship, that they should come and help them. And they came,

and filled both the ships, so that they began to sink (Luke 5:5–7, KJV).

Zwemer went on to say that he and others had toiled in the Muslim world all night, and had taken next to nothing. He could count the Muslim converts on his fingers. But, he said, we have the command of Christ to obey, and that, if we are faithful, the time will come when so many Muslims will come to Christ that, like the problem with the overloaded boats, there will not be room in the churches to hold them. The people at the Keswick Convention were so touched that they asked Dr. Zwemer what they could do. His answer was, "Pray!" This was the beginning of the Fellowship of Prayer for Muslims which has conducted special times of intercession ever since.[4] For example, days of prayer for Muslims are now held several times a year in Philadelphia and in the Los Angeles area. They also produce and distribute literature which encourages prayer.

Praying that God will change our hearts

© Caleb Project

## PRAYER: TOOL OF THOSE CALLED

It was the Student Volunteer Movement that also influenced Dr. William M. Miller (1892–1993) to give his life for missions. While he was studying in seminary, he put a map of the world on the wall of his dormitory room. He would then kneel by his bed in front of it and would pray, "Lord, I am willing to go anywhere in this world for you. Show me where." It was then that he heard Dr. Zwemer share the challenge of the Muslim world. God,

through him, called Bill Miller to go to Mashad in Eastern Iran near the border of Afghanistan.

Bill Miller then started a daily prayer meeting in his room to ask God for missionaries in accord with Christ's command, "Ask the Lord of the harvest, therefore, to send forth workers into his harvest field" (Matt. 9:38). Through prayer, he was able to get more than a hundred to be willing to be missionaries. Among those were Dr. Philip Howard, the father of Elizabeth Elliot, whose husband Jim was killed by the Auca Indians. He also was the father of David Howard, who has been a missionary in Colombia, Latin America; has headed up two of the Urbana Student Missionary Conventions; was Director of the Lausanne Congress in Pattaya, Thailand; then was Executive Secretary of the World Evangelical Fellowship, and later vice president of the David C. Cook Foundation. Through

Bill Miller's challenge, my parents also went as missionaries to Iran. Thus we see the results in the Muslim world that came through prayer following the great awakening of 1858.

## RESULTS OF PRAYER FOR AFGHANISTAN

I was born in Iran where my parents were missionaries. As a little boy, I heard them praying for a country to the east which had no Christians. It was Afghanistan. I do not remember this incident, but my mother told me that our Iranian pastor, Stephen Khoobyar, once asked me what I wanted to be when I grew up. I said that I wanted to be a missionary to Afghanistan. He replied that missionaries were not allowed in that land. I said that was the reason I wanted to be a missionary there.

Not only did the missionaries and Christians in Iran pray for the closed nation of Afghanistan, but dedicated men and women of God on the borders of that country, in India, later in Pakistan, and in Russia, also interceded. For example,

## TIPS FOR PRAYERWALKING

"Focusing on the same subject can be tough while sitting in a circle in a room," say Steve Hawthorne and Graham Kendrick.[1] Walking down the street surrounded by prayer needs can help. It raises your level of concern and ability to focus. "Prayers can be razor sharp for specific families with names and faces. Perception is heightened, and thus prayer can be far more directed by the Spirit of God."[2]

Prayerwalking is a quiet way to minister to your neighbors while learning to care about them. It also breaks down spiritual barriers by honoring God's kingdom where it is not being honored. Prayerwalking lays the groundwork for further ministry. Hawthorne and Kendrick provide this advice for prayerwalkers:

**Before you begin—**

1. Prepare your heart, gather your mind, and ask God for guidance.
2. Make sure your relationships with others are right.
3. Organize prayer teams (typically twos and threes).
4. Designate areas, routes, or sites. Maps may be helpful.
5. Agree on an appointed time to re-gather for debriefing.
6. Review background and Scriptures that may fuel your prayers.

**During the walk—**

1. Pray for the things you see and ask God to show you the city through his eyes.
2. Pray out loud, so your partner(s) can hear and agree with you, but not in such a style that will draw the attention of others on the street.
3. Pray together, listening to each other and agreeing. Do not skip from one topic to another, but pray conversationally and responsively. Short prayers help.
4. Pray with the Scriptures. Allow the words of the Bible to teach you to pray.
5. Pray with sensitivity to the people and places you are seeing. What does the Lord want to do for them?

Flora Davidson from Scotland lived in a two-story adobe house in the town of Kohat on the Northwest Frontier. In front of a window which looked out on the mountains of Afghanistan in the distance, she had a little bench. There she would spend hours on her knees praying that God would open that country to the gospel.

She also started a circle of prayer for Afghanistan. She would regularly distribute requests for intercession to believers who were concerned about reaching that nation for Christ. Later Margaret Haines, the sister-in-law of Dr. William Miller, worked with Flora Davidson in Kohat. She edited and published a quarterly prayer bulletin called "Missions on the Borders of Afghanistan." When she returned to the Philadelphia area because of poor health, she continued to encourage intercession for Afghanistan, and for years put out monthly prayer letters for the work in that country.

After I finished my studies, Afghanistan was still closed to regular missionaries. Therefore, I signed a contract with the Ambassador at the Afghan Embassy in Washington, D.C., to teach English in that country. After arriving there in 1951, while reading my Bible, I saw that this was what the apostle Paul did (Acts 18:1–4). Following him, I became a self-supporting missionary.

When my wife, Betty, and I arrived in Kabul, our main ministry was prayer. We also met with other Christian teachers for intercession. This was the way a house church began in our home. I used to pray every day for my Afghan Muslim students in the government school where I taught. One of these for whom I interceded went abroad for further study. He belonged to the royal family of Afghanistan. Later on, I received a letter from him telling how he had put his trust in Jesus Christ as his Savior. He also had joined an evangelical church and was teaching a young people's Sunday school

(cont. from p. 442)
**After prayerwalking—**

1. Share your topics of prayer with the rest of your group. Look for patterns and keep a journal of what you prayed.
2. Evaluate your prayerwalk. What do you want to do differently next time?
3. Consider the things you saw and prayed about and what they might mean for further ministry efforts. Did God reveal anything to you?
4. Decide how, when, and where to continue prayerwalking.

### FOR FURTHER STUDY
Steve Hawthorne and Graham Kendrick, *Prayerwalking: Praying On Site with Insight* (Lake Mary, Fla.: Creation House, 1993), pp. 23–39.

1. Steve Hawthorne and Graham Kendrick, *Prayerwalking: Praying On Site with Insight* (Lake Mary, Fla.: Creation House, 1993), p. 37.
2. Ibid., p. 38.

class. He enclosed a check to help out with God's work in Afghanistan.

## ANSWERED PRAYER: A SIGN AND WONDER

Not only is prayer for Muslims effective, but also, prayer with them for their felt needs can be a sign and a wonder when they see the answer, which then can lead them to accept Jesus Christ as their Lord and Savior. On one occasion, an Afghan friend came to me with his uncle who needed a cataract operation. They had just been turned away from the government hospital, where they were told that a bed for him to have the operation would not be available for three months.

My friend explained to me that this made it very difficult, since his uncle came from the central highlands, which was a journey of several days each way. Therefore, it would be difficult for him to make the trip and come back in three months. On the other hand, it would be very hard for him to stay in Kabul, the capital, away from his family for three months. He asked me whether I knew the head of that government hospital. I said that I did. He then asked me kindly to write a note explaining the situation, and asking whether it might be possible to admit his uncle sooner. I replied that I did not have to write a note but would personally speak to the head of the hospital.

The friend then asked me what the name was of the one in charge of the hospital. I answered, "His name is the Lord Jesus Christ. He is the head of every hospital." I then said, "Let us talk to him now." Praying in their language, I explained

the situation to the Lord and asked him to help. I then told them to go back to the government hospital. But they were reluctant to return there, since they had just been turned away. I said to them, "You asked me to intercede with the head of the hospital, and I did this. Now go back." Finally, they agreed to try again.

Several hours later, my friend returned to see me and he was all excited. He exclaimed, "You do know the head of that hospital!" He went on to explain that as soon as they returned, a patient was just being discharged, and they admitted his uncle immediately, putting him in the bed which had just been vacated. And they would perform the needed operation soon. This Muslim became a believer in Jesus Christ as his personal Lord and Savior.[5]

A Muslim convert to Christ in Europe has found prayer to be an effective means of evangelism. He finds out what needs people have, and then challenges them to pray to Jesus to help them with these needs. When the Lord answers, they see a sign and a wonder in response to their prayers. Many Muslims then also pray to Christ to forgive them their sins, and receive him as their Savior and Lord.

## THE WEAPONS OF OUR WARFARE

As the apostle Paul reminds us, "The weapons we fight with are not the weapons of the world. On the contrary, they have divine power to demolish strongholds" (2 Cor. 10:4). He also brings this out when he writes,

> Finally, be strong in the Lord and in his mighty power. Put on the full ar-

mor of God that you can take your stand against the devil's schemes. For our struggle is not against flesh and blood but against the rulers, against the authorities, against the powers of this dark world, and against the spiritual forces of evil in the heavenly realms (Eph. 6:10–12).

Pray for Christ to shepherd all peoples

© Frontiers

Our real foe is Satan and all of his evil forces. In the same way, Jesus Christ has taught us to petition daily, in the Lord's prayer, that we might be delivered from "the evil one" (*tou ponerou* in Greek, Matt. 6:13).

Notice that Paul says our struggle is not against flesh and blood or people. We need constantly to love our Muslim friends. Our Lord loves them infinitely, and this is the reason he has not only died for them, but has commanded us to take his Good News of forgiveness and eternal life to them. We must see that we are really fighting against the spiritual powers behind Islam. For this reason, the passage adds that, along with being strong in the Lord and putting on the whole armor of God so that we can stand against the devil, we also need to "pray in the Spirit on all occasions, with all kinds of prayers and requests" (Eph. 6:18).

## THE REAL ENEMY WE BATTLE

It is interesting to see how certain cults also trace their origins to a vision of an angel or a special messenger who they claim came from God. For example, Joseph Smith Jr., the one Mormons follow as their prophet, claimed that the angel Moroni appeared to him and gave him his commission three times.[7]

Also Sun Myung Moon, who started the Unification Church, claims that Jesus Christ appeared to him in Korea on Easter Day in 1936 and called him to be a special messenger.[8] The apostle Paul warns us that at times "Satan himself masquerades as an angel of light" (2 Cor. 11:14).

The apostle John tells us in the Bible that "the reason the Son of God appeared was to destroy the devil's work" (1 John 3:8b). He also tells us to "test the spirits to see whether they are from God" (1 John 4:1). He then reveals the test for determining the source: "This is how you can recognize the Spirit of God: Every spirit that acknowledges that Jesus Christ has come in the flesh is from God, but every spirit that does not acknowledge Jesus is not from God" (1 John 4:2–3). In other words, true divine revelation acknowledges the incarnation of Christ. The Qur'an throughout denies that Jesus is God, or the Son of God. Furthermore, Islam also denies that Christ died on the cross for our sins.

It was through seeking the real forgiveness of his sins that Haji Sultan Muhammad received Jesus as his Savior. He writes his testimony in the booklet, *Why I Became A Christian*.[9] After being an Islamic leader, a scholar, and one who had performed the pilgrimage to Mecca, he finally concluded that only in the death of Christ was there atonement for his sins.

## CLAIMING THE NATIONS FOR THE LORD

In his book, *The Last of the Giants*, George Otis points out that, just as Joshua and his armies had to fight warriors of great size before the Promised Land was occupied, so we today have awesome forces that hinder the evangelization of the world. He says that the greatest of these giants is Islam.[10] John Wimber states that Jesus Christ has won the war for world evangelization, but we, through his strength, need to do the mopping up and win the battles. The way we are to do this is not through our own strength, but through prayer to the Commander of the Lord's army, even as Joshua did (Josh. 5:15–18).

We should be greatly encouraged with the present revival of prayer around the world. The Concerts of Prayer Movement is gaining faithful groups of intercessors on every continent. Dr. C. Peter Wagner, who is coordinator of the AD 2000 Prayer Track, writes, "It is becoming clear that the real battle for world evangelization is a spiritual battle."[11] Campus Crusade's Dr. Kim Joon-Gon of Korea writes, "The Lord Jesus has the keys to open what no one can shut. I believe, in the next ten years, history's greatest revival will take place."[12]

In 1993 and 1994, Youth With A Mission encouraged Christians to fast and pray in a special way for Muslims during the Islamic lunar month of Ramadan. They plan to continue this practice on a yearly basis. Also, October 1993 was set aside as a time for focused prayer for more than sixty countries of the 10/40 Window, over two-thirds of which are Islamic.

God the Father gives the promise to God the Son: "Ask of me and I will make the nations your inheritance, the ends of the earth your possession" (Ps. 2:8). We too can claim this promise for Muslim peoples. As our Lord said, "Until now you have not asked for anything in my name. Ask and you will receive, and your joy will be complete" (John 16:24). Worldwide awakening will come through what Jonathan Edwards called "explicit agreement and visible union of God's people in extraordinary prayer for the revival of religion and the advancement of Christ's kingdom on earth."[13] In this way, all unreached people groups, including the Muslim peoples, will be reached. Then, as the Bible has promised, "The earth will be filled with the knowledge of the glory of the Lord, as the waters cover the sea" (Hab. 2:14).

### ENDNOTES

1. Patrick Johnstone, *Operation World*, 5th ed. (Grand Rapids: Zondervan, 1993), p. 72.
2. J. Edwin Orr, *The Eager Feet*, Evangelical Awakenings, 1792 and 1830; *The Fervent Prayer*, Evangelical Awakenings, 1858–; *The Flaming Tongue*, Evangelical Awakenings, 1900– (Chicago: Moody Press, 1975, 1974, 1973). The specific reference for this is in *The Fervent Prayer*, p. 160.
3. Luis Bush, ed., *AD 2000 and Beyond Handbook*, 3rd ed. (Colorado Springs: AD 2000 and Beyond Movement, 1993), frontispiece.

4. Address of the Fellowship of Faith for North America is: P.O. Box 65214, Toronto, Ontario, Canada M4K 3Z2. They put out a prayer bulletin every few months on needs in the Muslim world.

5. For further similar accounts, see my chapter in the book edited by J. Dudley Woodberry, *Muslims and Christians on the Emmaus Road* (Monrovia, Calif.: Missions Advanced Research and Communications Center, 1989), pp. 323–36.

6. *The Glorious Qur'an, Text and Explanatory Translation*, by Mohammed Marmaduke Pickthall (Mecca, Saudi Arabia: The Muslim World League, 1977), pp. 689–90.

7. *The Pearl of Great Price, Writings of Joseph Smith*, sect. 2, vv. 29–54.

8. J. Isamu Yamamoto, *The Puppet Master* (Downers Grove, Ill.: InterVarsity Press, 1977), p. 16.

9. Sultan Mohammed Paul, *Why I Became A Christian* (Bombay, India: Gospel Book House, n.d.).

10. George Otis Jr., *The Last of the Giants* (Tarrytown, N.Y.: Chosen Books, Fleming Revell, 1991).

11. Bush.

12. Bush.

13. Jonathan Edwards, *A Humble Attempt to Promote Explicit Agreement and Visible Union of God's People in Extraordinary Prayer for the Revival of Religion and the Advancement of Christ's Kingdom on Earth* (New York, 1844).

# PRAYER AND WORSHIP: OUR TOOLS FOR RESPONDING TO ISLAM

*by John Haines*

Of all the tools we find helpful in testifying of our faith to our Muslim neighbor, one is fundamental. And I believe that anyone witnessing to Muslims will agree with what I continually rediscover. The instrument most needed is prayer.

Imagine that you are building an object from rough wood. You work from a preconceived plan, a design, because you want to get into the mind of the designer. In our case, the designer is our Father in heaven. God directs the final appearance of our work in the people he brings across our path, and we work with them through his Spirit's skill. But God also designed the individual tools for the building process. These are the principles of evangelism set forth in the Bible.

In prayer, we discover both the master plan and the method. All of the other tools depend upon our effective use of this fundamental instrument. Without prayer, we will make only a half-hearted start.

## ISLAM'S CONCEPT OF WORSHIP

At the very heart of prayer, we find the biblical doctrine of worship. We bow before our great and holy God, our Father. We come before God on behalf of our Muslim friend. And only then do we speak. Our communication is at risk almost immediately, however, because of the very different concepts of worship in Islam and Christianity.

The Muslim Creed is fundamental to what any Muslim believes. It states: "I testify that there is no god but Allah, and that Muhammad is the Apostle of God." Here, as elsewhere in the Qur'an, the names of God and Muhammad are placed side by side. No other prophet receives such honor in Islam. Yet our friend claims to believe in the equality of all prophets under God. This link of the name of Muhammad with that of God is seen often in the Qur'an.[1] In the actual practice of popular Islam, the use of the Creed can bring the Muslim dangerously close to shirk, which means the association of another with the one unique God.

## THE BIBLICAL CONCEPT OF WORSHIP

We, then, need to do some serious thinking about the nature of worship. What are the implications of our concept of worship? Or of our Muslim neighbor's actual practice of worship? God intended from the beginning of history that we

---

John Haines, along with his wife Margy, has proclaimed the gospel to Muslims for more than thirty-two years. They began their service with Arab World Ministries in North Africa in 1970. Since then, they have been ministering to Muslim immigrants in France.

Adapted from John Haines, *Good News for Muslims* (Upper Darby, Pa.: Middle East Resources, 1998), pp.17–25. Used by permission. *www.awm.org*

should worship him and his Son, Jesus Christ. John was the great apostle of the deity of Christ. He shows us Jesus' deity very clearly in the climax of his writings, the book of Revelation. In Revelation 4, we are directed toward the eternal God, seated on his throne. Worship is offered to him. The scene suddenly changes in chapter 5. Now the Lamb, Jesus, is on center stage. He also receives worship (Rev. 5:12–14). All of the capacities and achievements of mankind are to be poured out like the ointment of Mary at the feet of Jesus. In the flow of the sentence structure in Greek, suddenly one word stands out: "worthy" (*axion*). Jesus is worthy. Why? "Because you were slain" (5:9). No other prophet can claim this. Our Lord Jesus Christ merits the sevenfold offering described in verse 12: he receives "'power and wealth and wisdom and strength and honor and glory and praise!'" As we grow in worship of Christ, and bring this kind of offering daily to his feet, we put on spiritual armor for ministry. Our hearts

## PARADISE AND HELL

The Qur'an demands that people believe in God. God will judge, and he promises paradise or hell. Righteousness and obedience lead to the garden of paradise.

> As to those who believe and work righteousness, verily we shall not suffer to perish the reward of any who do a (single) righteous deed. For them will be gardens of eternity; beneath them rivers will flow. They will be adorned therein with bracelets of gold, and they will wear green garments of fine silk and heavy brocade. They will recline therein on raised thrones. How good the recompense! How beautiful a couch to recline on! (Sura 18:30–31, YUSUF ALI)

Paradise is a place that offers both physical and sensual delights, whereas hell is a place of fire and torture.

> But the sincere (and devoted) servants of Allah, for them is a sustenance determined, fruits (delights); and they (shall enjoy) honor and dignity in gardens of felicity, facing each other on thrones (of dignity). Round will be passed to them a cup from a clear-flowing fountain, crystal-white, of a taste delicious to those who drink (thereof), free from headiness, nor will they suffer intoxication therefrom. And besides them will be chaste women, restraining their glances, with big eyes (of wonder and beauty). As if they were (delicate) eggs closely guarded. (Sura 37:40–49, YUSUF ALI)

> (Can those in such bliss) be compared to such as shall dwell forever in the fire, and be given to drink boiling water, so that it cuts up their bowels (to pieces)? (Sura 47:15b, YUSUF ALI)

> For the rejecters we have prepared chains, yokes, and a blazing fire. (Sura 76:4, YUSUF ALI)

In the Qur'an, there is no provision for deathbed repentance.

> Of no effect is the repentance of those who continue to do evil, until death faces one of them, and he says, "Now have I repented indeed"; nor of those who die rejecting faith: for them have we prepared a punishment most grievous. (Sura 4:18, YUSUF ALI)

Source: Annee W. Rose, *www.frontiers.org*.

© Caleb Project

"I Am the Bread of Life" (John 6:35)

prayer. Yet I began to realize that we were falling into a very predictable rut. Our Bible study time would always fill its allotted period, or, spill over. Little by little, worship and intercession were squeezed out.

Yet "always keep on praying" is the last weapon on the list in Ephesians 6:10–18. Look at the Great Commission itself. In Matthew's Gospel, it is preceded by a time of spontaneous, Spirit-guided worship (Matt. 28:17). How could we have missed the point? Yet we did, and we do. It is essential also to restore the broken walls of worship in our lives.

focus on Christ in worship. Then we move into action in prayer.

What is our goal in this prayer? We have seen that Christ is not at the center of our Muslim neighbor's vision. Christ will become that vital spiritual focal point only as Muslims center their worship on him. This is because the Lord Jesus alone is worthy of it, as the Lamb of God. As his witnesses, we come to God in worship and intercession. Then God's Spirit breaks up the hard soil of the heart of our friend.

## WORSHIP AND PRAYER: OUR PROTECTION

One summer a youth team met to prepare for outreach to the many Muslims in a large city. Each morning we aimed at putting on our armor for the spiritual battle through a time of Bible study and

During the eight years my wife and I spent in Grenoble, France, I was the only non-Frenchman among the elders of our church. There were many times when we came to our Monday evening prayer meetings burdened with some daily concern. We were sometimes aware of a difference of opinion. Yet there was never any open, lasting breach of unity. The basic reason was that the Holy Spirit had drawn us to Christ and to one another in our worship of him. Our opening seasons of adoring Christ so often melted us together.

## WORSHIP, THE GUARD OF THE CENTRALITY OF CHRIST

Our various Muslim ministry teams in Europe and elsewhere deliberately allow adequate time for worship. In so doing, we guard the centrality of Christ in our life and witness. After the apostle John tells us that the Lamb is worthy, he spells out in sevenfold detail exactly what this means: "Worthy is the Lamb who was slain, to receive power and wealth and wisdom and strength and honor and glory and praise!" (Rev. 5:12).

As we wait before our heavenly Father in worship, often we are led to action. For example, we may be made aware that our riches are not being used in the right way. Perhaps our attitude toward another person has not been honoring to the Lord. God may give us new wisdom in developing a relationship with a Muslim friend.

Worship opens spiritual doors. Learn anew to worship Jesus the Son of God. That worship will inevitably reach out to the Muslims whom God, in his providence, has placed at your doorstep.

Now I want to underline three aspects of this vast, biblical doctrine of prayer which I have found pertinent to my own ministry in friendship evangelism.

## THE CONFLICT OF PRAYER

Have you ever had this experience? You have just come to the place of prayer. You anticipate beginning a time of communion with the Lord. Suddenly, you remember a little chore that needs finishing. Or a nagging inner voice tells you of the note that you must jot down before something is forgotten. Before you know it, your mind has begun to wander. Suddenly you realize that you have wandered aimlessly down some corridor of thought. We all have experiences like that daily. Why?

The answer is found in Ephesians 6. Paul describes a great battle going on between us and a satanic host of "spiritual forces of evil in the heavenly realms" (vs. 12). Our victory in the fight involves taking the armor that is provided for us. It also requires us to "pray in the Spirit on all occasions, with all kinds of prayers and requests" (vs. 18). When you begin to intercede, the diversion you experience is a deliberate assault by the enemy.

Prayer involves conflict! How easy it will be to ease up in your advances against Satan's stronghold in the heart of your Muslim friend. So many good activities will compete for the essential one: prayer. The Lord Jesus Christ must make each of us his "good soldiers" in the incessant daily warfare. Then we become like Paul who said: "For I would have you know in how severe a struggle I am engaged on behalf of you" (Col. 2:1, WEYMOUTH).

## THE MINISTRY OF PRAYER

Does not each of us long to be of some practical use to the Lord? Yet we wonder if our prayers are really important. Do you honestly feel that the time spent before the throne of God is a ministry?

You may remember Paul's lesser-known friend Epaphras. Paul said that Epaphras was "always wrestling in prayer" and "working hard" for the church at Colosse (Col. 4:12–13). He had a special burden for the believers in this small, declining town in Asia Minor, so he worked fervently in prayer for them. Where was Paul at the time? In some comfortable office? No, he and Epaphras were prisoners in a Roman jail. Did their restricted circum-

stances keep them from any kind of a ministry to the Colossians? No, in fact, God's servants had a very real and important work among them right from their prison cell: "We have not stopped praying for you and asking God to fill you" (Col. 1:9). Paul and Epaphras faithfully performed a solid, lasting ministry by prayer and saw a great work of God accomplished.

William Carey once spoke of his field in India as a spiritual gold mine in which he planned to dig. But he was quick to add: "You at home must hold the ropes." Your witness to a Muslim friend is like digging for gold or hunting lost treasure. Yet it must begin with prayer. Prayer is a real ministry, however invisible it may be to those around you. It is certainly neither a waste of time nor an exercise in futility.

## THE REWARD OF PRAYER

We are often tempted to think that it does not really pay to spend time in prayer. There are so many other demands upon our time. Yet our Great High Priest gives us great dividends as we come to God by him. Not the least of these is the absolute delight of actually seeing God answer our prayers. Several days before we first sailed for Casablanca in 1964, my wife and I were reading the daily devotion, *Daily Light*, together (for April 16). We saw three tremendous Old Testament illustrations of answer to prayer. Pause for a moment to consider Jabez, Solomon, and Asa.

Jabez prayed and God gave him protection from his enemies and enlargement

of his portion in the Promised Land. Solomon prayed and God so answered that he remains unequaled in human history for wisdom. Asa prayed and God struck a mighty Ethiopian army before him. Talk about answers! Our prayers often seem quite feeble and faithless. Then we are pleasantly surprised as God repeatedly allows us to see him specifically answer. Perhaps God smiles then at our low estimate of ourselves—and himself.

No effective evangelism can progress against the great stronghold of Islam without the heavenly view brought by worship and prayer. This is especially true for the spiritual conflict going on in the lives of our Muslim neighbors. If Christ is not given his proper place, a vacuum is formed deep within a person. Some other person or thing must rush in to fill it.

The first essential tool, then, is to examine the heart of the Designer. We discover what is in the heart of our Heavenly Father through prayer. We enter anew into a ministry of prayer for others. Remember that the ministry that God has given you in prayer is an authentic one. It is just as real as the ministry which he has given you when you are off your knees, talking to your Muslim friend.

 **End of Key Readings for Lesson 12. See** RECOMMENDED READINGS & ACTIVITIES **on p. 465.**

## ENDNOTE

1. For example, in Sura 9 we often find the expression, *Allah wa rasulihi*, "God and his Prophet," that is, Muhammad.

# WHAT WILL IT TAKE TO WIN MUSLIMS?

*by Patrick O. Cate*

Just over a century ago (1890), Samuel Zwemer began his work among Muslims in the Middle East, when there were perhaps some 300 million Muslims worldwide. He labored in the cause of Muslim evangelism for more than fifty years and fully expected to see the collapse of Islam, but it did not come. After the Gulf War, some other people predicted a sudden collapse. However, no such crumbling has occurred. Rather, today there are almost one billion Muslims, and their religion continues to thrive.

After these disappointments, what will it finally take to win Muslims? More persistent prayer, of course, but also more of the right kind of missionaries and new action and more commitment to Muslim evangelism among our western church and mission agencies.

## REVISING OUR PRIORITIES

One of the basic reasons Muslims have not come to faith in Christ is that they have not heard of Christ, and one of the basic reasons they have not heard of Christ is that missionaries have not gone to tell them about Christ. One of the basic reasons missionaries have not gone to tell them about Christ is that the church has not seriously prayed to the Lord of the harvest to press laborers forward, out into the Muslim fields. Are Muslims, who make up one out of every five people in the world, on our daily prayer lists?

Of course, some people automatically think of all the barriers to Muslim evangelism, especially the political ones, such as the inability to obtain visas for work in predominantly Muslim countries. But in countries where Muslims are a minority, one can easily get and keep a visa. And you can spend one hundred percent of your time working with these Muslims. You do not have to use a tentmaking job that restricts your time for evangelism. Sometimes these Muslim minorities are more responsive to Christ than they are in their home countries, so we need to do some sharp thinking about reaching displaced or immigrant Muslims.

Mission agencies also need to think about developing new ministries in countries where Muslims constitute the majority. Some agencies work in such countries, but are not doing anything to reach Muslims. They are reaching professing Christians, or other minorities, the "easier people." We will never know about some doors, unless we knock, shake, or kick them a bit. We always ought to be pushing on doors to see what will happen. Sometimes, after years of pushing, they open.

Dr. Patrick O. Cate is president of Christar, formerly International Missions, Inc. (IMI). Christar has been working with Muslim peoples in twenty countries for more than seventy years. *www.christar.org*

Adapted from Patrick O. Cate, "What Will It Take to Win Muslims?" *Evangelical Missions Quarterly*, 28, no. 3 (Wheaton, Ill.: Evangelical Missions Information Service, July 1992), pp. 230–34. Used by permission. *www.billygrahamcenter.org/emis*

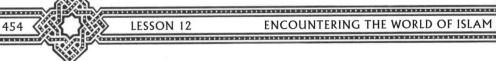
We have workers among Muslims who recently had to leave their country after twenty-three years. In their first fifteen years they did not see a single one of them come to faith in Christ. But they did not quit because they were called by God to be faithful. Between their fifteenth and twenty-third years, hundreds of Muslims made decisions for Christ. Today 4,500 people in that needy Muslim country are taking Bible correspondence courses because of their ministry. A church, comprised of Muslim converts with indigenous leadership, has been planted. What if they had quit earlier? It is going to take prayer, shaking some doors, perseverance, and trust in God to see the harvest.

## RECRUITING LONG-TERMERS

Mission agencies focusing on Muslim lands need to figure out how to capture a new generation of missionary recruits to work in countries where quick, easy responses are not forthcoming. These people do exist; in my visits to churches and schools I have found some who believe that God's standard is faithfulness, not immediate results. Missionary recruiters need to ask what it will take to enable workers to have the long-term commitment needed to reach Muslims. What will it take for workers to gain the attitude of leaving their bones on the mission field, if God would so permit?

One of the keys to reaching Muslims is relationships. It takes time for relationships to develop, and repeated visits. On the other hand, we need to be careful of only developing friendships but never sharing Christ.

We also must recognize that some people with tentmaking skills tend to go out with only a three- to five-year commitment. Sometimes, sadly, they are more interested in developing professionally than in using their skills to penetrate the culture and the country with the gospel. Sometimes their desire for career security and professional development can make them too timid in witnessing. Tentmakers need to be trained in the how of Muslim evangelism, in biblical and theological foundations, and in the ethics of tentmaking.

## FACING OTHER CHALLENGES

We need to mobilize prayer, not only for Muslims to believe and for more workers, but also for religious freedom and human rights. Mission agencies and churches could sponsor days of prayer and fasting for the Muslim world.

One of the challenges in the Muslim world is that the good is often the enemy of the best. It is so easy to spend our time doing good things. This is true any place, of course, but it seems to be intensified in the Muslim world. We can give ourselves to the mechanics of living, to our jobs, to team responsibilities, to mission paper work, and really end up not logging very many hours, either in language study during the first years, or in ministry to Muslims later on.

We need accountability. What level have we reached on the language proficiency checklist? How many hours a week do we study the language during our first years? After that, how many hours a week do we spend with Muslims? What is the quality

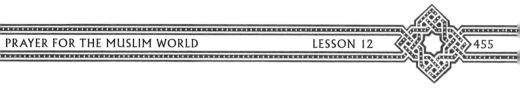
of our relationships and the quality of our sharing Christ with Muslims?

## UNDERSTANDING THE MUSLIM MIND

There is another pitfall we must avoid: always studying Islam and never evangelizing Muslims. It really can be said that Islam is the most studied and least evangelized religion. The number of books on comprehending Islam is phenomenal. Much has been said and written to help us understand the Muslim mind, but we need to be careful, lest we merely become scholars, divorcing our scholarship from the Great Commission.

On the other hand, before they go and while they are on furlough, people need to sharpen their biblical, theological, and ministry skills, and sometimes their secular skills as well. In his book, *America, Oil, and the Islamic Mind,*[1] Michael Youssef says, "The crisis is the gulf between our ways of thinking." If we will give ourselves to better understanding the Muslim mind, we will gain valuable help in sharing Christ with Muslims. This means not just understanding classical Islam, but also animism, because each Muslim is to some

## ENCOURAGING MUSLIM FRIENDS TO PUT THEIR TRUST IN JESUS CHRIST

We want our Muslim friends to put their faith in Jesus Christ, and we know only God can effect that decision, but what is our part in this? We encourage, we pray, we answer questions, we even gently persuade and encourage them to decide, but ultimately we rely on Jesus Christ and entrust our friends to him. Our confidence in Christ and his sovereign will frees us to be constructive patient friends.

- Pray! God can redirect a heart.
- Share how God is changing you.
- Pray with them for their needs.
- Encourage them to pray with you about their needs.
- Listen carefully to their questions.
- Pray that God will give you wise answers.
- Encourage them to read the Bible.
- Pray that God will enable them to understand his Word.
- Patiently claim God's promises of mercy and grace.
- Pray that God will allow them to receive his gift of new life through Christ.

Many times we are apprehensive about asking our friends if they want to believe in Jesus. We may fear that they will reject Jesus and our friendship, so we repeatedly postpone asking until another time. As a result, we present Christ, we share the gospel, we give our testimony, but we neglect to offer the gift of the gospel and ask them to accept it. Despite our awkwardness and fear, we who have experienced peace in Christ can invite others to believe: trusting the Holy Spirit's prompting, ask, "Do you want to accept Jesus Christ as your Lord and Savior?"

Source: *Encountering the World of Islam*

degree animistic. Animism has influenced the whole fiber of Islam.

As we grow in our understanding of Islam, we learn that it is quite pluralistic, with differing shades of religious and political beliefs. For instance, many Muslims are against Islamic fundamentalism and Shari'a law.

Sadly, one of the reasons more Muslims do not respond to the gospel is that some missionaries have not really learned the Muslim mind. They may have read one or two books or taken a course on Islam, but that is not enough.

## Sending our Best Quality

One worker who has spent a lifetime in the Muslim world, and who has nurtured and led more than two hundred missionaries to work among Muslims, made an interesting observation. He said that although we have many more workers than in the days of Zwemer and the other pioneers, in terms of quality, Zwemer and company beat us hands down. Today, he

said, we do not have people like Temple Gairdner (1873–1928, Church Missionary Society, Cairo), or Samuel Zwemer, who combined their sharp minds with a love for people and a passion for God.

He suggested that we generally ignore some of the best sources of candidates and said we should recruit Christian students at Harvard, Yale, Princeton, the University of Chicago, the University of California at Berkeley, and so on. Some feel we should also recruit more at seminaries, because not only do we need sharp minds, we need workers who can handle some of the theological issues that separate one billion Muslims from faith in Christ. Some seminary students possess secular degrees and secular professional backgrounds. We need to encourage these people to pursue opportunities in Muslim countries.

## Managing Discouragement

What about power encounter in winning Muslims? It is surprising for many evangelicals to learn that a large percentage of Muslim converts have had a dream in

## Faithful Witness

On a trip to Pakistan, Voice of the Martyrs director Tom White met an elderly gentleman who quietly, almost apologetically, shared this testimony:

> Every morning I get on a bus in our city. As the bus begins to move, I walk down the aisle and hand out gospel tracts. These have the simple message of Jesus, our Savior, who he is and why he came. People sitting in the bus have nothing to do. Many read them. Sometimes the Muslim men beat me. Usually by then, I have finished my outreach and am near the back door. They do me the great favor of throwing me out the door. I might bleed, but I have a handkerchief. So I find another bus, and begin again.

Courageous members of the persecuted church—Christians who risk their lives to share their faith—do not have to evangelize. They choose to witness.

Source: *www.cmmequip.org*

which Christ appeared to them and said something like, "I am the Way," or "Follow me." This has led them to find a Christian or a Bible, where they learned more about Jesus and put their faith in him.

However, we need to caution against going into Muslim areas expecting miracles to occur right and left. Thank God for the miracles we have seen and heard of, but some workers have left the field discouraged after four or five years because they saw no miracles, could not raise anyone from the grave, nor see anyone healed. They reasoned that they were not properly related to God, not properly gifted, or not called, and therefore quit.

Missionaries to Muslims have to believe that the gospel is the power of God unto salvation to everyone who believes (Rom. 1:16). Their faith must not rest in their ability to execute miracles and healings. Being filled with the Holy Spirit does not equal the ability to perform signs and wonders. Christ crucified is God's power (1 Cor. 1:22–24).

## REVIVING THE HISTORICAL CHURCHES?

Throughout most of the Muslim world there are historical churches, not made up of Muslim converts, such as Roman Catholics, Greek Orthodox, Armenians, Assyrians, and Copts. Some come from Hindu backgrounds. It could be argued that, over the last two centuries, a majority of missionaries going to the Muslim world to evangelize Muslims have

"I stand at the door and knock..." (Rev. 3:20)

© Caleb Project

spent most of their time evangelizing and discipling people from these historical churches. Compared to Muslims, they are easier to reach and more responsive. But the danger is that we will spend all our time trying to revive these churches and ignore the Muslims.

On the other hand, there is a tiny minority of people in some national churches who do work at Muslim evangelism. There is much we can learn from them. We should listen to them, work with them, and have them speak in our weekly mission gatherings, monthly meetings, and annual conferences. We cannot take a know-it-all attitude; we need to come as learners.

For example, I know of one national elder who has baptized about two hundred Muslim converts. We can learn much from people like him. A worthy goal would be to find at least one promising person in the national church. Have that person teach us culture and language, while the missionary teaches Muslim evangelism, praying that the national will catch the vision for it.

## Using Media for Penetration

We need to keep asking which media best communicate in the Muslim world and into specific countries. I lived in a middle-class (and near a lower-class) neighborhood in the Muslim world, and three video stores operated within two blocks of our home. Most Muslims read little, but they watch videos and television for hours. A Christian TV network, broadcasting from a satellite, could penetrate Muslim walls and be received by many more Muslims once they get receiving dishes.

The *Jesus* film possibly has been the medium used by God to lead more Muslims to faith in Christ in recent years than any other media tool. It has been translated into almost every major Muslim language.

However, better-trained workers and the latest technology will be of no avail unless mission agencies and churches consider their part in reaching Muslims. Agencies and churches need to look at their budgets and personnel, and ask what percentage is dedicated to reaching the one billion lost Muslims around the world. What part of their prayer life is devoted to asking God to open closed Muslim hearts and doors, and to send out new laborers? We need to take a hard look at our prayers, priorities, and preparation if we want to see Muslims won for Christ.

### Endnote

1. Michael Youssef, *America, Oil, and the Islamic Mind: The Real Crisis Is the Gulf Between Our Ways of Thinking* (Grand Rapids: Zondervan, 1991), page not cited.

# IBERO-AMERICANS REACHING ARAB MUSLIMS

*by Steven Downey*

"When you are called to report to the police in North Africa, you start packing. If you are lucky, they make you leave the country within twenty-four hours. If you are not so lucky, they put you in prison."

Rev. Marcos Amado, who leads Partners International, a Latin American mission agency, was relating a story about Carlos, a Partners International worker who had started a basketball team for disabled people in a North African country.

"So I guess my time is up here." The day came when Carlos had to report to the police chief in the capital city. The chief asked him if he was working in the country. Carlos said yes. The chief asked if he was helping the disabled; yes again. The police chief said, "I have called you here because my daughter has been helped by this program, and I want to thank you."

Carlos could hardly believe it. He had been having problems with his residency permit. The next day a policeman came to his house and delivered the permit.

Carlos is one of 6,500 Ibero-Americans—defined as Latin Americans, Portuguese, Spaniards, and North American Hispanics—who serve in more than one hundred countries from Albania to Zimbabwe. But in the post-September 11 world, perhaps the most significant place where Ibero-American missionaries serve is in Muslim-majority countries. Some also serve among Muslim people groups in countries such as India, where Islam is not the majority religion.

## SUITED FOR ARAB MUSLIM MINISTRY

The Ibero-American affinity with Muslims, at least superficially, is a natural one. The Ibero-American racial complexion is closer to that of Arabs than it is to North Americans and Europeans. Culturally, too, they are closer in how they perceive time, the concept of family, the importance of the group (versus individualism), and the preeminence of the spiritual over the material world.

"We can't say that it is the same in Latin America as it is in Jordan or Tunisia, but, generally speaking, most Latins are closer to Arab Muslim cultures than are people from western ones," Amado says.

Mr. Hugo Morales, partnership training coordinator for Cooperacion Misionera Iberoamericana (COMIBAM), a movement that mobilizes Ibero-American

Steven Downey is vice president of communications and marketing at Partners International, Spokane, Washington. *www.partnersintl.org*

Adapted from Steven Downey, "Ibero-Americans Reaching Arab Muslims," *World Pulse* 38, no. 5 (Wheaton, Ill.: Evangelical Missions Information Service, March 2003), pp. 1, 3. Used by permission. *www.billygrahamcenter.org/emis*

© Frontiers

Poise, elegance, and modesty are traits of Muslim women

through this training myself," Amado says. "It is five months of living in the country where the person is going to work, living with indigenous Muslim families, traveling by oneself, and studying the language four or five hours a day. It is tough, but in the end worth it. Some missionaries asked how I had learned so much after only five months in the country. A few had never taken a taxi or bus, nor traveled around the country."

mission work, believes there are historical, colonial, and economic reasons too. In A.D. 711, the Muslims of North Africa launched an invasion across the Strait of Gibraltar, occupying most of the Iberian Peninsula for more than seven centuries. The colonial ties of the peninsula stretch across to Latin America. Latin America and North Africa are closer to each other in living conditions than to those of the super-wealthy nations of the United States and Western Europe. Finally, "Ibero-Americans don't carry the political baggage of superpower status like U.S. citizens do," Morales says.

But Morales is quick to point out that, while these similarities make entry into North African cultures relatively easier, the longer Ibero-American missionaries stay, the more they realize that the challenges are almost as great as those faced by any missionary: learning the language, understanding cultural cues, dealing with hostility, educating children, and so forth.

It was partly this realization that led Partners International (PMI) to develop cross-cultural immersion training. "I went

The intense training pays off. On average, 50 percent of Ibero-American missionaries stay longer than three years; it is 90 percent for PMI missionaries. In 1999, Amado spearheaded the formation of the first Ibero-American Institute of Islamic Studies, a program that unites eighteen missionary organizations to train Spanish-speaking missionaries.

## ROOTS OF IBERO-AMERICAN MISSIONS

The roots of the movement that transformed Latin America from a mission field into a mission force go back to COMIBAM '87. This movement remains instrumental in mobilizing Ibero-American churches for global mission, and now operates with most of its resources coming from Ibero-America. In 1996, there were 3,900 Ibero-American missionaries; today there are 6,500. According to Ted Limpic of OC International, five hundred work in the Muslim world, ninety-two among Hindus, and eighty-seven in Buddhist countries.

Because most Muslim-majority nations forbid missionary work, tentmaking ministry is the best option. The type of work a missionary does determines the group of people among whom they will minister. "A good example is a Partners International worker, an engineer by trade, who designs water purification systems for needy communities," Amado says. "This puts him in contact with people of various social levels, principally the needy, and gives him a chance to share his faith."

Partners International recognizes that, to do ministry in poorer countries, one must engage in holistic witness. But Amado says, "We are not involved in community development projects only because they give us the opportunity to go into Muslim countries. We are involved in them because we believe that it is part of our mission as Christians. At the same time, we speak about Christ."

PMI's holistic projects, such as community outreach centers, water wells, and vocational training, are funded by Partners International and others. Partners International raises their worker support from Latin America, which Amado admits is a growing challenge. "Latin American economies are very unstable. Argentineans are suffering, and the Brazilian economy is not good. Churches are making the extra effort, but it is hard to keep up with 450 percent devaluation," Amado says. He recently sold his car to make ends meet.

In spite of the economic and spiritual challenges, the missions movement among Ibero-Americans is healthy. PMI has put teams in additional North African

## HOSPITALITY

Smiling faces greeted me along my morning walk to the palm grove—faces of the Bedouin women of this desert town in a poor African country. One lady, leaning on her hoe, greeted me from her garden, and we spoke of the weather as the cool of the morning lifted. We each wore a *malahfa*, eight yards of cotton wrapped from head to foot, and offering little protection from the heat. Guiltily, I realized that by lingering to talk, I had obligated her to invite me into her tent. I lay back on the floor mats and cushions, and we talked as she prepared *zrig*, a special drink made with costly canned milk instead of yogurt, mixed with warm water and sugar, and served from a goatskin flagon.

Many Muslim cultures value highly acts of kindness, hospitality, and generosity. A visit in a Muslim home is unforgettable: guests are treated as royalty and given the best the family can offer. Those who befriend Muslims may receive many such instances of hospitality, as well as opportunities for reciprocation.

Women guests need to act modestly, observing and imitating how other women behave in the home. (See "The Hijab" on p. 53.) We will not be heard, or even invited into Muslim homes, if, because of our dress or inappropriate interaction with men, we are judged to be untrustworthy women.

Source: Annee W. Rose, *www.frontiers.org*.

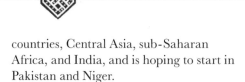

countries, Central Asia, sub-Saharan Africa, and India, and is hoping to start in Pakistan and Niger.

Morales points to a new trend: Ibero-Americans are hearing God's call to India, especially to the Dalits (untouchables).

"As a continent that has known poverty and the oppression of an unspoken class system, we are able to identify with and speak to the spiritual and material plight of the Dalits. Ibero-Americans are waking up to the reality of doing mission in the difficult places of the world."

# OVERCOMING A MILLENNIUM OF HATE

*by Luis Bush*

Mina was born into a religious Jewish family in Israel. Her parents never allowed the name of Jesus to be spoken in her home, and she was taught that Arabs want to hurt Jews and cannot be trusted.

In her early twenties, Mina spent a year traveling in South Africa. Near the end of her journey, she surrendered her life to Jesus Christ. Upon returning home to Haifa, she was led to join Carmel Assembly, where she grew in the Lord.

Eight years later she took a job marketing cosmetics door to door, including many Arab homes. To her surprise, many Arabs welcomed her, and she even made new friends. But not so with Muslims who were militant about their faith. The mutual distrust and clashing of spirits made her very uncomfortable.

One day, while in prayer, she told the Lord, "I hate the Muslims, and I don't want to go see them again." The Lord made it clear to her that she should love everyone. "If you want me to love everyone," she replied, "I pray that you will do that by the power of the Holy Spirit, because I cannot do this myself."

A year later, the Lord led her to attend the Israel College of the Bible in Jerusalem. One day while she was touring the Old City an amazing thing happened. She overheard a Muslim merchant arguing with another man. She went up to him and asked why he was yelling.

He replied, "Because he didn't want to buy from me!" She asked again and the merchant glared at her in speechless anger. She saw in his eyes all the cultural and religious hatred that was tearing apart their homeland. He spun around and stormed away, shouting, "We will get your country one day!"

Mina's Israeli side recoiled in fear, but to her great amazement, she was filled with compassion and the love of the Lord for the angry merchant. Catching up with him, she said, "I don't hate you. Why did you speak to me like that? You really hurt me." When the merchant saw the kindness in her eyes, his anger faded. "I am so sorry I hurt you. My name is Ibrahim." She introduced herself and offered to come visit him some day.

---

Born in Argentina and raised in Brazil, Luis and his wife Doris moved to El Salvador to pastor a local church. Luis coordinated an Ibero-American mission-mobilization initiative called COMIBAM, after which he served as CEO of Partners International. He then became the International Director of the AD2000 & Beyond Movement and currently serves as the International Facilitator for Transform World: Indonesia 2005.

Adapted from AD2000 & Beyond Movement, "One Person's Journey: Mina's Story," *Shalom-Salam: The Pursuit of Peace in the Biblical Heart of the 10/40 Window* (Colorado Springs: AD2000 & Beyond Movement, n.d.), p. 10. Used by permission. *www.ad2000.org*

On that day, the Lord had answered her prayer for love. His love had cut through generations of pent-up hatred and mistrust. Ibrahim's eyes were opened to the light of Christ's love shining through the eyes of an Israeli woman. And Mina's heart had been filled with godly love for Arabs, including Muslims.

Through that encounter, Mina also saw the answer to the troubles infesting her homeland—the great power of God's love. As Mina herself says, "The only way Arabs and Jews can be united is through belief in the Lord Jesus Christ. We can only pray that more and more Muslims and Jews will come to know him."

**End of Basic Readings for Lesson 12. See** RECOMMENDED READINGS & ACTIVITIES **on p. 465.**

**Go to:** *www.encounteringislam.org/ readings* **to find the Full Readings for Lesson 12.**

## Muslim Widow Arrives for Divine Appointment

*by G. Johnson*

I was asked to preach at a small church. The service went well, but a flat tire delayed my leaving. As I waited for repairs, an elderly Muslim widow with her two orphaned grandchildren shyly entered the church. She had come to seek Jesus, and told me she had two unusual dreams the week before. In the first, she was among other Muslims praying, and one man had the Qur'an open. On the other side of a river, she saw Christians holding the Bible and beckoning her to come and hear the Word of God. She wanted to cross the river, but the Muslims told her she would be thrown out of her family and society.

As she crossed the river to the Christians, she looked back and saw that the Qur'an had turned totally blank. The Christians shared the Word with her, and when the Muslims began to seek her, she found safety among the Christians.

In her second dream, she had just completed her final prayer of the day and fallen asleep when she was approached by a man in a hat, carrying a stick (a typical shepherd). This man called her to come to him so he could pray for her. She did not understand everything he said, but there was bright light everywhere, and she felt deep joy. She knew this shepherd must be Jesus, the Messiah.

When she shared her dreams with her late husband's brother, he ran her and the children out of the house. On this morning, she happened to pass by the church and decided this was the time to come to Jesus Christ. She prayed and accepted Jesus as her Savior! She has no idea how she will survive on her own, but says she needed to be faithful to the one who had come to her in her dream.

Source: *www.sim.org.*

# DISCUSSION QUESTIONS

1. Think of a time when you really worked at prayer. What helped you focus in that situation and energized you to enlist others to pray?

2. What keeps you motivated to pray?

# RECOMMENDED READINGS & ACTIVITIES*

Read: J. Christy Wilson, *More to Be Desired Than Gold*, 4th ed. (South Hamilton, Mass.: Gordon-Conwell BookCentre, 1998).

Bilquis Sheikh, *I Dared to Call Him Father* (Grand Rapids: Chosen Books, 2003).

Watch: A Caleb Project video highlighting a Muslim people group, *www.calebproject.org.*

Pray: Use the book *Operation World* to pray for Muslim countries.

Visit: Invite a Muslim friend to your home for tea or dessert.

Surf: Discover related web sites at *www.encounteringislam.org/lessonlinks.*

* For expanded details on these Recommended Readings & Activities, visit *www.encounteringislam.org/lessonlinks.*

# APPENDICES

# Appendix 1

# 99 Beautiful Names of God (Al-Asma Al-Husna)

The list is often memorized by Muslims and begun by saying "There is no God but one God" (Allah-la-ilaha-ila-Allah). Consider studying these biblical references to God's attributes with your Muslim friends.

| | ATTRIBUTE | ARABIC NAME | QUR'AN REFERENCE | BIBLE REFERENCE |
|---|---|---|---|---|
| 01 | The Gracious | Ar - Rahman | 1:1 | Ps. 103:8 |
| 02 | The Merciful | Ar - Rahim | 1:1 | Ps. 86:16 |
| 03 | The Sovereign King | Al - Malik | 59:23 | Zech. 14:9 |
| 04 | The Holy One | Al - Quddus | 59:23 | Ezek. 39:7 |
| 05 | The Source of Peace | Al - Salam | 59:23 | Isa. 9:6 |
| 06 | The Guardian of the Faith | Al – Mu´min | 59:23 | Lam. 3:22-23 |
| 07 | The Protector | Al – Muhaymin | 59:23 | John 10:1-18 |
| 08 | The Mighty Friend | Al - `Aziz | 59:23 | Ps. 24:8 |
| 09 | Omnipotent | Al - Jabbar | 59:23 | 2 Chron. 20:6 |
| 10 | The Most Great | Al - Mutakabbir | 59:23 | Deut. 33:26 |
| 11 | The Creator | Al - Khaliq | 59:24 | Gen. 1:1 |
| 12 | The Originator | Al – Bari´ | 59:24 | Mal. 2:10 |
| 13 | The Fashioner | Al - Musawwir | 59:24 | Col. 1:15-20 |
| 14 | The Forgiver | Al - Ghaffar | 38:66 | 2 Chron. 7:14 |
| 15 | The Subduer | Al - Qahhar | 12:39 | Deut. 9:3 |
| 16 | The Bestower | Al - Wahhab | 3:6-8 | Dan. 2:21-23 |
| 17 | The Provider | Al - Razzaq | 51:58 | Ps. 127:2 |
| 18 | The Opener | Al - Fattah | 34:26 | Rev. 3:7-8 |
| 19 | Omniscient | Al - `Alim | 6:71 | Ps. 139:1-2 |
| 20 | The Withholder, The Binder | Al - Qabid | 2:245 | Rev. 3:7-8 |
| 21 | The Expander | Al - Basit | 2:245 | Job 36:16 |
| 22 | The Abaser | Al - Khafid | 58:5 | Ps. 94:10 Matt. 7:22-23 |
| 23 | The Exalter | Ar - Rafi´ | 40:15 | 1 Sam. 2:7 |
| 24 | The Honorer | Al - Mu`izz | 3:26 | 1 Sam. 2:30 |
| 25 | The Dishonorer | Al - Muzill | 3:26 | 1 Cor. 1:27 |
| 26 | The All-Hearing | As - Sami` | 2:127 | Isa. 59:1 |
| 27 | The All-Seeing | Al - Basir | 17:1 | Deut. 11:12 |
| 28 | The Judge | Al - Hakam | 22:69 | Ps. 7:11 |
| 29 | The Just | Al - `Adl | 6:115 | Deut. 32:4 |

Continued

| 30 | The Kind One | Al - Latif | 6:103 | Rom. 2:4 |
| 31 | The Aware One | Al - Khabir | 6:18 | Gen. 16:13 |
| 32 | The Forbearing | Al - Halim | 2:225 | Jer. 15:15 |
| 33 | The Mighty One | Al - `Azim | 2:255 | Jer. 32:18 |
| 34 | The All-Forgiving | Al - Ghafur | 2:225 | Dan. 9:9,10 |
| 35 | The Most High | Al - `Ali | 2:255 | 2 Sam. 22:14 |
| 36 | The Appreciator | Ash - Shakur | 35:30 | Rom. 2:29 |
| 37 | The Great One | Al - Kabir | 34:23 | Ps. 145:5 |
| 38 | The Preserver | Al - Hafiz | 11:57 | John 10:28 |
| 39 | The Sustainer | Al - Muqit | 4:85-88 | Ps. 136:25 |
| 40 | The Reckoner | Al - Hasib | 4:6-7 | Heb. 11:18 |
| 41 | The Sublime One | Al - Jalil | 55:78 | Ex. 15:11 |
| 42 | The Bountiful One | Al - Karim | 82:6 | Deut. 28:12 |
| 43 | The Watchful | Ar - Raqib | 4:1 | Gen. 28:15 |
| 44 | The Responsive [to prayers] | Al - Mujib | 11:61-64 | John 14:14 |
| 45 | The All-Embracing | Al - Wasi` | 5:54 | John 3:17 |
| 46 | The Wise | Al - Hakim | 59:24 | 1 Cor 1:25 |
| 47 | The Loving | Al - Wadud | 11:90 | 2 Cor. 13:11 |
| 48 | The Most Glorious | Al - Majid | 11:73 | Jude 25 |
| 49 | The Resurrector | Al - Ba´ith | 22:7 | John 11:25 |
| 50 | The Witness | Ash - Shaheed | 4:33 | Rev. 1:5 |
| 51 | The Truth | Al - Haqq | 22:6 | John 14:6 |
| 52 | The Trustee | Al - Wakil | 4:81 | Gen. 1:16 |
| 53 | The Most Strong | Al - Qawi | 11:66 | Prov. 18:10 |
| 54 | The Firm One | Al - Matin | 51:58 | Ps. 102:25 |
| 55 | The Protecting Friend | Al - Wali | 3:68 | John 15:15 |
| 56 | The Praiseworthy | Al - Hamid | 14:1 | Rev. 19:5 |
| 57 | The Reconcilor | Al - Muhsi | 19:93-95 | 2 Cor. 5:18 |
| 58 | The Originator | Al - Mubdi | 10:34 | Gen. 1:1 |
| 59 | The Restorer | Al - Mu`id | 10:34 | Luke 6:10 |
| 60 | The Giver of Life | Al - Muhyi | 10:34 | John 11:26 |
| 61 | The Giver of Death | Al - Mumit | 2:28 | 1 Sam. 2:6 |
| 62 | The Alive | Al - Hayy | 2:255 | Rev. 1:17-18 |
| 63 | The Self-Subsisting | Al - Qayyum | 2:255 | John 17:5,24 |
| 64 | The Finder | Al - Wajid | 16:45-46 | Ps. 89:20 |
| 65 | The Noble | Al - Majid | 85:15 | Job 22:12 |
| 66 | The Unique One | Al - Wahid | 12:39 | John 1:14 |

| 67 | The One | Al - Ahad | 112:1 | Eph. 4:6 |
| 68 | The Eternal | Al - Samad | 112:2 | Gen. 21:33 |
| 69 | The Able [Capable] | Al - Qadir | 30:54 | Jer. 32:17 |
| 70 | The Determiner | Al - Muqtadir | 54:42 | Acts 2:23,24 |
| 71 | The Expediter | Al - Muqaddim | Hadith | Isa. 10:5-7 |
| 72 | The Delayer | Al – Mu´akhkhir | 71:4 | 2 Peter 3:8,9 |
| 73 | The First | Al - Awwal | 57:3 | Isa. 44:6 |
| 74 | The Last | Al - Akhir | 57:3 | Rev. 2:8 |
| 75 | The Manifest | Al - Zahir | 57:3 | Rom. 1:17-20 |
| 76 | The Hidden | Al - Batin | 57:3 | Col. 1:26 |
| 77 | The Governor | Al - Wali | 13:11 | Ps. 66:5,7 |
| 78 | The Most Exalted | Al - Muta`ali | 13:9 | Phil. 2:9 |
| 79 | The Source of All Goodness | Al - Barr | 52:28 | Ps. 84:11 |
| 80 | The Acceptor of Repentance | At - Tawwab | 2:37 | Rom. 2:4 |
| 81 | The Avenger | Al - Muntaqim | 32:22 | Ps. 94:1 |
| 82 | The Pardoner | Al - `Afuw | 4:43 | Mic. 7:16 |
| 83 | The Compassionate | Ar - Rauf | 2:143 | Ps. 116:5 |
| 84 | The King of Kings | Al - Malik Al - Mulk | 3:26 | 1 Tim. 6:15 |
| 85 | The Lord of Majesty and Bounty | Dhul - Jalali Wal - Ikram | 55:78 | Ps. 8:1 |
| 86 | The Equitable | Al - Muqsit | 3:18 | Prov. 11:1 |
| 87 | The Gatherer | Al - Jami´ | 3:9 | Isa. 56:8 |
| 88 | The Self Sufficient | Al - Ghani | 60:6 | Ps. 50:9,10 |
| 89 | The Enricher | Al - Mughni | 9:28 | Col. 1:27 |
| 90 | The Preventor | Al - Mani` | 5:24-26 | Mal. 3:11 |
| 91 | The Propitious | An - Nafi` | 10:107 | Gen. 6:8 |
| 92 | The Distresser | Al - Dharr | 2:155-157 | Judg. 2:15 |
| 93 | The Light | Aln - Nur | 24:35 | Isa. 60:19 |
| 94 | The Guide | Al - Hadi | 25:31 | John 16:13 |
| 95 | The Purpose Setter [the Originator] | Al – Badi` | 2:117 | Rom. 8:28 |
| 96 | The Everlasting | Al - Baqi | 55:27 | Ps. 102:27 |
| 97 | The Inheritor | Al - Warith | 15:23 | Josh. 13:33 |
| 98 | The Guide to the Right Path | Ar - Rashid | 11:78 | Ps. 25:9 |
| 99 | The Patient One | As - Sabur | Hadith | 1 Tim. 1:16 |

For Further Study: David Bentley, *The 99 Beautiful Names of God: For All People of the Book* (Pasadena, Calif: William Carey Library, 1999) and J. K. Mellis, *Abu Sharif: The Mystery of the Hundredth Name* (Netherlands: Goël Publishing, 2000)

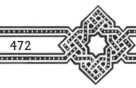

# READING THE QUR'AN CHRONOLOGICALLY

Reading the Qur'an or the Bible, neither of which are chronologically arranged, can be difficult until we gain a greater familiarity with their arrangement and content. While there is not a universally agreed upon chronology of either book, we have included this chronological Sura order to help familiarize Christians with the Qur'an and encourage its reading.

## EARLY MECCAN PERIOD: A.D. 610–612

1. 96
2. 74
3. 111
4. 106
5. 108
6. 104
7. 107
8. 102
9. 105
10. 92
11. 90
12. 94
13. 93
14. 97
15. 86
16. 91
17. 80
18. 68
19. 87
20. 95
21. 103
22. 85
23. 73
24. 101
25. 99
26. 82
27. 81
28. 53
29. 84
30. 100
31. 79
32. 77
33. 78
34. 88
35. 89
36. 75
37. 83
38. 69
39. 51
40. 52
41. 5
42. 70
43. 55
44. 112
45. 109
46. 113
47. 114
48. 1

## MIDDLE MECCAN PERIOD: A.D. 613–614

1. 54
2. 37
3. 71
4. 76
5. 44
6. 50
7. 20
8. 26
9. 15
10. 19
11. 38
12. 36
13. 43
14. 72
15. 67
16. 23
17. 21
18. 25
19. 17
20. 27
21. 18

## LATE MECCAN PERIOD: A.D. 615–621

1. 32
2. 41
3. 45
4. 16
5. 30
6. 11
7. 14
8. 12
9. 40
10. 28
11. 39
12. 29

## MEDINAN PERIOD:
### A.D. 622–623

| | | | | | |
|---|---|---|---|---|---|
| 13. | 31 | 1. | 2 | 12. | 59 |
| 14. | 42 | 2. | 98 | 13. | 33 |
| 15. | 10 | 3. | 64 | 14. | 63 |
| 16. | 34 | 4. | 62 | 15. | 24 |
| 17. | 35 | 5. | 8 | 16. | 58 |
| 18. | 7 | 6. | 47 | 17. | 22 |
| 19. | 46 | 7. | 3 | 18. | 48 |
| 20. | 6 | 8. | 61 | 19. | 66 |
| 21. | 13 | 9. | 57 | 20. | 60 |
| | | 10. | 4 | 21. | 110 |
| | | 11. | 65 | 22. | 49 |
| | | | | 23. | 9 |
| | | | | 24. | 5 |

# ARAB WORLD MINISTRIES

*www.awm.org*

**Motto**
Expressing faith in Christ through love for Muslims.

**Ministry emphasis**
Team-oriented ministries in media (radio, TV, and video), web sites, Bible correspondence courses, literature production and distribution, church planting, tentmaking and professional skills opportunities, transformational development, direct outreach, literature distribution, children's clubs, administrative support staff, and medical clinics and midwifery.

**Ethnic focus**
Peoples of the Arab world, including Arabs, Berbers, Kabyles, Kurds, Arabs in Europe and North America.

**What does your organization look for in those who will work among Muslims?**
Flexibility, long-term view, commitment to language acquisition and life-long training, proven ministry skills in home countries, ability to think and work "outside the box," a love for Muslims and a passion to share Christ with them.

**What is your most usual prayer request?**
First, for laborers to be sent to reap in the harvest fields. Next, for God's provision for new Muslim-background believers as they grow in their faith and adapt to the realities of living for Christ in an Islamic context.

**What is your greatest challenge in reaching Muslims?**
To find people who are willing and ready to do whatever it takes to see Muslims reached.

**Story of One**
The most exciting thing was to see how God is moving among the Kabyle Berbers in Algeria! I have never seen such joy and freedom in worship as in their meetings.

Most tell people boldly that they are Christians, heedless of opposition. Over the past twenty years the Holy Spirit has been bringing people to know Christ in many different ways. It seems that no one person or method is responsible for this movement. Rather, individuals spread the Word from town to town, village to village, with the result that people turned to Christ, and church groups sprang up all over the Kabyle mountains.

One man, a pastor and Christian leader, told me he thought there were probably one hundred churches there now, but no one really knows exactly sure how many churches there are, or how many converts.

Established in 1881; now with more than 200 workers.

# CALEB PROJECT

*www.calebproject.org*

## Motto
Equipping the church to reach the nations.

## Ministry emphasis
Mobilization–informing and educating about unreached people groups, providing resources (videos, prayer guides, training courses and manuals, and much more) to the church to help believers gain understanding, and facilitating short-term research trips that gather critical information to equip long-term workers.

## Ethnic focus
Any of the unreached people groups, many of them particularly Muslim, who have yet to hear of salvation in Jesus.

## What is your greatest challenge in reaching Muslims?
Just as with the greater task of reaching all remaining unreached people groups, communicating to the church the responsibility each believer carries for completing the Great Commission. In the current environment (post 9/11), the challenge is to help believers respond with love and courage, as opposed to fear.

## Story of One
Yousuf found the most precious gift of his life in the refugee center while waiting for permission to stay in the country. He has been reading the Bible and growing close to God while living in relative safety compared to the ongoing chaos, civil war, and atrocities in his African homeland of Sierra Leone. His body still bears scars of the inhumanity of humans, and his prospects for refugee status look good as he nears completion of the residency approval process.

Yousuf has been meeting with some fellow Muslims from West Africa and exploring with them the holy Injil and the idea of relationship with God through Jesus Christ. Some of his African brothers are beginning to respond to God's Word as well. Yet lately God has been tugging at Yousuf's heart through dreams, showing him the spiritual needs of his brothers and cousins back home. "Perhaps this is God's plan for me," Yousuf says. "I have found the precious gift of Jesus here. Maybe now Jesus will send me back with that gift for my family and people."

Excerpt from *Immigrants and Refugees: The New Faces of Europe Prayer Guide.*

Established in 1980; now with more than 75 workers.

# CHRISTAR

*www.christar.org*

## Motto
Bringing light to the least-reached.

## Ministry emphasis
Evangelism and church planting, medical, educational, and business ventures.

## Ethnic focus
Arab World, Turkic World, Eurasian, Chinese, Malay, Indo-Iranian, Indo-Aryan, Muslims in Europe, and Muslims in the United States.

## What is your greatest challenge in reaching Muslims?
Prayer for the Holy Spirit to convict people of the sin of unbelief in Jesus Christ as the Savior of the world.

## Story of One
One of our workers—through prayer, faithfulness, hard work, an education and medical ministry—has seen 646 Muslims make decisions for Christ over thirty years spent in one Asian town. This single woman teaches throughout Christar's one month al-Minar, or STOP (Summer Training and Outreach) program in Muslim Evangelism.

CHRISTAR®
Bringing light to the least-reached

Established in 1930; now with 200 workers.

# CRESCENT PROJECT

*www.crescentproject.org*

## Motto

Sharing the Hope with Muslims.

## Ministry emphasis

Equipping Christians, outreach through the local church, literature production.

## Ethnic focus

Muslims in the United States.

## What does your organization look for in those who will work among Muslims?

Faith that God can and will save Muslims, dedication and enthusiasm, commitment to loving Muslims through personal relationships.

## What is your most usual prayer request?

That Muslims would find salvation through Jesus Christ as Christians reach out to them in love.

## What is your greatest challenge in reaching Muslims?

Educating Christians that Muslims can be reached if we take the initiative to share the gospel appropriately.

## Story of One

Walid grew up in a Muslim family in Saudi Arabia. From an early age, a deep sense of spiritual emptiness consumed him. Once, while driving home from a pilgrimage to Mecca, he stopped his car along the side of the road, gazed out at the barren mountains, and in desperation prayed, "God of Abraham, reveal yourself to me!"

Walid continued his spiritual search after moving to the United States eight years ago. Several close Christian friends prayed faithfully for him, and two years ago he accepted Christ as Savior and Lord. Now he is on a mission to reach the hundreds of thousands of Muslims in Michigan. In his home church he leads a group of believers meeting weekly to reach out to Muslims nearby. While giving one of our staff a tour of his home church, he smiled and proclaimed, "God has given me a vision that this section of the sanctuary will one day be filled with Muslim-background believers like me!"

## CRESCENT
### PROJECT

Established in 1993; now with 11 workers.

# FRONTIERS

*www.frontiers.org*

## Motto

Our passion is to glorify God by planting churches among all Muslim peoples.

## Ministry emphasis

Our goal is to form communities of Jesus' disciples who demonstrate his love and serve their neighbors. Our singular focus enables us to pour our resources, experience, and growing expertise into this one objective.

## Ethnic focus

All Muslim peoples.

## What does your organization look for in those who will work among Muslims?

Our members are followers of Jesus practicing their professions in Muslim lands and sharing their faith when Muslims want to hear about it, as any believer would anywhere. We believe that young, relatively inexperienced people can, by God's grace, see Christ-like communities formed in the Muslim world—provided they are eager for accountability, teaching, counsel, and advice from those who are more experienced.

## What is your most usual prayer request?

We pray that God will open the hearts of Muslims to the same newness of life in Jesus that has reached through history—from the Middle East, across many cultures—and touched our hearts.

## What is your greatest challenge in reaching Muslims?

Prejudice. Centuries of misunderstanding between Islam and the West have clouded relationships on the streets and in coffee shops all over the world to this very day.

## Story of One

The imam was canvassing the neighborhood, inviting everyone to the mosque. When he discovered I wasn't Muslim, we discussed the Bible a bit and he left, saying, "May God guide you into Islam." I said, "May God lead you into truth as well."

A week later, he returned, saying he had been touched by my response. We talked more and made another appointment. When two of his colleagues arrived without him the next day, I was disappointed. I had felt a real connection with the imam. Late in their visit, I felt God's Spirit nudge me to ask, "Would you mind if I prayed for you?" Thanking him for our time together, I asked Father God to bless them each by name. In response, they muttered prayers of cleansing, as though they wanted to wipe away the contamination of my prayers in the name of Jesus.

Each time I pass by his mosque, I pray for Abu Suleiman.

Established in 1982; now with more than 90 teams living throughout the Muslim world.

# OPERATION MOBILIZATION

*www.om.org*

**Motto**
Bringing hope to the peoples of the world.

**Ministry emphasis**
Evangelism, relief and development, discipleship, church planting.

**Ethnic focus**
Arab world, Turkic world, Indo-Iranian peoples, Indo-Aryan peoples; Muslims in Europe, Australia, and South America.

**What is your greatest challenge in reaching Muslims?**
We have more opportunities than recruits.

**Story of One**

Where are you? You who are fortunate enough to know what it means to be saved? Where are you who have been washed in the blood of Jesus Christ?

Where have you been? Can't you see, that we are in agony?

Didn't Christ command you to come to us?

"The world is perishing in its darkness. Thousands are dying in the flames of hell. Have mercy, and come to us; we beseech you to come!

We are clad in the rags of ruin, totally bankrupt. Only God can help us now!

But will we also have a chance to hear his voice? His peace and his salvation?

Will we also have access to them?

"Where are you? Where are you bearers of light?

We call out to you, but there is no answer. Have you perhaps fallen asleep?

Where are you?"

A poem written by a young Central Asian girl on behalf of her people to Christians everywhere.

Established in 1957; now with more than 800 workers among Muslims.

# PIONEERS

*www.pioneers.org*

**Motto**
Reaching forgotten peoples.

**Ministry emphasis**
Church planting.

**Ethnic focus**
Arab world, Turkic world; Eurasian, Chinese, Malay, Indo-Iranian, Indo-Aryan, and Sub-Saharan peoples; Muslims in Europe and in the United States.

**What is your greatest challenge in reaching Muslims?**
Finding workers.

**Story of One**
"What is the cost of a soul?" Chris and Grace, two indigenous coworkers, asked that question as they discovered that their house-sitter —who was also a seeker—had run up a large phone bill and refused to pay for it. Their Pioneers coworker wrestled with the cost of the bill. Grace, however, wrestled with the cost of a soul.

Another local worker, Thomas, is thinking about the cost of another bill. He hopes to open a business—the first of its kind—in an unreached area. His business proposal asks for $10,000, but the life story of this future business owner has already cost a great amount. Consider the fact that God had rescued Thomas from some railroad tracks at about the same time he called Grace from an orphanage, and then he set both of them on a journey that led them to become the first workers in a group that has not heard the gospel—yet.

"What is the cost of a soul? We ask for eyes that see the costs—whether in prayer, finances, or relationships—as Christ would.

Established in 1979; now with more than 1250 workers.

# SERVING IN MISSION (SIM)

*www.sim.org*

## Motto
By Prayer.

## Ministry emphasis
Church planting, evangelism, discipleship, women's and children's ministry, sports ministry, literature, media, medical, leadership training, vocational training, literacy, outreach to prostitutes and street children, youth camps, HIV/AIDS ministries, relief and development, ESL teaching, and translation.

## Ethnic focus
Sub-Saharan, Indo-Aryan, and Chinese peoples; Southern Africans; Muslims in Europe and North America.

## What does your organization look for in those who will work among Muslims?
Some training in Muslim outreach, a clear sense of God's guidance, a close walk with the Lord, a strong involvement in a home church, a commitment to (and current involvement in) evangelism and discipleship, Bible knowledge, and commitment to prayer. We want people who can work well on a team, are flexible and emotionally stable, and have servants' attitudes—not for those who are "already perfect," but for those who are willing to grow and learn.

## What is your most usual prayer request?
For God to move in the hearts of Muslims, and in the hearts of the Christians who live near them, so that Muslims will be brought to saving faith and established in missionary-minded churches.

## What is your greatest challenge in reaching Muslims?
Being people of God, so that the Holy Spirit can move through us to communicate with his power, discernment, and love—this quality of godliness is greatly needed for ministry among people who are often resistant.

## Story of one
Recently God gave us a precious time with seven semi-literate Muslim-background women who came for training. We met upstairs in a home. From Sunday to Tuesday we sang, prayed, and listened to God's Word.

One of our workers had pictures of the Creation, the Fall, Cain and Abel, and so forth. Using chronological storying, we took turns teaching stories and having the women retell them to us. We also taught two stories from Jesus' life, showing how he interacted with women so differently than how the typical local religious men do.

Hanna, one of the seven, is so devoted to the Lord that her worship made us cry. Pray that she would be able to start meeting regularly with other believing women.

Serving In Mission

Established in 1893; now with more than 1000 workers.

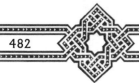

# TEAM EXPANSION

*www.teamexpansion.org*

**Motto**
Determined to make a difference.

**What is your greatest challenge
in reaching Muslims?**
Definitely the pressure put on inquirers by
the Muslim community.

**Story of One**
In the Middle East, the father is the most
important figure in the social structure.
He sets the attitudes, values, and political
orientation of the family. Fatherhood does
not end when the children marry. The
grandfather is still there to be an example
of fatherhood to a new father.

When I tell locals, "I am here because
my father sent me to you," suddenly I'm
one of them. It makes sense in the Middle
East that the father gives an instruction
and the son obeys, but people here know
western society doesn't function like that.
When I say, 'My father sent me to you,'
suddenly people want to know about this
father. They want to know why my father
would consider them so special that he
would send his son. "Why would a father
send his only son to a people?"

The spiritual realities are probably obvious to you, but this also has a personal
reality to me. When we were sent out, I
stood before the elders of the church as
they prayed over us. There was my dad
standing among them. He acknowledged
that God was the author of this endeavor,
so my father sent me.

Established in 1978; now with 50 workers among Muslims.

# THE EVANGELICAL ALLIANCE MISSION (TEAM)

*www.teamworld.org*

## Motto

From Everywhere to Everywhere.

## Ministry emphasis

Helping churches and missionaries to establish culturally relevant, sustainable, and reproducible churches among the nations through literacy, literature, media, medical (both preventive and curative), TESOL, and business ventures that provide contact with people and facilitate establishing relationships. The purpose of these relationships is for Muslims to meet real Christians, who share their faith in a contextually relevant way; to hear what the Bible teaches, and understand it more fully, and then make their own decisions.

## Ethnic focus

Arab world, Turkic world; Eurasian, Indo-Iranian, Indo-Aryan, and Sub-Saharan peoples.

## What is your greatest challenge in reaching Muslims?

Not enough personnel to deploy to opportunities in every area.

## Story of One

In Central Asia a man in prison came across a leaflet from one of our TESOL programs which advertised the "Christmas program" and gave very basic information. As his interest was piqued, upon release from prison, he asked his teenage son to find a Bible.

No local bookstores carried any Bibles and the teen was harassed for even trying. Eventually one shopkeeper told him about a "foreigner" who might be able to help him. The teen came to our TESOL worker who gave him a Bible.

Through reading the Bible and having conversations with our worker, this father came to believe in and follow Isa. Ten others in his family also believed. They meet weekly in this Central Asian city for mutual encouragement, teaching, and praising God.

Established in 1890; now with more than 70 workers among Muslims.

# YOUTH WITH A MISSION (YWAM)

*www.ywam.org*

**Motto**
To know God and make him known.

**Ministry emphasis**
Extensive mercy ministries, including medical treatment, community develop-ment, services to street children, counsel-ing, midwifery, and disaster relief. Also, discipleship, evangelism, church planting, ethnomusicology, literacy training, evan-gelical film showings in local languages, and the like.

**Ethnic focus**
Ministering in 140 countries, with more than 900 operating locations.

**Story of One**
It has been said that one can say anything, or preach any truth to a Muslim through a song, and John, a worker in Central Asia, has found this to be true. He started a simple recording studio in 1994 to record some of the first Christian music in the Central Asian Turkic languages. Building slowly, adding one piece of equipment at a time, his one-room studio—which began recording with a four-track tape deck—now uses high quality recording equipment.

John recalls the first recording they made of Central Asian worship music. "I had never known of a song that was written by a Uyghur believer. Then, in 1995, I met a Uyghur farmer who had become a believer and had started writing songs, expressing his faith and love for God. We spent the afternoon in his home sharing songs with each other. What a day!"

The words to the first Christian song written by a Uyghur:

  "You, Creator, were among your
      creation,
    But people didn't know it.
    Although you did many miracles,
    We still didn't recognize you.
    All praise and glory to you!
    We truly repent;
    It is such a shame
    That we are so late in believing."

*YOUTH WITH A MISSION*

Established in 1960; now with more than 11,000 workers and 100 teams working among Muslims.

# GLOSSARY

# GLOSSARY

Note that in transliteration from Arabic to English, there are variations in spellings. For example, many words may end in either *a* or *ah*, such as "mulla" or "mullah." Other variations may be: *a* or *u*, *al* or *ahl*, *al* or *ul*, *d* or *t*, *h* or *t*, *i* or *e*, *k* or *q*, *u* or *i*, *u* or *w*, *y* or *i*. Where multiple transliterations are provided; they are alternate spellings readers may encounter in other reading, some of which came from our authors' originals. We have conformed all occurrences in EWI to the first spelling listed. Diacritic marks in Arabic words are not shown, with the exception of Ka'aba, Qur'an, Shari'a (Shari'ah), Shi'a, Shi'i, da'wa, du'a, jam'a.

The glossary follows the standard convention of alphabetizing words under the first letter of the noun, rather than under the first letter of the preceding definite article: for example, "al-Islam" is listed under *I*, not *A*. Note that in Anglicizing Arabic words to make plurals (with *s*), the resulting word forms are no longer strictly Arabic.

The wide geographic spread of Islam has led to differing usage. Therefore, a word can have more than one meaning, and some words may share a common definition (e.g., "adan", "azan").

In general, italics indicate the literal meaning or that a word is cross-referenced herein. See the Common Word List, p. xli, and the Arabic Pronunciation Guide, p. xl, for more details.

Common Words are indicated with this symbol †.

# A

**abaaya** (ah-bah-**yah**) – female dress, black covering robe, head to ankle; cf., burqa, chador (chadris), hijab, jilbab.

**abangan** (ah-bahng-**ahn**) – the less orthodox Muslims of Indonesia; the "red people."

**Abbasid Dynasty** (ah-**bah**-sihd) – formed by al-Abbas (750–1258); the second Islamic dynasty, which ruled in Baghdad, "Golden Age of Islam." See "The Quraysh Family Tree," p. 15; Map, "The Abbasid Period of Consolidation (A.D. 732–1250)," p. 47.

**abd** (ah-**bid**), **abdal, abdu, abduhu** – *servant* or *slave*; *submission*; worshipper of Allah, his servant; common prefix of names. See "Unity, Submission, and Community," p. 355.

**Abd Allah** (ahbd-ah-**lah**), **Abd Ullah** – *slave of Allah*; father of the Prophet Muhammad, of the *Hashim* family of the Quraysh tribe. See "The Quraysh Family Tree," p. 15.

**Abd al-Muttalib** – cf., Muttalib.

**ablution** – cf., ghusl, wudu.

**Abraham** – *Ibrahim*; *Khalil Ullah*, Friend of Allah (intimate friend, Sura 4:125), prophet (Sura 3:67); Muslims trace

Muhammad's lineage back to "Abraham the True [hanif]" (Sura 2:135) through Ishmael (by Hagar); they believe Abraham was to sacrifice Ishmael (Sura 37:99–113), not Isaac, Abraham's son by Sarah (Gen. 22:1–19); also that Abraham and Ishmael (Sura 37:99–113) rebuilt the altar originally built by Adam at the same site, which became the Ka'aba in Mecca; cf., Books of God, Suhoof. See "God's Promise to Muslims," p. 70; "The Feast of Sacrifice," p. 168.

**abrogated, abrogation** – in the Qur'an, newer revelations cancel out (repeal or abolish) earlier revelations; prime example is abrogation of Sura 2:235 ("Let there be no compulsion in religion" (YUSUF ALI), by Sura 9:5, "Kill those who join other gods with God wherever ye shall find them" (RODWELL); "Fight and slay the pagans wherever ye find them, and seize them, beleaguer them, and lie in wait for them in every stratagem (of war)" (YUSUF ALI); cf., mansukh, nasikh.

**abu** (ah-**boo**) – *father of.*

†**Abu Bakr** (ah-boo **bah**-kuhr)**, Abu Bakr al-Siddiq** (ah-boo **bah**-kuhr ahl-sah-**dehk**) – a rich, respected merchant of Mecca; first man to believe in the Prophet and embrace Islam, the Prophet's closest friend and *Companion*; Muhammad married his teenaged daughter, Aisha; Abu Bakr became the first Caliph (632–634) according to Sunni; cf., Qur'an, al-Siddiq, Zayd. See "Quotes," p. 69.

**Abu Talib** (ah-boo **tah**-lib) – (d. 619) Muhammad's uncle, chief of the *Hashim* family of the Quraysh tribe; he brought up Muhammad after the death of

the boy's father, *Abd Allah*. See "The Quraysh Family Tree," p. 15.

**Abyssinia** – modern-day *Ethiopia* in Africa; cf., Monophysite.

**Acre** – port city of northern Palestine which changed hands many times during the Crusades.

**adan, adhan** (ah-**dahn** or ah-**zahn**) – *announcement*; the call (*azan*) to public prayer, made five times a day by the *muezzin* (*muadhdhin*) from the mosque's minaret; *Adan of the Fajr* (*early morning*) is at dawn.

**adat** (ah-**daht**), **adah** – the indigenous system of customary law, or local guidelines; practices having the force of law; governs ceremonies, traditions, rites of passage; cf., kejawen.

**adha** (ahd-**hah**) – *sacrifice*; cf., Id al-Adha; the Bible, even that part called Injil by Muslims, teaches Jesus is the true Adha, Lamb of God, sacrificed for sin.

**afkhar al-umam** (ahf-**khahr** ahl-oo-mahm) – *noblest of nations*; Arab's concept of his ancestry.

**afrit** (ahf-**riht**) – from root meaning *to roll in the dust*; species of jinn, described by the effect of its attack.

**Aga Khan** (ahg-ah **khahn**) – title of Nizari Ismaili Imams; direct lineal descendents from first Shi'i Imam, Ali (and Fatima); cf., Khojas.

**agape** – *love* (Greek); purely selfless love, not demanding or expecting reciprocation. See "Agape Love," p. 58.

**A.H.** – *after Hegira, anno Hegirae (in the year of [Muhammad's] Hijra)*; abbreviation for the year in the Muslim *lunar calendar*, used to designate date since the flight or Hijra of Muhammad (July 16, 622); established by Umar; cf., Hegira, Hijra. See "The Muslim Calendar," p. 162.

**ahad** (ah-**hahd**) – the oneness and absolute uniqueness of Allah; there is no likeness to Allah among all things and beings; ahad supports the negation of any other number, as in the three of *Trinity*, and the denial that Allah has any partner or companion associated with him; also, *wahid*, "The One, Same God for All"; tawhid. See Appendix 1, p. 472.

**Ahadith** (ah-hah-**deeth**) – Hadith.

**Ahl al-Bayt** – "people of the house"; cf., Sayyid, sharif.

**Ahl al-Dhimmah** – cf., dhimmi.

**ahl al-Kitab** (ah hahl ahl-kih-**tahb**) – "*People of the Book*," designation in the Qur'an for Jews and Christians, the people who have "holy books"; cf., aman, dhimmi, jizyah.

**ahl al-Sunnah wa-l-Hadith** (ah hahl ahl-**soon**-nah wahl-hah-**deeth**) – "*the people of Sunna and Hadith*"; official title of those who adhere to orthodox Islam.

**Ahmad** (**ah**-mahd) – another name for Muhammad (Sura 61:6); cf., Names of the Prophet.

**Ahmad** (**ah**-mahd), **Mirza Ghulam** (**mihr**-zah ghoo-**lahm**) – cf., Ahmadi.

**Ahmadi** (**ah**-mah-dee), **Ahmadiya** (**ah**-mah-**dee**-yah), **Ahmadiyya**, **Mirzari** – a small but vocal, heretical sect of Islam, and personality cult, from Punjab, India (1889); named for the founder, *Mirza Ghulam Ahmad al-Qadiani* (1835–1908), who claimed to have superseded Muhammad and was regarded as Mahdi and Messiah. Ahmadi follow a modern, progressive interpretation of Sunni Islam, but are regarded by most Muslims as not orthodox due to their belief in another prophet; two factions, Qadiani, Lahori.

†**Aisha, Ayisha** (ah-**ee**-shah) – Muhammad's favorite wife, his third; she was the daughter of Abu Bakr.

**Alhaji, Al-haji** (ahl-**hahj**-ee) – cf., Hajji.

†**Ali** (ah-**lee**) **ibn Abi Talib** – Muhammad's first cousin, son of *Abu Talib*, father of Hasan and Husayn; Ali married Fatima, the youngest daughter of the Prophet; recognized by Shi'a as the true successor of Muhammad, from whom came the succession of Imams, he being the first; he was the fourth Caliph of the Sunnis (655–659; assassinated 661), opposed by *Muawiyah* of the *Umayyad*. See "The Quraysh Family Tree," p. 15.

**Aligarh** (ah-lee-**gahrh**) **Muslim University** – founded by Sayyid Ahmad (or Syed Ahmed) Khan ("Sir Syed") in India.

**alim** (**ahl**-ihm) – a knowledgeable person or religious scholar.

†**Allah, Ullah** (**ahl**-lah) – *The God*; *The One True God*; the creator, sustainer, supreme being for Muslims. "Allah" is the only word for "God" in Arabic; prior to the rise of Islam, the principal deity of the Quraysh tribe, owner of the Ka'aba. The One True God was the only deity not represented by an idol in the Ka'aba; the term "Allah" was also used generally to refer to any supreme deity recognized by the many Arab tribes of Persia. Cf., Al-Ilah, Rasul-Ullah. See "Should Christians Use Allah in Bible Translation?" p. 20; "Is Allah God?" p. 89. See Appendix 1, p. 471.

**Allah al-Hayy** (ahl-**lah** hay) – "*Allah the Living*"; exclamation used in *dhikr* rituals. See Appendix 1, p. 472.

†**Allahu Akbar** (ah-**lah**-hoo **ahk**-bahr) – *takbir.* **1.** phrase meaning, "*Allah is the*

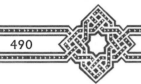

*Most Great* (or *the Greatest*)," or "*God is Great* (or *Greater*)," which begins, and is repeated as part of, ritual prayer. **2.** the phrase may be used in affirmation, or as a slogan to express defiance: "God is sovereign; we are on his side (and you are not)!"

**Allah wa rasulihi** (ah-**lah** wah rah-**soo**-lah) – "*Allah and his Prophet*" (Muhammad).

**alms** – cf., zakat.

**aman** (ah-**mahn**) – safety (of person and possessions) for foreign residents, decreed by the Muslim community; cf., dhimmi, jizyah, kharaj.

**amil** (ah-**mihl**), (**plur., amalah**) (ah-mah-**lah**) – official who supervises collection and distribution of the zakat.

**al-Amin** (ahl-ah-**mihn**) – *the trustworthy*; name by which Muhammad was known; cf., Names of the Prophet.

**Amina** (ah-**mee**-nah) – mother of the Prophet Muhammad.

**amir** (ah-**meer**) – *prince*; leader; *amir al-muminin, commander of the believers*, a Caliph's title.

**amr** (**ahm**-ehr) – *decree*; command of Allah.

†**amulet** – charm, talisman; believed to protect from harm, cancel offensive magic, or reverse sickness; types: udha (*to protect*), hajab (*shield like a curtain*), hariz (*guard against evil*), nafra (*flee*), wadh (*make distinct*), tamima (*be complete*); cf., du'a, evil eye, Hand of Fatima, nazar, Seven Covenants of Suleiman. See Picture, p. 199; "Another Source of Power," p. 202; "Types of Magic," p. 204.

**Anatolia** – geographic name for modern Turkey. See Map, "Where Is the Middle East?" p. 56; "Where Is the Middle East?" p. 57.

**angels** – God's messengers; guardians over humans; the doctrine of angels authenticates a species of being to whom ordinary Muslims may appeal for assistance; some traditional Muslims hold that belief in angels is an article of faith; cf., archangel, Azarel, Gabriel, Israfel, Michael.

†**animism** – **1.** the religious belief that all creation is pervaded by (alive with) spirits that are manifested in persons, objects, or places; they are contacted or controlled by the *shaman*, witchdoctor, or medium; cf., popular Islam. **2.** animism is largely based on fear and desire for control of influences on one's life; animism is also manifested as the worship of spirits.

**Ansar** (ahns-**sahr**) – *helpers, supporters*; inhabitants of Yathrib who became Muslims and asked the Prophet to come live with them; *Companions* and followers of Muhammad in Medina.

**Apostle of Allah, -of Arabia, -of Islam** – cf., The Messenger of God, The Prophet, Muhammad.

**aqida** (ahq-**ee**-dah) – statement of religious belief, a creedal affirmation.

**aqiqa** (ahq-**ee**-qah) – naming sacrifice (substitutionary) and ceremony, on seventh day after birth.

**al-Aqsa** (ahl-**ahq**-sah), **al-Masjid al-Aqsa** (ahl-mahs-**jeed** ahl-**ahq**-sah) – the *Mosque of Umar* (*Omar*) in *Jerusalem*, next to *Dome of the Rock* (*Sakhra*), the third most important pilgrimage destination for Muslims; from which Muhammad reputedly ascended to the heavens (*Lailat al-Miraj*); cf., Haram (al-Sharif).

†**Arabia** – Southwestern Asian peninsula between the Red Sea and the Persian Gulf. See Map, "The Arabian

Peninsula and the Surrounding Region in the Sixth Century," p. 31.

†**Arabic** – Semitic language of numerous dialects; principle language of Arabia, Jordan, *Syria*, Iraq, Lebanon, Egypt, and parts of North Africa. Language of Qur'an. For centuries the most important scientific language for the depository of the wisdom of antiquity.

†**Arabs** – native speakers of Arabic; Semitic people of Arabia, whose language and Islamic religion spread widely over Southwest Asia and northern Africa from the seventh century; cf., Qur'an. See Map, "The Arab World"; "The Arabic-Speaking World," p. 51.

**Arafat, Mount** – mountain outside Mecca; cf., Hajj, Umrah; ceremony of standing on the Plain of Arafat, Wuquf; Mina, jamra.

**archangel** – one of four: *Azrael, Israfel*, Gabriel (*Jibril*), and *Michael*; cf., angel.

**arkan al-Islam** (ahr-**kahn** ahl-**ihs**-lahm) – the Pillars of Faith (of Islam), the five religious duties.

**arraf** (ahr-**rahf**), (female, **arrafa**) – one who *knows*; diviner, fortune-teller.

**Ashab al-Nabi** – cf., Companions.

**al-Ashari** (ahl-**ahsh**-ahr-ee) – (d. 935) founded *Nizamiyah School*.

**Ashari** (ahl-**ahsh**-ahr ih), **Ithna Ashari** (**ihth**-nah ahl-**ahsh**-ahr ih), **al-Asharism** (ahl-**ahsh**-ahr-**ihs**-ihm) – anti-*Mutazalite* movement; named for *al-Ashari*; prevalent viewpoint on man's freewill in Islam today; Ashari hold that the Qur'an is the uncreated words of God; cf., Imam, Imamate, Imami, Shi'a, Twelvers.

**Ashura** (ah-**shur**-ah) – *the tenth*; tenth of the month of *Muharram*, the day Husayn's martyrdom is mourned by Shi'a; cf., Karbala Rawzah Khami, taziya.

**asr** (ah-**suhr**) – afternoon or third prayer, salat.

**Assassins** – *Hashashian*, or *Nizari*, "consumers of Hashish," followers of Hasan al-Salah (Hasan-i Sabbah); from Ismaili-type Shi'i Islam, quasi-Islamic sect; today this movement's survivors are called *Khojas*; the Crusaders mistakenly associated the Nizari with hashish addiction and political murder, and began the Assassins legend.

**associate** – cf., partner, shirk, wahid; the worst sin is associating another god or other gods with Allah.

**astaghafr Allah** (ahs-**tahg** fuhr ahl-**lah**) – "*I ask forgiveness of Allah*"; formula continually repeated by the Muslim and in his daily prayers in hopes of forgiveness for sins.

**Ataturk** (**Ah**-tah-toork) – "*father of the Turks*"; *Mustafa Kemal Ataturk* (1881–1938), founder of the modern, officially secular republic of Turkey (1922); formerly an Ottoman general; Ataturk abolished the Caliphate.

**awliya** (ahw-lee-**yah**) – *friends*; the saints of Allah (Sura 10:62).

†**aya, ayah, iyah** (ah-**yah**), (**plur.**, **ayat, iyat**) (ah-**yaht**) – *sign*, **1.** the signs, proofs of Allah; natural phenomena, his mighty acts in nature; miracles, evidence of Allah's divine mercy revealed within qur'anic texts. **2.** a single verse in the Qur'an.

†**Ayatollah, Ayatullah** (ah-yah-**tohl**-lah) – *sign of Allah*. **1.** honorific title of a high-ranking Shi'i legal scholar; **2.** a highly educated authority on observance of Islamic law, selected from the Ulama.

**Ayisha** (ah-**ee**-shah) – cf., Aisha.

**ayn** (') (**ie**-n)– Arabic diacritic, to indicate a constriction at the back of the throat, as in Ka'aba. The term "ayn" is pronounced with a long *i*, as in "Einstein."

**Ayyub** – Job.

**azan** (a-**zahn**), **azawn** (a-**zahwn**) – the Muslim call to prayer; cf., adan, minaret, muezzin, muadhdhin.

**Al-Azhar** (ahl-**ahz**-hahr) **University and mosque** – renowned Islamic university in Cairo, founded 970; university and mosque considered guardians of the faith.

**azima** (ah-**zee**-mah) – *incantation*; exorcism used most often when a person is struck (made ill) by an unnamed jinni.

**az ma bihtaran** (**ahz** mah **biht**-ahr-ahn) – *"those better than ourselves"*; common allusion used to refer to jinn indirectly in order to avoid inciting them (Iran).

**Azrael** (**ahs**-ray-eel) – one of four *archangels*, with Gabriel (*Jibril*), *Israfel*, and *Michael*; cf., angel.

# B

**Bab as-Salaam** (bahb **ahs**-sah-lahm) – *Gate of Peace*; through which pilgrims enter the sacred area (*Haram*) around the Ka'aba in Mecca.

**Babur** (bah-**buhr**) – (1483–1530) first of India's *Mughal* Dynasty rulers (1526–1530), descended from *Timur Lang* (father's side), and *Genghis Khan* (mother's side); cf., Mongol.

**Badr, Battle of** (ba-**duhr**) – in 624, first great battle in Islamic history, eighty miles south of Medina; 300 Muslims led by Muhammad defeated 950 Quraysh of Mecca; the first time Muhammad used the sword to advance his cause;

he interpreted his victory as Allah's vindication of his prophethood.

**Bahaism, Baabism** (bah-**hie**-ihs-ihm) – a pacifist, ecumenical sect, which became an independent, non-Muslim religion in mid-nineteenth century; many followers in U.S.; considered heretical by Muslims.

**Bahira** (bah-**hihr**-ah) – Nestorian monk who lived in the desert city of Basra, on the Quraysh caravan route to *Syria*; he supposedly recognized Muhammad's prophethood and the continuity of his teaching with Jewish and Christian Scriptures.

**Baitullah, Beit-Allah, Bayt al-Lah** (**bayt** ahl-lah) – *house of Allah*, mosque, masjid. A mosque is frequently called *Baitullah*. Cf., Al-Aqsa (Al-Masjid al-Aqsa, which is the Grand [Great] Mosque, in Jerusalem; Sakhra); also, Al-Masjid al-Haram, the Grand Mosque in Mecca which contains the Ka'aba.

**Bait-ul-Midras** (bayt-ool-mihd-**rahs**) – a place; a Jewish center in Medina.

**Bani Hashim** (ba-nee **hah**-shihm) – Muhammad's family, belonging to the Quraysh tribe; cf., Hashim.

**Banu Nadir** (ba-**noo** na-dihr) – Jewish tribe living in Khaibar (fifty-four miles from Yathrib) during Muhammud's time, defeated by the Muslims.

**Banu Qainuqa** (ba-noo qay-**noo**-qah) – Jewish tribe living in Yathrib, defeated by the Muslims.

**Banu Qurayza** (ba-**noo** qoo-rayz-ah) – Jewish tribe living in Yathrib when the Prophet arrived, later defeated by the Muslims; the men killed, the women and children sold into slavery.

**al-Baraa, Lailat; Laylat al-Barrah** (lay-**laht** ahl-bahr-ah) – *Night of*

*Liberation*; fifteenth of the month of *Shaban*, *Nisfu Shaban*. See "The Muslim Calendar," p. 162.

**baraka** (bah-**rah**-kah), **barakat** (bah-rah-**kaht**) – **1.** *blessing*, ultimately, of Allah; special power; that charisma which characterizes the person with exceptional spiritual powers to bring results; possessed by a *marabout*; **2.** positive magic force available from holy persons, places, or objects; obtained or conveyed by touch; sought as cure for evil eye; used to influence people, business, life in general; found in popular Islam, Sufi Islam; opposite is *hasad*. See "Why Is Baraka Needed?" p. 211.

**Barelvi** (bah-rehl-**vee**) – adherents of Sufi practices, including music (*qawwali*) and intercession by their *pir*; Indian sub-continent.

**batini** (bah-ah-**tih**) – esoteric, hidden, or inner meaning of Allah's word in the Qur'an, as opposed to *zahir*, the literal or apparent meaning.

**Battle of Badr** (**bahd**-ehr) – cf., Badr.

**Battle of the Trench** (**Allies**) – cf., Trench.

**Battle of Uhud** – cf., Uhud.

**al-Baydawi** (ahl-**bay**-dah-wee)**, Abd Allah** (ahb-dahl-**lah**) – *Shafi'i* jurist, *Ashari* theologian; author of what is considered to be the standard and most authoritative of all commentaries on the Qur'an (died late thirteenth century).

**beautiful names** – cf., ninety-nine names of God.

†**Bedouin** – nomadic Arab tribes of the desert, usually shepherds.

†**Believers** – monotheists; in the Qur'an, believers in Allah.

**Berbers** – Muslim peoples living in North Africa.

**"the best nation"** – "the best nation [community] revealed [sent down] to humanity" (Sura 3:110); "*khayru ummaten 'unzilat linnas*," "Islam is the best economic, social, religious, legal, and political system on earth." See "Muslim Community," p. 181.

**bida** (**bihd**-ah) – *innovation*; heresy, extra-legal interpretations of Shari'a law when the *ijtihad* technically ceased, and was replaced by the ijma.

**bin** (**bihn**), **ibn** (**ih**-bihn) – *son of*; **bint, bent** – *daughter of*.

**birr** (**buhr**) – *righteousness*; for the Muslim, obedient belief, generosity, consistency in rituals and requirements, and calm patience in adversity.

†**Bismillah, Basmahah, The** (bihs-mihl-**lah**) – the phrase, "*Bismillah al-Rahman al-Rahim*," "*In the name of Allah, the Merciful, the Compassionate*"; general invocation of Allah which prefaces each sura of the Qur'an (except 9); often used at the beginning of an undertaking, at the beginning of written documents, or as a protective formula. See "What Does the Qur'an Say?" p. 8; "Why Is Baraka Needed?" p. 211; Appendix 1, p. 471.

**Black Stone** – cf., Holy Black Stone.

**Book, the** – **1.** the Qur'an, *al-Kitab*. **2.** reference in the Qur'an to the Hebrew Scriptures, as in "the Books given to Moses…and the Prophets" (Sura 3:84, YUSUF ALI). **3.** this verse also cites "the Book given to…Jesus," or Injil. Cf., People of the Book, Taurat. See "Holy Books," p. 55.

**Books of God** – the five books which God has sent down to man. The book *Suhoof* (*Suhuf*, *pages* of Abraham), revealed through *Abraham*, has been lost;

the other four are *Taurat, Zabur,* Injil,
and Qur'an; cf., tanzil.

**al-Bukhari** (ahl-boo-**khah**-ree)**, Sahih**
(sah-**hih**) – (810–870) one of the two
original and premier collectors of hadith; he examined more than 600,000
potential hadith and retained as authentic 7,397 (divided into ninety-seven
chapters), known as *Sahih al-Bukhari.*
With *al-Muslim,* recognized as canonical
and authoritative; the two are known
as *The Two Sheiks* (*al-Shaykhan*), or *The
Correct Two* (*al-Sahihan*); cf., al-Kutub
al-Sittah, as-Sittah. See "Quotes," p.
69.

**Buraq** (boo-**rahq**) – winged animal
ridden by the Prophet Muhammad on
his ascension to heaven, *Lailat al-Miraj*;
it had the unveiled face of a beautiful,
well-dressed woman, wearing cosmetics
and ornaments.

**burqa, burka** (**buhr**-kah) – cf.,
abaabya, chador (chadris), hijab, jilbab.

†**Byzantine Empire** – eastern
Greek-speaking part of the late *Roman
Empire,* from 330, when Constantine
renamed *Byzantium* Constantinople,
to 1453, when Constantinople fell to
the Ottoman Turks. See Map, "The
Arabian Peninsula and the Surrounding
Region in the Sixth Century," p. 31.

†**Byzantium** – **1.** the ancient Greek
city of Thrace on site of modern
*Istanbul*; **2.** Byzantine Empire which
competed with Persia and *Ethiopia* prior
to Muhammad's time; cf., Chacedonian
orthodox.

# C

†**Cairo** – al-Qahira (alh-**qah**-heer-rah,
*victorious*), capital of Egypt, major

cultural and educational center for the
Arab and Islamic worlds.

†**caliph, khaliph, kalifah** (khah-**lihf**)
– *representative.* **1.** the vicegerent (Sura
2:30) of Allah, his administrative
deputy, undermaster; his representative
on earth to reflect the divine names and
qualities, and to fulfill the divine will;
the ruler of every Muslim; **2.** former
political and spiritual Islamic ruler who
was a close associate of Muhammad
or the descendant of one, and
Muhammad's successor as head of
the Muslim community; **3.** politically,
the succession of Muslim rulers with
secular authority, from the first, Abu
Bakr (632–634), to 1924; cf., Caliphate,
Imam.

†**Caliphate** (**kay**-lih-fayt) – the Muslim
state headed by a caliph; last Caliphate
abolished in 1924 by *Mustafa Kemal
Attaturk,* with the collapse of the
Ottoman Empire and Turkey's bid to
become part of secularized Europe.

**Carey, William** – (1761–1834) English
Baptist pastor, missionary, serving in
India for forty-one years, including
translating the Bible.

**Caucasus Mountains** – between Black
and Caspian seas; see Map, "The
Caucasus Mountain Region," p. 192;
"Eurasian Peoples," p. 193.

**chador, chadris** (chah-**dohr**) – **1.**
scarf or shawl, woman's head covering
in Iran. **2.** full-length flowing garment
worn by Saudi Arabian women; cf.,
abaaya, burqa, hijab, jilbab.

**Chalcedonian** – orthodox Christian sect
who believed Jesus had two natures (human and divine) united in one person;
cf., Byzantium Monophysites, Nestorian
Church of the East.

†**charismatic** – type of Christianity that emphasizes personal religious experience and supernatural gifts (healing, prophecy, tongues).

**China, Muslims of** – see "The Muslims of China," p. 342.

†**Christendom** – **1.** Christianity as a geographical entity. **2.** Western Europe under the Pope's spiritual jurisdiction.

**Chronicle of Seert** – a history of the Nestorians, written as early as the ninth century by an unknown author.

**colonialism** – western nations developing trade for their own benefit with, maintaining control over, and imposing their cultures on, foreign countries (colonies). See "Divergent Values," p. 135.

**Companions** – *Ashab al-Nabi*, or *Sahaba*; those closest to Muhammad in his lifetime; memorized and transcribed the oral revelations given to Muhammad, later assembled into the written authoritative version of the Qur'an; also preserved the hadith; cf., hafiz.

**compulsion** – "Let there be no compulsion in religion" (Sura 2:256, YUSUF ALI); *abrogated* by Sura 9:5; cf., "Law of Apostasy."

†**Constantinople** – former name of Istanbul (since 1930), city on both sides of Bosporus in northwest Turkey; founded in ca. 660 B.C. as Byzantium; renamed by Constantine who made the city the capital of the Eastern *Roman* or Byzantine empire; attacked by Crusaders in 1204; taken by Turks in 1453.

**contagious magic** – use of a person's hair or fingernail trimmings for cursing him.

†**contextualization** – process by which a local indigenous community of believers in Jesus Christ becomes an ongoing relevant witness within its own culture; the resulting witness is both biblically formed and culturally appropriate, including the careful reforming of all aspects of the culture by the local indigenous community of believers, with biblical guidance, into newly framed values, beliefs, and practices. See "The Church Contextualization Spectrum," p. 379.

**Copts** – Coptic Church; orthodox Christians of the Coptic Church in pre-Islamic Egypt; one of Muhammad's wives, Mary, was a Coptic Christian slave given to him by a Egyptian ruler.

**Covenant of Umar** (**Omar**) – probably first comprehensive attempt to detail the status of dhimmi (Christians and Jews) under Islam; spelling out terms of subjection, annual tribute tax, *jizyah*; cf., aman, kharaj.

†**Creed** – cf., Shahada.

†**Crusades** – Christian campaigns to reconquer the Holy Land, especially Jerusalem, in 1200s to 1300s.

**culture** – See "Diagram of Culture," p. 96.

**"cutting the Qur'an,"** *istikhara* (ihs-tee-**khah**-rah) – common method of divination; opened at random, qur'anic words are interpreted to assist person in decision-making.

# D

**Dajjal** (dahj-**jahl**) – *liar, deceiver*; name for the anti-Christ or pseudo-messiah who will appear at the end of time; prominent in hadith, not mentioned in Qur'an.

**Dalail al-Khayrat** (dah-**leel** ahl-**khah**-raht) – *Signs of Blessing*; a litany by poet al-Jazuli, in which Muhammad is exalted, and acclaimed as sole intercessor and channel of communication between the Muslim and Allah; popular at *Maulid al-Nabi* celebrations.

†**Dar al-Harb** (dahr ahl-**hahrb**), **Darul-Harb** (dahr-rool-**hahrb**) – "house that is not yet Muslim," territory presently outside of Islamic supremacy, of the infidels (non-Muslims), where jihad wars are permitted, or which is at war with Muslims.

†**Dar al-Islam** (**Darul-Islam**) (dahr ahl-**ihs**-lahm), **Dar as-Salaam** (dahr ahs-**sah**-lahm) – *territory of Islam, house of peace*; area of Muslim supremacy; lands in which technically no war is permissible; once Islamic, land is sacred and should always be Islamic, with Islamic government.

†**da'wa, da'wah** (dah-**ah**-wah) – *invitation*. **1.** calling all people to the path of Allah, to follow divine guidance. **2.** Muslim missionary work.

**Dawud, Daoud** (dah-**wood**) – David; cf., rasul, Zabur.

**Day of Atonement** – Yom Kippur; Jewish holy day for fasting, prayer, for atonement of sins.

**deen, din** (**deen**) – Muslim religious practice (such as reciting the Creed, praying, fasting, and giving alms), as distinct from belief, *iman*.

**Deen wa dawla** (deen wah **dahw**-lah) – union of the state and religion (or doctrine), life, and politics, to include all aspects of the life of individual and of the nation; all-inclusive and comprehensive Islamic system; characteristic of Muslim Fundamentalism.

**dervish, darwish** – Sufi mystic who often engages in whirling dance, trances, and singing or chanting of the names and attributes of Allah.

**dhikr** (**thih**-kuhr), **or zhikr** (**zih**-kuhr) – *remembering*. **1.** Sufi spiritual exercises, in which one is remembering Allah, in order to become mystically one with him (*tauhid, tarika, haqiqa*) or to perceive the oneness of all being, by concentrating on one of his names or attributes. **2.** chanting in recitation style with intense emotion.

†**dhimmi** (**thihm**-mah or **zihm**-mah), **ahl al-dhimmah** (**ah**-hahl ahl-**thihm**-mah) – *peoples*; people of the Covenant, Jews and Christians, monotheists, who were living as protected subjects (*aman*), and paid an annual tribute tax (*jizyah; kharaj*), under an Islamic government; this protection was prescribed by the Qur'an and codified by *Covenant of Umar*; cf., ahl al-kittab, People of the Book.

**Dhu al-Hijja, Dhul-Hijja** (thoo-ahl-**hihj**-jah) – the twelfth month (the seventh to the tenth), set aside for the Hajj, the formal pilgrimage; Id al-Adha is on the tenth. See "The Muslim Calendar," p. 162.

**din** (deen), **al-din** (**ahl**-deen) – *religion*; religion in general, and sum total of the faith and practice of Muslim religious duties in particular, including the five Pillars of Faith, good works, the complete way of life given in the Qur'an and Hadith. See "What Is Forbidden?" p. 102.

**divination** – *occult* attempts to direct and protect one's life in a complex universe, widely practiced by Muslims; efforts to discover cause and remedy, as well as the future; cf., istikhara, popular Islam.

**djellaba** (jehl-lah-**bee**-yah) – cf., jal-labiya.

**Dome of the Rock** – Qubbat al-Sakhra; cf., Al-Aqsa, Haram, Jerusalem.

**Druze** – an *Ismaili* sect (named after al-Darazi) so divergent from orthodoxy that it ceased to be Muslim; in the tenth century this sect deified a *Fatimid* ruler, rejected the Qur'an, and adopted an exclusive doctrine; found in Lebanon and *Syria*.

†**du'a** (**dah**-ah-wah) (**plur., adiya**) (ahd-**ee**-yah) – *to call*. **1.** supplication, informal prayer; a special prayer (often for healing), consisting of a magical prescription of *occult* words and symbols. **2.** charms written by du'a-writers, specialists in composing these written prescriptions. See "Prayer," p. 184.

**dukun** (doo-**koon**) – shamans; cf., kebatinan.

# E

**Easter** – Id al-Qiyama. See "Feast of Sacrifice," p. 168.

**Eid** – cf., Id al-Fitr.

**emigration** – cf., Hegira, Hijra.

**endogamy** – marriage within the extended family, first cousin preferred; common as a method of keeping wealth within family control.

**Ethiopia** – formerly *Abyssinia*, in Africa; Monophysite empire in Muhammad's time; had been competing with Persia and Byzantium prior to Muhammad's time; destination of some of first Muslims to escape from persecution in Mecca; cf., Horn of Africa.

**Eurasian peoples** – see "Eurasian Peoples," p. 193.

**Europe, Muslims in** – see "European Immigrants," p. 380.

†**evil eye** – envious glance bringing evil; in popular Islam, spiritual power is thought to be a potent contributor to the calamities and disintegration of life; valuable persons or things are constantly vulnerable to harm or destruction caused by other people's envy (*hasad*) or jealousy, projected through the eye by a mere look. Various types: salty eye (incurable); bad or unclean eye (both transitory); cf., baraka, nazar. See "Women and Power," p. 198; Picture, p. 199.

# F

**fajr** (**fa**-juhr) – first salat, or prayer (of five per day), at dawn or before sunrise.

**fakir, faqir** (**fah**-qeer) (**plur., fuqara**) (fah-qah-**rah**) – *poor wanderer*; religious or poor man who solicits alms in the name of Islam; a mendicant of a Sufi order (Sri Lanka).

**faqi** (fah-**kih**), **faqih** (**plur., fuqaha**) (foo-**kah**-hah) – *theologian*; cleric or sheik who can give religious verdicts; Islamic jurists, who form the Ulama. In popular Islam (Sudan), a mendicant dealing in divination and folk remedies. Cf., fuqaha.

**fard** (**fahrd** or **fahrth**), **fard ain** (fahrd **ien**) – *obligatory*; canonical duty or obligation of faith imposed on each individual; cf., wajib.

**fard kifayah** (fahrd kee-**fie**-yah) – collective duty; if performed by one, suffices for all.

**Farsi** – Persian language, dating from the ninth century, written in Arabic alphabet; language of modern Iran.

**fasad** (fah-**sahd**) – *decay*, spoiled, corrupt; political disorder.

**fasiq** (**fah**-sihq) – transgressor, reprobate.

**fatawa** (fah-**tah**-wah) – casuistries, the ethical rules by which conduct is deemed right or wrong; (not to be confused with fatwa).

**fatawi** (fah-**tahw**-ee) – cf., fatwa.

†**al-Fatihah, al Fatiha** (ahl-**fah**-tee-hah) – *the opening one*; opening Sura of the Qur'an, which is repeated several times during each salat, the five required times of prayer each day; it contains in condensed form all the fundamental principles of the Qur'an; spoken as an incantation for protection from the evil eye or because of its powerful, intrinsic *baraka*; cf., Bismillah. See "What Does the Qur'an Say?" p. 8.

†**Fatima** (fah-**tee**-mah) – the daughter of Muhammad and his first wife, Khadija; the wife of Ali, the fourth Caliph; as a female relative of Muhammad, she is thought to be a potential mediator with Allah; cf., Hand of Fatima. See "The Quraysh Family Tree," p. 15.

**Fatimid Dynasty** (**faht**-ee-mihd) – (909–1171) Ismaili Shi'i (descendants of Fatima) empire in Egypt and parts of North Africa; rival of the *Abbasid* for religious and political supremacy.

†**fatwa** (**faht**-wah) (**plur., fatawi**) (fah-**tahw**-ee) – legal ruling or verdict on an issue of canonical jurisprudence, or any religious edict made by an expert scholar, *mufti*, or Islamic authority; cf., Shafi'i.

**Feast** – cf., Id al-Adha, Id al-Fitr.

**fellah** (fehl-**lah**) (**plur., fellahin**) (fehl-lah-**heen**) – member of laboring class in Arab country who lives off the land; the farmers of Egypt.

**festivals** – public affirmations of commitment to Islam; festivals meet the everyday life needs of Muslims; prescribed, Id al-Fitr and Id al-Adha; optional, *Maulid al-Nabi.*

**Fiqh** (**fihq**) – the corpus of Islamic legal interpretation or jurisprudence; cf., ijma, madhhab, Shari'a.

**fitrah** (**foot**-rah) – natural state of purity or submission to the will or law of Allah; innate, pure nature possessed by all people at birth; the pattern according to which Allah has created all things (Sura 30:30); cf., sin.

**five Pillars of Faith, of Islam** – cf., Arkan al-Islam, Pillars of Faith, Shahada.

†**folk Islam** – cf., popular Islam.

**Fundamentalism** – cf., Islamic Fundamentalism. See "Progression to Violence," p. 145.

**fuqaha** (**foo**-kah-hah) (**sing., faqih**) (fah-**kih**) – *jurists*; doctors of Islamic law who compose the Ulama, early writers of dogmatic theology; cf., faqi.

# G

†**Gabriel** – *Jibril.*

**Genghis Khan** (**Jenghiz Khan**) – (d. ca. 1227), by uniting Mongol and Turkish tribes, he created a military force (horde) that conquered northern China, northern Iran, and southern Russia, the *Mongol Empire*; furthered by his descendeants *Babur* and *Timur Lang*, stretching from the Mediterranian to the Pacific, the *Mughal Empire.*

**Ghassanid** (**ghahs**-sah-**nihd**) – Christian, Arab, tribal buffer state, Byzantine Empire protégé, on preIslamic *Syrian*-Arabian border;

rivals of *Lakhmids*; later forced to submit to Islam, and allied with rivals to participate in destruction of Byzantine and Persian empires.

**al-Ghazali** (ahl-ghah-**zahl**-ee) – (1058–1111) Sunni theologian, called "The Proof of Islam"; main catalyst in a synthesis of orthodox theology and mystic teachings; major work, *The Revival of Religious Sciences*; became a committed Sufi.

**ghazi** (**ghah**-zee) – a Muslim fighter returned from jihad (holy war).

**ghul** (**ghool**) – *destroying*; species of jinn, described by the effect of its attack.

**ghusl, ghusul** (**ghahs**-sool) – full *ablution* ceremony (bathing), involving the entire body, in the prescribed manner, to cleanse of major impurity; cf., wudu.

**†gospel** – Jesus' message; Injil; cf., Ahl al-Kitab, People of the Book.

**Gospel of Barnabas** – a medieval (about 1300) forgery designed to authenticate Islam; thought to be written in revenge by a Spanish Muslim forced into Christianity by the Inquisition.

**Gospels** – the four Gospels: Matthew, Mark, Luke, and John of the New Testament (Sura 21:7); cf., Holy Book, Injil, People of the Book. See "Holy Books," p. 55.

**Greater Pilgrimage** – cf., Hajj.

**gurudwaras** (goo-ruhd-**wah**-rah) – Sikh places of worship.

# H

**hadath** (**hah**-dihth) – a type of defilement which would invalidate the ritual prayer.

**hadd** (**had**) (**plur., hudud**) (hoo-**dood**) – *limit, prohibited*; Allah's boundary limits

for halal (lawful) and haram (unlawful), or against the rights of Allah; punishments stated in the Qur'an; cf., sin.

**†hadith, Hadith** (hah-**deeth**) (**plur., ahadith**) (**ah**-hah-deeth) – *sayings, prophetic Traditions*; expressing Muhammad's Sunna ("that which has been transmitted," *said*), and complementing and standing alongside the Qur'an; Muslims believe Muhammad received *wahy ghayr matlub* (unread revelation), by which he made authoritative declarations. A massive number of these sayings, teachings, practices, and approvals of the Prophet Muhammad, and those things said or done in his presence of which he approved, were passed on through oral tradition by his eyewitness *Companions* after his death, and later transcribed (*matn*, or texts), and edited by Muslim authorities into great collections, the Hadith, resulting in contradictions, disagreements, and confusion over authenticity. Gradually six collections, *the Six Books, Sihah Sittah*, or *al-Kutub al-Sittah*, won universal recognition and remain authoritative. Hadith interpret Islam by defining appropriate actions, elucidating parts of the Qur'an, and expressing distinctive theological emphases; reinforce popular-Islamic cosmology and justify many popular practices. Cf., al-Bukhari, al-Muslim; Sihah Sittah. (In English, hadith is both singular and collective.)

**hadr** (**hah**-thuhr) – from *hadara, to bring down*. **1.** the bringing down of Allah to his worshipers as they remember him through the power of *dhikr*. **2.** public trance-dance performed by devotees of possessing *zar* spirits; **3.** Sufi ceremonial dance of healing from striking or possession by jinn.

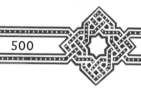

**haduk al-nas** (hah-**thook** ahl-nahs) –
*"those people there"*; common allusion used
to refer to jinn indirectly, in order to
avoid inciting them.

**hafiz** (**hah**-feez) (**plur., huffaz**) (**hoof**-
fah-ahz) – *guardian*. **1.** Muhammad's
*Companions* who memorized the revelations; **2.** title of respect given to those
who have memorized the entire Qur'an;
**3.** professional reciter.

†**Hagar** (**hay**-gahr) – mother of Ishmael,
father of the Arabs. See "God's Promise
to Muslims," p. 70.

**al-Hajar al-Aswad** (ahl-**hah**-jahr ahl-
**ahs**-wahd) – *Black Stone*, the Holy Black
Stone; symbol of the hereafter or divine
presence; a black meteorite, in the outer
east corner of the Ka'aba, the cubical
shrine (*"House of God"*) in Mecca; it is
to be ritually kissed or saluted by Hajj
pilgrims as they circle the Ka'aba.

†**Hajj** (hahj) – *setting out*; Greater
Pilgrimage to Mecca, required of all
Muslims once in their lifetimes, if they
are physically and financially able; the
fifth Pillar; usually initiated between
the seventh to tenth of *Dhu al-Hijja*, the
twelfth month, set aside for the Hajj;
described in Sura 2; cf., Hajji, Ihram,
Manasik al-Hajj wal-Umrah, Rukn,
Umrah. See "The Muslim Calendar,"
p. 162.

**Hajj-al-Ifrad** (hahj-ahl-**ihf**-frahd) –
pilgrim enters Mecca in the state of
*Ihram*, intending to perform Hajj only.

**Hajj-al-Qiran** (hahj-ahl-**qee**-rahn) –
pilgrim enters Mecca in the state of
*Ihram*, intending to perform *Umrah* and
Hajj together; cf., Qarin.

**Hajj Mabrur** (hahj mahb-**roor**) – Hajj
accepted by Allah for being perfectly
performed according to the Prophet's
Sunna, and with legally earned money.

**Hajji** (**hahj**-jee), **Alhaji** (**ahl**-hahj-jee) –
term of respect for man who has
performed the pilgrimage to Mecca, a
source of prestige; **Hajjah** (**hahj**-jah),
**Alhajjah** (**uhl**-hahj-jah) – term of
respect for a woman who has completed
the Hajj.

†**halal** (hah-**lahl**) – **1.** *loosed*, allowed or
free from restrictions unless specifically
prohibited by Qur'an or Hadith; **2.** *permitted*, what is lawful under the Shari'a;
cf., hadd; **3.** Meat that is properly
butchered in the name of Allah (Sura
22:34), with the animal's head facing
Mecca and its throat slit, allowing the
blood to drain out; cf., haram. See
"What Is Permitted?" p. 84.

**al-Hallaj** (**ahl**-hahl-**lahj**) – great
Muslim Sufi who denied Islam; his
request to die as did Christ resulted in
his crucifixion on a pole.

**HAMAS** – acronym for *Harakat al-
Muqawamah al-Islamiyya* (Movement of
Islamic Resistance); Palestinian Islamist
organization born in December 1987, at
the beginning of the Palestinian uprising (*intifadah*), or anti-Israeli resistance.

**"Al-hamdu-lil-lah"** (ahl-**hahm**-doo-
lihl-**lah**) – *"Praise to Allah"*; often said as
an expression of thanks.

**hamza** (') (**hahm**-zah) – Arabic diacritic
which signifies a glottal stop or catch,
as found in Scottish-accented English,
replacing *t*, as in "bi'er" (for "bitter"), or
"Sco'ish" (for "Scottish").

**Hanafi** (**hah**-nahf-ee), **Hanifi** (**hah**-
nihf-ee) – earliest and most widespread
*madhhab* or school of law, which places
a relatively liberal interpretation on the
Qur'an; emphasizes *qiya* (analogical
reasoning), *ray* (opinion), and *istihsan*
(preference) in forming law; founded

by al-Numan ibn Thabit ibn Zutu Abu Hanifah (d. 767).

**Hanbali** (**hahn**-bahl-lee) – fourth, smallest, and most conservative *madhhab* or school of law, which rejects innovation beyond the literal Qur'an and Hadith; founded by Abu Abdillah Ahmad Ibn Hanbal (780–855); modern Wahhabi are of the *Hanbali* school.

**Hand of Fatima** – protective talisman made of imprint or shape of a hand, often with an eye in the palm, as a trinket, or design painted on surfaces; used to ward off the evil eye; cf., Fatima.

†**hanif** (hah-**neef**) – *the pristine faith*; title of pre-Islamic Arab monotheist, thinker, and pious man of intelligence dissatisfied with pagan idolatry and sectarianism, and concerned with the political and religious situation in Arab territories; hanifs regard *Abraham* as their ancestor and first hanif; Arabic form from *Syriac* word meaning *heretic, rejected, separatist*.

**haqiqa** (hah-**qee**-qah) – *divine truth*; Sufi goal is the absorption of one's being into the *haqiqa* or *tarika*, or Ultimate Being.

**Harakat al-Muqawamah al-Islamiyya** – *HAMAS*, Movement of Islamic Resistance.

†**haram** (hah-**rahm**) – *unlawful, that which is forbidden*. **1.** prohibited and punishable by the Shari'a; an action which is canonically forbidden, blasphemous; cf., hadd; **2.** As an exclamation over bad news, "Haram!" means "God have pity!" See "What Is Forbidden?" p. 102.

**Haram** (hah-**rahm**) – *sacred*: a hallowed area, especially around the monuments of Medina, Mecca (the Haram or Grand [Great] Mosque, *Al-Masjid al-Haram*), and Jerusalem (*Al-Masjid al-Aqsa* and *Qubbat al-Sakhra* [*Dome of the Rock*]);

both in the *Haram al-Sharif*, the Noble Enclosure); cf., halal, Muharram.

**"Haram, fosh!"** (hah-**rahm fahs**-hah) – "God forbid! Blasphemy!"

**hasad** (**ha**-sad) – *envy*; tangible evil force, conveyed by the evil eye (Sura 113:5).

†**Hasan, Hassan** (hahs-**sahn**), **al-Hasan** – oldest son of Ali, Muhammad's grandson, brother of Husayn, who, for Shi'a, became second Imam after Ali's murder; for Sunnis, fourth Caliph, forced to resign role of Caliph in 661 by *Muawiyah*, fifth Caliph. See "The Quraysh Family Tree," p. 15.

**Hashashian** (hah-sha-**sheen**) – cf., Assassins.

**Hashemite** (**hash**-eh-miet) – another name for Hashimi, of the *Hashim* family; Hashemite Arabs claim descent from Muhammad.

**Hashim** (**hah**-shihm), **Hashimi** (**hah**-shihm-ee) – *Banu Hashim*, Muhammad's family, of the Quraysh tribe; also, Hashim was Muhammad's great grandfather, grandfather of *Abd Allah*. See "The Quraysh Family Tree," p. 15.

**hashish** (hah-**sheesh**) – purified resin from cannabis plant, smoked or chewed as a narcotic.

**al-hasud la yasud** (ahl-hah-**sood** lah yah-**sood**) – *"the envier will not overcome"*; a rhymed inscription; form of protective measure against the evil eye.

**heaven** – cf., Paradise.

†**Hegira** (**hihj**-rah) – cf., Hijra; *A.H.* See the "The Muslim Calendar," p. 162.

**Hejaz, Hijaz** (heh-**jahz**) – northwest coastal region of Arabia, on the Gulf of Aqaba and the Red Sea, linked to caravan routes, including pilgrimage cities, Mecca and Medina; first region to come under Islamic control.

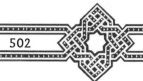

**hell** – *Jahannam*. Ahmadi believe hell is not everlasting; cf., Judgment Day. See "Paradise and Hell," p. 449.

**Hellenistic** – postclassical Greek history and culture, from death of Alexander the Great to accession of Augustus.

**henna, hinna** (**hehn**-nah) – dye often used by Muslim women on their hair and to draw intricate designs on their hands, particularly on special occasions.

**hidayah** (hee-**die**-yah) – Allah's divine guidance or instruction, revealed to mankind through his prophets.

**hijab** (hee-**jahb**) – *curtain*; from *hijaba*, to conceal, or shield, so as to be invisible. **1.** "the veil"; acceptable Islamic clothing for women. **2.** a long dress prescribed to cover the whole body from head to feet; cf., abaaya, burka, chador (chadris), jilbab. See "The Hijab," p. 53.

**Al-Hijr** (ahl-**hihj**-uhr) – spot in Mecca from which Muhammad began his *Night Journey, Lailat al-Miraj*, or ascension to heaven.

**†Hijra, Hijrah** (**hihj**-rah)**, Hegira, Hejira, Hidjra** – *change of direction, emigration*. **1.** Muhammad's flight from Mecca to Yathrib (Medina) in 622; the *Islamic lunar calendar* commences from the beginning of this year, signified by the letters *A.H.* (*anno Hegirae, in the year of* [Muhammad's] *Hijra*), when Islam was launched as a state and movement. **2.** to leave one's place of residence for Allah's sake. See "The Muslim Calendar," p. 162.

**Hira** (hie-**rah**) – a mountain near Mecca where, in a cave, Muhammad first received his revelation of the Qur'an from the *archangel* Gabriel; or the cave itself.

**Hizb ut Tahrir** (**Hizb al-Tahrir**) (hihz-boot-**tah**-reer) – Islamic Liberation Party (1953), founded to re-vive the Islamic nation, to be governed by Shari'a law, purge it of colonialism's traces, and uphold the Caliphate.

**hoja, hodja** (**hoh**-jah)**, hoca** – **1.** term for major cleric among Turks. **2.** in popular Islam, the village sorcerer.

**†Holy Black Stone** – *al-Hajar-al-Aswad*; cf., Ka'aba.

**Holy Book** – Qur'an; other "holy books" accepted by Muslims are the Law (*Torah, Taurat*), the Prophets (*Psalms, Zabur*), and the Gospels (Sura 5:68; 21:7); cf., Ahl al-Kitab, Injil, People of the Book. See "Holy Books," p. 55.

**†Holy City, the** – Mecca.

**†Holy House, House of Allah** – Ka'aba.

**honor** – prized as a part of a Muslim's identity, and commonly viewed as indicating God's approval; evidenced by chastity of women, family solidarity, and admirable personal and cultural qualities; cf., shame. See "Honor and Shame," p. 119; "View of Western Women and Christianity," p. 136; "A Visual Model of the Muslim Worldview," p. 159; "Women Protecting Honor," p. 164.

**Horn of Africa** – Projection on eastern coast of Africa into Gulf of Aden, Arabian Sea, and Indian Ocean; countries of Kenya, *Ethiopia*, Djibouti, Somalia, Eritrea, Sudan; this region's history was dominated by Ethiopia, characterized by struggles between Muslim and other herdsman, and Christian farmers, for resources and space. See Map, "Where Is the Middle East?" p. 56; "Sub-Saharan Peoples," p. 258.

**houri** (hoh-**ree**-yah) (**plur., hur**) (**hohr**) – Allah's female creations especially provided for the sexual enjoyment of

Muslim men in Paradise (Sura 56:22–23, 35–37; 38:50–53; 44:51–54; 55:71–76; 52:17–20).

**Hubal** (ha-**bahl**) – a Moabite statue or idol, chief of the many gods in the Ka'aba in the pre-Islamic *Period of Ignorance*; cf., Jahiliyyah, al-Uzza.

**huda** (**hoo**-dah) – *guidance*; revelation which guides man.

**Hudaibiyya, Hudaybiyah** (**hah**-dah-bah) – the treaty between the Meccan Quraysh and the Muslim umma (named for the place where the treaty was made), permitting Muslims to make pilgrimage to Mecca.

**hudud** (hoo-**dood**) – cf., hadd.

†**Husayn ibn Ali** (hoo-**sayn** ihb-bihn ah-**lee**)**, Husain, Hussein** – the younger son of Ali (Muhammad's grandson), who, for Shi'a, became third Imam after the murder of Ali's oldest son, Hasan; Husayn was murdered (with his sons and companions) at *Karbala* (680, by troops of Yazid, son and successor of *Umayyid caliph, Muawiyah*, fifth Caliph). Shi'a deeply mourn his martyrdom on *Ashura* (the tenth of *Muharram*), *taziya*, and pilgrimage is made to his tomb in *Karbala*. Husayn's death gave Shi'a their sense of suffering, leading to a history of political resistance, fighting against social injustice, and eschatological hope, cf., Mahdi. See "The Quraysh Family Tree," p. 15.

**I**

**ibadah** (ee-bah-**dah**)**, (plur., ibida )** (ee-bah-**daht**) – *worship*; acts of worship required to fulfill the devotional rites of Islam; the last four of the five Pillars of Faith are called *al-ibadat*.

**Ibadi** (**eh**-bah-dee)**, (plur., ibadah)** (**eh**-bah-dah) – cf., Khariji.

**Iblis** (ihb-**lees**) – *devil*; Satan, the source of all evil and temptation; qur'anic name for the Devil (from *diabolos*); used interchangeably with *Shaytan*; cf., Jamrat, al-Shaytanul-Kabir. See "Why Is Baraka Needed?" p. 211.

**ibn, bin** (**ihb**-bihn, bihn) – *son of.*

**Ibn-Ishaq** (ihb-bihn-**ihs**-hahq) – the earliest, most trustworthy of Muslim biographers of Muhammad (eighth century).

**"Ibn is sabil"** (**ihb**-bihn **ihs**-sah-beel) – "son of the road," wayfarer, wanderer, passerby, traveler.

**Ibrahim** (ihb-rah-**heem**) – *Abraham*.

†**Id al-Adha, Eid al-Adha** (eed ahl-**ahd**-hah) – Feast of Sacrifice, Sacrificial Feast; the major four-day festival in Islam, marks the end of the Hajj on the tenth day of the twelfth month, *Dhu al-Hijja*; the sacrifice, *qurban*, obligatory for any Muslim who can afford it (of rams, or other animals), is made in memory of *Abraham's* offer to Allah to sacrifice his son Ishmael, and Allah's provision of a ram instead; part of the Hajj rituals, as well as in every Muslim community, the meat shared with the poor; also, *Id al-Qurban* or *Id al-Kabir* (Great Festival); *Id al-Hajj* (Feast of Pilgrimage); *Bakr Id* (India); *Kurban Bayram*, or *Buyuk Bayram* (Turkey). See "The Feast of Sacrifice," p. 168; "Muslim Calendar," p. 162.

†**Id al-Fitr, Eid al-Fitr** (eed ahl-**fooh**-tihr) – *breaks the fast*; *Feast* of Breaking the Fast, the major three-day festival to mark the end of the fast at the conclusion of Ramadan, on first of *Shawwal*; also, Little Id, *Id al-Saghir* (Minor Feast), *Id al-Sadaqa* (Feast of Alms),

*Sekar Bayram* (Sugar Holiday, Turkey), *Idul Fitri* (Indonesia). See "The Muslim Calendar," p. 162.

**Id al-Qiyana (ihd**-uhl-kee-**yah**-nah) – Arabic for *Easter*; cf., adha. See "The Feast of Sacrifice," p. 168.

**iftar (ihf-**tahr) – meal eaten at the break of the fast, right after sunset, during the month of Ramadan; often shared in the community.

**Ignorance, Period of** – cf., Jahiliyyah.

**Ihram (ih**-hrahm) – **1.** state of ritual purity and peace (with self and others) entered by pilgrim intending to perform the Hajj or the *Umrah* (in which certain activities are prohibited); **2.** two seamless sheets (*izar* and *rida*) donned by all male pilgrims (modest clothes for women), on the Hajj or *Umrah*, when they reach Jidda (on the Saudi Arabian coast, forty miles from Mecca).

**ihsan (ih**-sahn) – *right doing*; proper conduct; a moral duty enjoined by Islam; the perfection the individual strives to achieve, as if he sees Allah, or Allah sees him.

**ijaz al-Qur'an** (ah-**jahz ahl**-quhr-ah-ahn) – *miraculousness of the Qur'an*; the doctrine that the Qur'an confirmed Muhammad's prophethood (Sura 10:37–39); that the Qur'an was not created in time, cannot be replicated, and that the Arabic text is sacred (Sura 16:103); therefore, the Qur'an's exact meaning is hidden and cannot be translated accurately from the Arabic; cf., mujiza.

†**ijma, ijmaa (ahj**-mah) – **1.** consensus of group of Muslim legal scholars, introduced in the eighth century to standardize legal theory and practice, as opposed to *ijtihad*, independent reasoning; **2.** currently, the general consensus of a group of Islamic judges representing the community, who know Islamic dogma; **3.** the third source of Islamic law, the first being the Qur'an, and the second, the Hadith.

**ijtema (ihj**-teh-mah) – gathering of *Tablighi Jamaat*, evangelizers and rejuvenators of the faith; second largest gathering of Muslims (after the Hajj).

**ijtihad (ihj**-tee-hahd), (**adj., ijtihadi**) – *to endeavor, exert effort*; independent reasoning or individual interpretation of the tenets of the faith by an Muslim scholar, as opposed to ijma, or *taqlid*; cf., mujtahid.

**Ikhwan al-Muslimun (ihkh**-wahn ahl-**moos**-lee-meen) – contemporary reform movement within Islam, started by Hasan al-Banna (1906–1974) in Egypt; cf., the Muslim Brotherhood, Wahhabi.

**Al-Ilah, Ilah, Illah (ahl**-eel-lah) – *the deity*; variant of Allah.

**ilm (ahlm)** – *knowledge*; intellectual knowledge of theology, as opposed to *marifah*, inner experimental knowledge (Sufi Islam).

**ilm al-tabir (ahlm ahl-tah**-ah-beer) – *science of interpretation*; particularly divination by the interpretation of dreams.

†**imam (ee-mahm)** – *leader*; **1.** lay religious leader, or professional cleric of a Muslim community or mosque; leads in Friday salat (noon congregational prayers); the imam *khatib* is the cleric who delivers the sermon, *khutbah*. Arab Shi'a have always referred to their religious authorities as imams; in North America, it is a title of religious standing; **2.** for the Sunni, prominent jurist; an authoritative scholar who founds a school of theology.

†**Imam** (ee-**mahm**) – *leader*; for the Shi'a, a pure and sinless, divinely appointed leader (ruler, Caliph, combination spiritual and political leader who rules by Islamic law), successor of Muhammad, granted same divine knowledge and light Allah gave Muhammad; considered by Shi'a Muslims to be the only authoritative interpreter of the hidden meaning of the Qur'an. Shi'a accept the *Imamate*, the succession of Imams who trace their genealogy to the Prophet. The twelfth Imam went into hiding (*occulation*), and the source of authority was transferred to the *fuqaha*, experts on Islamic jurisprudence (or *fuqh*), or the jurists of the Ulama, who are considered to be collectively the representatives of the hidden Imam; cf., Mahdi.

**Imamate** (**English**) (ee-**mah**-maht), **Imamah** (**Arabic**) (**ee-**mah-mah) – religious-political leadership; the Shi'i belief that the same divine knowledge and light Allah granted Muhammad continues through a succession of "rightly guided" sinless leaders, Imams; only these leaders (now in hiding) possess understanding of the hidden meaning of the Qur'an; meanwhile, the temporal authority for interpreting the religion rests with the jurists, fuqaha, of the *ulama*; cf., Imami.

**iman** (ee-**mahn**) – *faith* (conviction), *belief*; the Muslim Creed; formal belief (such as in Allah, *angels*, prophets, final *Judgment Day*), as distinguished from Muslim practices, *deen*. See "Ask Good Questions," p. 218.

**Imami** (ee-**mahn**-ih) – *Ithna Ashari*, *Twelvers*, Shi'a who accept the *Imamate* succession through Ali and believe the twelfth Imam (who went into *occultation* in 939), will return as the Mahdi

(Messiah-like leader), to institute divine rule on earth; *Ithna Ashari* believe an Imam is necessary in order to set up the ideal Muslim community.

**Indo-Aryan peoples** – See "Indo-Iranian Peoples," p. 80.

†**infidel** – non-believer, polytheist, idol worshiper; person who does not believe in the religion of Islam; cf., Dar al-Harb, mushrikun.

†**Injil, Indjil, Injeel** (ihn-**jeel**) – usually refers to the Christians' religious book, the present-day New Testament, or sometimes to the four Gospels. More accurately, Injil is the qur'anic term primarily understood by Muslims to refer to an original, uncorrupted gospel that God revealed to and through Jesus (Sura 3:84; 5:46–48), which Jesus taught, and which is lost (and secondarily, to the four Gospels, the New Testament, the Bible, or Christian Scriptures); Muslims believe that subsequently, the Injil became the greatly corrupted text (*tabdil, tahrif*; by *interpolation*, Sura 5:13–15), now known as the New Testament by Christians; also called *Injil Sharif*, or Noble Gospel; cf., The Book, the Book of God, Holy Book, People of the Book (Ahl al-Kitab).

**Insha Allah, insha-al-Lah** (ihn-**shah** ahl-lah) – *"If Allah wills"*; phrase commonly said as plans are made, or in hopes of something happening in the future; reminds believer that nothing happens unless Allah wills it, and that only what Allah wills will happen; (Sura 6:125; 76:30–31); cf., kismet, maktub, ma sha Allah, qadaa, qisma. See "Why Do Muslims Say, '*Insha Allah*'?" p. 237.

**interpolation** – inserting extra material into an existing document, altering or

falsifying the meaning, thus corrupting the original; cf., Injil, tabdil, tahrif.

**intifada** (ihn-tee-**fah**-dah or ihn-tee-**fah**-thah) – *uprising*; launched by Palestinians in 1987 against Israel, designed to lead to establishment of Palestinian state and homeland.

**Iqamat-as-Salat** (ee-**qah**-maht-**ahs**-sah-laht) – the performing of salat (prayers) by every Muslim: men in congregation in the mosque, women at home, five times a day, and in just the same way (by all the rules and pattern of postures) as did the Prophet Muhammad.

**iqra** (**ihq-**rah) – *recite*; the recitation of divine revelation.

†**Isa** (**ee**-sah) – Arabic for Jesus, *Isa ibn Maryam*, son of Mary; in the Qur'an (Sura 3:42–63; 4:156–59; 5:46–48; the Sura of Maryam, 19), Jesus is called *Kalimat Allah*, "the Word of God," *Isa al-Masih* ("Jesus, the Messiah"), righteous prophet, sign, Spirit from God, "the Breath from God," conceived miraculously (Sura 3:45), and "a prophet of the Book" (Sura 19:30); and is considered by Muslims to be one of the five or six authentic prophets (*rasul*), or *Nabi Isa* (prophet Jesus), a great spiritual leader, and teacher. For Christians, Jesus is God's Son, which is an offensive concept for Muslims (Sura 19:35), and which the Qur'an denies (Sura 9:30), along with his death. Muslims deny his crucifixion and resurrection (Sura 4:157–58; except 3:55 and, 5:117; cf., adha). The Qur'an claims Christ's chief mission was to confirm the law of the prophets before him, and to proclaim the coming Apostle, *Ahmad*, Muhammad (Sura 61:6); cf., Yesua. See "Is Allah God?" p. 89; "The Feast of Sacrifice," p. 168; "I Saw Him in a Dream," p. 200; "Jesus in the Qur'an," p. 299; "Jesus' Death," p. 312.

**Isa al-Masih** (**ee**-sah ahl-mah-**seeh**) – *Jesus the Messiah*.

**Isawa** (ah-**sahw**-wah), **Isawiss (disciples of Isa)** – a sect of Islam in northern Nigeria which exalts Jesus (Isa); cf., Millat Issawi, Muslimun Issawiyun.

**isha** (**ah**-shah) – *evening meal*; time of the fifth ritual prayer (salat) of the day; late evening, from one and a half hour after sunset, to the middle of the night.

**Ishak** (**ihs**-hahk) – Isaac, prophet (for Muslims).

†**Ishmael** (ihs-mah-**eel**) – *Ismail, God hears* (Gen. 16:11); father of the Arabs and the first son of *Abraham*, by his wife's maid, Hagar of Egypt (Gen. 16:1–16; 17:18–27; 21:9–21); Muslims believe Ishmael, not Isaac, was the son of God's promise to Abraham (Gen. 22:1–19; Sura 37:100–107), that he and his mother moved to the Valley of Mecca, where Abraham joined him to rebuild the Ka'aba. See "God's Promise to Muslims," p. 70; "The Feast of Sacrifice," p. 168.

**islam** (**ihs**-lahm) – *peace, purity, submission, obedience*; submission or surrender to the will of Allah.

†**Islam, al-Islam** (**ihs**-lahm) – *submission*; Islam is the monotheistic faith and practice of Muslims, as revealed to Muhammad and in the Qur'an, with both official, theological, ethical, and organizational expressions, and extensive, pragmatic, indigenous, informal constructs of beliefs and practices; cf., popular Islam.

**Islamic lunar calendar** – lunar calendar, started at 622 as the year *A.H.* 1; cf., Hijra.

**Islamic Fundamentalism** – Muslim militant movement; resurgence or revolution in doctrine, politics, and life, advocating return to the union of orthodox Muslim religion and the state, based on Shari'a law. It has arisen in response to disenfranchisement, secularization, and Westernization; and is variously evidenced by the call for idealistic reforms, or rebellion against government, fanaticism, dogmatism, or antagonism; cf., Islamist, Muslim Brotherhood, Wahhabi. See "Progression to Violence," p. 145.

†**Islamist** – radical Islamic political or social activist. See "Progression to Violence," p. 145.

**isma, ismah** (**ehs**-mah) – *preservation*; in particular, the preservation of the prophets from all *sin*, or at least from all major *sins*; their faithfulness to divine commands, impeccability, and inerrancy.

**al-isma al-husna, al-asma al-husna** (ahl-**ihs**-mah ahl-hoos-**nah**) – *"the nicest names"*; the *ninety-nine beautiful names* (or attributes) *of God*, mostly derived from the Qur'an; for many Muslims, belief in Allah devolves largely into magical use of his names; cf., subha. (As distinguished from Muhammad's more than one hundred Noble Names.) See Appendix 1, p. 471.

**Ismail** – Ishmael.

**Ismaili, Ismailiya, Ishmaeli** (ihs-mah-**ee**-lee) – a sect of the Shi'a, also called the *Seveners*, who split over the identity of the seventh Imam; named after Ismail, eldest son of Imam Jafar al-Sadiq (d. 765); one of the two branches (the other is Mustali), the *Nizari*, call the *Aga Khan* their Imam; also called *Khojas*.

**isnad** (**ihs**-nahd) – witness or chain of authorities through whom (by oral and written narration) the Traditions of the Prophet Muhammad were handed down from his lifetime; those who transmitted the hadith.

**al-Isra al-Miraj** (ahl-**ihs**-rah ahl-ma-a-**rahj**) – celebration of *Lailat al-Miraj*, when Gabriel took Muhammad from *Al-Masjid al-Haram* (Mecca), to *al-Masjid al-Aqsa* (Jerusalem), Sura 17:1.

**Israfel** (**ihs**-rah-feel) – one of four *archangels*, with Gabriel, *Michael*, and *Azrael*.

**Issawiyun** (ahs-**swah**-yoon) – the word used to describe a Muslim who exalts Jesus; can be translated "Jesus-ite."

**istihsan** (ihs-**tihh**-sahn) – juristic preference; the principle that permits exceptions to strict or literal legal reasoning in favor of the public interest; used for reforming Islamic law; cf., Hanafi, ray.

**istikhara** (ihs-tih-**khah**-rah) – *asking favors*. **1.** a salat appealing to Allah for guidance in a certain venture; **2.** a divinatory practice of opening the Qur'an at random, or counting out prayer beads (*subha*).

**Ithna Ashari,** (ahth-nah ahl-**ahsh**-ahree) – cf., Ashari, Imam, Imamate, Shi'a, Twelvers.

**ittakala** (iht-tah-**kahl**-ah) – *trust*; the trust of commitment to Christ.

**iyah** (**ee**-yah) (**plur., iyat**) (ee-**yaht**) – cf., aya (plur., ayat).

**izar** (ih-**zahr**) – seamless white cloth, wrapped around loins to knee level, by the male pilgrim on the Hajj or *Umrah*; cf., Ihram, rida.

# J

**Jacobites** – *Syrian* Monophysites (sixth century), Syrian Orthodox Church.

**Jahannam** (jah-**hahn**-nahm) – *hell*, hellfire; place of eternal punishment after death; cf., Judgment Day.

**Jahiliyyah** (jah-hihl-**lee**-yah) – *ignorance*; the *Period (Times) of Ignorance*, infidelity in pagan, polytheistic, nomadic Arabia, before Islam, before the revelation of Allah to Muhammad; or practices that existed then or were inherited from that time; cf., Hubal, Al-Uzza.

**jaiz** (jah-**ihz**) – canonically permissible deed, *mubah*.

**al-Jalil** (ahl-jahl-**leel**) – *Most Majestic*; one of the names of Allah. See Appendix 1, p. 472.

**jallabiya** (jehl-lah-**bee**-yah), **djellaba** – long dress worn by men and women in Arab countries.

**jam'a** (jah-**mah**-ah) – *mosque*; Muslim house of worship; cf., Baitullah, masjid.

**Jamaat-i Islami** (jeh-**mah**-ah-tee his-**lah**-mee) – Community of Islam, founded 1941 as a revivalist party in India before Pakistan partition; sought to reform, educate, and revive Islam.

**Jamaat al-Jihad, or al-Jihad (Islamic Jihad Community)** (jah-**mah**-ah ahl-jee-**hahd**) – Egyptian fundamentalist Islamic group founded in late 1970s; active in cities in Upper Egypt; allied with Islamic Community (al-Jama ah al-Islamiyyah, 1980); cf., Muslim Brotherhood.

**Jamra** (**jahm**-rah)**, (plur., Jamrat or Jimar)** (jah-ma-**raht**, **jih**-mahr) – during the Hajj, the ceremony at *Mina*; a ritual stoning with pebbles of one of three small stone stele representing *Iblis* and his powers of temptation;

recalls *Abraham's* turning from the devil's suggestion that he not sacrifice Ishmael; cf., Iblis, Shaytan, al-Shaytanul-Kabir.

**Janna** (**jehn**-nah) – *Paradise*; abode of peace, Islamic understanding of heaven, where Adam and Eve first lived, and the place to which the true slaves of Allah will return; cf., Yawm al-Akhir.

**al-Jazuli** (ahl-ghah-zah-**lee**) – poet who wrote the litany, *Dalail al-Khayrat*.

**Jerusalem** – third of Islam's holiest cities, focus of the Crusades; direction of prayer until the second year of the Hijra in Medina, when the break with the Jews became complete, and the Muslims began to face Mecca to win the favor of the Quraysh; cf., al-Aqsa (al-Masjid al-Aqsa); Qubbat al-Sakhra, Dome of the Rock, Haram; Saladin.

**Jesus, Prophet** – cf., Isa. See "Ask Good Questions," p. 218.

**Jewish tribes** – cf., Banu Nadir, Banu Qainuqa, Banu Qurayza.

**Jibril, Jibrieel** (jahb-**reel**) – Gabriel; *archangel* by whom Allah sent down his Book, the Qur'an, to Muhammad (Sura 2:97–98); protector of Muhammad (Sura 66:4).

**al-Jihad** (**ahl** jee-hahd) – cf., Jamaat al-Jihad.

**†jihad** (**jee**-hahd) –*struggle* for the faith. **1.** an inner struggle for remembrance of Allah, or expenditure of effort for his way; includes warfare against jinn; **2.** Islamic religious or holy war ("Lesser Jihad"), fighting with word or sword for the cause of Allah against his enemies or unbelievers, to extend the umma; sometimes regarded as the sixth Pillar of the Faith; Sura 2:135, 190–93; 9:29. See "What Is Jihad?" p. 148.

**jilbab** (**jihl**-bahb) – generic term for woman's outer cloak, wrap, or shawl, to be worn per qur'anic directions (Sura 33:59); cf., abaaya, chador (chadris), burqa.

†**jinn, jinni** (**male**) (**jihn**-nee)**, jinniya** (**female**) (jihn-**nee**-yah) (**plur., jinn**) (**jihn**) – separate species of spirits, below *angels* and above humans, created by Allah from fire; some evil, like demons, but others helpful; strong component of popular Islam. Intensely jealous of humans, jinn seek opportunities to injure them; they inhabit the human domain and are specifically territorial, having subtle bodies that can change by metamorphosis or enter people and things; described by effect (khafi [concealed], *ghul* [destroying], *afrit* [rolls in the dust], *ghashi* [one who faints]); or whether the person is struck or possessed (madrub, *majnun*, maklu, maqyus, *marid*, maskun, masqut, *matrush*, mushar [plur. musharum]); or given specific names (al-Karisi, *Umm al-Subyan*); cf., az ma bihtaran, haduk al-nas. See "Women and Power," p. 198; "Why Is Baraka Needed?" p. 211.

**jizyah** (**jihz**-yahh) – *tribute, tax;* a head tax imposed on Jews and Christians or non-Muslims living in an Islamic state and enjoying its protection (*aman*, dhimmi).

**Job** – Ayyub, Job.

**Judgment Day, Day of Final Judgement, Last Day** – cf., Munkar, Nakir; iman, Yawm al-Akhir. See "What Is Permitted?" p. 84.

**Juma, Jumah, Jumuah** (**joom**-ah) – Friday congregational prayer at noon; *salat al-Jumah,* prayer assembly; *Yawm al-Juma,* day of assembly.

**juzw** (**jooz**) – one of the divisions of the Qur'an into thirty equal parts for memorization purposes.

# K

†**Ka'aba, Ka'bah, Ka'ba** (**kah**-ah-bah) – *cube;* cubical shrine (*Baitullah, House of God*) inside the Al Masjid-al-Haram (the Grand [Great] Mosque) in Mecca, with the Holy Black Stone, *al-Hajar al-Aswad,* a black meteorite, in the corner, which was kissed by Muhammad, and Muslims since his time who make the Hajj; the *House of Allah* or the Holy House is believed to have been built by Adam, and repaired by *Abraham* and Ishmael; for Muslims, the center of the universe, toward which they turn in prayer.

**kabira** (keh-**beer**-ah) – great sins; cf., hadd, kufr, mushrikun, shirk, sin.

**kaffiyeh** (kah-**fee**-yah) – headdress, secured with a band around the crown, usually worn by Arab men.

†**kafir** (**kah**-fihr)**, (plur., kuffar)** (koof-**fahr**) – *ungrateful, unbeliever,* or *infidel;* one who rejects the message of Islam, or blasphemes; opposite of *mumin,* believer; cf., mushrikun.

**kalimah** (**kah**-lee-mah) – *the word;* bearing witness; the Creed or confession of the Muslim, as in, *kalimat al-Shahada, the word of testimony;* cf., five Pillars of Islam, Shahada.

**Kalimat Allah** (kah-lee-**maht** ahl-lah)**, Kalam Allah** (kah-**lahm** ahl-lah) – "*Word of God*"; one of Jesus' (Isa's) titles in the Qur'an; not a term used by Muslims to refer to the Bible.

**kampung** (kahm-**poong**) – neighborhood (Indonesia), source of community, support, and accountability; urban and rural; cf., lurah.

**karama** (kah-**rah**-mah) – *miracle;* authenticating sign of a saint.

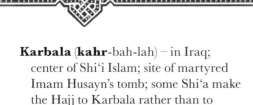

**Karbala** (**kahr**-bah-lah) – in Iraq; center of Shi'i Islam; site of martyred Imam Husayn's tomb; some Shi'a make the Hajj to Karbala rather than to Mecca; cf. , Ashura.

**al-Karisi** (ahl-kah-**ree**-see) – *the Red*; name of a *jinniya* (Turkey).

**kebatinan** (keh-**bah**-tee-**nahn**) – discipline of inner life; informal belief system (Javanese), including animism and various spirit beliefs, and *dukun* (Shamans); distinctive trait is practice of *ngelmu*, which explores the relationship between the natural and supernatural; thought to offer path to spiritual power.

**Kedar** (**kee**-dahr) – section of Arabian desert. See "God's Promise to Muslims," p. 70.

**kejawen** (keh-**jah**-wehn) – Javanese *adat*, customary law.

**Kemal Ataturk** (ka-**mahl** aht-tah-**tuhrk**) – cf., Ataturk.

†**Khadija, Khadijah** (khah-**dih**-jah) – Muhammad's first (when he was twenty-five) and only wife (wealthy widow about forty) until her death; first to believe in the Prophet and accept the message he brought from Allah; their two sons died, four daughters lived.

**Khalid Ibn al-Walid** (**khah**-lihd ihb-nihl-**wah**-leed) – a great warrior who planned the Meccans' defeat of the Muslims at *Uhud* (625); later converted to Islam, and became one of the most famous Muslim generals.

**Khalil Ullah** (**khah**-lee lool-**ah**) – Friend of Allah (Sura 4:125), *Abraham*; 2 Chron. 20:7, Isa. 41:8, James 2:23. See "God's Promise to Muslims," p. 70.

**khalifah, khaliph** (khah-**lee**-fah) – cf., Caliph.

**khamsa** (**khahm**-sah) – *five*; refers to five fingers of the human hand, used in a protective gesture: extended toward the potential inflicter of the glance of the evil eye.

**kharaj** (**khihr**-rahj) – land tax, paid by non-Muslims living under Islamic rule; cf., aman, dhimmi.

**Khariji, Khawarij** (khah-**wah**-rihj)**, Kharajiya** (khah-rah-**jee**-yah) – first puritanical and militant sect of Islam; Seceders, Exiters; named after Abdullah bin Ibad; descendents are today's *Ibadi*, who are much more moderate in their views.

**khatam al-anbiya** (**khah**-tahm ahl-an-**bee**-yah)**, khatimah** – *end*; *seal*; the last and greatest of all prophets, Muhammad.

**khatib** (khah-**teeb**) – cleric who delivers *khutbah*.

**khimar** (**khih**-mahr) – cloth worn by woman to cover her head and neck.

**khitan** (khah-**tahn**) – *circumcision*; rite of passage.

**Khojas** (khoh-**jah**) – cf., Assassins, Ismaili, Nizari; titular head is Aga Kahn.

**Khomeini** (khoh-**may**-nee)**, Ayatollah** (ah-yah-too-**lah** roh-**hohl**-lah) **Ruhollah** – (1900–1989) Iranian Shi'i cleric, leader of Islamic revolution (1979); emphasized strict enforcement of traditional social practices, and Shari'a law; issued fatwa against *Salman Rushdie* (1989).

**"khudh al-baraka min al-mawlid"** (khooth ahl-**bah**-rah-kah mihn ahl-**mahw**-lihd) – *"take the baraka from the mawlid"*; reason for celebrating the birthday or deathday of a holy man.

**khumrah** (**khoom**-rah) – kneeling mat of sufficient size to accommodate the face and hands during the prostrations of salat.

**khutbah** (**khoot**-bah) – sermon delivered to the congregation by the imam *khatib*, usually at the Friday prayers; cf., imam.

**kiai** (**kee**-ie) – Muslim leader and teacher (Java).

**kismet** (**kihs**-maht, Turkey) – *fate*; cf., qisma; maktub, qadaa, Insha Allah. See "Why Do Muslims Say, '*Insha Allah*'?" p. 237.

**kitab** (**plur., kutub**) (kee-**tahb**, **koo**-toob) – *book*; the religious books; *al-Kitab*, the Qur'an, *The Book*; the doctrine of Allah's books has largely turned into the practice of bibliolatry among Muslims.

**al-Kitab** (**ahl**-kee-tahb) – *The Book*; the Qur'an.

**Koran** (**quhr**-ah-ahn) – less preferable spelling of Qur'an.

**kudiya** (kah-**dee**-yah) – female practitioner; interpreter of dreams.

**kufi** (**koo**-fee) – *skullcap*.

**kufr, kufur** (**koo**-fuhr) – *blasphemy*; the ultimate evil of disbelief in God, his signs, and any of the articles of Islamic faith; ungodliness or lack of faith; rejection of revelation, thanklessness, atheism, apostasy, or infidelity; cf., hadd, kabira, kafir, mushrikun, shirk, sin.

**al-Kutub al-Sittah** (ehl-**koot**-oob ehs-seet-**tah**) – cf., Sihah Sittah.

# L

**"La ikraha fil-dini"** (**lah** ihk-rah-**hah** fihd-**deen**) – "There is no compulsion in religion"; the qur'anic saying (Sura 2:56), and Islamic ethos against an insistent, dogmatic orthodoxy.

**"La ilaha illa al-Lah"** (**lah**-eel-lah-**hah** il-lah **lah**) – confession of faith, or recitation of the Creed; first part of the liturgical expression, the Shahada: *"There is no God but Allah."*

**Lailat, Laylat** (lay-**laht** ) – cf., al-Baraa (Lailat), al-Miraj (Lailat), al-Qadr.

**Lakhmid** (**lahkh**-mihd) – Persian Empire protégé, Christian tribal buffer state, in preIslamic southern Iraq; rivals of *Ghassanids*; later, under Islam, and allied with rivals, participated in destruction of Persian and Byzantine empires.

**Last Day** – *Judgment Day, Yawm al-Akhir*; cf., iman.

**"Law of Apostasy"** – deterrent to Muslims' conversion to Christianity in countries where orthodox Islam prevails; advocation of application of Sura 4:88–89, 5:57, and 16:106, leading to imprisonment, torture, even death, of Christians, as of other infidels; cf., compulsion.

**Lesser Hajj** – Lesser Pilgrimage; cf., Umrah.

**Levant, the** (leh-**vahnt**) – former name of East Mediterranean geographical area (modern-day Israel, Lebanon, parts of *Syria* and Turkey).

**Love** – cf., al-Wadud; the loving; forty-seventh name of Allah.

**Lull, Raymond** – (1232–1315) first significant Christian witness to Muslims; martyred when past eighty years of age.

**lunar calendar** – cf., A.H. See "The Muslim Calendar," p. 162.

**lurah** (**loo**-rah) – *kampung* official whose position is a combination of mayor and sheriff (Indonesia).

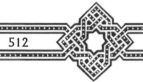
# M

**ma'bud** (**mah**-bood) – God accepted as God, the proper object of worship, reverence, loyalty, and obedience.

**madhhab** (**mahd**-hahb, or **mahth**-hahb)**, (plur., madhabib)** (mah-tha-**hihb**) – judicial system or rite; school of law, or interpretation, for ordering religious and community life; Sunni, Shi'a, and Sufi are in each group; there are four: *Shafi'i, Hanafi, Hanbali,* and *Maliki.*

**Al-Madina** (ahl-mah-**dee**-nah), **Madinah; Madinat al-Nabi** (mah-dee-naht-ahl-**na**-bee)**, Madinat al-Rasul ("city of the Prophet")** – Medina.

**†madrasa, madrasah** (mahd-**rah**-sah) – school; originally, school of cannon law; then secondary school; generally, refers to an Islamic school, one that emphasizes qur'anic studies, for children or those older. See Picture, p. 68.

**magha** (**mah**-ghah) – coffee house (India).

**Maghreb, Maghrib** (**mahgh**-rihb) – *sunset.* **1.** Arabic for the direction west; generally applied to West North Africa, centered on Algeria, Morocco, and Tunisia. **2.** *maghrib,* fourth or evening sunset salat. See Map, "Where Is the Middle East?" p. 56.

**†Mahdi** (**mahh**-dee)**, al-Mahdi** (**ahl**-mahh-dee) – *the rightly guided one;* the coming Imam, a Messiah-like world leader who will return or appear, to fill the whole earth with righteousness and cause it to embrace Islam; Sunnis still await his initial appearance, while Shi'a hold that the last Imam, Muhammad al-Mutazar, who disappeared in 874 (or 878), will someday reappear as the Mahdi; cf., Ahmadi.

**Mahmud of Ghazna** (mah-**mood**, **ghuhz**-nah) – (d. 1030) "Mahmud the idol smasher" invaded the Punjab (northwest India), furthering Islam's advance; a Muslim governor was set up in Lahore (ca. 1000).

**mahr** (**mah**-har) – form of dowry, a normal stipulation of a marriage contract, paid by bridegroom or his family.

**Majma al-daawat** (**maj**-ma ahl-**dahw**-aht) – *Collection of Invocations,* by Muhammad Ibn Kiyas al-Din; book dealing with the meaning and interpretation of dreams.

**majnun** (**maj**-noon) – *possessed by;* **1.** generic term for the state of being harmed by jinn; **2.** crazy, funny, or a maniac; used in jest to indicate such a person.

**Makkah** (**mah**-kah or **meh**-kah) – Mecca.

**maktub** (mahk-**toob**) – *written;* that which is fated for a person; determinism, fatalism; indicating responsibility for calamity; official Islam holds that existence for Muslims is fixed; in reality, through pragmatic activities, they seek to rewrite their destinies; cf., Insha Allah, kismet, qadaa, qisma. See "Why Do Muslims Say, *'Insha Allah'?"* p. 237.

**malak** (mah-**lak**)**, (plur., al-malaik, malaikah)** (ahl-**mah**-lihk) – *the ones in authority;* angels, created out of fire, faithful servants of Allah; cf., Archangel.

**Malay** (Mah-lay) **peoples** – See "Malay Peoples"; Map, "Southeast Asia," p. 127.

**Malik** (**mah**-lihk) – *angel* that guards the gates of hell and to whom one may appeal for assistance.

**Maliki, Malik** (**mah**-lihk-ee) – *madhhab;* a school of law, or judicial system based essentially on the hadith using *ray* and *qiyas*, especially those attributed to Muhammad's closest *Companions* in Medina; founded by Malik ibn Anas al-Asbahi (d. 795).

**malvi** (mahl-**vee**) (**plur., malvis**) – Muslim teacher.

**Mamluk** (mahm-**looks**) – dynasty in Egypt (ca. 1390), in which Cairo became center of the Muslim world.

**Manasik al-Hajj wal-Umrah** (mah-**nah**-sihk ahl-**hahj** wahl-**oom**-rah) – full ceremonial acts connected with the Hajj or *Umrah*: *Ihram, Tawaf, Say, Jamrat.*

†**man of peace** – community leader, or man of influence in his extended family, who welcomes Christians and may bring others (Luke 10:5–9).

**mansukh** (mahn-**sookh**) – that which is *abrogated*; that which *abrogates* is *nasikh.*

**manzil** (mahn-**zool**) – one of seven portions into which the Qur'an has been divided, so as to be recited in seven days.

**Maqam Ibrahim** (mah-**qahm** ihb-rah-**heem**) – the sacred stone on which *Abraham* stood while he and Ishmael were building the Ka'aba.

**marabout** (**mah**-rah-boo) – *one who has joined himself* to Allah; Sufi holy man; North or West African cleric possessing exceptional spiritual powers; religious saint (dead or alive); a charismatic leader of a Muslim religious order; if petitioned, his baraka is available; cf., murabit, pir, wali.

**marid** (mah-**rehd**) – very strong, aggressive type of jinn who try to kill their victims.

**marifah** (**mah**-ree-fah) – doctrine of inner experimental knowledge, or spiritual truth from ecstatic experience (Sufi); as opposed to *ilm.*

**Marionites** – eastern branch of Roman Catholic church, in *Syria* and Lebanon.

**Martel, Charles** – the Franks' general who stopped Islam's advance into France from Spain, at Poitiers and *Tours,* in France.

**Martyn, Henry** – (1781–1812) English pastor; went to India (1805) as a chaplain of the East India Company; a brilliant linguist, in under five years he had translated the New Testament into Urdu and Persian, and supervised its translation into Arabic; died tragically in Armenia at the age of only thirty-one; his life inspired missions vocation, translation, and scholarship.

**Maryam** (**Mary**) – Mary, mother of Jesus (The Sura of Maryam, Sura 19).

**Ma sha Allah** (mah **shah** ah-lah) – "*What Allah wills*"; **1.** expression used to protect others from the evil eye; added to every compliment or pronouncement of success, to prove one's sincerity, or cancel a possible curse; indicates a good omen; **2.** the protective substitute name given the newborn child, to mislead the jinn; cf., Insha Allah.

**Mashaf** (moos-**hahf**) – another name for the Qur'an in handwritten form.

**mashhad** (**mahsh**-hahd) – martyrium (Iran), shrine built in memory of a martyr.

**al-Masih** (ahl-mah-**seeh**) – in the Qur'an, "the Christ"; cf., Isa; Acts 10:38.

†**masjid** (**mahs**-jihd) – *mosque*; the place of bowing down, the Muslim place of worship; cf., Baitullah, jami.

**Al-Masjid al-Aqsa** (ahl-**mahs**-jijd ahl-**ahqs**-sah)**, (Bait-ul-Maqdis)** – the Grand (Great) Mosque (of *Omar*[*Umar*]) in *Jerusalem*; cf., Al-Aqsa, Dome of the Rock, Haram, Sakhra.

**Al-Masjid al-Haram** (ahl-**mahs**-jihd-ahl-hah-**rahm**) – the Grand (Great) Mosque in Mecca, inside the *Haram*, which contains the Ka'aba.

**Masjid Issawi** (**mahs**-jihd ees-**sahw**-ee) – a Jesus mosque.

**matn** (**miht**-ihn) – texts of hadiths, put in book form; Hadith.

**matrilocal** – society in which residence for new families is with wife's kin group.

**matrush** (mah-**troosh**) – state of being slapped by jinn.

**maulid, mawlid** (**mahw**-lihd or **mahw**-lood) – *birthday*; of a saint or prophet; such annual celebrations (with fairs, concerts, animal sacrifices, and offerings), occur especially at the shrines of pirs.

**Maulid al-Nabi, Mawlid al-Nabi** (**mahw**-lihd ahl-**nah**-bah-wee) – *birthday of the Prophet*. **1.** festal celebration of Muhammad's birthday, on twelfth day of third month, *Rabi al-Awwal*. **2.** a poem (*qasida*) by *Al-Mirghanni*, popular at celebrations of the Prophet's birthday.

**mawlana** (mahw-**lah**-nah) – from *protector*; official versed in Islamic theology; theologian of the orthodox hierarchy, employed to give religious instruction.

**mazar** (mah-**zahr**) – *place of pilgrimage*; site of religious visits; usually a shrine, as in the tomb of a Muslim saint; also *mashhad* (martyrium); *turba* (mausoleums).

†**MBB** – abbreviation used to refer to a Muslim-background believer; in many places, calling a convert a Christian would cause offense or even endanger the MBB's life. See "Barriers to the Gospel," p. 294; "The Steady Loss of Witness," p. 315; "Putting the Bible in Their Hands," p. 425.

†**Mecca** (**makh**-kah) – *Makkah, Bakka, Baca*; the birthplace of Muhammad, located in Saudi Arabia; "Mother of Cities" (Sura 42:7), considered the most *Holy City* of Islam, home of the Ka'aba; it must be visited by those Muslims physically and financially able, at least once in a lifetime, on the Hajj or *Umrah*.

†**Medina** (mah-**dee**-nah) – *Al Madina, Madinah, Madihat al-nabi*, City of the Prophet, formerly named Yathrib; city to which Muhammad fled (Hijra, 622), 290 miles north of Mecca, where he established the Islamic state, and where he is buried under the dome of the mosque; second holiest city in Islam.

**Mesopotamia** – geographic area; ancient name of modern Iraq.

**messehy** (mehs-seeh-**hee**) – *Christian, mujedadiin*, "The regenerated ones," possible name for believers.

†**Messenger of God, The; -of Allah, -Last** – Muhammad (Sura 33:40, 53:1–18); the Prophet, the *Apostle of Arabia, of Islam*; a messenger or prophet is rasul, or *nabi*.

**meunasah** (muh-**nah**-sah) – community building used for prayer, Islamic teaching, and civil meetings (Indonesia); cf., lampung.

**Michael** – one of four *archangels*, with *Azrael*, Gabriel, and *Israfel*.

†**Middle East** – Southwest Asia: Iraq, Israel, Jordan, Lebanon, Palestine, and *Syria*. See Map, "Where Is the Middle East?" p. 56; "Where Is the Middle East?" p. 57.

**mihrab** (**mih**-rahb) – prayer niche in the *qibla* wall of the mosque, indicating the direction of the Ka'aba in Mecca, toward which the Muslim should bow in prayer.

**Millat Issawi** (**mihl**-laht ees-**sahw**-ee) – churches as Jesus fellowships; cf., Isawa, Muslimun Issawiyun.

**Mina** (**mee**-nah) – pilgrimage site outside of Mecca on the way to *Arafat*; cf., jamra.

†**minaret** (min-eh-**ret**) – tower of the mosque from which the *adhan* (*azan*) is made by the *muezzin* (*muadhadhin*).

**minbar** (**mihn**-bahr) – the raised pulpit in the mosque, on the *qibla* wall, from which the Friday sermon is delivered.

**miqat** (**mih**-qaht), (**plur., mawaqit**) (mah-wah-**qeet**) – prescribed stations on the approach to Mecca for performing preliminary rites (assuming *Ihram*), in preparation for the Hajj or *Umah*.

**al-Miraj** (**Lailat**) (lay-**laht** ahl-ma-a-**rahj**) – *Night of Ascension*; al-Isra; Nocturnal or *Night Journey* of the Prophet Muhammad from Mecca (on *Buraq*), to *Jerusalem*, then ascension (*miraj, ladder, way of ascent*) into the "Seventh Heaven" (Sura 17:1; hadith), on the twenty-seventh of *Rajab*; supposedly confirming Islam's continuity with Judism and Christianity; Jerusalem became Islam's third holiest city; celebrated as *al-Isra al-Miraj* with prayers, sermons, and a vigil ending with a banquet for the family and sweets for the children; cf., Al-Aqsa, Haram, Jerusalem, Sakhra.

**Al-Mirghanni** (ahl-mihr-**ghah**-nee) – writer of *qasida*, *Maulid al-Nabi*, subtitled, "The divine secrets about the birth of the most honorable human creature."

**mirza** (**meer**-zah) – title indicating one's ancestors who came into India with conquering Mughals.

**Mohammedan, Mohammedanism** – misnomers for Muslim and Islam, based on mistaken idea that the religion of Muslims is the worship of Muhammad ("Mohammed"), a concept vehemently denied by Muslims.

**Mongol** – **1.** *n.* member of the peoples of nomadic origin who inhabited Mongolia, and established the Mongol Empire in the thirteenth century; **2.** *adj.* pertaining to Mongolia, or the Mongols, or their culture and language; cf., Babur, Genghis Khan, Mughal Empire, Timur Lang.

†**Monophysite** (mon-**nof**-ih-site) – one who believes that Jesus Christ has a single inseparable nature that is both human and divine; *Ethiopia* was Monophysite in Muhammad's time.

**Moors** – Berbers of Northwest Africa; conquered Iberian peninsula in 711.

**Moses** – *Musa*, Speaker with God, and a prophet (Sura 19:51), recipient of God's Book, *Taurat* (Sura 17:2, 23:49); cf., rasul.

†**mosque** (**mahsq**) – western form of Arabic masjid, the Muslim house of worship, especially for Friday prayers.

**Mothers of the Believers** – Muhammad's wives; Sura 33:6, 53b. See "The Ideal Women," p. 372.

**moussem** (moh-oos-s**ehm**) – "occultic fairs" in Morocco; "satanic signs and wonders conferences," to witness supernatural feats, offer blood sacrifices, and receive *baraka*.

**muadhdhin** (moo-**ahth**-thihn, or moo-**ahz**-zihn) – *caller of the adhan* (*azan*); the one who calls to prayer; cf., minaret, muezzin.

**Muawiyah ibn Abi Sufyan** (moo-**ah**-wee-yah ehb **nah**-bee **soo**-fee-yahn) – relative of Uthman, governor of *Syria*, leader of *Umayyad* tribe (at the time of the murder of the fourth Caliph, Ali, 611), who became the fifth Caliph,

according to Sunnis, causing a major split in Islam, as the Shi'a, or followers of Ali, separated from (and warred against) the *Umayyad*; marking the shift to an imperial age, he established the Umayyad Caliphate as an absolute monarchy in Damascus (661–750); d. 680; eventually succeeded by his son, Yazid (680–683). See "The Quraysh Family Tree," p. 15.

**mubah** (moo-**bah**) – canonically permissible deed, *jaiz*.

**muezzin** (moo-**ahth**-thihn or moo-**ahz**-zihn) – the cantor who gives the call to prayer from the minaret of the mosque; cf., adhan, azan, muadhdhin.

**mufti** (**moof**-tee) – superior judge, interpreter of Islamic law for Sunnis.

**Mughal (moo**-gahl)**, Mogul, Moghul Empire** – Urdu *mughal*, Persian *mugul*; empire founded by *Babur* (of *Mongol* origin), which in 1526 ruled in a section of India, until 1857, when the British overthrew the last emperor; known for outstanding expressions of Islamic culture, especially architecture; cf., Genghis Khan, Timur Lang.

**Muhajir, Muhajirun** (moo-**hah**-jihr, moo-**hah**-jihr-roon) – *emigrants*. 1. those who went from Mecca to Yathrib with Muhammad or in his lifetime. 2. one who emigrates for Allah's sake, or quits all that Allah has forbidden.

†**Muhammad, Mahomet** (moo-**hahm**-mahd) – *praised*; the Chosen One, Allah's Apostle, the Prophet and founder of Islam, considered by Muslims to be *khatam al-anbiya*, the *Seal* (last) and greatest of the Prophets (Sura 33:40), or Last Messenger of Allah (*Rasul-Ullah*); born 570; died 632; sometimes spelled, *Mohammed*; cf., Ahmad; Maulid al-Nabi, nabi, nadhir, Prophet of Allah, Quraysh, rasul. See "The Quraysh Family Tree," p. 15, "The Life of Muhammad," p. 34.

**Muharram** (moo-hahr-**rahm**) – *that which is forbidden*, therefore, sacred; the first month of the Islamic calendar; New Year's festival is on the first day of *Muharram*; cf., haram, Husayn, taziya. See "The Muslim Calendar," p. 162.

**mujaddid** (moo-**jahd**-dihd) – *renewer*, of the faith; according to hadith, one comes each century to correct Muslim practice, free it of innovations

†**mujahid** (moo-**jah**-hihd)**, (plur., mujahideen, mujahidin)** (moo-**jah**-hah-deen) – a Muslim who exerts himself on behalf of the faith, especially a fighter in a holy war, or jihad.

**mujedadiin** (moo-**jeh**-dah-**deen**) – *"the regenerated ones"*; term for generic identity of MBBs; cf.k messehy.

**mujiza** (moo-ah-**jee**-zah) – a special miracle granted to a prophet in confirmation of his mission; cf., ijaz al-Qur'an.

**mujtahid** (mooj-**tah**-hihd)**, (plur., mujtahidun)** (mooj-tah-hee-**doon**) – religious jurists who follow only those interpretations of Islamic law proved through independent reasoning (*ijtihad*) from the Qur'an and the Sunna.

†**mullah, mulla** (**moo**-lah) – **1.** term for major cleric among Persians, Iranians, northern Indians, and Pakistanis. **2.** Shi'a Muslim religious leader. **3.** in popular Islam, the practitioner of magic and crisis rites.

**multazam** (mool-**ta**-zahm) – *that to which one is attached*; part of the wall of the Ka'aba to which pilgrims try to "attach" themselves in embrace.

**mumin** (**masc.**) (**moo**-mihn)**, mumina** (**fem**), moo-**mihn**-na – *believer*; in contrast to an unbeliever, kafir.

**Munafiqun** (moon-ah-fee-**qoon**) – hypocrite Muslims, a Medinan party tolerated by Muhammad.

**munajat** – prayer posture; kneeling, arms partly raised in prayer. See "The Postures of Prayer," p. 91.

**Munkar** (**moon**-kahr) – with *Nakir*, the two *angels* who subject men to fearsome questioning about their faith after their deaths (Sura 47:27); cf., Yawm al-Akhir.

**murabit** (mah-**rah**-biht) – *one who has joined himself to Allah*; a living saint; cf., marabout, wali.

**murid** (moo-**rehd**) – a Sufi novice, or aspirant, under the guidance of a *murshid*; or a member of a Sufi brother-hood or *tarika*, founded by a pir (saint) whose function is to give guidance on all matters.

**murshid** (**moor**-shihd) – *guide*; Sufi spiritual guide who has himself achieved communion with God and is the preceptor of those who aspire to such, especially in Pakistan and India; cf., pir, sheik, tarika, ustadh.

**Musa** (**moo**-sah) – *Moses*, Speaker with God; the prophet of God through whom the *Taurat* was revealed; cf., rasul.

**Musa Ibin Uqba** (**moo**-sah ibn-bihn ahqah-**bah**) – third generation biogra-pher who deliberately accelerated the process of idealizing Muhammad.

**mushrikun** (**moosh**-ree-koon) – those who worship other powers besides Allah, thus repudiating Islam; *polytheists, pagans*, idolaters, unbelievers; cf., kabira, kafir, kufr, shrik, sin.

†**Muslim** (**moos**-lihm) – *one who submits*; one who is surrendered to Allah; a fol-lower of Islam, a believer in Allah and Muhammad as his Prophet; sometimes written *Moslem*.

**al-Muslim** (ahl-**moos**-lihm) – Muslim ibn al-Hajjaj al-Nisaburi (817–875); one of two original and premier hadith collectors (with *al-Bukhari*; referred to as *al-Sahihan, the Correct Two*, or *al-Shaykhan, the Two Sheiks*); his important collection, *Sahih al-Muslim*, contains 12,000; cf., al-Kutub al-Sittah, al-sahihah, as-Sittah.

**Muslim Brothers, Brotherhood** – cf., Ikhwan al-Muslimum.

**Muslim League** – founded in 1906 to focus political aspirations of Muslims in India, "spiritual founder of state of Pakistan."

**Muslimun Issawiyun** (**moos**-lee-moon **ees**-sahw-ee-**yoon**) – submission to Jesus movement; cf., Isawa, Millat Issawi.

**al-Mustafa** (moos-**tahf**-ah) – *the Elect; the Chosen One*, one of the names by which the Prophet Muhammad is com-monly known; cf., names of the Prophet.

**Mustafa Kemal** (moos-**tahf**-ah kah-**mahl**) – cf., Ataturk.

**muta, mutah** (**moot**-a-ah) – in early Islam, temporary marriage, especially for those soldiers away at war; arranged by contract according to specific guide-lines; sanctioned by Shi'a as having qur'anic validity (Sura 4:28); thought by others to be cancelled (*abrogated*).

**Mutazali** (moo-tah-**thahl**-lee or moo-tah-**zahl**-lee) – opposed and did not overcome the Ashari over criteria for determining the correctness of an act; they hold men have free will and human responsibility, as opposed to the unqualified sovereign free will of God; rationalists in developing philosophical methodology in Islamic theology;

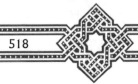

"italaze," the root word for *Mutazela*, means to secede.

**al-Muttalib** (ahl-**moot**-tah-lihb) – Muhammad's family, from his paternal grandfather, Abd al-Muttalib (d. 578), who raised Muhammad from age six to eight. See " The Quraysh Family Tree," p. 15.

**muttaqi** (moot-**tah**-qih)**, plur., muttaqun**) (moot-tah-**qoon**) – righteous person who fears and loves Allah much (does many good deeds, abstains from evil).

# N

**nabi, nebi** (**nah**-bee) – *prophet*; informant sent by Allah with his message, or to proclaim the will of Allah; cf., Maulid al-Nabi, Nabi Isa, Nur i-Muhammad, Rasul-Ullah.

**Nabi Isa** (**nah**-bee **ee**-sah) – Prophet Jesus; cf., Isa.

**nadhir, nadhr** (**nah**-duhr) – *warner*; Muhammad, who predicted dire consequences if idols, and not God alone, continued to be worshiped in Mecca, in the Ka'aba.

**Nakir** (nah-**keer**) – with *Munkar*, the two *angels* who subject men to fearsome questioning about their faith after their deaths (Sura 47:27); cf., Yawm al-Akhir.

**namaz** (nah-**mahz**) – *prayers*; the daily salat in India.

**names of God** – cf., ninety-nine "most beautiful names of God."

**Names of the Prophet, Noble** – more than one hundred Noble Names of the Prophet, selected from the Qur'an and hadith; cf., Ahmad, al-Amin, al-Mustafa; ninety-nine names of God.

**Naqshbandi** (nahksh-**bahn**-dee) – one of the four major orders of Sufi Islam (India).

**al-Nasai** (ahl-nah-**sah**-ee) – (830–915) one of six compilers of hadith, a collection of precedents (*sunan*); cf., al-Kutub al-Sittah, al-sahihah, as-Sittah.

**nasikh** (nah-**seek**) – *that which abrogates*; that which is *abrogated, mansukh*.

**Nation of Islam** – Black nationalist movement in the United States; moved toward Sunni Islam.

**nazar** (nah-**zahr**) – glass replica of a blue eye, worn or hung to ward off the evil eye (popular Islam). See Picture, p. 199.

**Nazarenes** – Christians mentioned in Sura 5:82 (YUSUF ALI): "Nearest among [men] in love to the Believers" are those "who say 'We are Christians [Nazarenes]'"; at that stage, empathetic to Muslims, and thought to be Muslims at heart.

**Nejran** (nehj-**rahn**) – territory in southern Arabia, modern-day *Yemen*; chief Christian center of southern Arabia at the time of Muhammad.

**†Nestorian Church of the East** – Christian group which maintained a vigorous presence in Persia (its largest religious minority), just prior to the rise of Islam; largely responsible for the missionary work which took the gospel to Arabia, India, Turkistan, and China; named after fifth century bishop who was wrongly alleged to hold that Christ had two distinct natures–not united–one human, one divine, which was the position held by the Nestorians; cf., Chalcedonian, Monophysite.

**ngelmu** (**ngehl**-moo) – cf., kebatinan.

**Night Journey** – cf., al-Miraj (Lailat).

**Night of Power** – cf., al-Qadr (Lailat).

**nikah** (nee-**kah**) – *conjunction*; legal marriage contract, or the social-religious rite which, according to Islamic law, validates the marriage.

**ninety-nine names of God** – the "most beautiful names of God," describing his perfection, chosen from the Qur'an (Sura 7:180, 17:110, 20:8) and Hadith; recited with aid of *prayer beads*; cf., Rahim, Rahman; al-Wadud. See Appendix 1, p. 471.

**Nisfu Shaban** (**nuhsf** shah-bahn) – *Middle of Shaban*; al-Barea (Lailat) the fifteenth of the month of *Shaban*. See "The Muslim Calendar," p. 162.

**Nizamiyah School** (nihz-ah-**mee**-yah) – cf., Al-Ashari.

**Nizari** (nee-**zah**-ree) – cf., Assassins, Hashashian, Ismaili, Khojas.

**Noah** – c.f. *Nuh*.

**North America, Muslims in** – see "Muslims in North America," p. 413.

**Nosrani** (**plur., Nasara**) (nahs-rah-**nee**) – *Christian*; the root word is from *Nazarene*; designates the European, or conqueror, in North Africa; also has the connotation of one's being a second-class citizen.

**Nuh** (noo-**eh**) – *Noah*; Preacher of God; cf., rasul.

**Nur al-Nur** (noor **ahl**-noor) – *the Light of Light*; name of Allah (Sura 24:35); refers to divine guidance (Sura 5:44–46). See Appendix 1, p. 473.

**Nur Muhammadi** (noor **moo**-hah-mehd-ee) – *Light of Muhammad*, the first creation of Allah, the manifestation of divine consciousness, and which each prophet preceding Muhammad manifested to a certain degree, each deriving their prophetic ability from Muhammadan light; concept in Sufi and Shi'i cosmology; cf., nabi, rasul.

**nusub** (na-**sahb**), (**plur., ansab**) (ahn-**sahb**) – stone altars on which sacrifices are offered to obtain favor from, or to honor, pirs, saints, *angel*s, jinn, etc.

# O

**occult** – *hidden*; supernatural realm of magic or witchcraft; practiced in Sufi Islam, and popular Islam.

**occultation** – *hiding*; cf., Imam, Shi'i, Twelvers.

**Omar** (ooh-**mahr**) – *Umar*

**Omar Khayyam** (**ooh**-mahr khie-**yahm**) – (d. 1131) well-known as mathematician, astronomer, philosopher, author of *Rubaiyat*; created a more accurate calendar.

**omissions** – removal of text passages from the original, thus corrupting it.

**One True God, the** – cf., Allah.

**†Ottoman Empire** – Turkish Muslim sultanate (1250–1700 at its height), established in the late thirteenth century in Anatolia, superseding the Byzantine Empire in the east, eventually extending over Southwest Asia, Northeast Africa, and Southeast Europe; its capital, Istanbul, was formerly Constantinople; ended in 1922 by *Mustafa Kemal Ataturk*. See Map, "The Ottoman Period of Resurgence (A.D. 1250–1700)," p. 48; "Quotes," p. 69.

# P

**pagans** – polytheists; *mushrikun*.

**Pahlavi** (pah-**lah**-vee) – **1.** scholarly language of pre-Islamic Persia in reign of the *Sasanid*; *Zoroastrianism* was the state religion; **2.** Pahlavi dynasty in Iran.

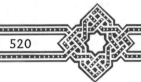

**Pan Islam** (pahn ihs-**lahm**) – ideology of political-social solidarity of all Muslims, rose in late nineteenth century with the spread of European colonialism; led by Jamal al-Din al-Afghani (1839–1897), a political reformist who emphasized united opposition to the Christian West and colonialism.

†**Paradise** – reward after death, *heaven*; place the souls of good people go after death, *Janna*; a garden (Sura 2:82, 3:133–36, 42:22), with feasts and compliant maidens (*houris*) to enjoy; cf., Yawm al-Akhir. See "Paradise and Hell," p. 449.

**partner** – Allah does not have a partner or *associate* (Sura 2:135; 9:30–32; 28:68–70; 30:40; 42:21); cf., shirk, wahid.

**Path** – The Path (Sura 1:6–7; 5:16; 17:72), The Right Path, The Straight Way, which Muslims must find and follow.

**pbuh, PBUH** – abbreviation of the term for the *tasliya*, which is, *"Salla Allah al-ayhi wa sallam" (s.a.w.)*, a phrase of blessing meaning literally, "May Allah bless him and grant him peace," or "Peace be upon him." Used by English-speaking Muslims when reference is made to the name of Muhammad or another prophet; since *pbuh* does not give the full meaning, some recommend using *s.a.w.* in writing.

†**People of the Book, -of the Scriptures** – translation of the qur'anic phrase, *Ahl al-Kitab*, which refers to the Jews and Christians, those who have "holy books" (Sura 5:68, 21:7), and, at first, counted as friends (Sura 5:82); cf., aman, dhimmi, jizyah, tabdil, tahrif. See "Holy Books," p. 55.

**Period of Ignorance** – cf., Jahiliyyah.

†**Persia** – remnants of ancient empire in Southwest Asia (500–300 B.C.; it once stretched eastward from the East Mediterranean Sea to the Indus River in present-day Pakistan); in Muhammad's day, present-day Iran and Iraq; occupied by Sasanid dynasty from 224–651, when *Umayyid* Muslims took over; largest religious minority was Nestorian. See Map, "The Arabian Peninsula and Surrounding Region in the Sixth Century," p. 31.

**Pilgrimage** – Hajj.

†**Pillars (Arkan) of Faith, Five Pillars of Islam,** Arkan al-Islam (ahr-**kahn** ihs-**lahm**) – the five religious duties: Creed, Prayer, Fasting, Alms, Pilgrimage.

  **1.** The witness or recitation of the Creed; Shahada.

  **2.** The saying of prayers at the five specified times of day; salat.

  **3.** The keeping of the fast during the month of Ramadan; saum.

  **4.** The giving of 2.5 percent of one's income to the poor, or for religious causes; zakat.

  **5.** The pilgrimage to Mecca and its environs at least once in one's lifetime; Hajj.

  **6.** Sometimes, an additional Pillar is the jihad, struggle for the faith or holy war.

†**pir (peer)** – *elder, wise person*; holy man; Sufi saint, spiritual guide, medicine man; founder of a Sufi brotherhood (*tarika*), especially in Pakistan and India; functions are to make intercession and bestow *baraka*; position often hereditary; cf., marabout, murshid, ustadh. See "Which Pir Do You Follow?" p. 217.

**polytheism** – worship of more than one deity; Christians are thought to be polytheists, worshippers of three Gods, Father, Son, and Holy Spirit; cf., pagans, shirk, mushrikun, kufr, sin.

†**popular Islam** – common practices addressing issues of power for the ordinary Muslim; also called folk Islam. As official faith and hierarchy fail to address everyday problems, fears, and felt needs, substitute authorities are found in the local, accessible, pragmatic practitioners of popular Islam, individuals with proven abilities in manipulating and controlling alternative forces of power and spiritual beings; a complex, all-embracing explanation of causality, requiring protective measures (charms, amulets, or other forms of prophylaxis), diagnosis by divination, and cures; components are local myths, folklore, traditions, customary rites, *animistic* practices; the worldview (both non-ethical and not accountable) of the Hadith, rather than that of orthodox Islam, or the Qur'an. See "Women and Power," p. 198; "Types of Magic," p. 204; "Belief and Practice," p. 206.

**pos** (**pohs**)– significant meeting place for young men of the *lampung*; a small elevated hut (Indonesia).

†**power encounter** – confrontation of evil powers in a visible manner, through prayer; demonstration of God's power over Satan primarily through healing and exorcism.

**power evangelism** – premeditated use of *power encounters* and miracles in evangelism as a method to convince people of the truth of the gospel.

**practitioner** – informal leader (male or female), healer who oversees crisis and cyclical rites for Muslims; makes up charms, talismans, herbal medicines;

writes prayers; deals with spirits; cf., popular Islam.

**prayer beads** – *subha*; used to count prayer repetitions, or recite *ninety-nine names of God*. See Picture, p. 191.

†**prophet** – person who is divinely inspired, a warner (Sura 43:23); prophets (Sura 2:136, 3:84); includes O.T. prophets and Jesus; cf., rasul, al-rusul, al-wahy. See "Jesus in the Qur'an," p. 299.

†**Prophet of Allah, The, -of Arabia, -of Islam** – Muhammad, Messenger of Allah (Sura 33:40; 53:1–18); cf., Rasul-Ullah.

**Psalms** – in the Qur'an, the revelations sent to the Prophet *Dawud* (David). See "Holy Books," p. 55.

**purdah** (**puhr**-dah) – *curtain* or *veil*; refers to various seclusion practices, designed to protect women from the time of puberty, so they will not mix with anyone but close relatives and women friends; supported in Islamic Scriptures, and upheld in law, but declining with education and economic opportunity.

# Q

**qadaa** (kah-**thah**), **qisma** (**khihs**-mah) – *measuring*; the determination of all things by Allah; his decree of good and evil as expressed in the hadith; the Islamic understanding and doctrine of predestination, that the timeless, divine foreknowledge of Allah anticipates events (*maktub, taqdir*); cf., Insha Allah, kismet, qadar (qadr). See "Why Do Muslims Say, '*Insha Allah*'?" p. 237.

**qadar, qadr** (kah-dr), **jabr** (jah-br) – fate; destiny predetermines all events; they take place according to Allah's

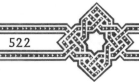
exact knowledge, and he is the power behind *qadar.*

**qadi** (**kah**-thee)**, (plur., quda) (koo**-dah) – *judge*; religious judge in both Islamic religious and civil courts; often compose Ulama; cf., fatwa, fuqaha, fuqh, ijma, Imam, imam.

**Qadiri** (kah-**dee**-ree) – one of the four major orders of Sufism.

**al-Qadr** (**Lailat**) (lay-**laht** ahl-**qah**-duhr) – *Night of Power*; "Night of Power and Excellence," "-of Destiny"; date Muhammad received his first revelation from Allah, when Gabriel commanded him to recite (Sura 96:1–5); twenty-seventh day of Ramadan. See "The Muslim Calendar," p. 162.

**Qarin** (ghah-**reen**) – one who performs *Hajj-al-Qiran.*

**qarina** (**female**) (keh-**ree**-neh)**, qarin** (**male**) (keh-**reen**)**, (plur., qarinat)** (keh-reen-**eht**) – *the one united.* **1.** the spirit double, or counterpart, born into the supernatural world at the birth of the human baby. **2.** a familiar spirit.

**qasida** (kas-**see**-deh) – traditional Arabic poem, usually having a rigid, tripartite structure; extols the Prophet and is used in festival devotion; cf., Al-Mirghanni, Maulid al-Nabi.

**qawwali** (khahw-**wahl**-ee) – music; cf., Barelvi.

**al-Qazwini** (ehl-kahz-**wee**-nee)**, Ibn Majjah** (ehb-ehn **mahj**-jah) – (822–887) one of six compilers of hadith, a collection of precedents (*sunan*); cf., al-Kutub al-Sittah, al-sahihah, as-Sittah.

**qibla** (**kehb**-leh) – *anything opposite*; the direction of salat, or of any significant official rite, toward the Ka'aba in Mecca; provided by the *mihrabs* (prayer niches) in the *qibla* wall of the mosque.

**qisma** (**kuhs**-meh) – *dividing*; lot, fate, destiny; cf., kismet, qadaa, qadar, maktub. See "Why Do Muslims Say, 'Insha Allah'?" p. 237.

**qiyas** (**khee**-yah) – *analogical reasoning*; principle of jurisprudence, derived from reason and analogical judgment, for the deduction of new rules; applications of principles from past cases, usually by analogy, without reliance on *ray* or unsystematic opinion; the fourth source for the Shari'a; *Qiyas* are the body of opinions; cf., Hanifi, Maliki.

**Qubbat al-Sakhra** (koo-**baht** ehl-**sahkh**-rah) – cf., Sakhra.

†**Qur'an** (**Koran**) (kohr-**aahn**) – *recitation*; Holy Book, the sacred Scriptures of Islam; its sacred text is said to be the uncreated, final, complete (and without errors), inspired word of Allah ("Divine Speech"); his final revelation to mankind, superceding all other revelation, sent down (*tanzil*) from heaven (Sura 15:9), to be "a guidance and a mercy" (Sura 16:64); revelation transmitted to the Prophet Muhammad by the *archangel* Gabriel over a period of twenty-three years; corresponds perfectly to the eternal original (or part of it) in heaven. Arabic text is sacred (Sura 16:103), so its exact perfect meaning cannot be captured by *translations*, called interpretations, or commentaries; first collected from Muhammad's *Companions* into book form by *Zayd*, Muhammad's aide, under the first caliph, Abu Bakr, in 634; official version, approved 657; powerful in its intrinsic *baraka* to protect; cf., batini, ijaz al-Qur'an, Mashaf, mujiza, zahir. See "What Does the Qur'an Say?" p. 8; "What Is Permitted?" p. 84.

†**Quraysh, Quraish** (koor-ray-**ihsh**) – the descendants of Ishmael, son of

*Abraham*; financially dominant tribe in Mecca prior to Islam; the tribe of the Prophet Muhammad; responsible for the Ka'aba. See "The Quraysh Family Tree," p. 15.

**qurban** (**koor**-bahn) – the sacrifice offered at Id al-Adha the day after pilgrims stand on Mount *Arafat* in Mecca.

**qutb** (**khuh**-tuhb) – human manifestation of divine consciousness (only one per age), through whom spiritual knowledge is gained, symbolized by the sheik of the Sufi order; term has come to indicate any holy man.

# R

**al-Rabb** (**ahl**-rahb) – *Lord*; most commonly used title for Allah; often in, *"Lord of all the Universe (Worlds)."*

**Rahim** (rah-**heem**), **al-Rahim** – *Most Merciful*; the second of the ninety-nine most beautiful names of God; cf., Rahman. See Appendix 1, p. 471.

**Rahman** (**rah**(kh)-man), **al-Rahman, Ya-Rahman, Raman** – *The Gracious*, or *Merciful*; the first of the ninety-nine most beautiful names (qualities) of God; cf., Rahim. See Appendix 1, p. 471.

†**rakat** (rah-**kat**) (**sing., rakah, raka**) (**roo**-koo-uh') – *set* of ritual prayers; from *ruku*; the salat or full cycle of prayers, or sets of *rakat*, composing a particular service—ascriptions of glory to Allah, recitations, and various movements and gestures consisting of bowings (*ruku*), and prostrations (*sujud*); a total of seventeen *rakat* are performed daily. See "The Postures of Prayer," p. 91.

**raksi** (rahk-**see**) – compilation of the numerical values of people's names, as spelled in the Arabic alphabet; used for divination, such as in matching potential husbands and wives (Malaya).

†**Ramadan** (rah-mah-**dahn**), **Ramazan** (rah-mah-**zahn**) – sacred month of saum, the fast (the ninth in the *Islamic lunar calendar*, "the best of all months"), when the Qur'an began to be revealed to Muhammad; cf., Lailat al-Qadr; now devoted to the saum, the third Pillar, during which a Muslim is supposed to fast from sunrise to sunset; Ramadan means *the scorcher*, suggesting it originally fell in summer; the last ten days of Ramadan are thought to be a time when Allah listens, either directly, or through the *archangel* Gabriel, to requests concerning the altering of one's fate (*qisma*); cf., tarawih. See "The Muslim Calendar," p. 162.

**ramal** (reh-**mehl**) – **1.** fast walking by men (not women) in first three rounds of *Tawaf*; **2.** diviner (Afgan Turkistan).

**ramy** (**rah**-mee) – throwing pebbles in the *Jamrat* at *Mina*.

**rapal** (**rah**-pahl) – use of prayers as magic formulas (Java).

†**rasul** (rah-**sool**), (**plur., rusul**) – *apostle*; messenger; a prophet sent as messenger with a revelation from God; Sura 2:136, 3:84, 6:83–86; 4:163–65. Muslim tradition lists 124,000 prophets, but five or six are the most prominent: Muhammad (*Rasul-Ullah*, Messenger of Allah), Apostle of God, *Seal* (Last) *of the Prophets*; Noah (*Nuh*), Preacher of God; Abraham (*Ibrahim*), Friend of God; Moses (*Musa*), Speaker with God; and Jesus (*Isa*), Word of God, Prophet of the Book; some add Adam, Chosen of God; Isaac (*Ishak*), Ishmael (*Ismail*), Jacob (*Yacub*), Jonah, David (*Dawud, Daoud*),

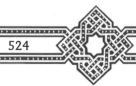
and Soloman; cf., the Book, Books of God, nabi, Nur Muhammadi; al-rusul.

**Rasul-Ullah** (rah-**sool**-ool-**lah**) – *messenger of Allah*; Muhammad.

**al-Rauf** (ahl-rah-**oof**) – *the Merciful*; name which applies to Allah and by which Muhammad may be invoked. See Appendix 1, p. 473.

**Rawzah Khani** (**rah**-oo-dah-**khah**-nee) – narratives of the martyrdom of Imam Husayn, read at events on deathday anniversaries of Imams and others, which may include the passion play of Shi'i martyrdoms at *Karbala*. cf., Ashura.

**ray** (rah-**ee**) – unsystematic reasoning or personal opinion in the field of Islamic law; cf., Hanafi, istihsan, Maliki, qiyas.

**Resurrection** – *Yawm al-Akhir*.

**rida** (ree-**dah'**) – seamless white sheet worn around upper part of body by the male pilgrim on the Hajj; cf., Ihram, izar.

**Ridwan** (rihd-**wahn**) – *angel* that guards Paradise and to whom one may appeal for assistance.

**Rome** – capital of Roman Empire, "center" of the known world.

**Rukn** (roo-**kehn**) – the essential ceremonies of the Hajj.

**ruku** (**roo**-koo-uh) – prayer posture; *to prostrate oneself*; from *rakaa, to bow down*; kneeling in obeisance during prayer; part of a rakat, composing the salat, ritual prayers. See "The Postures of Prayer," p. 91.

**ar-ruqyah** (ahr-**rahk**-yeh) – recitation of any Sura of the Qur'an ("Divine Speech"), while blowing one's breath with saliva over the sick person, as a means of curing disease.

**Rushdie Affair** (**Salman**) – English author of controversial novel, *The Satanic Verses* (1988); resulting in a fatwa calling for the death sentence, issued by *Khomeini*, in 1989 (revoked in late 90s).

**al-rusul** (ahl-rah-**sool**) – *apostles*; *prophets*; the doctrine of Allah's apostles mainly deals with their interaction with the supernatural world; for many, prophets (rasul) are more appealing than *angels*, because of their reputed willingness to intercede with Allah.

# S

**sahaba** (sah-**hah**-bah) – cf., *Companions*.

**Sacrifice, Feast of** – cf., Id al-Adha, Id al-Fitr.

**sadakat (pl.), sadaqah (sing.), sadaqat, sadaga** (**sah**-dah-kah, sahd-ahk-**aht**) – *true, sincere*; whatever is sanctified to Allah's service; charity; voluntary alms to the poor, or obligatory tax required by the government; given to acquire merit; cf., waqf, zakat.

**Safavid** (sah-fah-**veed**) – Muslim empire in Persia.

**Sahel** (sah-**hehl**) – semi-arid region of eastern north-central Africa, south of Saraha Desert. See Map, "Where Is the Middle East?" p. 56.

**sahil** (sah-**heel**) – *sound*.

**sahhara** (sah-**hah**-rah) – *sorceress*; popular practitioner (especially in Africa).

**sahih** (sah-**hee**) – *sound*.

**al-sahihah** (**ahl**-sah-**hee**-eh) – *veritable, verified* (from *sahih*, sound). Muslim scholars qualify hadith (the Prophet's Sunna) as *al-sahihah*, to separate the reliable from the spurious or weak; cf., al-Bukhari; al-Muslim.

**Sahih al-Bukhari** (sah-**hih** ahl-boo-**khah**-ree) – cf., al-Bukhari.

**al-Sahihan** (**ahl**-sah-hih-**hahn**) – cf., al-Shaykhan.

**sahn** (sah-**hehn**) – great open space or courtyard of the mosque.

**sahur** (suh-**hoor**) – meal eaten before dawn, at the start of the fasting period, during the month of Ramadan; also spelled *suhur*, which has an alternate meaning.

**Sakhra** (**sahk**-rah)**, Qubbat al-Sakhra** (koo-**baht** ahl-**sahkh**-rah) – *the Rock*; *the Dome of the Rock*, built on the sacred rock in Jerusalem, next to the *Mosque of Umar, Al-Aqsa*; or *Al-Masjid al-Aqsa*, from which Muhammad reputedly made his ascent to heaven (*Lailat al-Miraj*); held to have the impression of Muhammad's footprints.

†**salaam** (sah-**lahm**) – *peace*; a greeting of peace. **"As-salaam alaikum wa rahmatul-Lah"** (ahl-sah-**lahm** ah-**leh'**-koom wah **rahgh-mah**-too-lah) **or "Al-salaam**(**u**) **alaikum**(**u**) **wa rahmatul-Lah"** (ahl-sah-**lahm**-oo ah-**leh'**-koom-oo wah **rahgh-ma**-too-lah); meaning *"Peace be with you and the mercy of Allah"*; the response is "Wa-alaikum al-salaam" (wah ah-**leh'**-koom ahl-sah-**lahm**) ("Peace be upon you also"); cf., salam. See "Why Is Baraka Needed?" p. 211.

**Saladin, Salah al-Din** (ssah-**lah**-hahw-**deen**)**, Salah Eddin** (ssah-**lah** ehd-**deen**) – (1137–1193) the outstanding Kurdish Muslim (Sunni) general who defeated the Crusaders at Hattin, near the Sea of Galilee, and captured Jerusalem (1169).

**Salafi** (seh-lah-**fee**) – back to the roots reform movement, early twentieth century; emphasized overcoming stagnation, and replaced *taqlid* with *ijtihad*.

**salam** (sah-**lahm**) – from *salima, to be safe*; kneeling in ritual prayer, saying *"Peace be with you and the mercy of Allah"*; terminal point in ritual prayer, recited by worshipper. See "The Postures of Prayer," p. 91.

†**salat, salaat, salah** (sah-**laht**) – ritual prayer; a format of liturgical texts, and fixed gestures and postures, for a total of seventeen prayers; required five times a day (*fajr, zuhr, asr, maghrib,* and *isha*), performed toward Mecca, either in a mosque or in private; the second of the five Pillars of Faith; cf., du'a, Iqamat-as-Salat. See "The Postures of Prayer," p. 91; Picture, p. 386.

**salat al-istikhara** (sah-laht ahl-**ihs**-teek-**khah**-rah) – *prayer for conciliating favor*; special prayer for divining favorable future through dreams.

**salat al-jumah** (ssah-**laht** ahl-**joom**-'ah) – *prayer assembly*; Friday noon congregational prayer.

**salwar kameez** (sahl-**wahr** kah-**meez**) – baggy trousers and tunic, worn with the head scarf or schawl; Pakistani women's dress.

**sanduq al-nudhur** (sahn-**dook** ahl-noo-**duhr**) – *box for vows*; box at a saint's shrine into which are placed written vows of supplicants.

**Sanskrit** – classic literary language of India.

**Saracens** – **1.** pre-Islamic, nomadic people of *Syrian*-Arabian deserts. **2.** term referring to Arabs and Muslims during time of the Crusades.

**Sarafiel** (sah-rah-**fee**-yuhl) – the being closest to Allah, closer even than the *archangel* Gabriel; his intercession with Allah offers the ordinary Muslim hope.

**Sasanid** – Sasanian Dynasty (224–651) in Persian Iran, with main admin-

istrative capital in Ctesiphon, Iraq; Sasanian Empire competed with the *Roman Empire*; overthrown by Islamic armies (636f.); cf., Pahlavi, Umayyid, Zoroastrianisn. See Map, "The Arabian Peninsula and the Surrounding Region in the Sixth Century," p. 31.

**Satan** – cf., Shaytan.

**al-Saud** (ahl-sah-**ood**) – *House of Saud*, dominant clan in Arabia; its chief, Muhammad bin Saud, was patron of *Ibn Abd al-Wahhab*; Saudi Arabia means "the Arabia belonging to the Saud family."

†**saum, sawm** (**suh**-woom) – *the fasting*; the third Pillar; from before dawn (the *Adan of the Fajr*) to sunset; performed during Ramadan and at other times; implies abstinence and the moral inspiration derived therefrom; Sura 2: 183–88.

**s.a.w.** – abbreviation of the *tasliya*, which is "*Salla Allah al-ayhi wa sallam*," words of honor and salutation attached to the name of Muhammad; literally means "May Allah bless him and grant him peace"; cf., pbuh.

**Say** (ahl-**sah**-'ee) – ceremonial running seven times between the hills Safa and Marwah outside of Mecca during the Hajj or *Umrah*, in honor of Hagar and Ishmael; here Hagar pleaded with God until he caused water to spring from the Well of *Zamzam*.

**Sayyid, Seyyed** (say-yihd) – *master*. **1.** A title for Shi'i descendants of Muhammad *Ahl al-Bayt*, "people of the house"; considered spiritually and socially superior; cf., sharif. **2.** One who has a possessing *zar* spirit (not normally exorcised).

**Seal of the Prophets** – the Last Prophet, Muhammad (Sura 33:40).

**Semite** – speaker of a Semitic language, including Arabic, Amharic, Aramaic, and Hebrew.

**Seven Covenants of Suleiman** (soo-**lay**-ee-mahn) – amulet, supposed to protect against evil, to win love, to bless one's business activities, and to produce health and prosperity; the *jinniya, Umm al-Subyan*, states for the Prophet *Suleiman* the covenant terms by which she will refrain from touching the sons of Adam and the daughters of Eve.

**Seveners** – cf., Shi'a.

**shafaah** (shah-fah-'**ah**) – an advocate or intercessor for justice.

**shafi** (**shah**-fee) – *intercessor*; an intercessor for healing, in the case of illness; a saint because a mediator with Allah for ordinary Muslims; special permission to be intercessor (which passed to others) was granted to Muhammad, as the Qur'an names him to be "a mercy to mankind."

**Shafi'i** (ahl-shah-**fee**-'eh) – the *madhhab*, or school of law, founded by Muhammad ibn Idris ibn al-Abbas ibn Uthman ibn Shafi'i (d. 819), which applies a more liberal interpretation of the Qur'an, and stresses ijma (consensus), and the rights of the umma, determined by the Ulama, who issue *fatawi*; prefers hadith directly attributed to Muhammad; cf., qadi (plur., quda).

†**Shahada, Shahadah, Ash-Shahadah** (shah-**hah**-deh) – *testimony*; *to bear witness*; *The Witness*; confession of faith, or recitation of the Creed in the liturgical expression, the Shahada; "*La ilaha illa Allah, (wa) Muhammad rasul Allah*"; that is, "*There is no god* (none has the right to be worshiped) *but Allah, (and) Muhammad is the Prophet* (Apostle, Messenger) *of Allah*," or "*his Prophet*"; first

of the five Pillars of Faith; making this confession before two witnesses initiates one into Islam; repeated in the salat; cf., tashahhud.

**shahid, shaheed** (shah-**heed**) (**plur., shuhada**) (shoo-**hah**-dah') – *witness, martyr*; one killed fighting for the faith, witnessing by his death.

**shamans** (**shah**-muhnz), **shamanism** – popular Islam practitioners, such as medicine men or witch doctors; shamanism is the activities of such specialists, involving magic, prayers to saints, use of charms, amulets, curses, and incantations; cf., dukun, kebatinan. See "Types of Magic," p. 204.

**shame** – intense sense of disgrace produced by anything that threatens *honor*. See "Family and Children," p. 107; "Honor and Shame," p. 119; "Women Protecting Honor," p. 164.

**Shams al-Maarif al-Kubra** (**shamz** ahl-**mah'**-rihf ahl-**koo**-brah) – handbook of al-Buni (d. 1225), which continues to influence the practice of magic in the Arab world.

†**Shari'a, Shari'ah, Sharia** (shah-**ree**-ah)**, Shariat** – *the straight path*; ideal Islamic law; codification of rules and principles; fundamental law of Islam, the constitution of the Islamic community; the divine will applied to every situation in life. Derived from the Qur'an, the Hadith, and the Sunna of the Prophet Muhammad; the ijma, or general consensus of judges representing the community; and *qiyas*, analogically reasoned principles derived from preceding cases.

**sharif** (sheh-**reef**) – Sunni Muslim in direct line of descent from the Prophet Muhammad; *Ahl al-Bayt*, " people of the house"; one who inherits Muhammad's

*baraka*; and is, therefore, of noble descent; cf., Sayyid.

**shayatin** (shay-**ah**-teen), (**plur. of shaytan**) – devils, demons, evil spirits; *Suleiman* (Solomon) is known as Lord of the *shayatin*, having control over them (Sura 38:37).

**shaykha** (**shay**-khah) – female *zar* practitioner, thought to have power over the spirits; oversees the crisis and cyclical rites of popular Islam, especially for women. See "Women and Power," p. 198.

**al-Shaykhan** (ahl-**shay**-khahn) – *the Two Sheiks*; the two premier compilers of hadith, *al-Bukhari* and *al-Muslim*, referred to as *al-Sahihan* (*the Correct Two*), emphasizing their authority in Islamic literary heritage; cf., Sihah Sittah, as-Sittah.

**Shaytan** (**shay**-tahn) – *adversary, the one who opposes*; *Satan*; used interchangeably with *Iblis*, the devil; scholars hold that the term represents at least the principle (if not the personification) of evil; cf., Jamrah, al-Shaytanul-Kabir. See "'I Saw Him in a Dream,'" p. 200; "Why Is Baraka Needed?" p. 211.

**al-Shaytanul-Kabir, al-Shaytan al-Kibir** (ahl-shay-**tahn**-ahl-keh-**beer**) – *the Great Devil*; third small pillar (stele), representing Satan, at which seven stones are thrown, an integral part of pilgrimage procedure; cf., Hajj, Iblis, Jamrah.

†**sheik, sheikh, shaikh, shaykh** (**shaykh**) – *old man, chief, head, leader*. **1.** title of respect for Muslim cleric or leader. **2.** leader of a tribe, Sufi order, or religious brotherhood.

**Sheiks, the Two** – al-Shaykhan.

**Shema** (**Sh'ma**) (sheh-**mah**) – liturgical expression of the creed of the Jews:

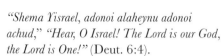
"*Shema Yisrael, adonoi alaheynu adonoi achud,*" "*Hear, O Israel! The Lord is our God, the Lord is One!*" (Deut. 6:4).

†**Shi'i** (**shee**-ee), (**plur., Shi'a**) (**shee'**-ah) – *followers*; from *Shi'at Ali* (fourth Caliph), *the Partisans of Ali*, minority Islamic sect (15 percent); the branch of Islam (in contrast to Sunni) that holds that the true leadership succession from Muhammad is from Ali, Muhammad's son-in-law and first cousin, and of the twelve Imams descended from Ali; also called *Ashari* (*Ithna Ashariyah*), the *Twelvers* (Iran, Iraq, *Syria*, Yemen, Pakistan, and Lebanon); other Shi'a are *Seveners*, or *Ismaili*, who conclude with a different seventh Imam, Ishmael (*Ismail*), whom they believe will return as the Mahdi (India and East Africa); or *Fivers*, who hold that the *Imamate* passed to Zaid, second son of the fourth Imam, Ali (North Yemen). (Note: "Shi'ites" and "Shi'ism" are anglicized forms used in popular media to refer to Shi'a and Shi'i Islam.)

†**shirk** (**shuhrk**) – *association*, or associationism; associating *partners* with Allah or worshipping other deities, so as to impugn the one God's, Allah's, absolute uniqueness and oneness; the unforgivable *sin* in Islam, considered *polytheism*, pantheism, or *Trinitarianism* (Sura 9:30–32); cf., kabira, kufr, mushrikun.

**shukr** (**shook**-kuhr) – gratitude, thankfulness; to deny *shukr* is *kufr*, disbelief in Allah.

**al-Siddiq, Siddiqun** (ahl-ssah-**dehk**) – *truthful*, those followers of the prophets who were first and foremost to believe in them, like *Abu Bakr as-Siddiq*, the martyrs and the righteous (Sura 4:69a).

**Sihah Sittah** (ahl-ssih-**hah** ssiht-**tah**) – the six collections of the six compilers of hadith; cf., al-Kutub al-Sittah, Sittah, as-Sittah.

**Sijjin** (**sih**-jihn) – from *sijn, prison*; a deep pit in which is kept the book in which the actions of the wicked are recorded.

**al-Sijistani** (ahl-**see**-jee-**stah**-nee), **Abu Daud** (ah-boo **dah**-wood) – (817–888) one of six compilers of hadith; his is called a collection of precedents (*sunan*); cf., al-Kutub al-Sittah, al-sahi-hah, Sihah Sittah, as-Sittah.

**Silk Road, the** – term referring to the ancient trade routes from Europe and the Middle East, across Central Asia, to China, India, and Indonesia (more accurately called central Eurasia), promoting transnationalization and Islamization; major route for exchange of ideas and goods between India and China and the West.

**sin** – in Islam, original sin does not exist; sin is over-stepping Allah's boundaries, but sins are mistakes that can be offset by good works; only unforgivable sin is shirk; cf., adha, hadd, kafir, kabira, kufr, mushrikun. See the "Feast of Sacrifice," p. 168.

†**Sind** (**sind**) – **1.** region of southeast Pakistan; **2.** a river in India.

**Sirah** (**see**-rah), **Sirat** (see-**raht**), **Seerah** (**see**-rah) – **1.** account of Muhammad's conduct in his wars and activities, as recorded first by his *Companions*; since then continually issued in various forms for use in evangelism and education, or to reinforce policy objectives; **2.** Sirah, a literary genre of biographies of Muhammad, his *Companions*, and saints.

**sirat, seerat** (sih-**raht**) – the bridge over hell, sharper than a sword and thinner than a hair; metaphorically, the narrow path to heaven; those judged not to have accomplished enough good deeds will not be able to successfully complete the transverse of this bridge to Paradise, and will be thrown off into Hell.

**as-Sittah** (ahs-seet-**tah**) – the six compilers of the hadith: *al-Bukari, al-Muslim, al-Tirmidhi, Abu Daud al-Sijistani, al-Nasai,* and *al-Qazwini*; their six collections are called *al-Kutub al-Sittah*, or *Sihah Sittah*.

**Six Books, the** – cf., hadith, al-Kutub al-Sittah, Sihah Sittah, as-Sittah.

**slamatan** (slah-mah-**tahn**) – ritual meal used to protect one from evil spirits (Java).

**standing ceremony** – Wuquf, Hajj ceremony of halting for prescribed prayers, in the Valley of *Mount Arafat,* to sense the presence of Allah and the forgiveness of sins.

**Southwest Asia** – area comprising modern Iraq, Israel, Jordan, Lebanon, Palestine, and *Syria*; cf., Middle East. See Map, "Where Is the Middle East?" p. 56; "Where Is the Middle East?" p. 57.

**subha** (**sehb**-heh) – prayer beads, designed to assist in recitation of the *ninety-nine beautiful names of God*, but more commonly used in the divination, *istikhara*. See picture, p. 191.

**Subhan Allah** (soob-**hah**-nah-lah) – "Glorified is Allah."

**sub-Saharan peoples** – see "Sub-Saharan Peoples," p. 258; Map, "Percentage of Muslim Population in Sub-Saharan Africa," p. 259.

†**Sufi** (**soo**-fee), (**plur., Sufis**) (**soo**-feez) – Muslim mystic (pir, *ustadh*) who renounces worldly attachments, and seeks and claims direct communication with, experiences of, and spiritual union and relationship with, Allah; through a series of special rites and ecstatic awakenings of his inherent, but dormant, emotional spiritual faculties. In contrast to orthodox Islamic monotheism, Sufi Islam tends toward pantheism (Allah is in all things), absorption (becoming one with Allah, *dhikr, tauhid*), and deification of Muhammad. (From the word for the coarse woolen mantle, *suf,* worn by early ascetics.) Cf., haqiqa, marifah, murid, murshid, Suhrawardi, tarika.

**Suhoof, Suhuf** (**suh**-hoof) – *pages of Abraham*; cf., Books of God.

**Suhrawardi** (**soo**-hoo-rah-**wahr**-dee) – one of the four major orders of Sufi Islam (Iran).

**suhur** (suh-**hoor**) – **1.** meal at dawn at start of period of the fast; cf., sahur; **2.** witchcraft, sorcery.

**sujud** (soo-**jood**) – *prostration*; prayer posture, part of a rakat; high point of ritual prayer (salat). See "The Postures of Prayer," p. 91.

**Suleiman** (soo-**lay**-ee-mahn) – Solomon; prophet, lord of the *shayatin*; stands out because of his power over demons and jinn; cf., Seven Covenants.

**Sultan** – cf., Ottoman.

**sunan** (soo-**nahn**) – *precedents*; cf., al-Qazwini; al-Sijistani (Abu Daud).

†**Sunna, Sunnah** (**soon**-nah) – *said, custom.* **1.** the established, normative precedent based on the legal orders, practices, and actions–the concrete example–of the Prophet Muhammad, as transmitted and recorded in the hadith. The Hadith, the corpus of these Traditions, is considered the authoritative model to be followed, and supplements the Qur'an; therefore, the Sunna is the straight *path, manner of life; the way* of faith and conduct as expressed in hadith and followed by the Islamic community; cf., al-sahihah. **2.** sunna

(lowercase) refers to a practice or custom.

†**Sunni** (soon-**nee**) – the major orthodox branch of Islam (about 85 percent), who follow the sunna of their forefathers; in contrast to the Shi'a, they believe that the true leadership succession from Muhammad is found in the four Caliphs: Abu Bakr, Umar, Uthman, and Ali; in the nineteenth century, the *Wahhabi* Sunni started a major reform movement in Arabia.

†**Sura, Surah** (**soo**-rah)**, Surat** (soo-**raht**) – *row* or *series*; one of a series of revelations; a chapter of the Qur'an; there are 114; divided into verses or *ayat, iyat* (sing., aya, *iyah*).

**sutra** (**suht**-rah) – *that by which something is concealed*; an article placed in front of a person who is engaged in prayer toward Mecca, used to prevent invalidation of prayers by an unbeliever or evil spirit.

**Syria** – country of Southwest Asia on eastern Mediterranean coast; ancient Syria (Roman, Byzantine) included Lebanon, most of present-day Israel and Jordan, part of Iraq, and Saudi Arabia. Syria had a large Monophysite population prior to Islam's introduction in seventh century.

**Syriac** – ancient Aramaic language of *Syria* (third to thirteenth centuries); liturgical language of several Eastern Christian churches.

# T

**tabdil** (tahb-**deel**)**, taghyr** (tah-**ghie**-yuhr) – *change*; used especially of a textual change or corruption in the biblical text, *tahrif*; cf., Injil.

**Tabi** (tah-**bee**-ee)**, (plur., al-Tabiun)** (ahl-tah-bee-**yoon**)– the successors, those who met or accompanied any *Companion* of the Prophet; took an important part in transmission of the hadith.

**Tablighi Jamaat** (tahb-**lee**-ghee jah-mah-**aht**) – Indian reform (of personal faith and religious practices) or evangelical movement, founded in 1927, now transnational; calls for defense of Islam and Muslim minorities; cf., ijtema.

†**ta ethne (Greek)** (**tah** ehth-nay)**, kol goyey (Hebrew)** (kohl **goh**-yee) – *all the nations; all the peoples, Gentiles, tongues, languages, tribes, clans, families of the earth*; Gen. 12:1–3, 18:18, 22:18, 26:4, 28:14; Ps. 67; Isa. 49:6; Dan. 7:14; Matt. 24:14, 28:19–20; Gal. 3:8; Rev. 5:9–10, 7:9–10, 15:4; distinct ethnic groups, linguistically and culturally separate, each with a unique worldview, including behavior, values, and belief system.

**tafsir, tafseer** (**tehf**-seer) – *explaining, exegesis*; commentary on the life of Muhammad, and especially on the Qur'an, and by which it is interpreted; conducted in linguistic, judicial, and theological areas.

**taghut** (tah-**ghoot**) – anything worshiped other than Allah; all the false deities; thought by some to include saints, graves, and leaders, as falsely worshipped and followed; cf., baraka, wali.

**tahrif** (**tahh**-reef) – the Islamic doctrine that Jews and Christians have corrupted (by interpolation, *tabdil*) the original text of their Scriptures, the *Taurat* and the Injil.

**takbir** (**tak**-beer) – *magnification*; exaltation of Allah in salat: recitation of, "Allahu Akbar," *"Allah is the Most Great."*

**Takbir as-Sijdah** (**tak**-beer ahs-**seej**-dah) – prostration; prayer posture with knees and arms bent. See "The Postures of Prayer," p. 91.

**Takbir i-Tahrimah** (**tak**-beer ee-tah-**ree**-mah) – prayer posture of standing with arms partly raised. See "The Postures of Prayer," p. 91.

**talaq** (t'**ah**-lakh) – form of divorce, usually carried out over a period of time and under certain conditions, but also by the husband's statement, "You are dismissed," repeated three times.

**talim** (**teh'**-leem) – divinely inspired teaching (through the Imam) which offsets inadequacy of human reasoning for understanding Allah.

**tanzil** (tehn-**zeel**) – *sending down.* **1.** revelation of the Qur'an, verbatim to Muhammad, from heaven (Sura 15:9); **2.** divine guidance through the prophets, from Adam to "the Seal of the Prophets," Muhammad.

**taqdir** (tahk-**deer**) – Allah's subjection of all mankind and history; cf., maktub, qadaa.

**taqiya** (tah-**ghee**-yah) – *dissimulation*; practice of hiding one's religion, formally sanctioned by Shi'i Islam, for protection from periodic persecution (Sura 3:28; 16:106) by Sunni majority.

**taqiyya** (**tah**-ghee-**yah**) – skull cap.

**taqlid** (tahk-**leed**), **taqlidi** (tahk-lee-dee) – literalist approach, unquestioning imitation of precedence, as opposed to the ijtihadi approach of modernizing reform movements.

**taqwa** (**tahk**-wah) – *piety*; of a pious or virtuous character, being god-fearing.

**tarawih** (tah-rah-**wee**-yeh) – special optional prayers in the evening, in sequences of twenty, said during the month of Ramadan, usually corporately.

**tarika, tariqa** (tah-**ree**-gha) (**plur., turuk**) (**too**-ruhk) – *way, path; complete submission to divine way*; Sufi order or path followed to achieve direct experience (gnosis) of Allah; *haqiqa.*

**tashahhud** (tah-shah-**hood**) – *the testimony*; giving of one's testimony, the Shahada; professing the faith, the Creed, the first Pillar.

**tasliya** (tahs-**lee**-yah) – term for the phrase, "*Salla Allah al-ayhi wa sallam*," "*Allah bless him and grant him peace*," used when reference is made to a prophet; cf., pbuh, s.a.w.

**tasmi'** (tahs-**mee'**) – prayer posture, standing. See "The Postures of Prayer," p. 91.

**Taurat, Tawrat** (tah-oo-**rah**) – the Law, or *Torah*, from the Jewish Scriptures, considered by Muslims to be true revelation from God through and to *Moses (Musa)*; *not* the Old Testament or Pentateuch; cf., tabdil, tahrif.

**Tawaf** (ahl-tah-**wahf**) – circumambulation (walking around) of the Ka'aba seven times during the Hajj or *Umrah.*

**Tawaf al-Ifadah** (tah-**wahf** ahl-ee-**fah**-thah), **Tawaf ul-Wada** (tah-wahf ahl-weh-**dah'**) – the *Tawaf* made before leaving Mecca after performing the Hajj or *Umrah*, heralding pilgrimage's end.

†**tawhid, tauhid** (tahw-**heed**) – term used to express the existence of and unity of Allah, the only God; the absolute oneness of Allah; Islamic monotheism, its fundamental basis; in orthodox Islamic terms, proclaiming the unity of Allah. Salvation for the Muslim is the purity or totality of this belief, the expression of personal and

social integration under Allah's will; including three aspects of belief: in the oneness of the lordship, worship, and names and qualities of Allah; for Sufi Islam, absorption or unity with Allah, or man's integration by means of the realization of the One God; cf., ahad, wahid. See "Unity, Submission, and Community," p. 355.

**taziya** (tah'-**zee**-yah) – *a consolation.*
**1.** the annual Shi'a procession and passion play in *Karbala* commemorating Husayn's martyrdom; participants in the commemoration rites are *taziyas*;
**2.** a model of his tomb carried in the procession at the feast of *Muharram.*

**Timur Lang** (tee-mur **lang**) – (1336–1405) "Timor the Lame," or Tamerlane (in the West); adventurous tribal chief, supported by local Muslim leaders, who rose to power in Iran by military force; later took northern India, *Anatolia*, and northern *Syria*; brought religious leaders into the government; cf., Babur, Genghis Khan, Mongol, Mughal.

**al-Tirmidhi** (ahl-tuhr-**mee**-dee) – (824–892) one of the six compilers of authoritative hadith collections (*jami*); his is called *Jami al-Tirmidhi*; cf., al-Kutub al-Sittah, al-sahihah, as-Sittah.

**Torah** – the first five books of the Hebrew Scriptures; the Qur'an (Sura 5:46; 61:6) regards the original as true revelation that preceded the Gospels and the Qur'an. Muslims believe the Taurat now is not complete and is corrupted; cf., tabdil, tahrif.

**Tours** – cf., Charles Martel.

†**Traditions** – cf., Hadith.

**translations** – Muslims consider translations of the Qur'an inferior to the sacred Arabic text; many think that various Bible translations are merely contradicting Bible versions; cf., tabdil, tahrif.

**Transoxania** – see Map, " The Arabian Peninsula and the Surrounding Region in the Sixth Century," p. 31.

**Trench** (**Allies**), **Battle of the** – (627) battle won by Muhammad's forces over Meccans and their mercenaries, which were led by Abu Sufyan, the same powerful leader of the troops at *Uhud* and *Badr*; the Muslims' defense, a trench dug in front of their positions, prevented this last attempt to stop Muhammad by force.

**Trinity, Tri-unity** – Christian doctrine that God is one and manifest in Father, Son, and Holy Spirit; for Muslims, often a major objection, considered *shirk* (Sura 9:30–32); the Qur'an asserts that Christians believe in a triad consisting of God, Mary, and Jesus (Sura 4:17); cf., associate, partner, wahid.

†**truth encounter** – confrontation of unbelief with the Bible.

**Tuareg** (too-**wahr**-ehg) – *the abandoned of God*; nomadic, Muslim, Saharan desert tribe.

**turba** (**toor**-bah) – mausoleum.

**Turkic peoples** – See "Turkic Peoples," p. 282; Map, "The Turkic World," p. 283.

**Twelvers** – cf., Ashari, Imam, Imamate, Ithna Ashari, Shi'a.

**Two Sheiks** – *Al-Shaykhan.*

# U

**udha** (**ood**-hah) – from *to protect*; protective amulet.

**Uhud, Battle of** (oo-**hood**) – (625) Muhammad and Muslims, led by *Khalid Ibn al-Walid*, were defeated by Meccans.

†**Ulama, Ulema** (ahl-**lah**-meh), (**sing.,** **Alim**) – *the learned*; **1.** for Shi'a, the collective body of Islamic scholars trained in theology and law, the custodians of Islamic dogma; makes legal interpretations for (and regulates the lives of) the community, and have the temporal authority (since the *Imamate*), to interpret the Qur'an; in Iran, power is centralized in the Ulama; **2.** for Sunnis, the authoritative principles of Islamic theology and law determined by the consensus of Muslim scholars; **3.** today, refers to imams, those trained in religious sciences, operating in mosques and madrasahs.

**um, umm** (**oom**) – *mother of.*

†**Umar, Omar, Umar ibn al-** **Khattab** (**oo**-mahr eh-**behn** ahl-**khah**-tahb) – one of the bravest and most important men of the Quraysh, an early convert to Islam, Muhammad's father-in-law (his daughter Hafsah was married to Muhammad), and principal advisor to the first Caliph, Abu Bakr; later, the second Caliph (634 to 644), according to Sunnis; he greatly expanded the conquered regimes, influenced the course of Islam, established the *lunar calendar*, transmitted many particularly authoritative hadith, and authorized assembly of the first codification of the Qur'an; cf., Covenant of Umar; Al-Aqsa, Al-Masjid al-Aqsa, Qubbat al-Sakhra, Sakhra. See "Quotes," p. 69.

**Umayyad, Umayyid** (oo-**mie**-yehd) – first Islamic dynasty, 661–750; after the murder of the fourth Caliph (Ali, in 659), the Sunni mantle returned to this tribe and its leader, *Muawiyah*, of the Umayyah clan, the fifth Caliph (661–680); he established the Caliphate in Damascus (661), the Umayyad

Dynasty ruling there until 750, when overthrown by the *Abbasid* Dynasty. See Map, "The Abbasid Period of Consolidation (A.D. 732–1250)," p. 47; "The Quraysh Family Tree," p. 15.

†**umma, ummah** (**oom**-mah) – *community*; the unified, equal people of Islam; the worldwide Muslim community; the essential unity and theoretical equality of all Muslims (Sura 6:159); *umma dun al-nas*, "a community apart or distinct from other men" (Sura 3:104); as in, *al-Umma al-Islaamiya*, or *The Muslim Nation*; cf., best nation. See "A Visual Model of Muslim Worldview," p. 159; "Muslim Community," p. 181; "Unity, Submission, and Community," p. 355.

**Umm al-Subyan** (**oom** ahl-**soob**-ee-yahn) – named *jinniya*; a loathsome, invisible female *jinniya* whose presence destroys; chief voice in the *Seven Covenants of Suleiman* (amulet).

**Umrah** (**oom**-rahh) – the "lesser Hajj"; visit to Mecca at a different time from the designated month of obligatory Hajj (*Dhu al-Hijja*), during which *Tawaf* and *Say* are performed; cf., Ihram, Manasik al-Hajj wal-Umrah.

**urs** (**'uhrs**) – *marriage.* **1.** the union between a pir and Allah at the time of his death; celebrated by his disciples on the anniversary date; **2.** the annual religious meeting held by a living pir.

**ustadh** (oo-**stahd**) – cf., murshid, pir, tarika.

†**Uthman** (**'ohth**-mahn) **ibn Affan** – Muhammad's cousin, member of *Umayyad* tribe, one of the first Muslim believers, and the third Caliph (644–656), succeeded by Ali; final canonical editing of the Qur'an took place under Uthman; married to Muhammad's daughters, Ruqayyah

and Umm Kulthum. See "The Quraysh Family Tree," p. 15.

**Al-Uzza** (ahl-'ooz-zah) – pagan goddess worshiped in the *Period of Ignorance*; most venerated idol of the Quraysh tribe; received human sacrifices.

# W

**wadi** (**wah**-dee) – channel of a water course, normally dry, except in the rainy season.

**al-Wadud** (ahl-wah-**dood**) – *the loving*; forty-seventh name of Allah; cf., names of God, ninety-nine names of God. See Appendix 1, p. 472.

**al-Wahhab, ibn Abd** – cf., Wahhabi.

†**Wahhabi** (wah-**hah**-bee)**, (plur., Wahhabiyin)** ( wah-**hah**-bee-yeen) – conservative branch of Sunni Islam (founded by Muhammad ibn Abd al-Wahhab, 1703–1792, Arab sheik, Muslim reformer), dedicated to strict interpretation of Islamic law, especially strict social codes; responsible for strong, contemporary reform movement throughout the Islamic world, such as the *Muslim Brotherhood* (Egypt), and Islamic Society (Pakistan); today, the holy places of Mecca and Medina (Saudi Arabia) are under Wahhabi control; cf., Hanbali.

**wahid** (wah-**heed**) – *The One*; the single, sole, one (with no second) "Same God for All"; sometimes used interchangeably with *ahad*; the Islamic negation of any number other than one (as in the three of *Trinity*); and the denial that Allah has any *partner* or *associate* associated with him; cf., tawhid. See Appendix 1, p. 472.

**al-wahy** (ahl-**wah**-hee) – divine *revelation*; inspiration by Allah of his prophets.

**wahy ghayr matlub** (wah-hee **ghayr** maht-**loob**) – *unread revelation*; received by Muhammad, by which he was able to make authoritative declarations, which became the hadith.

**wajib** (**wah**-jihb) – omission of duties that are obligatory (*fard*).

**Walaka** (wah-**lah**-keh) – "Woe upon you!"

**wali** (**wah**-lee) – sheik.

**wali** (wah-**lee**), **(plur., awliya)** (ahw-lee-**yah**) – *a near one*; protector, guardian; "friend of God"; a saint; saint veneration, shrine visitation, and vow-making to saints are important in Islam; also, *shafi* (*intercessor*), pir (*wise person*), *marabout, murabit* (*one who has joined himself to Allah*), or *murashid* (*guide*); cf., baraka, taghut.

**Wali Allah Shah** – (1702–1762) Muslim reformer in India; sought to rid Islam of encroaching Hindu elements and restore Muslim government under a Sufi worldview.

**waqf** (**wahk**-ehf) – *to dedicate to*; the endowment a Muslim leaves at his death for a specific charitable purpose; in Turkey, *evkaf*; the Ministry of Waqfs is the system established in Islamic countries for the administration of alms and supervision of endowments; cf., sadakat, zakat.

**wasilah** (wah-**see**-lah) – means of approach or achieving closeness to Allah by acquiring his favors.

**Western culture** – see "Divergent Values," p. 135; "View of Western Women and Christianity," p. 136; "Barbed Wire," p. 228; "Cultural and Social Barriers That Turn Away Inquirers," p. 229.

**Witness, The** – cf., Shahada.

†**worldview** – system of values, consisting of a person (or group's) general and comprehensive concepts and unstated assumptions about life, or view of the basic makeup of his (or their) world. See "Diagram of Culture," p. 96; "How Do You See the World?" p. 97; "A Visual Model of Muslim Worldview," p. 159; "Worldview Pictured in Everyday Life," p. 160; "Ask Good Questions," p. 218; "Storying in Ten Steps," p. 393.

**wudu** (woo-**thoo'**) – *ablution*; limited ceremonial cleansing, obligatory before prayers (or circumambulation of the Ka'aba), in which the hands up to the elbows, feet, and head (face, ears, nose, mouth, hair) are cleaned with water (or sand). See Picture, p. 90.

**Wuquf** (woo-**koof**) – station before Allah; most important phase of Hajj or *Umrah* ceremony, held on the ninth day; the standing ceremony, a ceremonial pause for prayers on Plain of *Arafat*.

# Y

**Yacoub** (yah'-**koob**) – Jacob; for Muslims a prophet.

**yaqin** (yahk-**keen**) – perfect absolute faith.

†**Yathrib** (**yehth**-rihb) – destination of the Hijra; renamed Medina after the arrival of Muhammad.

**Yawm al-Akhir** (**yahw**-oom ahl-ahkh-**heer**) – *The Last Day*; Day of Justice; Day of *Judgment*, *Yawm al-Din*; Day of *Resurrection*, *Yawm al-Qiyamah*; when the world has ended and the dead risen, the final trial, based on records kept, will occur; when the reward (Paradise, *heaven*), or punishment (*hell*, not eternal)

is meted out; cf., iman, Janna, Munkar, Nakir. See "What Is Permitted?" p. 84.

**Yawm al-Juma** (**yahw**-oom ahl-**joom**-ah') – *day of assembly*; Friday.

**Yemen** – country on tip of southwest Arabia; conquered by Muslim Arabs in seventh century; formerly, *Nejran*.

**Yesua, Yesuua** (yah-**soo**-eh'), **Yesus** – name for Jesus, transliterated from Greek; Isa is the qur'anic name for Jesus; considered a prophet as taught in the Qur'an; cf., adha.

# Z

**Zabur** (zah-**boor**) – *the Psalms*; name applied to the Scriptures (or the book) God revealed to the Prophet David (*Dawud, Daoud*); Muslims call the Zabur "the Prophets"; cf., Sura 21:105 and Psalm 37:29.

**zahir** (zah-**huhr**) – literal or apparent meaning of the Qur'an, as opposed to *batini*, the hidden meaning.

†**Zaid, Zayd** (**zay**-eed), **Zayd ibn-Harithah** – Muhammad's freed slave and adopted son; Muhammad married Zaid's wife Zainab (Muhammad's cousin) as his seventh wife (Sura 33:37–40); apparently, she and her noble family regarded Zaid, the former slave, as her inferior, so they divorced.

†**zakat, zakah, zakaat** (zah-**kaht**) – *to grow, to be pure, purification*; to purify one's soul and express gratitude for God's provision, statutory religious offering or alms tax, "poor-due," which must total 2.5 percent of one's yearly income, given for the cause of Islam and to the needy, and in expiation of what a Muslim retains; fourth of the five Pillars of Faith; cf., sadakat. See Picture, p. 79.

**Zamzam** (**zehm**-zehm) – the famed sacred well on the grounds of the *Al-Masjid al-Haram* of the Grand (Great) Mosque of Mecca; every pilgrim on the Hajj desires a drink or to take away a portion; traditionally, the lifesaving spring of water God provided for Hagar and her son Ishmael when they were wandering in the wilderness; *Zamzam* water, considered holy, is used in various purification rites; cf., Say.

**zar** (**zahr**) – **1.** a possessing spirit keeping one in bondage, not normally exorcised but part of everyday life and decision-making; *zar* spirits determine the form of feminine spiritual experience in popular Islam; cf., Sayyid. **2.** a ceremony connected with exorcism, commonly practiced in Egypt.

**Zayd b. Thabit** (**zayd** eh-behn **thah**-biht) – Muhammad's aide and scribe; assembled the first codified revelations to Muhammad, as the first text of the Qur'an (634), under the first Caliph, Abu Bakr; from scattered sources, chiefly the memories of the *Companions*, the *huffaz*; cf., hafiz.

**zhikr** – cf., dhikr

**zij** (**zeej**) – astronomical tables.

**zindiq** (**zihn**-duhk), (**pl., zanadiqah**), (zah-nah-**deerk**) – atheist.

**ziyara** (zee-**yah**-rah) – *visitation*; visit to tomb of Muhammad or grave of any saint.

**Zoroastrianism** – religion in ancient Persia founded by the Prophet Zoroaster; preserved in the Avesta (sacred writings), as monotheistic worship of Ahrura Mazda (Lord Wisdom), and an ethical dualism between truth and lie; almost totally supplanted by Islam; cf., Pahlavi, Sasanid.

**zuhr** (**zoo**-huhr), dhuhr (**thoo**-huhr), – noon salat; midday, second ritual prayer of the day.

**Zwemer, Samuel** – (1867–1952) "Apostle to Islam," student volunteer; instrumental in opening the eyes of churches to the need for Muslim evangelism. See Ruth A. Tucker, "Samuel Zwemer," pp. 320–325; "Our Personal Path to Muslim Hearts," p. 403.

# BIBLIOGRAPHY FOR GLOSSARY

Accad, Fouad Elias. *Building Bridges: Christianity and Islam.* Colorado Springs: NavPress, 1997.

Ali, Abdullah Yusuf, translator. *The Meaning of the Holy Qur'an.* Beltsville, Md.: Amana Publications, 2001.

*The American Heritage Dictionary of the English Language* 4th ed. Boston: Houghton Mifflin, 2000.

Esposito, John L., editor. *The Oxford Dictionary of Islam.* (New York: Oxford University Press, 2003.

————, editor. *The Oxford History of Islam.* New York: Oxford University Press, 1999.

Farah, Caesar E. *Islam.* New York: Barron's, 2003.

Geisler, Norman L., and Abdul Saleeb. *Answering Islam: The Crescent in the Light of the Cross.* Grand Rapids: Baker, 2002.

Kateregga, Badru D., and David W. Shenk. *A Muslim and a Christian in Dialogue.* Scottdale, Pa.: Herald Press, 1997.

Livingstone, Greg. *Planting Churches in Muslim Cities.* Grand Rapids: Baker, 1993.

McCurry, Don M., editor. *The Gospel and Islam.* Monrovia, Calif.: Missions Advanced Research and Communications Center, 1979.

McDowell, Bruce A., and Anees Zaka. *Muslims and Christians at the Table.* Phillipsburg, N.J.: P & R Publishing Co., 1999.

Musk, Bill. *The Unseen Face of Islam.* Grand Rapids: Monarch Books, 2003.

Parshall, Phil. *Beyond the Mosque.* Grand Rapids: Baker, 1985.

————. *Muslim Evangelism: Contemporary Approaches to Contextualization.* Waynesboro, Ga.: Authentic Media, 2003.

Saal, William. *Reaching Muslims for Christ.* Chicago: Moody, 1991.

Shorrosh, Anis A. *Islam Revealed: A Christian Arab's View of Islam.* Nashville: Thomas Nelson, 1988.

Woodberry, J. Dudley, editor. *Muslims and Christians on the Emmaus Road.* Monrovia, Calif.: Missions Advanced Research and Communications Center, 1989.

**On-line dictionaries of Islamic terms are available at these web sites:**

*http://dictionary.al-islam.com*
*http://www.usc.edu/dept/MSA/reference/ glossary.html*

# BIBLIOGRAPHY

# BIBLIOGRAPHY

A. H. "Discipleship of Muslim Background Believers." In *Ministry to Muslim Women: Longing to Call Them Sisters*. Edited by Fran Love and Jeleta Eckheart. Pasadena, Calif.: William Carey Library, 2000.

Abdalati, Hammudah. *Islam in Focus*. Beltsville, Md.: Amana Publications, 1998.

Abdul-Haqq, Abdiyah Akbar. *Sharing Your Faith with a Muslim*. Minneapolis: Bethany House, 1980.

Accad, Fouad Elias. *Building Bridges: Christianity and Islam*. Colorado Springs, Colo.: NavPress, 1997.

Adeney, Miriam. *Daughters of Islam: Building Bridges with Muslim Women*. Downers Grove, Ill.: InterVarsity Press, 2002.

Ahmed, Leila. *Women and Gender in Islam*. New Haven, Conn.: Yale University Press, 1992.

Akhter, Javeed. "Schisms and Heterodoxy among Muslims: An Etiological Analysis and Lessons from the Past." International Strategy and Policy Institute, November 23, 2003. *www.ispi-usa.org/currentarticles/schism.html*

Al-Faruqi, Ismail R. *Islam*. Beltsville, Md.: Amana Publications, 1998.

Al-Munajed, Mona. *Women in Saudi Arabia Today*. New York: St. Martin Press, 1997.

Abdullah Yusuf Ali. *The Meaning of the Holy Qur'an*. Translation. Beltsville, Md.: Amana Publications, 2001.

Ali, Abdullah Yusuf, translator. *The Meaning of the Holy Qur'an*. Beltsville, Md.: Amana Publications, 2001.

Ali, Shah, with J. Dudley Woodberry. "South Asia: Vegetables, Fish, and Messianic Mosques." *Theology, News, and Notes*. Pasadena, Calif.: Fuller Theological Seminary (March 1992), pp. 12–13.

Allport, Gordon. *The Nature of Prejudice*. New York: Doubleday Anchor Book, 1958.

Anderson, John D. C. "The Missionary Approach to Islam." *Missiology* 4, no. 3 (1976), p. 295.

Anonymous. "Bringing Home New Faith in Christ." *Charisma Magazine* January 29, 2004. *http://www.charismanow.com/a.php?ArticleID=8518*

———. "Faithful Witness." *Intercede* 19, no. 2 (March/April 2003), p. 4.

———. "Filling the Gap: One Couple's Diary During Six Months in Central Asia." *Frontiers Frontlines* 4, no. 3 (September–October 2003), pp. 1, 3–6.

———. "Healing for Body and Soul." *Serving in Mission Together* 102, p. 4.

———. "Just Imagine." *Serving in Mission Together* 102, p. 6.

———. "Media Reaches Restricted-Access Nations." *Intercede* 17, no. 5 (September/October 2001), p. 5.

———. "The Reconciliation Walk." *SOON Magazine. http://www.soon.org.uk/page15.htm.*

———. "Which Pir Do You Follow?" *Serving in Mission* 102, p. 12.

Armstrong, Karen. *Islam: A Short History.* New York: Modern Library, 2000.

———. *Muhammad: A Biography of the Prophet.* New York: Harper Collins, 1992.

Barrett, David B., George T. Kurian, and Todd M. Johnson, editors. *World Christian Encyclopedia.* Oxford: Oxford University Press, 2001.

Blincoe, Robert. *Ethnic Realities and the Church: Lessons from Kurdistan.* Pasadena, Calif.: Presbyterian Center for Missions Studies, 1998.

Bridges, Erich. "Into the Hungry Heart of Islam." *TC Online.* International Mission Board (January–February 2003). *www.archives.tconline.org/trends/jan03t.html*

Briffault, Robert. *Rational Evolution: The Making of Humanity.* New York: MacMillan, 1930.

Brooks, Geraldine. *Nine Parts of Desire: The Hidden World of Islamic Women.* New York: Anchor Books, 2004.

Bukhari, Sahih. *The Collection of Hadith.* Translated by M. Muhsin Khan. Vol. 1, bk. 57, no. 19.

Bush, Luis. "One Person's Journey: Mina's Story." In *Shalom-Salam: The Pursuit of Peace in the Biblical Heart of the 10/40 Window.* Colorado Springs: AD2000 & Beyond Movement, n.d., p. 10.

Caleb Project. *Hope and a Future for Azerbaijan*. Littleton, Colo.: Caleb Project, 1999.

————. *Immigrants and Refugees: The New Faces of Europe*. Littleton, Colo.: Caleb Project, 2003.

————. *The Madurese of Indonesia*. Littleton, Colo.: Caleb Project, 1996.

————. *Turkey: A Time for Harvest*. Littleton, Colo.: Caleb Project, 1997.

————. *The Uyghurs of Central Asia*. Littleton, Colo.: Caleb Project, 2003.

Caner, Ergun Mehmet, and Emir Fethi Caner. *Christian Jihad*. Grand Rapids: Kregel Publications, 2004.

Cate, Mary Anne, and Karol Downey. *From Fear to Faith: Muslim and Christian Women*. Pasadena, Calif.: William Carey Library, 2002.

Cate, Patrick O. "Gospel Communication from Within." *International Journal of Frontier Missions* 11, no. 2 (April 1994), pp. 93–97.

————. "What Will It Take to Win Muslims?" *Evangelical Missions Quarterly* 28, no. 3. Wheaton, Ill.: Evangelical Missions Information Service, (July 1992), pp. 230–34.

Catherwood, Christopher. *Christians, Muslims, and Islamic Rage*. Grand Rapids: Zondervan, 2003.

Center for Ministry to Muslims. "Folk Islam: The Muslim's Path to Supernatural Power." *Intercede* 18, no. 5 (September–October 2002), pp. 1, 4–5.

Chapman, Colin. "Biblical Foundations of Praying for Muslims." In *Muslims and Christians on the Emmaus Road*. Edited by Dudley Woodberry. Monrovia, Calif.: Missions Advanced Research and Communications Center, 1989.

————. *Cross and Crescent: Responding to the Challenge of Islam*. Leicester, UK: InterVarsity Press, 1995.

————. *Islam and the West: Conflict, Co-Existence, or Conversion?* Carlisle, UK: Paternoster, 1998.

————. *Whose Promised Land?* Grand Rapids: Baker Books, 2002.

Colgate, Julia. *Invest Your Heart: A Call for Women to Evangelize Muslims*. Mesa, Ariz.: Frontiers, 1997.

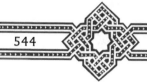

————. "Muslim Women and the Occult: Seeing Jesus Set the Captives Free." In *Ministry to Muslim Women: Longing to Call Them Sisters*. Edited by Fran Love and Jeleta Eckheart. Pasadena, Calif.: William Carey Library, 2000.

Conn, Harvie. "A Muslim Convert and His Culture." In *The Gospel and Islam: A Compendium*. Edited by Don McCurry. Monrovia, Calif.: Missions Advanced Research and Communications Center, 1979.

Cooper, Anne, and Elsie Markwell. *Ishmael, My Brother: A Christian Introduction to Islam*. Grand Rapids: Monarch Books, 2003.

Crawford, Trudie. *Lifting the Veil: A Handbook for Building Bridges across the Cultural Chasm*. Leesburg, Va.: Majesty Publishers, 1997.

Detwiler, Gregg. "Honoring Strangers." *Discipleship Journal* 137 (2003), p. 31.

Dixon, Roger L. "The Major Model of Muslim Ministry." *Missiology: An International Review* 30, no. 4 (October 2002), pp. 443–54.

Downey, Steven. "Ibero-Americans Reaching Arab Muslims." *World Pulse* 38, no. 5. Wheaton, Ill.: Evangelical Missions Information Service (March 2003) pp. 1, 3.

Dretke, James P. *A Christian Approach to Muslims*. Pasadena, Calif.: William Carey Library, 1979.

Esposito, John L. *What Everyone Needs to Know about Islam*. London: Oxford University Press, 2002.

————, editor. *Oxford Dictionary of Islam*. Oxford: Oxford University Press, 2003.

Evans, Wendell. *Church Planting in the Arab-Muslim World*. Upper Darby, Pa.: Arab World Ministries, 1986.

Fagerland, Dale. "Another Source of Power." *Intercede* 17, no. 1 (January–February 2001), p. 5.

Fellure, Jacob M. *The Everything Middle East Book: The Nations, Their Histories, and Their Conflicts*. Avon, Ma.: F+W Publications, 2004.

Friedman, Thomas L. *From Beirut to Jerusalem*. New York: Anchor Books, 1989.

————. "War of Ideas, Part 6." *New York Times* (25 January 2004), p. 2.

Fry, C. George, and James R. King. *Islam: A Survey of the Muslim Faith.* Grand Rapids: Baker, 1982.

Garrison, David. *Church Planting Movements: How God Is Redeeming a Lost World.* Midlothian, Va.: WIGTake Resources, 2004.

———. "Obstacles to CPMs." In *Church-Planting Movements.* Richmond, Va.: International Mission Board, 1999, pp. 49–52.

Gaudeul, Jean-Marie. *Called from Islam to Christ.* London: Monarch, 1999.

Geisler, Norman L., and Abdul Saleeb. *Answering Islam.* Grand Rapids: Baker Books, 2002.

George, Timothy. *Is the Father of Jesus the God of Muhammad?* Grand Rapids: Zondervan, 2002.

Gilchrist, John. *Facing the Muslim Challenge.* Cape Town, South Africa: Life Challenge Africa, 2002.

Gilliland, Dean S. "Modeling the Incarnation for Muslim People: A Response to Sam Schlorff." In *Missiology: An International Review* 28, no. 3. Scottdale, Pa.: America Society of Missiology, 2000, pp. 332–333.

Greig, Kim. "Praying for Muslim Women." In *From Fear to Faith.* Edited by Mary Ann Cate and Karol Downey. Pasadena, Calif.: William Carey Library, 2002.

Haines, John. *Good News for Muslims.* Upper Darby, Pa.: Middle East Resources, 1998.

Hawthorne, Steve, and Graham Kendrick. *Prayerwalking: Praying On Site with Insight.* Lake Mary, Fla.: Creation House, 1993.

Hewly, Debra. "Hosting amongst Muslim Homes." In *Al Jummah* 13 no. 4 (July 2001), pp. 14–15.

Hoskins, Edward J. *A Muslim's Heart: What Every Christian Needs to Know to Share Christ with Muslims.* Colorado Springs: Dawson Media, 2003.

Jabbour, Nabeel T. "Islamic Fundamentalism: Implications for Missions." *International Journal of Frontier Missions* 11, no. 2 (April 1994), pp. 56–58.

Issa, Fuad. *Adha in the Injeel.* Indianapolis: Arab International Ministry, 1995.

Johnson, G. "Muslim Widow Arrives for Divine Appointment." *Serving in Mission Together* 96 (2001), p. 6.

Johnstone, Patrick, and Jason Mandryk. *Operation World*, 21st Century Edition. Waynesboro, Ga.: Paternoster USA, 2001.

Karen. "Pioneering in the Muslim World from a Woman's Perspective." Unpublished paper, 1980.

Kateregga, Badru D., and David W. Shenk. *A Muslim and a Christian in Dialogue.* Scottdale, Pa.: Herald Press, 1997.

Kingsriter, Del. *Questions Muslims Ask That Need to Be Answered.* Springfield, Mo.: Center for Ministry to Muslims, 1991.

Livingstone, Greg. *Planting Churches in Muslim Cities: A Team Approach.* Grand Rapids: Baker Books, 1994.

Love, Fran. "Church Planting that Includes Muslim Women." *International Journal of Frontier Missions* 13, no. 3 (July–September 1996), pp. 135–38.

Love, Rick. *Muslims, Magic, and the Kingdom of God.* Pasadena, Calif.: William Carey Library, 2000.

———. "Power Encounter among Folk Muslims: An Essential Key of the Kingdom." *International Journal of Frontier Missions* 13, no. 4. El Paso, Tex.: International Student Leaders Coalition for Frontier Missions, 1996, pp. 193–95.

Mahoumet, Fatima. *The Zwemer Institute Newsletter* (Spring 1981).

Mallouhi, Christine A. *Miniskirts, Mothers, and Muslims.* Grand Rapids: Monarch Publications, 2004.

Marsh, Charles R. *Share Your Faith with a Muslim.* Chicago, Ill.: Moody Press, 1980.

Marshall, Paul, Roberta Green, and Lela Gilbert. *Islam at the Crossroads.* Grand Rapids: Baker Books, 2002.

Martin, E. J. "Why Am I a Missionary to Muslims?" *Mission Frontiers* (September–October 2003), pp. 12–13.

Massey, Joshua. "Hometown Ministry as Prefield Preparation." *Evangelical Missions Quarterly* 38, no. 2. Wheaton, Ill.: Evangelical Missions Information Service (April 2002), pp. 196–201.

———. "Should Christians Use Allah in Bible Translation?" *Serving in Mission Together* 104 (2003), p. 15.

McCurry, Don. *Healing the Broken Family of Abraham*. Colorado Springs: Ministries to Muslims, 2001.

McDowell, Bruce A., and Anees Zaka. *Muslims and Christians at the Table*. Phillipsburg, N.J.: P & R Publishing, 1999.

Miller, Roland. *Muslim Friends: Their Faith and Feeling*. St. Louis, Mo.: Concordia Publishing House, 1995.

Miller, William M. *A Christian's Response to Islam*. Phillipsburg, N.J.: Presbyterian and Reformed, 1980.

———. *My Persian Pilgrimage*. Pasadena, Calif.: William Carey Library, 1995.

Moffett, Samuel H. *A History of Christianity in Asia*, vol. 1. New York: Orbis Books, 1998.

Moucarry, Chawkat. *The Prophet and the Messiah: An Arab Christian's Perspective on Islam and Christianity*. Downers Grove, Ill.; InterVarsity Press, 2001.

Muller, Roland. *Honor and Shame: Unlocking the Door*. Philadelphia: Xlibris, 2000.

———. *Tools for Muslim Evangelism*. Belleville, Ontario, Canada: Essence Publishing, 2000.

Musk, Bill. "To Save a Soul." In *Touching the Soul of Islam: Sharing the Gospel in Muslim Cultures*. East Sussex, UK: Monarch Publications, 1995.

———. *The Unseen Face of Islam*. London: Monarch Books, 2003.

Nassar, Waleed. "Ten Stumbling Blocks to Reaching Muslims." *Ministries Today*, (July–August 1994), p. 80.

Nehls, Gerhard. *Muslim Evangelism*. Cape Town, South Africa: Life Challenge Africa, 1991.

Newbigin, Lesslie. *The Gospel in a Pluralist Society*. Grand Rapids: Eerdmans, 1989.

Nickel, Gordon D. *Peaceable Witness among Muslims.* Scottdale, Pa.: Herald Press, 1999.

Oksnevad, Roy, and Dotsey Welliver. *The Gospel for Islam: Reaching Muslims in North America.* Wheaton, Ill.: Evangelical Missions Information Service, 2001.

Open Doors. "World Watch List." *Open Doors* (January 2004).

Parshall, Phil. *Beyond the Mosque.* Grand Rapids: Baker, 1985.

———. "God's Communicator in the 80s." *Evangelical Missions Quarterly* 15, no. 4. Wheaton, Ill.: Evangelical Missions Information Service (October 1979), pp. 215–221.

———, editor. *The Last Great Frontier.* Philippines: Open Doors with Brother Andrew, 2001.

———. "Lifting the Fatwa." *Evangelical Missions Quarterly* 40, no. 3. Wheaton, Ill.: Evangelical Missions Information Service (July 2004), pp. 288–293.

———. *Muslim Evangelism: Contemporary Approaches to Contextualization.* Waynesboro, Ga.: Authentic Media, 2003.

———, and Julie Parshall. *Lifting the Veil: The World of Muslim Women.* Waynesboro, Ga: Authentic Media, 2002.

Payne, Tony. *Islam in Our Backyard.* Kingsford, Australia: Matthais Media, 2002.

Pickthall, Mohammed Marmaduke and Arafat Kamil El-Ashi, translators. *The Meaning of the Glorious Qur'an: Explanatory Translation.* Beltsville, Md.: Amana Publications, 1996.

Poston, Larry A., with Carl F. Ellis Jr. *The Changing Face of Islam in America.* Camp Hill, Pa.: Horizon Books, 2000.

Racey, David, with Erik Nubthar. "Contextualization: How Far Is Too Far?" *Evangelical Missions Quarterly* 32, no. 3. Wheaton, Ill.: Evangelical Missions Information Service (July 1996), pp. 304–10.

Riddell, Peter G., and Peter Cotterell. *Islam in Context: Past, Present, and Future.* Grand Rapids: Baker Academic, 2003.

Rockford, Jim. "Is Planting Churches in the Muslim World 'Mission Impossible'?" *Evangelical Missions Quarterly* 33, no. 2. Wheaton, Ill.: Evangelical Missions Information Service (April 1997), pp. 156–65.

Rowland, Trent, and Vivian Rowland. *Pioneer Church Planting.* Littleton, Colo.: Caleb Project, 2001.

Royal Embassy of Saudi Arabia. "Islam and Knowledge." *Islam: A Global Civilization.* Washington, D.C.: The Royal Embassy of Saudi Arabia, n.d.

Sa'a, Yehia. *All the Prophets Have Spoken.* Durham, Canada: Good Seed International, 2001.

Scoggins, Dick, and Jim Rockford. "Seven Phases of Church Planting: Phase and Activity List." *Evangelical Missions Quarterly* 33, no. 2. Wheaton, Ill.: Evangelical Missions Information Service (April 1997), pp. 156–165.

Shakir, Mohammedali H., translator. *The Qur'an Translation.* Elmhurst, N.Y.: Tahrike Tarsile Qur'an, Inc., 1999.

Sheikh, Bilquis. *I Dared to Call Him Father.* Grand Rapids: Chosen Books, 2003.

Shenk, David W. "Conversations Along the Way." In *Muslims and Christians on the Emmaus Road.* Edited by J. Dudley Woodberry. Monrovia, Calif.: Missions Advanced Research and Communications Center, 1989.

———. "Islam and Christianity: A Quest for Community." Unpublished paper, January 14, 1983.

———. *Journeys of the Muslim Nation and the Christian Church.* Scottdale, Pa.: Herald Press, 2003.

Sidebotham, Bruce. *The Reveille Shofar* 6, no. 1. (First Quarter 2002).

Smith, Jay. "Courage in our Convictions." *Evangelical Missions Quarterly* 34, no. 1. Wheaton, Ill.: Evangelical Missions Information Service (January 1998), pp. 28–35.

Smith, Marti. *Through Her Eyes: Perspectives on Life from Christian Women serving in the Muslim World.* Waynesboro, Ga.: Authentic Media, 2005.

———. "The Volga Tatars." *Echo Magazine* (Winter 1999).

Smith, Michael Llewellyn. "The Fall of Constantinople." In *History Makers.* London: Marshall Cavendish, Sidgwick & Jackson, 1969.

Sproul, R. C., and Abdul Saleeb. *The Dark Side of Islam.* Wheaton, Ill.: Crossway Books, 2003.

Steffen, Tom A. *Passing the Baton: Church Planting That Empowers.* La Habra, Calif.: Center for Organizational & Ministry Development, 1997.

Terry, John Mark. "Approaches to the Evangelization of Muslims." *Evangelical Missions Quarterly* 32, no. 2. Wheaton, Ill.: Evangelical Missions Information Service (April 1996), pp. 168–73.

Thomas, Lyndi Parshall. "The Valley of Decision." In *The Last Great Frontier.* Edited by Phil Parshall. Philippines: Open Doors with Brother Andrew, 2001.

Tozer, A. W. *The Pursuit of God.* Camp Hill, Pa.: Christian Publications, 1993.

Travis, John. "The C1 to C6 Spectrum." *Evangelical Missions Quarterly.* Wheaton, Ill.: Evangelical Missions Information Service (July 1996), pp. 304–10.

Taber, Shirin. *Muslims Next Door: Uncovering Myths and Creating Friendships.* Grand Rapids: Zondervan, 2004.

Tucker, Ruth A. *From Jerusalem to Irian Jaya: A Biographical History of Christian Missions.* Grand Rapids: Zondervan, 1983.

VanderWerff, Lyle. "Mission Lessons from History: A Laboratory of Missiological Insights Gained from Christian-Muslim Relationships." *International Journal of Frontier Missions* 11, no. 2 (April 1994), pp. 75–79.

Watt, W. Montgomery. *Mohammad at Mecca.* Oxford: Oxford University Press, 1953.

———. *Muhammad: Prophet and Statesman.* Chicago, Ill.: Kazi Publications, 1996.

Willis Jr., Avery T. "Storying in Ten Steps." *Following Jesus Series. www.fjseries.org* (2003).

Wilson, J. Christy. *More to Be Desired than Gold.* South Hamilton, Mass.: Gordon-Conwell BookCentre, 1998.

———. "Undergirding the Effort with Prayer: Muslims Being Reached Foremostly through Extraordinary Prayer." *International Journal of Frontier Missions* 11, no. 2 (April 1994), pp. 61–65.

Woodberry, J. Dudley, editor. "Forms of Witness: Here Is How I Share." In *Muslims and Christians on the Emmaus Road.* Monrovia, Calif.: Missions Advanced Research and Communications Center, 1989.

———. "The Relevance of Power Ministries for Folk Muslims." In *Wrestling with Dark Angels.* Edited by C. Peter Wagner. Ventura, Calif.: Regal Books, 1990.

———, and Russell G. Shubin. "Muslims Tell: 'Why I Chose Jesus.'" *Mission Frontiers* (March 2001), pp. 28–33.

Yancey, Phillip. "The Back Page: Letter from a Muslim Seeker." *Christianity Today* 45, no. 15 (December 2001), p. 80.

Zeidan, David. *Sword of Allah: Islamic Fundamentalism from an Evangelical Perspective.* Waynesboro, Ga.: Authentic Media, 2003.

Zwemer, Samuel. *The Muslim Christ.* London: Oliphant, Anderson, and Ferrier, 1912.

# INDICES

# BIBLICAL REFERENCES

# QUR'ANIC REFERENCES

# TOPICAL INDEX

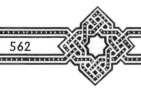

# ABOUT THE EDITOR

Keith Swartley has had a heart for Muslims since first befriending them in the old town of Mombasa, Kenya, East Africa in 1983. Since then Keith has enjoyed learning from and sharing with Muslims in Turkey, Korea, Kyrgyzstan, Kazakhstan, Indonesia, London, and Philadelphia. Keith hopes to one day retire in the Muslim world, but, until then, he plans to continue motivating Christians to reverently and gently share the love of Christ with Muslims around the corner or across the globe.

Keith and his wife Ethel, an English as a Second Language professional, have two daughters: Margaret and Charis. In addition, their family has often included international students from Asia and Latin America whom they have hosted for up to two years.

From 1993 until 2002, Keith was on staff with the U.S. Center for World Mission outside Philadelphia, Pennsylvania. Keith worked with churches and universities training and leading short-term mission teams (including ten trips to Turkey). One of Keith's major projects since 1992 has been the development of this course, formerly titled *Perspectives on the World of Islam*. After September 11, 2001, in response to national and international needs, the course quickly became his main ministry focus. In the summer of 2002, the Swartleys joined Caleb Project in Littleton, Colorado, to further develop *Encountering the World of Islam*.

As a part of Keith's ministry with Caleb Project, he teaches *Encountering the World of Islam* and *Perspectives on the World Christian Movement* courses. You can contact Keith at *kswartley@encounteringislam.org*.

This resource is recognized as being part of the *Perspectives Family* of resources.

PERSPECTIVES
*Family*

*www.perspectivesfamily.org*